**Instructional
Technology**

Exploration Series in Education

Under the Advisory Editorship of John Guy Fowlkes

Instructional Technology

Its Nature and Use

Fifth Edition

of Audiovisual Materials: Their Nature and Use

Walter A. Wittich

Professor of Educational Communications, University of Hawaii

Charles F. Schuller

Director, Instructional Media Center, and Professor of Education, Michigan State University

Harper & Row, Publishers
New York, Evanston, San Francisco, London

Contents

v

2. Learning and teaching with media

3. Teaching with pictures and graphics

4. Three-dimensional teaching materials

5. Displays for learning 191

6. Community study 231

7. Maps and globes 269

8. Audio recording and playback 317

9. Audio-cued learning

10. Still projection

11. Motion picture film learning

12. Instructional television

13. Computers, simulation, and games

14. Individualized Instruction and technology

15. Multimedia Instructional Development

629

Appendix: Source lists

687

Index

715

Editor's introduction

I T is a pleasure once again to introduce a new edition of this significant work by Walter A. Wittich and Charles F. Schuller—a work that now has a history that stretches over two decades. In the early 1950s it was becoming apparent that future teachers should have some specific instruction in the use of audiovisual materials and the other nonverbal communications media that were increasingly coming into use. So in 1953 a book entitled *Audiovisual Materials: Their Nature and Use* was published by Harper & Brothers. This book is the fifth edition of that one. The need that this work has filled has been graphically demonstrated in its widespread use, not only throughout the United States, but also in other countries, in its first four editions.

This fifth edition of the book by Wittich and Schuller is called *Instructional Technology: Its Nature and Use*. This change of title reflects the great expansion of scope and emphasis of this edition—an expansion which in turn reflects the recent dynamic expansion of the field itself. Thus this edition includes in its augmented coverage a number of exciting new developments that promise much for the future, such as computers, simulation, and games, planetariums, visual literacy, and the Instructional Development system. The book also, of course, again thoroughly covers, in updated form, the familiar media that have proved themselves over the years, such as flat pictures, models, filmstrips, films, and television.

This book bridges the gap between theory and practice by constantly relating them to each other through practical, tested methods of application. In the course of accomplishing this function, the authors include many specific examples of applications of media and technology in actual teaching involving a variety of instructional strategies. The authors constantly keep two fundamental themes in mind: they emphasize throughout that the basic purpose of the use of instructional technology is the improvement of learning; they also emphasize throughout the impor-

tance of the role of the individual teacher in adding the human, personalized factors that are essential to the most effective use of instructional technology.

For all these reasons, I can express with great confidence my belief that this edition will be even more effective in aiding teachers and learners than were the previous four.

John Guy Fowlkes

Preface

AS we have prepared this fifth edition of our book, now called *Instructional Technology: Its Nature and Use* (formerly *Audiovisual Materials: Their Nature and Use*), we have analyzed the new demands on education that have arisen because of the many fundamental changes taking place in our way of life (some of which are described in Chapter 1). We have undertaken to address ourselves to these new demands in terms of the best that is known, both old and new, about the learning process and about the experimentation and development taking place across the nation in crucial efforts to upgrade the quality and the productivity of educational programs at all levels.

Central to all of this effort, of course, is the learner. As he succeeds or fails in terms that are relevant to him, so in effect do our educational programs succeed or fail. We see teaching and instruction, therefore, primarily as ways to make effective *learning* possible. Although this concept in itself is not new, the last few years have shown more tangible progress toward its attainment than the preceding several decades. We have new curriculums and new educational programs in reading, the sciences, the social studies, mathematics, English, and the foreign languages. We have hundreds of junior and community colleges with dynamic new programs; we have hundreds of school systems developing truly individualized instructional programs for the first time. In other words, we are beginning to feel a pervasive sense of excitement and change in education that promises much for its future and for the future of the society it serves.

It is in this context that we decided to change the name of our book. Though we have always been concerned with much more than audiovisual materials per se, the term ''instructional technology'' better reflects today's emphasis on the *process* by which learning can be improved. *Instructional technology,* in short, is a new way to think about problems of teaching and learning to find workable solutions. In this broad sense, the concepts of instructional technology become central to the whole educational process.

Instructional technology adds a new applied behavioral science approach to the problems of learning and teaching in that it makes use of pertinent scientific methods developed in psychology, anthropology, sociology, communications, language and linguistics, cybernetics, perception, and other related fields. It also incorporates the management principles of cost effectiveness and the efficient use of available learning resources and instructional personnel. Though instructional technology as a concept does not necessarily imply the use of machines, experience has shown that the newer learning systems of various kinds more often than not involve media, data processing, automated self-instruction, and related forms of equipment and resources. Individualized Instruction, for example, becomes financially practical in today's school systems only when effective large-group and medium-size group techniques can also be used; such group techniques frequently include television, films, and other forms of projection. Individualized Instruction typically employs a variety of print, audiotape, slide, filmstrip, and 8mm motion picture materials used by students independently, thus freeing teachers to generate materials and to work with individual students as needed. A significant example of the kind of scientific thinking embodied in instructional technology is Instructional Development, which is introduced in Chapter 3,

mentioned throughout the book, and discussed in detail in Chapter 15.

The foregoing does not mean that we have abandoned either the content or the convenient organization and methods of treatment that made the first four editions of the book so successful. Flat pictures, graphics, models, sound films, television, community study, and other familiar topics are all still here, though in thoroughly updated and revised form. In addition, there are substantial new sections on visual literacy, multimedia applications, outdoor laboratories, and planetariums, plus two entirely new chapters on Individualized Instruction and computers, simulation, and games. All this is presented within the broader context of instructional technology as a logical and powerful means of improving teaching and learning.

During the six years which have marked the development of this fifth edition, we have continued to be committed to many of the basic generalizations and guiding principles which have proved themselves throughout the first four editions. These include:

1 Effective learning begins with first-hand *or* concrete *experiences and proceeds toward more abstract experiences. Thus a student who has the advantage of reacting to well-selected and wisely used media and materials can learn more effectively than one who is provided with largely verbal information and materials.*

2 A learner profits most from instruction when he becomes involved through his own *interests and* desires. *Well-chosen educational media present concepts in such a way as to incite interest and stimulate involvement.*

3 A student who is knowledgeable and whose interests are aroused is better able to perform as a creative, inventive *human being.*

4 The most objective evidence that a

learner has accomplished his goal is to be found as one observes and evaluates the quality of the responses he makes to instruction. Observable behaviors shown by learners after they have responded to media instructional opportunities present tangible evidence that can be measured, evaluated, and used by teachers as the basis for continual replanning and improvement.

As we have noted, the most useful and still pertinent materials used in previous editions have been retained. As we have also noted, in revising the book we have taken full account of the many significant developments that have occurred in the last six years in the more effective organization and use of technology in instruction. For example, teaching by television, once thought to be somewhat questionable because of its passive nature, has been recycled as carefully planned multimedia instructional experiences which include provision for learners to engage actively in overt responses. Continued evidence shows that effective instructional television relies heavily on the teacher to provide the means for such learner response to television stimulation. Indeed, at its best, instructional television involves the participation not only of its creators, but also of the classroom teacher who guides its use, the students who respond to its use, and the parents who enter into the process in various ways. Current instructional television programs such as "Sesame Street" and "The Electric Company" (both discussed in this book) are good examples of systematic organization that incorporates the highest quality of contemporary instructional technology.

As we have mentioned, the concepts and principles of instructional systems development commonly becoming known as Instructional Development (I.D.) are introduced and discussed in this edition. The purpose here is not so much to help the student develop skills in this quite complex subject as to make him aware of its importance and its essential components so that he may be more ready to support and participate in the Instructional Development efforts that appear likely to come into wide use in schools and school systems across the country during the years ahead. Thus one goal of this fifth edition is to introduce the student to a way of thinking that can guide him in developing systematic plans for, and use of, instructional technology in the learning process.

A few words about the structure of this fifth edition:

The chapters are developed progressively, so that students can readily become acquainted with the latest in instructional technology. Relevant learning theories and teaching principles are discussed in the opening chapters and referred to repeatedly throughout the book as they relate to illustrative applications of the various forms of media use in learning situations. As the book proceeds through the chapter sequence, it provides the reader with explanations of procedures for identifying learner needs, objectives, and goals and methods of arranging for pupils an effective environment of alternative learning experiences made available through instructional technology. Such explanations produce threshold understanding, so that students who use this book will be prepared to proceed from there with progressively more effective applications and evaluations of media use with students in their own classes.

We should also note some specific features of the book that are intended to be helpful to both the instructor and students. In this fifth edition each chapter is preceded by a special type of new feature—a set of Objectives and parallel Performance Responses. The Objectives are suggested goals to be attained while studying the chapter; the Performance Responses are guides to methods of attaining the goals and applying the information and ideas acquired in meaningful ways. The Further Learner Response Projects at the end of each chapter are intended to provide suggestions for exploration of certain topics in more depth and for the development and refinement of skills in the effective use of instructional technology. Each chapter is followed by a summary and by References and Media References (and in most cases also by Source References) that list specifically relevant sources and materials. It should be noted that the captions for the illustrations do more than merely parallel content introduced in the text. Many of the captions present additional information; also, many of them include questions designed to elicit responses that will be helpful in self-evaluation or evaluation by the instructor or other students. As before, the book ends with an Appendix that consists of extensive lists of major sources of all pertinent kinds of instructional technology materials and equipment.

Still another new feature is a further guide to productive student activity in the form of a separate supplement, the *Student Production Guide,* prepared by us in collaboration with Jay C. Smith and David W. Hessler. This *Guide* is designed to reinforce the opportunities for the student to demonstrate the ways in which he can reorganize creatively and usefully the information he has gained as a result of studying and using this book. The *Guide,* which is action oriented, includes detailed and well-illustrated directions (many of them in a flow-process format) for producing simple and inexpensive mediated materials of various types; directions for operating and maintaining projection and sound equipment commonly found in schools; reference information on screens, projection lenses, types of film, and the like. The *Guide* also includes source lists of materials and equipment used primarily in production work.

As part of the current climate of change, education is being extended increasingly both downward and upward—to younger age groups and to adults. As education thus becomes a more continuing involvement for people of all ages, the varieties of readiness brought to the process become constantly more important factors in the educational scene. These varieties of readiness actually present exciting challenges to teachers and future teachers—challenges specifically to those who are eager to investigate learner reactions to instructional television, audio materials, projected and nonprojected visuals, games, individualized instruction modules, computer-based instruction, and the interrelated use of all of these through the means described in this book as Instructional Development. Within this climate of change, therefore, we present this fifth edition, entitled *Instructional Technology: Its Nature and Use.* The contents are the result of our joint study, experimentation, testing, and practical application of productive ideas in many years of our own and our colleagues' classroom teaching.

The materials in this book have been gathered and organized with the continuing help and suggestions of friends, professional colleagues, graduate students, and hundreds of students of education in our classes. The book as a whole has been tested, changed, and evaluated in terms of the behavioral responses that its various parts have elicited. Accordingly, this is a laboratory-tested book that is recommended to the instructor and his students as an experience in the *realities* of applying instructional technology to the solution of a wide variety of learning problems.

WE wish to express our gratitude once again to Dr. John Guy Fowlkes, Professor of Education (Emeritus) at the University of Wisconsin, for the original and continuing inspiration that he has brought to both of us. Further thanks are extended to professional colleagues who have actually used preliminary versions of portions of this edition in classroom contexts: Professors Lillian Lum, Lucius Butler, and Geoffrey Kucera of the University of Hawaii and Professors Bruce Miles, Wilfred Veenendaal, Elwood Miller, James Page, Donald Wilkening, Kent Gustafson, and Paul Witt of Michigan State University. We wish also to thank the many master's, post-master's, and doctoral students in Instructional Development and Technology at both the University of Hawaii and Michigan State University who assisted at various stages during the preparation of this edition. Particular thanks and recognition are due Mrs. Ruth Murphy, secretary to the coauthor at Michigan State University, for her dedicated and invaluable assistance on this and the preceding three editions. Special thanks are also extended to Mrs. Pamela Forcey, Special Projects Editor, Harper & Row, for her patience, professional competence, and untiring efforts during the editorial process.

Since this book is about instructional technology, it must of necessity rely heavily on photographs, charts, diagrams, and other visuals. We express our thanks in the Acknowledgments section to the various individuals and companies who supplied most of the illustrations. The quoted passages used to amplify our ideas are acknowledged in footnotes.

Walter A. Wittich
Charles F. Schuller

To the student

AS a teacher, either in service or in training, you are or will be working with pupils who vary widely in interests and abilities. One reason for the wide variations, of course, is that today virtually everyone of school age is in school. As we all know, one of the primary results of these variations is that many students are not satisfied with school plans for instruction which all too often are better suited to an earlier era than to an age of social and political unrest, information and population explosions, instant worldwide communication, and jet-space transportation. Nor should these students be satisfied with outmoded methods of instructions; they know, just as we teachers and future teachers know, that if their education is to be meaningful and revelant to them, it must keep pace with the changes in all other areas of our society.

The basic purpose of this book is to help you formulate and arrange more useful and acceptable learning experiences which will be interesting and challenging to these young people—young people who need, and deserve, to be interested and challenged.

At the outset, and as you study this book, you will want to be familiar with our frame of reference. The following, therefore, are four of the more important assumptions which we, the authors, have accepted and acted on as we have prepared this fifth edition of our book, now called *Instructional Technology: Its Nature and Use*:

1   New technological communication techniques that so well serve the needs of our out-of-school society have counterparts that can very effectively serve in-school learning programs.

Examples of how these counterparts actually have been, and may be, used in schools are described throughout this book.

2   Each learner is an individual with unique interests, personality characteristics, learning capacities, intellect, and creative potentials.
3   A learner must become involved before he can be expected to respond.

This book describes varied alternatives for arranging useful media experiences that will challenge and involve the *individual* learner. These experiences make use of pictures, graphics, audio and video equipment, projected motion and still images, maps and globes, three-dimensional materials, computers, simulation, and games, as well as combinations of these—all teamed with appropriate printed materials. Descriptive examples portray media use by large and small groups and in individualized classroom learning situations.

4   Systematic analysis of learner needs and systematic development of viable solutions to those needs are essential to significant improvement of today's educational programs.

Beginning in Chapter 3, periodically thereafter throughout the book, and particularly in Chapter 15, there are references to an instructional systems approach to solving teaching and learning problems; this type of approach is commonly becoming known as Instructional Development (I.D.). In discussing Instructional Development and describing some actual applications of it in this book, our purpose is simply to introduce you, the student, to the basic concepts and principles of this approach. We believe this is important both because of the potential values of I.D. and because it appears likely to come into wide use in school systems throughout the United States during the next decade.

As a student, you need to know what is expected of you. Thus at the beginning of each chapter you will find a set of Objectives and parallel Performance Responses. The Objectives are clearly stated goals that can be attained while studying the chapter. The Performance Responses are suggested ways to respond that will help you to (1) "fix" and clarify the information and ideas acquired and (2) apply them meaningfully to your teaching plans. Both the Performance Responses and the Further Learner Response Projects at the end of each chapter are very likely to include certain ones that really "turn you on"—that lead you, in other words, to pursue with enthusiasm the further questioning, discovering, and development of skills in the effective use of instructional technology that are the underlying purpose of this book.

There are other specific features of the book that are intended to be helpful to you. At the end of each chapter is a summary that will be useful for review. Also at the end of each chapter are References and Media References (and, usually, Source References) that list sources and materials that are particularly relevant to the chapter. The book ends with an Appendix that consists of extensive lists of major sources of all kinds of instructional technology materials and equipment other than those used primarily in production work. You will note that the captions for the illustrations do more than merely parallel content introduced in the text. The captions constitute a second line of interrogation and demonstration of concepts that relate to media learning. Many captions are independent statements that reinforce the meaning of the photograph, graphic, or diagram. Many captions include questions designed to elicit responses. The purpose of these questions is to facilitate your own self-evaluation of your grasp of the meanings associated with the visual message and also to facilitate evaluation by the instructor and mutual evaluation by you and other students during class sessions.

There is a separate supplement, the *Student Production Guide,* which you may purchase if you wish to. We have prepared this supplement (in collaboration with Jay C. Smith and David W. Hessler) as a further guide to student activity that is designed to reinforce the opportunities for the student to demonstrate the ways in which he can reorganize creatively and usefully the information he has gained as a result of studying and using this book. The *Guide* expands much of the specific information in the book and adds other specific information. Thus the *Guide,* which is action oriented, includes detailed and well-illustrated directions (many of them in a flow-process format) for: (1) the kinds of simple and inexpensive production that can easily be carried out by teachers and pupils within the school setting—methods for producing effective pictures, graphics, displays, exhibits, maps, audiotapes, and other mediated materials to supplement those acquired from outside sources; (2) the operation and simple maintenance of all major types of projection and sound equipment commonly found in schools; (3) reference information and suggestions on projection screens of various types, projection lenses in relation to image size, types of film suited to various conditions of use, and the storage and filing of types of materials that often present storage and filing difficulties. Also included are extensive source lists of materials and equipment needed in production work in individual schools. The *Student Production Guide* is a valuable supplement to this text and is coordinated closely with it but is made available separately so that it can be used or not in accordance with the particular needs and desires of the individual instructor and individual students.

Today's school environment should offer varied alternatives among instructional experiences. Thus the following chapters are organized to lead you through a wide variety of teaching-learning alternative experiences which may be identified with instructional technology. The arrangement of the chapters is such that you will become involved first with those aspects of instructional technology that are more or less readily acceptable and readily available to you in the beginning stages of application: flat pictures, the chalkboard, models, specimens, graphics, three-dimensional teaching materials, displays, maps and globes, and real-life situations in the community. Beyond this, the more truly technological aspects of media learning are explored. Included here are audio learning experiences, still and motion picture projected experiences, television, computer-based instruction, simulated learning, and individualized instruction opportunities. You are invited to go as far as you like— the further the better—until, finally, in the last chapter you will discover the fascinating types of learning experiences made possible by the interrelated use of *all* appropriate learning resources. This is multimedia learning systems utilization or multimedia Instruction Development—a type of teaching and learning which employs interrelated media only after a systematic new way of thinking about and solving learning problems has been explored.

We wish you good reading, enjoyable searching, and insightful involvement with instructional technology as you explore its nature and use.

Walter A. Wittich
Charles F. Schuller

Acknowledgments

THE authors wish to express their appreciation to the following companies, individuals, and institutions for their valuable assistance in supplying the fine photographs and other visual materials on which this book so heavily depends. All photographs and diagrams not credited in this list were supplied by the authors.

Figures

1.0 Eastman Kodak / *1.1a–b* NASA / *1.2* National Association Division of Research, 1967 / *1.3* Ad Hoc Committee on Preparation of Nursery and Kindergarten Teachers, American Association of Colleges for Teacher Education, 1970 / *1.4–1.6 Projections of Educational Statistics to 1979–80,* National Center for Educational Statistics, U.S. Dept. of Health, Education and Welfare, 1970 / *1.7* NASA / *1.9* Oakland, California, Public Schools / *1.15a–e* The Pennsylvania State University, Still Photography Studies / *1.16* Jerry Kemp and McGraw-Hill / *1.18a–d* Hawaii Curriculum Center, Honolulu

2.5 Oak Ridge, Tennessee, Public Schools / *2.9c* Oakland, California, Public Schools / *2.11a–b* Central Washington State College / *2.11c* Apple Valley School, Yakima, Wash. (Edward H. Marble & Assoc., Architects, A.I.A.) / *2.13* University of Hawaii High School / *2.15* University of Hawaii High School / *2.17 Parade* magazine / *2.18* Encyclopaedia Britannica Educational Corporation

3.0 United Nations / *3.1* Children's Television Workshop / *3.2* Eastman Kodak / *3.3–3.4* Michigan State University / *3.5a–c* Eastman Kodak / *3.6* Rand McNally / *3.7* Charles Beseler & Company / *3.8* Coronet Instructional Films / *3.9* Eastman Kodak / *3.10a–b* Cranham, Rapho Guillumette / *3.11* NASA / *3.12a–c* Eastman Kodak / *3.13* Cranham, Rapho Guillumette / *3.14a* Silvester, Rapho Guillumette / *3.14b* Titia Bozuwa / *3.15* Michigan State University / *3.16* Ray Atkeson / *3.17* Los Angeles City Schools / *3.18* U.S. Department of the Interior National Park Service / *3.19a–b* Michigan State University / *3.20* Denoyer-Geppert / *3.21a–c-3.22a–d* Michigan State University Graphics / *3.23* Michigan State University / *3.24* William C. Brown Co., Publishers / *3.25a–d-3.26a–d* Michigan State University Graphics / *3.27* Copyright © by the New York Times Company. Reprinted by permission / *3.28* *Educational Technology* magazine / *3.29* Copyright © 1971 United Feature Syndicate, Inc. / *3.30* TM ® All rights reserved 1971. Publishers-Hall Syndicate / *3.31* Santa Barbara *News-Press* / *3.32–3.35* Michigan State University Graphics / *3.36* Society for Visual Education, Inc. / *3.37* Michigan State University Graphics

4.0 Fisher Scientific Co. / *4.1a–b* Realistic Visual Aids / *4.2* A. J. Nystrom & Co. / *4.3* Society for Visual Education / *4.4* Michigan State University (Ken Kumasawa) / *4.5* International Harvester Co. / *4.6a* University of Wisconsin / *4.6b–c* University of Hawaii / *4.7* Denoyer-Geppert Co. / *4.8* Camera-Craft / *4.9* Long Beach Unified School District, Long Beach, Calif. / *4.10* Denoyer-Geppert / *4.11* Los Angeles City Schools, Audio-Visual Section / *4.12* Robert C. Ragsdale, Ltd. / *4.13* Singer, Link Division / *4.14* Michigan State University / *4.15a* Society for Visual Education / *4.15b* Oregon Museum of Science and Industry / *4.15c* Bloomfield Hills Public Schools, Bloomfield Hills, Mich. / *4.16a* Oregon Museum of Science and Industry / *4.16b* Bloomfield Hills Public Schools, Bloomfield Hills, Mich. / *4.17–4.20* Michigan State University Graphics / *4.21a, c* Mexican National Tourist Council / *4.21b* *Museo Nacional de Antropología,* Mexico City / *4.22–4.24* California Museum of the Sea Foundation / *4.25* Denoyer-Geppert Co. /

4.26 Revell, Inc. / *4.27–4.28* Los Angeles City Schools, Audio-Visual Section / *4.29* Oregon Museum of Science and Industry / *4.30* Museum of Science and Industry, Chicago

5.0 Seattle Public School System / *5.1* John Reeves / *5.2a* Alex Gray / *5.2b* E. F. Hauserman Co. / *5.3* Robert C. Ragsdale, Ltd. / *5.4* Hans Geerling Photography / *5.5a–c* Michigan State University / *5.6* Eberhard Faber, Inc. / *5.7–5.10* Michigan State University / *5.11a* Charles Mayer Studios / *5.11b* Michigan State University / *5.12* A-1 School Equipment Co. / *5.13a–b* Educational Aids, Inc. / *5.14a–c* Michigan State University / *5.15a–c* U.S. Plywood Corp. / *5.15d* Michigan State University / *5.16* Educational Aids, Inc. / *5.17a–b* Michigan State University / *5.19–5.20* Michigan State University / *5.21* Ben Kann / *5.22* Museum of Science and Industry, Chicago

6.0 Bob Samples / *6.1* Adlai Stevenson High School, Prairie View, Ill. / *6.2* The Seattle *Times* / *6.3* Hays from Monkmeyer / *6.4* Nation's Schools / *6.5* Adlai Stevenson High School, Prairie View, Ill. / *6.6* Los Angeles City Schools, Youth Services Section / *6.7* Stevens, Ford Foundation / *6.8* Adlai Stevenson High School, Prairie View, Ill. / *6.9* Milwaukee Public Schools / *6.10a–b* Olympia, Wash., Public Schools / *6.11a–c* Milwaukee Public Schools / *6.12a* Honolulu Newspaper Association Library / *6.12b* Titchen, Honolulu Newspaper Association / *6.13a–c* American Telephone & Telegraph Co. / *6.14b* American Telephone & Telegraph Co. / *6.15a–b* Three Rivers Commercial Newspaper, Lamphere Schools, Madison Heights, Mich. / *6.16a* Honolulu Channel 11 KHTV / *6.16b* Star Bulletin, Honolulu, Hawaii / *6.17a–c* Portland Community College, Ore.

7.0 Michigan State University / *7.1* Boeing Airplane Company / *7.2a* Julien Bryan, *Hunting Wild Doves* / *7.2b* Julien Bryan, *Building a House* / *7.2c* Julien Bryan, *Building a Bridge* / *7.2d* Julien Bryan, *Yugoslavia* / *7.2e* Julien Bryan, *Fishing on the Coast of Japan* / *7.2f–g* Julien Bryan / *7.3a–b* High School Geography Project / *7.4–7.5* Denoyer-Geppert Co. / *7.6* C. F. Schuller / *7.7* Michigan State University / *7.8* A. J. Nystrom & Co. / *7.9* Hubbard Scientific Co. / *7.10* Panoramic Studios / *7.11–7.12a–c*, & *f* Denoyer-Geppert Co. / *7.12d–e* A. J. Nystrom & Co. / *7.13* T. N. Hubbard Scientific Co. / *7.14–7.15* Copyright by R. Buckminster Fuller / *7.16a–d* Michigan State University / *7.17a* A. J. Nystrom & Co. / *7.17b* Richard Edes Harrison, copyright / *7.18–7.19a* A. J. Nystrom & Co. / *7.19b* Carnahan-Hanson Co. / *7.21a–c* Scott Foresman / *7.22* McKinley Publishing Co. / *7.23* Hammond Education Sales / *7.25* Los Angeles City Schools / *7.26* Aero Service Corp. / *7.27* Fisher Scientific Co. / *7.28* Wisconsin *Journal of Education* / *7.29* Denoyer-Geppert Co.

8.0 Norelco / *8.1* 3M Company / *8.3a* Concord / *8.3b* Califone / *8.3c* Sony / *8.3* Wollensak 3M / *8.4* Norelco / *8.5* North American Philips Corp. / *8.6* Shure Brothers, Inc. / *8.9a* Electronic Futures, Inc. *8.12b* Lamphere Public Schools, Lamphere, Michigan / *8.13a* Newcomb Audio Products / *8.13b* Rheem Califone / *8.16* Chicago Public Schools / *8.17* National Education Association / *8.17* Educational Equipment and Materials / *8.18* Kalart/Victor / *8.19a–d* Wayne State University

9.0 Pioneer School, Olympia, Washington (Ray Moffit) / *9.1a* S. N. Postlethwait / *9.1b* S. N. Postlethwait / *9.5* NHK Japan Broadcasting Corp.) / *9.6* St. Louis Public Schools / *9.7a* Chicago Public Schools / *9.7b* Wisconsin St. University at La Crosse / *9.8* 3M/Wollensak / *9.13* NEA

10.0 Shackman, Monkmeyer / *10.1a–b* Children's Television Workshop / *10.2* Eastman Kodak Company / *10.3* Society for Visual Education / *10.4* Sawyer's Inc. / *10.5a–b* Michigan State University / *10.6* Department of Education, San Diego County, California / *10.7a–b*, & *f* Society for Visual Education / *10.7c* Encyclopaedia Britannica Educational Corporation / *10.7d, e, g, h, i*, McGraw-Hill / *10.8a* Instructional Materials Center, Los Angeles / *10.8b* Viewlex, Inc. / *10.8c* Standard Projector & Equipment Co., Inc. / *10.9* Eastman Kodak Company / *10.10a–b* Imperial Film Company / *10.11a* BFA Educational Media / *10.11b* Guidance Associates for permission to reprint photographs from the full-color sound filmstrip program *Me, Myself, . . . and Drugs*, © 1971. Guidance Associates of Pleasantville, N.Y. / *10.12a* North American Philips Corp. / *10.12b* Audiscan, Inc. / *10.13* American Optical Corp. / *10.14a–b* Charles Beseler Company / *10.15* A. J. Nystrom & Co. / *10.16* Realistic Visual Aids / *10.17* Charles Beseler Company / *10.18a* Bausch & Lomb / *10.18b* Los Angeles Public Schools / *10.19* Dukane / *10.20–10.21* National Cash Register Co. / *10.22* Michigan State University / *10.23* Keystone View / *10.24* Michigan State University / *10.25* Young America Films, Inc. / *10.26* NASA / *10.27* Viewlex / *10.28* Carroll College News Service / *10.29a* Viewlex / *10.29b* Graflex, Inc. / *10.29c* Standard Projection and Equipment Co., Inc. / *10.30a* Viewlex / *10.30b* Graflex / *10.30c* Standard Projection and Equipment Co., Inc. / *10.31a* Eastman Kodak / *10.31b* Sawyer's / *10.31c–d* Spinler & Saupp / *10.32b* Charles Beseler Company / *10.32c* American Optical Corp. / *10.33b* Charles Beseler Company / *10.33c* Projection Optics Co., Inc. / *10.33d* Charles Beseler Company / *10.34* Michigan State University

11.0 A. V. Explorations, Inc. / *11.1a–b* Atomic Energy Commission / *11.1c* Tennessee Valley Authority / *11.1d* Consulate General of Japan / *11.2a* Technicolor, Inc. / *11.2b* Eastman Kodak / *11.3a* Society for Visual Education / *11.3b* Films Incorporated / *11.3c* Coronet Instructional Films / *11.4a* Coronet Instructional Films / *11.4b* Encyclopaedia Britannica Educational Corp. / *11.5a* Dr. H. E. Edgerton / *11.5b* Moody Institute of Science / *11.6a–b* Encyclopaedia Britannica Educational Corp. / *11.7* Division of Diagnostic Radiology, Univ. of Rochester Medical Center / *11.8a–b* Coronet Instructional Films / *11.9a–b* Western Woods Studios / *11.10* Ranic Audio Visual Limited / *11.11* Courtesy Rank Organization; TFC / *11.12a–c* Australian Commonwealth Film Unit / *11.15* W. A. Wittich & J. G. Fowlkes, *Audio-Visual Paths to Learning*, Harper & Row, 1946 / *11.20a–b* Eastman Kodak / *11.21a–b* Technicolor & M. Lefferts Photography / *11.22* Eastman Kodak

12.0 Coatesville Area School District and Educational Television (H. Eugene Hollick) / *12.1a–e* COMSAT / *12.2a–b* Children's Television Workshop / *12.3a* Kamehameha Schools, Honolulu / *12.3b* Burnt Hills–Ballston Lake Central Schools / *12.4* Reprinted with permission from Children's Television Workshop, © 1971 CTW / *12.5c* NHK (Japan Broadcasting Corporation) / *12.6a–c* Michigan State University / *12.8* Inner London Education Authority / *12.10a–c* Sony Corp. / *12.12a–c* Atlanta, Fulton County, Georgia Public Schools (Gil Tauffner) / *12.13a* Los Angeles County Schools / *12.13b* Bellflower Unified School District, Bellflower, Calif. / *12.13c* Alhambra City Schools, Alhambra, Calif. / *12.13d* Los Angeles County Schools / *12.15b* Stillwater Public Schools, Stillwater, Okla. (Wesley Beck, Jr.) / *12.16* Clark School for the Deaf and Education TV Magazine (Gordon Daniels) / *12.17a–b* Donald J. Cyr / *12.18 Educational Television Magazine* (H. Eugene Hollick) / *12.19a–b* Oral Roberts University and Bob Hawks, Inc. / *12.19c* Chester Electronics Laboratories / *12.21* Banks Alabama Model School (Edward Wood) / *12.22* Denison, Texas, Public Schools.

13.0 Kaplan, Black Star / *13.1a–c* Responsive Environments Corp. / *13.2–13.5* American Telephone and Telegraph Corp. / *13.6* Waterford Township, Michigan, School District / *13.7–13.8* Donald Bitzer and D. Skaperdas, "The Economics of a Large-Scale Computer-Based Education System: Plato IV," *Computer-Assisted Instruction, Testing, and Guidance,* Wayne H. Holtzman, ed., Harper & Row, 1970 / *13.9* MITRE Corp. / *13.10* The Detroit Free Press and Action Line / *13.11* Singer, Link Group / *13.12a–b* United Air Lines / *13.13* Allstate Insurance Co. / *13.14a–d* Society for Visual Education / *13.15* Wff'N Proof-Learning Games Associates (Christine Allen)

14.0–14.11 Instructional Development Division, United States International University, Corvallis, Oregon (Jack Edling AECT) / *14.12* Waterford Township, Michigan School District / *14.13–14.16* Instructional Development Division, United States International University, Corvallis, Oregon (Jack Edling)

15.0 Stashin, Rapho Guillumette / *15.1–15.2* National Special Media Institutes / USOE / *15.3* Michigan State University / *15.5a–j* Hawaii English Project / *15.6–15.10* Michigan State University / *15.11a–d* U.S. Department of State / *15.12a–b; 15.13* Lansing Community College, Lansing, Mich. / *15.14; 15.15; 15.16a–b* Oakland Community College, Bloomfield Hills, Mich. / *15.17* Planetariums Unlimited / *15.18a–c* Coldwater, Mich. Public Schools / *15.19* McDonald Elementary School, Warminster, Pa. (John Carver, Architect) / *15.20* Lansing Community College, Lansing, Mich.

Plates

3.1a–b A. J. Nystrom & Co. / *3.2* Shostal, The Agency for Color Photography (F. Schneider) / *3.3a* Courtesy of *Harpers* magazine / *3.3b* Courtesy of Tabori, Ltd., 1971, Dorothy E. Hayes, designer, Floyd Sowell, artist / *3.3c* Courtesy of Buddha Records / *3.3d* Courtesy of Braniff International / *4.1a* Circus World Museum, Baraboo, Wisconsin / *4.1b* International Harvester Company / *4.2a* Lawrence Bernstein and G. W. Hughes / *4.2b* Ward's Natural Science Establishment, Inc. / *4.2c* T. N. Hubbard Scientific Company / *4.3* Museum of Science and Industry, Chicago /

7.1, 7.2a–b A. J. Nystrom & Co. / *7.3–7.6* Denoyer-Geppert Company / *7.7* NASA / *11.1* Harper & Row film; animation by Travenol Laboratories, Inc. / *11.2a* E. S. Beckwith / *11.2b* Encyclopaedia Britannica / *11.3a* Larusson, Saga Productions / *11.3b* Encyclopaedia Britannica / *11.3c–d* Kaoch, Saga Productions / *11.3e–f* Moody Institute of Science / *11.3g* Coronet Instructional Films / *15.1* Courtesy National General / *15.2a* Edward B. Trovillion / *15.2b* E. S. Beckwith / *15.3* McGraw-Hill Educational Films

**Instructional
Technology**

ONE

The teacher and the communications revolution

Objectives	Performance responses
1	
To identify the social, curricular, and technological changes in our society and test your knowledge of them by making judgments about their effect on your own teaching responsibilities.	Observe students in class and identify several typical student responses to typical classroom learning experiences. Analyze the nature of and reasons for the responses. Describe and evaluate the responses in ways designated by a group leader or the instructor.
2	
To identify the basic process of communication and relate it to the psychological barriers ("noise") which occur during classroom learning and apply your resulting generalizations to your own teaching responsibilities.	Observe a classroom learning environment and analyze any evidence of the presence of any or all of the factors that contribute "noise" and thus interfere with the communication process. Describe and evaluate your findings.
3	
To identify basic generalizations evolved from research on the effectiveness of audiovisual media communication and evaluate the effect of the generalizations on your own teaching procedures.	Create a set of optimal changes in the classroom learning environment you know best, changes that reflect your awareness of several of the generalizations drawn from current educational communications research. Describe the changes by using either visual or verbal methods, or both.

WHEN man first stepped onto the moon on July 20, 1969, nearly 2 billion people on earth participated in a historic learning experience. In its brilliant reporting of the event, the National Aeronautics and Space Administration achieved what most teachers know they should do and hope to do; that is, NASA presented current and useful information by a combination of audio and visual methods—media, as they are usually called. Media, collectively, are a powerful and effective means of educational communication. They are what this book is about.

The moon landing reports are therefore a remarkable example of teaching. The moon landing was by its very nature of almost universal interest. Nevertheless, the many ways used to report it increased both interest in the event and understanding of it. Consider the media used: Today's mass communications technology made possible reports relayed by communication satellites to earth television that originated aboard the Apollo 11 command module, aboard the lunar module, and finally on the surface of the moon. There also were audio voice messages; still photography explained by accompanying accounts in the world press; and countless graphics, used first to show what would happen and later to redescribe the landing. In addition, there were the specimens brought back by the astronauts that are still being examined and analyzed by scientists.

Consider the learning impact of this multifaceted "teaching example": All the media—television, audio messages, models, still pictures, charts, diagrams, maps, tape recordings, and specimens—reinforced each other to produce a gripping experience that held the attention of millions for hours on end, making each feel almost as though he were participating (see Figure 1.1).

A new technological vocabulary was introduced, used, and soon widely understood: "escape velocity," "translunar course correction," "attitude orientation," "retrorocketing," "lunar orbital insertion," "docking," "reentry," "communications blackout," and so forth. This example of verbal teaching and learning is indeed a model to investigate for school use.

A new realization of the worldwide unifying power of multimedia communication was dramatically brought about as an international audience saw, understood, and appreciated the accomplishment of an almost unbelievable feat by three of their fellow men. They also came to appreciate the cooperative efforts of the thousands who planned the moon journey and designed and produced the complex equipment needed.

To teachers, all of this represents a reaffirmation of the power of interrelated media utilization in achieving learning goals. And all of this leads to two important questions that must be answered: How can we bring appropriate parallel methods into the classroom? In other words, how can we help learners of all ages to profit from this systematic "media way of learning"?

These questions are addressed to those who are responsible for teacher education;

FIGURE 1.1

When man first stepped onto the moon, millions of earthbound watchers observed. History was created and communicated simultaneously through television via space satellites and surface relays. What impact does all of this have on teacher-learner expectations about in-school communications? An astronaut stands on the moon. In the other photograph, taken from the command and service module, the two astronauts who landed, riding in the lunar module ascent stage, make their docking approach to the CSM —on their way home. The earth is seen rising above the lunar horizon.

those who administer and supervise elementary, high school, and college educational programs; and those who administer programs of in-service professional education.

For many years educators have worked to find answers to such persisting questions as: How can we determine the needs of learners? How can we provide learners with effective experiences that will truly help them to learn? That these and related needs have been met in a less than perfect way is shown by the opinions of some teachers themselves. In Figure 1.2 are summarized teachers' assessments of the apparent value of pre-service professional educational experiences provided to them before

they began teaching. Most of the teachers reported that their pre-service training was adequate in helping them acquire subject knowledge, understanding of the psychology of learning, and general teaching methods. The important point, however, is that their teacher training programs did not help them understand the nature and use of audiovisual media. We must conclude, with reluctance, that many who administer and teach in pre-service training programs neither emphasize nor demonstrate adequately the selection, use, and evaluation of new media learning resource materials (audiovisual materials) as a means of improving the education of the young.

This is a disturbing conclusion because it is imperative that teachers understand both the nature and the uses of audiovisual media and instructional technology in general. For instance, the Educational Policies Commission of the United States, describing "the creative teacher," states that he uses a wide variety of interrelated media to assure quality instruction; he uses films, filmstrips, television, pictures, maps, globes, models, museum materials, and audio recordings to improve learning opportunities.

The following chapters of this book describe the characteristic uses of and ways to evaluate mediated learning resources. First, however, one should understand some of the social and environmental circumstances of our time—for it is these circumstances that have created the urgent need to use media in instruction.

Effective teaching: some current dilemmas

G REAT social and technological changes now confront and inevitably affect teachers and their relationships with learners and learning problems. Some of these changes are the growing school population and its impact on the nature and needs of learners; the rapid development of new information and the expanding curriculums

FIGURE 1.2

This graph summarizes assessments by teachers of the adequacy of their pre-service professional education in the four areas indicated. The survey results show that teachers themselves are aware of the necessity for adequate educational communications through the proper and sufficient use of media.

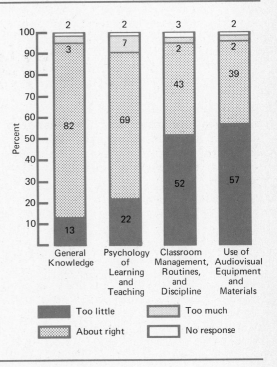

organized to cope with it; the impact of new communication tools and techniques as they relate to pupil expectations and responsiveness. The teacher is faced with three primary and somewhat conflicting needs: the need to keep up to date about information in his field of learning; the need to deal with individual differences, accentuated by the school population explosion; and the need to understand and apply the best of classroom-oriented communication techniques. It is obvious that in our current society the task of teaching is becoming more exacting and more complex. Nevertheless, and partly for the same reasons, it is also becoming more stimulating and more rewarding.

The changing school population

Walk through the corridors of almost any of our schools and you see evidences of the schools' population explosion. You see old, outdated buildings that are still in use unchanged. You see sections of other older buildings that are torn apart where new wings are being added; you see temporary classrooms. You also see new schools in use or under construction. In some areas you see entirely new campuses that are being built on the growing edges of expanding cities. This expansion of school facilities must continue into the foreseeable future, for the following reasons:

It is true that the upward trend in the birthrate has leveled off recently. Nevertheless, this leveling off, at first deceptively reassuring, will actually not affect the expected upward trend in school enrollments. For one thing, the actual numbers of young children are expected to continue to increase, though more slowly (see Figure 1.3). In any case, the birthrate factor will be offset by both the holding power of the school and the *downward* as well as the *upward* expansion of school programs. The downward extension of education is marked by the increasing percentage of children attending kindergarten, preschool, Head Start, and nursery school programs.

The upward extension of education is even more dramatic. Increasing proportions of high school students stay on to graduate, and, having thus qualified, elect to enter the nation's junior colleges, community colleges, four-year colleges, and then graduate schools. The numbers of high school and college *graduates* project themselves upward year after year (see Figure 1.4). These projections accompany estimates that by 1980, approximately 3½ million teachers will be needed to instruct nearly 64 million students who will be enrolled in formal educational programs, as well as related special ones (see Figure 1.5). Expenditures for American education, which were a mere $2.7 billion in

FIGURE 1.3

Actual and projected numbers of children from newborn through kindergarten age, in millions.

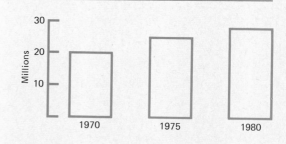

FIGURE 1.4

Actual and projected numbers of high school
graduates and earned bachelor's and higher
college degrees, in thousands.

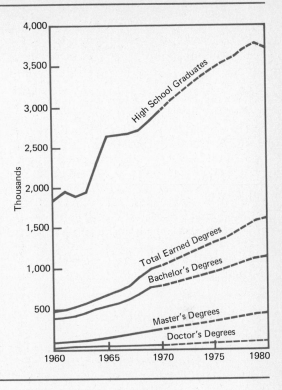

FIGURE 1.5

Actual and projected enrollments, in millions.
(a) Enrollment in grades K–12 of regular day
schools, by institutional control and organizational level. (b) Degree-credit enrollment in
institutions of higher education, by control and
type of institution.

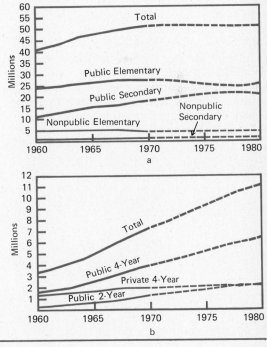

FIGURE 1.6

Actual and projected expenditures for regular elementary and secondary day schools and institutions of higher education, in billions of 1970 dollars. These figures do not include pre-school and child care costs.

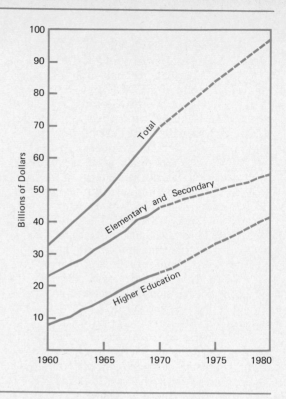

1942 and had risen to $70 billion in 1970, are expected to exceed $97 billion in 1980[1] (see Figure 1.6).

Teachers who contemplate this burgeoning role for the education profession see in it mixed blessings. On the one hand, there will be no shortage of opportunities —economic, social, and personal—within the foreseeable future for anyone who is professionally qualified and trained to make accomplishment in the field of education his lifelong pursuit. On the other hand, complicated learning and instruction problems accompany such increases in school populations. Larger classes present problems to teachers as it becomes more and

more difficult for them to relate to individual students and their needs. Furthermore, the larger classes include students ranging over a continually wider spread of backgrounds, interests, and aptitudes. The result is that the teacher is less able to arrange suitable learning experiences and utilize appropriate communication techniques that will challenge this widening spread of interests and abilities. To meet these formidable teaching challenges, the best of an increasingly diverse array of learning materials must be understood and used to their fullest extent by those who plan to teach in the currently changing educational scene.

[1] *Projections of Educational Statistics to 1979–80,* National Center for Educational Statistics, U.S. Department of Health, Education, and Welfare, Washington, D.C., 1970, p. 7.

The changing curriculum

Recently one of the authors was involved in measuring the effectiveness of new media in the teaching of physics at 102 high schools. An initial survey of existing practices revealed that, though all the high schools used one of six widely used physics texts, not one of the teachers reported being able to "cover" the entire text during the semester course. When asked why, teachers gave such typical responses as these: "There is too much science material to cover in a single semester." "Science concepts are becoming so complex that we can't hope to cover all of the topics included in today's text." "Even though our text makes no mention of atomic physics, we haven't time to cover the traditional physics contents in a semester."

Since this survey, even more new physics information has been developed. To give only a few examples: there are new data about the earth's gravitational field and the nature of the layers of ocean water and their effects on ocean currents; there is the invention of the rotary piston engine, as contrasted with the traditional reciprocating engine; there is space physics information developed by those few people who have successfuly planned and accomplished the journeys to the moon.

Biological knowledge, when compared to its extent in 1900, is reported to have increased four times by 1930, 16 times by 1960, and 30 times by 1970; furthermore, it is estimated that it will have increased 100 times by the year 2000.[2] It is reported that in certain areas of the physical sciences knowledge doubles about every 15 years. As a result of all this, the teacher is confronted by a dilemma: should he return to school for a complete subject-oriented reeducation every 10 to 15 years? Or should he seek current avenues of information in an effort to keep up to date? How the latter may be done is discussed in later chapters.

There have been parallel curriculum developments in the field of social studies. At the turn of the century the subject "history" was the sole representative of what today comprises social studies. Later, in 1917, the Committee of Seven originated the social sciences curriculum as such: European History or Geography in grade 7, American History in grade 8, Civics in grade 9, European History in grade 10, American History in grade 11, and Problems of Democracy or The Study of the Government of America in grade 12. This organization seemed to be adequate until about 1960. During the 1960–1970 decade, however, social studies teachers brought about their own explosion of knowledge by abandoning the traditional curriculum that covered only European backgrounds in favor of inquiries into worldwide human interrelationships: South America, Africa, Asia, the Pacific countries, India, the Near East, and so forth.

How does one acquire valid specific information about political, social, and economic developments in such Southeast Asian countries as Laos, Cambodia, North and South Vietnam? How does one become informed about these places and others where the people, who are searching for their place in the developing world, are currently enmeshed in war and in countless economic, educational, and social problems? How does one give students meaningful information about such countries? Quite obviously, older forms of communications are not enough. What is needed is a means of information-giving that will bring the world of reality—the world as it is actually developing—to the student. How new educational media may be used to accomplish this is explained in later chapters.

Because it is so relevant to the questions we have just asked, we will, however, briefly describe here an interesting teacher interchange program at the East-West Center at the University of Hawaii. The aim of this

2 Frederick R. Smith and C. Benjamin Cox, *New Strategies in Curriculum in the Social Studies,* Rand McNally, 1969, p. 11.

program is to attempt not only to shift the emphasis of content of social studies more to Asian peoples, but also to investigate the use of new media in bringing current, useful information to learners. In this teacher training program, which at first was experimental but now is one of the continuing options available to grantees, social studies teachers from U.S. mainland school districts are invited to the University of Hawaii to study side by side with social studies teachers from such Pacific and Asian countries and territories as Japan, Taiwan, Hong Kong, Thailand, India, Australia, New Zealand, and so on. Discussing the necessity for this project, one of its planners commented: "The speed with which Pacific nations are growing in industrialization, population, and communication is almost unbelievable. It is long past time for *Asian* social studies courses to be included in mainland high school curricula."

During the course of this program, teachers not only evaluate and plan to use existing films, filmstrips, tapes, and related materials; more important, they actually engage in the production of transparencies, maps, charts, and 2×2 slide sets and in the collection of models and specimens. Each also collects his own materials to be used when he returns to mainland work and brings new media information opportunities to his students.

The knowledge explosion and the changing social world of man, then, are reflected in curriculum changes in our schools. A half-century ago, the curriculum was rather rigidly divided into 24 subject units in the fields of grammar, Latin, mathematics, history, and rhetoric. By contrast, when the U.S. Office of Education released a few years ago the results of a survey on what high school pupils study, a wide

sampling of American high school students reported their enrollment in nearly 1,000 distinct and identifiable courses, divided into these broad areas:[3]

English, 137	*home economics, 73*
mathematics, 91	*business, 143*
foreign languages, 44	*health and physical education, 87*
science, 74	*vocational education, 65*
social studies, 203	
music, 82	*unclassified, 73*

Two specific examples of the expansion of curriculum areas in terms of contemporary information are enough to give a concrete picture of the effects of the knowledge explosion. The expansion in the field of social studies has brought about such new courses as international relations, problems of modern living, public affairs, radio and television broadcasting, world cultures, and world governments and the United Nations, to name only a few.[4] In the more technologically oriented area of industrial arts there are such new courses as air conditioning, audiovisual technician, census and polling, industrial cooperative training, modern plumbing, gas turbine maintenance, appliance maintenance, and many others.

In other words, it is obvious that the school today finds itself with constantly more and more subject information to teach. Of necessity, the child spends more time in school. But while he is there, he and his teachers face a problem: "No longer can one small head [that of the teacher] carry all that a student must learn. We must do something drastic to better enable us to handle the staggering buildup of new knowledge"[5] (see Figure 1.7). Nor can the textbook, so far the

[3] Edith S. Greer and Richard W. Harbeck, "What High School Pupils Study," Bulletin No. 10, OE 33025, U.S. Office of Education, 1962.

[4] J. Minor Gwynn and John B. Chase, Jr., *Curriculum Principles and Social Trends*, 4th ed., Macmillan, 1969.

[5] B. Frank Brown, "Education," *Honolulu Star Bulletin*, February 27, 1965.

FIGURE 1.7

Can one teacher be expected to "know all" at a time when man's knowledge is exploding through new frontiers with every tick of the clock? What alternatives are there? (One of the first two men on the moon sets up a solar wind composition experiment.)

chief instructional medium, be relied on much longer to communicate with efficiency. This does not mean that in teaching all this new information our old techniques should be eliminated; what it does mean is that something must be done about using new communication techniques—educational media—to "backstop" the teacher in his task of communicating current, useful, and accurate information to learners. New instructional materials must be utilized in sufficient measure to provide pupils with the needed concrete or quasi-concrete experiences that make both old and new material understandable and interesting. It is only through the use of the very newest instructional materials—films, filmstrips, slides, charts, models, and other audiovisual media—that such adequate experiences with the modern world may be provided.

THE INQUIRY METHOD AND LEARNING MATERIALS An important change in

teaching procedures in part complicates the curriculum content shifts already described, but it also presents exciting new potentialities for media use. Science teachers for some time have employed a student-centered learning procedure called the *inquiry method*. This method is a workable means for helping learners to achieve intellectual development beyond that possible through old memorization and response procedures. It is, in fact, a way to help learners to achieve the ability to search for and locate information, to analyze information, and to use this new-found information in creative and inventive ways.

"Inquiry," in other words, is a term used to describe the process by which a learner becomes interested in developing and investigating his own questions or goals as he interacts with a variety of information sources and experiences. In the area of science, it has been demonstrated that the inquiry method works best when the learner may respond to all kinds of learning resources—experiments, demonstrations, printed materials, 16mm sound motion picture films, film loops, graphics, charts, audio information, instructional television, etc. In the face of this convincing evidence of the effects of good teaching procedures as demonstrated by innovative teachers, far too often there still is a serious lack of proper learning resource materials and facilities with which the learner who is involved in inquiry can interact. But where the inquiry method can be fully employed, three definite advantages become apparent:

1. The learner is likely to become more interested in developing questions, ideas, or guesses about the learning resource experiences he encounters.

2. The learner helps pose questions that challenge him and he seeks to proceed further on his own.

3. The learner demonstrates initiative in delving individually into resource learning experiences within which he can find relevant information in his attempt to test his ideas, to satisfy his curiosity, and to find answers.

For the reasons just enumerated, the inquiry method in recent years has become very interesting to social studies teachers, who see in it valuable possibilities for their own field. Accordingly, during the 1960s many social studies inquiry projects, centered in colleges, universities, or in experimental curriculum projects, were set up and operated in the classrooms of certain school districts. On the basis of the results of such projects, it has been established that the same desirable results which become apparent when pupils employ the inquiry method in science also become apparent in the social studies—*provided that adequate media learning resources are available.*

When the successful inquiry projects in social studies are analyzed, one element in common is found to be materials for instruction that are carefully selected and presented. For example, in a study of the growth and development of cities, learning resource materials included 2-by-2 photographic slides that showed aerial views of American cities. Pupils posed questions, analyzed the slides for information, noted common elements and unique features, and then tested their observations until they could draw generalizations and conclusions from them.[6] In a creative high school social studies project, the instructor relied heavily on 16mm sound motion picture films, filmstrips, and study prints to present real-life situations understandably and graphically to learners. In this case also, the students were led to inquire, understand, test, and generalize about the interactions among people who live in far-off places.

Across the nation, more than 50 comparable social studies and history projects are in the process of changing the face and form of social studies instruction as pupils respond to the multimedia learning material packages of information. Such packages usually include statements of suggested goals, criteria for evaluation, plans for teaching procedures, and, above all, interrelated media learning resources. Media learning materials usually include "original documents," letters, charts, maps, graphics, picture sets, prerecorded tapes, 16mm sound films, and 8mm film loops. Topics cover a wide range: the Monroe Doctrine, the Discovery of the New World, the Culture of the Iroquois, national income and productivity, water resources, networks of cities, the "game" of farming, the role of citizenship, and others representative of the new and expanding social studies inquiry curriculum.[7]

What kinds of learning resources must be available if learners are to follow the

[6] Paul Griffin, "Oregon Geography Project: Report to the 1968–1969 University of Hawaii Experienced Teacher Fellowship Program," 1969.

[7] Smith and Cox, op. cit., chap. VII, pp. 130–152.

FIGURE 1.8

This is one of the Learning Resource Centers at the Kailua High School in Hawaii. During the scheduled times for independent study, students are free to come in and examine and respond to learning experiences through which they seek information that will help them accomplish previously worked-out goals. How do these facilities compensate for the lack of homogeneity among students? What opportunities do you see for both slow and gifted learners when they work in an environment like this one? If you believe that the search for information is a highly individualized quest and should proceed at the pace and intensity the learner determines, what effect may this environment have on his progress?

inquiry method to its successful conclusion? See Figure 1.8 for one answer. Traditional verbal learning resources are not enough. The child who is alive in the late twentieth century has limited opportunity to gain background experiences needed to unlock understandings of words used in a social studies book to describe events, personalities, political circumstances, and places that existed centuries ago, or even 50 years ago. Such events can become understandable, however, if they are presented through media that give information in visual or audio format: simulated learning experiences presented in the form of dramatic reenactment on audiotape, or, better still, 16mm sound motion picture format, pictorial sets of information, or 8mm single-concept loops.

In centers where the inquiry method has been used successfully, traditional library organization has been adapted to make possible the students' independent search for knowledge. That is, such a library includes not only printed materials, but media learning resources as well. The Media Learning Resource Center established within the Oakland (California)

Public Schools—a learning library arranged for individual inquiry—is a good example. In this resource center students have access to all kinds of interrelated learning experiences: films, recorded tapes, picture sets, slides, charts, maps, and printed materials (see Figure 1.9). The student is free to locate these for his own use, either in the library or in his classroom. He may take any media equipment and materials to his home for the weekend to be viewed and discussed with parents and friends.[8]

Other examples of how such learning centers may contribute to the inquiry method are discussed in detail in Chapter 15, "Multimedia Instructional Development."

The changing extraschool communication world
It is important to use new and effective ways of communicating to learners the basic

[8] George Noone, "Oakland Public Schools: Report to the 1968–1969 University of Hawaii Experienced Teacher Fellowship Program," 1969.

FIGURE 1.9

Students at the Sobrante Park School of the Oakland school system have unlimited access to all kinds of media-oriented learning experiences with which they may interact. Here a teacher shows two children what the tiny pictures on a super 8mm film look like before they view the film. How large a gap between the ideal of unlimited access and actual practice is there in your school? What are some of the changes that must be made to give all students free access to learning opportunities?

knowledge, skills, understandings, and concepts they need in order to move intelligently into a citizenship role. An unfortunate gap still exists between this *idea* and its practice. Therefore, to try to close this gap—to establish further the need for greater use of new media learning resources in our schools—we now discuss communication processes used in the extraschool world.

Modern communications have made our word a "global village."[9] To appreciate this vividly, think of some of the communication changes and innovations since 1950: television, voice writing, satellite visual scanning transmission, printing and photographic refinements, and satellite communications through INTELSAT (see Chapter 12, Figure 12.1). Schoolteachers and learners live and work in an environment marked by half hourly and special event newscasts around the clock. Information—political, economic, and human interest—comes from "everywhere" in "instant" audio and visual form.

As if this were not enough to arouse one's interest in how best to become informed *inside the classroom,* one should note

the less spectacular changes in more traditional areas of extraschool communications. Table 1.1 shows the growth in various forms of extraschool media since 1950, projected to 1980. Most striking, of course, is the growth in the number of television receivers. But the increase in the number of

TABLE 1.1

Trends in extraschool communications media in the U.S.

[9] *This Is Marshall McLuhan: The Medium Is the Massage,* 16mm film sound, color, 53 min., McGraw-Hill, 1968.

radios, though less marked, is still impressive. During the early years of television, there were those who predicted that it would cause the virtual demise of radio; the figures on radios show that they obviously were wrong.

The picture-story format is worthy of special note as an example of the adaptation of a successful type of extraschool communication for formal school purposes. This type of communication, made possible by advances in photographic and printing techniques, was originally introduced in this country in the 1930s in magazines intended for a general mass audience. *Life,* the first of this type, was followed by *Look* and other imitators; all rapidly attained huge circulations. In recent years, however, the competition of television, with its mass appeal, has caused these magazines to change quite radically (or cease publication, as a number have, including *Look*). Although they still make extensive use of pictures, they have generally abandoned the traditional picture-story format, and they now include a high proportion of textual content. In other words, they have been forced by huge losses in advertising revenues—revenues that now go to television advertising—to leave the mass-market field to television. Nevertheless, the picture-story technique pioneered by these magazines remains in effective use in publications intended for schoolchildren. Briefly, a picture story summarizes and presents, in an integrated combination of pictures and short captions, information in such a way that almost any reader's attention is arrested and held for about 12 to 15 minutes. Magazines about current events which employ this technique are used by thousands of teachers and millions of primary- and intermediate-grade students. Similar publications are read widely by high school students in science and social studies classes. The total circulation, in fact, of instructional magazines for both elementary and secondary levels is esti-

43,000,000	51,000,000	62,000,000	67,000,000
52,000,000	59,000,000	63,000,000	66,000,000
8,000	9,000	10,000	10,500
99,000,000	156,000,000	305,000,000	400,000,000
10,000,000	55,000,000	105,000,000	200,000,000
19,000	13,000	10,000	9,000
3,000	5,000	4,000	4,000

Note: All figures rounded to nearest thousand or million.
a *World Almanac,* 1950, 1960, 1969.
b *Newspaper and Periodical Directory,* N. W. Ayers, 1968.
c *UNESCO Statistical Yearbook,* 1968.
d *World Almanac,* 1950, 1960, 1969.
e *International Motion Picture Almanac,* 1968.
f Projections based on 10-year moving averages.

mated to be more than 25 million during each school year. Many of these magazines, most of which are weekly, use picture stories to a greater or lesser extent.

Other relevant social communication methods, however, are not being adapted as effectively to school use. Extraschool radio communication, as measured by set ownership, nearly doubled during the 10-year period 1960–1970. Forecasters predict that within the 1970–1980 decade, radio sets owned will reach 400 million. Although radio communication obviously has demonstrated its appeal and value in the social world, very few of the nation's schools employ comparable audio-radio learning communication, even though it is a proved low-cost means. Exceptions are noted in Chapter 9, "Audio-Cued Learning."

In 1950 the U. S. Bureau of the Census was so unsure of the status of television that a national count was barely considered worthwhile. The count was done, however, showing that in that year about 10 million sets were in use in the United States. By 1960 television ownership had mushroomed; 55 million sets were in use. During the next decade, television set ownership nearly doubled; 105 million black-and-white and color sets were in use in 1970. A modest extension of this indicates that it is highly probable that 200 million sets will be in use in the United States by 1980 (see Table 1.1).

When television's amazing growth and development became apparent, there were those who predicted that the motion picture entertainment film would be doomed to a secondary role. This has proved to be far from the case. Indeed, the motion picture film has demonstrated its appeal to the public's need for this kind of communication through reruns on television every day of the week (many of them during evening prime time); in fact, at least several and often as many as 20 to 30 full-length motion pictures are available to viewers in any one area in any 24-hour period. As part of this trend, an increasing number of entertainment films are being made specifically for television. Furthermore, the traditional motion picture theater, although experiencing a slow decrease in number in this country (see Table 1.1), can by no means be ignored. UNESCO's statistics show that today the production of the full-length motion picture film is a worldwide communication activity. The United States, which used to be in first place in production of feature-length motion pictures for theater showing, is now behind, as shown in this list of titles produced per year: Japan, 719; India, 316; China, 257; Italy, 245; Hong Kong, 171; United States, 168.

Extraschool communication has had a strong effect on our children. By the time the typical first-grader arrives at school, he has become a devotee of television, perhaps owns his own radio, helps to purchase millions of comic books, and no longer sleeps in the back seat when his parents go to an outdoor theater. Also, most children have begun to read by the time they come to school. Table 1.2 shows how the communications sophistication of

TABLE 1.2

Percentage of children who had begun to use each medium at each age

our children increases year by year. (Comic books are discussed in Chapter 3.)

The influence of these factors on our schoolchildren is very real; in fact, it has generated forces outside the classroom which seriously affect the efficiency of classroom communication techniques. The teacher constantly finds himself battling to get and keep the attention of the learner. The significance of this struggle is made particularly clear when we consider the amount of time the learner spends in school as compared with the time he spends out of school under the influence of nonschool-oriented communication devices and messages. The division of the child's time (figured on a 180-day, 6-hour-a-day school attendance schedule) looks like this for an average year:

in-school living   *1080 hours*
out-of-school living   *4395 hours*
sleep (9 hours per day)   *3285 hours*

Thus, for every hour the student is exposed to classroom information and media, he spends more than four under the influence of nonschool communications. For example, an outdoor-theater manager reports, "The number of young children who come in to see the movies—just tall enough to look over the back of the front seat—what impressions they get." And one junior high school teacher tells of the invasion of the portable radio:

Occasionally someone answers my questions in a very loud voice. Then I realize— the student grins—and quickly removes the pocket radio ear plug. He has been listening surreptitiously to the morning news. It was more fascinating than I or the book. "Solid-state" radios are everywhere. I am not always sure who's really listening to me!

Similarly, the testimony of the newstand operator reveals the power of comics: "The new comic books are selling better than ever—why not? Color, action, excitement —better than most school books. . . ."

The interference with classroom communication that derives from nonschool media shows no tendency to diminish (see Table 1.1). Actually, the various interference factors, as they grow, reinforce one another in a kind of spiraling way that results in constantly increasing desires for ex-

Age	TV	Radio	Maga-zines	Comic books	Movies	Books		Newspapers	
						Read to them	They read	Read to them	They read
14	11	3	1	1	38	0	0	0	
37	20	11	6	8	58	0	0	0	
65	27	20	17	21	72	2	4	0	
82	40	33	35	39	74	9	9	0	
91	47	41	50	60	75	40	12	9	
94	53	53	61	70	75	73	12	44	
95	62	59	68	76	75	86	12	59	
96	65	62	70	77	75	89	12	71	

Source: New Teaching Aids in the American Classroom, Office of Education, U.S. Department of Health, Education and Welfare. OE 34020, 1960.

posure to them; in some cases, indeed, these desires become almost compulsive—think of the child who "must" have his transistor radio playing constantly, wherever he is (sometimes even at school, as we have seen!). To sum up, the powerful and effective demands for attention made by non-school media seriously challenge the communication techniques employed in the classroom.

In the light of this, what are we, as teachers, doing for the children of the modern age to help them continue some of their communication expectations once they arrive in the classroom? In too many cases we accept these learners into our school-rooms and then literally shut out the rest of the world and its influences. Too often the classroom teacher finds himself relying on communication methods which cannot effectively compete with methods currently employed in the extraschool environment. Out-of-school communication media are skillfully devised to snare and hold the attention of the individual, whether he be child or adult; yet too often we teachers try our best to satisfy the natural interest and enthusiasm of children by using outworn and outmoded communication tools.

These facts should lead all teachers, supervisors, and administrators of schools to ask themselves these fundamental questions:

1   *Is the voice of the school being lost amid the influence of current mass communication techniques?*
2   *Are today's school communication methods the best that can be employed?*
3   *Are better educational materials and methods available through which the school may communicate more effectively with learners?*

It is time teachers realized that the school must have effective means of communication if it is to be held responsible for successfully commanding the attention of schoolchildren and youth and for arranging suitable instructional opportunities. The realization of this situation makes imperative a new role for the teacher—one in which he assumes responsibility for providing classroom communications that are adapted to the needs of the students and used in ways that will allow learners to reach the recognized goals of instruction successfully. In other words, the teacher must decide not merely to put up a defense against the forces of extraschool communication interference; rather, he must decide to take active constructive steps to counteract these forces.

The basic communication process

I N order to know the world, one should be able to experience it fully and at first-hand. As we seek to lead learners into new fields of inquiry, we run the risks inherent in departing from known backgrounds unless, in the process, we provide new, appropriate, and dependable firsthand experiences. But, of course, as the world becomes increasingly more complex, it becomes increasingly impossible to provide children with actual firsthand experiences. Obviously, some compromise in the form of substitute experiences must be evolved and used to enable children to conceptualize their world. This is the essence of communication as an essential part of teaching.

Yet in order to select appropriate media which will best provide these substitute experiences, one must understand what is involved in the process of communication itself. The basic communications model shown in Figure 1.10 involves most often an informational or interpretive process.

FIGURE 1.10

A basic communications model. What influences
the channel of messages?

Students | MESSAGES | Teacher and Educational Media

Messages, information, or reactions to information travel from that which initiates and sends them toward that which receives them. The route along which the messages travel may be thought of as a "communications channel." The message (stimulus) may be a statement made by the student or the teacher or it may be provided in a film, chart, picture, or chalkboard illustration. The receiver of this stimulus reacts in some way; that is, he may listen or see or examine through touch or taste. These reactions can lead to active responses. A question can lead to an answer or suggestion; examination of a film, specimen, or object may lead to a spoken observation or a smile; or the response may be no more than passing the message on to another student. A message communicated by the teacher may bring forth interested responses from some pupils—questions, possible answers, or suggestions—and nothing from others. Ideally, the communication channel carries both messages and countermessages; it involves initiation, re-

ception, response, or, as it is sometimes called, "feedback."

This communications channel must be kept wide open so that informational and interpretive messages relating to the subject being considered can be revealed and made understandable to the pupil. It is only when the teacher and pupil are able to communicate clearly and without interference that valid understandings about the social and scientific world can be acquired and recorded correctly in memory for later use.

In an ideal learning environment, either within the classroom itself or outside the classroom—as, for example, in field-study situations—the communication process travels along a channel clear of any interference. Usually, the more varied and appropriate the sources from which messages originate, the stronger and more valid are the responses and countermessages that occur between teachers and students or among students. As we have seen, out-of-school communications media and tech-

FIGURE 1.11

Extraschool interference sometimes obstructs
clear classroom communications. Do these
factors affect your own teaching?

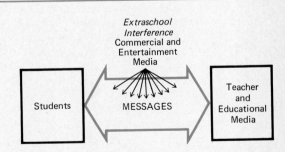

Extraschool Interference Commercial and Entertainment Media — Students | MESSAGES | Teacher and Educational Media

niques are often sufficiently varied and very appropriate to the student, so much so that they make a greater impact on him than school media and techniques (Figure 1.11). Obviously, however, not all barriers to effective communication come from out-of-school interference: some formidable barriers—psychological ones—originate during the interactive classroom process itself.

Psychological barriers to effective teaching

E VEN the best teaching plans and procedures may be ineffective when they come up against communication barriers that originate in the classroom. Our rapidly expanding knowledge of human behavior and learning has enabled us to describe specifically one important group of obstacles to effective teaching. Like antiquated and outworn methods of classroom communications, psychological barriers to learning and teaching have certainly always existed; however, as more and more research into human behavior and learning exposes these barriers and points to means of overcoming them, it becomes highly important for the teacher to acquaint himself with both the barriers and the techniques by which they may be removed. Thus, although these are of a different nature than the teaching-learning impediments we have previously discussed, they too are subject to the teacher's control.

Success in classroom learning is closely related to the clarity and understandability with which messages are communicated by the teacher, either directly or by the information sources he has chosen for use. The educational psychologist describes this basic communication process as one that enables messages that pass between sender and receiver to be clearly recognized and completely understood by both. However, as we have said, many psychological barriers may lie in the channel area; some are caused by outside-of-school conditions (home life, etc.), but others arise from conditions generated within the classroom itself.

The teacher bears the burden of achieving clarity in classroom communications; thus he must always be alert for recognizable "interference" or "noise." The teacher must not only recognize interference possibilities, but also know the means by which a clear channel of communication may be established and maintained with efficiency, for he is usually the only one who can improve the nature and strength of the messages or remove the barriers to receiving these messages. As long as messages are transmitted with clarity, unchanged or uninterrupted by interfering factors, pupil-teacher communications will proceed efficiently.

Experience indicates, however, that many changes do occur as the messages presented by a teacher—or through the media chosen by him—pass to and are interpreted by the pupils. As a result, classroom learning experiences are frequently so altered as to lower the general efficiency of instruction. As indicated in Figure 1.12, the clarity and understandability of the messages transmitted and received in a classroom depend on the avoidance of the following five, often overlooked, barriers to effective classroom communication: verbalism, referent confusion, daydreaming, limited perception, and actual physical discomfort.

Verbalism

The human organism is remarkable. For example, it automatically sets up defenses against annoying stimuli. Most of us have

FIGURE 1.12

Psychological barriers obstruct efficient classroom communications, in addition to extraschool
interference. What are your experiences with the
realities of these barriers?

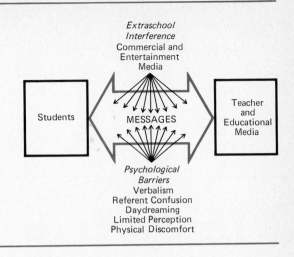

found ourselves in a noisy committee session or a gathering at which almost everyone speaks at once and makes continuous
demands for our attention. In such situations, we discover how amazingly simple it
is to shut out psychologically unwanted
noise or unattractive appeals for attention. We concentrate our mental attention
on what is interesting and desirable—a
stimulating private conversation or a point
of agreement taken by a fellow committee
member. On occasion, we may completely
"shut out" unwanted audio stimulation,
letting our mind occupy itself with
thoughts of pleasanter experiences we have
had elsewhere.

Similarly, many learners in the classroom find it very easy literally to "tune us
out" when our teaching approach becomes
too repetitious, "noisy," uninteresting, or
unattractive. Experienced teachers report
that continued use of any one kind of device or stimulus results in its decreasing
efficiency. Certainly the learning efficiency
of words actually declines as more and
more words pour forth endlessly. Just as
a muscle tires when overused, so interest
and attention lag before a never-ending
barrage of words. As one seminar partici-
pant reported:

*During the first five or six weeks of school,
pupils listen to me. They seem very interested in my descriptions and directions.
Then comes a curious change. As week
follows week and more words follow
more words, interest lags and finally even
I realize that it is time for a change, a
change in the methods I use to get across
the ideas I so urgently seek to teach.*

And many a guidance counselor has run
into such pupil complaints as the following:

Counselor: You were telling me you can't
get interested?
Pupil: If you were in the classroom, you'd
know what I mean. It's just talk,
talk, talk. Every once in a while there
is a big shout, "Listen, listen to me,
while I explain again." He's always
telling us to listen. I try to listen—but
it's always just more words, words,
words.

Further, it has been demonstrated repeatedly that unless learning experiences
are within the learner's interest and comprehension levels, little or no progress is
made toward achieving goals. The teacher
knows from experience that he must be
aware of the learner's readiness to accept

TABLE 1.3

Estimated number of items of audiovisual
materials and equipment owned by
U.S. public schools, July 1969

Selected equipment

Screens	919,000
Record players	698,000
Earphones	576,000
Overhead projectors	453,500
Slide and filmstrip projectors	426,000
Tape recorders	320,000
16mm projectors	251,000
Learning carrels	171,000
Slide or filmstrip viewers	163,000
Reading devices	98,600
Opaque projectors	91,600
Transparency makers	71,200
8mm projectors	58,600
35mm slide cameras	27,200
Rear screen projectors	22,200
16mm cameras	14,100
Drymount presses	11,750
8mm cameras	7,200
Microprojectors	6,180

Selected materials

Filmstrips	21,700,000
Still and flat pictures	12,400,000
Disc recordings	7,200,000
Overhead transparencies	5,230,000
Maps and globes	4,200,000
2-by-2-inch slides	2,400,000
Tape recordings	2,020,000
16mm films	1,315,000
Reading programs	336,000
8mm films	104,000

Source: Loran C. Twyford, New York State Education
Department, 1969.
Note: The total number of public schools operating in
1969 was estimated at 92,500.

planned learning experiences. Yet many
pupils have not been adequately prepared to
meet the excessive verbalism with which the
school typically communicates information.
It has been found that, particularly among
the lower socioeconomic strata of our population, a large number of children have
received their preschool training from parents and others in the home who themselves
have limited verbal ability. Thus, unac-
customed to the barrage of words that
pours forth from the teacher and that con-

fronts them in their readers and textbooks,
these children are not equipped to comprehend the teacher's endless verbal messages.
In short, excessive verbalism can no longer
be condoned, particularly in today's world
of communication, which offers much more
effective alternatives.

Excessive verbalism, therefore, may
create a psychological barrier that can
seriously interfere with effective classroom
communication. To alleviate this problem in
planning continuing classroom experiences

in the language arts, the social studies, science, and mathematics, one may draw from a variety of instructional materials which use the best of the communications techniques to transmit a great deal of solid subject content. These include sound motion picture films, models, specimens, filmstrips, charts, diagrams, tapes, records, transcriptions, television, and many others, all of which will be discussed at length later in this book. Most public schools already have much of the equipment and many of the materials needed by a teacher who wishes to improve his communication techniques (see Table 1.3). Furthermore, a teacher should remember that he can make use of educational media and equipment even more effectively by allowing his students to take part in selecting, using, and interpreting modern instructional materials. The extension of teaching techniques to include a variety of audiovisual materials and equipment chosen by the teacher in itself increases student interest and attention. Nevertheless, student participation in choosing and using such communication aids makes it even more likely that the disinterest and boredom that result from monotonous teaching techniques will be overcome (see Figure 1.13).

Referent confusion

It is natural for us, in the absence of adequate background experiences, to turn automatically to seemingly related experiences for help in understanding something new, hoping to draw conclusions that may then apply to the new problem. When such reference to previously learned material is successful in helping us comprehend the new materials, it is referred to as *transfer* or *positive transfer*. Often, however, attempts to transfer previously acquired understanding to new problems result in confusion because such needed similar understandings seldom are available at the time in the minds of both teacher and student. Such an impasse is called *referent confusion*.

Referent confusion can best be illustrated by examples; for instance, a teacher was explaining to a group of students in the southwestern United States a unit which had to do with beach and sea animals. "How many of you have seen a sea horse?" asked the teacher. "What are some of its characteristics—color, size, and texture, for example? From your general information about sea animals, fish, and crustaceans, can you make a guess?" A pupil volunteered the thought that a sea horse

FIGURE 1.13

The children have searched, inquired, and learned. Now they happily present evidence of their new-found understandings and concepts. What types of learning resources do you think have probably been made available to individual members of this group?

must be a swift, powerful animal capable of predatory raids on other sea creatures. As the teacher continued questioning, it was revealed that the student, not having had any firsthand experience with sea horses, quite naturally drew on past experience with creatures of the nearly similar name—''horses.''

In another classroom, the word ''tarantula'' was being explored. A pupil had come across it during his reading and had raised the question of its structure, size, and deadliness. Other learners, not having had any firsthand experiences with the creature, made estimates of its size—which varied from inches to feet—and invented qualities of size and function which not even this remarkable creature could live up to. When the teacher then displayed a specimen tarantula, the enthusiasm with which the learners corrected their impressions was delightful to see.

Referent confusion is common in reading. An author attempts to express his meaning by choosing a series of words which describe experiences he seeks to recreate in the imagination of his readers. Yet how can he be sure that the reader will have similar, or even nearly similar background experiences and resulting understanding when he attempts to interpret the words that the author has chosen? In similar fashion, a teacher attempts to describe an experience in appropriate words. However, as these words are heard and interpreted by 25 pupils, is there any reason to assume that the backgrounds of each of these 25 pupils are as uniform and as dependable as that of the teacher who has chosen words based on his individual experience?

Referent confusion is particularly likely to occur in verbal communication, for differences in frame of reference make it possible for two people to use the same words and yet to arrive at completely different interpretations. In this way, a whole set of communication interference factors

is created. Indeed, it is usually the case that the pupils draw on their own experiences that are related to but often much different from those of the teacher and, consequently, the interpretations the pupils are likely to evolve are colored if not altogether confused.

No teacher can ever be entirely sure that the words he chooses to describe an idea or a process will convey adequate meaning to every one of his students. Each student's unique background influences his interpretation and understanding in a unique way. It is logical that the greater the abstractness or remoteness of the subject described, the less similarity there will be between the meaning the teacher intends and the understanding achieved by the pupil. For example, on crossing the state line into Vermont, a geography teacher's son expressed great surprise at seeing forests of trees instead of the never-ending ''forests of chimneys'' which he had *read* characterized heavily industrialized New England. And a second-grader reported that she had ridden up and down on an ''alligator'' (meaning escalator or elevator) while on a field trip. A high school student was incensed when his grade in English was lowered because he quoted Poe's famous line as ''Quoth the Raven nevertheless.'' Such misstatements made by pupils are, in most cases, caused by referent confusion.

Daydreaming

Another rather common, yet avoidable, block to efficient communication occurs when the learner daydreams; that is, when the pupil turns away from the flow of classroom communication and dwells upon his own private experiences and fantasies. Often these are more interesting, more exciting, and thus more preoccupying than those that are identified with classroom activities. An introspective ''playback'' of last Friday's television thriller or a week-

FIGURE 1.14

Reputation: a quiet, well-mannered child—a "good" pupil. What in-school or out-of-school thoughts might be responsible for this somewhat detached look?

end movie or the reconstruction of scenes from a comic magazine can completely override a pupil's attention to classroom discussion or text assignments. For, in daydreaming, the strongest, the most immediate, or the most completely understood sequence of experiences crowds out the less interesting and the not-so-well understood. Classroom experiences that depend too consistently on verbalism, for example, may be completely rejected, with daydreaming as the inevitable result.

Daydreaming is thus a remarkable defensive device by which the pupil can protect himself against the tedium and boredom of a humdrum classroom environment. Many pupils are remarkably adept at it; some can even smile pleasantly in seeming classroom attention, while actually they are escaping into their private thoughts. Many a daydreamer is thought of as a "good" pupil, since he causes no disrupting influence and no trouble and is just as quiet and orderly as can be (Figure 1.14).

Nevertheless, daydreaming obviously interrupts a pupil's association with the stream of information communicated in the classroom and thus completely thwarts learning from planned classroom activities. The alert teacher is aware of those students who have a tendency to daydream; rather than trying to take punitive measures to prevent it, however, he searches for classroom-generated causes of such behavior. Certainly the daydreaming barrier can be lessened or obliterated through increasing the understandability and interest level of classroom communication by using techniques such as those discussed in the following chapters.

Limited perception

The expressions "Do you see?" and "Do you understand?" have become virtually synonymous. Although strictly speaking, of course, the words "see" and "understand" refer to different psychological processes, it is not by accident that the former is often used in place of the latter in every day conversation. This characteristic of "seeing" what one understands has to do with the cognitive (intellectual) aspects of perception rather than with the physiological acuity of seeing and hearing. Most students have normally functioning sensory mechanisms. Nevertheless, the effects of these mechanisms are influenced by certain psychological aspects of understanding the meanings of perceived data and of learning, aspects that warrant further discussion.

Psychologists have often pointed out that we receive through our sensorimotor apparatus a great deal more than we are aware of. Within our span of vision at any given moment, for example, lie many more objects than we consciously perceive. This limitation of conscious perception is connected with the intellectual aspects of perceiving; it has little to do with the mechanical ability to take in sensory data.

It is well known that appropriate training can increase both visual and auditory learning to a surprising extent merely through enlarging the span of intellectual awareness to match more closely the span of physiological perception. It is possible to more than double a student's ability—indeed, anyone's ability—to acquire factual information from an experience through just such appropriate training. Reading-improvement programs offer a good example of the principles by which the intellectual field of perception may be widened. Ordinarily the eye span—that is, how much a person "sees" instantaneously of a word, a group of words, or a line—directly affects the speed and comprehension with which he reads. Most people can train themselves to increase their visual recognition span, and hence their speed of reading, without loss in comprehension. There are various ways to accomplish

this. In one effective method, the pupil progressively limits the time he takes to recognize a printed word or phrase. Or he increases the length of the word or phrase he can recognize in a fixed interval of time. Another method of increasing one's skill in seeing is to organize one's visual grasp or perception into units. The airline pilot has trained himself to sweep his eyes across the instruments, systematically focusing on each instrument in sequence. Next he moves his field of vision across the horizon of the sky, perhaps following a figure-eight line of sight so as to include sky areas above and below the horizon, and from extreme left to right. All of this is carried out systematically and at precalculated time intervals so that the pilot may note immediately any changes in flight conditions, approaching aircraft, radar signals, or warning and all-clear light signals. The bus driver has a similar visual perception routine to follow.

Several techniques have been developed which have also improved the "seeing" efficiency of pupils. One teacher assembled his pupils outside a hardware store window and instructed one third of them to observe as many objects as possible as they walked by and then to record their observations. The pupils in the next third were also instructed to record the objects they noted as they walked by the window, but, in addition, they were told to classify their perceptions according to large and small objects. The last third were told to walk by the window, to note the objects, to classify them, and then to sweep the window area twice according to the lower and upper halves. This last group recorded more than twice the items reported by the first group and half again as many as had been noted by the second group. In such a way, the span of awareness can be expanded.

When proper listening and viewing techniques are made as much a part of the study situation as is consideration of content, there is a notable increase in the amount of information that pupils can observe and understand.

Physical discomfort

As we all know, one's physical environment can produce either a favorable or an inhibiting emotional tone. Yet for decades little or no attention was given to the physical comfort of the student in the classroom. What thought was given to physical conditions at all tended to be expressed as the dictum, "Learning is a painful process anyway, and some discomfort is good for the pupil." In contrast, private industry has come to recognize that comfortable and efficient working conditions have a definite economic value; witness the many new office buildings with their striking interior decor, air conditioning, soundproofing, carpeting, and lighting systems that can be precisely controlled to supplement—or replace—the available natural light. Chatting with her colleagues over lunch, one teacher remarked to them, "I've just transferred my checking account to the new bank. I like to do business there—air conditioning, wonderful acoustics, and the decor of the interior—just beautiful."

The fact that the need for comfortable physical surroundings applies to classrooms as well as to business establishments has been generally acknowledged only in recent years. In other words, the modern classroom must be thought of as providing a comfortable environment for learning. One expert put it this way:

Classrooms must be carefully remodeled for comfort and pleasantness. The new concept of a learning laboratory instead of a classroom for reluctant learners has a number of merging characteristics:

1 *It must be air conditioned in order to assure greater physical comfort for tense, frustrated learners.*
2 *The floor should be carpeted for improved acoustical effects.*

3 *Color is important and decor makes a notable difference to apathetic students who have been carelessly educated through indifferent attention to their requirements.*[10]

The classroom environment should also be characterized by light control that permits the use of projected materials; temperature control that encourages mental alertness; acoustical treatment that deadens reverberations and permits speaking and listening in comfort. The temperature and acoustics particularly should be automatically controlled.

Specific planning of the physical facilities that are best suited to effective classroom communications will be considered in detail in later chapters. It is worth mentioning briefly here, however, some important developments that have become increasingly widespread in the past few years: Classrooms everywhere are being equipped with the mechanical means of shifting instantaneously from verbal instruction to the use of audiovisual materials and methods. Colleges and universities are constructing entire centers devoted to audiovisual learning. Universities are applying the results of research by building lecture rooms designed to capitalize on the benefits of using the new communications media. For example, the auditorium building shown in Figure 1.15 incorporates many of these innovations, permitting the selection and use of any needed combination of media: slides, films, projectuals, tapes, and others.

The task of the teacher to communicate is of prime importance. To attempt to communicate without taking into account the factors that interfere with efficient communication in our classrooms, however, is to court disaster.

[10] Dr. Frank Brum, Atlantic City Education Seminar, Carnegie Corp., *Honolulu Advertiser*, p. Bl, February 27, 1965.

FIGURE 1.15

An outstanding example of a multimedia facility is the Forum Building at Pennsylvania State University. This building was specifically planned to provide a functional learning environment for large groups through visual media and the maximum use of technological innovations. (a) As the plan shows, the circular building contains four wedge-shaped auditoriums, each seating almost 400 students. Four different presentations may be projected simultaneously from four clusters of equipment in the central core to four rear-projection screens, each facing into one of the auditoriums. Each cluster consists of a 16mm sound motion picture projector, two 2″ × 2″ slide projectors, and two 3½″ × 4″ slide projectors. The building is also equipped with four television projectors, audio mixers, amplifying units, audio recorders, and overhead projectors. Various types of lighting are available, including spotlights and fluorescent lamps. Chalkboard instruction is possible at any time: when an auditorium is dimly lighted, the instructor uses ultraviolet light and fluorescent chalk. (b) In one of the auditoriums, an instructor is using one slide projector to present a specific learning experience; next, he may use two projectors simultaneously. Below the rear-projection screen is the chalkboard. A roll-down front-projection screen for use with an overhead projector is mounted above the chalkboard. (c) Within the central core, the film and slide projectors are positioned above the rear-projection screens. The television projectors on the floor present live studio teaching, videotape recordings of various kinds, or off-the-air telecasts on the screens. (d) Carefully worked-out media experiences are "triggered" by the instructor as he operates the podium controls that activate the projectors. (e) The cross-section diagram shows how each cluster of equipment projects images on the screen across from it. In the level below, instructors prepare and store their instructional materials.

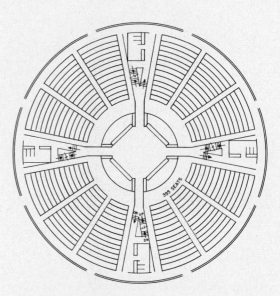

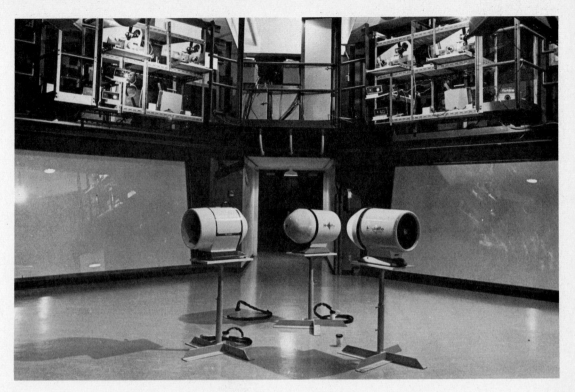

CROSS SECTION
INSTRUCTIONAL AUDITORIUM BUILDING
THE PENNSYLVANIA STATE UNIVERSITY

The toll of inadequate educational communications

NEAR the little village of Clam Lake in northern Wisconsin, there has been installed for use by the U. S. Navy a remarkable underground antenna that can transmit signals over long waves. Because these waves pulsate very slowly, they are so far-reaching that the signals they carry can penetrate the depths of the ocean. This means that instantaneous communication is now possible with deep-running atomic submarines—submarines cruising at depths that used to cut them off from all communication with the surface. Thus one technological leap has extended man's range of communication through hitherto impenetrable barriers.

By contrast, what goes on in the schools? How extensively is man's technological and psychological knowledge used there to break through the barriers to communication discussed in the previous section? In many schools across the United States, more than half of the school day— 58 percent in elementary schools and 53 percent in secondary schools, to be exact— is devoted to instructional experiences and pupil responses that depend on *verbal* stimuli. In these two situations, a large proportion of the time is occupied in listening, and of this time as much as two-thirds is spent heeding the words of the teacher. Nevertheless, when a number of schoolteachers were asked which language skill they judged the most important to teach, only 16 percent of them said they thought listening was essential.[11] Similar conclusions were reached in another study: learners still acquire most of their information through reading.[12]

Thus we are led to a basic question:

11 "Listening," *Encyclopedia of Educational Research*, 4th ed., Macmillan, 1969, p. 747.

12 William S. Gray, "The Sociology of Reading," *Encyclopedia of Educational Research*, 3rd ed., Macmillan, 1960, pp. 1088–1095.

How much time is spent each day in seeing and responding to *media-related* learning experiencies—experiences presented in ways that even to a small degree reflect the sophistication that has been achieved in the out-of-school world? The answer to the question obviously is: "too little time." We must then ask another basic question: How soon will the schools begin to make adequate use of the many kinds of information communications that already exist —the kinds that enable them to transmit certain desired concepts and understandings effectively to learners as they seek their places in the present and future world? This question, unfortunately, is difficult to answer. But it must be answered. More and more people agree that because the schools are *not* heeding the message of the current communications revolution, they are literally driving from their classrooms large numbers of students who otherwise would continue their formal education. These students driven from classrooms are the "dropouts."

The authors strongly believe that though there are many reasons for school dropouts, high on the list is the impasse created when the extraschool communication experiences of learners collide with the antiquated and unchallenging teaching methods that are still used in far too many classroom. It is unrealistic to expect the learner who is in tune with worldwide intercommunication of sight and sound to perform with interest and consistent attention in a classroom dominated by traditional verbal and printed communication techniques. Every time a student drops out, those responsible for the conduct of teaching must look to themselves as the only ones who can analyze the reasons—the only ones who can suggest constructive ways to correct the deficiencies in communication that inevitably are among the reasons.

Although there have been great gains

in the last 20 or so years, the statistics on dropouts nevertheless are alarming. For example, in 1967, 23 percent of those students who had been enrolled in the ninth grade earlier had dropped out of school before graduating from high school. If any business or industry discovered that nearly a quarter of their services or products were ineffectual or defective, one can easily imagine what would happen. At the very least, an immediate meeting of the board of directors would be called, and the fundamental procedures and processes would be closely questioned, thoroughly analyzed, and then changed. Obviously, this is not the case with the public schools; for whatever reasons, the lag in making widespread and concerted efforts to deal with this alarming dropout rate continues.

An analysis of the characteristics of more than a million high school dropouts showed that IQ is not the factor it once was thought to be. The following figures were reported for this group:

IQ of 80 and less—18 percent
IQ of 80 to 89—14 percent
IQ of 90 to 109—47 percent
IQ of 110 and above—11 percent

It has been pointed out repeatedly that the single most important resource any country possesses is its youth. Many people have also pointed out that unless this group in our country acquires a full understanding of their role in the ongoing society, great sociological upheavals may be expected. Many sociological changes are necessary in our society, but if they come about only as the result of upheavals, they are likely to be neither lasting nor effective, and the upheavals themselves are likely to cause grave damage to our social structure and institutions. Leaders are needed who advocate constructive changes but who also work to bring them about through accepted democratic, nonviolent procedures. Such leadership roles usually are expected to be taken by those from the

higher IQ groups; indeed, they usually are. This brings us back to the dropouts and a searching question that must be asked: What do educators have to say when they are confronted with the report that 11 percent of a large group of dropouts had IQs of 110 or above?

It is hard for anyone to explain or justify the fact that about 1 in each 10 dropouts is probably of superior intelligence—a potential leader. Nevertheless, there are several well-known and logical explanations to account for dropouts in general. When teachers are asked why students drop out, they give a number of reasons. For one thing, there are economic pressures. It is true that often one's time and energy may be put to immediate financial use by dropping out of school. On the other hand, as economists point out, the economic advantages of staying in school are great—two and three times the expected life-span earning power of the dropout. Guidance counselors report, on the basis of interviews with students, that boredom, daydreaming, and classroom discipline problems are among the principal impediments to good adjustment to classroom work. Teachers know, of course, that such frustrations severely obstruct the educational process and greatly increase the temptation to drop out.

One investigator recently attempted to describe the typical dropout in terms of a case history:

Mike's problems seemed to have begun when he failed first grade and then eighth grade. Since that time, he has changed schools frequently, he is often tardy, and his attendance has been irregular, with his excuse usually being vague illness. His performance has consistently been below his potential, and most of his grades have been below the average. Mike seems to have feelings of not belonging; he rarely participates in extracurricular activities. His behavior has required disciplinary measures.

Mike's case is descriptive of noninvolvement in the ongoing nature of instruction. Quite obviously, he has found little to challenge his interest and few reasons for taking any initiative. One who observes such behavior realizes that there has been a twofold failure: the goals of teaching and learning have not been successfully communicated to the student; nor has he been confronted with the kind of learning experiences that will challenge his interests.

Often, when remedial work is undertaken, the learner is given the opportunity to individualize his search for information; he is confronted with a wide variety of learning experiences, including 16mm films, picture sets, charts, diagrams, maps, slide sets, tape-recorded information. The inevitable result is a quickening of interest in learning as such. Most teachers realize that the repetitious use of single stimuli may quickly produce disinterest and boredom. Many teachers have learned by experience that variation in classroom procedures and in the selection and use of teaching materials ordinarily heightens the interest and enthusiasm with which pupils approach their work. Because communication techniques available today are so varied, it is unthinkable for a teacher to

delay the introduction of new and effective techniques and materials. The influence of the knowledge explosion has brought dramatic changes in textbook publishing. These changes include increasing varieties of text materials, some of which appear in new formats, including paperbacks; cluster systems or series of related books, programed materials, and texts; and texts that rely on accompanying prerecorded audio materials, filmstrips, or picture sets. All of this is to the good.

As the variety of materials used increases, many textbook publishers have created subsidiary divisions that are exploring and creating programs that interrelate text materials with teaching tapes, language laboratory materials, film and filmstrip sets, programed instructional materials, and series of 8mm and 16mm motion picture films. Supported by the findings of researchers called "new media experts," publishers now produce multimedia learning materials that are "packaged" with textbooks and other educational reading materials. Thus sets of films and filmstrips are produced to accompany tape-recorded materials and taped materials are produced to accompany textbooks. Such multimedia learning packages or learning

FIGURE 1.16

Such media materials as these make it possible to provide the interrelated experiences through which students can use the inquiry method. Depending on the nature of the learners' goals, the appropriate experiences are audio, visual, or tactile, or combinations of these. When the learner can have such multimedia experiences, he is free to move at his own pace toward achieving his self-known goals of investigation. To what extent are such opportunities available to the pupils with whom you work? What barriers might prevent you from giving this kind of learning experience opportunity to your pupils?

kits (see Figure 1.16), when used in their entirety, make it possible for the learner to respond to an interrelated series of media and verbal learning experiences which have proved to be highly productive. All of these developments have come about largely be-cause it has been found that in multimedia learning, each experience, provided that it is appropriate and needed, adds to *and* reinforces those that have preceded it and that each experience prepares learners for *and* thus reinforces the next one.

Some media research generalizations

THOUSANDS of research studies in media-learning relationships have been carried out since 1955. The work of summarizing the accumulated studies has been undertaken by a number of scholars, including Dr. William Allen, University of Southern California; Dr. Wilbur Schramm, Stanford University; Dr. Ray Carpenter; Dr. Loran C. Twyford, New York State Education Department.

A systematic overview of the results of media research supports such generalizations as the following nine:[13]

Generalization 1
The carefully planned classroom use of appropriately selected 16mm and 8mm teaching films can lead learners to greater acquisition of information, understanding, and concepts, identifiable with recent and

accepted curriculum plans and statements of goals.

Generalization 2
The carefully planned classroom use of appropriately selected graphic materials—including charts, diagrams, graphs, flat pictures, and combinations of these—gives to pupils increased conceptualization and understanding, that is, more than they usually gain from verbal explanations.

Generalization 3
The carefully planned use of appropriately selected audio materials—including records, transcriptions, prerecorded tapes, and tape modules—significantly and effectively helps pupils to achieve sought-after learning goals, particularly in social studies, language arts, and foreign languages.

Generalization 4
The carefully planned and systematic classroom use of educational television can accomplish significant increases in learning, particularly in foreign languages, social studies, science, and mathematics.

Generalization 5
The carefully planned use of projected still images—including slides and filmstrips, particularly when integrated with supporting verbal instruction and explanations

[13] The terms "audiovisual materials," "instructional media," and "educational media" are synonymous. The term "media" includes all three of these terms and therefore now usually refers to the broad range of audiovisual materials, programed instruction, and television. The use of this term in this way is supported by *Standards for School Media Programs* (1970), a joint publication of the American Association of School Librarians and the Association for Educational Communications and Technology. More specifically, "media" thus refers to films, filmstrips, recordings, posters, maps, charts, and flat pictures, as well as the newer media learning materials and methods discussed in later chapters, such as programed materials, television, remote-access retrieval systems, computer-assisted instruction, etc.

available either in print or in audio-recorded format—can help learners to accomplish significant increases in learning associated with social studies, science, language arts, and industrial education.

Generalization 6
The carefully planned use of appropriately selected models, specimens, and realia can bring pupils to levels of insights and understandings of relationships and processes in mathematics, social studies, and science above and beyond those possible through verbal explanations.

Generalization 7
Programed instructional learning participated in by pupils who are compatible with the demands of the process produces significant and accelerated learning outcomes.

Generalization 8
Individualized learning modules can be devised which permit learners to proceed at their own pace and learn significantly more information through self-tutorial involvement than if they were bound to keep to the pace of large-group instruction.

Generalization 9
The interrelated use of media selected in terms of goals to be achieved facilitates learning outcomes which reflect with significance the reinforcing effect of such multimedia learning systems.

To sum up, by means of carefully selected and wisely used instructional media, learning experiences may be created that can be used with each other in an interrelated way so as to achieve reinforcing effects in the mind of the learner. Such procedures are discussed and described in the following chapters. These procedures have been and will be referred to by a variety of terms: "multimedia instructional development," "multimedia learning systems," or "media learning systems." Of these terms, we prefer "multimedia instructional development"; this term, in fact, is the title of an entire chapter (Chapter 15) devoted largely to a discussion of actual examples of the achievement of such interrelated organization of learning experiences.

Some trends to be explored

WE have discussed some of the recent developments that are drastically affecting education in the United States: more and more pupils to teach; more content to learn; the necessity to adapt extra-school communication developments to school use; the application of educational communications research to school use. Educators have developed systematic procedures for attempting to handle the new tasks these developments obviously involve. The changing manner of meeting these tasks may be described in terms of two basic media utilization trends:

Trend 1—using media to communicate information and using teachers to teach
In the light of the increasing and more sophisticated use of audiovisual or educational media learning materials, the teacher no longer should consider himself the sole source of information in the classroom. Media have proved beyond all doubt their ability to communicate appropriate content information with efficiency. The result is that the teacher now has time to *teach;* he has time to plan, arrange, and evaluate; even more important, he has time to encourage and counsel pupils.

The teacher-visitor looked up from the pupils' guide to content learning objectives which he had been studying.

"You've taken all the mystery out of teaching," he exclaimed to the teacher. "You've listed openly all that the students want to achieve. You even describe where the information is—prerecorded tapes, film loops, models, and specimens. What's left for the teachers to teach?"

The teacher smiled and then started to reply.

"Let me explain *my* concept of teaching," he began. He waited for his visitor to nod assent and then continued. "Teaching is helping the learners decide, with suggestions from me, what they wish to accomplish—what their goals will be. For example, in this unit on 'Ocean Life Along the Shore,' it's all stated right here." He pointed to the goals listed. "We worked out these goals at the very beginning—the pupils and I—and later we may add or discard some." He turned to the next page. "Here we've tentatively decided what learning experiences we need if we really expect to accumulate enough information to make judgments, draw conclusions, or formulate generalizations about life in the tide pools." He paused.

The visitor studied the two pages. He examined the "experiences needed" list and noted the information source experiences suggested: Visit the shoreline at low tide to collect tide pool specimens; study the film *Carnival of the Sea;* study the 8mm film loops *Coral Colony* and *Sea Hare and Mollusks;* examine specimens of diatoms; listen to prerecorded tapes in *Life in the Tide Pools, Anatomy of a Coral Reef . . .*

"Why, what's left for the teacher? When do you lecture?" the visitor asked eagerly.

"What's left for the teacher?" the instructor repeated, smiling; then he answered the question: "A dozen searches to help organize, a hundred half-truths and discoveries to help straighten out, planning further searches with the few who want to dig deeper on their own, keeping others 'inventing' new ways of using their new-found information or reporting it to their classmates."

"Yes, I agree with you. There are very effective new ways of communicating information. And I can see there still is plenty left for a good teacher to do. But what about you? You've spent years study-ocean science and marine biology, so I should think it would be pointless for you to use all these other ways to communicate information when you're teaching a unit like this one that deals with your own specialty."

"Of course I constantly use my content knowledge as I plan with students and evaluate their work. And I can do that with ease when the unit relates to marine biology. But in that area, as in all science areas, I gratefully rely on learning materials for the actual communication of information. For instance, with words I can't possibly convey the motion and color of reef life the way a well-made 16mm sound motion picture film can. My patience wears thin after I've explained the life cycle of the coral polyp for the fifth time—and some learners need such repetitious explanations! But an 8mm continuous loop film can provide an exact and dependable explanation endlessly. Instructions which I record on tape and evaluate before giving them to students are much more certain to convey meaning about an experimental procedure for studying diatoms than my repeated, on the moment, verbal explanations."

The instructor paused to note the reactions of his visitor, then continued. "It's been a new experience to select and use new learning materials to present information—and I haven't escaped guilt feelings—the feeling that I should be 'teaching it all myself.' But I'm convinced now that information as such can be learned depend-

FIGURE 1.17

The relative roles of the pupils and teacher in the five steps of media learning and the roles of media and the teacher in helping children achieve terminal goals are summarized in these two diagrams. (In the first diagram, black indicates relatively greater emphasis of role than green.) Can you analyze the extent to which you act on the central ideas expressed? Do you approve of all of them or do you have reservations about some?

RELATIONSHIP AND RELATIVE EMPHASES OF
TEACHER AND PUPIL ROLES IN MEDIA LEARNING:

1. Planning the Enviroment   T ⟷ P

2. Interaction with Media   T ⟷ P

3. Response to Media Stimuli   T ⟷ P

4. Evaluation   T ⟷ P

5. Recycling as Needed   T ⟷ P

LEARNER OBJECTIVES

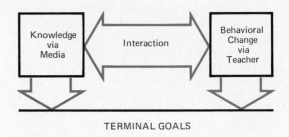

TERMINAL GOALS

ably and efficiently by studying audiovisual materials or by examining things at first-hand while listening to a prerecorded tape 'talk-through.'

"Teaching, to me, is helping learners discover what they need, surrounding them with opportunities for experiencing and discovering useful information, and, most important, being able myself to concentrate on helping them plan their schemes for *using* or *applying* their new-found information."

Seeing a fleeting wrinkle of doubt cloud the face of his visitor, he added, "It's hard to change one's long-practiced ideas isn't it?"

Research evidence has established that information can be communicated more efficiently by using appropriate new media —audiovisual or learning materials—than by using traditional verbal means. When teachers accept this fact and act on it, they discover that they can easily find the time to perform the vital and basic functions of a teacher—those that only a teacher can accomplish: pupil-teacher planning, giving learners access to needed audiovisual or media learning experiences, and, finally, guiding each learner in ways to use his new-found information in creative and inventive manners. Figure 1.17 summarizes the roles of pupils and teacher in media learning and shows how the teacher interacts with media learning.

Trend 2—creating multimedia learning environments

It once was considered almost astonishing if one teacher said to another, "We used a film today" or "Tape recorders are quite remarkable." In other words, it was thought to be an event of some innovational import when a teacher used one of these new media channels. During the last decade, however, not only has the use of these media become fairly common, but much has been learned about the reinforcing effect of interrelated or multiple use of media teaching materials.

"Multimedia learning" refers to the basic strategy underlying the constructive use of a variety of interrelated learning experiences—the strategy that is also referred to as "multimedia instruction" or "multimedia instructional development," the term used as the title of Chapter 15. All three of these terms refer to the selection and use of appropriate sequences of interrelated audiovisual or instructional media learning experiences which reinforce and strengthen one another in furthering the progress of the learner.

The principle of reinforcement is vitally important. If learning experiences are not arranged with reinforcement constantly in mind, there is danger of overwhelming the learner with a kaleidoscope of experiences that do not focus on terminal goals. Thus the use of media in a reinforcing context means that learners are given opportunities to respond *logically*—in a planned way—to stimuli that challenge their senses: seeing, hearing, touching, sometimes even tasting and smelling.

It is obvious that the manner in which interrelated audiovisual or educational media learning experiences are presented to the student is of utmost importance. Strategies have already been mentioned, and others will be described in more detail later, through which media experiences may be presented to students for their greatest possible benefit in large groups and small groups and in self-tutorial situations. Self-tutorial, or independent study, techniques have proved to be highly effective, particularly when information is presented to the learned in many different ways: tape cartridges, 8mm continuous film loops, slide sets, audio tapes, filmstrips, programed instructional packages, sequences of diagrams, displays of specimens or realia, photographs, collections of flat pictures, charts, maps, and so forth.

Children who participate in the kindergarten-through-grade-3 self-tutorial multimedia programs in the public schools of Hawaii spend the first days in learning how to operate simple new media equipment—cassette tape recorders, 8mm film loop projectors, filmstrip projectors, audio card readers, and so on. Once this is accomplished, the children, who range from 5 to 8 years, become self-sufficient as they pursue their own interests in exploring the varied experiences made available through the media equipment.

The applications of these methods in connection with the language skills program in Hawaii are described in detail in Chapter 15, but it seems worthwhile to summarize them briefly here as a specific example. In this program, children working alone, or in some cases with a classmate, learn the sounds of English by manipulating independently 35 sets of magnetic card-reader cards. Later each child learns about prepositions or pronouns or name words by consulting other sequentially organized sets of these cards. Word recognition and phrases and short sentences are learned in the same way. During continued self-tutorial learning, 8mm film loops and plastic-coated exercise books are used to master cursive letters and letter combinations. Prerecorded tapes, in easily identified and used cassettes, enable each child to understand fully certain children's books and at the same time almost automatically improve his reading ability by "visualizing words" (reading) and hearing them spoken at the same time. Stories that greatly interest young children are carefully chosen for recording, stories that become the foundation for the later study of a broad range of literature. Children also begin to discover how to go about creative writing by responding to cassette-taped instructions that lead them ultimately to the effortless

FIGURE 1.18

These children aged 5–8 easily master the
manipulation of equipment and learning materials
used in individual or small-group self-tutorial
learning. (a) This child is engaging in independent mastery of typing skills. He begins this
even before he knows how to read, following
cues from the manual next to him, which gives
all the necessary information in diagram form. By
following pictorial directions, children in the
Hawaii English Project have been successful
in gaining enough skill in typing to compose
original stories. (b) This child is using an audio
magnetic card reader to identify simple word
families by seeing visual cues and at the same
time listening to their spoken counterparts. He
begins by identifying families of similar short
words, then moves on to short phrases and,
finally, simple sentences. As language skills
grow, this child, like many of his classmates,
will become involved in peer teaching. (c) Children use the audio card reader to listen to
simple stories, written and spoken phrase
by phrase on illustrated card groups like
these. (d) Using a cassette tape recorder-
playback, a child reads a prerecorded book as
he listens, matching what he hears
to the identical words in the book. To
provide such experiences, the classroom is
reorganized to include semiprivate work-study
areas for individuals or small groups. Note the
absorption of the children in these pictures as
they pursue and become involved in the activities
of their choice. Unlike adults, these children
have no fears or fixed behaviors to overcome.
What advantages do you see in more widespread
use of this kind of instruction? What new responsibilities are implied? What role do you see
for yourself?

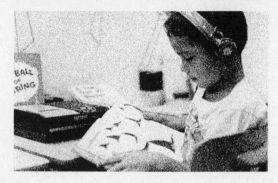

use of electric typewriters, machines that then make it easy for them to put on paper their own thoughts and experiences (see Figure 1.18). During all these activities the teacher is always there to help when help is needed, to evaluate the children's progress, and to advise the learners as they make plans to use their new information in small discussion groups, creative dramatics, creative art, and so forth.

The entire program is continually changing and continually being recycled. The interrelated self-tutorial media learning experiences are constantly improved and reorganized on the basis of professional judgments of significant gains to each learner in terms of content knowledge mastery, manipulative skills, involvement, and creative performance. When a learner fails to learn or when his interest flags, the teacher becomes involved both as an evalu-

ator and a humanitarian. By using his own judgment, the teacher must find alternatives for the student. Thus it is the human teacher who is always the central force in arranging to meet the special needs of each child.

The following chapters of this book are devoted to specific descriptions of ways to select and use media so as to create this type of responsive environment. Thus this chapter has given a preview of theory which will be demonstrated more completely in the rest of the book. Many examples will be included throughout that illustrate the shift toward teacher and student involvement through new ways of using new media. In other words, this book describes the intelligent selection and use of media that can lead to maximum learner involvement and creative response.

Summary

The twentieth century has seen more changes in scientific, technological, and communications developments than had been achieved during all the earlier centuries. The teacher finds himself in the midst of a revolution in communications, classroom strategy, and the very nature of his students.

Never before have virtually all the children of all the people crowded into our schools. Inside the classroom, they reflect both contemporary progress and contemporary dilemmas; thus they reflect both good and bad conditions in our society. These conditions result in dilemmas that confront the teacher who attempts to communicate with efficiency and interest, who attempts to evoke the responses from and produce the favorable behavioral changes in students which are necessary if they are to achieve their goals. Among these dilemmas are the changing school population, the changing curriculum, and the impact of

an exciting, dramatic, almost overwhelming extraschool communication environment.

The basic communication process involves messages traveling from sender to receiver and responses and countermessages traveling from receiver to sender. This process frequently is impeded and even completely obstructed by persisting psychological barriers to effective teaching—verbalism, referent confusion, daydreaming, limited perception, and physical discomfort.

Inadequate educational communications result in boredom with school, dropping out, and entering society ill prepared for the tasks that must be assumed.

Research studies have established definitely that through selection and use of appropriate new educational communications materials—audiovisual media—many of the obstacles to the creation of an environment for effective learning can be overcome. Educational research supports the generalization that instruction can be significantly improved through the wise selection and use of sound motion picture films, filmstrips, programed learning materials, educational television, and the interrelated use of appropriate filmstrips, slides, models and specimens, maps and globes, and charts, all of which are closely related to the reading resources we have learned to use so effectively during the past decade.

The total teaching task is complicated finally by the teacher's realization that he has not been adequately prepared during his professional training to understand, select, and use new instructional materials with efficiency. It is the purpose of this and the following chapters to remedy this situation.

The goal is to describe how media may be used to communicate information, thus freeing the teacher to do what only teachers can do—engage in the humanization of instruction and learning. A second goal is to describe and explain how multimedia environments may be arranged to create lifelike, realistic, and interesting information and skill-learning experiences.

Further learner response projects

1

To supplement the experiences you have read about in this chapter, you should make a real effort to view one or more of the films listed in the References. Report some of your high-point reactions to your fellow students.

2

Arrange a visit to a nearby school, either elementary or secondary. Interview some of the senior teachers and ask them what influences they have felt from the outside-of-school communication world. Ask them also what problems are created by the changing nature of the student group and by changes in the curriculum. Report your findings to your fellow students.

3

Arrange to visit a classroom in order to observe the communication techniques used. As they occur, list any communication barriers that you see within the student group or between the teacher and the students. After the class, discuss some of these with the teacher so as to gain further insight through his comments and reactions. Report your own reactions.

4

Interview some of your fellow students and a sampling of high school students, asking such questions as:
a How many newspapers do you read regularly? Which ones?
b How much time do you spend each day listening to the radio?
c How much time do you spend watching television?
d How much time do you spend reading magazines?
e How many motion pictures do you see each month?
What conclusions do you draw from these interviews?

As their weekly meeting started, the Supervisor of Beginning Teachers asked the group of teacher interns, "What happened this week as you continued the experiment?"

The experiment involved having ready for the arrival of the intermediate graders at the beginning of the school day an *interest-awakening or readiness-arousing event*—insofar as such awakening or arousing is possible. The event was to communicate in and of itself to the learners.

Now the interns began their reports. One started in: "Over the weekend, several friends and I went out on the reef at low tide to net up some diatoms, which is easy. My idea was to set up right on a tabletop near the classroom entrance—where students would practically fall over it when they came in—a microprojector, all focused and projecting a clear image of one or two of the best specimens. As it turned out, we captured a beautiful sea hare in one of the tide pools, and I used this along with the diatoms."

"You got everything all set up before the children got there Monday morning?" the supervisor interjected.

"We surely did." The intern continued, "The diatoms were just beautiful, or so I thought, and the sea hare stayed very much alive in the saltwater aquarium I borrowed from the science lab."

"So—enter the 'learners' and the action begins?" the supervisor encouraged.

"You should have been there. I took up my 'observation post' and—what do you suppose? The first three who came in went right by—even grumbled a little about the way being blocked. And then Tim— noisy Tim we call him—came 'boiling' through the doorway, practically knocked over the whole display, then stopped as if rooted in his tracks. He couldn't get enough of it. Even now, each time I look around, there he is—dipping out a drop of seawater, focusing, drawing—coralling his friends to 'come-see.' Well, the details are on this chart—six, maybe eight, of the 27 'intermediates' were really 'turned on' and ready to search and discover on their own. But, all that work! How can I light a fire under the rest?—if anything will—"

During the rest of the session the seven other interns described their efforts: a current events display of news items, along with a new and very colorful physical-political map of Africa; a sand table forest with a remarkable model of an Algonquin Indian winter home placed dramatically within it; a daylight view unit, all set up with earphones plugged in, ready for the viewing of a new 16mm film, *Visit to Antarctica;* a round table and chairs inviting anyone to sit, pick up an attractive book, switch on the cassette playback, put on the earphones, and respond to a story presented simultaneously in printed and spoken-playback form.

As the discussion developed, one generalization became acceptable to the members of the group: It takes more than one "event" to awaken and engage the interest of *all* the learners who ordinarily make up a normal classroom group. In other words, each learner possesses his own and entirely unique pattern of interests, stages of readiness, and receptor and response capacities.

The implications of this generalization are endless. One of the most important conclusions to be drawn, however, is that the teacher who proposes to investigate the use of media in producing active involvement and desirable behavioral responses in students should expect to experiment endlessly with classroom environments arranged for these purposes. Just as the interns continued their experiments to discover what varieties and patterns of audiovisual communications must be provided if the varied readiness thresholds and interests of individual learners are to be engaged, so must the classroom teacher.

Six tenets of media-related learning

THIS chapter discusses six vital tenets of learning which are so closely related to the effective use of audiovisual communication that they should be considered before we proceed to specific descriptions of media and their nature and uses.

One of the central points made in Chapter 1 is that the broad and varied use of modern communication devices can effectively offset a host of impediments to learning. Nevertheless, no matter how well the devices or the combination of devices seem to serve, *from the teacher's point of view,* if they are to be truly effective for each *learner,* the teacher, in selecting them and the subject matter they are to communicate, must take into account at least the following important tenets of learning:

1. Each learner is unique, particularly with respect to the efficiency of his receptor mechanisms and his response capabilities.

2. Perception is the foundation of learning.

3. The learner must become involved. He must be aware of his purposes and conduct much of his own search for information, skills, and understandings. He must know what performance is expected and become involved in all aspects of the media learning process.

4. Content and the media used to communicate it must be suitable to the learner.

5. Teaching strategies must be appropriate.

6. Creativity is the goal of learning. Creativity becomes evident through the observable responses of learners.

For most effective integration of these tenets into his teaching, the teacher must do the following: (1) determine the learner's level of conceptual attainment as rooted in his previous experience; (2) evaluate the subject matter to be communicated in terms of the level of pupil conceptual ability; (3) select concrete learning experiences which will be best suited to—have the best chance of "reaching"—the pupils at their own levels; (4) select those media which will best provide needed concrete or quasi-concrete learning experiences and at the same time transport the learners higher up the abstraction scale without sacrificing true meaning and understanding in the process; (5) organize the use of media learning experiences in such a way that the pupils' own inventiveness and creativity will be invoked, thus providing a basis for evaluation.

In confronting these tasks, the teacher must start with the students' observable behaviors as prime points of reference. "The proof of the pudding is in the eating"; in other words, the teacher must constantly observe the students' responses to learning experiences and attempt to assess realistically the kinds of knowledge, information, and interpretations the pupils have acquired; the skills they have acquired; and the beliefs which may underlie their observable behaviors. The degree of the completeness or accuracy of the conceptualizations that pupils hold will be demonstrated as they write, discuss, and respond in other ways during class discus-

FIGURE 2.1

These junior high school students are preparing a report on their own plans and discoveries. At this point, what are the most important functions of their teacher? What are some of the judgments she is probably making?

sions, laboratory or creative work sessions, related school activities, and observable out-of-school situations. The observable behavior of learners provides the only reliable measure of the relative efficiency and accuracy with which the subject matter has been assimilated, conceptualized, and used by each learner (see Figure 2.1).

1. Each learner is unique

Because each learner is a unique bundle of receptor and response capacities, many challenges are created as one goes about providing a dynamic environment for learning which can be depended on to achieve at least predetermined goals. This uniqueness is shown in a description of the reactions of a group of suburban adults and young people who had decided that none of them would be truly involved with "relevancy" unless they went together to see a performance of the play *Hair*:

The group, varying in age from middle-aged couples to youngsters in their teens, discussed with keenness the anticipated event. Beforehand, they had learned that the play differs—sometimes the cast takes off its clothes at a point in the play, sometimes it doesn't.

After we had gone through this amazing company of sight and sound, we came out and were walking across the parking lot, and our middle-aged spinster friend said, "Well, I guess the cast didn't feel like taking off their clothes today."

And we looked at her in utter horror and surprise; all of us then said, "But they did!" And for 15 or 30 seconds, there they were—completely motionless, completely nude, in front of the audience. She had not seen it.

A little later, as we were driving home, I began to talk about the chickens. I raised the question as to how they could have kept so calm. Toward the end of the play, the chickens were back on the scene wandering about very peacefully, and I assumed that they had been drugged.

Steve, our 16-year-old boy, said, "What chickens?"

We had had enormously different individualized experiences.[1]

[1] John I. Goodlad, "Providing Dynamic Environment and Learning," *Educational Broadcasting Review*, Vol. 3, 1969, Convention Report, Special Issue, p. 53.

Many of you will say, "But we all know people react differently to experiences." Nevertheless, the *degree* to which variations exist should constantly be kept in mind by teachers, particularly by those who seek and use intelligently clear-cut, dynamic media learning materials.

Another example of individual differences in reception is provided in the delightful story of a young child who had been placed by his father on the back of a mule, the better to watch a wonderful circus. After the performance, the father asked the child, "What did you like the most of all you saw at the circus?"

"The two long ears of the mule," the child answered.[2]

The interests and purposes of the father who placed the child on the mule and the child who observed the circus were entirely different and obviously unknown one to the other. How often do such circumstances pervade the classroom, where they multiply in complexity as *one* teacher and *his* goals and purposes may be accepted or ignored by each one of the 25 to 35 pupils who confront him?

Why were there such variations in responses to seemingly similar stimuli among the people who saw *Hair* and between the adult and child at the circus? This is a good time to examine Figure 2.2, which gives a partial explanation. After you have studied the figure, consider another example of variations in responses —this time among the members of a typical classroom group involved in a study trip learning experience:

The junior high school students stood before the amazingly complicated assembly line at an automobile assembly plant. As they watched a frame being moved into place, the body being swung into position

above it, the advance and retreat of automatic screw and bolt tighteners securing the two together—all this produced visual, auditory, and even olfactory stimuli which flooded into the "receptors" of the watching learners. As the receptors responded, stage after stage, one could imagine the scene of activity within the various zones of the eyes, ears, and noses—perhaps even the pressure-sensitive tactile cells of the skin became involved—as wave on wave of chemically and pressure-induced nerve impulses and corresponding electronic counterparts constantly flowed, crisscrossed, and interacted on their ways to the conceptualiza-

FIGURE 2.2

Any individual responds to audio and visual stimuli in ways that both produce and reflect the marks of his own personality. At any or all stages of reception, endless variations may occur among learners. Similar individual differences occur in tactile, olfactory, and gustatory reception-response systems. What implications do these variations have for a teacher's expectations of students' reception of and response to classroom learning experiences?

[2] G. Mialaret, *The Psychology of the Use of Audio Visual Aids in Primary Education*, United Nations Educational, Scientific and Cultural Organization, Paris, 1966, p. 53.

tion, storage, or response zones of the inner brains of the learners.

Some knowledge was gained. This was evident when the group was back in the classroom and given the opportunity to respond. Responses through verbal discussion and proposals for graphics (diagrams, pictures, a mural, etc.) and for further study and search showed the nature of and manner in which the field study experiences were interpreted by each of the learners. No two learners responded in the same way. Indeed, there was an astonishing number of variations in what individual pupils had seen, thought they had seen, and had not

seen. As a result, omissions, careful observation of details, and desire to search further were all among the responses.

The implications of such incidents are well known to most teachers: wide variations in reception, perception, and response, due to individual differences, may be expected from a group of learners during their interaction in any learning experience. The teacher soon realizes that it is folly to expect that learning experiences presented to large groups of students may accomplish uniform mastery of skills, concepts, or understandings or that such learning outcomes may be uniformly applied as

Stages of visual reception

Stages of audio reception

1

Light waves enter the eye
Individual differences occur as light beams become refracted and distorted on way to retina.

Sound waves reach the eardrum
Individual differences occur as chain of ossicles alters waves to pressures which are transmitted to the cochlea.

2

Creation of optical nerve impulses
Individual differences occur as retinal cells transform light energy into electrical energy.

Creation of audio nerve impulses
Individual differences occur as inner-ear corti cells respond to create nerve impulses by lengthening and contracting.

3

Transmission of nerve impulses
Individual differences occur as nerve impulses are passed inward over a series of nerve relays.

Transmission of nerve impulses
Individual differences occur as nerve impulses are passed inward over auditory nerve.

4

Cortical perception
Great individual differences occur in little-understood inner-brain mechanisms which suppress or select and process impulses for perception and possible response.

Cortical reception
Great individual differences occur in the efficiency of inner-brain mechanisms which suppress or select and process impulses for perception and possible response.

5

Response
Great individual differences occur in response-conditioning factors: physical skills, existing inventories of concepts, principles, interests, etc.

Response
Great individual differences occur in response-conditioning factors: physical skills, existing inventories of concepts, principles, interests, etc.

FIGURE 2.3

These pupils are about to respond individually to media-originated stimuli. Why does individual use of media reduce the errors usually experienced in traditional large-group learning situations? How does the use of learning materials such as these enable us to take advantage of what we know about individual differences in reception and response?

students attempt to solve problems or attain uniform performance goals. Nevertheless, the teacher may attain greater control over the efficiency of planned learning arrangements if he follows these suggestions:

1. Organize learning in such a way as to acknowledge the presence of individual differences of reception, perception, and response; that is, use individualized and small-group instruction, as well as the traditional large-group instruction ordinarily associated with teacher and classroom organization.

2. Arrange for a variety of alternative and varied, though appropriate, learning experiences that are used and responded to by learners; that is, make avail-

able printed sources, diagrams, motion pictures, charts, flat pictures, filmstrips, audio tapes—all to provide reinforcement as choices are made by pupils, each in terms of his own pattern of interests.

3. Organize instruction to allow frequent responses of individuals so as to reveal better the nature and accuracy of their conceptualizations and understandings.

Specific procedures will be described and illustrated later for organizing learners for individualized instruction or into small groups, the members may have similar interests, more uniform background, and some of the skills necessary to interpret their new-found information (see Figure 2.3).

Now let us examine the next very closely related tenet.

2. Perception is the foundation of learning

The eyes, the ears, the nerve endings of our nose and mouth that respond to odors and tastes, and the nerve endings of our skin that respond to pressure and heat and cold—these are the means through which we come to perceive and understand our environment. As has been said, the efficiency of these receptive mechanisms varies among individuals as much as the individuals themselves vary. Nevertheless, since these perceptor sensory mechanisms are the continuing contact with our world of things and events, we must take into account and understand the limitations of reception per se.

Our receptive mechanisms do nothing more than feed us data—sensory impressions—and thus are not responsible in themselves for the coherent ''pictures'' we receive of the objects and events that take place in the outer world. Once the processes of reception per se have been accomplished, the bewildering processes of the perceptual mechanisms of the internal brain—about which we know relatively little—receive and interpret the various impressions, which then become organized into meaningful understanding. Thus it is that any

given perceptual event is a pattern composed of the multiple sensory messages that are sensed by all or any of the learner's perceptual mechanisms that have been stimulated by external occurrences. Because perceptual events do not occur in isolation from one another but, rather, are continuously occurring as a result of constant sensory stimulation, there are also constant shuffling and reshuffling, arranging and rearranging, and selection and reselection of sensory impressions and patterns of these into still larger combinations of patterns. This process leads ultimately to an organized thought pattern which we may call a ''concept.'' Kingsley summarizes it thus:

In perception we apprehend objects or events. When we perceive, we translate impressions made upon our senses by stimuli from our environment into awareness of objects or events. . . . The objects and events of which we become aware are regarded in perception as present and going on. This activity of perceiving is such a universal and intimate feature of our mental life that it is often difficult to realize that objects of the physical world do not merely present themselves and that we do anything more than open our minds to receive them as they really are. It is easy to overlook the fact that we construct our world of things and events out of our sensory processes and that physical objects as we know them through sight, sound, taste, smell, and touch are products of our own perceptions. . . .
Widely differing qualities of sensory experience depend upon the organs of sense and upon the nervous system. They are the basis of our knowledge of the world about us. Without them, there would be no awareness of anything.[3]

In general, the more thoroughly one experiences his environment and assimilates received messages into understand-

[3] Howard L. Kingsley, *The Nature and Conditions of Learning*, Prentice-Hall, 1947, p. 262.

ings and concepts, the more sophisticated he becomes as a learner. Ordinarily, learners who have accumulated more and more complete inventories of understandings and concepts have these working tools available to them as they seek to apply their experiences to the solutions of problems, for example, the interpretation of words or symbols. Having acquired understandings about reality ordinarily enables the learner to become aware of how real experiences may be referred to through words, symbols, or colors.

The factory worker who has burned himself or cut himself on accidentally coming in contact with portions of machinery painted red understands that future contacts with red-marked machinery parts are likely to cause pain and suffering. To this worker, "redness" becomes a "cue" associated with real experiences with pain. The American driving in Europe understands and acts on the international highway symbols by associating his own background experiences with the pictured symbols he sees on signs: stopping for an open bridge, skidding across a tight curve, narrowly avoiding a collision with another car entering the main highway from a side road, and so on.

The process of associating understandings gained from real or partly real experiences with word symbols is dramatically illustrated by the remarkable vocabulary developed by young learners who avidly follow television, radio, and picture-story magazine descriptions of current space events. Merely listen to such imaginative play as this, as it takes place on countless playgrounds, to realize the extent to which vocabulary can be developed *if* learners are able to experience appropriately:

"This is lunanaut[4] Freddie to spacecraft command module, Apollo 14."

"I read you, lunanaut, prepare for lunar module touchdown" (not football!).

"Lunar touchdown coming up at about eleven hundred minus thirty."

"To lunanaut Freddie! To lunanaut Freddie! Touchdown recorded. Slight moonquake shows on my computer screen."

"I report very little moon dust. I repeat, very little moon dust."

"Good work, lunanaut Freddie. Prepare for EVA at exactly eleven hundred plus fifteen."

"Extra-vehicular activity preparation about to begin."

The creative "play" goes on in this vein for some minutes, but then, to paraphrase an old joke, the children stop playing and return indoors to take up their seat work in intermediate readers in which an additional 50 words chosen from the 1955 edition of one of the standardized word lists are the focus of the lesson.

Similar implications are reported by Robert M. Gagné as he describes the manner in which a learner who has had many experiences and acquired resultant understandings and concepts may apply these to later problem-solving processes, particularly reading:

The sophisticated learner has little difficulty in learning concepts and principles, in any content field, under learning conditions that include verbal representations of stimuli. But the inexperienced learner may have serious difficulty. This is because the experienced learner is well aware that words are merely representations of reality; that it is the referents of the words that are the true stimuli, not the words themselves. The inexperienced learner may not have acquired this basic strategy, and therefore may fall into the trap of learning mere words or word sequences.[5]

---

[4] *Encyclopaedia Britannica Book of the Year— New Words of the Decade,* 1970, p. 797.

[5] Raymond V. Wilman and Wesley C. Mierhenry, eds., *Educational Media: Theory into Practice,* Charles Merrill, 1969, p. 105.

Considering what has been said, one may generalize that any understanding or conceptualization has its basis in reality—concrete experiences or reasonable portrayals of them. Aspects of this generalization may be associated with all avenues of content learning. It is apparent in the statement of the art teacher who reports that when pupils have mastered some of the skills—manipulation of charcoal, brush, or clay—it is the child who has experienced widely, has traveled, and who has observed at firsthand people, places, and things who is most likely to use his new-found skills to express himself through creative drawing, mural painting, ceramics, and so on. The language arts teacher reports that the child most able to engage in creative writing is one whose head teems with understandings and conceptualizations gained from reading, play-going, televiewing, film viewing, picture study, travel, continuing observation of the community through which he moves, and so forth.

In other words, as one acquires concepts, this learning, in turn, enables him to cognize additional aspects of his objective environment and to build even larger, more encompassing concepts; similarly, these abstract concepts provide the experiential background needed by the individual to perceive and to understand increasingly less tangible aspects of his objective world, which lead to ever more abstract concepts, and so forth. It should be noted, however, that where the *concrete* basis for abstract conceptualization is lacking, acquisition by the individual of the concept involved will be inadequate at the least and perhaps may not take place at all.

Athough most primary teachers acknowledge that before the word must come the idea, the teachers of upper grades, high school, and even college must also assume the responsibility for being sure that the background experiences which underlie comprehension of the printed word are provided for the student's conscious experience and understanding. This is as true of the college freshman enrolled in biology, mathematics, or the social history of the United States as it is of the second-grader in a social studies class. For without a sufficient conceptual foundation, not only is the learning process likely to be severely impaired, but also the thinking process itself will be severely limited (see Figure 2.4).

To sum up, perception refers to "the

FIGURE 2.4

Can you describe the receptor-response processes that occur as this child observes and handles the baby chick? What relationship may this event have to later experiences with abstract references during language arts discussions, reading, writing, art expression, and so forth?

ways in which man senses or becomes immediately aware of his environment."[6] The process of understanding must begin with perception. If perception is to lead to *valid* understandings, however, the following three generalizations, which have resulted from research studies, are among those that must be taken into account:

1. The better an object, person, event, or relationship is perceived, the better it can be understood (and remembered).[7]

2. Correct initial perceptions facilitate learning; misperceptions impede it.[8] Thus a student who correctly perceives the intent or content of a picture, graphic, or paragraph has a distinct advantage; if he misperceives it, he may not only misunderstand but also learn false or irrelevant information.

3. Where it is desirable, as in most of education, to substitute vicarious for firsthand experiences—for example, as with drawings, pictures, textbooks, and films—it is important that these substitutes (surrogates) adequately represent reality from a perceptual standpoint.[9]

PERCEPTION AND THINKING When confronted with a learning problem, the

[6] Malcolm L. Fleming, *Perceptual Principles for the Design of Instructional Materials*, Final Report, Project 9-E-001, Grant No. OEG-5-9-245001-0016 (010), Bureau of Research, U. S. Office of Education, 1970, p. 1.

[7] Bernard Berelson and Gary A. Steiner, *Human Behavior: An Inventory of Scientific Findings*, Harcourt, Brace & World, 1964, p. 18.

[8] Julian E. Hochberg, *Perception*, Prentice-Hall, 1966, p. 2.

[9] Ibid. Any student, whether or not he has taken a course in educational psychology, will find it valuable to review at this point some of the theories of the stages of cognitive development and of perception by means of ikonic and symbolic signs in a standard educational psychology text; for example, Herbert J. Klausmeier and Richard E. Ripple, *Learning and Human Abilities: Educational Psychology*, 3rd ed., Harper & Row, 1971, pp. 405–429.

learner becomes involved in the thinking process. If the problem is clearly understood, if it is interesting and challenging to the learner, and if it is not so difficult as to discourage him, the learner will begin to search his mind for and to select appropriate information and concepts which may apply to the solution of the problem. He may be able to recall such background knowledge or he may have to search beyond his own mind for new information. He may do the latter through reading, discussion, or interviews or, if his concrete background for the learning task is insufficient, he may seek new perceptual experiences through observation, examination, or experimentation. If the pupil is rewarded in his search, he will blend the newly acquired information into an answer to the learning problem or, failing to do this, he may give up and leave the task unfinished.

Adults, of course, are generally better thinkers than children, for they have had broader and deeper experiences with both the concrete and the abstract foundations of thought. Teachers are all too quick to forget how limited their pupils are in the number, variety, and scope of perceived experiences in relation to their own. It is unlikely that many, if any, of a teacher's pupils have it within their ability to draw on as wide a variety of background experiences which can be recalled as easily on exposure to mere verbal cues as can the teacher. Indeed, it is too often the case that, although the pupils may have learned the *words* used by the teacher or the textbook, they may not have the corresponding firsthand experience necessary to understand the true ideas behind the words.

We are still teaching mainly with a rapidly increasing abundance of reading and verbal materials. In addition to stacks of books such as those shown in Figure 2.5, there is also the recent emphasis on programed learning materials, most of which demand reading skills; television instruction in which the televised teacher mostly

FIGURE 2.5

Printed words are intended to communicate the author's experiences and ideas by cuing the reader's existing store of experiences, facts, and concepts. The teacher's responsibility is to provide the experiences that will give the readers the ability to understand the author's meaning.

talks; and a wide variety of workbooks and pupil manuals which are based on the ability to read and write. As a consequence of this heavy reliance on verbal materials, many seemingly successful pupils spend more time learning new word patterns than they do new *idea* patterns. They become adept at recognizing parts of speech and sentence construction and they easily record verbalized facts in their memories; consequently, it is not difficult for these pupils to answer a test question in such a way that it *seems* as if they truly comprehend the idea behind the question. In actuality, however, the real significance of the facts and their relationships may be quite vague in these pupils' minds, in which case the true thinking or problem-solving process is severely limited.

The orderly process of thinking, then, involves the learner's selection of his own background experiences and concepts that apply to the solution of a problem and the discarding of those that do not apply. Conceptualization and understanding are the outcomes of perceptual or real experiences with events or things. Clearly, the basis for thinking is a broad background of perceptual experiences.

One important goal of education has been reached when individuals have acquired sufficient conceptual understanding of a wide scope to be able to handle reflective thinking and problem-solving with respect to a wide range of objective phenomena by means of symbols—words, numerals, and other cues—rather than having to refer continually to the direct experi-

FIGURE 2.6

The interrelationships of concrete, quasi-concrete (or simulated), and abstract learning experiences with concept formation. What generalization can you propose which would serve as a reliable basis for your own teaching procedures?

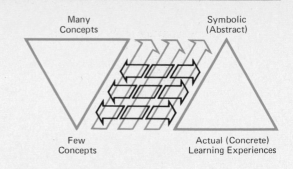

Many Concepts

Symbolic (Abstract)

Few Concepts

Actual (Concrete) Learning Experiences

ences for which these symbols stand. But without a sufficiently broad base of direct experiences, this goal cannot be achieved.

Figure 2.6 depicts graphically how this concrete-to-abstract learning takes place. The triangle at the left reveals how the pupil begins with few or no true concepts and gradually builds from primitive concepts—which are narrow in scope and simple in nature—to a larger range of increasingly complex and inclusive concepts. The means by which the pupil acquires this learning proceed in a reverse manner (right-hand triangle). He must have many and diverse opportunities for concrete and direct experience from which to build concepts. Only gradually does he become less dependent on these experiences in order to acquire new concepts. Finally he can expand his understanding of his world through indirect experiences derived from symbols.

Ideally, the teacher recognizes that pupils who are relatively low on the concept scale need to have a maximum of new learning opportunities presented in concrete situations. As pupils advance higher on this scale, more abstract experiences provided through more abstract symbolic or verbal experiences may prove to be appropriate. Progress in the concept scale may move in varied directions. Often a student's progress seems to be arrested when in fact the pupil has only temporarily returned to basic, direct experiences in order that he may fill important gaps in his understand-

ing. It is unlikely, for example, that a musically gifted student might try to improvise his own musical arrangements from simple aspects of his learnings rather than to proceed directly to more advanced material.

It is worth mentioning at this point that, during recent years, much has been written about "education for excellence," "accelerated study programs," and increasing "challenges." Unfortunately, in many cases, teachers have interpreted this movement as a signal to lengthen assignments, to increase homework, or, in general, to move ahead by increasing the pace so as to invade course content formerly designated for a grade or two beyond. This has taken its toll, as efforts to "get tough" usually do. Often the results are pupil maladjustment, irate parental reactions, and teacher frustration. Most attempts to meet the demands of modern educational-improvement programs have failed to accommodate the pupils' needs for the sequential steps that lead to this advanced and accelerated learning. Or if theoretically these steps have been built into the new curriculum "ladder," teachers have not provided sufficient time for the pupils to assimilate the information they are supposed to learn from each step. More than likely the teacher, in his efforts to cram in the required subject matter, has failed to draw on the pupils' own experience and has perhaps proceeded too quickly to the abstract levels of information-giving instead of providing the necessary opportunities for concrete experience.

Yet, in most cases, accelerated curriculum programs can be utilized within the suggested period of time with no loss in learning efficiency—in fact, they can result in greater learning efficiency—when the subject matter is presented in terms of the students' existing interests and background knowledge. Indeed, the teacher may find that he can proceed quite rapidly and with great teaching success; but this can only be possible after he has paid due attention to the levels—or thresholds—of interests, ability, and conceptual development among the learners.

It is particularly helpful, both to the teacher and to the pupils, if the teacher includes in his evaluation of pupil readiness those extraschool aspects of the pupils' lives that are usually overlooked by school personnel as irrelevant to class activities. The special world of childhood is always of much more interest and relevance to the pupils themselves than is the world adults know; yet adults, including teachers, typically ignore its intriguing facets as trivial and meaningless. The alert teacher pays due respect to these more immediately interesting aspects of the pupils' world, noticing the concepts the children have acquired from their experience with their own world and drawing on these concepts and experiences to lead the children toward those which are involved in classroom learning goals.

An understanding of the relationship between known concept levels and needs in terms of direct or increasingly sophisticated learning experiences enables the teacher to help his class move steadily toward the top of both of the scales shown in Figure 2.6. The goal is to employ such classroom plans, materials, and techniques as will permit students to advance upward on the achievement scale, starting from their own levels. Significantly, between the base and the apex of the right-hand triangle in Figure 2.6 lie various levels of communication devices which range from the most basic and direct perceptual experience with people, objects, and events; upward through simulated firsthand experience provided through appropriately selected motion picture films, recordings, slides; still higher through semisymbolic media such as graphs, diagrams, charts; and finally to symbols which have little visible relationship with their referents—numerals, math symbols, and words (Figure 2.7).

FIGURE 2.7

A graph showing Japan's imports and exports was the outcome of a pupil project. What learning activities preceded the completion of this project? Where on the two scales of the concept-media diagram (Figure 2.6) would you place these pupils? Where do they go from here?

PERCEPTION AND ATTITUDE FORMA-
TION Integrally bound up with the thinking process, and exerting a strong influence
on the outcomes of this process, are the attitudes the learner acquires as he proceeds
up the ladder from the concrete to the abstract levels of learning and thinking. Although an attitude is not the same thing
as a concept, the learner acquires attitudes
toward his perceptions at the same time
that he acquires concepts of them; and just
as one's store of concepts provides the basis
for his further cognition of the world, so
his previously acquired attitudes provide
the basis for acquiring additional attitudes
or changing old ones. These attitudes can
even serve to influence what aspects of his
perceivable world the learner will select to
include in his further perception and learning. Thus attitudes can strongly color what
the learner comes to know, the thinking
process by which he comes to know it, and
any further learning that is based on his
acquired knowledge. Indeed, the attitudes
one acquires along with facts and concepts
can exercise a strong influence on his orientation to *learning itself*.

But what is an attitude? There are
many descriptions of attitudes which might
be given, but one which serves our purpose
well has been voiced by Gordon W. Allport:
"An attitude is a mental and neural state
of readiness, organized through experience,
exerting a directive or dynamic influence
upon the individual's response to all objects and situations with which it is related."[10]

The formation of attitudes can take
place in many ways: through the concomitant pleasure or pain that accompanies perception and cognition; as a result of rewards or frustrations that seem to the
learner to follow the learned information or
its application; through a lack of sufficient

[10] Gordon W. Allport, *Attitudes: A Handbook of
Social Psychology*, Clark University Press, 1935,
p. 810.

facts and concrete experience needed to
round out one's conceptual understanding
of something; or as a consequence of exposure to the attitudes held by influential
people in the learner's social sphere. One
illustration of attitude formation is provided by a group that was studying Japan.
At the beginning of the unit, Japan was
to the students a vague, contradictory place
of cherry blossoms, bound feet, strange music, aggressive militarism, and fawning pas-
sivity. "Strangeness" and "quaintness"
best represented the overall attitudes of the
learners toward the country and its people.
In all probability, these feelings had been
acquired from attitudes that prevailed in
the students' homes, from inadequate or
half-truths believed by the parents as a result of the parents' own only partially adequate school experiences.

Attitude formation may start during
conversations around the dinner table as
children listen to parental views. Parents'
expressions about history, for example, may
arouse or deaden the child's desire to investigate American history. Specifically, a
child's awareness of the idea of "frontiers-
men" or "pioneers" may spring from
purely emotional experiences gained in
home conversations about the subject or
perhaps from television viewing. Today's
schools must acknowledge the attitudes with
which pupils enter their classes and provide
the means by which erroneous attitudes can
be replaced by those which square more
accurately with the facts. Simulated realistic experiences can be collected and arranged for pupils by a teacher who has been
carefully trained or, better, one who has
participated in many firsthand experiences
himself. One advantage the Japan study
group enjoyed was that the teacher had
been to Japan and had observed for himself
the modern Japanese culture, and thus he
was able to provide his class with his own
realistic attitudes in addition to the materials he selected for fact learning and
concept building. While we can't send all

teachers around the world, it is the present-day responsibility of the teacher to investigate current communication materials that are most likely to foster realistic attitudes as well as accurate and complete information.

The diagrammatic representation in Figure 2.8 shows the multidirectional relationships that exist among concrete experiential backgrounds, recalled perception, attitudes, and thinking. Although the diagram shows three levels of development—*perceptual, thinking,* and *attitudinal*—all are endlessly intermeshed and interrelated. As a learner attacks a learning problem, his thinking may be influenced by an attitude that has been well established in his mind, if only on an emotional basis. As he seeks further information through discussion, additional concrete experiences, interviews, and reading, he will quite automatically select those aspects of the data that are most in keeping with this attitude and screen out those that do not fit into the previously established matrix of his accumulated experience. Clearly, such "colored" thinking can be detrimental to the accuracy of the final outcomes of his learning.

In the classroom the teacher has an opportunity to modify or influence the pupils' attitudinal background and actually to build new attitudes. The alert teacher will be as aware of the faulty or undesirable attitudes held by his pupils as he will be of the inaccuracy of their factual understanding. It should be noted, however, that in too many cases teachers themselves perpetuate and reinforce faulty pupil attitudes because of their own attitudes. Yet, by supplying positive and concrete opportunities for perceptual experience, the teacher can help children to transcend their inadequate attitudes and to acquire those which are at once socially desirable and realistically oriented to the objective environment.

Inappropriate attitudes toward the "pioneer" idea, for example, can be altered through classroom study situations which give realistic experiences of pioneer life, thus fostering a clearer conceptual understanding. Concrete experiences provided in school may include exposure to models of pioneer villages and trips to a museum (or a restored village, if possible) to examine pioneer home construction, costumes, utensils, and other tangible aspects of frontier

FIGURE 2.8

Reflective thinking is a more useful basis for developing realistic attitudes than emotion.

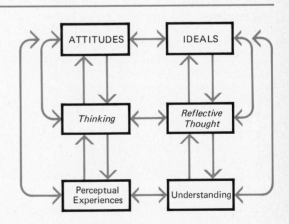

living. A well-planned bulletin board with illustrations can help to visualize pioneer life. A motion picture film often shows, in an interesting but not overly romanticized presentation, a reconstructed frontier village complete with people who talk in the pioneer manner. These added experiences and understandings can alter a pupil's original attitude, or even replace it with an entirely new one, as attitudes based on imitation or emotion give way to those the learner himself forms on the basis of his new concrete experiences, thinking, and conceptualization.

3. The learner must become involved

The idea that the learner, to be successful, must interact with the elements of the environment among which he searches and explores is one of the central areas of agreement among specialists in the psychology of learning. The learner must know what he is expected to do. He should, whenever possible, have a hand in establishing the purposes of the learning experience and be given the opportunity to search, discover, and experience on his own and at his own rate. It is fortunate that the very nature of new media instructional learning experiences makes it feasible for the learner to become deeply involved in his own purposing, questing, and discovering.

As teachers explore the use of media in the improvement of learning, they should consider and apply such guidelines as these, which have been evolved from research and experience:

1. Learners usually participate whole-heartedly in any activities they help to plan.

2. Learners are likely to exhibit apathy and "learn" to escape responsibility if direction by the teacher is excessive.

3. Learners tend to progress toward the completion of a learning activity in terms of their own purposes. Usually, the greater the learners' participation in set-

ting purposes, the higher is the level of achievement each seeks.[11]

All of the above may be identified as reasons for engaging in so-called pupil-teacher planning, a process which, despite its name, all too often actually consists of planning by the teacher, with little or no pupil involvement. Since the teacher is ultimately responsible for seeing that adequate progress is made in his classroom, he must, of course, make sure that broad agreements on curriculum goals are followed. When he has made this clear to the pupils, however, genuine pupil-teacher planning can take place if the teacher encourages learners to engage in planning, particularly of the kind that reveals pupil thresholds of interest, information about the subject, curiosity about further inquiry and discovery, and, most important, eagerness to participate in the location, evaluation, and use of media learning experiences. Consider an example:

A teacher of English literature had informed the pupils that their next adventure would be to learn more about Shakespeare by reading and researching the play *A Midsummer Night's Dream*. The teacher had spent most of the period reading passages that introduced several of the main characters and gave a hint or two of the plot. Then he made it known that it was to be the privilege of the group to plan for special ways to continue the study. Such a transferring of responsibility sometimes is not accepted at once. However, there usually are a few students in any group who will lead the way. In this case, the process had been developed over several semesters, with the result that the activities and projects that finally survived the pro and con evaluations of the students and their teacher stimulated the formation of small groups, which searched, reported, and cre-

[11] Adapted from Goodwin Watson, *What Psychology Can We Trust?*, Teachers College Press, Columbia University, 1961, p. 5.

ated in terms of their own specific interests.

Individuals and teams of students spent hours searching for materials in the English learning resource center and the community library—many more hours than the teacher, planning alone, would ever have dared suggest. Soon the results of the search were evident in the classroom. Picture and poster displays showing life in Shakespeare's time were exhibited by one group. A short film on the Shakespearean theater was introduced, shown, and explained by another. Recordings of selected passages from the play read by several great Shakespearean actors were played. Other pupils read passages themselves. Finally, plans were completed and set in motion for several of the groups to stage their own creative re-enactment of episodes that could be presented in today's social setting. To sum up, this teacher reported that such pupil participation in planning accomplished levels of activities that no possible number of suggestions from him alone could have brought forth.

Research studies on pupil involvement in goal-setting in connection with the use of audiovisual learning experiences yield clearly defined evidence that justifies the following generalization: When students are encouraged to set forth their *purposes* for viewing a motion picture film, listening to prerecorded audio tapes, participating in community study activities, and so forth, not only will significantly greater understanding and conceptualization occur, but learners will also be more likely to use such new-found information in creative and inventive ways.

In the social studies, a group of junior high school students helped in developing purposes for their study of the Navajos. Their search for materials in their library media center revealed the usual filmstrips, recordings of chants and songs, a few artifacts, and several sound films. Then members of one of the planning groups decided that to really understand these people and

particularly their children, they should pay them a visit.

"And we did just that," their teacher reported. "The fact that we live in Hawaii and the Navajos 3,000 miles to the east across the Pacific and the mainland made no difference to them. No one ever told these kids they couldn't do it—so they did." The cost of the trip at first seemed an almost insuperable obstacle, but the children worked at extra jobs at home, in the neighborhood, and in the community to raise money; some made small withdrawals from their savings. Parents contributed, and local businessmen who heard about the project made voluntary contributions. Quite soon, enough money was available. (For further details, see Chapter 6.)

During this time of the explosion of knowledge, if for no other reason, the opportunities of questing through the increasing number of outstanding new media learning materials in school learning resource collections must be shared with those students who possess the interest and ability. As students share in this, they gain the sense of being involved, of planning and of creating—creating opportunities that not even the best and most experienced teacher can always anticipate.

The benefits that come to learners who become truly involved in learning experiences are implied in this statement:

The best way to help pupils form a general concept is to present the concept in numerous and varied specific situations, contrasting experiences with and without the desired concept, then to encourage precise formulations of the general idea and its applications in situations different from those in which the concept was learned.[12]

4. Learning experiences must be suitable

By "suitable" learning experiences we mean that both the subject matter to be

---

[12] Watson, op. cit., p. 7.

learned and the media learning materials by which it is to be learned must be geared to the pupils' interests, abilities, and readiness to become involved in the situation. Even when a teacher has put much effort and thought into the planning of learning experiences, he may find himself quite discouraged by the lack of pupil responsiveness, a lack that is caused simply by the fact that the pupils are not ready for or interested in the particular experiences.

Take, for example, the teacher who returned to his midwestern community school inspired by the year he had spent in Asian studies at the University of Hawaii.[13] Preparing to teach a new semester course in Asian culture, this man selected for the children's basic reading three survey texts that included information on Japan, Korea, Taiwan, the Philippines, Indonesia, Malaysia, Burma, Cambodia, and Vietnam. He then obtained from the Asian Study Society very appropriate sound motion picture films. From a variety of source books, he patiently prepared a series of hand-drawn maps, historical-event chronological tables, and related tabular charts and graphs. He selected from among the pictures he had taken during his own tour of Japan those he thought gave a real feeling of the interesting places he had visited. Finally, he selected and brought to school a collection of recordings of Haiku poetry. Thus armed with a wide variety of audiovisual materials to introduce what to him had been the exciting adventures of his year abroad, he confidently began the new semester.

At first, the teacher's enthusiasm was infectious. Soon after the beginning of the

semester, the students were still eager. But as the days wore on, the teacher began to notice with dismay that the initial sparks were dimming and that the students seemed more and more preoccupied and less and less concerned with what he was attempting to help them do and learn. Discouraged, the teacher fell back on his traditional approach—he distributed textbooks, issued prescribed readings, gave assignments, and announced the schedule of exam dates.

What had happened, of course, was that the plan was totally teacher-dominated, disregarding the pupils' interests and the suitability of materials, the selection of which might well have involved pu-

FIGURE 2.9

These students are helping to select learning materials: (a) filmstrips for use in their social studies class; (b) prerecorded reading-story tapes for their small group to use in second-grade language arts (c) disc recordings for use in social studies. These students not only help select materials for class use but also are allowed—and encouraged—to take audiovisual materials and equipment to their homes over the weekend.

[13] This is the Asian Studies Program carried out by the East-West Center at the University of Hawaii which is described in Chapter 1. Students for this program are selected according to the ratio of two Oriental teachers for every U.S. mainlander. The program consists of two semesters of course study climaxed by a tour of the United States for each Asian teacher and a tour of the Orient for the American teachers.

pil planning and action. But, beyond this, the teacher finally realized that in his enthusiasm over his own year of experience —traveling among the people and places of Asia and obtaining a host of exciting new conceptual experiences for himself— he had misjudged the readiness of his class to accept and profit from the materials he had so enthusiastically collected. He had misjudged the level of their background experiences, forgetting that they lacked any preliminary interest in the Orient, which really was essential for the learning experiences he had assembled, to be effective. In brief, he had "missed the mark."

Successful teaching with media involves the determination of the concept level already attained by pupils and the subsequent use of new experiences by and for the pupils that lead from that concept level and thus become experiences that provide continuing avenues for additional conceptualization. As indicated, it is the teacher's task to know his pupils well enough to assess their levels of ability, background learning, and interest; it is not the pupils' task to adapt their interests and abilities to the learning situations presented by the teacher. The teacher must understand when subject content is suitable for the pupils' levels of readiness or how

to adapt the subject content, for which he is responsible, to meet these levels. He must also understand what kinds of communications media and what concrete conceptual experiences are most suitable and appropriate for the learners' readiness stage and which will be most likely to arouse the pupils' interest sufficiently to lead them to search further for, and use creatively, new information. To start below the pupils' responsive levels actually leads to pupil boredome; to start too far above these levels often leads to pupil frustration or failure; and to overlook the innate desire of the learner to become involved at the planning stages presents a hazard no teacher should permit to exist.[14]

The selection of learning materials is complicated by the fact that such large numbers of excellent films, filmstrips, slides, prerecorded tapes, models, specimens, charts, flat pictures, and so forth, are available. However, the task of selecting materials need not be up to the teacher alone. Once pupils have planned and know their purposes, they are in a unique position to help search for those experiences that will be of greatest use. The task of selection can profitably become an integral part of pupil involvement. Fortunately for the teacher at work today, learning resource centers organized by subject matter or, in smaller schools, for a sequence of grades or subjects, make it possible for pupils to participate in the selection and evaluation of the very learning material which they, as a result of their auditioning and previewing, believe will be helpful to their classmates (see Figure 2.9).

5. Teaching strategies must be appropriate

Traditional school organization practices have, unfortunately, "standardized" the "egg-crate" school building. For years such school buildings have housed, with alarming conformity, 35 pupil-teaching stations where 30- to 45-minute subject time slots have been observed. Into such inflexible programing, 45 million pupils are inexorably absorbed for a kind of safe-keeping. Difficulties presented by this type of organization have been discussed in Chapter 1.

In the face of this, most psychologists who are specialists in learning agree that proper school organization should encourage space and scheduling strategies that follow such precepts as these:

The right-sized group for any activity depends on both maturity of the individuals and the nature of the activity. Hundreds of thousands may be spectators at a film, a television presentation, or a spectacle. Working, interacting groups seem to do best when composed of five to eight members. If the group is larger, some become performers and others spectators. At age 6, spontaneous groups seldom exceed two, three, or four children. Sizes now accepted for school classes are much too large for good cooperative work.[15]

With the growing availability and use of new educational media learning experiences, the way has been cleared to make changes that accord with these precepts. No longer is there any defense for marshaling all learners through uniform large-group experiences, *a technique that has never been supported by valid research evidence.* Rather, the variations now include large-group instruction (which is still, of course, very useful and justifiable), provisions for small-group instruction, peer teaching, and self-tutorial learning (individualized organization for learning), and all manner of interrelated aspects of these. An example follows:

Nearly 200 seniors had assembled, as

[14] For further study of creativeness concepts, see E. Paul Torrance, *Education and the Creative Potential,* University of Minnesota Press, 1964.

[15] Watson, op cit., p. 15.

they were accustomed to twice a week, in a small auditorium. They were meeting, on this occasion, to listen to a report by a representative of the Department of State. A teacher introduced the guest speaker.

The speaker began by describing the prisoner of war dilemma in Vietnam at the close of 1970. Next he explained that in order to understand the setting of the events, the students should know something of the culture of the people and the nature of places and things in Vietnam. To help them, he continued, he would show a 12-minute sound motion picture film that would give them some realistic experiences about that area of the world. The film was shown, and the speaker continued by describing many of the problems involved in fighting a war in Vietnam and, more important, in becoming a prisoner of war in Southeast Asia.

"Never before," the speaker concluded, "have so many Americans been held as prisoners of war for so long a time and in violation of the Geneva Convention."

After this large-group session, the pupils reorganized themselves, as was their usual procedure, into small groups. Several groups shared the supervision of a teacher-leader. While discussion was begun usually by the teacher, the impact of the lecture and film soon triggered lively responses, suggestions, and next-step plans from the students.

"How can this happen today?" one pupil asked, urgency in his tone.

"How can a nation just ignore the Geneva Convention?" another student added.

"What's the Geneva Convention? Seriously, I should know about it, and I intend to find out."

Other students volunteered:

"How does the Red Cross fit into all of this?"

"What can the Department of State do?"

"I'd like to find out about the Paris Peace Talks and what they have done about the P.O.W. problem."

As the small-group meetings disbanded, one social studies teacher pondered, "Quite a list of purposes. The theory seems to be working. General background information of use for all—that's the function of the large group. Then small groups to encourage involvement through pupil-teacher planning. Most of the next steps I would have offered were anticipated by the students! And that's good! Several of these ideas I hadn't even thought of—look at this list."

Following procedures now well established, the social studies teacher went down the hall to the Social Studies Learning Resource Center (similar to eight other such centers in the school, one for each of the academic content areas: mathematics, industrial arts, home economics, language arts, sciences, etc.). On entering, the teacher went to the schedule board and, under the card identifying his small groups, attached the statement of questions previously approved. He then turned to discuss with the supervisor of the resource center procedures that would permit the individual learners to come in and pursue their own inquiries by referring to the varieties of resource materials available to them. During the rest of the week, pupils enrolled in the Problems of Democracy course would spend whatever time they chose in pursuit of background material which would yield information to be applied to the inquiries they individually chose to pursue (see Figure 2.10).

The Social Studies Learning Resource Center represents an environment in which the motivated learner may become completely absorbed studying source information as the first step in the process of self-discovery evaluation, and application of new information to his own purposes. Immediate access to materials by the learner is almost guaranteed; this is a key factor

FIGURE 2.10

This is the Social Studies Learning Resource Center at Kailua High School in Hawaii, shared by hundreds of students. During scheduled times students are free to come to this center to pursue individual or small-group study. They have easy access to all kinds of learning resources: film-strips, recorded materials, films, pictures, news-paper files, books, and pamphlets. (a) Students locate filmstrips (b) they study the pictures, charts, and related data; (c) they meet to discuss, evaluate, and plan to search further through other materials available in the center. How do your learning resource facilities compare? What are your reactions?

in the learner's feelings of achievement and success. Within the learning resource center, the student may locate immediately and study individually current events material in filmstrip form, prerecorded tapes, map projectuals, chart sets, picture sets, newspaper clipping files arranged in order of central topics, and so forth. Because students have ready access to materials and flexibility of time to study them, a high percentage of students are able to learn more in less time than if they were held to the pace which the traditional classroom organization imposes. The inevitable result is a degree of heterogeneity which teachers have long recognized as being desirable, but about which they often felt frustrated when they were forced to ask, "What can I do with a student who quickly exhausts all the available supplies and sits impatiently while I struggle to help the laggards?"

The essence of evolving trends in teaching strategy, then, is this: Present basic background learning materials to large groups of students; reorganize the large groups into smaller groups for purposes of discussion, planning, reporting, and evaluating; make available countless individualized or self-tutorial learning resource opportunities to students who choose to pursue their own plans at their own pace.

Through such strategies, the individual is permitted to plan, to inquire, to become involved, to engage in a self-directed search to discover and know, and, finally, to apply his new-found information in patterns which he can develop, usually, with the help and guidance of a skillful subject-oriented teacher (see Figure 2.11). Examples of ways media can be arranged and identified with such emerging new patterns of teaching strategy are discussed in later chapters.

6. Creativity is the goal of learning

Learning for learning's sake is not enough. As has been said earlier, the degree to which one may learn information per se as a result of interacting with well-chosen mediated learning experiences greatly exceeds what may be learned through involvement with more traditional verbal experiences. Nevertheless, teachers who wish to use audiovisual communication experiences for their fullest benefit should encourage pupils not to be satisfied until those who are able to have experimented with endless *creative* and *inventive* ways of employing newly learned skills and information. Three widely accepted learning precepts support such purposes:

1 *Opportunity to plan and develop fresh, novel, and stimulating experiences is a kind of reward which is quite effective in stimulating learning.*
2 *A sense of achievement and satisfaction develops within the learner as he transfers learned information into self-conceived applications of his own creation.*
3 *Behaviors which are rewarded or reinforced through the sensation of self-accomplishment which occurs as one invents, creates, or applies new learning to the solution of self-initiated projects are more likely to recur in the future.*[16]

These precepts in no way diminish the desirability of arranging learning experiences which yield skills and information as such. Rather, they suggest that *the teaching-learning act is not complete unless learners become involved in planning and accomplishing creative activity.*[17]

An example follows:

[16] Watson, op. cit., pp. 2–7.

[17] See Chapter 1, pp. 33–39, for a discussion of ways new media learning materials can accelerate learning of factual information, which then becomes the basis for science and social studies discovery and inquiry methods, processes which cannot be completed until the students have applied learned information and skills to testing hypotheses or drawing conclusions and generalizations.

The teacher of creative art arranged for the members of the senior high school class to attend regularly scheduled laboratory periods during which the immediate purposes were to master skills involved in textile design, preparation of textile dyes, identification of textiles, and, finally, batiking (the applying of brilliantly colored designs to textiles, using wax to control the process). Students acquired information as they observed demonstrations by the instructor, sound motion picture films, and batik specimens; they also reviewed a step-by-step explanation of batik skills as presented in a sound filmstrip. Next, during laboratory sessions, they practiced and evaluated the batik skills they had learned and corrected their failures.

The instructor then announced: "Now that you've learned some of the basic skills, I'll expect you to figure out what you'd like to do with them."

The next day a number of students responded, displaying to the group and the instructor trial patterns, textiles, and dye samples to be used to produce finished batiks. Some were encouraged to go ahead on their own. Others needed more planning time and advice from classmates and the instructor.

"Too often we consider the task completed when skills are mastered," the instructor explained later to a visitor. "Actually, it's at that point the real learning takes place." He paused and directed attention to the finished projects: dresses, purse covers, swimsuits, pillows, and so forth. "The days weren't long enough. Once they were free to proceed on their own, some of those who had least to say or do during skill instruction came up with some of the most original and best executed batiks."

The type of environment that leads to creative learning can be provided for any subject area. For example, a science film on the nature of solids, liquids, and gases raises as many questions as it answers. The

FIGURE 2.11

Variations for desired teaching strategies are possible when appropriate facilities are provided, that is, adequate school buildings. These photographs and diagram show a school plant designed for a variety of teaching strategies: (a) independent study, (b) small-group study, in this case, listening to taped learning materials, and (c) large-group learning areas located around a central resource center. Such planned interrelationship must involve administrators, teachers, community representatives, and media personnel. How do your facilities compare?

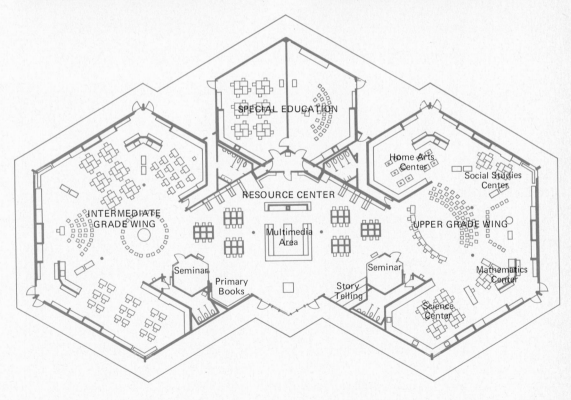

SPECIAL EDUCATION

RESOURCE CENTER

Home Arts Center

Social Studies Center

INTERMEDIATE GRADE WING

Multimedia Area

UPPER GRADE WING

Seminar

Primary Books

Seminar

Story Telling

Mathematics Center

Science Center

FIGURE 2.12

questions can be explored best when the quest for additional information is "triggered" by encouraging students to formulate their own hypotheses, search out ways to test them, devise their own equipment, observe their experiments, and, on the basis of their results, to make generalizations. Throughout this process, the teacher guides, encourages, evaluates—and by so doing, is engaging in teaching at its best.

It is obvious that the concept of learner-centered inventive teaching is much easier to illustrate in operation than to describe as a process. Inventive or creative experience and accomplishment by learners seem to involve the reshuffling of acquired information patterns into entirely new expressions and accomplishments. For one learner, inventiveness might be expressed in the creation of an original story; for another, it might be expressed through the fashioning of a musical instrument out of tin cans, wires, and wood. For others, invention may be more complex—perhaps the initiating of new organizational plans for the school student body in which ideas and activities normally limited to a class group are expanded to the entire school or even to community participation (see Figure 2.12).

Many pupils, if the learning situations presented to them are conducive to it, are capable of some degree of creative invention. This is well demonstrated by a high school Asian culture study group that was exploring the possibilities of gaining a better understanding of Oriental culture. As a unit on Japan progressed, the students learned by listening to recorded explanations and examples of Haiku poetry. This kind of poetry, they learned, is a closely prescribed form of poetic expression. The Haiku poet seeks to express a central idea through a poetic word picture which, by esthetic tradition, is limited to 17 syllables. It is not impossible to transfer this same task to English. The teacher described the

These pupils are watching a creative dramatization presented by members of another class. Such activity represents the culmination of planning, searching, experiencing, conceptualizing. What do you "read" from this picture? From what you see, can you make any evaluative judgments? Could this be the response to some of your own teaching plans?

mechanics of Haiku poetry, played additional recorded translations, and then encouraged several pupils to experiment on their own.

"It's harder to use fewer words than many, isn't it?" one pupil commented after a few trials.

"Writing a letter to the embassy is nothing compared to getting across one idea in 17 syllables," a second volunteered.

"I've been at this for two study halls now—but I've got a start!" a third exclaimed happily.

Before the end of the week, several students were able to present to the rest of the group a number of poetic word pictures in the Haiku style. Two were particularly good, "Waves" and "Lapping Tide"; a

third, "Bird at Dawn," was truly outstanding:

> Early yellow light;
> wings circling against
> low clouds;
> dawn bird's silent flight.

Inventive creativity can be manifested in a variety of ways: through the traditional channels of artistic expression—literature, drama, painting, photography, sculpture, pottery, music, dance, and so forth; through mechanical channels, such as carpentry, electrical work, machinery manipulations, and the like; through social channels, such as group leadership, helping, understanding, or providing spontaneous entertainment for others; and in the purely ideational realm, as exhibited in discussion or writing.

Often, a pupil's inventive potentialities are revealed in ways not considered desirable by the teacher. For example, the pupil who constantly disrupts the class with humorous remarks may be showing a real talent for comedy which, if encouraged through more appropriate channels, might prove to be of considerable value both to the class and to the individual's further development. Similarly, the pupil who seems to have a strong but negative leadership influence on his fellow class members may have talents that an alert teacher can develop into those that are actually an aid to him in his role as teacher. Or the absent-minded child who seems to be preoccupied

FIGURE 2.13

The gifted learner often produces much less than his best. How may the teacher tap hidden sources of inventive creativity?

with matters other than his classwork may be manipulating profound scientific or mathematical ideas (see Figure 2.13). Even the child who seems to have difficulty expressing himself verbally may actually have an unusually good aptitude for imagery which careful attention and help from the teacher can develop into true literary talent. Many teachers who have worked with culturally deprived pupils have found inherent in their pupils' compositions a great deal of poetic imagination and vision, talent which might easily have been overlooked if the teacher had noticed only the children's limited vocabulary, poor grammar, and slang-ridden expressions. Thus the teacher should be prepared to meet positively even "negative" pupil behavior, on the chance that it might be symptomatic of true inventive creativity.

A teacher who encourages creativity strives to provide a classroom environment replete with understandable and useful experiences that will capture the imagination of students and inspire *them* to creative response. The teacher at work in this day of burgeoning audiovisual materials has available to him a rewarding opportunity to explore and experience the joys of working in a learning environment that can be so rich in appropriate learning experiences as to capture the creative imagination of curious and motivated pupils. This is a high-sounding statement of purpose, but it is amply justified. Certain specifics involved in achieving it are described more completely in later chapters, but they are introduced briefly here to serve as basic guidelines to help the teacher plan for this kind of activity.

Creative teaching as such is most apt to occur when the classroom can be characterized as a media-related environment for learning. The implication of this is that the teacher realizes the opportunities for bringing comprehensive learning experiences into the classroom through the means of audiovisual materials. A diagrammatic representation of a creative learning environment is shown in Figure 2.14. The term "messages" refers to information transmitted by a person—teacher to pupil, pupil to teacher, or pupil to pupil—or by an audiovisual learning medium. Regardless of its origin, a message must affect the interests and accumulated knowledge of the person to whom it is directed if teacher-learning communication is to take place; for this reason, such a message may be referred to as an *affector*. If the message affects the receiver in such a way as to elicit a *responding* message, this response may be termed an *effector*. It is through the effector messages of the pupils that the teacher may judge the degree of involve-

ment that has occurred as a result of an affector message. Pupil responses usually occur in proportion to the number of useful affector messages which are created within the classroom by the teacher, by educational materials and media, and often by the pupils themselves.

As stated, maximum learner involvement in creative thinking and doing is most likely to result when there are many carefully selected and wisely presented opportunities for firsthand learning experiences or for simulated concrete experiences such as those provided through films, filmstrips, models, mockups, television, pictures, graphics, community study trips, and so forth. A rich learning environment must also, of course, include a well-stocked book library of resource materials and many opportunities for pupil-teacher exchange of ideas and conclusions. Indeed, the opportunity for free interchange of ideas, interpretations, questions, and possible solu-

FIGURE 2.14

The affector and effector communication process.

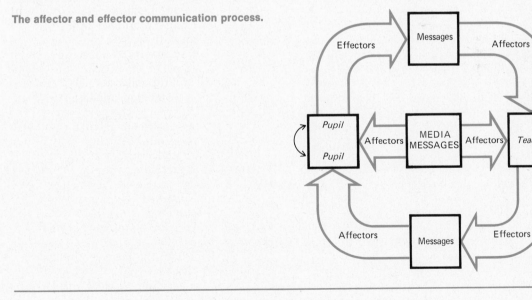

FIGURE 2.15

Why, when, and by whom should this experiment in viscosity be conducted? Whose creativity is being evidenced here?

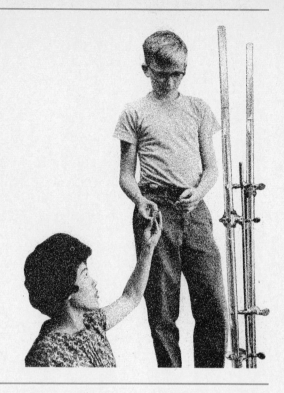

tions to problems between pupils and teachers and among the pupils themselves is a most important ingredient of an inventive and creative learning environment. Media materials themselves and appropriate ways of making them readily available for the independent search and inquiry of the student are discussed more completely later (see Figure 2.15).

Finally, the most reliable form of evaluation can be achieved when the learner responds to instruction through means that reflect his own inventive information or skills he has acquired. Evaluation is more sure to be valid when the nature and extent of learner responses are *observable* and thus may be judged and valued.

Summary: systematizing the use of media for learning

Powerful tools for the improvement of learning are now available to teachers and learners. It is the purpose of the following chapters to present to teachers the systematic procedures through which assessment of learner needs, strategies for pupil in-

volvement and instruction, and the interrelated use of mediated learning experiences may be employed in the interests of better learning—an approach now often referred to as *multimedia instructional systems.*

74

What has been said in this chapter may be incorporated into the following plan for constructively using media learning experiences. This plan of action may be useful as a point of reference as succeeding chapters are read and applied (see Figure 2.16):

1. Analyze the thresholds and needs of learners. Each learner is unique in terms of his interests, abilities, levels of readiness, and capacity to adapt and create. Pretests are extremely desirable in helping to reveal the thresholds at which learners are likely to begin their quest for learning experiences (media-related experiences).

2. Help pupils understand what is to be taught, what information is to be learned, and what skills are to be acquired. Make it possible for these understandings to be the result of pupil participation and involvement.

3. Decide as soon as possible what behaviors are expected to be observable among learners when instructional experiences have been completed. Sometimes referred

FIGURE 2.16

This is a closed-loop continuous instructional development plan. Within this diagram, which highlights ways to systematize the use of media for learning, are incorporated the basic learning tenets discussed in this chapter. It is suggested that you refer to it as you proceed through the following chapters.

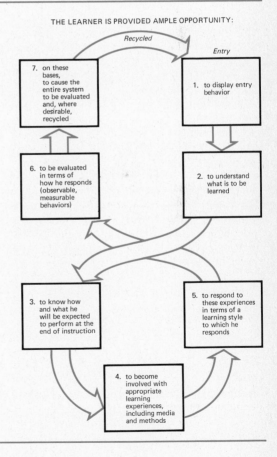

THE LEARNER IS PROVIDED AMPLE OPPORTUNITY:

Recycled

Entry

7. on these bases, to cause the entire system to be evaluated and, where desirable, recycled

1. to display entry behavior

6. to be evaluated in terms of how he responds (observable, measurable behaviors)

2. to understand what is to be learned

3. to know how and what he will be expected to perform at the end of instruction

5. to respond to these experiences in terms of a learning style to which he responds

4. to become involved with appropriate learning experiences, including media and methods

to as *behavioral objectives* or *terminal objectives*, these should be described in terms which will permit the learner to know what he should be capable of doing and on what basis he will be evaluated (mastery of information, performance of skills, and inventive and creative outcomes).

4. Select suitable learning experiences. Wherever possible, this should involve the learners' participation. The object is to select those learning experiences which, because of their nature, will communicate with greatest efficiency the information or skills that are to be conceptualized and employed creatively by the learner. The final question: does the selected learning experience communicate effectively to the learner?

5. Select the most appropriate teaching strategy or organization for learning. The alternatives are large group, small group, self-tutorial, peer teaching, and interrelated variations of these. Teaching strategies are needed which will permit learners easy access to media learning experiences and self-involvement in responses to them.

6. Provide for evaluation by observing the final creative behaviors and accomplishments of students. Remember that "the proof of the pudding is in the eating" —the success or failure of any teaching strategy is apparent only in the inventive behaviors and accomplishments which students show at the close of actual instruction.

7. Use the results of evaluation by reorganizing through addition or deletion, a process sometimes referred to as *recycling*. No curriculum plan, no instructional procedure, no strategy for instruction is ever constant or fixed. On the contrary, change, revision, and improvement are inevitable outcomes of multimedia instructional system utilization.[18]

[18] Based on analyses of media systems by Diamond, Barson, and Lange. See Robert M. Diamond, *The Use of Multimedia Instructional Materials Within the Seminar*, University of Miami, 1965;

The responsibility for planning, utilizing, implementing, and evaluating multimedia learning experiences rests not only on the teacher, but also, more fundamentally, on all of those who participate in the planning and execution of teacher programs. Thus in addition to the teacher's responsibility, there is the responsibility assumed by media coordinators, school administators, school board members, librarians, lay persons, and supervisors. All these types of responsibility have been charted in terms of a new approach to the improvement of learning referred to as *Instructional Development*. Instructional Development is a more sophisticated approach that incorporates what has been said about learning systems to this point and carries it forward into a systematic training program for teams of teachers, administrators, and educational specialists. Because the I.D. process is somewhat complex, we have chosen to introduce it in simple terms in conjunction with the selection and use of pictures and graphics in the next chapter; we refer to it thereafter at various points in the succeeding chapters and develop it in further detail in Chapter 15, "Multimedia Instructional Development."

We should emphasize that in using multimedia learning experiences, it is most important to arrange to involve the learners themselves, for they, after all, are the participants, the consumers, the ultimate users of what is being arranged. The chapters that follow are devoted to defining and describing specific media channels and presenting examples of ways they may be employed in accomplishing multimedia instruction.

John Barson, *A Procedural and Cost Analysis of Media in Instructional Systems Development*, Michigan State University, 1965; John Barson, *Instructional Systems Development: A Demonstration and Evaluation Project*, Michigan State University, June 1967; Phillip C. Lange, "Technology, Learning and Instruction," *Audiovisual Instruction*, Vol. 13, No. 3, March 1968.

Further learner response projects

As teachers we have become so accustomed to the presence of all kinds of limitations to effective learning that we are in real danger of accepting them—particularly those that cause us to forget the problems confronting learners as they explore new areas of cognitive learning. For this reason
the following six projects are suggested. Select one or two of these and carry them out either with some of your fellow teachers who work with you but who are not necessarily enrolled in this class or with some or all of the pupils you teach.

1

Imagine that you are about to learn to read and that you are making your first acquaintance with the alphabet. Study the following alphabet for no more than a minute or two:

aɪ	*(as in aisle)* aɪl	e	*(as in data)*	de̱tə
ɑ	*(as in calm)* kɑm	ə	*(as in data)*	detə̱
aʊ	*(as in now)* naʊ	i	*(as in unique)*	unik
ʊ	*(as in put)* pʊt	ɪ	*(as in in)*	ɪn
u	*(as in true)* tru	j	*(as in your)*	jur
ʌ	*(as in cup)* kʌp	ð	*(as in these)*	ðiz

Presumably you are now prepared to read with comprehension the following primer story:

> aʊr sṭʌdɪ ʌv wʊl
>
> *wi kom ðə wʊl.*
> *wi juz kardz tu kom ðə wʊl.*
> *wi kom ðə wʊl tu mek jɑrn.*
> *wi mek jɑrn aʊt ʌv komd wʊl.*

As you read this story, were you able to make sense out of the words? How many times did you have to refer to the alphabet? The chances are that even repeated reference to this alphabet did not help you understand the words and that few, if any, "pictured" concepts or understandings of familiar objects were called to mind by the word cues. Yet the experience you just went through is not unlike that which beginning readers face as they attempt to attach meaning to verbal symbols used to refer to real things. What is needed?

2

Locate a verbal description of some little-known animal or thing, for example, a sea horse, octopus, squid, star fish, tarantula, platypus, or aardvark. To begin with, you would probably consult an encylopedia for a concise description. If you chose the aardvark, you would find a description similar to the following (an actual description from the Encyclopaedia Britannica) :

The body is stout, with arched back; the limbs are short and stout, armed with strong, blunt claws; the ears long; and the
tail thick at the base and tapering gradually. The elongated head is set on a short thick neck, and at the extremity of the snout is a disc in which the nostrils open. The mouth is small and tubular, furnished with a long extensile tongue. A large individual measured 6 ft., 8 in. In color it is pale sandy or yellow, the hair being scanty and allowing the skin to show.

Now ask your fellow teachers or students to sketch their visualization of this description. Examine the sketches for evidences of differing background experi-

FIGURE 2.17

These three drawings were inspired by the same verbal description of an aardvark.

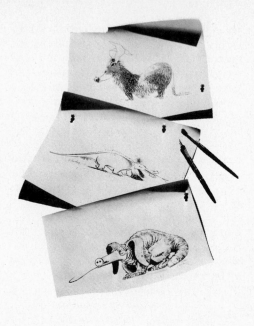

ences. *Then compare them with those produced by three professional artists (see Figure 2.17). What generalizations do you arrive at which relate to the universal nature of learning problems?*

3

In order to demonstrate the manner in which new media materials can provide valuable background learning experiences, select for use a short portion of some appropriate sound motion picture teaching film. Now consider how you might engage in a role-playing situation similar to the following, which occurred during a faculty meeting devoted to exploring the means of improving learning opportunities. In this case, an excerpt from a film on Eli Whitney was used. Your excerpt should be from a comparable film.

In order that the attending teachers themselves might benefit from concrete experience, the chairman utilized the role-playing technique, asking the group members to consider themselves pupils in an upper-grade social studies class that was about to begin a unit on American inventors.

"Can any of you think of some great American inventors?" the chairman asked of his "class." The teachers came up with Edison, McCormick, Fulton, Bell, and Whitney, the last being the most frequently recalled name.

"Obviously, to most of you, Whitney is an outstanding inventor, so we'll begin our study with him," continued the chairman in his role of teacher. "What do you already know about Eli Whitney?"

The cotton gin was overwhelmingly the largest response; only two of the teachers credited Whitney with having formulated the principles which underlie mass production. The chairman next asked the group members to close their eyes and to indicate with their hands what they remembered to be the approximate size of this famous cotton gin, and to maintain this pose as they reopened their eyes and looked around them. When the teachers compared their estimates of the cotton gin's size, they saw that the smallest estimate was about a foot wide, another was about two feet high, and one so big that the particular member's arms were not long enough to convey his idea of its proportions. The chairman then showed a 2-minute film excerpt in which the actual size of the cotton gin was revealed to be about 15 feet by 4 feet (Figure 2.18).

"Let's consider the implications of this experiment," continued the chairman. "What are your reactions?"

"Most of us were way off," remarked one "pupil."

"Yet you all studied Eli Whitney and his cotton gin in grade school, again in high school courses, and perhaps even later, in college courses. Surely you should have a fairly good memory of its size."

The teachers thought about this for a moment and then one volunteered, "But we never had a chance really to visualize it."

"What information sources did you recall just before you indicated the size of the cotton gin?" asked the chairman.

"Well, I remember reading about Eli Whitney, but my idea of the size of his invention was way off," said one teacher.

"I saw a drawing of it," said another, "but apparently I got a wrong impression."

The discussion continued on the efficiency of learning that stems solely from verbal description. The teachers agreed that verbalization is not sufficient to impart a true concept of unfamiliar objects or events.

FIGURE 2.18

This reconstruction of Eli Whitney's cotton gin reflects careful and authoritative historical research. How does it compare with your own mental image of the machine you learned to associate verbally with Eli Whitney?

4

Examine the learning objectives listed in a typical unit of work in a course of study in a subject area in which you are interested. (As an alternative, analyze some of the study questions at the end of a typical chapter from a textbook.) State the background perceptual experiences a learner must have in order to respond intelligently to the activity in question.

5

Arrange to visit a nearby school which includes a subject or departmental learning resource center in its programing. If possible, interview a teacher, supervisor, or principal and ask such questions as these:

a   Under what circumstances are pupils free to use the learning resource materials?

b   Does planning for the use of learning resources include pupil initiative or participation?

c   During about what percentage of the school day are pupils able to conduct their own questing of cognitive information or skill information in the learning resource facilities?

d   To what extent does the person you interviewed believe that the learning resources available fulfill the questing and research appetites of average learners? of the more gifted learners?

What conclusions were you able to draw on the basis of criteria statements made in Chapter 2? What plans do you have in terms of your future teaching roles and goals?

6

Interview a primary-grade reading teacher and ask the following questions:

a   What readiness activities do you help children engage in before attempting beginning reading?

b   What is the relationship of readiness activity to success in reading?

c   Are home backgrounds (presence of good books in the home, family travel, family group conversation) reflected in children's reading success? Report your interview to your classmates. What conclusions do you draw? Conduct similar interviews with teachers of art, social studies, and so on. Formulate similar but appropriate questions for your interviews.

As an alternative, ask similar questions of a high school teacher of social studies, science, and so on.

References

ALLPORT, GORDON W. *Attitudes: A Handbook of Social Psychology.* Clark University Press, 1935.

Asian Studies Program, The. East-West Center, University Hawaii.

BARSON, JOHN. *A Procedural and Cost Analysis of Media in Instructional Systems Development.* Michigan State University, 1965.

BARSON, JOHN. *Instructional Systems Development: A Demonstration and Evaluation Project.* Michigan State University, June 1967.

BERELSON, BERNARD, and GARY A. STEINER. *Human Behavior: An Inventory of Scientific Findings.* Harcourt, Brace & World, 1964, p. 18.

BLOUNT, NATHAN S., and HERBERT J. KLAUS-MEIER. *Teaching in the Secondary School.* 3rd ed. Harper & Row, 1968.

DIAMOND, ROBERT M. *The Use of Multimedia Instructional Materials Within the Seminar.* University of Miami, 1965.

FLEMING, MALCOLM L. *Perceptual Principles for the Design of Instructional Materials,* Final Report, Project 9-E-001, Grant No. OEG-5-9-245001-0016 (010), Bureau of Research, U. S. Office of Education, 1970, p. 1.

GOODLAD, JOHN I. "Providing Dynamic Environment and Learning." *Educational Broadcasting Review,* Vol. 3, 1969, Convention Report, Special Issue, p. 53.

HOCHBERG, JULIAN E. *Perception.* Prentice-Hall, 1966, p. 2.

KINGSLEY, HOWARD L. *The Nature and Conditions of Learning.* Prentice-Hall, 1947, p. 262.

KLAUSMEIER, HERBERT J., and RICHARD E. RIPPLE. *Learning and Human Abilities:*

Educational Psychology. 3rd ed. Harper & Row, 1971.

LANGE, PHILLIP C. "Technology, Learning and Instruction." *Audiovisual Instruction,* Vol. 13, No. 3, March 1968.

MIALARET, G. *The Psychology of the Use of Audio Visual Aids in Primary Education.* United Nations Educational, Scientific and Cultural Organization, Paris, 1966, p. 53.

NERBOVIG, MARCELLA H., and HERBERT J. KLAUS-MEIER. *Teaching in the Elementary School.* 3rd ed. Harper & Row, 1969.

TORRANCE, E. PAUL. *Education and the Creative Potential.* University of Minnesota Press, 1964.

TRAVERS, ROBERT M. W. *Essentials of Learning.* 3rd ed. Macmillan, 1972.

WATSON, GOODWIN. *What Psychology Can We Trust?* Teachers College Press, Columbia University, 1961.

WILMAN, RAYMOND V., and WESLEY C. MIER-HENRY, eds. *Educational Media: Theory into Practice.* Charles Merrill, 1969, p. 105.

Media references

Aaaark—Something About Communication, 16-mm film, sound, color, 18 min. U. S. National Audiovisual Center.

Changing Attitudes Through Communication, 16mm film, sound, color, 23 min. BNA Films.

Communications Primer, 16mm film, sound, color, 22 min. Charles & Ray Eames.

Let Them Learn, 16mm film, sound, color, 27

min. Encyclopaedia Britannica Educational Corp.

Making Sense Visually, filmstrip, sound, color. Eastman Kodak Company.

No Reason To Stay, 16mm film, sound, b/w, 29 min. National Film Board of Canada.

A Visual Fable, filmstrip, sound (record), color, 18 min. Eastman Kodak Company.

THREE
Teaching with pictures and graphics

Objectives	Performance responses
1 To be able to differentiate between visual literacy training and students simply taking pictures.	View and critique the films *Hey, Look at Me* and *Visual Literacy* (see Media References) from the standpoint of Objective 1.
2 To be able to design a learning experience that encourages the visual sequencing of ideas.	Use (or take) a set of pictures and write a plan for a legitimate learning experience in a subject and at the grade level of your choosing which will require your students to use the pictures in an ordered sequence.
3 To be able to select from a group of flat pictures and graphics those that are good for teaching purposes and to justify the selection.	From a set of pictures and graphics provided by the instructor (or by yourself from magazines or other sources) select two each to illustrate (a) good composition; (b) clear interpretation; (c) effective color; (d) desirable contrast and sharpness. Be ready to discuss and justify your selections.
4 To be able to illustrate two ways each in which (a) an impression of depth and (b) an impression of motion can be conveyed in a flat picture.	Identify a teaching situation in your own area in which flat pictures showing depth are important for needed understanding. Find pictures illustrating two means of providing the needed depth concepts and be ready to describe how the depth effect is achieved. Do the same with a set of still pictures which portray motion by two or more means.
5 To be able to list the principal steps in the Instructional Development approach to teaching and learning problems.	Write the four general steps in the Instructional Development approach, with a brief explanation of what is involved in each step.
6 To be able to mount three pictures (or graphics) of different proportion by at least two methods.	From a group of mounted pictures or graphics, select three that are mounted effectively for teaching purposes. Be ready to defend your selections before the class.

FROM the moment we open our eyes in the morning until we fall asleep at night, our senses are literally bombarded with thousands upon thousands of sensory stimuli. In one way or another, we process these, sifting out most, attending casually to others, and focusing our attention on those which, for whatever reason, may interest us.

It is only from those on which we focus our attention that we are likely to learn anything. Teachers, therefore, regularly expend much energy and ingenuity in attempting to focus students' attention and interest on the lesson at hand, that is, to *motivate* them. We all recognize the vital importance of motivation in learning. There is much more to learning, of course, than merely being motivated, but little learning is likely to take place without the initial drive that comes from being self-motivated.

A key problem in today's schools arises from the fact that many students perceive little relationship between what they are called upon to do in school and the world they see outside of school. That world is a highly visual one—our students, before they even begin school, are accustomed to expertly designed visual messages of many kinds. As they grow older, they find the mass media ever more insistently seeking and competing for their attention. Powerful visual communications are an inherent part of their out-of-school environment, and they respond readily and naturally to them (see Figure 3.1).

Our more successful students are able to develop and maintain a kind of perspective which enables them to take their school-ing as it is. Others—including ever greater numbers of disadvantaged youth—tend, for many reasons, to be less successful from the beginning of school, to fall farther behind as time goes on, and eventually to drop out. A common characteristic of many of these culturally deprived youngsters is difficulty with the language, both oral and written. The language used in their homes and neighborhoods is apt to be more different from the language they experience in school than is the language used in most middle-class homes. Thus they are handicapped at the outset, and unless something other than conventional language methods and materials is used, the future success in school of such pupils is, at best, in jeopardy. Commonly, these are the youngsters who by the time of adolescence have developed a feeling of apathy about ever achieving success in school. Is it any wonder that they get "turned off" and tend to lash out at the "establishment"?

Visual literacy

"*Visual literacy* refers to a group of vision-competencies a human being can develop by seeing and at the same time having and integrating other sensory, verbal, and learning experiences."

A recent development of growing promise is *visual literacy training,* which is explicitly designed to give students motivation and skills in expressing themselves, first in visual terms and later in spoken and written language. The children are given simple Instamatic cameras and film

FIGURE 3.1

"Sesame Street" and "The Electric Company" are two children's television programs that bridge the gap between pure entertainment and education. Produced with adequate funds and professional talent, these programs have achieved marked success in stimulating preschool and middle-grade reading. In this scene from "Sesame Street," "Big Bird," one of the program's featured performers, discusses the letter "M" with one of his human colleagues— one way visual examples help achieve "literacy."

and are taught how to use them to tell picture stories (see Figure 3.2). Reports from a number of school systems indicate considerable success both with average students and, more particularly, with youngsters from economic and culturally deprived environments.

Several years ago, a six-week summer project was conducted with 100 first-, second-, and third-grade children of migrant workers to determine the impact visual literacy training might have on language skills. Half of the children were given visual literacy training and half traditional training in language skills. The results at the end of the summer indicated a clear superiority in oral language for the experimental group, as well as some important fringe benefits:

The excitement implicit in any visual literacy project is difficult to describe to anyone who hasn't seen the wonder on the faces of youngsters when they see their newly-processed pictures. The migrant pupils in the experimental classes became so excited that many of them spent time after school discussing their pictures with teachers and the project staff. Such interest in school is highly unusual for such pupils. The quality and frequency of their oral language responses were among the most important results of the project. Even the most silent, recalcitrant pupil will jabber about pictures, but he'll really "go on and on" about his own pictures . . . for they are the most meaningful pictures he can show you.[1]

Another investigator did a study on teaching grammar and composition in a college preparatory high school with visual literacy techniques. His control group learned by traditional means, but the experimental group primarily used visuals and cameras. At the end of the experiment, both groups had improved in grammar at about the same rate, but the quality of the film group's composition work was much superior to that of the control group. The traditional group generally turned in the minimum amount of work, whereas the film

[1] Roger B. Fransecky, "Visual Literacy and Teaching the Disadvantaged," *Audiovisual Instruction*, October 1969, pp. 28–31 ff.

group worked long and hard at revising their narrations and generally submitted excellent work. The researcher summed up the results thus:

Motivation: This is the key. While both groups "learned grammar" equally well, the film group enjoyed it and, as a result, was easier to work with. The traditional group dreaded composition and did little or no revision. Revision to them meant "copy it over on good paper." However, the film group wrote compositions that they wanted to write; they used a thesaurus because they wanted "that right word"; they wrote compositions and enjoyed the effort. They found that learning could be relevant and fun.[2]

What is visual literacy?

Although visual literacy is attracting increasing attention, there is still uncertainty about its precise nature and significance. As one writer puts it, "When I say visual literacy, what I have in mind is a great dim

[2] Gerald W. Jaromin, "Teaching Grammar and Composition Using Cameras," in *Proceedings of the First National Conference on Visual Literacy*, Pitman, 1970, p. 196.

shape, the outlines and importance of which are not yet clear."

Much of the original work on visual literacy was done by John Debes and his associates at Eastman Kodak. Its development as an increasingly specific concept is based on a confluence of knowledge, theory, and technology in many areas, including general semantics, structural linquistics, transformational grammar, psychology, and philosophy. Experience thus far seems to indicate that visual literacy training, through providing nonverbal as well as verbal means of communication for today's children, can help alleviate some of the more critical instructional problems facing today's schools.

But what, actually, is visual literacy? Debes has undertaken to formulate a definition that he describes as tentative but as one having some consensus behind it:

Visual literacy refers to a group of vision-competencies a human being can develop by seeing and at the same time having and integrating other sensory experiences. The development of these competencies is fundamental to normal human learning. When developed, they enable a visually literate person to discriminate and interpret

FIGURE 3.2

Students at both elementary and secondary levels apear to benefit significantly from creating their own communications through pictures. Before they go out "in the field," these children discuss their cameras with their teacher.

the visual actions, objects, and symbols, natural or man-made, that he encounters in his environment. Through the creative use of these competencies, he is able to communicate with others. Through the appreciative use of these competencies, he is able to comprehend and enjoy the masterworks of visual communication.[3]

Some psychological foundations for visual literacy training

As suggested by the definition just quoted, certain fundamental learning concepts underlie the principles of *visual literacy training.*[4] These can be summarized in three brief statements:

1   *A child's conceptions emanate naturally from a progression of experiences, at first very largely physical or kinesthetic in nature, which form a framework on which much of his later learning takes place.*

An infant, for example, instinctively and avidly seeks his mother's breast and, in the process, experiences a total sensory involvement along with the reinforcement and rewards of being fed. Thus, through hunger and the expression of it, the impulse to search and find and be rewarded is established and reinforced almost from the beginning of life. The significance of this impulse to seek and find and be rewarded in the process is, of course, fundamental to all learning.

2   *A child begins early to develop a visual vocabulary which takes on meaning to the extent that he can interact with*

and have some effect on the items or processes seen.

Contrary to earlier thought, we now know that babies can make subtle depth discriminations by the time they are 60 days old.[5] Long before he learns to talk or to interact selectively with people and objects around him, the baby stores up visual images that are meaningful to him to the extent that interactions with them have had meaning in a physical sense. When he sees his mother warm the bottle or move the

[5] T. G. Bower, ''The Visual World of Infants,'' *Scientific American*, December 1966, pp. 80–92.

FIGURE 3.3

Very young children learn to communicate effectively long before they learn a spoken language. Unfortunately, we tend to minimize nonverbal communications skills later on.

[3] John L. Debes, ''The Loom of Visual Literacy,'' in *Proceedings of the First National Conference on Visual Literacy*, Pitman, 1970, p. 14.

[4] See John Debes, ''Some Foundations for Visual Literacy,'' *Audiovisual Instruction*, Vol. 13, No. 9, November 1968, pp. 961–964.

high chair close to the table, he knows that food is coming and responds accordingly. Further, he learns early how to get action to bring about these desirable events (see Figure 3.3). In the process he develops understanding and skills in what two researchers call "visual language," one element of which they call "body language" —the actions we make, consciously or otherwise, by which we transmit ideas or feelings to others.[6] Both by crying and by other actions, the baby thus learns to make his

[6] Weldon Kees and Jergen Reusch, *Non-Verbal Communications,* University of California Press, 1964, pp. 16–20, 36–41, 189–193.

needs known and to respond by expression and other means when they are met. He likewise learns early to be aware of and respond to the attitudes and actions of people around him. Whether they are affectionate, neutral, or negative, there seems little question that these visual images are organized and that they become the basis for his development of verbal skills later on. He not only learns to interpret but to use body language, and by the time he is 2, he has become pretty sophisticated at it, with an extremely active and effective visual vocabulary through which he achieves success and happiness in his own little world.

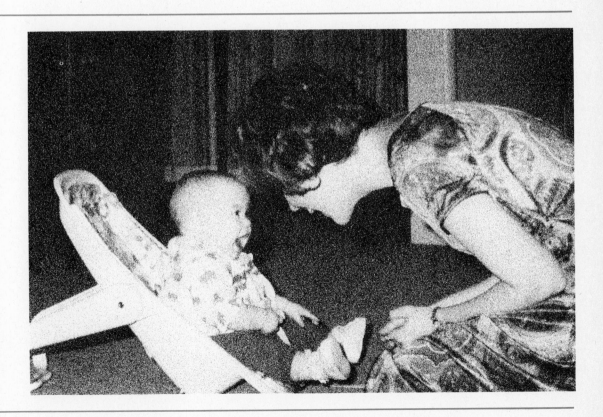

3 *In the process of developing a visual
language, children need much practice
in ordering and sequencing things
visually if they are to order and sequence ideas verbally later on.*

This ordering takes place naturally and
normally in home environments in which
infants have opportunities to select and
attend to a continuous stream of visual
images with which they can react in terms
of their needs and their interests at the moment, whether hunger, curiosity, or other
interests. The point is that in their own
world, babies, like adults, must become selective in what they attend to in terms of
what interests them at the moment or, as
they grow older, for longer periods. In
such acts they attend to certain things and
ignore others and, in the process, begin to
make sense in their own terms of what they
see. Were it not so, the child would develop
with a hopeless kaleidoscope of visual images without order. Instead, he concentrates
on his mother, on his blocks, or on whatever may attract him for the moment. In
so doing he tends to exclude other things
and in that process begins to provide a kind
of order and sequence to what he sees.

Deterrents to visual sequencing

Preschool children used to get continuous
practice in ordering things visually and in
choosing what or what not to attend to, but
now they begin at an early age to become
heavily involved with television viewing
over extended periods of time (see Figure
3.4). The television programs, usually designed for older children or adults, tend to
preclude visual selection or ordering. You
either look or you don't look. Furthermore, it is difficult to interact meaningfully
with a TV mother, toy, or glass of milk.
The child may in fact respond, but nothing he does has any effect on what happens
on the television tube. From the standpoint
of both visual choice and kinesthetic re-

sponse, therefore, the child tends to become a passive receiver of the visual ideas
of others, rather than practicing the selection and ordering of his own visual perceptions.

Whatever their considerable benefits
might be, television, films, and other pre-
programed visual sequences may have a
deterrent effect on the child's readiness and
development of verbal skills—particularly
in the ordering and sequencing of ideas.
The need for such experiences apparently
is very real. For example, two specialists
who have done considerable work with
children with learning disabilities say that
the one factor common to such children is
their incapacity to *order* ideas. In consequence, they recommend that visual sequencing be practiced assiduously.[7]

Other influences on verbal development and skills frequently compound the
problem. The family and home environment, as we know, are highly important
factors in the child's development and can
have marked effect both on his perceptions
and on his chances for developing verbal
skills. Thus, coming from a home environment where there is little conversation or
where conversation is in language forms
different from those used in school, the
youngster is clearly at a disadvantage when
moving into a school environment that is
very largely verbally oriented from the beginning. As Debes puts it, "In the nonverbal family, there's not much talk anyway. In the television family, there's even
less. Therefore, opportunities to communicate verbally are relatively few; the chances
of a child becoming articulate grow dim."[8]

[7] Marianne Frostig and Phyllis Maslow, "Language Training: A Form of Ability Training,"
Journal of Learning Disabilities, February 1968,
pp. 15–24.

[8] Debes, "Some Foundations for Visual Literacy," op. cit., p. 963.

FIGURE 3.4

Unquestionably there are many benefits here, but also some handicaps to child development. How can we maximize the former and minimize the latter?

What is involved in visual literacy training?

In the context just described, among others, visual literacy training appears to hold much promise. For whatever reasons a learner's opportunities may have been limited, when he comes to school he should be given practice in selecting and attending closely to visual phenomena of importance to him. Second, he needs opportunities to interact in his own way with what he is looking at. Third, he should have opportunities to create meaningful visual statements of his own. Finally, he should be encouraged to arrange ideas visually in the way he wants to arrange them. Such activities are elements that are inherent in effective visual literacy training.

More specifically, visual literacy training undertakes to develop the following competencies:

1 To read visuals with skill.
2 To "write" with visuals, expressing one's self effectively.
3 To know the grammar and syntax of visual language and be able to apply them.
4 To be familiar with the tools of visual literacy and their use.
5 To appreciate the masterworks of visual literacy.
6 To be able to translate from visual language to verbal language and vice versa.[9]

The Educational Projects Division of Eastman Kodak has produced a series of teachers' guides and filmstrips intended to help teachers who wish to try the visual literacy route.[10] The pictures in these materials are designed to help the learner develop a hierarchy of specific skills and discriminations so that he may learn to "read" pictures skillfully as a basis for creating and "telling" his own picture stories (see Figure 3.5). Representative skills and activities to be developed usually include the following:

1. Perceive visual differences and similarities in a group of pictures—lightness and darkness, brightness, shapes, sizes, color, depth, movement, and so forth.

2. Perceive common characteristics in a group of pictures—objects normally seen together; like processes (general: walking, playing, working, running, fighting, smiling; specific: walking to school, playing ball, driving a truck, riding a bicycle, etc.); like emotions (anger, happiness, affection, pleasure, excitement, etc.).

3. Perceive sequential relationships in

[9] Debes, "The Loom of Visual Literacy," op. cit., p. 13.

[10] Initial publications include *A Visual Fable, How Does a Picture Mean? Making Sense Visually* (see Media References), and *Rhetoric of the Movie,* plus Photo Discovery Sets of pictures which students can manipulate to tell a variety of stories.

FIGURE 3.5

Involvement is the key here. What are three ways that visual literacy training can help these pupils better achieve traditional school objectives?

a group of pictures—"read" a sequence of objects or expressions arranged so as to communicate an intended idea, a story, an emotional reaction.

4. Put together a series of pictures arranged to express an idea or emotion so

that others may understand it and add the words necessary to explain it.

    5. Create the pictures or drawings and the verbal explanation necessary to communicate effectively an idea, a story, and/or an emotion to others.

It should be noted that though these skills and activities fall into a natural and logical progression, it is *not* essential that they be dealt with in that logical order. To insist on doing so might well take all the fun out of what must be an exciting and stimulating new learning experience if it is to produce the results which it appears remarkably capable of producing. The teacher should concentrate instead on (1) developing and maintaining a high level of motivation and (2) developing and expanding each individual's ability to "read" pictures and to communicate his own ideas through them.

Although there are still many questions about visual literacy, it does seem clear that through the development of certain visual skills, learners can be provided with an important additional means of interpreting and communicating about themselves and their environment. Visual literacy appears to have special benefits for those with limited verbal skills; nevertheless, it probably has equal or greater potential in a variety of subjects and grade levels for competent and articulate students as well.

It should be noted also that though much of the work in visual literacy so far has been done through still and motion picture photography, there would seem to be good reason for not limiting our thinking to pictures in this restricted sense. What we are really talking about is enhancing the learner's ability to *communicate* visually. Along with photographs, various forms of drawings, graphics, and displays, for example, are familiar ways of expressing ideas and concepts; furthermore, dramatizations and demonstrations have elements conducive to visual literacy training. We shall frequently refer to visual literacy implications as we discuss the various media in the chapters that follow.

Nature and characteristics of flat pictures

ALTHOUGH visual literacy may appear at first blush to be a unique area—and perhaps it is—that uniqueness consists primarily in how the media are generated and employed in the teaching process. Actually, the teacher using the visual literacy approach finds it necessary to know a good deal more about the media themselves—pictures, graphics, slides, films, and so forth —than most of us typically do. The reason for this is that the crux of the visual literacy idea is for students to communicate by means of pictures or *other* visual media. Ultimately, they translate or interpret those pictures and media with articulate, verbal language.

To do this, the student must be led to discover the difference between good and bad pictures and how to design and put visuals together so that they will tell the story he wants to communicate. Thus it is essential for the teacher to understand the characteristics of good pictures and graphic forms so that he may select and apply them effectively in whatever context he chooses, including that of the visual literacy approach. Let us turn, therefore, to an analy-

FIGURE 3.6

Study prints are widely available in color in sets like this one and in large sizes from school supply companies.

sis of flat pictures and graphic forms which can be helpful in interpreting and communicating ideas.

Definition of flat pictures

A *flat picture* is a still, opaque representation of a scene or object—such as a photograph, drawing, painting, or textbook illustration.

We use the term "flat pictures" to describe illustrations in magazines and books, photographs, study prints, and the like—pictures that can be examined and used as they are without a projector or viewer (see Figure 3.6). "Still pictures" is a broader term that refers to all nonmotion pictures in either opaque or projected form. In other words, slides, transparencies, and filmstrips are included along with flat pictures as "still pictures."

We should note that the term "still pictures" can be somewhat misleading in that many such pictures present scenes where motion is clearly evident, even though the picture itself does not, of course, move; as we shall see, there are many cues in a dynamic picture which portray the motion actually present. The term "motion pictures" is also, strictly speaking, inaccurate, since the illusion of motion is created both in films and on television by a series of still pictures projected on the screen or tube in a progression too rapid for the eye to detect (this is discussed in Chapter 11). Both terms have the advantage, however, of being universally understood in functional terms, and we will continue to use them in that sense.

But we also need a term to distinguish between projected and nonprojected still pictures. Although many of the same selection and use considerations apply whether a picture is projected or not, we use the term "flat pictures" to provide that distinction and thus identify this part of the powerful picture medium more specifically and accurately.

Advantages of flat pictures

Like any other instructional material, flat pictures have some unique characteristics that produce advantages, as well as other

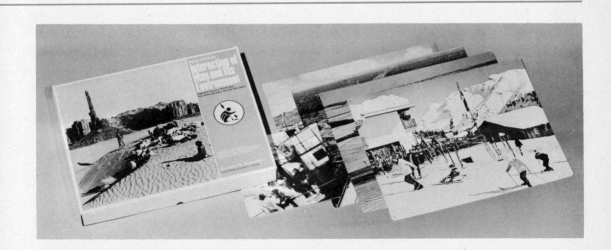

characteristics that produce limitations in their use for teaching purposes.

LOW COST AND READY AVAILABILITY One of these advantages, of course, is ready accessibility on an almost unlimited range of topics. Literally thousands of good pictures appear each year in magazines, newspapers, and advertising brochures of many kinds which can be acquired at little or no cost. In addition, modern textbooks normally include large numbers of good illustrations, and there are many excellent sets of study prints available for purchase by any school.

EASE OF USE   A second advantage of flat pictures is the ease with which they can be used. Special equipment is unnecessary, though a filing system of some sort is essential so that specific pictures can be found when needed. If they are large enough, they can be held up in front of a whole class. Students, individually or in small groups, can use them for a variety of purposes. They can be mounted in study displays or put together in any order so as to fashion a visual message.

EASE OF MAKING   Finally, a teacher or students can rather readily draw simple pictures or graphics or take pictures with cameras, thus generating the right ones for immediate and specific classroom purposes. This, of course, is not only an essential element of the visual literacy program, but also is a useful procedure in many other teaching contexts as well.

Limitations of flat pictures
All teaching materials have advantages for some kinds of teaching tasks and limitations or disadvantages for others. Just as a teacher becomes skilled at selecting suitable reading materials, so should he become competent at choosing media and materials that will be most effective for each lesson.

FIGURE 3.7

Small pictures can easily be shown to a whole class by using an opaque projector.

In part, this choice depends on the inherent strengths and limitations of the various available materials; in part, on teaching purposes; in part, on methods of use. Let us examine some limitations of flat pictures with these factors in mind.

SMALL SIZE   The vast majority of the pictures in books, magazines, and newspapers are too small to be used effectively in front of a class. Unless enlarged or projected by some means, they simply cannot be seen well enough by everyone in the class to justify using them in this way. Thus size is an inherent limitation for one type of use. This limitation can be overcome, however, if an opaque projector and adequate light-control facilities are available (see Figure 3.7). Moreover, study prints can be obtained which are large enough to be used in front of a whole class-

room if attention does not need to be focused on small details in the pictures. Size is not necessarily a limitation in study displays, because if the overall effect of the display is good enough, students will go up to examine the display—and the small pictures—at close range.

LACK OF DEPTH When accurate perception of depth is essential to learning a particular concept or skill, a model or the object itself may be preferable to a two-dimensional flat picture. Accordingly, stereo pictures are often used in medical schools, along with models and actual laboratory dissection, to ensure accurate understanding of the precise relationships of body tissues. Aerial mapping services use precision instruments in matching flat aerial stereo photographs to provide a basis for accurate contour maps of surveyed areas. Technicians' manuals frequently contain complex diagrams of the assembly or disassembly of a machine; in some cases, small sections are blown up, or "exploded," for detailed examination. In these cases, where depth perception is of critical importance, flat pictures are used as supplementary rather than as primary sources of information. Other visual forms, plus considerable experience on the part of the viewer, are necessary if the viewer is to read picture depth with precision.

What then is a teacher to do? The *first* thing is to recognize that there is a problem. Few teachers appear to realize that picture-reading is indeed a real skill that must be acquired before a child can learn effectively from pictures. The development of picture-reading skills, of course, is one of the important functions of visual literacy training. The selection and use of pictures with good depth and motion cues clearly constitute a second important step

FIGURE 3.8

The breathtaking beauty and awe-inspiring immensity of the Grand Canyon are apparent in this picture to one who has seen it in person, but much less so to one who has not. Why?

a teacher can take; helping the students to interpret these cues is still another.

It must be recognized that there is a syntax or arrangement of elements in a good picture, just as there is a syntax of grammatical elements in the construction of a good sentence. Both the quality of the elements themselves—for example, the cues —and how well they are put together are critical to the readability of pictures. In other words, though we tend to assume that pictures communicate more or less automatically, we must remember that this is not the case—pupils need to learn how to read pictures, just as they need to learn how to read words.

There is considerable evidence that uninitiated learners have particular difficulty in reading three-dimensionality into flat pictures. The perspective cues we use to provide depth in pictures are relatively unintelligible to a large majority of children from cultures other than our own; indeed, only about half of our own children read depth properly in flat pictures by the time they enter the first grade. For some reason, boys seem better than girls in this respect in both American and African cultures. In any case, though both boys and girls in the United States have normally mastered reading such cues by the fifth grade, it is clear that we cannot assume the reading of depth in pictures to be automatic.[11]

For scenes with which the observer has some familiarity—and to which he brings a sufficient degree of experience—these factors provide the cues that enable him to sense rather accurately the actual depth in the scene being pictured. When scenes contain few familiar elements, however, the accuracy of one's depth impressions may be considerably reduced. Thus the vastness of the Grand Canyon is extremely difficult to grasp from a picture unless

---

11 Ruth H. Monroe and Robert L. Monroe, "Reading Pictures—A Cross-Cultural Perspective," Claremont Reading Conference Yearbook, Claremont College, Claremont, Calif., 1969, pp. 67–72.

one has actually seen it in person (see Figure 3.8). Youngsters who have never seen mountains or skyscrapers have difficulty in sensing their true dimensions from flat pictures.

LACK OF MOTION Since flat pictures by definition are "still" pictures, we can use them readily to communicate ideas about essentially motionless subjects. Such scenes as landscapes, mountains, forests or trees, buildings, objects, animals, or people in still positions are natural subjects for flat pictures. The general implication for teachers is that flat pictures are well suited to the teaching of concepts in which motion is not important to understanding (see Figure 3.9).

FIGURE 3.9

The power of a picture to capture emotions and portray feelings as well as meanings is often overlooked. Think of four ways in which you could make effective use in your teaching of pictures such as this one.

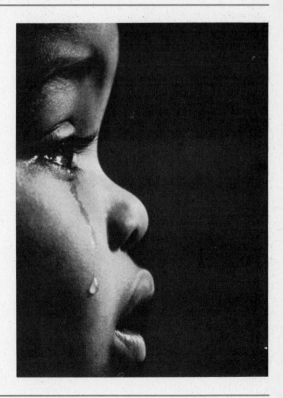

FIGURE 3.10

(a) Stop-motion photography enables both coach and athlete to analyze a performance in detail.
(b) The strobe shot of a tennis player "freezes" his motions in succession.

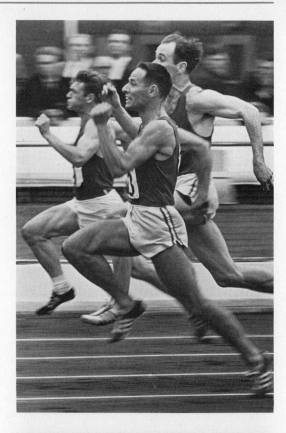

Flat pictures of moving subjects also have great value when they are used for study purposes. Stop-motion photographs of a hurdler, for example, help him and others to analyze good points or flaws in his form as he clears the hurdle. A special technique, strobe photography, produces pictures that really consist of a series of stop-motion photographs superimposed on one another. Such pictures also are very useful in analyzing an athlete's form (see Figure 3.10). Identification of machine parts is better done with still pictures than with motion pictures (the reverse is usually true if the purpose is to explain how the machine operates).

Again, however, we must note that the lack of motion in flat pictures is only relative. Still pictures can depict motion very satisfactorily for many purposes. For example, most students have seen television coverage of moon rocket launchings from Cape Kennedy. Thus they bring to a flat picture of a rocket launching a complete awareness of the motion represented by the outpouring of smoke and flame and by the rocket itself as it moves slowly upward from the launching pad (see Figure 3.11). To a viewer with such experience, the picture at once assumes a dynamic rather than a static quality.

Further, still pictures often contain clues to motion actually present. One is a blurring of the image of a moving object,

FIGURE 3.11

Pictures such as this one have become almost routine in our Space Age. Does this mean that they are no longer valuable in teaching? (The men who were to be the first on the moon begin their mission on July 16, 1969: a Saturn V rocket launches Apollo 11.)

FIGURE 3.12

Motion can be shown in various ways in still
pictures. In these examples, see how many cues
to motion you can identify.

with a succession of blurred contours behind the path or motion, as in Figure 3.12. The blurring device is logically based on the fact that a moving image on the retina actually produces a blurred impression of the object. Instead of actually blurring— or in addition to it—artists frequently use symbols such as the wake behind a boat or clouds of dust behind a stagecoach to suggest motion. Typically, such symbols are exaggerated somewhat to be more sure of getting the idea and the degree of motion across to the viewer. Since these symbols often have no exact counterparts in nature, they must be learned; there is, in fact, a reasonable amount of evidence that children do not normally detect the dynamic or active qualities of pictures before the third grade.[12] One significant and still largely unexplained finding in some research studies, however, is the fact that the use of color substantially facilitates the perception by young children of the dynamic features of pictures.

Another type of clues to motion in still pictures is that provided by objects in positions that cannot possibly be maintained. A tree falling, an airplane taking off, a man with both feet almost off the ground, or an athlete in mid-air cannot remain that way, and thus are seen in motion (see Figure 3.13). Again the experience of the viewer is an essential ingredient in reading motion into such scenes.

Finally, combinations of these clues in one or more still or static pictures showing a process that is going on force the viewer to recognize that something has happened, is happening now, and is going to happen. For example, consider a series of scenes showing cows being milked, tank trucks taking milk to the dairy, milk being bottled, delivery by the milkman, and children drinking milk at the breakfast table—such

[12] Robert M. W. Travers, *A Study of the Advantages and Disadvantages of Using Simplified Visual Presentations in Instructional Materials.* Final Report on USOE Grant No. OEG–1–070144–5235, 1969.

FIGURE 3.13

Here is another still shot of an action scene. What are the motion cues here?

FIGURE 3.14

These pictures were selected as examples of good composition. What elements make them so? Where is the focal point of each picture?

a series makes it easier for the viewer to interrelate the various components and integrate them into a dynamic whole. Interpreting such a series does, however, require a fairly complex and sophisticated level of perception of the kind that usually is necessary in using flow or process charts. That is, the level of perception involved is higher than that needed to interpret, for example, comic strips. A comic strip tells its story in straight linear fashion, but a series of scenes taking milk from cow to breakfast is more abstract in that the series requires the viewer to fill in the gaps and apply interpretive processes in order to grasp the meaning. Nevertheless, the fact that pictures requiring this sophisticated type of perception are being successfully used with quite young children in visual literacy projects suggests that under certain conditions they may have greater skills in interpreting and communicating through pictures than research studies to this point would appear to indicate.

Picture quality

Thus far we have been concerned with the more extrinsic characteristics of flat pictures—their ready availability, ease of use or of making, and their inherent limitations of size, depth, and motion. These are fundamental. But we also need to be concerned with the qualitative characteristics of pictures. As one biology teacher put it:

I'm a camera fan myself and take a lot of pictures. In the process, I have come to have a great deal of respect for people who can take really good pictures. There's a lot of difference between ordinary pictures and good ones, and I try hard to find the good ones to use in my biology classes.

What are "good" pictures in the sense meant by this science teacher? And why are such pictures better than ordinary pictures for teaching purposes? An art teacher had this to say in answering the second question:

Well, what we're really talking about is visual communication, isn't it? In my art teaching, I try to instill in my pupils an appreciation for such things as color, line, and composition in good pictures so that they can apply these fundamentals as they make their own sketches and designs. But the same principles apply to any visual material which is intended to communicate. The better a picture is from an art standpoint, the better it is likely to transmit what it has to say to anyone looking at it.

In other words, good art and good visual communication go hand in hand. Let us take a closer look at four of the characteristics found in effective pictures—*good composition, clear communication, effective color,* and *good contrast and sharpness.* In the process, we can equate these four and one other—size—with the teaching functions that flat pictures can fulfill.

GOOD COMPOSITION The fundamental characteristic of any effective picture is composition or good overall organization, such as is shown in Figure 3.14. Usually an effective picture has a clear-cut center of interest to which the rest of the picture contributes by such means as the balance of the picture as a whole, the position and direction of lines, and the use of light, shadow, and color. The focus of attention is rarely in the center of the picture—a position other than the center is usually more pleasing to the eye. The presence of a good focal point can readily be ascertained by allowing the eye to travel naturally over the picture until it fixes on a point of key interest. Look away from that point, and your eyes tend to go back to it if a strong center of interest is there.

Occasionally, there are pictures of huge crowds, geometric patterns, or a large number of similar objects that do not have a center of interest in the usual sense. In these pictures, the overall effect is the objective—a general impression rather than specific detail. Thus 100,000 people in a public square, row on row of dilapidated houses, or rolling fields of grain extending as far as the eye can see may have a powerful effect on the observer. Such a mass subject is difficult to photograph effectively, however, because it does not have a visible center of interest around which composition can be built. The center of interest in such pictures is an idea, rather than a physical thing; thus their effectiveness is determined by how well this idea is communicated. Figure 3.15 illustrates this problem.

CLEAR COMMUNICATION The principles of good composition apply to all pictures. Those to be used in teaching, however, should also clearly communicate the intended message or idea. One of the most difficult skills for the visual designer to learn is that he must first clearly define *what* he wishes to convey and then control his medium so that *how* he presents the message effectively communicates it. The good photographer typically plans each shot carefully so as to focus on a single

FIGURE 3.15

Although lacking some elements that go to make up a good picture, this scene represents something very "real" in many of our lives. Is there a communication value in such pictures?

idea and to eliminate all details that are not important to that idea. When this is done effectively, the resulting pictures are simple rather than complex and consist of large, clear images.

In general, the simple, direct picture, uncluttered with unnecessary details, communicates its message more clearly and directly than the complex picture. In fact, for complex subjects, it is usually better to use a series of pictures rather than to try to include too much in any one picture. This principle of *selective simplicity* applies both when making and selecting pictures; it applies as well to other kinds of visual designs such as study displays and graphic materials. A good rule of thumb to follow when considering whether something should or should not be included in a picture or display is this: unless it contributes something significant to the meaning or intent, do not include it. When in doubt, leave it out!

EFFECTIVE COLOR The use of harmonious and effective color is a third mark of good art. Colored pictures selected for use with children should generally be true and natural in color. Color values in nature are seldom primary reds, blues, greens, and violets; rather, they are composed of infinite and subtle variations of these colors. Thus, where color is important in a teaching situation, it should obviously be as true as possible (see Plates 3.1 and 3.2, following page 132).

According to a study of the use of drawings to convey ideas to illiterate farm workers in Venezuela, color seems to add to the communication potential of illustrations if it adds to the realism, but it detracts if used unrealistically.[13] This researcher also suggests that color is valuable in increasing interest. Another investigator

adds a further and significant consideration: "Color poor in quality offends the sensitive viewer and prevents the development of good taste by the less sensitive."[14]

Color is a part of our natural environment. It follows that *good* color in pictures adds realism as well as attractiveness to a pictured scene. Illustrations of particularly effective color use are found in Plates 3.1 and 3.2, following page 132. As color film has improved and as color reproduction processes have become more flexible and less expensive, color pictures of excellent quality are being used with increasing frequency in textbooks and reference books of all kinds. A number of well-illustrated magazines, advertising brochures, and trade journals make extensive use of full-range color reproductions.

In this connection it is worth pointing to the use of color pictures in this book itself. We have chosen our color illustrations very carefully to illustrate situations of various types where color is essential to convey the full meaning. As a result, the color illustrations relate to certain passages in only six of the chapters. In the rest of those chapters and in the other nine chapters, the illustrations convey very well what they are intended to, we believe, in black-and-white form. In other words, as teachers ourselves, we have used color in this book where it adds understanding; we have not used it merely to make the book more attractive. This does not, of course, mean that we deny the esthetic value of color pictures; it would be nice to have color throughout if cost would permit. The point is that there are many cases when color is not necessary for effective communication.

It is important to note that black-and-white photography, despite its name, can provide a wide variety of *color* impressions. Study of the gray scale (a scale of uncol-

[13] Seth Spaulding, "Communication Potential of Pictoral Illustrations," *AV Communications Review*, Winter 1956, pp. 31–33.

[14] Catherine M. Williams, *Learning from Pictures*, Department of Audiovisual Instruction, National Education Association, 1963, pp. 5–17.

ored shades from black to white) suggests the many subtle variations in value that are possible with black-and-white film (see Figure 3.16). Because of this greater flexibility, many photographers actually prefer working with black-and-white film whenever color is not an essential element of the picture. For the same reason, it is often well for the teacher to select good black-and-white photographs rather than mediocre colored pictures.

GOOD CONTRAST AND SHARPNESS
Sometimes we say in judging its quality, that a picture is "flat." This may mean several things, one of which is that the important parts do not stand out enough from the rest of the picture. Consequently, the picture as a whole lacks luster and vitality. More skillful lighting, exposure, and developing will result in blacker blacks, whiter whites—and a picture that is more interesting and effective as a whole. It is also possible to have too much contrast; this produces a harsh effect. Therefore, the good photographer or artist strives to achieve just the right amount. And as discriminating selectors, teachers should look for this important quality in the pictures they choose for classroom use.

FIGURE 3.16

The full range of the gray scale is included in this beautiful shot of Mount Hood at sunrise. What advantages can you see for some kinds of study in the many subtle gradations in tone which are possible with black-and-white pictures?

Clarity and sharpness are also important in communicating information and ideas. Although softness of focus is effective in portrait work and for the portrayal of certain moods, most educational subjects are better illustrated by pictures that are clear and sharp. The sharp picture with strong contrast provides better opportunity for accuracy in detail—a better representation of reality—and thus is preferable when information is the primary objective in using pictures.

Nature and characteristics of graphics

MOST students initially are less familiar with graphics than with flat pictures. Nevertheless, graphic materials of various kinds are a valuable means of communicating certain kinds of information that are, in fact, learned relatively early in life. By the time students reach the middle grades, they are making extensive use of graphic forms in school; many simple graphic forms, however, such as traffic signs, word-picture and number-object combinations (as in the ''Sesame Street'' programs and storybooks), and some commercial advertising displays are probably understood by the time a child first comes to school.

Definition of graphics

Graphics are instructional materials that summarize significant information and ideas through some combination of drawings, words, symbols, and pictures.

Drawing or sketching, of course, is used to make the original copy for all kinds of diagrams, graphs, and most charts such as the one in Figure 3.17. Sketches in rough

FIGURE 3.17

Charts, like other illustrative materials, have some distinctive values in teaching and also some limitations. Identify two of each.

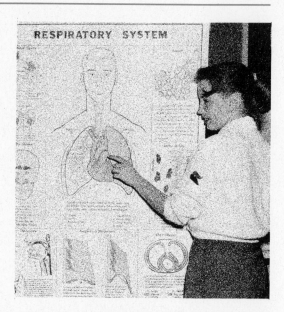

FIGURE 3.18

Words themselves are symbols, but we have devised many shortcuts through pictorial and graphic symbols to communicate concepts and information which is often of a fairly complex order.

form are used for most layouts and in more refined form are basic to the figures and symbols used in posters, cartoons and comics, and pictorial graphs. Symbols such as those in Figure 3.18 are a form of visual shorthand which is used extensively on many diagrams (such as blueprints) and signs, as well as on all maps. Words and numbers are used in practically all graphics to supplement and clarify meaning or, as in graphs or tables, to present quantitative information. Pictures or lifelike sketches are key elements in many charts and posters. Cartoons or comics are specialized kinds of drawings with words added as needed to convey the idea or story represented. Thus the term *graphics* involves a variety of visual forms, principal among which are draw-

ings and symbols in some form. Figure 3.19 gives an idea of the variety of charts and graphs in common use. The specific types are discussed in the next sections of this chapter.

The instructional values of graphic materials lie generally in their capacity to focus attention and to convey certain types of information in condensed, summarized form. A biology chart on cell division, for example, quickly summarizes the complete process of mitosis (see Figure 3.20). A diagram of office organization typically indicates departments, functions, and channels of responsibility. A graph of automobile production shows at a glance whether more or fewer cars are being produced this year than in preceding years. In each of

FIGURE 3.19

Which of the graphics in these illustrations can
you identify as to specific type—that is, bar
graph, line graph, flow chart, and so forth? As
you read the following sections on graphs,
diagrams, and charts, refer back to these
examples and see if you can identify them more
precisely.

FIGURE 3.20

these cases the essence of the graphic message is brevity, sharp focus on key information, and—if well executed—a heightened level of viewer interest (see Figure 3.21).

Maps and globes are also a form of graphic materials in that they are products of a highly specialized order of drawings known as cartography. Maps and globes and map-reading skills are of such importance in education and have such distinctive features and requirements in teaching that we devote an entire chapter to them (Chapter 7). In the present chapter, we discuss the other principal types of graphics—graphs, diagrams, charts, posters, cartoons, and comics.

Graphs

A *graph* is a visual representation of numerical data.

A table of figures may contain a wealth of valuable information, but a graph of the same data presents the gist of that information quickly and effectively. Further-

more, graphs reveal important relationships in the data, such as trends and variations from normal. Finally, and of particular significance for the teacher, graphs are inherently more interesting than numerical tabulations, however well arranged the latter may be.

When a teacher wants to keep interest in library-reading running high among his pupils, he may post a *progress graph* showing the number of books read by each pupil in the class. Progress graphs—which can be purchased from school supply houses —have a number of bright-red bars that are revealed by removing small sections of the overlaying paper. The pupils' names are inserted on the chart and one section of the overlay is removed for each completed project.

The appeal of graphs is not limited to youngsters. For example, who is not familiar with the large pictorial thermometers used to register progress in fund-raising campaigns for the Community Chest or the new church that is to be built on the

FIGURE 3.21

(a) This is a good, clear graph. (b) This, obviously, is a confusing and cluttered graph. (c) Here are the main criteria for good graphics —in graphic form.

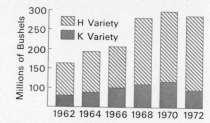

Rice Yields in Kawane County

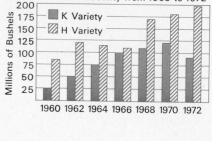

Comparative Rice Yields in Various Villages and Towns in Kawane County from 1960 to 1972

Criteria for Good Graphics

- Simple
- Bold
- Legible
- Brief
- Adequate Margins

corner? The businessman is especially dependent on graphs to show trends in sales volume, and he refers continually to them for information on business in general.

It is well to remember that the major purpose of graphing is to present comparative quantitative information *quickly* and *simply*. When a graph is intricate and difficult to read, it loses its chief advantage. Complex graphic concepts are more effectively presented, as a rule, in a series of simpler graphs than in a single intricate composite. Even when a composite graph is desirable, it should follow a series of supporting graphs.

TYPES AND ADVANTAGES OF GRAPHS
There are many kinds of graphs. Among those most commonly used are line, bar, circle, or "pie," and pictorial graphs. Each has certain advantages and applications.

Line graphs The line graph is potentially the most *precise* or accurate of all graphs; it is therefore particularly useful in plotting trends or relationships between two sets of data. A line graph should be used when a considerable number of data are to be plotted or when the data comprise a continuous series which, over a period of time, clearly shows the progress or development taking place. The line graph shown in Figure 3.22 was plotted from continuous data. Numerous variations and combinations of the simple line graph are used, including shaded-surface graphs of several types and silhouette graphs.

Bar graphs Bar graphs are among the simplest of all graphs to *read* (Figure 3.22). They also are easily constructed, as

FIGURE 3.22

These are four of the most commonly used types of graphs.

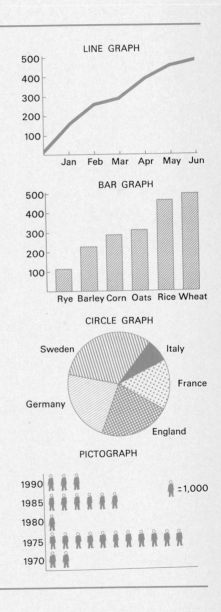

each of the several groups of data to be plotted is represented by either vertical or horizontal bars. The length of the bars is used to express the percentages of the data, while the width of all the bars remains the same. The bar graph is employed to best advantage when the number of values to be compared is small—usually no more than six or eight. Occasionally, more bars are used, but, in such instances, additional elements such as color or pictorial representations are needed to make the graph more readable and interesting. The bar graph provides direct comparison of quantitative data at specified intervals of time.

Circle, or pie, graphs The circle, or pie, graph is divided into sectors, each of which is used to represent a component *part of a whole*. The essence of the circle graph is that its combined parts must always add up to 100 percent. To put it another way, two characteristics are common to all circle graphs: (1) They always present totals or whole amounts and (2) their parts or segments are calculated in percentages or fractional parts of this whole. When the intermediate-grade teacher introduces the subject of fractions, he may begin by cutting an apple into halves and quarters. He may apply a similar technique with the feltboard, fitting segments of a circle together to form the complete circle.

Research indicates that circle graphs are the most accurately read of all common graph forms when used to compare parts of a whole. For example, if a nation produces 10,000,000 tons of coal per year and 7,500,000 tons are bituminous, 2,000,000 anthracite, and 500,000 lignite, this information can be shown on a circle graph by shading 75 percent of the circle to represent bituminous production, 20 percent for anthracite, and the remaining 5 percent for lignite. The resulting "pie" is a natural and easily understood visual device with which to present this data. Such information as the sources of the school

dollar, the distribution of expenditures of a municipality, or the proportional sources of the world's petroleum supply can likewise be well represented by pie graphs. A good example is shown in Figure 3.22.

Pictorial graphs Much of the eye-catching appeal of figures that give a three-dimensional effect is attained by the flat, simplified, and representational figures that are used in pictorial graphs. Simplified drawings give the graph *realism* and *interest* appeal. This type of graph is actually an adaptation of the bar graph and is usually employed to present the same kinds of data. Used widely in magazines and newspapers, the pictorial graph is easily read and has the added advantage of using realistic representational figures to convey meaning.

Pictorial statistics were first popularized in Vienna by Otto Neurath, a renowned sociologist who sought a means of conveying significant statistical information in a way that would be both interesting and readily understood by peoples around the world. He achieved this by developing simplified outline figures of such subjects as a man, woman, child, cow, ship, or sheaf of grain and using them to represent graphic data. Neurath termed his figures "isotypes"; variations of his original figures are now used in most countries of the world. *Pictorial statistics* thus refers to any graphic form employing such figures, as, for example, those shown in the pictograph in Figure 3.22. Compare the four types of graphs shown and note the relative degrees of interest and readability of the several types.

RESEARCH ON READABILITY OF GRAPHS AND TABLES There have been a number of studies over the past two decades on the relative readability of various types of graphs and tables. A synthesis of the findings suggests a number of points of interest to teachers:

(1) The circle, or pie, graph is the

easiest of all graphic forms to comprehend. Such graphs, however, are useful only for comparing parts of a whole; therefore, we need to examine the other graph types. (2) Horizontal and vertical bar graphs, in that order, are probably the next most comprehensible graphic forms. A three-dimensional effect in the way the bars are drawn does not of itself make for less accurate reading of a bar graph. (3) Line graphs are probably the best type in presenting precise, detailed information or in showing significant trends. (4) Comparative-area graphs—squares, circles, rectangles, and so forth—tend to be the least accurately read of any of the various types of graphs. (5) Either bar graphs or short simple tables are more effective when reinforced with text than without. (6) Long tables—even if reinforced with text—are less effective than other graphic forms. (7) Simply casting figures into a prosaic text form, as in a paragraph, is probably the least effective means possible of presenting quantitative information. (8) Pictorial graphs have essentially the advantages of the graphic forms with which they are combined. Best are pictorial horizontal bar graphs. In addition, if well designed, such graphs are probably more interesting to the nontechnical reader than other types of graphs.

Diagrams

A *diagram* is a condensed drawing consisting primarily of lines and symbols designed to represent the outline, interrelationships, or key features of a process, object, or area.

Although graphics in general are condensed visual summaries, the diagram is the most condensed of all. It depends almost entirely upon lines and symbols to convey information and, accordingly, may be highly abstract. This means that a background of knowledge and experience in the subject of the diagram is necessary before it can be read intelligently. Construc-

tion diagrams usually reproduced as blueprints provide a good example of the complexity to which diagraming can go and the difficulties we may face in interpreting them. If you have the necessary technical background and experience to read a blueprint such as the one shown in Figure 3.23, you have no problem. If you do not, however, it can be totally confusing and meaningless. Yet such diagrams are so essential that modern construction, engineering, and manufacturing would be impossible without them.

There are many simpler types of diagrams, of course, such as those used in learning to thread a motion picture projector (see Figure 3.24) or those used with dress patterns to enable women who make their own clothes to fit the pieces together properly. Toy manufacturers use diagrams to help children and their parents assemble wagons and model planes, ships, and railroads. (As many fathers know, such diagrams are often something less than clear!) We frequently sketch out simple diagrams to help someone find his way to our home, to the right freeway entrance, or to the airport.

Diagrams can be important visual tools in teaching, as well. English teachers for generations have used diagrams in teaching the relationships among subjects, predicates and other parts of speech. We use process diagrams in the social studies to show how a bill becomes a law; cross-section diagrams in science to show how jet engines, pumps, and hydraulic systems work; and other diagrams in shopwork to lay out jobs to be done. Clearly, diagrams are a valuable means of synthesizing certain kinds of information.

On the other hand, we need to realize that a diagram can *impede* learning if its meaning is unclear to the learner. This suggests that whenever diagrams are used, we need to be sure that our students can read them. Reading difficulties in diagrams may range all the way from the meaning of the symbols used to a lack of understanding of the purposes the diagram is intended to serve. Whatever the reason, learning can be effectively blocked right there unless we clear it up before going on.

Charts

A *chart* is a combination of pictorial, graphic, numerical, or verbal materials designed to present a clear visual summary of an important process or set of relationships.

The term "charts" has a number of interpretations. To the navigator, a chart is a specialized kind of map. To the businessman, it can be a graph or a tabular arrangement of sales data. To the engineer, it may be a technical diagram. Thus "chart" is likely to have different meanings for different people. For our purposes, however, we can be more specific because charts for teaching have certain values and characteristics of their own.

The principal steps in the production of steel, the organization of Congress, the parts of a flower, the phases of the moon, parts of speech, or a historical time line are typical of the many and varied subjects suitable for treatment on charts. Many charts are available commercially in sets, but valuable simplified charts can also be made by teachers and students. Because of heavy printing costs involved, commercial producers frequently combine several related charts on one large sheet. When designing your own charts, however, it is easier and usually more effective to keep them simple and relatively uncrowded. Specific steps that should be followed in making charts and other graphic forms are described in the accompanying *Student Production Guide*.

TYPES OF CHARTS   As suggested by the definition of charts, charts may be made up of almost any combination of visual and verbal elements. Their distinctiveness and

FIGURE 3.23

Technical fields rely heavily on diagrams to communicate detailed, precise information. Without such diagrams as this blueprint, our construction and manufacturing industries could not function.

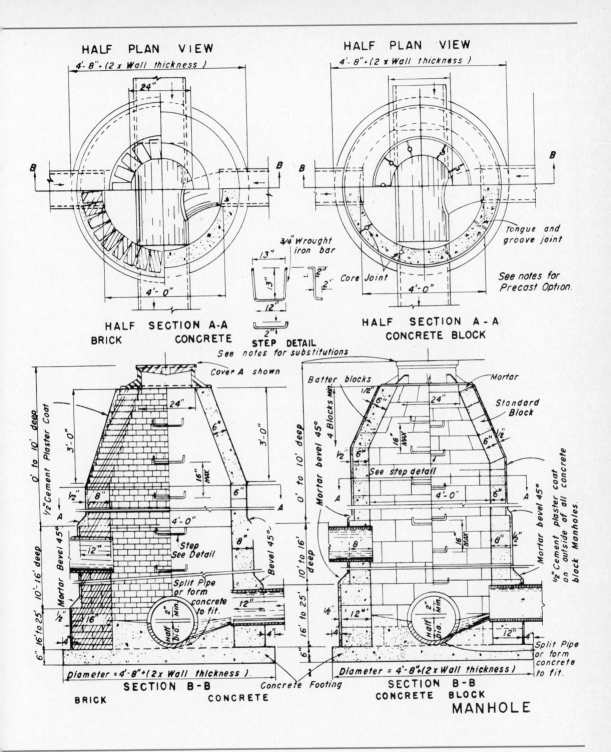

HALF PLAN VIEW
4'- 8" + (2 x Wall thickness)
24"
B   B
4'- 0"

HALF PLAN VIEW
4'- 8" + (2 x Wall thickness)
B   B
Tongue and groove joint
Core Joint
4'-0"
See notes for Precast Option.

3/4" Wrought iron bar
13"
13"
12"
2"
2"
2"

STEP DETAIL
See notes for substitutions

HALF SECTION A-A
BRICK   CONCRETE

HALF SECTION A-A
CONCRETE BLOCK

Cover A shown
½" Cement Plaster Coat   0' to 10' deep
24"
3'-0"
6"
3'-0"
16" MAX
8"
6"
½"
4'-0"
Step See Detail
8"   Bevel 45°
12"   0' to 10' deep
Mortar Bevel 45°   10'-16' deep
Split Pipe or form concrete to fit.
16   Half 2" Dia. Min.
½"   16' to 25'
6"   12"   4"
Diameter = 4'-8" + (2 x Wall thickness)
Concrete Footing
SECTION B-B
BRICK   CONCRETE

Batter blocks   Mortar
½"   Standard Block
4 Blocks Min.   24"
Mortar bevel 45°   16" MAX   6"   ½"
½"   6"
See step detail
4'-0"   6"   A
A   8   16" MAX   6"
½"   ½" Cement plaster coat on outside of all concrete block Manholes.
10' to 16' deep   Mortar bevel 45°
½"   12"   Half 2" Dia. Min.
6"   16' to 25'   Split Pipe or form concrete to fit.
12"   4"
Diameter = 4'-8" + (2 x Wall thickness)
SECTION B-B
CONCRETE BLOCK
MANHOLE

119

FIGURE 3.24

Open-reel motion picture projectors, regardless of specific type, are threaded in this way.

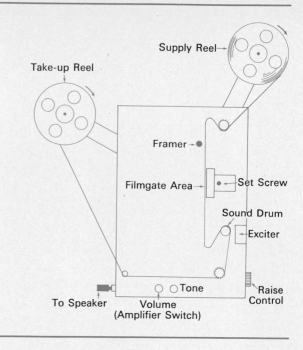

ways of classifying them derive more from their functions than from the kinds of visual or verbal materials used on them. In a functional context, one graphic arts expert has identified some 50 different classifications of charts. For classroom purposes, however, we need note only four groups of these: outline and tabular charts; flow, organization, and process charts; tree and stream charts; time-line charts.

As we consider these four basic chart forms, it will be helpful to keep in mind the following characteristics of good charts for teaching:

1. Clear and well-defined purposes. Usually a chart concentrates on one main idea, concept, or process.

2. Use of whatever visual, verbal, or other materials are needed to achieve the purpose or purposes specified.

3. Summary treatment of information. Good charts typically do not provide large amounts of information. Rather, they summarize the key points to be learned.

4. Adequate size for principal features to be seen across a room, if needed.

Outline and tabular charts The organization of content into an *outline* of key points and subpoints which a teacher may letter on the chalkboard results in a useful chart form (Figure 3.25). The content may range from simple parts of speech, phonetic words and syllables, and number sets to traffic safety or field trip rules and regulations. *Tabular* charts, as the name implies, present information in columns (Figure 3.25). Common uses include vocabulary or spelling lists, arithmetic exercises, production or sales figures, and the Table of Atomic Weights in chemistry.

Flow, organization, and process charts The organization of a student council or a unit of government, the development of a manufacturing process, or the steps whereby a bill becomes a law can be shown to advantage in a *flow* chart (Figure 3.25)

120

FIGURE 3.25

These are four of the most commonly used types of charts.

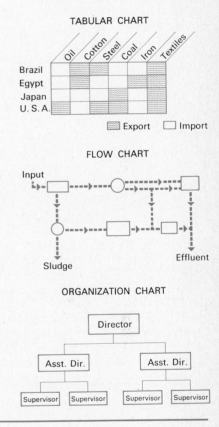

OUTLINE CHART
Graphic Criteria

1. Simple
   a. Eliminate the nonessential
2. Bold
   a. Make bars dominate
3. Legible
   a. Large open letters
4. Brief
   a. Precise title
5. Adequate Margins
   a. Top and sides equal, bottom larger

TABULAR CHART

Oil Cotton Steel Coal Iron Textiles

Brazil
Egypt
Japan
U.S.A.

Export   Import

FLOW CHART

Input

Sludge   Effluent

ORGANIZATION CHART

Director

Asst. Dir.   Asst. Dir.

Supervisor Supervisor   Supervisor Supervisor

or *organization* chart (Figure 3.25). This type of chart is well suited to showing functional relationships and is used widely in industry and government for that purpose.

Tree and stream charts   As its name suggests, the *tree* chart is developed from a base composed of several "roots" that lead into a single "trunk." The "branches," in turn, represent developments and relationships. A good example is a genealogy chart in which two individuals are the roots from which a family "tree" grows. The *tree* chart is useful in showing developments resulting from a combination of ma-

FIGURE 3.26

These are four of the most commonly used types of charts and diagrams.

TREE CHART

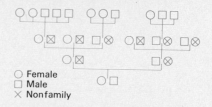

○ Female
□ Male
✕ Nonfamily

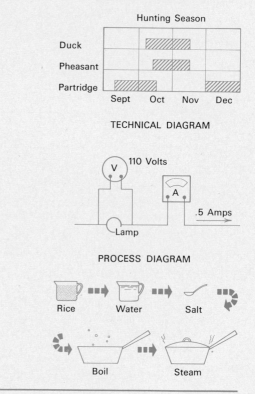

TIME-LINE CHART

Hunting Season

	Sept	Oct	Nov	Dec
Duck		░░		
Pheasant		░░		
Partridge	░░			░░

TECHNICAL DIAGRAM

V 110 Volts
A
.5 Amps
Lamp

PROCESS DIAGRAM

Rice Water Salt

Boil Steam

jor factors (Figure 3.26). For example, such a chart is suitable for showing the many by-products obtainable from coal. It is similarly effective in showing how iron ore, limestone, coke, and various chemicals may be combined to produce a variety of types of steel. Sometimes a reverse form of the tree chart is useful in showing how a great variety of elements are combined to form one important product. This type of chart, known as a *stream* chart, can be used to illustrate an industrial nation's dependence on other countries for strategic materials.

Time-line charts Time lines are helpful for summarizing sequences of events or for making chronological comparisons of comparable developments in various countries (Figure 3.26). Wheat production in a given year in a number of Western nations might best be shown in a bar graph or a pictorial bar graph; but a *time-line* chart would be better for comparing wheat production in those countries at 10-year intervals from 1900 to 1970.

Technical diagrams As the name implies, the *technical* diagram (Figure 3.26) is used for functions that are essentially technical in nature—electric circuit layouts, construction blueprints, fuel systems, and similar complex assemblies. To facilitate the required precision in communicating the complexities involved, many standard symbols are used which are often unintelligible to the layman. For the diagram to have meaning, the symbols must, however, be clearly understood by the engineers, contractors, and other specialists employing them.

Process diagrams The *process* diagram shown (Figure 3.26) is a simple one, but such diagrams can be highly detailed and complex, as when the numerous steps in a manufacturing process are illustrated. A process diagram implies a flow of activity as well as an orderly sequence of separate steps. When the ''flow'' rather than the individual steps is emphasized, such diagrams are frequently referred to as flow charts, or flow-process diagrams.

Student- and teacher-made graphics

Much of what has been said about graphic communications materials relates to the *interpretation* of graphics—that is, graphs, diagrams, charts, posters, comics, and cartoons—by the pupil. In making and designing their own graphics, pupils are provided with a quick, sure, and interesting way of gaining useful information and understanding. Graphics can be constructed by pupils and teachers to organize and present reports, demonstrations, how-to-do-it explanations, and so forth. For example, in English the pupil can prepare and use a chart to visualize the story line and action of a short story or novel. The science student may rely on his creative diagram to explain the mechanism and operation of the retrorockets used in space docking. The home economics student might present charts to show the interrelationship of calories and weight with various methods of meat cookery.

As teachers, we must become more concerned with the creative ability of students to express and apply their knowledge. The inventive use of graphics which the pupils themselves produce to meet their own needs is an area of instruction which should be more emphasized. To begin in this direction, we should be concerned primarily with the student's understanding of graphics as a means of expressing information and ideas. His decision to use a chart, graph, or poster in the first place should be based on the determination that it will communicate something important and perhaps unique. Accordingly, one circumstance in which it makes sense to *construct* a graphic is where one is needed that is not otherwise available.

Another circumstance in which graphics-construction activities are warranted is when the act of preparing in itself will contribute significantly to the student's understanding of the subject under study. In the preparation of a time line, for example, the process of locating significant events in juxtaposition on the chart may help the pupil to fix important time relationships in his mind more clearly than studying someone else's time line, reading a verbal summary, or getting the requisite information from another source, such as class discussion. It becomes a matter of good judgment by the teacher of when and for whom preparation activity is desirable to bring about desired understandings.

A related and important consideration is the fact that one learns a good deal about *interpreting* graphs, diagrams, posters, cartoons, and some chart forms through the experience of *making* them. Development of students' abilities to interpret these graphic forms readily and intelligently is clearly an important function of our schools. Accordingly, to the extent that such experience is needed for improving the interpretive skills of students, construction activities are certainly justified.

In this connection, there is a close relationship between the student's ability either to make *or* to interpret graphics and his grasp of related concepts. Thus the ability to count and some concept of scale are necessary for constructing the simplest bar graphs; percentage and the calculations necessary to convert information to more complex scales are required for most circle or line graphs and for time lines. In the course of such applications, the pupil both firms up his math and develops insights into the meanings of comparable graphics.

It is also important for the student to learn how graphics can *misrepresent* information by various techniques. When students become alert to distortions, interrupted scale, and changes in size of symbols as examples of how false impressions can be conveyed on graphs and sequence charts, they gain in the ability to do critical thinking. In constructing the chart or graph for himself, the student often becomes more conscious of these pitfalls than he does through mere exposure to ready-made graphics. Attention to the source of the data (which should always be noted) is another useful factor in critical evaluation which students need to learn in order to deal intelligently with the profusion of graphics used for communication in the world around them.

SCHOOL-MADE CHARTS Any of the types of charts described are available from commercial sources (see the source lists in the Appendix), but many of them can be made by teachers or pupils. Elementary teachers have suggested the following possibilities, each named according to its teaching function rather than type of chart:

1. *Experience charts* A trip to the library, bakery, museum, and so forth, will be long remembered if some of the salient points are put down on charts.

2. *Achievement charts* Charts setting down principles of spelling, of arithmetic, or of science that have been mastered by the class.

3. *Charts recording plans and class rules* A field trip plan can be outlined on a chart to give in advance special emphasis to some of the important sights that will be seen.

4. *Instruction charts of wide variety* *Number* charts help bridge the critical step to the gradual realization that numbers are abstract ideas. *Phonetic* charts are enormously helpful in establishing familiarity with common syllables and words and introducing the link between writing and speech. *Work* charts list series of problems or questions to be answered. They also help develop reading skill and speed.

At higher grade levels, of course, the possibilities are almost unlimited.

As already noted, specific suggestions on methods and materials for making graphs, diagrams, and charts are in the accompanying *Student Production Guide*.

Posters

A *poster* is a visual combination of bold design, color, and message intended to catch and hold the attention of the passer-by long enough to implant or reinforce a significant idea in his mind.

Posters have existed in primitive form since the invention of movable-type printing in the fifteenth century. The first posters, which consisted almost entirely of text, carried notices of royal proclamations, tax assessments, fairs, markets, and newly printed books. Some of them did have wood-cut illustrations. But it remained for lithography—the printing process developed in the mid-nineteenth century which made possible the first cheap and brilliant color reproduction—to bring the modern concept of posters into being.

The modern poster was born in 1867 in Paris, when Jules Chéret, the first of the great modern poster artists, was commissioned by the actress Sarah Bernhardt to prepare a poster announcing her appearance in the play *La Biche au Bois*. Chéret's use of color, design, and bold lettering was striking, and his posters started a new trend in graphic communication. As the poster idea caught on, many fine artists experimented with it in Europe and the United States. The best of these posters combined simplicity and visual force with emotional impact or wit; many became famous. During both world wars, the major powers used large-scale poster campaigns to recruit military enlistments, sell war bonds, build morale, and boost the war effort generally. U. S. Treasury officials regarded posters as highly significant factors in the success of the war-loan drives during both wars. In the meantime, industry adopted the poster idea on a massive scale for advertisements in newspapers and magazines and on billboards throughout the world. Developing nations find posters useful in promoting malaria control, improved agricultural practices, sanitation, and family planning, and in political campaigns.

UNIQUE CHARACTERISTICS OF GOOD POSTERS If they are to achieve their purpose, good posters must have a dynamic, compelling quality. They must essentially be simple, for there is no time to try to involve the viewer in detailed study. They need to be striking enough to attract attention and convey their message quickly; they must also be good-looking enough to be pleasing to the eye.

The element of dramatic simplicity is well illustrated in the civil rights poster in Figure 3.27. The eye-catcher in that poster is the clenched black fist symbolizing black militancy which leads the eye to the clasped black and white hands in the background which symbolize the cooperative efforts necessary to achieve solutions to our civil rights problem. Originally, the poster was used in an advertisement for a filmed history of the civil rights movement, with the clenched fist carrying the eye to the following message printed at the top: "To understand today's black militancy, your students must understand yesterday's civil rights struggle." The design is so strong, simple, and impelling, however, that the poster communicates its basic message powerfully without words. Thus it is an outstanding poster. See Plate 3.3, following page 132, for other outstanding posters.

POSTER APPLICATIONS IN SCHOOLS There are two types of useful poster applications in schools. One is the professionally prepared posters available from such sources as the National Safety Council, the National Dairy Council, the Community Chest, and other agencies that emphasize good safety and health habits, consideration for others, and the like. (A listing of sources of such posters is in the Appendix.) Such posters are valuable at all age levels. Industry has found, for example, that there is a direct relationship between safety records and safety campaigns, one important element in which is reminder posters. The same is true in schools. Learning an idea, learning a good safety or health habit is one thing; practicing it is another. We need reminders, and good posters can serve this reinforcement purpose well.

A second important use of posters in schools is in the creative possibilities of student-made posters. The discussion of visual literacy brought out the importance of pupils being able to express themselves visually through pictures. The same can be true for some youngsters through their ability to draw and sketch ideas in graphic forms. Any student who makes his own posters has the opportunity of expressing what he has learned. Some students in a class in English literature, for example, may prepare posters for a Shakespearean display. History students can trace interesting parallels in the political posters used in political campaigns and then make their own that relate to general elections or school elections. Social studies committees and student councils analyzing current school problems such as playground safety, lunchroom conditions, recreational programs, and corridor traffic between classes may find well-prepared posters an effective means of expressing their conclusions.

Campaign or advertising posters made in connection with school and community activities are an important outlet. Campaigns for electing members of the student council, class plays, athletic contests, clean-up campaigns, music festivals, forensic contests, hobby shows, and the like are ''naturals'' for the preparation and use of posters. Poster-making enables the school to capitalize on the natural drives of pupils to accomplish socially important and desirable objectives that interest them.

Cartoons and comics

A *cartoon* is a pictorial representation or caricature of a person, idea, or situation, designed to influence public opinion.

A *comic* is a form of cartooning in which a cast of characters enacts a story in a sequence of closely related drawings designed to entertain or inform the reader.

FIGURE 3.27

The attention-holding quality of this poster is based on its stark simplicity and the dynamic strength of its contrasting symbols—the clenched fist and the clasped hands.

FIGURE 3.28

A succinct idea sharply rendered—usually with a bit of humor—is one of the marks of the good cartoonist.

Hal Money

"School let out early--there was a power failure at the ETV station."

Although they have some similar characteristics, cartoons and comics have quite different origins. The use of the cartoon to lampoon man and his foibles goes back to the sixteenth century, when Renaissance artists began to caricature one another with deftly drawn sketches. Archaeologists have uncovered on the walls of ancient buildings many drawings that poke fun at the great and the pretentious. Medieval manuscripts contain similar evidence of refreshing humor directed at persons and groups prominent in the contemporary society. In fact, an interesting analogy can be drawn between the king's jester in medieval times and the modern cartoonist. The modern political-social cartoon came into prominence in the 1860s, when Thomas Nast conducted his famous cartoon campaign against the notorious Tweed Ring in New York—a campaign that was credited with doing much to arouse public indignation and public support of the eventually successful efforts to overthrow Boss Tweed.

Cartoons are widely used today in newspapers and magazines in two rather distinct ways. In one use, cartoons have a political-social purpose: to present a point of view or a position on an important issue, often in an attempt to influence public opinion. In the other use, which is somewhat more recent, cartoons provide a more or less sophisticated form of entertainment by poking fun at the attitudes, values, and activities of various groups and institutions within our society (see Figure 3.28). Both types of cartoons are very much a part of the visual world from which we and our students come.

Comics or comic strips came into use somewhat later than cartoons, during the newspaper war between William Randolph Hearst's New York *Journal* and Joseph Pulitzer's New York *World* in the mid-1890s. The two newspapers used many techniques, often unscrupulous ones, to build circulation, but a significant part in the contest was played by strips of funny drawings involving an innocent character known as "The Yellow Kid" from the

FIGURE 3.29

Comics vary widely in their appeal to different age levels. A few, such as *Peanuts*, have exceptional appeal to a wide range of readers both young and old. What accounts for this?

color of his clothes. The comic strip, started by one paper, was soon copied by the other. The rival versions of the drawings in both papers and the notoriety arising from the sensationalized and often fabricated "news" the papers printed in their efforts to outdo each other in mass appeal led to the derogatory term "yellow journalism."

Today comic sections in newspapers are read daily by millions of people of all ages. There is sufficient variety to appeal to young and old alike. The *Peanuts* strip, for example, has a huge following at the adult level because of its whimsical but incisive human characterizations (see Figure 3.29). The comic strip format has also been successfully adapted to other uses such as the comic book and the more recent serious information pieces which now appear within the comic sections of Sunday papers.

COMIC BOOKS AND THEIR INFLUENCE
Although used successfully in promotional campaigns as early as 1911, comic books did not really come into their own until the mid-1930s. Once they had caught on, however, they rapidly developed into big business. At one point, some 50,000,000

comic books were published on a weekly, biweekly, or monthly basis in the United States and Canada. Until the middle 1960s, comic books were read almost universally by children in the intermediate grades, by nearly half of all high school pupils, and by approximately one-third of people between the ages of 18 and 30. It is probable that the widespread development of television viewing was responsible for much of the drop-off in comic book reading during the middle and later 1960s; comic book circulation was down some 5,000,000 in the United States at the end of the decade.[15]

During the 1940s and 1950s, in particular, there was much concern among educators and parents about the effect of undesirable comics emphasizing violence and even sadism on children and their reading habits. This widespread concern actually resulted in several cities barring certain comics from sale at various times. But, though there was general agreement during this period that the influence of

[15] Leonard Bray, ed., *Newspapers, Magazines, and Trade Publications*, Ayer, 1970, p. 1461.

comic books *was* extensive, the many research studies done to pinpoint the nature of this influence did not reach any consensus; some reported positive effects on children, others reported negative ones. In any case, after a careful study of all the research done in this area, two investigators concluded in 1954 that there was no valid basis for either strongly opposing or stoutly defending the comic medium.[16]

Whatever else they may have done, it was evident that comic books stimulated the reading habits of young people far more than any other single device to have come upon the American scene to that time. For example, an early study indicated that a child who read one comic book per month read about twice as many words per year as his reading books contained and that both the amount and the character of the vocabulary provided valuable practice for the young reader.[17]

A useful development arising from comic books is the instructional comic being produced by a number of companies, particularly in the popular science areas. Such comics, which attempt to capitalize on the popularity of the comic book format, have achieved some degree of success. Currently, many Sunday comic sections carry a science feature which highlights present and possible future developments in a wide range of fascinating areas such as oceanography, space travel, atomic energy, and

FIGURE 3.30

This is an example of one of the successful adaptations of comic art techniques.

power from the sun (see Figure 3.30). Far from being science fiction, these strips often carry the names of prominent scientists on whose work the features are based; they are read by millions of adults as well as children.

The selection and use of pictures and graphics

THERE have been many changes in textbook, magazine, and even newspaper publishing during the past two decades as

[16] Paul A. Witty and Robert A. Sizemore, ''Reading the Comics: A Seminar of Studies and an Evaluation,'' *Elementary English*, December 1954, p. 502.

[17] Robert L. Thorndike, ''Words and the Comics,'' *Journal of Experimental Education*, December 1941, pp. 110–113.

a consequence of the general trend toward more and better visualization in communications. A comparison of elementary and secondary textbooks today with those of 20 years ago shows marked increases in the use of illustrations, color, attractive cover designs, and more readable type faces and formats. This is true also of college textbooks. Though competition among publishers is undoubtedly a prominent factor

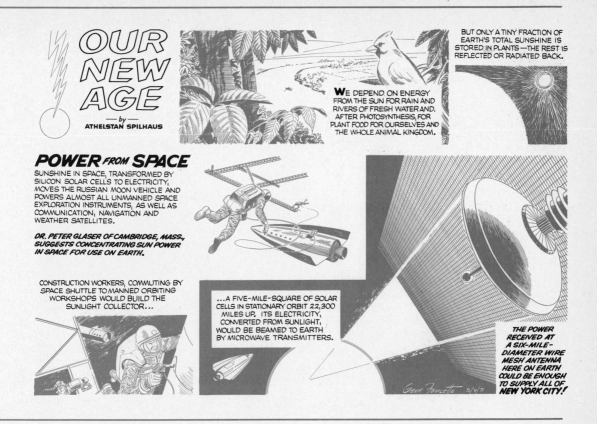

OUR NEW AGE
by
ATHELSTAN SPILHAUS

WE DEPEND ON ENERGY FROM THE SUN FOR RAIN AND RIVERS OF FRESH WATER AND, AFTER PHOTOSYNTHESIS, FOR PLANT FOOD FOR OURSELVES AND THE WHOLE ANIMAL KINGDOM.

BUT ONLY A TINY FRACTION OF EARTH'S TOTAL SUNSHINE IS STORED IN PLANTS—THE REST IS REFLECTED OR RADIATED BACK.

POWER FROM SPACE

SUNSHINE IN SPACE, TRANSFORMED BY SILICON SOLAR CELLS TO ELECTRICITY, MOVES THE RUSSIAN MOON VEHICLE AND POWERS ALMOST ALL UNMANNED SPACE EXPLORATION INSTRUMENTS, AS WELL AS COMMUNICATION, NAVIGATION AND WEATHER SATELLITES.

DR. PETER GLASER OF CAMBRIDGE, MASS., SUGGESTS CONCENTRATING SUN POWER IN SPACE FOR USE ON EARTH.

CONSTRUCTION WORKERS, COMMUTING BY SPACE SHUTTLE TO MANNED ORBITING WORKSHOPS WOULD BUILD THE SUNLIGHT COLLECTOR...

...A FIVE-MILE-SQUARE OF SOLAR CELLS IN STATIONARY ORBIT 22,300 MILES UP. ITS ELECTRICITY, CONVERTED FROM SUNLIGHT, WOULD BE BEAMED TO EARTH BY MICROWAVE TRANSMITTERS.

THE POWER RECEIVED AT A SIX-MILE-DIAMETER WIRE MESH ANTENNA HERE ON EARTH COULD BE ENOUGH TO SUPPLY ALL OF NEW YORK CITY!

Gene Fawcette 5/4/71

in these changes, there seems little question that better textbooks have been developed in the process.

One important criterion in textbook selection, therefore, is the quality and appropriateness of the pictorial and graphic illustrations used. In this connection, it is important to keep in mind the levels of abstraction and complexity involved in the illustrations in relation to the maturity levels of students. Graphic materials and, to a lesser extent, pictorial materials vary widely in the levels of abstraction represented and, accordingly, in the levels of experience required to interpret them readily. The cartoon in Figure 3.28, for example, would have little meaning to most students below the upper secondary level.

Such factors as these are important considerations in both the selection and the use of *any* instructional materials. A thorough knowledge of his students' abilities and limitations, plus a clear and specific determination of his objectives, will do much to help the teacher select the best available materials and to use them in the most effective ways.

In general, as we have seen, circle graphs, bar graphs, and line graphs are more easily read than other types. As we have also noted, diagrams are typically abstract by nature and often require background knowledge before they can be helpful. Some graphs and charts are more crowded or more complex and difficult to read than others. One picture may illustrate a point precisely and clearly while another may do it poorly or even be distracting. Two of the more important basic selection criteria to keep in mind are these: Is a visual illustration in fact necessary at all? If it is, how far does the one being considered contribute *significantly* to the desired understanding? The use of visuals merely for the sake of using visuals is pointless and may even retard rather than enhance the desired learning.

As we have examined the characteristics of good flat pictures and the strengths and limitations of each of the several types of graphics, we have, in effect, been establishing the criteria according to which they should be selected and put to use. In addition to considerations of pertinence and appropriate level, the physical quality of the materials themselves becomes important. Generally speaking, we remind ourselves that pictures that communicate well have a strong center of interest, good composition, good color where color is important, and a sufficiently sharp focus to provide the necessary detail.

Graphics, by definition, synthesize information at the same time pulling it together and pointing out its most significant elements. Normally, this kind of material is more useful after students have moved along in a subject than at the beginning;

pictures, on the other hand, can be useful at almost any point in the lesson. There are some graphics, however, that are very useful in motivational or developmental phases of a lesson.

In some cases, a teacher may want to have a carefully selected set of pictures available for his students to work with. In other cases, the students should seek out pictures from magazines and picture files to achieve a particular purpose—or take their own pictures. Picture-taking by students is particularly valuable for studies involving the local community and, as we have seen in the visual literacy discussion, is particularly useful, also, for enabling many students to express themselves in new and effective ways. In that connection, it should be noted that visual literacy training is not restricted to the very young, nor are its values limited to the academically deprived student. The well-known media philosopher Marshall McLuhan and the noted psychologist Jerome Bruner are among those who have pointed to the creative possibilities inherent in the "discovery" method and in opportunities afforded students of all ages to use modern methods of communication.

The Instructional Development approach to more effective teaching and learning

THERE are two general approaches to the selection and use of teaching materials and methods of any kind. The first, which is also most typical of what a good teacher normally does, is to take the materials readily at hand—textbooks and reference books, pictures, graphics, filmstrips, and other materials—select from them intuitively in terms of the pupils' and the teacher's own interests and abilities, and do the best with them that he can. This approach is reasonable and, of course, some-

times highly effective; in any case, it is probably representative of what most teachers have done for generations.

Today, however, there is a more promising and systematic approach that relies less on intuition, gives us, as teachers, a much better chance of being highly effective, and, most important, helps assure optimum learning on the part of our pupils. This is the *Instructional Development* approach, which we shall emphasize at various points throughout this book. It is a highly

PLATE 3.1

Highly effective large study prints in excellent color are available in various subject areas. Those shown here and in Plate 3.2 are selections from several series of pictures on Europe, North America, and Africa designed to illustrate key concepts in geography. They are laminated, 30 × 21 inches, and each set comes in a window-type case that serves for storage of the set or as a frame for individual pictures. (a) Rhineland, West Germany; (b) the pulpwood industry, Three Rivers, Quebec, Canada.

PLATE 3.2

Aside from strong esthetic appeal, what does color add to this striking view of the Swiss Alps? How does color contribute to an understanding of the landscape and its vegetation? How does it contribute to comprehension of life and the problems of living on a Swiss mountainside?

PLATE 3.3

The design of a poster is influenced by its subject, and subject and design together determine the character and impact of the poster. Some are strong and vibrant; others are quiet and peaceful. Each one, however, has a message, and the measure of its effectiveness is how well the message is communicated.

ATTICA!
SAN QUENTIN!
ANGELA DAVIS??

PLATE 4.1

Color is particularly important in dioramas
which create the illusion of reality in miniature.
(a) This diorama, in the Circus World Museum
in Wisconsin, takes us back to a farming community in the 1890s, when the arrival of the
traveling circus was one of the most exciting
events of the year. (b) This is a diorama of a
modern farm. (c) This diorama shows the ancient
cliff dwellers at Mesa Verde in Colorado.

PLATE 4.2

The colors used in models vary with the purpose of the color. To aid in understanding complicated medical models, exaggerated natural colors in bright hues with strong contrasts are often used. To emphasize certain points or distinguish among important parts of simpler models, a few colors in cool hues may serve the purpose very well.

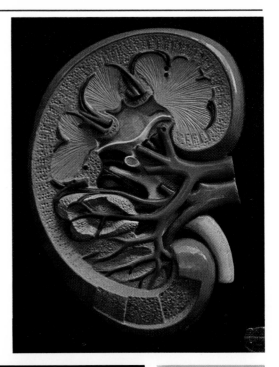

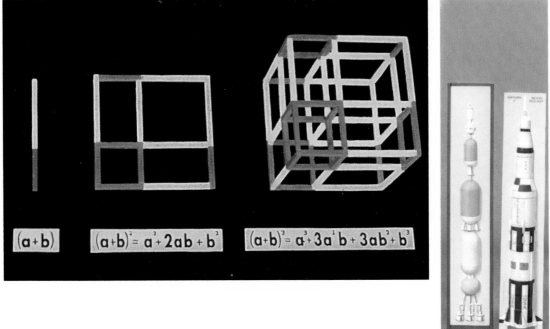

$(a+b)$

$(a+b)^2 = a^2 + 2ab + b^2$

$(a+b)^3 = a^3 + 3a^2b + 3ab^2 + b^3$

humanistic system in that it enables us as teachers to do those things that we can do best, accommodates individual differences in students, and helps better to assure that those key purposes that our schools exist to achieve are, in fact, accomplished.

Let us note at once that as an individual teacher you can hardly install an instructional system yourself. A complete system entails intensive, cooperative efforts by administrators, teachers, supervisors, and specialists in instruction, curriculum, technology, and other fields. But you can make a start and in the process not only improve your present teaching but also help pave the way for wider adoption of Instructional Development in your school and school system.[18]

There is no better place to start than with the selection and use of such readily available materials as flat pictures and graphics. Thus we begin with this chapter and develop the principles involved further as we proceed through this book. Much of what you will read and discuss in this context is not new. For example, we have talked about objectives for many years, though we have failed for the most part

[18] A carefully designed and thoroughly tested training program called the Instructional Development Institutes (IDI) has been developed by a consortium of the instructional technology departments in four major institutions to train teams of teachers, administrators, policy-makers, and specialists in curriculum, instruction, media, and subject areas in the process of developing instructional systems. These IDIs were developed over a two-year period under a USOE grant to the National Special Media Institutes Consortium consisting of Michigan State University, Syracuse University, the Teaching Research Division of the Oregon System of Higher Education; and the University of Southern California. Professional assistance in organizing and conducting IDIs is now available through numerous teacher education agencies in the several regions of the United States. For information address Dr. Charles F. Schuller, Director, National Special Media Institutes, c/o Instructional Media Center, Michigan State University, East Lansing, Michigan 48823.

to pin them down or find ways to make them work for us. Now, however, the rapidly increasing number and complexity of social and economic problems facing our schools mean that we have no choice but to find better answers than we have so far on how best to employ the dollars and resources we have to educate our young people.

It is interesting and relevant to note that industry and government have long since moved into use of the systems approach to find the best solutions to training and production problems. In fact, the field of engineering is where the systems approach originated, and its use spread from there into a variety of military, administrative, and production areas. In education, we have a more complex job to do than in any of these, but to the extent the systems approach can help us—and it can —we must attend to it.

In the simplest terms, application of the systems approach to the solution of teaching and learning problems is largely a matter of carefully analyzing what those problems really are and applying to their solution the best knowledge that we have about learning, methods, and instructional materials. If the process is to pay off, however, it must be applied in a far more systematic and rigorous manner than we typically use in attempting to solve educational problems today.

Let us do a quick rundown of the four principal steps involved in the instructional systems approach, relating them as we do so to the selection and use of flat pictures and graphics in teaching.

1. Analysis of the problem

Say you are teaching a general science course in the seventh grade and know from standard achievement tests that 30 percent of your class are from one to three years below where they should be in science for their age and grade level. Is this the problem? In a general way, yes, and as a committed teacher you are determined to do what you can to improve the situation. Before you can do much about it, however, you need to know much more than where your students stand now on achievement tests. You need to know the *reasons* why the problem exists. Is it that their science teaching in the lower grades has been poor? Perhaps, but we've already swept too many problems under the rug in education on that score and, besides, it doesn't really help us very much. Is it because these students of yours are poorly motivated? If so, why? Is it because they are deficient in reading skills? If so, in what respects and how deficient? Is it because a number of them come from culturally deprived homes and have already become used to failure or may see little relevance between what you are trying to teach and the world they live in?

Probably all these reasons apply to the problem in varying degrees. The point is, you need to find out as much as you can in order to avoid the trap of designing solutions to the wrong problems. Like a good doctor, you want to make a correct diagnosis first that will enable you to get at the underlying causes of the problem and not merely treat the symptoms. Most school systems today have fairly complete records on each child. These records are a good place to start. There are also specialists in guidance and counseling and others whom your principal can bring in to assist you. Even though you may never be totally satisfied with the results of your analysis, your efforts in this direction will not be wasted; they can pay substantial dividends in helping you to find valid solutions to the problems you face.

2. Definition of objectives

Much has been written about the nature and importance of clearly defined objectives. If you have not already become acquainted with Mager's or McAshan's in-

teresting and highly readable discussions of objectives, this would be a good time to take a close look at them.[19] The essence of their message is: (1) unless you know pretty specifically what it is you want your students to achieve in science (or any other subject), their chances of doing so are virtually nil; (2) they provide you the ways and means of spelling out your objectives in such a way that you *will* know without question whether or not you and your students have achieved them. Like careful analysis of what the problem really is, clear-cut and measurable objectives are essential to finding real solutions to our pupils' learning needs. These steps have been followed far too seldom in most schools and colleges today.

3. Selection of teaching strategies; weighing practical alternatives

Once you have analyzed the problem and spelled out your objectives, you're ready to get at the key question of practical solutions. One obvious but impractical solution is spending several hours a week with small groups or individuals in the deficient group. This might be ideal if you had the time, but the chances are that you already have a heavy schedule. There may be special remedial teachers to whom these students can be assigned, but the chances are there are not. In other words, you will find quickly that the alternatives open to you are limited in one way or another—by time, by available helping staff, and by lack of money or other resources.

You are still nonetheless determined to do the best that you can. So among the possibilities that are realistic and open to you, you make the best possible choices. If, for example, you find reading deficien-

[19] Robert Mager, *Preparing Instructional Objectives*, Fearon Publishers, Palo Alto, Calif., 1962; H. H. McAshan, *Writing Behavorial Objectives: A New Approach*, Harper & Row, 1970.

FIGURE 3.31

Students learn that escaped oil presents particularly difficult pollution problems. A tragic example was the Santa Barbara oil-well "blowout" in 1969. During the massive clean-up campaign, frantic efforts were made, as shown, to save birds covered with thick oil, but 4,000 birds died.

cies to be characteristic of the below-grade students, you may go to the librarian or resource center and get a selection of ungraded science reading materials that those students *can* handle. You may also develop several tracks, not only to accommodate the slower students, but also to provide more stimulating and challenging material for the above-average ones as well. In short, this is the stage where you really get down to business on what methods and materials should be used.

Because you know precisely what it is you want to achieve and with whom, you're also in a much better position to pick just the right pictures and graphics to do the job. Should you want pictures, say, on pollution, you will make a determination in terms of two basic considerations: (1) the availability of suitable pictures that illustrate the precise points you want to stress and (2) how good and appropriate those pictures are.

In the latter connection, you may well find that to make the subject of pollution real to your students, you and they need to go out and see polluted areas in the immediate vicinity at firsthand and take pictures as you go. Not only can such study trips and pictures help bring the subject alive, but they can also provide your students with new and exciting ways of expressing themselves and their ideas. A wide range of possible activities may suggest themselves, including committee reports incorporating audiotaped interviews with interested city officials; student-made graphs or charts showing the extent and seriousness of the pollution problem in your community; steps being proposed in the community to attack the problem; student initiation of or at least participation in clean-up campaigns with attendant student-made posters on litterbugs, waste, and other contributing factors in the problem (see Figure 3.31).

You may have noted that up to now we've said relatively little about media and technology. This is as it should be, for until we've really analyzed the problems and needs and have pinned down the objectives, we have little basis for determining either the specific methods or materials necessary to enable us to attack the problem and to attain those objectives. It is essential that you note this progression of events, for it is the only sound basis on which good decisions can be made on either the methods or the materials you should employ.

To put it another way, we make a strong case throughout this book for the great potential of many kinds of audiovisual materials and of techniques for their effective use. But optimum benefits to learning—and this is the only justifiable reason for whatever methods and materials we may use—come only from the kind of careful analysis of real needs, specification of objectives, and determination of possible and viable solutions suggested. If we've done those steps carefully, we have a good start—but we're not through yet!

4. Tryout, evaluation, revision, recycling

We have emphasized that objectives must be spelled out specifically enough so that we can in some way measure whether or not they have actually been achieved. Let's say that your learning objectives on a pollution unit include the following specific behavioral objectives for each student:

1. Identify and write the names of three major kinds of pollution.

2. Select from a picture file (or display) at least three examples of each of the three general types of pollution.

3. Pick from a list of 20 prepared items three contributing causes for each of the major types of pollution.

4. Take six pictures (or select from a prepared display or file) of two examples of each of three kinds of pollution in your own community.

5. Take six pictures (or select from a prepared display or file) to illustrate contributing causes for each type of pollution in your own community.

6. Identify at least two things that need to be done to help solve each of the three kinds of pollution problems in your own community.

7. Pick from a list three statements by officials in your community which accurately describe efforts made to date to solve pollution problems.

These objectives suggest the degree of specificity necessary for you to ascertain whether they have, in fact, been achieved.

FIGURE 3.32

This is a popularized version of an Instructional Development model developed and validated by the National Special Media Institutes (NSMI) for use by classroom teachers and administrators for the improvement of instruction. (The actual model is shown in Figure 15.1.)

There would be many others, of course, some of them (*enabling* objectives) preliminary to broader (*terminal*) objectives which would demonstrate understanding of the subject at a contextual level. For each of these, you would have ways of measuring whether or not each student had actually achieved it and for each objective you would have designed a set of experiences which would help him to achieve the indicated learning.

It is very likely that the first time through, you would find quite a number of your experiences that worked very well and others that did not. Those that did not work well you would revise and try again. You might also find that the areas covered by your objectives were not comprehensive

enough. You might discover that the interviews you had scheduled with local government officials were something less than satisfactory, possibly because they were unaware of or unconcerned about pollution problems in the community or, for various reasons, felt that the local government could do little about them. If this was the case, you might find it necessary to expand your horizons and use materials from other cities where active steps *were* being taken to fight pollution or to enlist the support of local civic leaders in your own area who were really concerned. Otherwise, your long-range objectives of developing awareness and concern among your own students about pollution problems might fail to be realized. In any case, on

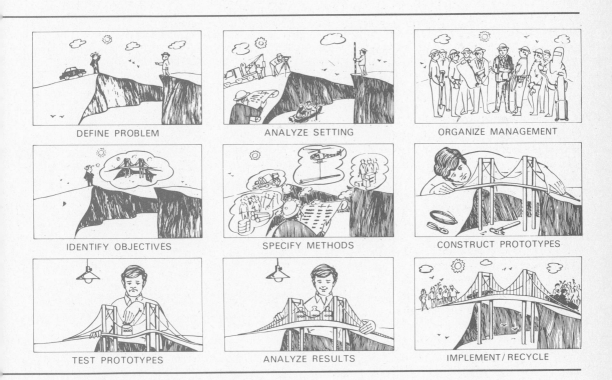

DEFINE PROBLEM

ANALYZE SETTING

ORGANIZE MANAGEMENT

IDENTIFY OBJECTIVES

SPECIFY METHODS

CONSTRUCT PROTOTYPES

TEST PROTOTYPES

ANALYZE RESULTS

IMPLEMENT/RECYCLE

the basis of your tryout and evaluations you would revise your materials and techniques in certain instances and try them out a second time with another group of students. You would continue this *recycling* until you were relatively certain that you had a series of learning experiences which in fact achieved the goals for your students which you and they had set out to achieve.

Within this broad context the selection and use of pictures, graphics, or any other kind of teaching materials are seen in proper perspective. For unless all or nearly all your students successfully achieve the objectives that have been established in a given unit of work, there is something wrong with the objectives themselves or with the methods and materials used to achieve them—or both.

Your job as a teacher is to arrange the educational experiences your students have in such a way that each of them has an optimum chance of succeeding and progressing as well as you both can manage. The Instructional Development approach provides the best opportunity that has been conceptualized in education so far for that happy combination to be brought about (see Figure 3.32).

After you have been exposed in the chapters that follow to the various types of media, their characteristics, and their uses in teaching and learning, we shall go into more detail on Instructional Development principles and techniques as we begin putting media together in integrated patterns in Chapter 15, "Multimedia Instructional Development."

Mounting of flat materials

T HE very profusion of pictorial, graphic, and related materials, such as small maps and pertinent news clippings, presents problems of care and of storage when not in use. Most new schools today have good libraries or learning resource centers where well-organized central files of pictures and similar materials are maintained. This system is very helpful to the teacher, but where, for whatever reason, you wish to maintain a file of your own, some ideas on organizing and maintaining such files may be helpful. Further, because most such flat materials are more often damaged from inadequate storage than from actual use, we offer some suggestions for mounting and other protective techniques. Library and resource center personnel can be most helpful here, and their services, if available, should be used. Nonetheless, it is well for you or your assistants to be able to function on your own if necessary.

We place relative values on pictures

and graphics just as we do on other available teaching materials—in terms of how useful they are for our particular purposes. Outstanding or unique pictures that are just right and perhaps difficult to replace should be mounted to protect them from damage. Less valuable pictures and those of purely transitory or one-time value may be filed unmounted or discarded. When used in class or in study displays, such materials can, if desired, be quickly and easily placed on temporary mountings. (Several temporary mounting techniques are described on pages 140–142.)

Some guidelines for mounting flat materials

Some general considerations that should be observed in mounting pictures include the following:

1. USE GENEROUS MARGINS   Generous margins are not merely a matter of artistic

FIGURE 3.33

The value of generous margins and of proper margin proportions is illustrated here. Note that the bottom margin is always wider than the top or side margins.

taste; they embody the direct application of the principles of attracting and holding attention. Any object tends to attract more attention when it is by itself than when it is crowded in among a number of other, similar objects. Moreover, an appropriate mounting makes a good teaching picture more attractive, just as an appropriate frame enhances a photographic portrait or a painting.

Correct proportions for mounting pictures of various shapes are shown in Figure 3.33. Note the width of the margins used. The width of the top and bottom margins is determined by the shape of the picture, as the illustration shows. Note also that the bottom margin is *always* wider than the top one. The side margins are always equal and usually in between the size of the top margin (smallest) and the bottom (largest).

2. USE COLORS THAT DIRECT ATTENTION TO THE PICTURE AND NOT TO THE MOUNTING This means that, as a rule, it is best to select for the mounting a color that appears in the picture in a relatively minor degree. This repetition of color creates a pleasing harmony in the total effect given by the mounting and picture together. It is usually not wise to use a color for the mounting which predominates in the picture itself because of the resulting loss of desirable contrast. A picture of a field of ripe grain will not appear to the best advantage on a yellow mounting, nor will a picture with a broad expanse of blue sky look well on a light-blue mounting. In such cases, the picture loses definition because, from a short distance away, it tends to merge with the mounting itself.

In general, neutral tones for mountings are more satisfactory than primary or brilliant colors, although there are notable exceptions. Bright-red or green mountings look well with Christmas pictures, orange mountings with Halloween subjects, and gay pastel mountings with Easter decorations. The idea here is to emphasize a gay and festive spirit; the purpose of these mountings may be primarily decorative, which is entirely appropriate in such cases. As a general rule, however, where informational purposes predominate, the principles mentioned above should apply.

3. USE BORDERS AND TEXTURE EFFECTS ON OCCASION Often a narrow border will help to set off the picture from the mounting. Sometimes an inked line around the picture is effective. A similar border effect is obtained by inserting, immediately behind the picture, a sheet of mounting paper slightly larger than the picture and of a different color from that used for the mounting itself. Since this sheet extends slightly beyond the edges of the picture, it provides a border in a contrasting color. White used for a border of this kind is often highly effective because it brings out the color in the picture.

Although colored drawing paper is inexpensive and probably the most readily available material for mounting, you may occasionally want to use other materials for variety or special effects. Tag ends of wallpaper in subdued all-over patterns or with textured surfaces are one good possibility. Others include fabrics of various kinds, dress and suit boxes, and even corrugated cardboard. Your art teacher can help with ideas. The help of teacher aides and, even better, some of your students can make such projects feasible and worthwhile.

Temporary mountings

There are various relatively simple ways to mount pictures and other flat visuals on a backing surface. *Rubber cement* has long been used; a few dabs will usually suffice. Because rubber cement tends to soak into some of the more porous materials and can

FIGURE 3.34

Examples of satisfactory and effective methods
of fastening pictures on various surfaces.

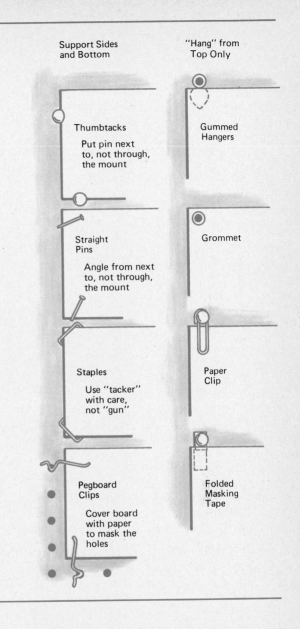

Support Sides
and Bottom

"Hang" from
Top Only

Thumbtacks

Put pin next
to, not through,
the mount

Gummed
Hangers

Straight
Pins

Angle from next
to, not through,
the mount

Grommet

Staples

Use "tacker"
with care,
not "gun"

Paper
Clip

Pegboard
Clips

Cover board
with paper
to mask the
holes

Folded
Masking
Tape

be a bit messy, some convenient substitutes are being widely used. One of these is a *spray adhesive* which comes in an aerosol can and is simply sprayed on. Another is a commercial *waxer,* some of which are quite inexpensive and highly practical for school use; the wax backing serves as an adhesive. *Gummed tapes* can also be used without difficulty; particularly useful is a double-surface masking tape which can be applied to the back of a picture and simply pressed on the mounting surface. A synthetic waxlike adhesive called *Bulletin Board Styx* is also used for mounting; this is particularly useful for displaying mounted pictures on solid, rough, or glossy surfaces. Small bits of the wax are sufficient to hold the mounted picture in place for as long as desired.

When pictures or graphics are to be displayed on a cork or other porous display surface, the fastest and simplest method of temporary mounting is to use *straight pins,* as many art teachers do. The pins, which hold both the mounting and the picture in place, cannot be noticed more than a few feet away; this fact makes pins preferable to thumbtacks, which detract from the effectiveness of the display if many are used. Several types of mounting and fastening devices are shown in Figure 3.34.

Permanent mountings

When flat visual materials are to be used repeatedly or handled regularly by students, some type of permanent mounting is desirable. A fairly stiff backing material is used for the mounting, and any of several good permanent mounting techniques is employed. Most schools today have dry-mount presses and Thermofax machines; many, in addition, are acquiring laminating machines. All of these are useful for mounting.

Dry mounting requires a special tissue material that is affixed by means of a dry-mount press or hot iron. The dry-mount tissue can be obtained in rolls or sheets from photographic supply stores. A piece of the tissue is trimmed to picture size and put on the back of the picture. The picture and the tissue backing are then placed on the mounting material and covered with a piece of plain white paper. When put in a dry-mount press (or applied firmly with an iron heated to about 300 degrees), the picture fastens firmly to the mounting. The picture is then sprayed with a clear flat lacquer to protect it.

Lamination seals mounted or un-

mounted visuals in a clear, nonglossy plastic covering that permanently protects them from dirt, moisture, and tearing. Laminating machines are needed for this kind of mounting, but there are useful substitutes where such machines are not available. One of these is a clear plastic film that can be applied to a picture by putting it through a Thermofax machine. Also available are inexpensive clear vinyl sheets that can be

FIGURE 3.35

A three-part picture is shown in a sectional mounting, as displayed and as filed.

purchased in many household supply stores and applied with a hot iron. School- and art-supply houses carry clear plastic sheets especially designed for picture protection. Some are applied with heat and pressure; others are self-adhesive and can be applied by hand. Although they are not as strong or permanent as machine lamination, these processes are useful substitutes. Large pictures may be readily and inexpensively pro-

tected by spraying them with a coat of clear lacquer.[20]

Sectional mountings

It often is advantageous to use a series of identical mountings for magazine-fold pic-

[20] See Herbert Scuorzo, "Plastic Picture Protection," *Grade Teacher*, September 1963, pp. 12 ff., for details on the process.

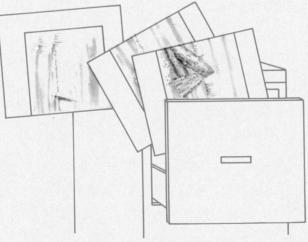

tures or murals that are too large for a single mounting. When displayed, the series is a unit, for the individual sections are identical in size and coloration and when fitted together look like a panel; they are separated for filing and storage (see Figure 3.35). In another method of sectional mounting, lightweight sections are fastened together with masking tape or cloth tape and accordion-folded when not in use. Either method is a practical solution for handling the ever-increasing number of excellent two- and three-fold materials in such magazines as *Life, Holiday,* and a few others.

The permanent and temporary techniques described above are those most commonly used. During the past decade or so, with increased funding for education at all levels, business and industry have addressed themselves seriously to the development of better equipment and materials for the teacher and the learner. Progress in picture-mounting techniques is one example of this, and further improvements may be expected. You should be on the alert for them as you visit the exhibits at your conventions and scan the advertisements in your professional journals. (See also the source lists in the Appendix.)

Storage and retrieval of flat materials

TEACHERS who go to some trouble to find and use good pictures and graphics know the importance of proper storage and filing of such materials.

The filing system
The simplest filing system involves grouping pictures and related flat materials according to the teaching units or topics in which they are used. When rather large numbers of pictures are involved, subheadings are helpful. For example, pictures on *Greece* may be subdivided as follows: Greece—Mountains, Greece—People, Greece—Farming, and so forth. Tabbed or color-coded separators should be used, the pictures in each section being listed in pencil on the separator. Other indexing systems include notebook lists, with identification of pictures by numbers or topics for quick location; similar lists in lesson-plan folders; and a simple card file, with related groups of pictures listed on each card. The filing and indexing system should be as simple as possible but still flexible enough to accommodate additional pictures and sections. Further, the system of classifica-

tion and labeling used needs to be geared to the maturity level of the pupils using it. The school materials center staff can be of assistance in setting up a practical and workable filing system for your visual materials.

The visual file as a learning experience
In our discussion of visual literacy, we stress the importance of having learners express themselves visually. The visual files may provide some elements of visual literacy experience if students themselves are involved in the development of such files. In the process, they can gain valuable experience in the selection of good visuals and in using them to communicate ideas. In the same process, over a period of several years, succeeding groups of students can be a decided help to you, as well, in developing and organizing a file of good visuals.[21]

The idea is to begin with a teacher-

21 Suggested by Professor Wilfred Veenendaal of the Instructional Media Center, Michigan State University.

provided nucleus of pictures. These can be loose examples in envelopes or folders from which the students can select examples to fit the particular purposes of the topic being studied. After some instruction, they can mount the better pictures and graphics and use them in whatever ways appear suitable. At an appropriate point, questions can be raised on how good and suitable the selected pictures are, and the students should be encouraged to bring additional or more appropriate examples of their own. In a subsequent evaluation session, have the students select the best of the pictures that have been brought in, then repeat the mounting exercise, perhaps using backing materials the students themselves bring in. The evaluation and selection process can be repeated each year—perhaps accompanied by a lesson on mounting pictures to facilitate that aspect of the activity.

You can make judgments as you go along on how many topics or subjects to work with in this way. It is important to keep the proper perspective: though an exceptional file of pictures and graphics may, of course, be assembled and mounted in this manner, the more significant gains come from the learning experiences of the students themselves (see Figure 3.36). By working closely with visuals in this process, students may learn better how to read pictures and to communicate ideas with them. Through the selection and evaluation process, they will gradually learn to discriminate between good and poor pictures and perhaps begin to appreciate those that are exceptional. They are very likely also to learn important content, though actually the learning that results from working directly with visuals may prove the more lasting and beneficial.

Storage facilities

In addition to a workable filing system that helps locate materials readily when needed, some kind of storage facilities are essential. These can range from fairly elaborate built-in classroom facilities to simple but workable portable substitutes.

FIGURE 3.36

Sometimes the teacher helps, but often he leaves the children to their own devices. What determines?

FILING CABINETS   Modern classroom facilities usually include built-in drawers and cabinets in which various instructional materials and supplies can be stored. Standard, letter-size filing cabinets are suitable for small mounted pictures in folders, but legal-size files are better, since they accommodate material up to 11 × 14 inches; such vertical filing cabinets are now available in sizes up to 14 × 18 inches. Horizontal flat files with a number of shallow drawers are particularly good for larger materials up to 40 × 60 inches. When such facilities are not available, various types of cases, cartons, and boxes are often used; particularly useful among these are the strong and inexpensive plastic and laminated cardboard cartons and cases made specifically for storage that are now available (see Figure 3.37).

PORTFOLIOS   Portfolios are also an excellent means of protecting pictures when not in use or while carrying them; they have been used by artists and art teachers for many years. A portfolio is nothing more than two pieces of heavy cardboard or similar material hinged with flexible tape on one of its long sides (see Figure 3.37). Pictures or graphic materials are laid flat in the open portfolio, the cover is closed and tied, and it is ready to go. A portfolio can be made up in any size desired; one 34 × 44 inches accommodates most pictures and small charts and still is easy to carry.

FIGURE 3.37

Here are a few suggestions for solving picture storage problems. Dimensions can be adjusted to suit your needs.

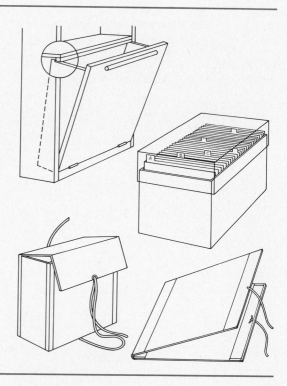

Summary

Visual literacy is a relatively recent and promising development in mediated learning. In brief, visual literacy training undertakes to develop students' abilities to read visuals and to express themselves through them. Experiments in which students make their own pictures to communicate ideas appear to provide strong motivation plus a positive influence on oral and written language as well.

Flat pictures are so readily available that it is easy to underestimate their importance in teaching and learning. The picture medium as a whole has a certain universality and versatility that no other medium of communication quite shares. Although somewhat less familiar than pictures, graphic materials combine readily with other media in summarizing significant information and ideas. Like other media we shall study, both pictures and graphics have intrinsic and extrinsic strengths and limitations that must be considered in their selection and use.

Although pictures and graphics combine rather naturally and effectively in a lesson, they have distinctive functions. Pictures illustrate or represent actual objects or scenes. Graphics, on the other hand, compress and distill information. They summarize significant quantitative information, as on graphs; show relationships, as on charts and diagrams; and illustrate some fairly complex and abstract ideas, as in cartoons, diagrams, and charts. Because of their summary nature, graphic materials typically require some background of information to be used effectively.

In general, it is better to use a few carefully selected pertinent pictures and graphics rather than many. The effective use of flat pictures also requires directing the viewers' attention to specific points or impressions to be looked for. Those that are large enough can be used in front of a class; those that are small can be projected in an opaque projector or incorporated in study displays. Both have great value, as well, for individual and small-group study.

Care in selection is the first essential for effective learning results with pictures or graphics. The starting point for effective selection and use is defining teaching objectives that are clear and explicit. The pictures and graphics chosen must be valid and directly pertinent to those objectives. They must also be suited to the maturity level of the students and be of good quality.

The application of Instructional Development principles provides the best basis yet discovered for assuring effective learning results. Although a complex and demanding process, its rewards are commensurately superior to conventional planning. The I.D. process will be referred to at pertinent points as we discuss various kinds of media in the following chapters; it will be dealt with further in Chapter 15, "Multimedia Instructional Development."

Some form of mounting increases the effectiveness of flat pictures and preserves them. Also important is a system of filing and storage for ready access and retrieval when needed.

Further learner response projects

1

Ask each student to bring in several examples of good flat pictures relating to their respective subject-matter fields. Have the class evaluate a selection of these pictures in terms of the principles discussed in this chapter.

2

Have a committee prepare an annotated and classified list of good sources of free

or inexpensive flat pictures for duplication and distribution to class members.

3

Ask each student to bring in a current issue of Life, Holiday, or a similar publication for use in a class discussion of the

qualities of good photographs. Draw up a list of suggestions on how to take good pictures.

4

Instructional pictures that are good from an artistic viewpoint can communicate more effectively than those that are not and can also help to improve esthetic taste.

Select a number of pictures from this chapter and other sources which seem to fulfill this dual requirement; be prepared to justify your selections.

5

Divide the class into committees and have the members of each committee select and evaluate the best examples they can find of one type of graphic material. Consider

such points as (a) standards to be observed in selection, (b) sources of suitable materials, (c) costs.

6

Have a committee of class members investigate sources of free or inexpensive graphic materials, prepare an exhibit of

sample materials, and make classified lists of sources for distribution to class members.

7

Ask members of the class to bring in graphic materials they have found particularly helpful in their teaching and explain their use of them.

References

ARNHEIM, R. *Visual Thinking.* Berkeley, University of California Press, 1969.

BRIGHAM, D. L. *Interdisciplinary Visual Arts in Learning.* Attleboro, Mass., Attleboro School Department, 1969.

BROWN, LES E. "Another Look at an Old Medium —Using Pictures in Social Studies." *Audiovisual Instruction,* November 1969, pp. 72–73.

CARPENTER, HELEN M. "Developing Picture Reading Skills." *The Instructor.* September 1964, pp. 37–38.

CATERINO, S. J. "Student Involvement in Making Visual Perception Materials." *Audiovisual Instruction,* November 1969, pp. 74–75.

CIEMBA, JOHN. "Photography: A Key to Learning." *Audiovisual Instruction,* November 1969, pp. 66–67.

CONLAN, KATE. *Poster Ideas and Bulletin Board Techniques.* Oceana, 1965.

CORRIGAN, R. E., and R. A. KAUFMAN. *Why Systems Engineering?* Fearon Publishers, Palo Alto, Calif., 1965.

Designing Instructional Visuals. Instructional Media Center, University of Texas, Austin, 1968.

DWYER, FRANCIS M. "Exploratory Studies in the Effectiveness of Visual Illustrations." *AV Communication Review,* Fall 1970, pp. 235–249.

EAST, MARJORIE. *Display for Learning.* Dryden, 1952, pp. 54–87, 210–237.

"Effectiveness of Family Planning Comic Books," *Information Education Communication in Population Newsletter,* East-West Communication Institute, Honolulu, January 1972, p. 11.

Elements of Visual Literacy. Eastman Kodak Company, March 1968.

FLEMING, MALCOLM L. *Perceptual Principles for the Design of Instructional Materials.* USOE Final Report, Project No. 9–E–001: Grant No. OEG 5–9–245001–0016 (010), January 1970.

FORMANEK, RUTH, and JOHN SWAYZI. "Teachers and Technology: Exploring Visual Literacy." *Audiovisual Instruction,* March 1971, pp. 86–87.

FRANSECKY, ROGER B., and JOHN L. DEBES. *Visual Literacy: A Way To Learn—A Way To Teach,* Association for Educational Communications and Technology, 1972, 32 pp.

FRASER, DOROTHY MCCLURE, and EDITH WEST. *Social Studies in Secondary Schools: Curriculum and Methods.* Ronald Press, 1961.

GIBSON, JAMES J. "A Theory of Pictorial Perception." *AV Communication Review,* Winter 1954, pp. 2–23.

GRIFFIN, PAUL F., and RONALD L. CHATHAM. "The Still Picture in Geography Instruction." *Journal of Geography,* May 1967, pp. 222–230.

HANGEN, NANA. "The Perception of Dangers in Action Illustrations." *AV Communication Review,* Fall 1970, pp. 250–262.

HORN, GEORGE F. *Bulletin Boards.* Reinhold, 1962.

JACOBY, SUSAN. "Photo Frenzy in the Classroom." *Audiovisual Instruction,* October 1969, pp. 37–39.

JENKINS, JOSEPH R., WESNER B. STACK, and STANLEY L. DENO. "Children's Recognition and Recall of Picture and Word Stimuli." *AV Communication Review,* Fall 1969, pp. 265–271.

KEMP, JERROLD E. *Planning and Producing Audiovisual Materials.* 2d ed. Chandler, San Francisco, 1968.

KEPES, G. *Vision and Value Series.* Braziller, 1966.

KNOWLTON, JAMES Q. "On the Definition of 'Picture.'" *AV Communication Review,* Summer 1962, pp. 157–183.

KRAMPEN, M. *Design and Planning.* Hastings House, 1967.

KRAMPEN, M. "Signs and Symbols in Graphic Communication." *Design Quarterly, 1962.* Minneapolis, Walker Art Center, 1965.

KRAMPEN, M. "The Psychology of Visual Communication." *Dot Zero I.* Glens Falls, N.Y., Finch, Pruyn & Company, Inc., 1966, pp. 12–15.

LAPOLT, RUTH. "A New Approach to Visual and Written Sequencing." *Audiovisual Instruction,* May 1968, pp. 477–479.

LAV, ANNE. "How To Start a Picture File for Your Classroom." *Grade Teacher,* September 1967, pp. 152–154.

Lettering Techniques. Instructional Media Center, University of Texas, Austin, 1965.

LIECATI, ALICE, and JACK CHAPPEL. *Making and Using Charts.* Fearon Publishers, Palo Alto, Calif., 1957.

MACKLIN, RONALD R. "Fitting Together the Visual Puzzle." *A-V Communications,* August 1967, pp. 13, 38–41.

MINOR, ED, and HARVEY R. FRYE. *Techniques for Producing Visual Instructional Media.* McGraw-Hill, 1970.

PARKER, J. E. "Visual Literacy for Minority Youth." *Audiovisual Instruction,* December 1969, pp. 24–26.

Planning a Photo Essay. Eastman Kodak Company, 1966.

ROSS, S. B. "Exploring the Concept of Visual Literacy." *The Independent School Bulletin,* October 1969, pp. 44–46.

SITES, RAYMOND S. "Bringing the Nation's Art Treasures to the Classroom." *Audiovisual Instruction,* March 1961, pp. 98–99.

TOOMEY, GEORGE. "Operant Techniques and Material Usage." *Journal of Education,* October 1969, pp. 69–71.

WILLIAMS, CLARENCE M., and JOHN S. DEBES, eds. *Proceedings of the First National Conference on Visual Literacy.* Pitman, 1970.

Media references

Bulletin Boards and Display, filmstrip. BFA Educational Media, 1966.

Chalkboards and Flannel Boards, 35mm filmstrips (4), color, 30 frames each. Bailey Films, 1967.

Charts for Creative Learning, 16mm film, sound, color, 10 min. Bailey Films, 1966.

Effective Visual Presentations, slide/tape, sound. Eastman Kodak Company, 1969.

Flannel Board Use, filmstrip, b/w or color, 30 frames. Bailey Films, 1966.

Graph and Picture Story Skills Kit. Science Research Associates, 1967.

Graphics, series of 17 transparencies from *Instructional Media Transparency Masters*— a series of 147. Keuffel and Esser Company, 1969. *Chalkboards* (4) and *Flat Pictures* (5) are also part of the series.

Hey, Look at Me, 16mm film, sound, color, 12½ min. DAVI/Screenscope.

How Does a Picture Mean?, filmstrip. Eastman Kodak Company, 1968.

Language of Graphs, 16mm film, sound, b/w, 13 min. Coronet Films, 1948.

Making Sense Visually, filmstrip, sound, color, 77 frames. Eastman Kodak Company, 1969.

Mounting Still Pictures, filmstrip, color, 58 frames. Visual Instruction Bureau, University of Texas, 1956.

Photo Discovery Sets, picture sets. Eastman Kodak Company, 1967.

Pictures for Teaching, slides, Chandler, San Francisco, 1965.

Posters, 16mm film, sound, color. ACI Productions, 1968.

Story Starters, super-8 cartridged film loops. Ealing Corporation, 1969.

Study Pictures and Learning, filmstrip, color, 63 frames. Teaching Aids Laboratory, Ohio State University, 1960.

Teaching with Still Pictures, filmstrip, color, 53 frames. Basic Skill Films, 1958.

Teaching with Visual Materials, filmstrip series, color, 35–40 frames each. McGraw-Hill, 1964. The Chalkboard, Parts I and II, and Posters for Teaching.

Using Charts and Graphs in Teaching, 35mm, filmstrip, color, 51 frames. Basic Skill Filmstrips, 1958.

Visual Fable, A, filmstrip, sound (record), color, 18 min. Eastman Kodak Company, 1969.

Visual Literacy, 16mm film, sound, color, 20 min. National Special Media Institutes, Michigan State University, 1971.

What Is a Graph?, filmstrip, b/w, 26 frames. Visual Education Consultants, 1965.

Source references

See source lists in the Appendix; particularly relevant sections are: Art Supplies; Comics; Flat Picture Sources; Free and Inexpensive Materials Sources; Graphic Materials; Photographic Equipment (Still Cameras); Reproduction Equipment.

See *Student Production Guide,* Chapter 3, "Graphics Techniques for Instructional Materials Production," particularly Design, Color, Bulletin Boards, Chalkboards, and Graphs; Dry Transfer Lettering, Wrico Lettering; Rubber Cement Mounting; Lamination.

FOUR
Three-dimensional teaching materials

Objectives	Performance responses

1

To be able to list five unique teaching advantages of models, objects, and specimens.

Divide your class into groups of four or five students each. From a selection of instructional models, objects, and specimens of several types, provide each group with one model for close examination and discussion of its particular advantages. After a few minutes pass the materials from group to group and repeat until all groups have examined several examples of each type. During the following report session, list and critique the advantages indicated.

2

To be able to demonstrate effective use of three-dimensional materials in a miniteaching situation.

Using groups and materials as in Response 1, but organized according to subject and grade level, each group should work out a teaching demonstration of up to five minutes involving 3–D materials of one or more types. Present the demonstrations before the class for discussion and critique.

3

To identify six or more useful sources for 3–D materials in your subject area and grade level.

Using source lists and your committee members' recommendations, prepare a selective source list in your subject area and grade level. Add brief annotations regarding distinctive items or features. Consolidate, classify, duplicate, and distribute copies to members of the class.

4

To discriminate between learning situations in which 3–D materials are and are not of significant value.

Prepare a list of 10 specific learning objectives for your own subject area and grade level and identify those objectives for which 3–D materials would be of significant value. Be prepared to justify the selections made in discussion with other members of your committee or class.

5

To plan an effective teaching display involving 3–D materials.

Using the group organization of Response 2, select a legitimate topic for a study exhibit involving 3–D materials. Then work out a specific layout design on a large piece of heavy paper and present it for a critique session in class. (You may want to consult the specific planning suggestions in Chapter 5, pages 217–226.)

6

To identify and explain four unique and significant learning values available through outdoor learning laboratories.

Set up a committee of three or more with particular interest in the potentials of outdoor learning laboratories in teaching. Visit a nearby outdoor laboratory, if one is available, or write and phone for information and examples of unique learning experiences available through outdoor laboratories in various subjects and at various grade levels. Follow up with a presentation or report to your media class.

HAVE you ever watched a baby play with his toys? As he sits in his high chair, his chubby little hands grasp whatever he can reach. Somewhat clumsily—but with great concentration—he pushes, pulls, and maneuvers his rattle around until he gets a grip on it. He bangs it on his tray for a while, samples its flavor when he can locate his mouth, and eventually dumps it overboard for the satisfying crash that follows. Pick it up for him and he will repeat the process, with many variations, again and again.

Now let us observe his mother on a shopping tour. At the vegetable counter she picks up and squeezes several heads of lettuce before finding one that is firm. She spies some cantaloupes and again she goes through the squeezing routine. She thoughtfully smells several which "feel" pretty good—and then walks on without taking any. The watermelons *do* look better today, so she briskly thumps several and finally buys one that produces a satisfactory hollow note.

Meanwhile, the baby's father stops in to see the new cars at the showroom on his way back to the office from lunch. He isn't really thinking of buying a new car, but, like most men, he likes to keep up with new developments in automobiles. So he goes in just to have a look. Subconsciously aware of the danger, he keeps a safe distance, circling casually to look at each car from several sides. Shortly, of course, he finds himself in the driver's seat of a gleaming sedan, turning the wheel just a little to get the feel and noting appreciatively the convenience of the wheel-tilt mechanism, the comfortable "give" of the seat cushion, and how readily the electric windows glide up and down as he touches the fingertip controls.

The baby and his parents in these familiar situations are learning and experiencing through their physical senses even as you and I do in various ways each day. As we noted in Chapter 2, although we "think" with the brain, the raw material for learning and thinking must come initially through one or more of the physical senses. We can learn nothing without sensory impressions. We know that the more complete, vivid, and accurate our sensory experiences are, the more effective the learning experience will be. Does this mean that we should bring all possible auditory, visual, and other sensory experiences to bear on every learning concept? The answer is No.

In discussing various media and materials, we stress the importance of three principles of selection and use: (1) We select only materials that can make a distinct contribution to carefully identified learning objectives; (2) we choose the best combination of these and other teaching materials to achieve the desired results; (3) we use these learning materials in the ways most likely to accomplish our specific learning objectives.

To put it another way, we choose teaching materials in terms of the kinds of communication that each type can best perform—we put together a "team" of several types of appropriate materials and we put the team to work in the way dictated by the specific purposes and circumstances of a particular lesson. Clearly, we are talking here about a *selective* experience, with materials and methods chosen to provide that experience. When sensory impressions can be utilized to improve learning—as they can in many cases—these, too, must be selectively used. Thus when sensory experiences are called for, we draw on those that are most pertinent and use them in whatever available ways seem most likely to attain the desired end. To illustrate, if familarity with a bakery is important as a part of community study, a field trip to a bakery, a suitable film, and related reading materials might well be used in combination. The film can provide an excellent overview of bakeries in general, the processes involved in baking, and the nature of the industry; the reading materials can provide considerable additional information. However, neither can convey an accurate impression of the heat of the great ovens or the delectable odors that are so much a part of a bakery.

The social studies teacher is continuously faced with the need for bringing realism into the study of the far places of the earth—mountains, plains, deserts, and jungles; people and customs of long ago; the trade, industry, agriculture, and government in the many sections of our own country. He has a great wealth of printed materials to draw upon and he uses them extensively, but he knows that he needs somehow to give added meaning to the words his pupils read. So he uses carefully selected films, maps, objects, field trips, and other devices that can help make the learning experiences more real and lifelike.

On the other hand, we know that many things of a physical character do not lend themselves well even to firsthand experience. One can visit the local waterworks and power plant without gaining much understanding of how the great pumps and generators work. One can get a thrill out of watching a giant diesel locomotive move a heavy train without having any idea of how it operates, and one can observe the moon for a lifetime without acquiring an understanding of its phases. The operation of some things like a pump, a generator, and an engine cannot be seen from the outside, but must be shown from the interior if one is to see how they work, and even then their intricate construction may be baffling. The solar system can be seen to some extent, but it is too vast to be conceptualized from direct observation alone. Teachers need somehow to modify direct experience in such cases if they are to help their pupils learn efficiently. One way of doing this is by using three-dimensional materials.

Types of three-dimensional materials

WE now consider six types of three-dimensional materials and areas which can provide opportunities for useful learning experiences when direct, firsthand experience is either impractical or impossible. These are models, objects and specimens, mock-ups, dioramas, outdoor laboratories, and museums.

Models

A *model* is a recognizable three-dimensional likeness or representation of a real thing. Models may represent real things that are infinitely large, like the earth or the solar system, or real things that are as small as an atom. The thing represented may be an inanimate object such as a mountain, a monument, or a mine shaft; or it may be a living organism or organ such as a paramecium, an elephant, or the human heart. The model may represent something as intricate as a jet engine, a nuclear-powered submarine, or a spacecraft, or something as simple as a counting device that can be depicted by spools on a string. It may be

FIGURE 4.1

Making a model can be "busy work" or a constructive, valuable learning experience. What makes the difference?

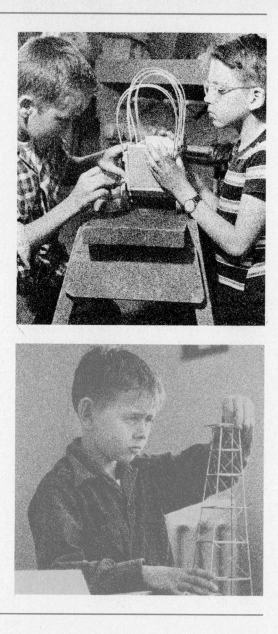

complete in every detail or considerably more simplified than the original.

The satisfaction obtained from models has been translated into a rapidly growing industry—the manufacture of model kits. Model kits for everything from insects to atomic reactors are available, and adults as well as children take to them with enthusiasm. Most are in precise scale, and many are accompanied by a manual that contains not only directions but also useful information on the subject. Models also, of

FIGURE 4.2

It is assumed when models such as this are used that (1) it is important to learn the relative positions of the several parts of the object being modeled, (2) 3–D is a necessary element for such learning, (3) students will be allowed to work with the model directly.

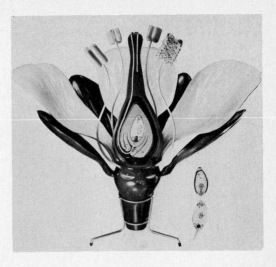

course, may be built from "scratch"—using materials at hand and consulting pictures or diagrams. The model itself may not be so authentic or effective as a kit model, but the result of the extra amount of research and thought children must put into it is likely to be an extra amount of learning. For example, when the children shown in Figure 4.1 have finished the covered wagon and the oil derrick, they will have acquired a substantial amount of related information and interest in the process.

CHARACTERISTICS OF EFFECTIVE MODELS In the light of what we know about the importance of sensory experience in learning, let us examine seven characteristics of models that make them effective for teaching purposes.

Models are three-dimensional Most objects around us have a third dimension; that is, they have depth or thickness as well as height and width. Depth is one of the unique characteristics of models which contributes significantly to their realism. (If the third dimension is unimportant to

comprehension, a model is probably unnecessary and a picture or chart may serve as well or better.) The model in Figure 4.2 is an example of three-dimensional representation that greatly enhances instruction. By working with such a model, along with appropriate visuals and related reading, a student can quickly understand the relationship of the pistil and stamens and how the pollen reaches the stigma to effect fertilization of the ovules in the ovary and thus develop new seeds.

Models reduce or enlarge objects to an observable size Even from a high-flying jet airliner we can see only a small portion of the earth's surface; the astronauts can see much more, but even they can view only part of the earth's surface at a time. A globe, however, is a model that enables us to picture the whole earth without difficulty. Conversely, the greatly enlarged model of an anopheles mosquito shown in Figure 4.3 enables these Indian children better to understand this enemy they must fight in the war against malaria.

Ideally, a model should be large enough to be seen readily by the whole class. Fre-

FIGURE 4.3

One advantage of models such as this is that greatly expanded size makes detailed study possible. Does the picture also suggest certain precautions the teacher should take in such cases? If so, what?

quently, however, the cost of large models and the problem of storage space for them enforce a practical compromise in the form of models smaller than we would like.

Models provide interior views of objects A cutaway model of the human tooth reveals the layers of enamel and dentine and the nerve which otherwise are difficult to visualize. The rapidly spinning parts of a generator, a steam turbine, or an automobile engine are completely enclosed, but a simplified working model with removable or cutaway sides makes it possible to see and to understand how they work. A model like that in Figure 4.4 is helpful to an industrial arts teacher in showing details of frame house construction which normally are invisible.

Models simplify complex objects As you lift the hood and look at an automobile engine, the impression you receive is apt to be complex and confusing because of the intricate array of wires, belts, hoses, and accessories in addition to the engine itself. But such a look may be more revealing if you have studied a cutaway model of such an engine. The electric motor, the jet en-

gine, and the giant pumps in municipal pumping stations are other examples of complex mechanisms which can readily be explained with the help of simplified models.

The advanced student, however, needs more complete models or the real thing. Students in technical or engineering schools usually have a variety of cutaway engines and models to study and manipulate, along with carefully done graphics such as the one shown in Figure 4.5. Agricultural-engineering schools test machinery of many types, frequently using cutaways and accompanying graphics for instruction. Equipment manufacturers also use this technique for dealer and customer training, as well as for advertising.

Models accent important features with color and texture Two allied instructional purposes are served by color. The first is identification of important or related parts, as in engine models. The second is increased comprehension of function or operation. In addition, color serves to make models more eye-catching, interesting, and in many cases more attractive. This does not suggest that color should minimize other features of a

FIGURE 4.4

This teacher-made model is used to identify and examine key elements in frame house construction. What are the particular benefits or learning advantages of such a model in an industrial arts class?

model. Effectively colored models have a balance in color harmony and intensity which emphasizes the parts and functions that are important to comprehension.

The role of color in models is illustrated in Plates 4.2 and 4.3, following page 132. In the algebra model, color serves primarily to enable the student to follow visually what happens when algebraic sums are squared and cubed. In an anatomy model,

FIGURE 4.5

This cutaway drawing of a diesel engine transmission shows the potential shift and gear positions that produce changes in the engine-to-wheels power-speed ratios. From a learning standpoint, is such a picture adequate to explain *how* these changes take place?

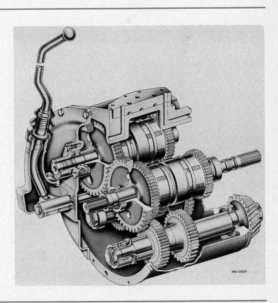

such as the kidney shown in Plate 4.1 or the heart shown in Plate 4.2, color furthers comprehension through readier identification of parts according to their location and function. Color plays a similar part in clarifying the "anatomy" of the Saturn rocket shown in model form in Plate 4.1. This role of color applies to models generally. That is, important and distinctive parts are colored so that each one stands out clearly. The colors may be natural (this is desirable in some anatomy and other models, of course), but more often they are made brighter or otherwise accented for better visibility. For example, one widely understood color convention is often used: in anatomy models arteries are colored bright red and veins bright blue, though actually there is no difference in the colors of these blood vessels and very little difference in the color of the blood within them. Conversely, parts of a model that are not essential for understanding are often neutralized by being shown in muted colors.

Varied surface textures are also used to differentiate parts of a model. The pistons and other moving parts in a cutaway engine may be chrome-plated for better visibility, whereas other areas are left rough or unpolished. Rough and smooth textures on relief-map surfaces have significant and distinctive meanings. Texture is also an important means of conveying accurate impressions from certain anatomy and biology models. Frequently, color and texture are used together with good effect, as in the kidney model in Plate 4.1.

Models can be created in class This section should not leave you with the impression that, to be useful in teaching, models must be complex and expensive. Many can be made rather easily from paper, papier-mâché, wood scraps, wire coat hangers, and other common materials. For example, the papier-mâché volcano shown in Figure 4.6 erupts convincingly from its cone. Ammonium dichloride crystals are used as fuel for the volcano. The crystals burn slowly, spitting sparks several inches high, emitting smoke, and spreading dark ashes down the sides of the cone as the eruption continues.

Students can make small weather vanes, anemometers, and similar models that are suitable for their needs and provide greater learning advantages than commercial models. Nevertheless, some of the new inexpensive commercial models now available are particularly valuable because with them it is practical for pupils to make their own models of quite complex organisms and structures such as molecules, cells, and motors of various kinds.[1]

Many models can be disassembled and reassembled The value of models in instruction lies not only in their three-dimensional realism, but also in the fact that they can be examined by touch as well as by sight. Piaget makes an important point about young learners which to some degree probably applies to all learners—namely, that though a child may observe an object, the object has little relevance or meaning for him until he has an opportunity to grasp or touch it or relate to it through his other kinesthetic response mechanisms.[2] The anatomy model in Figure 4.7 can be taken apart so that each part may be examined individually. Fitting each part back in its proper position gives the student a degree of familiarity with the structure of the human body which is difficult to achieve in any other way. Furthermore, the interrelationship of the several parts is made much more clear.

[1] See References, particularly the articles by Carboni, Hyer and Young, Kniskern, Larson, and Scuorzo, for a variety of related suggestions.

[2] Jean Piaget, *The Child's Conception of Physical Causality*, Littlefield, Adams, 1960, pp. 272–273, 281–287.

FIGURE 4.6

The specific learning objectives for which models are used vary according to grade levels. Combinations of 3–D and flat displays can often supplement and reinforce one another, as in this case.

FIGURE 4.7

Discovery of just how and where body parts fit together is critically important for the prospective physician or surgeon but can be of keen interest to any student. The assembly and disassembly of 3–D models of some complexity can both stimulate interest and facilitate increased learning.

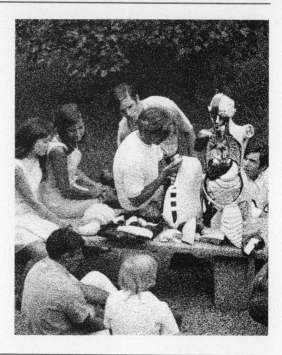

Objects and specimens

An *object* is the real thing, whereas a model is a recognizable three-dimensional representation of the real thing.

Specimens are objects that are representative of a group or class of similar objects.

There is little point in using a model if the real object itself can be brought to the classroom and if it is not too complex for easy observation (see Figure 4.8). You would not, for example, use models of Indian arrowheads, tools, and cooking utensils if you could secure the real objects. You might lead the children to make models of a wigwam and an Indian village if these were important elements in the concepts to be learned, but you would probably also have them bring Indian beadwork, arrowheads, tools, utensils, blankets, and other craftwork for display. Models and objects supplement each other in providing realism, authenticity, and interest.

It should be noted that collections of objects are removed from their normal setting so that they can be brought together for study and analysis. This means that the object is not seen in its natural surroundings and therefore may appear less "real" than it does in nature. A mounted hawk in a display case filled with other mounted birds loses some of its realism even though it may be a good example of taxidermy. Obviously, however, this limitation is much less important than the advantages of being able to examine a bird specimen at close range and in whatever detail desired.

"Specimen" and "object" are similar though not identical terms. Both terms refer to objects, but specimens, by definition, are objects that are typical or representative of a class of objects or things. An example of a specimen in biology would be a plant or an animal, entire or in part, which has been prepared and kept to illustrate a species or variety.

FIGURE 4.8

These children are learning what an ancient urn *really* looks like.

INSTRUCTIONAL APPLICATIONS There are significant advantages for learning in having objects and specimens available. First, even though removed from their normal surroundings, they are real things. This fact tends to make the learning situation more concrete, more authentic, and more interesting. The firsthand opportunity to observe the hatching of chicks, for example, can provide an unforgettable experience for the young student (see Figure 4.9).

Second, detailed closeup study can be made of birds, insects, and other specimens which would be next to impossible even if the time and money were available to take classes to where these specimens are accessible in nature. Some are inaccessible, in any case—living things in the sea and minerals deep in the earth, for example.

Finally, even though widely separated in nature, a collection of similar objects and specimens makes possible comparisons and generalizations that could not be made if

each example had to be seen separately in its natural habitat or location. For instance, imagine how long it would take to accumulate from observations in the field the essential information about minerals that is represented in a collection of rocks. Yet with the collection before you, you can readily begin to classify, infer, and generalize. This is also true, of course, of any collection of objects and specimens.

Most children are avid collectors, and teachers can sometimes channel this natural interest into useful learning experiences as they collect objects and specimens for the classroom. The objects and specimens that can be used to advantage in teaching are almost unlimited in number. The following list gives only a sampling of the range of content that can be taught with the help of objects and specimens:

Science Cocoons; rock collections; plants and flowers; fish, mice, worms, and other

163

FIGURE 4.9

When the real thing is available and easily
brought to the classroom, it may provide the
best and most vivid learning experience possible.
What can you see as useful outgrowths for these
children of watching eggs hatch?

FIGURE 4.10

When delicate or fragile specimens are em-
bedded in clear plastic, they can be handled
and studied at close range without risk of
damage—another example of how technology
can benefit learning.

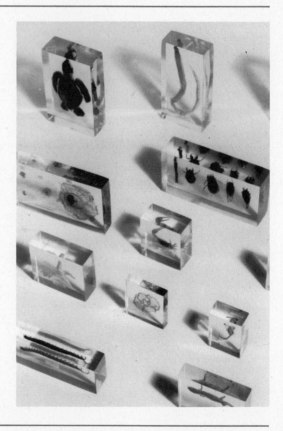

small animals (Figure 4.10); different kinds of coal, oil, and other fuels; samples of ore; seashells; a telegraph key, radio set, doorbell, telephone; dry cells and storage battery.

Social studies Locally manufactured products; period costumes; relics and souvenirs (as of political campaigns); coins and stamps; fuels; raw materials such as cotton, wool, flax, ores, and grains; Early American utensils, toys, tools, furniture, spinning wheels, pictures, and books; folk art materials such as those shown in Figure 4.11.

English Period costumes; clothing and

relics; letters and manuscripts; musical instruments; fabrics; stage props; tapestries; speaker's podium and microphone; printing type and layouts.

Mathematics Slide rule, micrometer, vernier scale, and other measuring instruments; transit; sextant, compass, timepieces, and navigation charts; bottles and other containers for volume measurements; coins; drafting tools such as dividers, T squares, and triangles; identical familiar objects for instruction in addition, subtraction, division, and multiplication.

Home economics Fabrics and sewing

FIGURE 4.11

Materials from a kit on Japanese folk art circulated in Los Angeles elementary and secondary schools. Such materials add an important dimension to students' understanding of cultures other than their own. (Some 200 kits on various subjects are used in Los Angeles schools.)

equipment; foods and utensils; period costumes to show trends in design; raw fibers such as cotton, wool, flax, and silk; wallpaper sample books; paint and papering tools; table settings.

Mock-ups

A *mock-up* may be defined as an operating model, usually at full scale, designed to be worked with directly by the learner for specific training or analysis.

A three-dimensional teaching device that has proved particularly useful in industrial and military training programs is the mock-up. The term ''mock-up'' suggests an imitation of a real thing—which in fact it is—but the imitation may or may not involve the similarity of appearance that

a model normally has. In addition, in a mock-up, some fundamental elements of the real thing may purposely be eliminated in order to focus attention on others. For example, an operable electrical system of an airplane may be laid out on a large panel so that trainees can become familiar with the cables and connections that normally are concealed in the fuselage and wings of the plane.

INSTRUCTIONAL APPLICATIONS   A simple kind of mock-up is frequently used by kindergarten and primary teachers when they have pupils build a grocery store, a flower shop, a Santa's toy shop, or a railroad train out of blocks or cardboard cartons (see Figure 4.12). The purpose of these activities is to train the children in

FIGURE 4.12

Precise realism is of little or no importance when young children are building their own house of boxes and boards, but 3–D *is* important to give their imaginations full sway.

FIGURE 4.13

Driver-trainer simulators of this type have been found to be highly effective for driver-education programs. As students respond to filmed problem sequences, their responses are recorded electronically, including reaction time. At what point or points in the training process would such trainers be valuable?

cooperative activity, reading readiness, or perhaps elementary number concepts.

A useful mock-up for industrial arts classes is an electrical wiring and fusebox installation that includes on one panel all the elements necessary for the lead-in wiring of a house. Placing these various elements on one panel makes it possible to show students the complete installation, whose parts are normally separated by a floor and walls. The students can see quickly just how the installation should be done.

Industries use mock-ups for streamlined demonstrations of steps in manufacturing processes, for analyzing possible new plant layouts, for orienting new employees regarding the interrelationships of their work with that of others, and for self-testing demonstrations of various types.

Mock-ups have many applications in training, including the well-known device for driver training shown in Figure 4.13

and the Link trainer for airplane pilots shown in Figure 13.11 Developed initially for fighter pilots, the Link trainer is used extensively by commercial airlines, not only for training pilots to fly new planes, but also for providing refresher courses for experienced crews. Various flying problems and emergencies can be simulated in the trainer at no risk to passengers, crews, or planes. Such trainers are further illustrated and discussed in the section on simulation in Chapter 13.

Dioramas

A *diorama* is a three-dimensional scene in depth incorporating a group of modeled objects and figures in a natural setting.

One of the most fascinating forms of three-dimensional materials is the miniature diorama. Its universal appeal is well known to everyone who has seen dioramas in museums, in advertising displays, or in classrooms. The diorama scene is usually set up on a miniature stage with a group of modeled objects and figures in the foreground which is blended into a painted realistic background (see Figure 4.14). The objects in a diorama—such as figures, buildings, and trees—are seldom made to scale. A building is made to look smaller at the far end in order to exaggerate depth. Thus as you look *down* at a diorama, a street may seem too narrow at the far end. These are among the methods used to achieve *perspective,* which is essential to any representation of depth. Figures of diminishing sizes and exaggerated perspective, in fact, can produce an effect of considerable depth in a remarkably small space. When this illusion is well carried out and when color is used in appropriate ways, a diorama has striking vividness and realism (see Plate 4.1, following page 132).

INSTRUCTIONAL APPLICATIONS Modern museums make extensive use of dioramic exhibits to show scenes involving distant places and historical periods. Teach-

ers in schools in the vicinity of such museums are well aware of the vast educational potential of dioramas. The Milwaukee County Museum, the Los Angeles County Museum, and the well-known Cleveland Youth Museum are among those that are doing outstanding work in coordinating historical and current materials with school programs by means of dioramas. Even though such museums are not available to many schools, the advantages of the diorama need not be lost. Good dioramas can be constructed by students from easily available and inexpensive materials. Paper leaves dipped in stained wax are good for some kinds of tropical foliage; fine sawdust stained green will do for grass; the furrows of a plowed field can be imitated by running a comb over a bed of wet clay; and pieces of green rubber sponge do very well for shrub and tree foliage.[3]

[3] Additional suggestions for constructing dioramas are illustrated in the film *How To Make and Use a Diorama* and the filmstrip *The Diorama as a Teaching Aid* (see Media References at the end of this chapter).

FIGURE 4.14

This diorama of otters in their natural habitat is taken from an actual setting in Michigan in which the area represented is over a mile in depth. Note how well it is reproduced here in a space only a few feet deep through techniques which greatly exaggerate depth and which blend actual materials in the foreground with a painted but highly realistic background. Identify three techniques used to create this depth.

One of the extremely valuable teaching opportunities accompanying diorama utilization results from the fact that the diorama itself provides the teacher with an interesting way to evaluate pupil learning. When one considers the combination of understandings and skills that pupils must possess before they are able to plan and complete a diorama successfully, it can readily be seen that the completion of such a project is the best evidence that the pupils really understand the concepts involved. The arrangement of a diorama's background, for example, must be inspired by information known to the learners. The planning and designing of objects in the middle and foreground also reflect the accuracy of the concepts the pupils have learned. The diorama as a whole thus becomes a "test" of the facts and conceptualizations the pupils have achieved, whether in social studies, science, or marine biology. Of course the actual construction of a diorama also provides the pupils with a concrete learning experience. Facts and concepts that might otherwise remain largely at the abstract level are likely to come alive in the pupils' minds as they embody them in the tangible diorama. Certainly the making of a diorama provides an excellent means of eliciting the pupils' creative involvement in the learning experience.

Outdoor laboratories

An *outdoor laboratory* is an exterior learning area on or adjacent to a school site which is suitable for environmental studies of one or more of the following types: aquatic (areas such as ponds, streams, marshes); terrestrial (areas such as farm, grass, woodlands); geological (areas such as boulder trails and displays of rock and mineral deposits and geological formations).

One of the highly significant changes taking place in education today has a reciprocal relationship to a significant recent trend in our society as a whole. This trend is the new emphasis on ecology—on fighting pollution and conserving our natural resources. Thus educating our young people to become influential in achieving these goals is now an important part of the curriculum at an increasing number of schools. In turn, these young people are motivated by each other and by the home, the community, and the mass media to be receptive to—even eager for—such instruction. Official recognition of the national importance of environmental education was shown by Congress when in 1970 it passed the Environmental Education Act for the purpose of making environmental education a basic element of the curriculum in our elementary and secondary schools.

Although educators have long been concerned with the need for better conservation and resource-use education and practices, a broad concerted effort has come about only with the awakening of the American people to what former Secretary of the Interior Stewart Udall has called "the quiet crisis."[4] One important expression of new efforts in this direction is the planning of school sites so that parts of them can be used effectively for environmental studies. The importance of what have come to be called "outdoor laboratories," "lands for learning," and "green islands" is suggested by the following quotation from the 1964 report of the American Association of School Administrators entitled "Conservation: In the People's Hands":

Due to the encouragement of far-sighted school board members and superintendents, school sites are becoming larger—increasing from a corner lot just off the village square or an acre in the corner of a cow pasture in a rural neighborhood to 20, 30,

[4] Stewart L. Udall, *The Quiet Crisis*, Holt, Rinehart and Winston, 1963.

FIGURE 4.15

or 40 acres and even more in some instances. This space has rich potential for outdoor laboratories in which plant and animal life can be studied. Yet in far too many school districts, these potential laboratories are underdeveloped and unused, while pupils in classrooms a few hundred yards away pore over dry, stale subject matter pertaining to rocks and plants and wind and rain in outdated books or pamphlets.[5]

In a recent report dealing with forward-looking school site policies, Russell Wilson, professor of education at the University of Michigan and school-planning expert, put it this way:

One rational approach to the tidal wave of concern for man's environment is through increased concentration on programs for the young on environmental education, and, more precisely, through opportunities for active learning and participating in ecological projects on school site outdoor laboratories.[6]

Under Dr. Wilson's leadership and with the support of the State Department of Public Instruction, many Michigan schools have established outdoor learning laboratories of several types (see Figures 4.15, 4.16). For example, in Parma and Coopersville there now are newly built, biologically valuable ponds within easy walking distance of the high school buildings; the Ann Arbor school system has systematically laid out and planted nature trails; Standish, Harper Creek, and Port Huron have used new and better criteria in choosing and selectively purchasing school sites, so that their new high school sites are already rich in varied natural learning resources—trees,

Who knows whence comes the spark that fires the mind of a future scientist—or simply projects an inquiring mind along new and productive channels? It may come from examining a plant under the guidance of an understanding teacher; it may come from studying deer tracks in the snow; it may come from walking purposefully through the woods to gather insect specimens. We *do* know, in any case, that without such sparks there is little true learning. These children are in the real world, but the real world is now giving them new and unique experiences. What implications do novelty and active involvement have for motivation, as well as for sustaining interest?

[5] *Michigan Journal of Secondary Education*, Spring 1965, p. 12.

[6] Russell Wilson, ''Opportunities for Environmental Education on School Sites,'' Preliminary Draft of a Report on Ann Arbor Board of Education School Site Policies, February 23, 1970.

FIGURE 4.16

When the real world can be studied at firsthand, as in these outdoor school laboratories, one in Oregon and one in Michigan, there are significant potential advantages for both learners and teachers. Identify two such opportunities for each group and describe how you would take fullest advantage of them.

shrubs, small mammals, birds, and streams or ponds. Ann Arbor, Coldwater, and Gwinn have brought together for school site planning purposes not only their own faculty and administrators, but also resource consultants including experts from the State Committee on School Sites, foresters, geologists, botanists, soil scientists, hydrologists, and conservation specialists.[7]

In addition to ponds and bogs and woodlots where a variety of biological specimens and phenomena can be studied, Wilson suggests a number of other more specific and very useful outdoor displays such as the following:

1. Bench mark A bench mark including latitude, longitude, elevation, township, section, and range can be useful in social studies and mathematics as well as science classes.

2. Base line A surveyed, straight, north-south, or east-west line at least 1,000 feet long can be used as a base line for mapping

exercises, range finding, pacing, and similar purposes. The line should be marked off in 100-foot intervals with one of the end intervals subdivided into 10-foot units.

3. Rock wall Construct a rock wall, possibly a retaining wall, containing a gradational pattern of rocks (see Figure 4.17). The specimens should be large, cut and trimmed, but unpolished (except for the building stone section, which should contain polished examples obtained from a local monument maker).

4. Boulder scatter field Large, native, uncut examples of boulders can be set on gravel or crushed stone.

5. Sundial A large class-sized sundial can be designed to fit the decor of the school.

6. Foucault pendulum Provide a pendulum support about 52 feet high. Since most modern schools do not have this height available inside, the pendulum must be outdoors, but the location should be sheltered from the wind as much as possible. Such a pendulum provides actual, visible proof that the earth is rotating.

7. Compass rose A large, class-sized com-

[7] Russell E. Wilson and June S. Wilson, ''School Site Development,'' unpublished report on the Title III Project, Croton-on-Hudson, New York, August 1968, p. 2.

FIGURE 4.17

To save time and energy, we can sometimes "improve on" nature by bringing examples of her handiwork together in one place, as in a rock wall that contains representative examples in natural form of all the principal rocks of the region. There should usually be separate sections of igneous, sedimentary, and metamorphic rocks, plus a section of polished building stone examples. In mountainous areas, an additional structure can show ripple marks, joints, faults, folds, geodes, concretion, and other types of mountain formations.

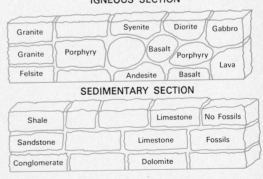

pass rose can be inset on the playground or located on a nature trail.

8. *Dynamic water basin* This 30-foot-by-30-inch artificial basin can be used to study many active geologic processes: waves and wave action on shores; sedimentation sequences and rate; beach structures; river systems; erosion. Half of the basin should have a constant 2-foot depth; the other half should grade from 1 foot to the surface (see Figure 4.18). A valve to regulate the water level and a drain are essentials.

9. *Erosion slope* An erosion slope should be divided into compartments, each 3 feet wide and 6 feet long, with a collection trough at the base (see Figure 4.19). The

FIGURE 4.18

Sedimentation and a variety of other geologic processes which naturally occur over considerable periods of time can be analyzed readily with a locally constructed dynamic water basin.

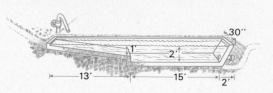

FIGURE 4.19

The study of erosion and erosion control can be greatly facilitated by an erosion slope.

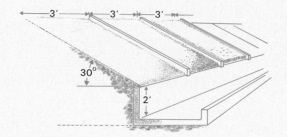

FIGURE 4.20

A cut through a natural or simulated soil bank provides a ready means of studying stratification or sedimentation phenomena or the current composition of soils in the local area.

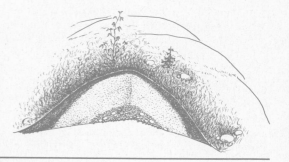

materials in each compartment can be varied for individual experiments (sand, loam, clay, grass, ground cover) ; the collection trough allows students to determine the amount of runoff, soil loss, and so forth. Conservation techniques can thus be studied under natural conditions subject to exact analysis.

10. Soil profile This is a natural, unsupported cut through a section of a hill. A 5-foot or 10-foot bank is sufficient. A natural bank facilitates the study of mass-wasting talus slopes and erosion patterns, as well as the soil profile itself (see Figure 4.20).

11. Footprint area Print a dinosaur track in concrete as part of a science terrace or patio. Print a collection of tracks of native animals useful in biology as well as paleontology. The tracks should be varied to show animals walking, running, and leaping.

12. Standard weather station A weather station can be purchased complete or the instruments may be collected and the shelter for them constructed as a class project.

It is obvious that outdoor displays can be of keen interest to young and old alike. Thus an important part of the overall site development plan for outdoor learning laboratories is to make these areas, as well as the more typical recreation and playground areas, available for widespread community use when schools are not in session.

Although it is more difficult and expensive, the "green island" concept can in some measure be applied in large-city settings where many of the nation's children live and go to school in "asphalt jungles."[8]

[8] For suggestions for improving and using the city school environment, see "The City: A Laboratory for Learning," *Conservation Education*, No. 11, Fall 1964, Conservation Foundation, 1250 Connecticut Ave., N.W., Washington, D.C. 20036. The Foundation also publishes the monthly *Conservation Foundation Letter*, available on request.

Museums

A *museum* is an institution that collects and preserves original objects and specimens and uses them both for scholarly research and for educational displays which often include replicas, models, dioramas, and other techniques designed to interest and inform the public.

No discussion of three-dimensional materials or displays could be complete without some consideration of museums. Although there were a few library-museums in Egypt and Greece even before the Christian era began, the origin of museums as we know them today came centuries later, during the Renaissance. In this period, princes, noblemen, and other wealthy men began amassing collections of art and objects connected with natural history or science. The earliest true museums all grew out of such private collections. The first of these modern-era museums probably was the Ashmolean, founded at Oxford University in England in 1677. The oldest of the great national museums is the British Museum, which dates from 1759. The first public museum in the United States was opened in Charleston, South Carolina, in 1773. Among the great museums of this country the oldest are the Smithsonian Institution in Washington, founded in 1846, and the American Museum of Natural History and Metropolitan Museum of Art, both in New York, founded in 1869 and 1870.

This bit of history is inserted simply to show that for centuries men have felt a need somehow to preserve evidences of their cultures. If they had not done so, much of what we know of earlier civilizations might have been lost or much less clear. Until the late nineteenth century museums were primarily repositories for indiscriminate and usually disorganized collections of materials of many kinds. Since then, however, they have changed radically. In their modern role they are visually articulate, diversified, and significant educational agencies. Today most cities of 100,000 or more—and many smaller cities—have one or more museums. Large cities often have many; New York, for example, has more than 40 public museums. Accordingly, wherever you may teach, there is likely to be a museum of some sort available somewhere in the area.

Teachers need to be aware of the fact that museums not only are places to go and see exhibits on a great variety of subjects but also are valuable sources of materials of instruction. The Los Angeles County Museum, for instance, has for many years sent out kits of materials to the area schools. The Washington State Museum at the University of Washington performs a similar service for schools in that state. The St. Louis Public Schools initiated a museum distribution service early in this century. A number of museums, such as the Milwaukee County Museum, produce and distribute visual materials and publications and also design and present fascinating programs for students in a variety of subjects and grade levels. All of these exemplify the efforts made by modern museum curators to take their programs *to* the public as well as to attract students and the adult public to their exhibits.

TYPES OF MUSEUMS There are literally thousands of museums across the United States and the world. Most of these concentrate on art or on historical or scientific areas, but within those categories are many specialized types of particular interest to schools such as the Museum of Modern Art in New York; the National Gallery of Art in Washington, which specializes in the art of the Western world; the Museum of Science and Industry in Chicago and similar museums in other cities which focus on the applied sciences; and natural history museums, historical museums, children's museums, folk museums, marine museums, and anthropological museums.

Among anthropological museums, the beautiful Museo Nacional de Antropología in Mexico City is recognized as the out-

standing museum of its type in the world. Exceptional display techniques are used, and thousands of people, including many groups of schoolchildren, visit the museum each week. The museum also attracts scholars from all over the world to what is believed to be the most complete analysis and documentation to be found anywhere of the origins of the early peoples who inhabited North, Central, and South America (see Figure 4.21).

THE MODERN FUNCTIONS OF MUSEUMS The early museums, as we have noted, were conceived of primarily as places where collections could be observed and perhaps studied by a select few. The modern museum, however, is specifically intended to "acquire and study objects of

historic and aesthetic value which serve to illustrate certain developments and trends, and from these to select objects and exhibit them in installations planned to inspire or educate the public."[9]

The important words here are "illustrate certain developments and trends." Most museums work closely with the schools if given the opportunity and try in every way possible to make their exhibits interesting and attractive so the general public, as well, will be drawn to them. But they recognize that to be of lasting value, museum experiences must *select* and *interpret* the exhibits in terms of man's more basic interests and needs. Thus we see presenta-

[9] Hans Huth, "Museums and Art Galleries," *Encyclopaedia Britannica*, Vol. 15, 1960, p. 991.

tions such as Conquest of Space, Pollution, Soil Erosion, Population Control, Highway Safety, Economic Development, and other broad topics relating man to nature as well as to history. The Museum of Science and Industry in Chicago, the Oregon Museum of Science and Industry in Portland, and science museums of various types in Los Angeles, Boston, Philadelphia, and other cities make a determined effort to interpret the applications of science to industry *in terms* of man's physical, social, and cultural needs.

The dynamic and varied nature of the experiences awaiting the visitor to the Chicago Museum of Science and Industry has been well captured by a *Time* reporter:

Amidst the casual atmosphere of a subdued

country fair, a visitor can "see" his voice, watch a working model steel mi'l, scramble through a captured German submarine, ride an elevator down to an operating coal mine under the museum, watch thousands of plastic balls fall into a probability curve, follow a feather and a penny as they fall at the same rate in a vacuum. Everywhere the visitor participates, pushing buttons, pulling levers, yanking chains, turning cranks, and talking into phones. He can play ticktacktoe with a computer, watch baby chicks hatch, walk through a throbbing 16-ft. model of the human heart, see a display that illustrates "everything to do with sex."[10]

The Queen Mary   One of the most striking and unusual museums in the world today is at Long Beach, California. This city purchased the beautiful old Cunard liner Queen Mary and gave the ship a permanent home in order to serve both as a museum and as a monument to an era of transatlantic crossing by sea that has now passed into history. The artist quoted in the caption for Figure 4.22, who helped to publicize the ship through sketches and drawings, has also described his reactions to the ship as an educational experience:

I want to share with you first impressions of the Queen as I recall them. At first hearing her name—Queen Mary—she is magical. Just the opportunity to know that she awaits all who choose to come and visit is in itself a satisfaction and tremendously exciting. To think: "What shall I find there?" And that which is to be found is something for every age group—every child—regardless of educational development—but certainly a richer experience awaits the highly developed individual—whether it be child, teenager, adult, or senior citizen.[11]

[10] Time, September 4, 1964, p. 63. The walk-through heart is shown in Plate 4.2.

[11] Morry Gabbe, letter to Lewis Saks, August 1971.

FIGURE 4.22

The British ocean liner Queen Mary made 1,001 crossings of the Atlantic between her maiden voyage in 1936 and her retirement in 1967. On war service from 1940 to 1946, she carried more than 765,000 military personnel and three times took Winston Churchill to conferences in the United States. Longer than three football fields (overall length: 1,019 feet), this majestic vessel is shown in Long Beach, where she has been since the end of 1967. An artist has eloquently described his initial reactions to the ship: "So first I saw her—Queen Mary—what excitement enveloped me! Here she was. Still afloat—her face rejuvenated—spanking clean and still proud: no woman has matured with greater grace. Her lines crisp—her decks solid—her lore bountiful. We had but met—only one day—such a short time for an acquaintance to develop, yet somehow her charm is enchantment—and when I left—I knew full well that I must return."

FIGURE 4.23

The Queen Mary at Long Beach is divided into museum and tour areas, as this diagram shows. Museum: 1. lobby and museum entrance; 2. the Queen Mary story; 3. engine room; 4. shaft alley, lowest part of the ship; 5. steering station, with hydraulic rams which moved the 140-ton rudder; 6. propeller room outside the hull where one of the four 18-foot-diameter propellers can be seen; 7. educational gift shop; 8. theater; 9. stern gallery for exhibits, originally crew's quarters. "The Living Sea," created by the noted oceanographer Jacques-Yves Cousteau, is a special educational marine exhibit in itself. Tour: 10. main lounge, with three-story-high vaulted ceiling; 11. promenade deck, featuring photographs of famous passengers taken on board; 12. cargo hatch; 13. bow, seven stories above water; 14. luxurious first-class passenger suite and, nearby, contrasting World War II soldiers' quarters; 15. quarters of ship's officers; 16. bridge, command station of the ship; 17. "top of the house," used for taking compass bearings; 18. sun deck for passengers; 19. one of the 24, 145-person lifeboats.

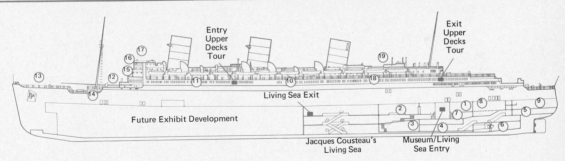

Entry
Upper
Decks
Tour

Exit
Upper
Decks
Tour

Living Sea Exit

Future Exhibit Development

Jacques Cousteau's
Living Sea

Museum/Living
Sea Entry

FIGURE 4.24

The bridge of the *Queen Mary,* the nerve center of the ship, provides many specific learning potentials—and many good photography opportunities.

Lewis Saks, long-time media director of the East Detroit Public Schools and visiting professor at the University of Southern California during the summer of 1971, initiated a project with his U.S.C. classes to prepare teacher-training materials designed to introduce teachers to the great potentialities of the *Queen* as an educational experience. He describes the project, in part, as follows:

You prearrange your visit with the City Fathers, with the ship's management, and, above all, secure a knowledgeable tour guide. You go aboard with students accompanied by a U.S.C staff that is ready with cameras and tape recorders. Some of these students find the ship a monumental thing to digest. It is. Some students bear down with the 2 × 2 slide cameras and the flow of reporting begins to happen. . . .[12]

An outgrowth of the continuing project is the shaping of an approach to the great liner that can lead on to effective classroom social studies, science, and fine arts teaching. The class members and staff undertook to assess the huge museum-ship and to photograph and sketch some of its significant learning areas, including its art and historical collections, palatial dining rooms, bridge, and engine room (see Figure 4.23). In the process they had to devise new methods of investigation and means of media documentation adequate to convey the vastness of the setting without losing the identity of the specific learning potentials in various parts of the ship (see Figure 4.24).

In addition to being a unique kind of monumental project (perhaps one might expect such an undertaking from the people of southern California!), the museum-ship is evidence, as well, of the growing public awareness of the important role of modern museums as significant educational agencies.

[12] Lewis Saks, memorandum, August 25, 1971.

Teaching with three-dimensional materials

A high school history teacher told a visitor after a class:

I would hardly know how to teach history without using the models and objects we have collected over the years I have taught in this school. They seem to help my pupils actually to live the events and times we are studying. One of the things that pleases me greatly is that many of our former students who have graduated keep coming back to see how our collection is growing.

One had only to watch this teacher at work for a short time to appreciate that her pupils' unusual interest in historical things stemmed in large measure from her own genuine and infectious enthusiasm. She was an excellent teacher. But her classroom also helped to bring history alive. Objects and models pertinent to the lesson were much in evidence. The teacher utilized pictures and old prints liberally, and there seemed to be an interesting story about each one. Objects were discussed in context and examined at close range and all but the most fragile were handled by the students. When questioned about damage and loss of articles, the teacher said that there was virtually none; the students were proud of their collection and treated it accordingly.

Selection in terms of learning needs

By this time, it should have become obvious that three-dimensional materials, like other audiovisual materials, should be used when they can make a unique contribution to the lesson. Three-dimensional materials are often more real to the student than pictures because they have depth and substance. They can be seen and handled and sometimes smelled or tasted, in this way providing a more complete perceptual experience. Thus in learning situations where the third dimension is important, a suitable model, object, specimen, or mock-up should be used (see Figure 4.25). Of course the real thing should be used when possible and feasible.

FIGURE 4.25

One function of models is to develop comprehension through tactile as well as visual impressions. Texture is clearly unimportant here, so how can the tactile sense be used to advantage?

In addition, when appropriate, the actual construction of a simple model or diorama should always be considered. For example, an English teacher may construct a model of the Globe Theater from cardboard. A mathematics class may be taught more efficiently with a set of cubes, some spools on a string, a nest of tin cans, or a shoestring and a circle of wood for demonstrating the meaning of π. Stockades, Conestoga wagons, and wigwams are practically standard equipment in the social studies classroom, and most of them can be made by the pupils. With a little help, pupils can easily construct models of various kinds (see Figure 4.26).

In all such situations, one question to be answered is whether the need is important enough to warrant the time and effort involved in making a model, mock-up, or diorama. The same question applies, of course, to collecting specimens and preparing displays. It cannot be answered categorically or in terms of subject-matter learning alone, because, as every experienced teacher knows, the values of such activities to pupils in terms of cooperative experience, individual recognition by the group, and satisfaction in accomplishment may far outweigh the value of the information acquired and the time spent in such activities.

Principles of effective use

As with all instructional materials, three-dimensional teaching tools will not serve pupil learning effectively—no matter how ideally suitable the materials themselves are *potentially*—unless the teacher presents and utilizes them properly in his teaching strategy. Three-dimensional materials do, however, have an intrinsic appeal that suggests some ideas regarding their effective use in instruction.

BE SURE ALL CAN SEE This principle applies, of course, to all visual materials being used with a group, but has particular reference here because many models and most objects and specimens are too small for detailed use with a class-sized group. Ideally, every model would be large enough to be seen easily by everyone in the class

FIGURE 4.26

Putting a model together from one of the fascinating educational kits now available can be an absorbing and concentrated kind of experience which combines the pleasure of accomplishment with a good bit of learning.

FIGURE 4.27

Although these objects are too small for the class to observe in detail from their seats, their interest potential is sufficient to attract students for a close look if needed to identify the items and answer the question.

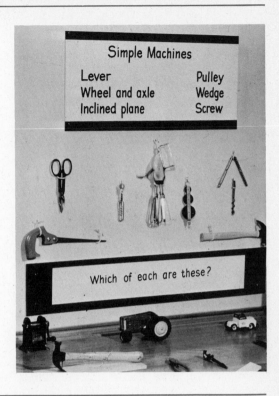

at one time. Though this is often impractical because of such factors as space, cost, and storage facilities, such materials should be large enough for all to observe the general features, closer examination being left for small-group and individual study (see Figure 4.27).

USE WITH OTHER MATERIALS   When you use a model of a flower, for example, to explain pollination to a biology class, you may wish to use a large wall chart for details so that the class can see it readily. You work back and forth between the two to establish clearly the relationship between parts and functions. At the appropriate point, you may also show sound motion picture film which uses animation to visualize the fertilization process. Flat pictures would be useful to establish natural sur-

roundings, and closeup shots of blossoms on 2×2 slides would be helpful in identifying the principal parts of various flowers. In spring or fall, you undoubtedly bring in some real flowers for concrete application of the information required. Or, better still, if an outdoor laboratory or nature trail is readily available, you have your students examine flowers of various kinds in their natural habitats.

In a word, as with other visual and auditory materials, for maximum benefits you use models or objects as part of a *team* of materials. Each part of the team is chosen for the distinctive job it can do well as a part of the overall effort.

PRACTICE USE BEFORE CLASS   Though this principle may appear obvious at first glance, teachers sometimes find themselves

FIGURE 4.28

Some firsthand experience with pulleys and weights in one of Los Angeles' Elementary District Science Centers. What learning advantages are there in such activities as compared with a demonstration in class using typical laboratory pulleys and weights?

stumbling through a presentation because they have not thought each point carefully or have not practiced sufficiently with the model and related materials. The more complex the material, the more important it is to practice the demonstration. The able and experienced teacher is willing to leave little to chance, for he knows that small things can make the difference between a well-planned presentation that "goes over" and one that "just misses."

When using three-dimensional materials in class presentations or demonstrations, the good teacher bears in mind the following points:

1 *The materials should be positioned so that all in the class can see.*
2 *The specific features to be observed or noted should be clearly indicated.*
3 *The teacher should have sufficient assurance in his own presentation so that he can be attentive to class reactions.*
4 *The teacher's movements must not obstruct the pupils' line of vision.*
5 *The presentation should not proceed too rapidly and should be flexible enough to accommodate review or repetition of points as necessary.*

PROVIDE FOR A CORRECT CONCEPT OF SIZE One of the dangers in using three-dimensional materials is that the pupils may get distorted ideas of actual size unless care is taken to guard against this in teaching. A curator in the Milwaukee County Museum tells of a case that illustrates this point. An intermediate class studying some Polynesian exhibits was particularly interested in a small-scale diorama of a native village. Actual coins used by the natives were included in the exhibit. Since the people in the diorama were only a few inches tall, some of the crude coins were nearly as large as the natives themselves. In evident perplexity, a number of pupils asked how the natives managed to carry their money around with them!

One way of emphasizing correct size concepts is by showing the actual object along with the model for the same object. Another is by making comparisons with familiar objects. For example, a picture of a large turbine in a power plant can be helpful when used with a small model if a workman is shown in the picture to indicate the relative size of the giant turbine.

ARRANGE FOR FIRSTHAND EXAMINATION Since one of the major appeals of objects, specimens, models, and mock-ups is their three-dimensional realism, this appeal should be used to stimulate curiosity, interest, and imagination. Unlike pictures,

184

such materials appear differently from every angle and hence should be examined from various points. One of the best ways of providing for this is to have students work directly with the materials (see Figure 4.28). Further, since the use of models offers an opportunity of providing well-rounded sensory experiences, there is good reason to let the students handle a model as well as look at it. To do so makes the experience more concrete, tangible, and memorable to the learner. Those models and specimens that are too fragile or too small to permit handling can be mounted in clear plastic (see Figure 4.10), thus making detailed examination possible from all angles without risking damage to the specimen.[13]

[13] For directions on simple and effective means of plastic mounting, see Herbert E. Scuorzo, ''Embedding Realia in Plastic,'' *Grade Teacher*, January 1963, pp. 10 ff.

Anyone who has seen intermediate-grade pupils making their own models, or junior and senior high school pupils concentrating on collections of insects will have little doubt of their ability to handle models and specimens with care. In any case, there is not much point in having these valuable tools of instruction if the students are not allowed to handle them. Experience with outdoor laboratories and nature trails likewise confirms the fact that the large majority of students will exercise responsibility and care in protecting the plant life and specimens provided there for their benefit. This attitude, as well as the learning that takes place, is further enhanced when students are encouraged to help in the selection of models and specimens and in collecting specimens and objects for use in class or laboratory (see Figure 4.29).

FIGURE 4.29

This high school student on an archaeological research team is beginning a "dig" on an Indian camp site in Oregon. Clearly there is an object lesson here which goes beyond whatever this girl may be learning about archeological techniques. What else does this picture say to you?

STORE WHEN NOT IN USE   Storage problems frequently lead to classrooms that are cluttered with all kinds of objects, specimens, and models. At the proper time they are hauled down and dusted off, used, and then put back on the shelf for another semester or year. Too often these collections are in full view of the students at all times, distracting attention and lessening their effectiveness when used for instruction.

Although some materials like aquariums, terrariums, and globes lend themselves well to continuing observation and interest as part of the classroom environment, most teaching materials are unsuited for this purpose. The enterprising teacher sees to it that they are stowed away out of sight until the psychological moment arrives for using them. He realizes that their interest value is thereby greatly enhanced and that attention can be focused more effectively if unrelated materials are not visible.

Like a good merchandiser, the teacher knows that he must catch and hold his pupils' attention before he can "sell" his ideas effectively. Some teachers cover the glass in their classroom storage cabinets with colored drawing paper, others ask the art department to use this space for simple, appropriate designs that have a decorative effect but are not distracting. When no cabinet or other storage space is available in the classroom, cartons or boxes may be used to store three-dimensional materials between uses.

School displays and exhibits

ASIDE from the classroom itself, three-dimensional materials are most widely used in educational displays and exhibits. Although we tend to think of displays and exhibits primarily in connection with retail selling, museums, trade shows, and fairs, they have many useful applications in schools as well. Most schools have parents' nights, hobby shows, or annual exhibits of some kind. Vocational schools and technical high schools make regular use of displays to show the work done by various departments. Most of the newer elementary and secondary school buildings have built-in display cases in the corridors for educational exhibits during the school year. In all of these, three-dimensional materials play a prominent part.

Principles of 3–D use in displays

In Chapter 5 we discuss the study display in detail. We shall point out here, however, that the effective use of three-dimensional materials in the learning display depends on the proper observation of several important principles.

APPROPRIATE BALANCE AND EFFECT The first consideration is to determine the relative importance of the three-dimensional material to the specific purposes of the display. If a model or mock-up is to play a featured role in the display, it should have prominence—but not so much as to obscure other materials in the display. If several objects and specimens are to be used, they should be arranged in such a way as to achieve appropriate balance and effect. As in all educational planning, the specific objectives for the display govern both the selection of materials and how they are used.

DESIGN AND COLOR   Sound principles of design and color use should, of course, be observed when using three-dimensional objects in a school study display. These are essentially the same principles as those discussed in connection with picture quality

FIGURE 4.30

Participation is "the name of the game" in effective professional exhibits. As far as is practical, the principle of viewer involvement should also be built into school exhibits and displays.

(pages 106–110)—good organization and composition plus effective use of color and contrast—applied to the overall design of the display.

LIGHTING AND MOTION   Lighting and motion are important additional features of effective study displays involving three-dimensional materials. Since they are discussed in some detail in the next chapter, we will merely say here that color and lighting go hand in hand in highlighting key features of a display as well as in attracting initial attention to it. Motion of figures in a diorama or of parts in a working model can likewise enhance both the attention-getting and interest-holding qualities of displays or exhibits.

VIEWER INVOLVEMENT   Any display or exhibit can profit from heightened viewer involvement by provisions made for him to engage in some activity other than merely looking at it (see Figure 4.30). Pushing buttons to activate a display, putting on headphones to hear taped explanations, responding to exercise questions by pushing more

buttons—all are simple representative ways of involving the viewer. These do not require intricate or complex mechanisms like those sometimes used in large exhibitions such as World's Fairs or in museums, but they are based on similar learning principles. One of these is that people at any age learn best when actively involved.

The working of this principle was vividly demonstrated by people in two Cleveland suburban communities who cooperated to build a model "safety town" on one of their school playgrounds. They constructed small buildings, laid out streets complete with traffic signs and lights, bought pedal-type cars and trucks, and even supplied a policeman to help with safety instruction for their kindergartners. Some children "drove" around the town while others were taken around as pedestrians by their teachers. Then the groups reversed roles. In the process all learned their safety lessons so well that there was a sharp reduction in the number of traffic accidents involving children.[14]

[14] "Teach Tots Safety with a Model Town," *School Management*, August 1962, pp. 42–43.

Summary

Much of the effectiveness of direct concrete experience in learning comes from the fact that such experience involves a well-rounded use of the physical senses. Although firsthand experience is impossible or impractical in many teaching situations, important segments of reality can frequently be brought into the classroom by means of models, objects and specimens, mock-ups, and dioramas.

These three-dimensional materials can help to make the learning situation more real, lifelike, and interesting to the student. Furthermore, they are frequently an improvement on reality itself. A model of the solar system or of a one-celled animal, for example, reduces the vastness of the former and enlarges the microscopic proportions of the latter to a size that can be seen and studied. Cutaway models provide interior views of objects which ordinarily cannot be observed. Among their other useful characteristics, models have the realism of three dimensions, they usually are simplified, important features are made to stand out clearly, and many have removable parts.

Models are defined as recognizable three-dimensional representations of real things; objects are the actual things. Specimens are objects that are typical of a class or group of objects. A mock-up is similar to a model, but is distinguished by rearrangement and condensation of essential elements so that they can be studied more readily. A diorama is a three-dimensional scene made with miniature objects and background with exaggerated depth.

With the modern emphasis on ecology and environmental studies, many school systems are providing excellent outdoor laboratories and nature trails where a variety of natural phenomena can be observed and studied at firsthand. Museums of all types provide potentially valuable learning experiences involving significant art, historical, and scientific concepts. These experiences often are presented in visually articulate and highly interesting forms that bring the past alive, interpret the present, and anticipate the future.

In order to use three-dimensional teaching materials effectively, it is of primary importance that they be seen clearly and examined from various angles. Students should accordingly be permitted to handle and work directly with them whenever possible. The instructor must be careful to avoid giving the class distorted size concepts when models are used. As in all effective teaching, he should combine pertinent materials in terms of specific lesson objectives. In general, three-dimensional materials should be stored out of sight when not being used for actual instruction.

Displays and exhibits are other highly effective means of using three-dimensional materials. Although good educational exhibits require careful planning and the application of artistic principles governing arrangements, color, and lighting, they can and should be cooperative projects in which the students participate actively. As in the construction of dioramas and the use of other three-dimensional materials, valuable concomitant learning can take place in addition to the information acquired.

Further learner response projects

1

From catalogs suplied by the instructor or your school library, select several three-dimensional items you would particularly like to have in your school. Describe how *they would help the children you teach (and perhaps others) in a memo to your principal requesting their purchase.*

2

With others, form committees to prepare lists of sources of three-dimensional materials that are supplied free or on loan to schools. Ask your instructor for suggestions and check such sources as the Elementary Teacher's Guide to Free Curriculum Materials, the Educator's Guide to Free Science Materials, and local libraries and museums. Organize the lists in terms of subject areas and grade level and have them duplicated for distribution to the class.

3

Examine a few effective window displays in your community and analyze them in terms of arrangement, use of color, and lighting. Take pictures, if feasible, or make simple sketches of the designs and layouts. Critique them with interested colleagues.

4

Survey the display and exhibit facilities in your own or a friend's school building. List ways in which these could be improved and bring your list to class so you can discuss your ideas with colleagues.

5

Select a suitable subject for a display or exhibit—for example, pollution control, career opportunities, drugs, community helpers. "Brainstorm" with several interested associates on how such a display could be designed and put together. Select the best ideas, make a plan and design, share it with the class or an interested group, note their suggestions, and file the amended plan for later use.

6

Storing three-dimensional teaching materials is a constant problem in many schools. Visit several schools in your community and gather information on how this problem is handled. On the basis of your findings, list practical suggestions for improving the storage of 3–D teaching materials.

References

CARBONI, REMO. "Plaster and Burlap—How To Make a Large Landscape Model." *School Arts,* September 1963, pp. 16–17.

EAST, MARJORIE. *Display for Learning.* Dryden, 1952, pp. 31–53, 255–280.

Educational Displays and Exhibits. Instructional Media Center, University of Texas, Austin, 1965.

HARDING, ROBERT G. "New Dimensions to School-Produced Media." *AV Instruction,* April 1969, p. 65.

HYER, JAMES E., and RICHARD G. YOUNG. "Making a Collection of Preserved Animal Specimens." *Grade Teacher,* March 1964, pp. 28–29 ff.

KEMP, JERROLD E. *Planning and Producing Audiovisual Materials.* 2d ed. Chandler, San Francisco, 1968.

KNISKERN, EDNA MAKI. "An Easily Made Cell Model." *The American Biology Teacher,* March 1964, pp. 191–192.

LARSON, G. OLAF. "Paper Stereomodels." *Journal of Chemical Education,* May 1965, pp. 274–276.

MINOR, ED, and HARVEY R. FRYE. *Techniques for Producing Visual Instructional Media.* McGraw-Hill, 1970.

MORLAN, JOHN E. *Preparation of Inexpensive Teaching Materials,* Chandler, San Francisco, 1963.

RUBY, DORIS. *4–D Bulletin Boards That Teach.* Fearon Publishers, Palo Alto, Calif., 1960.

SANDERSON, R. T. *Three-Dimensional Teaching of Chemistry.* Van Nostrand, 1964.

SCUORZO, HERBERT E. "Embedding Realia in Plastic." *Grade Teacher,* January 1963, pp. 10 ff.

SHEPPARD, D. "A Method for Assessing the Value of Exhibitions." *British Journal of Educational Psychology,* December 1960, pp. 259–265.

WITMEYER, STANLEY. "Display Is Visual Communication." *The Instructor,* May 1960, pp. 47–50.

Media references

Atomic Models, Valence and the Periodic Table, 16mm film, color, 45 min. University of Iowa, 1962.

The Diorama as a Teaching Aid, 35mm filmstrip, color, 58 frames. Ohio State University, 1957.

How To Make and Use a Diorama, 16mm film, color, 20 min. McGraw-Hill, 1956.

Models and Realia, series of 8 transparencies from *Instructional Media Transparency Masters—A Series* (of 147). Keuffel and Esser Company, 1969. Exhibits (2 transparencies) also part of the series.

Museums for School Children, 16mm film, b/w, 21 min. United World Films, 1950.

Relief Models, 16mm film, color, 10 min. David Lipscomb College, 1955.

Simple Exhibit Technique, 35mm filmstrip, color, 40 frames. Ohio State University, 1958.

Successful Exhibit Ideas, 35mm filmstrip, b/w, 81 frames. Pocket Films, 1958.

A Special Set of Models for Introducing Chemistry, 16mm film, color, 45 min. University of Iowa, 1962.

Source references

See source lists in the Appendix; particularly relevant sections are: Three Dimensional Materials; Display Surfaces and Supplies; Multimedia Equipment and Materials; Museums; Photography (Lighting).

See *Student Production Guide,* Chapter 3, "Graphics Techniques for Instructional Materials Production," particularly Design and Color.

FIVE
Displays for learning

We are consumers and producers.

Objectives	Performance responses

1

To be able to identify three basic functions of study displays.

Write a brief description of the basic purposes of motivational, developmental, and summary displays. Describe how they are created and who should create them. From illustrations in the chapter, pictures provided by the instructor, or displays in your school, identify two of each type and briefly explain the reasons for your identifications.

2

To be able to identify and list the distinctive physical and instructional advantages of six different types of study display areas or surfaces.

In two columns labeled "Physical" and "Instructional," respectively, briefly list the advantages of six types of study displays discussed in this chapter. Check your list with those of two or more of your fellow students.

3

To be able to apply the principles of effective design, color, and lettering in developing a study display.

Using a selected topic in your own subject area and grade level, do a layout sketch of a study display which you feel would have significant value in your teaching. Be ready to justify the display chosen in terms of (1) its appropriateness as a display subject and (2) the particular type of display selected from among those available to you.

4

To be able to explain and demonstrate the physical characteristics of effective displays.

Using the sketch made in Response 3, develop the display sufficiently to illustrate your grasp of the *physical principles* of effective display described on pages 186–187. Photograph the result in color and bring the prints or slides to class for a critique by the instructor and fellow students. (An alternative response is to select from a group of existing slides or pictures of study displays.)

5

To be able to describe and demonstrate four techniques of effective chalkboard use.

With several other students, take 35mm slides of chalkboard uses in your own schools and present them for a critique in your media class. Be ready to demonstrate in class four or more chalkboard techniques you have found to be effective.

6

To be able to relate specific display techniques to specific instructional purposes.

Using one or more of the layouts and photographs produced in Responses 3, 4, and 5, describe specific instructional uses to which they can be put.

DURING the period since the Soviets sent up the first spacecraft in 1957, much has happened to change the face and the feel of American schools. Once barely more than baby-sitting agencies, with rows of boxlike classrooms where knowledge was poured into the heads of students to digest, or more often to reject, the schools have started to become centers for learning where the nature, the needs, and the interests of young people are increasingly shaping both school buildings themselves and the curriculum, the methods, and the organization of the school program.

These are a few of the changes that are taking place: Instead of one lock-step schedule, we have flexible scheduling. Instead of a single teacher doing most of the teaching in each subject, we have teams of teachers, each doing what he can do best. Instead of classes usually of uniform size, we have combinations of large-group, small-group, and individualized instruction. And instead of libraries with nothing but printed materials, we have central learning resource centers well stocked with films, filmstrips, slides, audiotapes, and other media learning materials, in addition to books.

New environments for learning

As a result of changes in school programs, school designers have become much more conscious of the need for an environment that is conducive to learning. The institutionalized, sterile appearance of traditional boxlike classrooms, libraries, and corridors is giving way to warm, attractive, and flexible surroundings with learning resource centers as focal points and with a wealth of display spaces throughout the school area. There are extensive display board spaces in classrooms, halls, and the resource center. (Even in older schools, inventive use is frequently made of bare wall spaces, ceilings, and free-standing temporary display arrangements in appropriate areas.) In these newer schools there are lighted display cases in the corridors and in some classrooms (see Figure 5.1). In some of the larger, divided

classrooms, there are "teaching walls" which have multiple uses as rear-vision screens with sliding cover panels serving as chalkboards and display boards. Even the ceilings are used—free-form mobiles and models of the solar system hang from them and, in an increasing number of schools, planetariums project the stars and planets on them. The school grounds include such outdoor learning laboratories as carefully designed geological paths, erosion study slopes, botanical gardens, soil plots, and aquatic areas.

In short, when considering displays for learning, we need to think in much broader terms than merely "bulletin boards." We must now think of study displays as a part of the total learning environment which has been specifically designed to involve the students (see Figure 5.2). Although in less

FIGURE 5.1

To be effective, displays must be *seen*. Display areas such as these both enhance the effectiveness of displays and encourage their creative use.

FIGURE 5.2

In modern school buildings, various ways are used to increase display areas. The sliding panels shown folded against the wall and extended to form a partition in these pictures taken at different schools are one example.

comprehensive form, such a total environment is not unlike World's Fair exhibitions in which the intention is for the viewer to be surrounded, to walk through, to pass by, or to examine closely as his interest may dictate.

The presence or absence of attractive display areas is frequently a major factor in the general appearance and feeling that a school or a classroom provides pupils and teachers. All too often most of us have had the experience of walking into a classroom characterized by bare walls devoid of any evidences of pupil activity or the excitement of learning. In contrast, most of us also have the pleasant memory of classrooms where the walls gave dramatic evidence of the nature of pupil and teacher activities. Colorful displays—which both communicate information and incite interest and involvement—impart to a school and its classrooms a personality that suggests something of the vitality and excitement of what goes on there. Study displays, of course, are only one indicator of the level and quality of learning taking place, but they are of sufficient importance to merit our particular attention.

Study displays

A *study display* is an organized visual arrangement of learning materials, usually on a wall or a horizontal surface, which is designed to present significant information or ideas on a given topic.

An effective study display is a stimulating experience. It may include a wide variety of materials such as diagrams, photographs, pictures, graphs, news clippings, mobiles, and three-dimensional objects and specimens. It may be planned and developed by teachers or pupils or both. Today's teachers know that effective displays can help pupils learn, and they are always on the alert for new ideas and materials that will make possible even more productive uses of them.

Functions of study displays

Good study displays can help a teacher to achieve many different types of purposes. In the ways they achieve these purposes, displays may be broadly categorized into three basic types: motivational, developmental, and summary. (1) In the course of a unit of work, at the outset a display may be *motivational,* intended to elicit interest and curiosity. A motivational display usually is designed and put up by the teacher or his assistants. (2) As a unit of work proceeds, a display may be *developmental,* intended to add information and comprehension. A developmental display should actively involve the students in both planning and execution (see Figure 5.3). (3) At the end of a unit of work, a display may be *summary,* intended to pull together all of the key ideas in the unit. A summary display may be produced by either the teacher or students or both.

To some degree, any display tends to fulfill all three of these functions. Its success, however, depends significantly on which purpose is paramount and on the consequent steps taken to plan and develop the display itself. The important point is that a teacher needs to have clearly in mind the functions he wishes a particular display to serve. His specific objectives in terms of content, ideas, or behavioral outcomes must be clearly defined if desired outcomes are to be achieved.

In terms of the Instructional Development principles discussed in Chapter 3, we need to think of study displays as part of

FIGURE 5.3

Involvement in the form of some kind of active participation is necessary if learning is to take place. Helping to plan and develop a display can be an important kind of involvement with a real "payoff" in student learning.

a whole *team* of instructional materials and methods which are selected only after our objectives have been carefully specified and the various practical alternatives to achieving them have been well thought through. In other words, study displays, like any media or methods, should be incorporated in a unit of study on the basis of a systematically developed plan; this plan should take into account not only the content to be covered but also the abilities, needs, and interests of the pupils and the learning problems standing in the way of achieving specified objectives. Not until this point should a teacher make final selections of the materials and methods to be used as the best available means of attaining those objectives with his own students. Within that systematic planning context, the teacher then selects from those available the media, materials, and methods to be used in terms of their particular advantages and limitations for the jobs to be done, as discussed throughout this book.

Distinctive characteristics of study displays

Because study displays are composed of a variety of materials such as pictures, graphics, objects, and specimens, they quite naturally share with these materials their inherent advantages and limitations (which were described in Chapters 3 and 4). Nevertheless, when these elements are combined into an effective display, the total effect can and certainly should be something greater than the simple sum of its parts.

As one example, displays are uniquely suited for motivational purposes—much more so, as a rule, than the individual pictures and other materials of which they are composed. As another, developmental dis-

FIGURE 5.4

"Teaching walls" of various types provide
expanded amounts of useful display space, plus
versatility and attractiveness as well. The use
of such space, however, must be well planned
to avoid a cluttered or messy effect.

plays that are put together by students
require a level of planning and application
activity that has learning potentials beyond those normally associated with the
individual pictures, objects, and models
which may comprise the display. Further,
such displays can provide useful visual
literacy training opportunities for the
students participating in their development
to the degree that the students themselves
design the display, select or create the materials that are to go into it, and put them
together (see Figure 5.4).

A good display can attract and appeal
to the learner who is primarily visual-
minded, stimulate the curiosity and imagination of most of the pupils, and be of
particular assistance to the slow learner
who can absorb it at his own pace. The
study display can provide effective transitions from old to new materials, provide
opportunities for less verbal students to
communicate visually (and perhaps achieve
needed recognition in the process), and
provide practice for all students in the
ordering and sequencing of ideas.

On the other hand, the display medium
also has certain limitations. Good displays
take considerable time and effort to do well.
Furthermore, like any other medium or
technique, displays can be overdone and
lose their freshness and appeal. It stands to
reason, accordingly, that we should carefully select the topics on which to use them.

FIGURE 5.5

A commercial display must "sell" or it is worth-
less. As teachers, we also need to "sell."
Furthermore, our "product" is infinitely more
important than games or clothes or snowmobiles
or toasters—or anything else in store window
displays. Yet we can learn much from them in
terms of design, interest, and effective visual
communication. What ideas do you find in these?

There is a tendency, also, for displays to become cluttered and lose their effectiveness. Finally, we need to recognize that classroom displays may compete for attention when other learning activities are being conducted. Such factors as these must be taken into account in determining when and how to make best use of this versatile but demanding medium.

Some displays serve typically administrative purposes—reports on student activities, notices of events, regulations, and the like. For the most part, we are not considering that type of display here beyond observing that most administrative bulletin boards could profit materially from application of some of the same principles of organization and design as are suggested for the effective study display. There is no good reason why administrative bulletin boards should be the cluttered "mess" they usually are. With a little time and effort they can be made both more attractive and effective.

There are, of course, many examples of effective displays in the business world. The

selling display—which actually *must* communicate and convey information to be effective—is designed to encourage potential customers to buy goods or services. To find many excellent examples, merely stroll by some department store show windows or walk along the aisles of a supermarket. A successful commercial display must command attention, arouse interest, and involve the viewers sufficiently so that then or later they will be moved to take the action desired by the creator of the display—to buy the product.

In a real sense, the school display faces some of the same challenges. A motivational display, for example, is definitely intended to arouse interest—to "sell" an idea for a new unit of study. Many teachers, in fact, wisely consult advertising displays for ideas on interesting arrangements, attention-getting devices, uses of color, effective titles, and the like. One characteristic that is obvious in good eye-catching advertisements or window displays is that they are essentially simple and concise in conception and design—they reflect a single clear-cut idea (see Figure 5.5). Whether one is selling a product or a concept, it is well to keep this underlying principle of simplicity of definition in mind because it is relevant to all forms of effective visual display.

Provisions for display areas

B EFORE proceeding further into the planning aspects of study displays, let us look briefly at the various kinds of spaces which can be used to advantage for display purposes.

Spaces normally available

Display spaces are essentially of two types, flat and three-dimensional; sometimes, as in dioramas, both are used in combination. Flat display areas such as bulletin boards are typically installed on the walls in classrooms, corridors, and instructional resource centers. In newer schools, liberal amounts of these panels are usually provided in the classrooms, with up to a third of the usable wall area being used for this purpose, or a minimum of from 15 to 20 linear feet. In some cases, convertible panels are installed so that the same wall space may serve alternately for chalkboard, display, or projection screen purposes (see Figure 5.6). In addition, a map rail with sliding fittings is usually mounted above chalkboard areas. The fittings have hooks and clips on which

maps or charts can be hung. The rail also contains a narrow strip of cork or similar substance to which flat materials can be attached with thumbtacks or pins.

Three-dimensional displays or exhibits can be placed on tables or shelves or in display cases built into classroom or corridor walls (see Figure 5.1). Display cases are frequently located, as well, at strategic points near the school entrances so that visitors may be provided information and ideas on significant aspects of the school's program. Display cases, which may have several shelves, should contain built-in lighting so arranged as to light all areas adequately. Each case should also have an electrical outlet for supplemental lighting, for projection equipment which may occasionally be used in a display, and for devices employing small motors to provide motion.

The ceiling can likewise be used to advantage for certain types of displays where suspension is needed. An obvious example for small classrooms is the suspended globe, but inventive teachers have found overhead suspension effective for such "naturals" as

FIGURE 5.6

With limited visual display space, versatility becomes important. Here the same panel can be used for chalkboard, magnetic board, screen, or study display purposes.

a model of the solar system, models of space platforms, spaceships, and airplanes, a model of a section of the moon with astronauts on it, and mobiles of several types.

To teach the Great Circle and certain other concepts in geography, a sixth-grade teacher had his students create a wall map mural showing the curvature of the segment of the earth between New York and London. The children used models of jet aircraft, plus a globe and a piece of string. In the process of developing the mural, the students had to check back and forth constantly with the globe as the aircraft "flew" over it in order to achieve a relative degree of accuracy as well as the perspective necessary to show the earth's curvature on a flat surface. Needless to say, before they were done the students had acquired some important new insights about reading and interpreting the globe and flat maps of the world.

Supplemental "do it yourself" display spaces

When needed, as they frequently are in older school buildings, various methods and devices can be used to supplement available study display spaces. These range from simple panels of Celotex or similar porous material which can be set on the chalk rail or on an easel (see Figure 5.7) to free-standing or pole-mounted arrangements of panels and shelves which can provide entirely new and highly effective display areas whenever desired (see Figure 5.8). One or more of the following additional suggestions may also be applicable in buildings with limited display facilities:

1. Unused wall or chalkboard areas can be hung with coarse, loosely woven cloth or heavy paper suspended from a light strong wire that has been stretched above the chalkboard or other area to be used. The cloth provides a surface on which flat materials can be pinned. The heavy paper can be used either for the same purpose or for murals, with the pupils drawing directly on it with crayon or pastel chalk. The paper can first be spray-painted with a background water color if desired; if this is done, the corners should be fastened while the paint dries to avoid curling. These temporary display surfaces can easily be removed whenever desired.

2. Small areas of up to 4 × 6 feet can

FIGURE 5.7

A variety of useful display spaces can be added in most classrooms. This composite drawing suggests the possibilities from which practical selections can be made.

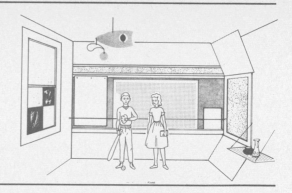

be converted for use as display spaces by fitting them with composition board or plywood veneer panels that have been covered with an inexpensive, loosely woven material such as burlap, hopsacking—both of which come in a wide range of colors— or monk's cloth. The material should be slightly larger than the panel so it can be folded over the edges and stapled on the reverse side. Start at the left edge, then staple the top and bottom edges, stretching and smoothing the material as you go until it is fastened around all four edges of the panel.

3. Free-standing panels of various sizes can either be purchased or constructed of inexpensive materials. Among the former are lightweight notched panels which fit together at an angle and provide their own support. Also available are lightweight

FIGURE 5.8

Shelving and vertical display areas on free-standing poles in arrangements such as this one are an inexpensive and interesting way to add flexible spaces for a variety of displays.

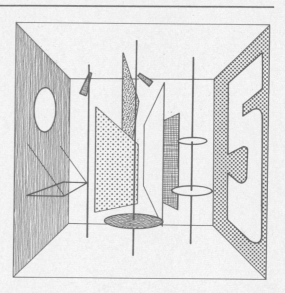

FIGURE 5.9

This diagram shows how pipe stands can be used to form versatile two-sided free-standing display panels or pegboard panels.

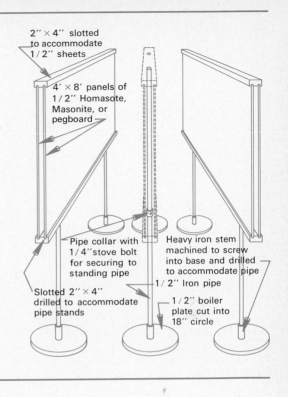

2″ × 4″ slotted to accommodate 1/2″ sheets

4′ × 8′ panels of 1/2″ Homasote, Masonite, or pegboard

Pipe collar with 1/4″ stove bolt for securing to standing pipe

Heavy iron stem machined to screw into base and drilled to accommodate pipe

Slotted 2″ × 4″ drilled to accommodate pipe stands

1/2″ Iron pipe

1/2″ boiler plate cut into 18″ circle

metal extension poles with adjustable fittings to which panels and shelving can be attached; two panels and three poles provide a free-standing unit, but many arrangements are possible, including squares, triangles, and even enclosed areas with walk-through traffic patterns for special occasions such as science fairs, art shows, or lobby shows. Free-standing panels or pegboards can also be mounted on pipe stands (see Figure 5.9).

4. Across a little-used corner of the room stretch clothesline from hooks mounted in the edges of the chalkboard frame or cabinets. Stretch the lines to form a zigzag pattern across the area, then to these zigzag supports attach large sheets of lightweight but strong cardboard cut from old mattress cartons, large grocery cartons, or card-table containers. Use these free-form areas as surfaces on which to display objects, specimens, pictures, graphics, or student work.

5. One of the simplest means of adding needed display space is to take any unused wall spaces in classrooms or corridors and mount materials directly on them. Double-surfaced masking tape or similar adhesives will hold most flat materials, and Bulletin Board Styx, a waxlike adhesive of considerable strength, can be used for heavier materials, raised letters, or even three-dimensional objects. The surface must be free of oily film or dust for such adhesives to work effectively. Although better suited for some purposes than others, unused wall spaces should not be overlooked as practical supplements to existing display areas. With a little assistance and direction, students at upper-grade or secondary levels can readily install most types of supplemental display areas.

Special display surfaces

I N addition to the kinds of display surfaces we have considered, there are several types of specialized display boards, each of which has certain unique advantages and applications for teaching purposes. These include such devices as pegboards, feltboards, hook-and-loop boards, and magnetic boards.

Pegboards

One of the more versatile surfaces for display purposes is the pegboard. Pegboards, which are made of tempered Masonite, have ⅛-inch holes punched in a regular pattern 1 inch apart over the entire surface.[1] These boards come in 4 × 8 foot sheets and can be cut to fit any desired space within those dimensions. Special metal hooks, clips, and other fittings, available from any hardware store, can be inserted in any pattern desired; they will support fairly heavy objects. To provide space behind them for insertion of the fittings, pegboards must be mounted ½ inch or so out from the mounting surface.

For display purposes such boards are particularly useful for combining flat and three-dimensional materials, the latter being placed on hooks or shelves which can be located anywhere on the surface. The ⅛-inch holes are also the right size for golf tees which can be used to punctuate or emphasize parts of the visual design or simply to support maps or charts fitted with grommets. Pegboards make a good backing surface for display cases as well. The regular pattern of holes is not unattractive as a background, but, when desired, the surface of the board can easily be covered with cloth or paper.

[1] Pegboard comes in ⅛-inch and ¼-inch thicknesses, with corresponding hole sizes. The ¼-inch pegboard is used primarily for grilles and other construction purposes. The lighter, ⅛-inch, board is preferable for most display purposes.

Feltboards

Because felt or flannel materials have a nap or fiber surface, similar materials will adhere to them; this simple fact makes possible another very useful display surface— the feltboard. Flat, lightweight teaching materials backed with pieces of garnet paper or flannel can be readily used on feltboards. Feltboards can be purchased or they can be made rather easily by stretching inexpensive cotton outing flannel or wool felt over flat panels of plywood, Masonite, or even heavy cardboard. Frequently both sides of such panels are covered to provide additional space.

This type of display surface is particularly convenient for use with sequential or additive kinds of learning materials (see Figure 5.10). In explaining the water cycle, for example, a teacher can begin with a diagram showing evaporation from bodies of water and land surfaces, add a second showing cooling and condensation into clouds as the warm air rises, and then a third showing clouds building up and condensing into rain falling back to the earth's surface and starting the cycle all over again (see Plate 5.1, following page 260). Another example is the teaching of fractions —overlay pieces of felt representing halves, thirds, quarters, and so on, are fitted onto base circles, squares, and rectangles.

Many materials of this type are available inexpensively from school supply houses, but you can also make your own by cutting desired shapes of felt or flannel or by pasting small pieces of garnet paper or flannel on the reverse side of pictures, cards, and similar flat materials. Some textured-surface papers like kraft paper have enough nap to stick to the feltboard by themselves.

Figures cut from a children's magazine or others made of kraft paper can be used for a creative story hour or for a demonstration on safety. The chemistry

FIGURE 5.10

Various flannel or felt symbols are convenient for cumulative kinds of learning exercises.

teacher finds the feltboard useful in explaining molecular structure, the meaning of valence, or formula development. The physical education teacher or band director uses the feltboard for demonstrating football plays and marching formations. The language arts teacher can use it to advantage in showing relationships between parts of a sentence, in vocabulary drill, and in similar exercises.

The feltboard thus can be useful in visualizing a variety of concepts in many subjects and at many grade levels. It is particularly well suited to situations calling for step-by-step development of a topic, but it is valuable as well for discussion or drill periods, for visual change during development of a topic, and for student involvement. Students can easily manipulate feltboard materials and enjoy doing so; this ready use by students can and should be utilized in a variety of drill, exercise, and demonstration situations.

Hook-and-loop boards

The hook-and-loop board is similar to the feltboard, but it is much stronger, permitting the display of relatively heavy three-dimensional objects, as well as pictures and other flat materials. The surface of the board is made of a special nylon fabric that consists of thousands of tiny but very strong loops. An adhesive-backed patch on which comparable numbers of tiny hooks are woven is affixed to the object to be displayed, and the object is then pressed onto the board surface. Though the supporting strength of the hook-and-loop board is really quite remarkable, objects affixed to it are very easily removed. Such boards can be used on easels but are better fastened to the wall for full advantage to be taken of their weight-supporting capacity (see Figure 5.11). The two types of fabrics, complete boards, and sets of materials for use on them are available from school supply houses (see the source lists in the Appendix).

In addition to their special three-dimensional capacity, hook-and-loop boards can be used exactly like feltboards with the additional advantage that materials will not shift or fall (see Plate 5.1, following page 260). Such accessories as precut letters of various sizes for titles or captions, pads of drawing paper, and even magnetic chalkboards to fit onto the surface—all backed with the necessary hook-on material—are readily available.

FIGURE 5.11

Display requires versatility. (a) The hook-and-loop board provides a strong support surface for 3–D materials of substantial weight. (b) It is also useful in displaying flat materials of substantial size which a feltboard would not hold.

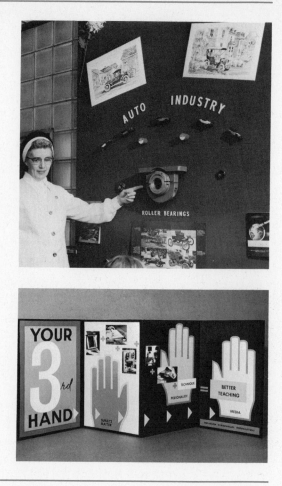

Magnetic boards

Magnetic boards are still another type of useful display surface. Any sheet of metal or screening which will attract a magnet can be used for magnetic board purposes. Such screening is sometimes used behind permanently mounted wall maps to serve as a base for various magnet-mounted symbols or cards bearing place names or other geographic features. Many schools have installed steel-backed chalkboards specifically to provide the added utility of a surface that can be used either for chalkboard or magnetic board purposes or both in combi-nation. Small magnets to which any appropriate symbols can be affixed will hold wherever they are placed on the surface.

The magnetic board is a "natural" for the driver education teacher portraying various driving problem situations; for the coach diagraming plays or defenses; or for the band director working out marching formations. Small models of cars or people or other objects with magnets attached will hold firmly to the surface but can easily be moved around as desired (see Figure 5.12). Further, when desirable, small magnets can also be used to hold papers, pictures, and

FIGURE 5.12

Another vertical surface with 3–D capacity is the magnetic board. Light objects with small magnets attached adhere to its surface but are easily moved. The medium thus is good for use in diagraming driver education problems, athletic team plays, band maneuvers, and similar motion situations.

similar flat materials against the surface of the board for specific immediate purposes.

Chalkboards

Chalkboards are such familiar parts of the school environment that they tend to be taken for granted. Consequently, many teachers tend to think only of the chalkboard's obvious general utility and thus overlook some of its unique potentialities. Consequently, also, though chalkboards themselves have changed considerably over the years (see Figure 5.13), their uses have not kept pace. Today in modern school buildings, classrooms are equipped with nonglare boards in soft green or other pastel shades, usually permanently mounted on two sides of the room. The chalk is relatively dustless and clean, and one or more of the board sections is likely to have a steel backing so that it may be used as a magnetic chalkboard, as discussed above and below. Let us take a quick look at a few of the uses to which the chalkboard can be put

and expand then to a discussion of some of its more unique potentialities.

THE ROLE OF THE CHALKBOARD IN INSTRUCTION Chalkboards have long been used in the primary grades for experience stories which the children themselves dictate and the teacher prints; this use continues, for it is still valuable. In the intermediate grades, the teacher may introduce a new unit of study by writing interesting questions on the chalkboard to capture the imagination of his pupils and channel their interests. As the unit continues, the chalkboard is useful in many ways such as lists of references to be consulted, further questions and projects developed by the students, and summaries of key points at appropriate intervals.

A combination of chalkboard techniques, including the use of color, is valuable in teaching arithmetic and mathematics at various levels, as, for example, in explaining the division of whole numbers in the primary grades and algebraic di-

FIGURE 5.13

Movable panels are among the newer ways to solve the problem of limited chalkboard space. The reverse side serves as a display board or screen.

vision at the secondary level. The covered chalkboard techniques (see Figure 5.14) is valuable for short tests or for drill exercises in arithmetic, spelling, vocabulary, or any other area that lends itself to brief and quick visual treatment.

Materials with much detail, however, such as accounting problems or other materials intended to be studied at some length, are better presented by other means —mimeographed sheets, prepared overhead transparencies or slides, charts, and pertinent printed materials. In other words, though the chalkboard can be used to real advantage on occasion by individual students, it is essentially a medium for use with a group or class working on transitory materials that can be quickly and conveniently placed on it.

The magnetic chalkboard, a very versatile teaching medium, is shown in use in four different subject areas in Figure

FIGURE 5.14

The chalkboard is still one of the more versatile and convenient means of visualizing concepts. Here a simple technique enables the teacher to expose items in sequence, revealing them at the most appropriate time for tests or exercises during class discussion.

FIGURE 5.15

5.15. Thus the magnetic board enables the teacher to explain quickly the theory behind equations or formulas having to do with areas, perimeters, and circumferences or the plotting of algebraic equations in graphic form. It has many applications in driver training and in home economics. The athletic coach may use such a board to lay out game plans and strategies. He can use one set of symbols to represent the players on offense, another for those on defense and, perhaps with colored chalk, can develop offensive and defensive plays, strategies, and alternative moves. By covering part of the chalkboard with an ordinary window shade or drape, he can also test his players' analysis and reactions to typical problem situations that may arise during a game. A chalkboard, in short, can be particularly useful to the coach in helping his players to gain some of the cognitive understandings necessary to improve their performance under actual game conditions.

Tips for effective use   In general, material should be placed on the chalkboard before class or while the class is otherwise occupied. When the teacher is using the chalkboard during a class discussion or similar exercise he is leading, he should remember the importance of keeping the pace moving. He should use an assistant or student to do the board work or, if he must do it himself, use brief phrases or abbreviations and turn toward the class frequently with comments or questions so as to maintain eye contact. A teacher should avoid turning his back on the class for more than a few moments at a time, since this tends to slow the action and reduce the concentration and interest of the students.

Although many of the uses just described are familiar ones, we should not take it for granted that knowing *about* them is tantamount to being able to apply them effectively. Teachers should use the chalkboard when it is the quickest, most effective way to visualize and clarify con-

The magnetic chalkboard opens up a host of possibilities. Any lightweight objects can be mounted with adhesive on small magnets for use on steel chalkboards and slid quickly from place to place. Semipermanent diagrams such as the basketball court can be drawn with chalkboard pen and ink and removed with a solvent whenever desired. Meanwhile, chalk may be used and erased at will.

cepts for better understanding. But when it is thus used as part of a learning experience, it should be used with some care. Also, within reason, the use should be planned in advance.

There are some important practical matters a teacher should keep in mind. Much chalkboard use is ineffective simply because the writing is careless, sloppy, cluttered, and even almost illegible. In the first place, the surface of the board should be kept clean, to provide good contrast. All material placed on the chalkboard should be readily readable from the back row. To achieve this, enough pressure should be applied to the chalk to produce bold and clear definition of lines and characters (see Figure 5.16 and also the mathematics prob-

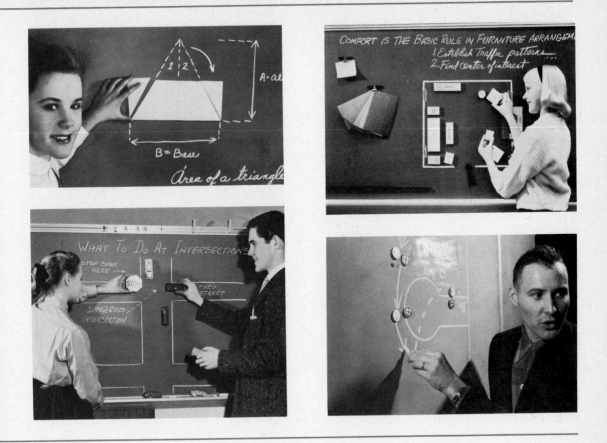

lem in Figure 5.15), and large letters and numbers should be used. Many teachers use printing rather than cursive writing on the chalkboard—particularly when their handwriting leaves something to be desired—and find, with practice, that they can print almost as rapidly as they can write longhand. With awareness of the need and a little practice, most teachers could materially improve the effectiveness of their chalkboard efforts for the myriad uses to which this convenient and versatile medium can be put.

On the other hand, we should not *overuse* the chalkboard as an instructional medium. As reiterated throughout this book, we need to vary our communications techniques from time to time in order to maintain their psychological effectiveness with learners. The instructor who intuitively and continually looks for new ideas and new approaches for improving learner interest, involvement, and understanding is reflecting a sound learning principle. This principle applies to the media the teacher uses as well as to the many other activities and interpersonal relationships involved in teaching. Applied to the chalkboard, this principle suggests both a need to avoid overdependence on it when other means can serve the learning purpose as well or better and a need, when it *is* employed, to seek a purposeful variety in methods of using it. A number of such variations are described

FIGURE 5.16

A simple but important part of good chalkboard technique is to use large enough letters and numbers and write with enough pressure so the material can easily be read from anywhere in the room.

in the examples and illustrations in this section. Another basic variation results when use of the chalkboard is combined with other techniques and materials. The chalkboard may and often should be used along with other teaching materials—models, experience charts, flash cards, and other devices—which contribute to an understanding of the relationships, concepts, and objects necessary for comprehension in a teaching situation.

The critical analysis deriving from the Instructional Development approach described in Chapter 3 is the best way to prevent overuse or misuse of the chalkboard or any other media alternatives. Short of this, your own intuitive "feel" for the needs of the teaching situation—when a change of pace is necessary, when you are not doing enough things in different ways to maintain interest, participation, and pupil in-

volvement at the desired levels—will help you avoid overuse of the chalkboard or other techniques and media in the course of your teaching.

SOME BUILT-IN ADVANTAGES   At the risk of oversimplification, we now summarize three of the most important advantages of the chalkboard in the classroom:

1. *It is always there, ready for use.* Whether used well or badly, this is clearly a convenience to the teacher.

2. *It is highly flexible.* Anything that can be drawn or written can be placed on the chalkboard. It is usable by either teacher or pupils and lends itself well to use with a variety of other media and techniques.

3. *Copy can be easily erased, replaced, or modified.* This is a valuable attribute in any developmental or explanatory work

with pupils during which refinements, corrections, or rephrasing may be desirable.

EFFECTIVE CHALKBOARD INSTALLATIONS As a teacher you may have an opportunity to suggest improvements in your present building or to recommend installations for new buildings being planned in your school system. Accordingly, let us look briefly at several important attributes of modern chalkboard installations. Not only in recommending improvements but also in order to take full advantage of the chalkboard as an integral part of classroom teaching, you should know the following characteristics of effective chalkboard installations:

1. They provide maximum contrast between background and material placed thereon. Part of this contrast is achieved by having clean boards, but an equally important part is placement so as to avoid glare from windows or lighting.

2. They are readily erased or cleaned without leaving ''ghosts'' or smudges with either light or colored chalk.

3. While the utmost in contrast can be achieved with the old black slate boards, a soft green (or in some cases another pastel color) has proved adequate for contrast and blends much better with the decor of the room.

4. The height of the board should be gauged to the average height of the pupils who are to use it. Typically, the height of the board is adequate to accommodate both the teacher and the pupils.

SOME ADDITIONAL CHALKBOARD AIDS In addition to the suggestions for effective use of the chalkboard that have already been made, there are a few other ideas and techniques which any teacher may find useful.

1. Lines and grids Many teachers tend to write uphill or downhill; an easy way to correct this is to draw fine, ruled parallel lines or dots as guides. These can be erased when the material has been lettered or drawn on the board. Music teachers find inexpensive staff-liners invaluable for teaching music theory. Mathematics and science teachers frequently use painted grid forms 36 inches square to facilitate the drawing of graphs and diagrams.

2. Outline forms or patterns Frequently used outlines such as state maps; circles, triangles, rectangles, and parallelograms for math; breakers, test tubes, and graduated measures for chemistry can be conveniently cut into patterns or templates for use whenever needed (see Figure 5.17). Templates can be cut from any thin lightweight material such as plywood or Masonite and held against the board to draw around. Chalkboard stencils also may be used for transferring map outlines to a chalkboard; these are described in Chapter 7, pages 303–304. Another means of transferring maps, graphs, or diagrams is to project them on the chalkboard with an opaque projector and trace the desired lines (see Figure 5.18). For temporary purposes, such as current events, this is a simple and effective means of providing necessary visual materials as a basis for discussion and examination. If no opaque projector is available, the ''grid'' technique produces the same result. In this technique, a grid of small squares is lightly drawn over the original material to be transferred; then a grid composed of the same number of larger squares is lightly drawn on the chalkboard. The original is duplicated on the chalkboard by copying what is in the corresponding squares, one square at a time, then erasing the grid lines from the board. Anyone can quite quickly become adept at using this technique.

3. Stick figures Although freehand drawings require above-average skills, anyone,

FIGURE 5.17

A clothing pattern is produced accurately by
means of a template. In mathematics, templates
assure accuracy even in quickly sketched figures
for theorems. In addition to those shown, what
ideas for the use of templates do you have?

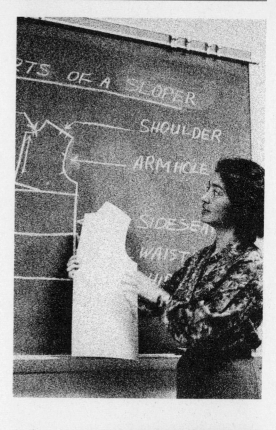

FIGURE 5.18

The diagram of the grasshopper has been projected by means of an opaque projector and the key lines sketched in. In another method, the map has been projected from a filmstrip and used as a guide for tracing. Under what conditions is the use of a projector to produce a chalkboard images more valuable than the image that is directly projected onto a screen?

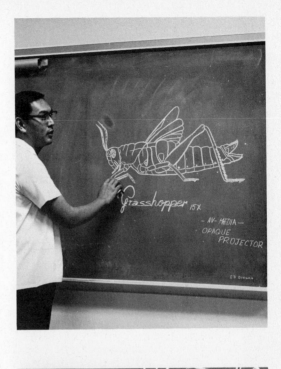

FIGURE 5.19

Stick figures are easy to draw, but they are more effective when the proper proportions, shown here, are approximated. Action is emphasized when the lines are slanted.

after a little practice, can draw simple, effective stick figures such as those in Figure 5.19. These can be useful in a variety of contexts besides adding touches of humor and interest and a change of pace to your chalkboard use.

(Outdoor laboratories and planetariums are two other important and distinctive learning areas which involve study displays. They have certain special characteristics not shared by other types of displays, however, and are therefore discussed in Chapters 4 and 15, where they fit more appropriately into the context of the discussions of three-dimensional materials and multimedia instructional development.

Planning and organizing the study display

I F what has been said so far suggests that preparing good displays can be time consuming and a lot of work, this is essentially correct and should be recognized. It suggests at once that aside from day-to-day chalkboard use, it makes sense to plan for a few really good displays during a term rather than many. It suggests further that ways should be found to distribute the work involved.

Plan ahead

In your planning, you should have a pretty good idea at the beginning of a semester of the units or topics during which study displays will be particularly appropriate and can add significantly to the learning experience. With such advance planning, you have the advantage of being able to get things started well ahead of time, to delegate responsibilities, and to set up a schedule so that when the proper time arrives, the display can be put together in its entirety and have optimum impact. In the interim, the materials can be stored before they are put together in final form. Not all displays will be done this way, of course; for example, the work-type developmental display is intended to be produced as an in-class experience. Motivational and many summary displays, however, can be planned sufficiently in advance to facilitate the work involved and probably to improve the result.

Distribute the work

Students can and should be involved in display preparation, as should teacher aides and other assistants. Students can help greatly, of course, in the collection and selection of materials for learning displays, but they can also benefit from time to time in helping to design and put displays together. As a starter, you can develop a model study display early in the year which can provide a good takeoff point for students to learn more as time goes on about planning visual sequencing and such other elements as layout, design, and composition. The student who is artistically inclined and who is interested in color, design, and form will become a particularly effective member of the learning display planning committee. As students progress, they will understand more about the mechanics of mounting pictures, preparing original diagrams, and arranging attractive layouts for the learning elements of a study display. As the teacher comes to know more about the interests and capacities of individual pupils and correlates these with the opportunities presented by study display work, the group will be more likely to realize the goals of involvement and creative expression.

As we have noted, students acquire considerable facility with visual language before they ever come to school. For them visual expression and interpretation in various forms are natural and normal means of communicating. These skills can be further developed and used both to enhance their understanding of content ideas and to assist in the development of verbal skills.

Although not everyone can or should follow a set plan in developing study displays, certain basic principles and requirements must be observed to achieve desired results. Naturally, there is some order, as well, to the steps involved. For example, it would be a waste of time to start selecting materials before having clearly defined the purpose of the display and the specific content it is to cover. Beyond that point, several steps may go on simultaneously. For discussion purposes, however, it is helpful to consider content elements and physical arrangements separately; thus these are the subjects of the next two sections.

Learning-content elements

Materials and devices selected for a study display must communicate understandable and relevant information and be sufficiently attractive to involve the learner in continuing search and creativity.

ESTABLISH YOUR PURPOSE As in any other educational endeavor, you must know first what you wish to accomplish and then plan how it is to be done. A museum exhibit expert has given some sound advice:

Exhibits are too often made with a minimum of clear thinking and planning. A vague idea is not enough and even a splendid one needs much detailed work. You would not dare to face a microphone without a script, or film a motion picture without a scenario. Treat your exhibit with equal respect. Put down its purpose in writing: describe the basic idea; be specific about the facts and figures to be used; the technique by which they will be shown. Your manuscript should also include complete copy.[2]

The goal may be to arouse interest, to explain a process, to report facts, or to pose a problem, or all of these. In any case, be-

[2] Bruno Gebhard, ''How To Make and Use an Exhibit,'' in *Exhibits: How To Plan and Make Them*, National Publicity Council for Health and Welfare Services, 1946, p. 5.

fore proceeding further, the primary purpose must be known. It is often helpful to incorporate this purpose in the title of the display itself, or it may be visualized in an attention-demanding graphic diagram or design.

GATHER CONTENT MATERIALS Decide on the nature of the content materials you will want to include. Usually, a good study display results from a wide search for a variety of materials—newspaper and magazine articles, photographs, charts, graphs, diagrams, and related three-dimensional materials, including objects and specimens (as discussed in Chapters 3 and 4). Of these, only the best and the most relevant should be chosen to appear in the final display; that is, only those content elements which are the most *meaningful, graphic,* and *colorful* should be selected for the actual display. Decisions must be made about the best headings to be used, what the captions should say, and which pictures or graphics should be mounted.

SELECT PROVOCATIVE CONTENT A good study display possesses much content and information which leads the learner to study the display in detail and, ideally, to inquire further on his own. A display that is merely attractive and impressive in its overall content does not achieve very much. Although we stress the importance of keeping displays simple, this simplicity is a relative thing—it is directly dependent on the objective for which the display is designed. Normally, a good display has the potential of arousing sufficient interest to make the pupils want to explore the subject further. This, of course, is particularly true of motivational displays that are designed to help launch a new unit of study; but it should also be true of developmental displays. Developmental displays actually have a kind of dual effect: during their preparation the students' research and active involvement produce added interest in the topic they are studying; and the added knowledge and experience thus gained tend to generate still more interest and a desire to explore further and find answers to new questions.

Thus the good study display selects for its principal components the most provocative information available and presents it in dramatic, attention-getting fashion so that the viewer will be drawn to examine the less prominent elements of the display as well. These, in turn, should provoke further questions in the viewer's mind which you can use as one means of stimulating further investigative activities on his part. Naturally, you do not rely on the display alone to achieve the desired level of motivation and activity, but the study display has real potential for stimulating and for imparting information—a capacity you should recognize and use.

Physical arrangements

The materials and devices selected for a display normally are selected because they are highly effective as individual pieces of teaching material by reason of their interpretive quality, visual layouts, use of color, captions, and the like. The trick is to combine these strong individual elements in such a way that they complement one another and enhance rather than detract from the overall effect. The total effect, in other words, should be greater than the simple sum of its parts.

ASSEMBLE THE NECESSARY SUPPLIES Your first step in implementing the mechanics of the display is to gather the raw materials with which you will put the elements of the display together. These supplies usually include kraft paper; large sheets of heavy paper for backgrounds or for paper sculpture; pastel chalk, wax crayons, and show-card colors; lettering

stencils and pens; three-dimensional cardboard, plastic, or ceramic letters with which words or phrases can be formed; and masking tape. Mounting must also be considered; wire, tacks, and pins may be used for this. (See the source lists in the Appendix for display materials; see also the Media References at the end of this chapter.) Supplies for study displays should be made easily available to both teacher and pupils.

MAKE A PLAN Your second step is to carry the plan to the "blueprint" stage. Work it out on paper, showing measurements, design to be followed, color scheme, lettering, and placing of materials. The art teacher can be helpful, because effective exhibits and displays always incorporate sound art principles, such as simplicity, good design or arrangement, and the proper use of color, lighting, and, sometimes, motion.

Because a good layout is a matter of imagination and creativity, one should experiment with arrangements. It is usually advisable before settling on a final plan to make copies of several parts of the display, lay them out on a table top, and try various arrangements until you are satisfied that you have the best one. Cutout paper forms may be used which can be moved across the desk top or over the surface of a piece of kraft paper which represents, in miniature form, the final display.

Plans may have to be modified as students search for and discover exciting and appropriate pictures, graphics, and related three-dimensional materials. For example, verbal information may be made more understandable by converting it to diagrammatic, graphic, chart, or comic-drawing form. As this occurs, the change-and-improvement process goes forward; as a rule, however, these changes should be planned in the "blueprint" stage before incorporating them in the final display.

FIGURE 5.20

The dark-toned areas suggest the eye-movement path of the viewer in each case. What layout ideas can you develop which will lead the viewer to examine all the elements included in your display?

In planning the layout of a study display, there are seven primary attributes of design which are essential to an attractive, attention-arresting display. These are (1) simplicity, (2) effective use of color, (3) wise choice of headings and captions, (4) clear and artistic lettering, (5) adequate lighting, (6) motion when feasible, and (7) provision for the viewer's participation.

1. Keep it simple It is useful to think of posters when planning a display. A poster must not be crammed with words and ideas; it must convey one central idea (as discussed in Chapter 3). So it is with displays. If you have more to communicate than one central idea, put it in another display.

The *design* itself should be simple. Basically, designs are merely arrangements based on various lines that lead the eye where you want it to go and at the same time produce a pleasing overall effect (see Figure 5.20). The good and bad arrangements shown in Figure 5.21 illustrate this point vividly.

A symbol, cutout, or bold and unique design provides an attention-demanding "device" or center of interest for a display. For example, if the subject relates to space exploration, a simplified, abstract representation of a rocket ship might be used as the key symbol. Of course, the pictures, graphs, diagrams, specimens, and the other two- or three-dimensional objects used should all help to bring about specific and concrete understanding of the information displayed. Attractive mountings, cartoons, diagrams, charts, and graphics should be employed generously in the overall layout (these materials were also discussed in Chapter 3).

2. Use color wisely Color is an important factor in any display or exhibit. It can be used for such purposes as attracting attention, emphasizing boundaries, indicating classifications and groups, and providing effective backgrounds for materials and lettering. In fact, color is one of the basic elements that are fundamental in displays and exhibits. Professional museum exhibit experts often cite a three-part formula as the first essential for successful exhibitions: sound architectural design, proper use of lighting, and good color effects.

Use color when color is clearly needed to bring out the essential elements which the study display is to communicate and when it will attract the learner's attention and interest him in studying the content of the display itself. The use of color in display situations has at least three purposes:

1. To dramatize or focus attention on key items or relationships. Study displays involving rules, directions, steps in a pro-

cess, time lines, important dates in history, and so forth, will profit from the judicious attention-demanding use of colors that help classify or differentiate.

2. To present visualized information accurately and comprehensively. Scenes, costumes, persons, and geography and science objects which have color in real life demand the use of color when presented in a study display. Thus a study display designed to portray wildlife effectively must of necessity be shown in its natural and authentic colors. Similarly, displays involving architecture, costumes, and geographical settings should be shown in natural color if the full truth is to be communicated to the learner.

3. To heighten interest. Study displays are most likely to attract attention when color is used as part of the design; that is, when pleasing combinations of colors are used in a decorative way for backgrounds, for frames for the graphics in the display, and so forth. Intense colors virtually demand the attention of the viewer, and displays set off against warm complementary colors usually appeal to the learner's esthetic sense and help interest him in further study of the display.

The selection of color combinations for displays, exhibits, picture mountings, graphics, and models is simplified by using a color wheel (see Plate 5.2, following page 260). A color wheel is made up of the three

FIGURE 5.21

primary hues—red, yellow, and blue—and three secondary hues—green, orange, and violet, which are mixtures of adjacent primary colors. Tertiary hues can be created by mixing a secondary color with one of its adjoining primaries; for example, yellow-orange, red-orange, yellow-green, blue-green, and so forth. Many additional colors are created by changing the value or intensity of primary, secondary, and tertiary colors; this is accomplished by adding black or white or by mixing the color with its complementary hue.

In choosing combinations of colors for a study display, poster, and so forth, it is wise to select colors that naturally go well together. These are:

1 *Complementary colors—colors directly opposite each other on the color wheel*
2 *Triads—any three colors equidistant from one another on the wheel*
3 *Split complementaries—any single color plus the two on either side of its complementary*
4 *Analogous colors—those colors that have the same primary base (red, yellow, or blue); these are usually found next to each other on the color wheel*

Some colors—reds, oranges, and yellows—are cheerful, warm, conspicuous. They are normally associated with fire, danger, excitement. The so-called "cool" colors, on the other hand—green, blue, and purple—are more soothing and restful. These are commonly used to represent grass, water, and sky. Color studies show that blue, green, and red—in that order—are the most *preferred*; orange, red, and blue have the greatest *attention* value; yellow, green, and orange have the greatest *luminosity* or brightness.

Color wisely used is an important consideration in deciding content and arrangement of effective study displays. Provided that colors which harmonize are used together, the principles illustrated by a simple color wheel may readily be applied

Note how arrangement, lettering, and contrast can make a difference in a display layout.

223

to any problem of color selection. However, good judgment and common sense are the teacher's best qualifications for using color intelligently in creating effective color displays. Several good examples are shown in Plate 5.3, following page 260.

3. Use appropriate headings and captions
Every display should have a central heading which states the general purpose and idea of the display. Be dramatic. Ask a question, pose a problem, make a direct claim or statement. Headings and captions are extremely important. The headline, or title, is usually one of the means by which attention is first directed to the display. The captions employed should be as clear, simple, and succinct as possible and carefully planned to enhance the viewer's interest as he steps closer to examine the display in more detail. Aside from that used for the heading, one letter size for identification of key elements and another smaller one for needed explanation or discussion will normally suffice. The quality of the captions will be determined by the directness and clarity with which they describe information relating to the materials used in the display itself.

4. Use good lettering Lettering for displays and exhibits in schools can be done in several ways. Hand lettering put in by capable students or teachers is distinctive and particularly desirable for large headings. Cutout plywood letters made in the manual arts shop are excellent. Three-dimensional letters made of cardboard and plaster are highly effective and can be purchased commercially. Gummed letters in various sizes and colors are also available at low cost. (See the source lists in the Appendix.)

Good lettering requires color know-how. The most important factor in lettering is the contrast in brightness between color of letters and background. This contrast affects both the distance from which the words can be read and the speed of reading. Research on color and lettering for highway signs is applicable here to some extent; for example, the most attention-commanding background colors for such signs are yellow, white, red, blue, and green, in that order.[3] Block lettering with bold, thick lines and open spacing provides optimum legibility.[4] Background and letter colors used on highway signs must accommodate a variety of weather, lighting, and background conditions which are not applicable to educational displays; however, the general requirements of *brightness* and *contrast* for optimum visibility and legibility *do* apply to both. Thus black lettering on yellow or white, dark green or blue lettering on white, or white lettering on green or blue backgrounds are all examples of effective combinations.

5. Arrange adequate lighting Lighting is a dominant factor in any exhibit or display. It serves not only to focus attention but also to bring out the effects that are created with design and color. Artificial light is often better than daylight because the latter varies and is unpredictable; furthermore, strong daylight tends to reduce contrast and thus weaken the character of a display. It is easy to appreciate the advantages of artificial light: simply make a mental comparison of the appearance of a well-designed store show window in daylight with its much brighter, more inviting appearance at night. The concentration of light within the window when there is no competing daylight is very important in drawing and

[3] P. Odescalchi, ''Conspicuity of Signs in Rural Surroundings,'' *Traffic Engineering and Control*, Vol. 2, No. 7, 1960, pp. 390–93.

[4] A. W. Christie and K. S. Rutley, ''Relative Effectiveness of Some Letter Types Designed for Use on Road Traffic Signs,'' *Roads and Road Construction*, Vol. 39, 1961, pp. 239–244.

Planning and organizing the study display
225

holding attention. The same is true of displays and exhibits.

Intricate and expensive lighting arrangements for study displays and other school exhibits are usually impractical and unnecessary. Spotlight and floodlight bulbs that screw into standard light sockets can be obtained in various colors. These can be used with pleasing effect in simple clip-on or self-standing fixtures which are quite inexpensive. For special occasions, such as a public exhibit in the gymnasium, a stage floodlight or two may be desirable for general illumination of displays and exhibits. (Whenever a number of fixtures of several types are to be used simultaneously, a sufficient power supply and enough separate circuits should be available to avoid overheating the lines or blowing fuses. Check beforehand with the school electrician or maintenance man on such matters.)

When exhibit cases are located in corridors, a fluorescent fixture concealed in each case increases the attention-focusing power of the materials displayed. If you want to experiment, you can get pleasing effects by using colored gelatin sheets over the lights. (Since fluorescent light is "cold" light, no danger of fire is involved.) Display boards located on inside corridors or in dark corners of classrooms need lighting to be effective. A shaded fluorescent fixture at the top of such a board is a good way of lighting the display surface evenly. Recessed fixtures in the ceiling over the display area are a decided advantage. Flush-type fixtures are good for general illumination; an adjustable fixture known as a "bullet light" is excellent for baby spots. (There should be standard plug-in outlets in all recessed exhibit cases and adjacent to corridor display surfaces.)

6. Use motion when feasible Motion can be very important to a display or exhibit, both to attract attention and to focus it on one or more elements within the design.

Movement can be actual motion provided by small electric motors, a motion picture film, or an automatic slide changer; or it can be simulated by changing light patterns. Changing light patterns can be achieved by such means as Christmas tree blinker-light fittings, a rotating color wheel in front of a floodlight, or polarized light such as that provided as special accessory equipment on an overhead projector.

Good judgment should be exercised in using movement in displays or exhibits. Your principal concern must always be to get the message across—to achieve the purpose for which the display or exhibit is designed. Accordingly, you should use those materials and techniques which are most appropriate to that end in any given instance, bearing in mind that overemphasis of one element, such as movement, may hinder more than it helps. It is possible, in other words, to enliven a presentation to the point where it intrigues but doesn't communicate. It is much more common, unfortunately, for displays and exhibits to be unnecessarily pallid and prosaic and, in consequence, to go unnoticed.

7. Involve the viewer The most effective exhibits frequently involve the viewer in some type of participation activity. Exhibits in the Chicago Museum of Science and Industry and other museums in which the viewer pushes a button or turns a knob to make something happen are extremely popular. Anyone who has visited the American Museum of Atomic Energy at Oak Ridge, Tennessee, will readily remember the part of the tour in which he can have a dime bombarded with neutrons so that it activates a Geiger counter, after which it is returned to him encased in a souvenir plastic disk. Driver demonstration or aircraft operation devices in which the observer operates controls are always popular because the viewer gets actively involved. At a simpler level, a viewer becomes in-

FIGURE 5.22

Their delighted involvement is clearly evident in the faces of these little girls listening to a taped description of Colleen Moore's Doll House at the Chicago Museum of Science and Industry. (This miniature fairy tale castle, created for the silent screen star Colleen Moore, took seven years to build. The castle, made of aluminum, is at a scale of 1 inch to 1 foot—its tallest tower rises 7 feet from the base. Water runs out of all its tiny spigots, and electricity illuminates light bulbs the size of grains of wheat.)

volved when he pushes a button and activates a taped explanation (see Figure 5.22).

Such devices may be costly or otherwise unsuitable for some study displays. Nevertheless, an attractive, attention-arresting heading and good content elements can lead the learner to become absorbed in the display itself even without active participation. The reduced size of the print in the captions used to describe highly interesting visuals helps to "pull the learner" closer to the display and further to involve his attention. Captions that ask questions or make suggestions are also useful.

The value of viewer participation in an exhibit is based on familiar principles of learning. Experienced teachers know that pupil involvement is closely related to learning and to retention of what is learned.

Carry out the plans

Planning, the key to a good exhibit or display, is well worth the time it takes. If your "blueprint" has been planned down to the smallest detail, you can proceed to execute these plans in the actual display with assurance and a minimum of waste motion. Your students should work with you on the planning from the beginning in most instances, and, with a little help here and there, they can carry much of the load in arranging the display itself. Helping to put on an exhibit offers another good opportunity for valuable learning above and beyond significant gains in factual information. The greatest profit for all, however, is derived from an exhibit that is planned and executed in terms of sound and effective educational principles (see Plates 5.3–5.5, following page 260).

Evaluating displays for learning

As is the case with most educational endeavors, the evaluation of study displays must center on how effective they are in terms of the specific purposes established for them.

Achievement of purpose

The first question to raise in evaluating a display is: Does the display have a clear, well-defined purpose, and is it designed for a specific group or audience? If the purpose is clear and the level of materials appropriate, a subjective judgment as to how well that purpose was achieved can then be made. It is probable that the display is only one of a series of learning experiences provided on any given unit of work. Thus it is likely to be difficult to evaluate it or any other single component in isolation. Nonetheless, within that overall context, the point of how well the display performs the function for which it was designed is fundamental.

As a corollary, it is well to keep in mind that the substance of a display should be of sufficient merit to warrant the time and effort involved. A display can sometimes be interesting without saying very much. Therefore these questions should be asked: Does the display say something or do something important for the viewer? Does the content relate clearly to the intended purpose? Do all the elements fit together?

Effectiveness of design

In considering design, these questions are important: Does the display have eye appeal? Does it attract attention? Is the lettering effective? Does the overall design have simplicity and unity?

Achievement of student involvement

The extent to which a display achieves student involvement is, of course, somewhat dependent on the type of display and how it is used along with other learning experiences. Nonetheless, the most useful and effective displays are those that actively involve the students, cause them to want to know more, and excite their interests. Students may be involved, first, through helping plan and execute displays. They may also be involved through opportunities to manipulate things or cause things to happen within a display such as lighting changes, a taped explanation, or movement of some kind. Judgments on these and comparable elements may be summed up in answering the question: Does the display elicit the desired reactions from the pupils?

Study displays are of many kinds and can serve many functions. No single display can achieve all of these functions—nor should it be expected to. But if its purpose is clear, its design appropriate and of good quality, and its subject suitable for display purposes, it will have the most important elements necessary for its success.

Summary

Teachers have a readily available opportunity to enrich instruction through the creation of study or learning displays. A study display is unique as a learning resource—it is more than simply pasting up parades of turkeys at Thanksgiving or bunnies at Easter. Rather, it is a collection of related and self-explanatory pictures, graphics, and three-dimensional objects which *together* convey useful information, visual explanations, and actual demonstrations in which the viewer can participate.

Displays are of three basic types according to the primary functions they can perform: motivational, developmental, summary. The design and implementation of each type are direct results of the specific purposes it is intended to achieve.

When engaging in the creation of effective learning displays, the teacher should follow carefully worked out and proved principles such as the following:

1. Study displays are learning experiences and should reflect this goal.

2. A good display is the result of a plan which presents informative pictures, graphics, models, and specimens in such an interrelated manner as to communicate meaning to the viewer.

3. Study displays must relate to the subject being studied and the interests and curiosities of the learner. The best study display involves the learner and entices him to engage in further search for related information.

4. The best learning displays command attention and study; communicate concepts, facts, and insights; and develop enthusiasm for the subject being studied.

5. A good learning display reflects good physical organization and layout.

Study displays that teach are the carefully planned creative efforts of the teacher and pupils. Such cooperation involves the pupils in the purposes and spirit of the study display, with the result that the pupils learn from displays as well as create their own to present information, demonstrations, and explanations to their classmates.

Study displays should be evaluated according to three primary criteria: achievement of purpose, effectiveness of design, and degree of student involvement.

Further learner response projects

1

In your teaching area, select four topics worthy of and suitable for study display development. Briefly write your reasons justifying the selection of each topic for this treatment, considering reasonable alternatives as you think it through. Exchange papers with several other class members and critique one another's selections in a small-group session.

2

Select one of your Project 1 topics and put together a plan for development of an effective motivational type of display. Include (a) specific purposes to be achieved; (b) type of display or exhibit to be developed; (c) materials to be employed (assuming for this purpose that needed materials are all available to you); (d) a simple layout or design showing the key elements of the display you would put together. Critique the plan with the same small group, noting helpful suggestions and ideas received. Refine the plan and file it for later use.

3

Take an interested group of your own pupils (if you are teaching) and start plans for an exhibit or display on another of your Project 1 topics. This time the display is to be student-planned (with appropriate help from you) and student- developed. Report back to your class or critique group on what you did to incite interest, how it worked, and what suggestions you have for initiating a project of this nature.

4

Begin to accumulate a file of photographs, diagrams, illustrations, specimens, and so on, which will be useful in creating motiva- *tional study displays for the subjects you teach or will teach.*

5

With one or two classmates (or teacher colleagues) do a survey of (a) study displays, (b) commercial product displays, and/or (c) advertisements. Take pictures *of both good and bad examples and use these later for report and discussion purposes in your class.*

References

Anyone Can Create a Lively Bulletin Board. Hayes School Publishing Co., Wilkinsburg, Pa., 1968.

BOUGHNER, HOWARD. *Posters,* Pitman, New York, 1962.

BOWMAN, WILLIAM J. "Graphic Communication." Wiley, New York, 1967.

"Bulletin Boards" (a monthly feature). *Grade Teacher,* issues from 1963 to present.

Cartooning. Higgins Ink Co., Brooklyn, N.Y. 11215.

COMBA, JOHN. "Photography: A Key to Learning." *Audiovisual Instruction,* November 1969, pp. 66–67.

CONLAN, KATE. *Effective Library Exhibits.* Oceana, 1962.

CONLAN, KATE. *Poster Ideas and Bulletin Board Techniques.* Oceana, 1965.

Daily Bulletin Boards for All Occasions. Hayes School Publishing Co., Wilkinsburg, Pa., n.d.

EAST, MARJORY. *Display for Learning.* Dryden, 1952.

Easy To Make Bulletin Boards. Hayes School Publishing Co., Wilkinsburg, Pa.

Educational Displays and Exhibits. Instructional Media Center, University of Texas, Austin, n.d.

Ford Foundation, The, *A Living School: Report of the Planning Group for Programming an American International School in New Delhi, India,* 1960.

Graphic Tips: Advertising Lay-Out Fundamentals. NuArt Company, Chicago, Ill., 1967.

GUMM, BEN, and JACK BLAKE. "Software," *Audiovisual Instruction,* June–July 1969, pp. 123–124.

HARTSELL, HORACE D., and WILFRED L. VEENENDAAL. *Overhead Projection.* Henry Stewart, Inc., Buffalo, N.Y., 1960.

HAYETT, WILLIAM. *Display and Exhibit Handbook.* Reinhold, 1967.

HORN, GEORGE F. *Bulletin Boards.* Reinhold, 1962.

Instructional Display Boards. Reinhold, 1962.

KELLEY, MARJORIE. *Classroom-Tested Bulletin Boards.* Fearon Publishers, Palo Alto, Calif., 1961.

KELLEY, MARJORIE, and NICHOLAS ROUKES. *Matting and Displaying the Work of Children.* Fearon Publishers, Palo Alto, Calif., 1957.

KEMP, JERROLD E. *Planning and Producing Audiovisual Materials.* 2d ed. Chandler, San Francisco, 1968.

Kindergarten and Primary Bulletin Boards. Hayes School Publishing Co., Wilkinsburg, Pa.

LAFLAME, PATRICIA J. *Exhibits.* Cooperative Extension Service, Michigan State University, 1969.

LEES, M. M. "Bulletin Boards Anyone? Try These Tips." *Business Education World,* September 1963, pp. 14–15.

LOCKRIDGE, J. PRESTON. *Better Bulletin Board Displays.* Visual Instruction Bureau, University of Texas, 1963.

MINOR, ED, and HARVEY R. FYE. *Techniques for Producing Visual Instructional Media.* McGraw-Hill, 1970.

MORLAN, JOHN E. *Preparation of Inexpensive Teaching Materials.* Chandler, San Francisco, 1963.

PHILLIPS, WARD, and JOHN H. O'LAQUE. *Successful Bulletin Boards.* F. A. Owen Publishing Co., 1966.

Planning a Photo Essay. Eastman Kodak Company, 1966.

PLUSS, R. "Sharpen Up Your Bulletin Board!" *Clearing House,* March 1964, pp. 437–438.

RANDALL, REINO, and EDWARD C. HAINES. *Bulletin Boards and Displays.* Davis Publications, Worcester, Mass., 1971.

RUBY, DORIS. *3-D Bulletin Boards That Teach.*

Fearon Publishers, Palo Alto, Calif., 1960.

SCHULTZ, MORTON J. *The Teacher and Overhead Projection.* Prentice-Hall, 1965.

THOMAS, DELLA. "Book Displays." *The Instructor,* November 1966, pp. 52 ff.

WITMEYER, STANLEY. "Display Is Visual Communication." *The Instructor,* May 1960, pp. 47–50.

Media references

Better Bulletin Boards, 16mm film, sound, color, 13 min. Indiana University, 1956.

Bulletin Boards: An Effective Teaching Device, 16mm film, sound, color, 11 min. BFA Educational Media, 1956.

Bulletin Boards and Display, 35mm filmstrips (2), color, 36 frames each. BFA Educational Media, 1966.

Charts for Creative Learning, 16mm film, sound, color, 10 min. BFA Educational Media, 1961.

Dry Mounting Instructional Materials, 16mm films (5), sound, color, 5 min. each. University of Iowa, 1966.

Exciting Bulletin Boards, 35mm filmstrips (2), color, 40 frames each. McGraw-Hill, 1963.

Flannel Board, The, 35mm filmstrip, color, 40 frames. McGraw-Hill, 1963.

How To Make and Use a Diorama, 16mm film, sound, color, 20 min. McGraw-Hill, 1956.

How To Make and Use the Feltboard, 35mm filmstrip, color, 54 frames. Teaching Aids Laboratory, Ohio State University, 1955.

Instructional Media, 136 sets of masters for transparencies, color. (Developed by Stanley A. Huffman, Jr., director, Learning Resources Center, Virginia Polytechnic Institute and State University.) Keuffel & Esser Company, 1969.

Lettering, 8mm films (7), sound, color, 3 min. each. Chandler, San Francisco, 1964.

Magic of the Flannel Board, 16mm film, sound, color, 19 min. Association Films, 1964.

Mosaics for School, 16mm film, sound, color, 10 min. BFA Educational Media, 1961.

Mural Making, 16mm film, sound, color, 6 min. Syracuse University, 1956.

Passe Partout Framing, 16mm film, sound, color, 10 min. Indiana University, 1956.

Poster, 16mm film, sound, color, 16 min. BFA Educational Media, 1969.

Poster Making, 8mm film, sound, color, 3 min. Heater and Associates, 1966.

Poster Making: Design and Technique, 16mm film, sound, color, 10 min. BFA Educational Media, 1953.

Successful Exhibit Ideas, 35mm filmstrip, b/w, 81 frames. Pocket Films, 1958.

Teaching with Visual Materials, 35mm filmstrips (6), color, 38 frames each. McGraw-Hill, 1964.

The Terrarium, 16mm film, sound, color, 12 min. BFA Educational Media, 1967.

Source references

See source lists in the Appendix; particularly relevant sections are: Art Supplies; Display Surfaces and Supplies; Graphics Materials; Free and Inexpensive Materials; Furniture and Facilities; Lettering; Multimedia Equipment and Materials; Museums; Three-Dimensional Materials.

See *Student Production Guide,* Chapter 3, "Graphics Techniques for Instructional Materials Production," particularly Design, Color, Bulletin Boards, Chalkboards, and Graphs; Dry Transfer Lettering; Wrico Lettering; Rubber Cement Mounting; and Chapter 4, "Producing Photo and Sound Materials for Instruction," particularly Photo and Sound Materials: Design and Use, Photographic Slide Production, and Audiotape Production.

SIX
Community study

Objectives	Performance responses

1

To identify the rationale for planning and using community study learning experiences as a means for providing relevance and precision in instruction.

Cite philosophical beliefs as well as school practices that support the idea that relevant learner involvement is achievable when appropriate extraschool learning opportunities are made the subject of pupil-centered inquiry.

2

To identify the variety of community study opportunities which are being used currently in achieving, with efficiency, such accepted learner goals as: understanding the structure and values of society, achieving economic self-sufficiency, and attaining self-realization.

Identify specific kinds of community study experiences cited in the text or known to you firsthand and associate these with the goals cited in Objective 2.

3

To understand and employ an evaluation process through which to judge the efficiency of one or more community study experiences.

Using either a community study learning example described in this chapter or, preferably, one which you plan and put to use, evaluate its efficiency according to the criteria given on pages 264–265. Present your outcome to your fellow students or colleagues and listen to their judgments.

4

To select the community study opportunities nearby or far afield which you judge (on the basis of Response 3) will increase the efficiency with which you "teach."

Survey and select one or more community study learning experiences which reflect your use of the criteria on pages 264–265.

DURING a sabbatical tour of centers of educational media innovation in the United States and Europe, we found ourselves in the quiet archives of the British Museum. We stood before the beautifully arranged Comenius exhibit, absorbing the thinking of this remarkable educational reformer who spent the greater part of the seventeenth century observing education and proposing and practicing educational change. This man, who believed in universal education, was certain that the old restrictions of time and place and narrowly conceived curriculum concepts should be broken down; he also was certain that the breaking down would be best done by giving students opportunities to voice their own interests, enthusiasms, and curiosities by seeking answers—by observing for themselves the activities of people, places, and things, no matter where they were. Nearby in the museum were displays devoted to the work of Pestalozzi, Herbart, and Froebel, also among the great ideological pioneers who prepared the way for new advances in educational theories and practices.

These four European leaders evolved many ideas about learning and teaching which were radically new in their time but which have since become part of the main current of educational thought in the United States. Some of their most important views about learning may be summarized as follows: *The most effective way to help students to become informed about their social and natural environment is to provide for them learning experiences which are real or lifelike and which are available to them for firsthand scrutiny, questioning, and cognition.*

When they were first made, such statements as these were dismissed as being highly philosophical and somewhat impractical. Since then, however, it has been shown over and over again that through such learning experiences and such methods understanding becomes relevant to the learners if they are involved as the seekers, the planners, and the participants.

We are currently in a period of much economic affluence and fast and easy transportation. Concrete evidence of this and also of the truth of the theories of the four philosophers we have mentioned was apparent as we continued our study tour. We encountered young people in groups of two, three, and four on their vacation migrations, traveling widely to see people, places, and things everywhere, limited only by the necessity to return to their jobs or classes. Huge numbers of young Americans now travel abroad each summer. During the summer of 1971, in fact, no fewer than 300,000 of them, between the ages of 15 and 25, followed their own inclinations to see other parts of the world. Evidences of this migration are obvious everywhere—the numbers of young people at airports, whether in Stockholm, Tokyo, Hong Kong, London, Copenhagen, Paris, or Rome; the large groups of them in city parks, at youth hostels, in museums and art galleries; the young Americans moving about not only by plane, train, and car, but also on motor scooters and bicycles and on foot, carrying backpacks and roll tents. The significance of all this, however, is not so much in the numbers of young people as in the fact that they constantly seek firsthand information, constantly search out ways to *experience* and thus *learn* about their world.

On the beaches near Calais, in northern France, there still are many grim signs of the Channel invasion of 1944. Also, spotted here and there amongst the upturned, blasted fortifications built and then so soon destroyed during the early 1940s are to be seen the tan and green tents of youth hostelers. A conversation with the members of one such group reveals much about their interests and purposes.

A youth, responding to the morning's greetings and our question, spoke with feeling: "I've read thousands of pages about World War II. But you've got to be here—you can almost feel it—it must have been brutal."

His companion chimed in, "Did you 'make' Ypres Ridge?"

I nodded that we had been there.

"It's unbelievable. How can man blow himself apart like that?"

As the conversation continued, we discovered that these high school graduates had planned their own tour of Europe. During a 10-week period they had visited farms, battle areas and monuments, the unique multipurpose communication towers that stud Europe, and the historic landmarks of Paris and Rome. Now they were reluctantly making their way back to Heathrow Airport in England, there to board a nonstop 747, over the Pole and back to the United States and school.

Later, while we were wandering through the remarkable Cathedral of Charlemagne in Aachen, we had a similar exchange with three young coeds who had pooled their resources and jointly planned their journey.

"There's nothing like this," said one, moving her hand expressively to indicate the magnitude and beauty of the cathedral.

"St. Peter's is bigger," another volunteered, "but not so elegant."

"This took over 500 years in the building. Why, that's incredible."

The third asked us, "Say, what have you seen that we ought to?"

Obviously, "seeing for themselves" was what life was all about for these girls. As we parted from them, we had the definite impression that even though they soon would be back, "hitting the books again," as one put it, college would not be the same for them. Now they—like all the other college students who had been traveling—had the background of countless self-selected readiness experiences that would help them find new meanings in their studies—new meanings that their minds could never have grasped or formulated before.

Fortunately, today the idea of expanding the experiential resources of the school to include community study or community resource learning is more widely accepted than ever in the history of public education, partly because the idea has received wide support among educators. As formulated by groups of influential educators over the years, the following are among the purposes and aims of learning experiences in general that relate to basic societal goals and thus to community study specifically: understanding social life, developing citizenship and civic responsibility, achieving vocational understanding and economic self-sufficiency, and, perhaps most important of all, self-realization by the individual. These objectives were stated as long ago as 1918 by the U.S. Office of Education. They were restated in 1938 by the Educational Policies Commission of the National Education Association and again in 1954 by the NEA; they have been restated still more recently by educators who have studied the influences on man of the ecological environment as it relates to social objectives.

In spite of the wide recognition of these objectives, community study experiences are not as integral a part of instruction as one would hope. Too often, school districts are enmeshed in the restrictions imposed by rigid bell-time schedules, narrowly compartmentalized subject and course offerings, and adherence to the traditional and all too customary arrangements that cause almost all learning experiences to go on within the four walls of the classroom.

There are exceptions, fortunately. For example, faculty members of the Walt Whitman School in Bethesda, Maryland, asked the students to help design the kinds of courses or projects *they* would like to pursue. Faculty and students of the Adlai E. Stevenson High School in Prairie View, Illinois, pursued a similar program which gave responsibility to students for defining experiences that would be relevant to the goals and objectives of students *and* faculty. Each school had its share of students who claimed they found little that was relevant in their usual activities; nevertheless, this program that directly involved the students was embarked on to benefit students and teachers in many general ways, not specifically to "cool down" activism.

The result of student planning in each school was a proposed schedule of learning experiences drawn from the surrounding community. Invitations were extended to people who were particularly knowledgeable in space science, banking, the stock market, the draft laws, psychology, religion, world politics, writing, music, and the arts. Where circumstances warranted it, the students made arrangements to leave the school building in order to participate in community experiences. As the program went forward in both schools, the experiences that were evolved included a combination of field trips, demonstrations and "rap" sessions, and special course offerings—dozens of opportunities from which each student could make his *own* schedule from the various activities presented. Nearly 3,000 students participated.

The results? Parents felt that the regular school program should incorporate greater use of community learning resources, community work experience opportunities for students, wider offerings of courses or electives, freer scheduling, and more individually elected learning opportunities.

Teachers felt that students gain from such programs a higher sense of responsibility, a heightened interest in learning, and awareness of new ideas gained from contacts with fields of knowledge entirely apart from what is available within the "walls" of the school itself.

Students felt that they thoroughly enjoyed having an opportunity to participate in programed planning. They described their feelings about the project by using such terms as "freedom," "variety," "new experiences," and "opportunity to choose for one's self." Students referred to "a sense of community between teachers and us" and "trust"[1] (see Figure 6.1).

Almost invariably, whenever students are given a voice in the management of the learning experiences provided by the schools, strong interests are expressed in investigating the community at firsthand. To give a third example, the Benjamin Franklin Parkway School in Philadelphia is another school where students move freely into the community to carry on "questing" and "discovery." Parkway is in the downtown area of the city, amid businesses, institutions, and museums. The basic philosophy developed at the school is that *how* students learn is closely related to *where* students learn. In applying the philosophy, the faculty and students make the city their classroom. This, of course, is quite a departure from practices at traditional high schools.

Each of the 500 students is given the opportunity to participate as one of the management group whose function is to decide the nature of Parkway's day-to-day operations, including the determination of the nature of their own program.

1 "Free Form Learners," *Nation's Schools*, Vol. 84, No. 3, September 1969.

FIGURE 6.1

These community representatives shown at the Adlai E. Stevenson High School are among many who were invited to "come to school" to provide experiences in contemporary living which could be made available in no other way as effectively. Other pupils "left school" to visit other "relevant" community activities and people. Are the learning activities you plan relevant? To whom? The learner, the teacher, the administrator? The members of the community?

Through "town meetings" once a week, the the entire school community becomes involved in discussing and resolving the problems of the nature of their academic curriculum. As a result, nearly 200 community agencies and persons are involved in the "academic" program. Students are permitted to make their own arrangements to enter into the community to observe, to question, and to participate. In the words of John Bremer, the Parkway program's director, "We acted to break down the walls and get the students out into the city—to use it, learn about it, live in it. Not only have the variety and type of learning resources been multiplied many-fold by expanding into the city, but the quality of the experiences is enhanced."[2]

It goes without saying that whenever as drastic a revision of a school program as this is undertaken, administrative and behavioral difficulties appear. Nevertheless, the important point is that such a program *is* possible. Though it is not reasonable to expect all schools to be able to reorganize immediately to this extent, *some breaking away and some loosening up of the traditional high school program of studies must be attempted*. Such school programs as the three just described show that this can be accomplished and that more and more learners can become *profitably* involved.

The scope of community resources

W HEN is a child old enough to participate in community activities?

For many years it was accepted practice for children to sit quietly at desks placed in rows while the authority figure —the teacher—communicated instructions from the front of the room. This idea has been undergoing violent change.

Occasionally, some adults now show remarkable trust in the judgment and wisdom of young learners. Recently, elementary-grade children of the Mercer Island Public Schools in the state of Washington were given an unusual opportunity by their

2 James D. Greenberg and Robert E. Roush, "A Visit to the School Without Walls: Two Impressions," *Phi Delta Kappan*, May 1970.

district superintendent. They were invited to work with school officials and architects in examining plans for the new high school which they would soon be attending. As the superintendent put it, "We want to get the students involved in the planning and design of the school so that when they go to their first high school classes, they will feel it's their building." Not all of the students responded to the challenge. But those who did gave thoughtful attention to the project, viewing it through the eyes of those who later would actually live and learn in the new facility and expressing their ideas[3] (see Figure 6.2).

[3] Paul J. Avery, "Students, Architects Team-up To Plan a New High School," *Nation's Schools,* Vol. 85, No. 6, June 1970.

If we accept what most learning psychologists believe, that most firsthand experiences with people and things are primary sources for learning, then we must be willing to reevaluate the nature of the learning experiences we provide on such a basis.

Up until his entrance into kindergarten or first grade, the child has spent most of his life probing, examining, questioning, and experimenting in order to gain understandings about his home, backyard, neighborhood, and other aspects of his immediate environment. He has taken walks or trips with his parents, wandered off with his age-mates, and pulled apart his toys; he has asked questions endlessly of the grocer, the plumber, or the automobile mechanic. Through this natural self-expression of

FIGURE 6.2

When can a young learner's wisdom contribute to solving important community problems? These fifth-graders have been invited to express their ideas about the high school they will attend— directly to the architect.

FIGURE 6.3

To explore for one's self is the most natural quality of inquiry. This child is learning what is relevant to *him.* Do you consider such self-initiated interest and wholesome curiosity as you plan learning experiences? What role do you arrange for the learner?

childhood, he has developed his innate curiosity and satisfied it through firsthand observation (see Figure 6.3).

Yet when he comes to school, this same child—who has spent so much of his life wiggling, crawling, and exploring—finds himself within the restraining walls of a classroom, confined to a chair, and restricted in his activities to those called for by the teacher! To expect the 6-year-old to conform to the restricted environment of a classroom for five hours a day, five days a week is to run counter to all we know about his mental, emotional, and physical makeup. But older children, too, have natural needs to explore, to be physically and mentally active, and to express themselves fully through the social channels open to them. Yet too often the school —a social setting deliberately provided for children—has thwarted these needs, demanding that children's natural physical and mental expressions be confined during the long school hours only to those that fit into a narrowly prescribed curriculum. Certainly such an approach to education is anachronistic, to say the least, when it is followed by those who claim to be students of the child, his nature, and his needs.

Arrangements should be made for the pupil to continue his natural exploring behavior in similar but more directed and appropriate community study activities which permit direct observation, touch, experimentation, and questioning. The child should be allowed to pry into every corner of his environment as he participates in carefully planned, school-controlled community study experiences. Instead of being confined to the four walls of a classroom, he should be "free" to investigate his "world": the school yard, his friends' homes, the business district, and the open country outside the area he lives in. The "schoolroom" for the child should include the caterpillars in the shrubbery and the small stream with its myriad wonders— water plants, wriggling insects and pupae, tiny fish, and the sparkling crystalline rocks and stones on the stream bed (see Figure 6.4). The school day should include talks and visits with community helpers— the mailman, the fireman, the policeman, and the people who are engaged in laundering, dairying, breadmaking, poultry raising, and the other commercial enterprises in the community. Older and more able learners should be permitted to range farther afield: For them, extended stays at school camps and overnight study tours, as well as visits to nearby governmental agencies, manufacturing plants, and public-works projects, are means of revealing the facts of and opportunities provided by the society they will enter as participating adult citizens.

One particularly valuable opportunity is provided by a program recently announced by the National Park Service. Park Service officials, increasingly concerned about the abuse of the country's parks as they constantly become more crowded, decided to put together a total experience that would show children and young people the causes and effects of pollution and how it can be overcome. The program, which is called National Environment Education Development (NEED), is used in conjunction with traditional curriculum courses in science and the social studies, in the elementary grades and in high school. The basic idea is to present preliminary information in the school but then follow it up with an *actual field trip*

into one of the National Parks. The purpose of the trips ranges far beyond merely identifying plants and animals; rather, the purpose is to create an attitude—to promote an understanding of how man both uses and abuses nature around him. Thus the program seeks to help young people to make value judgments about their environment and to show them what impact their own decisions and actions can have. In this case also, as the caption to Figure 6.4, puts it, are the desired outcomes cognitive? Or do they take the form of long-range affective impressions?

The traditional concept of the classroom is slowly changing, however. Fortunately, there are constructive alternatives to traditional classroom instruction in the form of plans which either can bring useful community learning experiences and resources right into the classroom or which permit the students themselves to go out into the community to observe, to question, and to learn. More and more the classroom is becoming a work-planning base from which learners can look in many directions

FIGURE 6.4

These learners are exploring part of their community "schoolroom." This "aquarium" is complete beyond anything that could be contrived within the school, yet parts of it were taken indoors for further study and reporting. With what "subjects" does this community study identify? Math? Language arts? Ecology? Are the outcomes cognitive? Affective? How much time should be allowed it? When?

FIGURE 6.5

To whom can we go to find out about communication through photography? What course does one take? The professional who makes photography his life work should be available to learners who "inquire." When an outside expert is brought to the classroom, is it a "put down" to the teacher? This is learning through direct involvement!

to gain the needed and useful experiences that exist in the social and physical community at large (see Figure 6.5).

The immediate community often provides extremely dynamic and interesting real-life opportunities for learning. It is the responsibility of the administrator and teacher alike to investigate the community, particularly the resources which seem most likely to help students gain a more clear-cut and fuller understanding of formal school experiences.

Community study defined

COMMUNITY study refers to the various learning situations through which pupils come into firsthand contact with the people, places, and things all around them. It includes visiting organizations, institutions, and neighborhoods or regions of the community; interviewing public officials and community leaders; participating in community affairs and planning; listening to and observing others plan and operate both public and private enterprises; examining the tools, machines, reports, and various other accouterments involved in the diverse business of the community; and questioning wherever and whenever the pupil's curiosity is evoked. In short, community study provides real-life opportunities to learn by doing and to gain understanding directly from the things, processes, services, and social and political activities that make up the stream of community life.

The terms used to describe the various forms of community study vary widely; *school journeys, excursions, tours, visiting-authority programs, field trips,* and *hostel trips* are but a few. However, many of these terms include activities not specifically designed to inform directly about community life, and many others are not directly useful in realizing the central work-study goals of the curriculum. For example, a community leader might be invited to talk at a school assembly on a subject that has no particular relevance to the specific units being studied by the pupils in their classrooms at that time. Many "visiting-authority" and other programs which involve the community at large are planned and carried out in connection with the *total* school—they have little or no articulation with individual courses of study. For this reason, *community study* is used in this chapter to cover only those excursions, field trips, "visiting-authority" programs, and other community activities that are implemented as *integral parts of* *specific units of curriculum instruction.* Toward this end, community study experiences are presented as that part of the formal school program which *extends the individual classroom into the community* or which *brings the community into the classroom* in order to give the pupil direct experiences with the people, places, and things they are studying.

Inquiry through community study

EDUCATION is the search for the truth of life. This is done best by observing and analyzing life experiences in terms of their values and meanings, strengths and weaknesses, social worth or lack of it, and interest to the individual. From experiences with things of the community, teachers and pupils can attempt to discover many of the values by which they wish to live.

This process relates closely to what has been referred to earlier as "inquiry study." Inquiry is the term used to describe the process by which the learner begins as an observer of all about him, evaluates what he sees, and, finally, selects or determines the values he wishes to live by. The implication is that the learner must be placed in "context" with life experiences if he is to respond to and understand them. The more concrete and therefore understandable these experiences are, the more likely the learner is to respond intelligently to the concepts he perceives. Thus one's study of the community can be a most helpful basis for "inquiry."

Community study opportunities are available through arrangements which bring either resource people or demonstrations *into* the school or which make it possible for students to leave the school to explore and to witness certain aspects of the neighborhood, other cities, the next state, or, when feasible and desirable, for-

eign countries. Walking trips, bus excursions, air tours, residence in school camping facilities, or extended study journeys all offer varied opportunities to learn.

The use of community study and community resources is a matter about which teachers make judgments in terms of what they observe to be the needs of the pupils for given experiences with reality.

One teacher states: "Students pose countless questions which make desirable our community study program. It opens vistas through which to investigate the 'world' itself. Through community study, learners develop enthusiasm for wanting to know, observing at firsthand, and for making judgments."

Walking trips

In the lower grades, it is quite easy to arrange visits to observe nearby community helpers—the workers in the post office, fire station, police station, food store, zoo, arboretum, and water-supply plant, for example (see Figures 6.6 and 6.7). Walking trips can also make it possible for pupils to watch simple demonstrations of the typical work activities of various community-service people who travel around the local district. Because these people often pass nearby, one of them—for example, a telephone lineman—might arrange to be near the school at a convenient hour. (In the

FIGURE 6.6

Walking trips are an easy and inexpensive way to give school children a wide variety of direct experiences with their community as well as with the concrete bases of their abstract learning. What concepts are taking shape in the pupils' minds as they observe the structures of a seedling tree at a nearby nursery?

lower grades, the "buddy system"—in which each child is paired off with a dependable fellow pupil—is one effective way of getting the class to a place within reasonable walking distance of the school. The teacher learns from experience that the best position for him to take is at the rear of the column. Experience also will reveal which children can be depended on to lead the column.)

Walking trips provide invaluable study experiences within the immediate vicinity of the school. Such opportunities are so obvious that they often are overlooked. Perhaps, also, some teachers are reluctant to be seen "walking around during school hours when we 'ought' to be inside working." Whatever their cause, it is high time for us to overcome the inertias that have prevented us from making use of the values

FIGURE 6.7

Seeing at firsthand this wild area near their school is an experience that can start these children on a quest for further information about ecology, leaf forms, and seasonal variations. Is such an inquiry related to science, social studies, or government? Or does it lead to an interrelated study experience?

of the immediate school environment— values that are available just by going there. Frequently, the students—teachers, too—are so preoccupied in getting from where they live to the school that they entirely overlook the fact that they can learn from the environment through which they pass. It certainly makes much more sense to ask a student to study the environment through which *he* walks or moves and to make judgments about it than just to read abstract textbook descriptions of a similar environment.

For example, a junior high school group was beginning their study of a unit entitled "Investigating Soil." During a preliminary discussion, the students expressed curiosity about the texture of earth, its chemical composition, the effect of heat and light and the seasons on the soil, and its fertility. The idea was developed that everything we are comes from the earth.

The young people had been thumbing through their books when their teacher asked, "If you could have your choice of ways to find answers to our questions, what would you really like to do?"

There was talk about library resources, encyclopedias, books, films. Then one student hazarded a very daring idea: "Maybe we should go out and dig around in the soil—do tests on it." The processes for getting out of the schoolroom and into the immediate environment had begun.

According to an earth scientist, we should

create instructional tactics and strategies that will enable students to use the resources of their own environment. This is the turning inside out of instructional practice. Instead of asking the student to respond to a textbook abstraction of his environment, the environmental studies program invites the student to invent the abstractions that describe what he finds around himself. Thus the students are more capable and sensitive to their environment. And, because they have gone

through the process of inventing abstractions, the students have a deeper understanding of the abstractions that their heritage has provided them.[4]

During such experiences in the nearby community pupils frequently record pertinent information by using Polaroid cameras. Why shouldn't young people today, who live in the midst of a technological revolution, develop facility in communicating through other channels than the traditional writing and speaking?

Walking trips make it possible for pupils themselves to watch important things happen, to be "there." One does not have to go very far from the school grounds to see some of society's most pressing problems as they occur and affect all of us—air pollution, inadequate waste disposal, noise pollution, and other violations of our immediate environment which greatly diminish our pleasure in living. All these adverse influences (and others) must be studied continuously by the upcoming generation if any positive and really effective controls are to be brought about when they reach their voting majority.

It is not always necessary to embark on community research as an entire class group. Rather, those students who demonstrate that they are able to asume responsibility should be given opportunities to leave the school grounds alone or in groups of two or three to investigate and to report what they found. If a pupil is dependable enough to get himself from home to school, he should be given the opportunity—provided that he has earned it—to carry on investigations which, because of their importance, make it desirable for him to venture out into the community during school hours. (Needless to say, parental and administrative support for such activities must be secured.)

[4] *Environmental Studies,* September 1, 1970, p. 1.

Field study

Field study usually involves automobile or bus trips to outlying areas—truck farms, dairies, sewage disposal plants, automobile wreckage yards, arboretums, television stations, banks, meat-packing plants, food preparation industries, water-supply facilities, the town hall, the legislature, meetings of the city council, traffic control courts, or other agencies that affect the welfare of the community.

When the social studies class was investigating transportation developments, this question came up: What will happen, during the next 10 years, to the eight million automobiles manufactured each year? The question was related to the fact that one student had brought to class a newspaper article describing the cost of removing junk automobiles from the streets of the community—a matter of 30 dollars each.

"Aren't auomobiles worth something —even as junk?" one student inquired.

"People ought to find some use for all the steel and metal in an automobile," another ventured.

Several students volunteered to search for answers in the community. As they did so, other questions occurred to them: What is the relationship of automobile exhaust to air pollution? What is the relationship of automobile taxes to highway building? Visits were made to local automobile distributors to find out what was being done about "cleaning up" the exhaust. As students dug deeper into each topic, more areas for investigation emerged, among them traffic problems, parking problems, increasing auto license rates, congestion on the freeways during rush hours, the costs involved in building new freeways and multilevel intersections, and the rate structure of driver insurance for young people.

FIGURE 6.8

These students are questioning a traffic court judge at the end of a session. They have listened to testimony by drunk drivers, "junkies," speeders, and the just plain careless. What is the relationship of such an experience to text source accounts?

Information was brought to school in various forms: borrowed 16mm motion picture films on traffic safety; Polaroid snapshots taken by committee members of traffic jams, pedestrians struggling to get through street intersections, dozens of junked automobiles parked in the weeds of a lot next to the school grounds; verbal reports on arrangements made with a highway patrolman and the school's driver-training director to meet with the group for a "rap" session on "teen-agers on wheels" (see Figure 6.8).

That learners generate great enthusiasm for acquiring information by visiting community resources is evident. Students achieve the thrill of discovery when they witness things for themselves, gain understandings from realities that they see actually exist, and set out to explore on their own. This kind of opportunity results in direct involvement in information acquisition. No intermediary steps need be fought through; rather, the learner is placed in direct confrontation with the living facts as they occur in real-life situations—with the persons who serve, with the processes, and with the problems that affect the life of the community.

As will be described later in this chapter, many communities have studied carefully the opportunities presented by field study learning. On the basis of such studies, authorized lists of community study situations are published for the use of teachers at work in the various curriculum areas.

Visits by resource persons

Visits by resource persons are a valuable means of bringing demonstrations and specialized information into the classroom, particularly when field study is not feasible within the rigidly defined time schedules that often exist in junior and senior high schools. Visiting authorities may be recruited from among parents of school pupils, friends of the school, and representatives of banking, communications, governmental, transportation, and local industrial groups. Resource persons can usually conduct demonstrations and supply answers that go beyond the teacher's more generalized fund of information. For example, as a group of eighth-grade children continued their study of the state in which they lived, they developed many questions about the nature of the land and about the manner in which it was utilized within their own community and the area adjacent to it. As their search continued, the pupils learned that the local farm-management director, the high school geography teacher, and the state aeronautics commission's educational officer were willing to visit the classroom. The men were invited to meet with the pupils, and the ensuing class discussion resulted in a walking trip over the terrain, further library study, and an aerial field trip—all planned by the pupils themselves.

Special learning trips

Special learning trips include as wide a variety of creative situations as the facilities of the school district will permit and the inventive imagination of the staff can encourage.

Special learning trips include those organized around facilities maintained for the purpose by the school district itself. The Milwaukee public school system, for example—which encourages teachers to participate with their students in a carefully organized wide range of community study experiences—owns a forest on the outskirts of the city. Teachers of kindergarten through twelfth grade schedule trips to this "outdoor school" for the study of nature, ecology, and related biological sciences. In the school forest is "the cabin in the woods," which contains a classroom where class sessions are held. There specialists, teachers, and students study specimens gathered right in the woods. The Mil-

FIGURE 6.9

waukee public schools also use the University of Wisconsin's Camp Upham Woods about 100 miles from the city. After careful planning and preparation by teachers and students, about 70 students at a time are taken to this 300-acre wooded tract on the bank of a river. During each encampment, which lasts for three days or more, teachers and staff members lead the children in firsthand nature and conservation study, outdoor activities, arts and crafts, and cooperative living (see Figure 6.9). On their return to school, the children engage in many activities directly related to their camping experiences. Other ''outdoor schools'' have been established by school districts across the United States, for example, near Racine, Wisconsin, San Diego, California, and Olympia, Washington (see Figure 6.10). Similarly, many school systems are establishing ''outdoor laboratories'' on or near school sites for the study of various scientific and ecological characteristics of the local region (see Chapter 4, pages 162–163 and 169–175).

In Milwaukee, community study also is emphasized. The public schools issue a list, revised each year, of available and appropriate facilities around which teachers can organize community study programs and trips. These include art museums, zoos, the air museum, hospitals, government agencies, local business and service organizations, and the state capital. When transportation is needed, the school buses are used. The board of school directors encourages the ''regular'' teachers to carry out the instructional program cooperatively with staff specialists. In all cases, the learning experiences are regarded as carefully organized opportunities for staff and students to work closely together. The experiences culminate in the development of learner-created inventive projects and related reports (see Figure 6.11).

More ambitious planning is necessary when a student group travels farther

This map of Camp Upham Woods is used by Milwaukee students and teachers as they prepare for their days of living and study at the camp. About 120 people are housed in the six cabins (Ihlenfeldt, Varney, Craig, Bible, Bewick, Ranger Mac), which contain double-decker bunks.

abroad to examine a more remote environment. One such community study experience was organized by a group of Teacher Corps students at work on the Leeward coast of Oahu, Hawaii.

''Why not,'' several of the teachers reasoned, ''make a study of useful experiences available here on the Waianae coast?'' As the program evolved, several

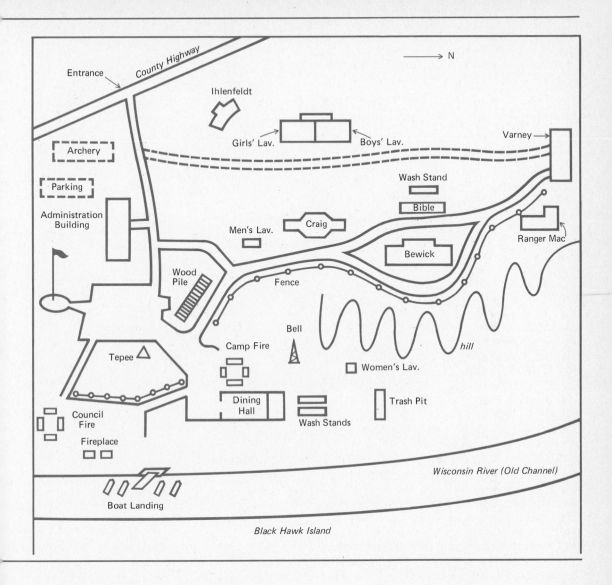

teachers and their pupils began by taking walking trips along the shore and up into the beautiful, arid western slopes of the Waianae mountain range. They talked to "old-timers," asking them about their cultural history—the economic and sociological beginnings of the small shore communities where they had been born and still lived. Their curiosity grew and expanded out-ward like the concentric rings formed in water when a stone is tossed in.

As the students expressed their wider and wider curiosity, they asked more and more questions. "What about the irrigation canals under and through the Waianae mountains?" "Do other people build canals like these to bring life-giving water to their fields?"

FIGURE 6.10

Olympia, Washington, students spend a portion of their fall or spring semester at the "outdoor school" under the direction of their regular teachers and the "outdoor staff." These pictures show some of them collecting specimens and analyzing soil. What advantageous opportunities does such a program give learners?

They discovered a Hawaiian heiau—an ancient place of worship where the first Hawaiians set up their altars. Then the question was: "Have other people developed religious ceremonies and places like these?" They discovered worn-down and abandoned railroad tracks and found that they had conflicting ideas about the explanation. Was it the automobile? The question that naturally followed was: "Do other people change their forms of transportation and communication? Why?"

The children found some partial answers shortly afterwards during a study of the civilization of the Navajo Indians. But the number of their questions increased, and they became very curious about the Navajos and their way of life. All of these questions, which were stimulated by the children themselves, rekindled in the mind of one of their teachers an idea that had long lain dormant. This teacher had a friend and colleague who was teaching at a Navajo reservation in Arizona. Carrying out his idea, the teacher asked the children, "Why not *go* to the mainland to see, learn, and find answers?" As he expected, their initial astonishment at the

FIGURE 6.11

Milwaukee public school students are given
many extraclassroom learning experiences.
(a) Children engage in actual conservation as
they plant tree seedlings in a state park. (b) Two
high school students try out information learned
in marketing classes in a school-related appren-
ticeship program. (c) What kinds of behavior
responses do you think took place among these
elementary-grade children after a series of
planetarium demonstrations? What parallel experiences would be valuable for the pupils with
whom you work?

idea of so long a trip was followed immediately by a flood of enthusiastic comments. Caught up in the spirit of adventure, some of the children carried it further. "Why couldn't some of those mainlanders visit us here in Hawaii?" one asked. Others chimed in, "They must be curious about a lot of things, just as we are."

So it was that teachers and pupils met with local school authorities to gain sanction for their creative and innovative dual plan. The cost of their own trip at first seemed to be an insurmountable barrier, but (as was mentioned in Chapter 2) money was made available through the work of the children themselves and through local business people, parents, other members of the community, and one local newspaper. (Such educational activities are, of course, the rightful responsibility of authorized educational agencies. Fortunately, there is evidence that such innovations are increasingly being financed directly by school district authorities who recognize the worth of such learning opportunities.)

Thus in the spring of 1970, several teachers and parents accompanied 20 Hawaiian schoolchildren as they traveled by air to the West Coast to begin a journey of discovery which took them to several cities, the Grand Canyon, and, for their longest stop, the largest American Navajo Indian reservation. While there, they lived with the families of their newly met Indian age-mates. Two weeks later, they were visited by 24 Navajo children who experienced, for the first time, life and living in Hawaii (see Figure 6.12). In this way the newly acquainted Navajo and Hawaiian students completed the exchange experience by living, exploring, and discovering together.

Such extended school journeys are gaining wide use; they are possible whenever pupils, teachers, parents, and administrators work cooperatively in planning them and carrying out the plans. To give another example, the principal of the Ox-

hey School in a suburb of London describes their successful plan as follows:

One of our most profitable expanded educational opportunities occurs when, after intensive planning by students and teachers, 90 of our upper-grade children embark from Heathrow Airport for an extended tour of Central Europe. Our longest stop is in Austria, where the children, by previous arrangement, have the opportunity of living with other children of their own age and, of course, within the family groups. While abroad, the children explore the places and processes, visit people, and respond with enthusiasm and excitement to what they see and learn about. To what better use can modern transportation and communication facilities be put than to further the education of the young?

Representative of similar tours in the United States is the annual exchange conducted by the Lessenger Elementary School in the small city of Madison Heights, Michigan. The members of the fourth grade engage in a kind of exchange learning problem with other fourth-grade children in Three Rivers, Michigan, a rural community about 150 miles southwest of Madison Heights. During a three- to four-day period of the spring semester, each group of students culminates weeks of preliminary planning, letter writing, and discussion by traveling by train and bus to visit their "fourth-grade friends" of the other community. The initiative taken by the Madison Heights and Three Rivers schoolchildren includes responsibility for planning the experience, arranging for transportation, stating their preferences about what they would like to see, learn, and understand, and most important, the responsibility for using their new-found information in some individually creative or inventive ways on their return. (The details of the actual steps accomplished during planning, visiting, learning, and responding are discussed more completely on pages 256–258.)

FIGURE 6.12

(a) When these Hawaiian youngsters "tried out" living in Arizona on a Navajo Indian reservation, they had the unexpected bonus of the first snow they had ever seen. (b) These are two of the Navajo children as they arrived in Hawaii shortly afterwards to return the visit to their new Hawaiian friends. Amazed discovery was the key to the adventure in learning for both groups. Do you hope you can arrange similar adventures for children in your own role as a teacher?

To give a final illustration, as upper grades or high school students complete their work in such subjects as American Government, Problems of Democracy, or United States History, they annually join thousands of others on extended visits to their nation's capital. On a recent visit to Washington near the end of the spring semester, one of the authors found his own hotel reservation preempted by eight high school boys who had converted the room into a temporary dormitory. The city's hotels had literally been taken over by thousands of high school students and their teachers. Available parking areas were jammed with school buses identified by their banners, many of which bore the names of communities as far as 2,000 miles away. Other high school student groups visit the nation's capital by train and plane. Needless to say, such study trips are costly; they also present certain risks to schools. They are accomplished successfully, however, as the result of careful planning and organization of the type that will be described later.

Research surveys

Research surveys are a highly valuable kind of community study activity. Community survey activities include fact-finding interviews with business, governmental, or community leaders in their normal work settings. This form of community study is usually engaged in by selected groups or by individual students who have given evidence of their ability to handle such opportunities. Gifted pupils, in particular, benefit from the opportunity to ask professionals questions about taxation, law, transportation, communications, art, literature, housing, and job opportunities.

To gain the most from a community survey or professional interview, the students must prepare carefully. They should discuss what they have read, formulate well-thought-out key questions and, with their teacher, list the names of authorities who they feel could best answer these questions. It is desirable to have the pupils write letters in advance asking each of these people for a date and hour that would be acceptable; when given ample time to schedule the interview, scientists, authors, judicial officials, and administrative department heads are more likely to participate.

Personal interviews with these leaders become more difficult as distance increases, and the cost of transportation usually makes

FIGURE 6.13

Two-way communication between students and an authority can be provided as a telelecture. (a) Audio telelectures are very effective and now can be arranged quite economically by using this newly developed portable conference telephone. The set, which can be plugged into any standard jack, is a telephone with a loudspeaker built in and two remote microphones added. The telephone is used to contact the speaker; then, using the microphones in turn, any or all students in the room can question him, and all hear his amplified replies. The teacher or a student moderator can control the microphones. Here high school students seeking vocational guidance are interviewing a local businessman, speaking from his downtown office. (b) In a New York State elementary school, telelectures are used successfully to stimulate greater interest in reading. Here a pupil using one of the microphones questions Jay Williams, author of a popular series of books for fourth- and fifth-graders. The author speaks to the pupils from his home in London. Thus this device takes on life when it is incorporated into the creative and inventive thinking of teachers and students. These students have discovered how easy it is to reach out into the community—or across the ocean—as they seek contemporary information that vitally interests them. How would you use this equipment in your own teaching? (c) When a video telelecture can be arranged, closed-circuit television adds an extra dimension—students can see the speaker as he answers their questions.

some of these experiences prohibitive. One unique way of solving this problem has been worked out at Stephens College, Missouri, where long-distance speaker-phone interviews are carried on. When the teacher and members of the class decide it is profitable to seek information of an expert thousands of miles away, a group-telephone interview may be arranged. Often in speaker-phone interviews the entire 40-minute class period is devoted to the interview. Depending on the distance involved, interviews of from 30 to 40 minutes range from $6.50 to $15.60 each. In view of the fact that these calls make possible authoritative answers to specific questions, the

preparation of which may have taken weeks of thoughtful effort, this cost is small (see Figure 6.13).

This kind of research survey can be done entirely by letter, of course, but at the expense of the give-and-take that normally characterizes conversation. A long-distance speaker-phone interview is much more spontaneous; it is personal rather than impersonal, and results in more information.

The results of speaker-phone interviews are impressive. In one case, students did more outside reading on the topics of the field studied and there was a 10 percent increase in enrollments in advanced courses in the same field. Further, participating students showed increased skill in asking questions and in directing inquiry toward pertinent ends.[5] Research community surveys also often have far-reaching effects. In Wisconsin, for example, a high school group actually initated a community housing project. In New York, action begun by a similar group led to a slum-clearance project. What better way is there of initiating pupils into their future role of responsible citizens?

[5] Harold Rubin, ''Telephone Network Courses,'' *Educational Screen and Audio Visual Guide*, March 1964.

Planning community study experiences

As is the case with all school *affairs,* the responsibility for planning community study learning experiences should involve cooperative interaction by the school board, the local school administrators, the teaching staff, interested parents, representatives of the community, and the pupils themselves. The role of the school board is extremely important. In the examples described in this chapter, the school board has definitely placed its stamp of approval on community study learning activities. With such assurance, school administrators, the teaching staff, and the pupils are free to proceed in developing the details they wish to pursue. Backed by such approval, the teacher may help initiate or support ideas that are then developed by members of his class and interested parents. With the knowledge that the school administrator approves and sanctions such activity, great creativity may be achieved.

Parent groups have a definite responsibility in considering and supporting the use of community study. In Manhasset, New York, a committee of interested parents and teachers set about to survey Manhasset's resources—its people and their specific skills and knowledges. In other words, this committee sought to discover the true wealth of the community in terms of the people in it. The committee began by interviewing professional and business people to discover what specific skills and abilities they had which would enrich learning situations in the classroom. This information was then catalogued for reference by interested teachers. In this way, the committee discovered, for example, that a very able lawyer could be available when the social studies class was investigating personal rights and the techniques and procedures of court action. A nurseryman who had developed certain grafting techniques would explain them to general science students. A ceramist was willing to explain and demonstrate glazing techniques to the art class. A music-shop proprietor who was also a skilled cello player was willing to help the members of the cello section of the school orchestra.

The Winnetka, Illinois, public schools long have had a committee of parents available to student groups that seek the advice of professional persons skilled in various life activities and pursuits. The Beloit, Wisconsin, public schools have a schedule of "community days" during which committees of teachers are invited by various local service organizations and businesses to visit, to explore, and to judge the relationship of these kinds of experiences to student-organized searches for information. Appropriate opportunities for community study are later arranged for students. As already mentioned, the Milwaukee public schools annually produce a revised list of community study experiences sanctioned by school authorities for use by teachers and student groups.

As a teacher considers the use of community study learning experiences, he should reexamine the existing authorized community study manuals produced by his own school district. If there are no manuals or lists, the teacher's own estimate of how the needs of his learner group can best be served by community study should become the basis for requests to the principal or subject supervisor that given community experiences be provided.

Pupil-teacher planning for community study

Because the modern world environment is so complex, the teacher can no longer consider himself able to contrive, within the classroom, all of the learning experiences judged to expedite the progress of learners toward the achievement of their goals. Rather, the role of the teacher is to exercise his skill as the arranger of an interesting and effective total learning environment—and, when desirable, to include within this environment community-wide learning situations.

With community study, as with all good learning activities, specific planning should reflect the thinking of both learners and teachers. The basic question that must constantly be kept in mind is this: *Is the community resource learning experience in itself the best means by which the learner may acquire desirable and needed understandings, skills, and conceptualizations?* If the question cannot be answered positively in relation to a community study experience, then the experience may become little more than a "stunt."

Just as the pilot of a jet aircraft has disciplined himself to carry on a rigorous preflight inspection and analysis of the conditions which should be present to make his flight successful, so should the teacher precheck to make sure that all systems are "go" before he leads children into a community resource learning experience.

The selection of a desired community study experience, as such, should be the business of both teacher and pupils. In addition, the learners should become involved during succeeding stages of planning: decisions on the goals and objectives of the experience; discussion of techniques for carrying on observation during the experience; *and, most important, anticipation of the kinds of creative response and inventive use to which learners will put their new-found information when the experience has been accomplished* (see Figure 6.14).

As one attempts to apply the meaning of Figure 6.14 to one's own instructional planning, the obvious initial beginning steps have to do with understanding what the learner group already knows about the given subject, what, in addition, they are curious to know about, and by what means one is best able to "find out." At this point, the comparative value of other learning experiences—films, filmstrips, prerecorded tapes, research in print materials, and so forth—should be considered in terms of where they promise to yield effective outcomes and thus which ones should be employed as related experiences, and when.

Without a plan, few learning experiences are successful. Thus preliminary discussion of *what* information is known and what answers are being sought should be carried on with maximum learner participation and initiative. Mechanical arrangements should be carefully thought out in advance—the setting of dates, the means of transportation, the determination of budget needs and resources, and, finally, safety precautions to be observed.

During the actual participation in the study situation, observing and recording are most important. Usually, community learning experiences confront students as a "kaleidoscopic view"; accordingly, the observing must be anticipated carefully as well as recorded. Taking notes is one way; asking questions and recording them and their answers on portable audiotape recorders is another. Alternatives include acquiring from appropriate officers or other people associated with the business, firm, or institution available descriptive charts, brochures, or reports. Wherever possible, visual recording—taking pictures along the way with a simple camera—is a highly reliable means of recapturing important but often fleeting impressions.

The final goal, of course, is *learner response*—that period in the study sequence where the student is expected to arrange the information he now understands and the concepts he has gained—to arrange these in some form which expresses his own creative and insightful grasp of the information and, at the same time, becomes an understandable explanation to others. This leads directly into the next step, evaluation, which must be based primarily on the degree to which learners have responded and the manner in which their responses

FIGURE 6.14

Pupil-teacher planning for learning through community study.

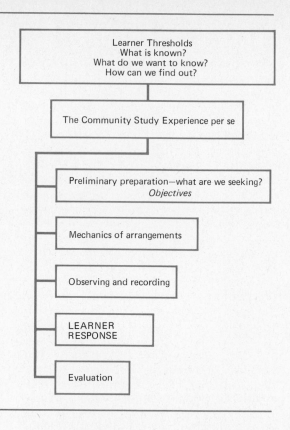

communicate what they themselves have learned, created, or arranged for their own use or for the use of others. Three examples of how these processes actually work in the stream of ongoing classroom instruction are now presented.

The fourth-grade students of the Lessenger Elementary School in Madison Heights, a suburb of Detroit, were confronted with the task of discovering how the people of Michigan lived, worked, and enjoyed the results of their labor. The broad curriculum plan for the community study outlined the general task. It was, however, up to the students and the teachers to select the learning experiences through which they would carry on their simple research and study and arrive at conclusions which would have meaning to

them now and in later life. First the usual learning materials of the school were examined and discussed—books, government publications, films on the state's resources and activities, sets of pictures, and so forth.

Then one student volunteered a suggestion: "In the summer, my parents take the family up into northern Michigan. We visit friends, take walks through the forest, go fishing in the streams, visit the cranberry farmers, even watch wild rice being gathered—we always *see* so many things and *do* so many things. Can't we make arrangements to *see* more of our state, even though we're in school?" Many other children enthusiastically agreed. And so it was planned to select a community where a few people were already known to several of the pupils and to arrange for a field trip which would become an integral part of the students' study of Michigan. By actually going there and living in the community, not for just an overnight visit, but for a week—if this could be arranged —the students would have time to "see," ask questions, explore, and discover answers to things they were curious about: how friends lived, played, and did chores, how farming and the government of the community were carried on, what the main industry was, what people did in their spare time, and so on. After some discussion, it turned out that a number of the children had friends or relatives in Three Rivers, a rural community about 150 miles to the southwest. Thus it was decided that this should be the place to explore.

Known skills were called on during the process of preparation: Letters were written to fourth-grade students at the Three Rivers school, letters that included questions about how lodging, food, and transportation could be arranged. Here was a real-life situation in which writing and language arts skills were being utilized to solve needs felt by the pupils themselves. Pupils arranged, completely, the details of transportation by school bus and train. They read schedules, collected money, and purchased the tickets. Housing was solved by offering to exchange with Three Rivers students, who were invited to return the visit later. Thus the Madison Heights children would be guests in Three Rivers homes, and when the Three Rivers children came, they would stay in Madison Heights homes. All this had the approval of parents and school authorities, of course. Arrangements were also made for food and entertainment during the week's visit.

Now the students could concentrate on the real purpose of the study trip, that is, by direct observation to discover the answers to the questions they had previously worked out, questions which were actually the learning objectives. At Three Rivers

the activities of the community were discovered by visiting the small business establishments; observing and interacting with routine farm activities, which gave students direct experiences with dairy herds, domestic animals, rotating crop procedures, harvesting and processing grain for storage or sale; visiting local industries—the cheese plant, the dairy, the lumber mill; visiting forests and recreational areas—streams, lakes, and winter sports facilities.

When the Three River students came for their visit in the metropolitan Detroit area, they toured museums, went through customs on a visit to Canada, toured the airport, saw the assembly line of an automobile plant, and visited other manufacturing plants (see Figure 6.15).

During both visits, school-planned programs projected far into the late afternoon and evening hours as discussions went on within the family groups about what the children had seen, what understandings had been gained, and what use they would make later of their new discoveries. During the experiences, several types of information-recording constantly went on. Ideas were recorded on tape and photographed with Instamatic and Polaroid cameras; notes were taken; descriptive pamphlets, color postcards, and printed diagrams and explanations were gathered together until suitcases were needed to carry back all the information.

Back in their respective classrooms, discussion of plans soon turned into the formulation of more group and individual projects through which information could be reported, not only through the medium of a classroom exhibition of information, but also as short editorial stories, a classroom newspaper which carried accounts of their experiences, a display of pictures taken during the tour and organized into a filmstrip story, and, along with it, explanations written and later recorded by the students. Displays of interesting ma-

FIGURE 6.15

Pupils from two Michigan communities exchange week-long visits to observe—and learn. Touching is essential to full perception, whether (a) city-dwellers are learning about a horse on a farm or (b) rural children are learning about mosaic religious art in a museum. Is such an exchange a "stunt" or a carefully planned and innovative learning experience?

terials picked up along the way were arranged in the classroom, and other pupils were invited to come in to see them. The worth of the activity is summarized as follows by Vera Bennett, principal of the Lessenger Elementary School:

What did the children do with all of their information? Many language arts experiences have resulted. Letters were written to all persons responsible for participating in the arrangements and accomplishments of the trip. In addition, the students write creative stories which they bind and place in a learning center—a learning center which is growing so rapidly and expanding so continuously that we live in it daily.

Another example illustrates the very worthwhile student involvement that can occur in the latter stages of a community resource project. Like their mainland counterparts, many students in the Honolulu public schools arrange a visit to a newspaper during their study of modern communication developments. Before such a trip, students are asked to describe what they already know about newspapers and how and why they are produced, but, more important, they are asked to describe what they are curious to know more about. As always, the teacher enters into this stage of the planning by offering some possibly more sophisticated purposes and goals of his own.

After their firsthand study of the newspaper, one group of students on their return to their classrooms developed some rather remarkable innovative uses for their new-found information. For example, they tied in their experiences with television and with reading (see Figure 6.16). Such experiences with a local newspaper often lead to a desirable long-range result: many students begin to develop a lifelong habit

—the careful and intelligent study of the newspaper as a main source of socially useful information.

A third example comes from the Portland Community College in Oregon. Here, under the leadership of Amo De Bernardis, the president, the school activities are organized as an integral part of the community itself. As the result of years of cooperative planning by teachers, the administration of the college, and representatives of local labor unions, business organizations, and service agencies, the curriculum of

FIGURE 6.16

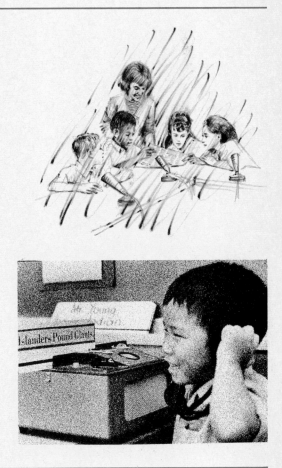

Teachers and pupils create very inventive ways to use information resulting from their visit to a newspaper plant and their continuing study of newspapers. (a) One group describes their experiences on a local television hour. (b) This primary grader, with his teacher's help, improves his reading skills by responding to headlines drawn from his favorite sport. Can you parallel such activities?

FIGURE 6.17

These students at the Portland Community College combine classroom study with on-the-job experience as (a) carpenter's apprentice, (b) dental assistant, (c) baker's apprentice. These students divide their time between school and the community, continuing their community activities as long as the experiences are relevant to *them* and their performance is acceptable. Do you accept these criteria as a basis for evaluation of community-related study?

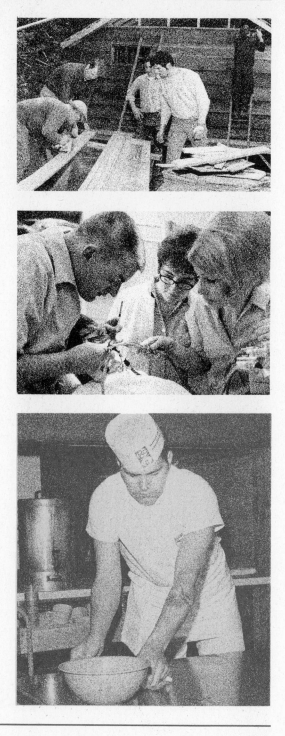

PLATE 4.3

Natural colors are important in the study of
anatomy, as is clear in this remarkable model of
the human heart in the Museum of Science and
Industry in Chicago. People become truly
involved in the exhibit—they walk right into the
model, see the heart valves function, and hear
the amplified beat.

PLATE 5.1

These display demonstrations of the water cycle
and the more complex photosynthesis and
respiration processes of plants illustrate one
value of the feltboard—it enables color symbols
to be rearranged quickly during classroom discussion. A hook-and-loop board was used to
display the heavier components of the hydrogen-
helium display.

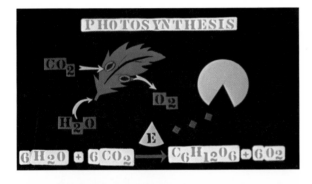

PHOTOSYNTHESIS

$$6H_2O + 6CO_2 \rightarrow C_6H_{12}O_6 + 6O_2$$

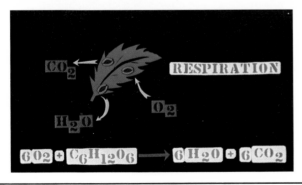

RESPIRATION

$$6O_2 + C_6H_{12}O_6 \rightarrow 6H_2O + 6CO_2$$

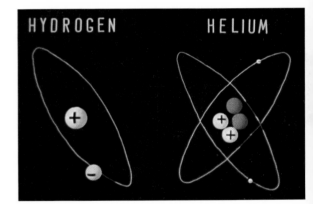

HYDROGEN   HELIUM

PLATE 5.2

The color wheel is an unlimited palette with
which to design your display materials. Use it
as a tool in your design laboratory as your visual
communications continue to grow in color effectiveness. The three primary hues are shown in
the central circle; the three secondary hues—
green, orange, and violet—form the middle circle.
Tertiary hues form the outer circle. The wheel
itself can be used to mix new colors and to select
harmonious color combinations.

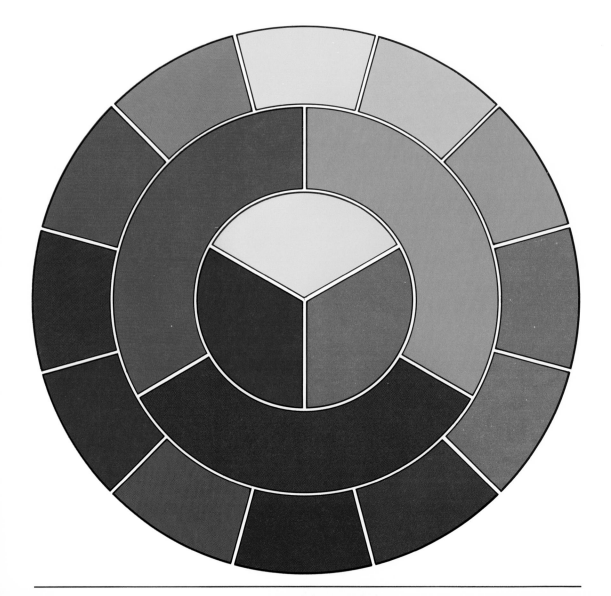

PLATE 5.3

Examine these five study displays carefully. To
what extent do they observe good principles of
layout, content selection, and color use?

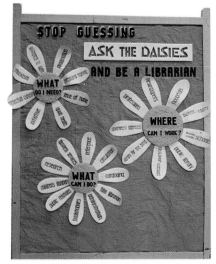

PLATE 5.4

The display of flat materials, fabrics, leaves, and other small specimens is enhanced by artistic arrangements such as these and also by the use of panels in various positions.

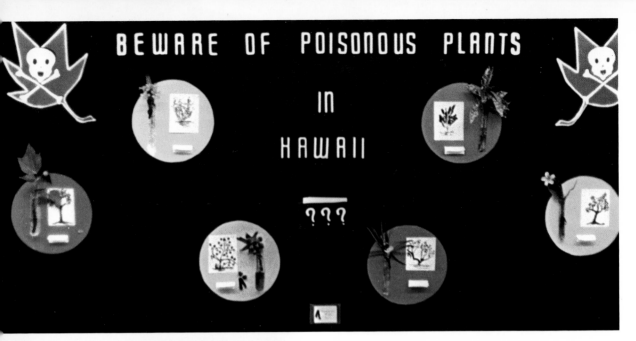

PLATE 5.5

These are two motivational study displays. Note that the wall part of the spider display leads the viewer to immediate sources of further knowledge—books and specimens (also shown in the detailed picture). Do these displays motivate and also accomplish their teaching objectives? How?

the school encompasses two kinds of opportunities: students are on the campus during specific organized class sessions, but also in every possible way they participate in activities in the community which bear a direct relationship to their immediate goals for life involvement. The administrators of this school believe that no student should be required or asked to participate in either an on-campus or a community-related activity if he does not find, within that experience, complete relevance in terms of his own interests, future vocational and social goals, and feelings of satisfaction (see Figure 6.17).

A final example of the integration of community study with classroom study comes from Madison, Wisconsin. For many years, teachers and administrators there have developed widely used community study opportunities. What makes this program particularly worthy of note, however, is its recent expansion. In 1970 the school system set up a unique center for the development and distribution of original local materials. The result has been the production of a number of interesting filmstrips accompanied by guidebooks and slide resource sets accompanied by narrative scripts. Examples of the filmstrips that show their wide range are: *A Citizen's Role in City Government, Legends of Lake Mendota, Madison's Food Industries, Geology of Wisconsin, Lake Pollution in the Yahara Watershed, Cherokee Marsh—A Wetland To Cherish.* Such a program might well be examined and emulated by other school districts (all of the materials are available for purchase or loan).[6]

[6] Information on this project, initially funded in part under ESEA Title III, and the materials may be secured from: Supervisor, Local Materials Office, Madison Public Schools, 545 West Dayton Street, Madison, Wisconsin 53703. A study of the project entitled *Local Materials Project: An Evaluation and Description, 1971,* is available from the same source.

Similar daring plans are being carried out across the nation, particularly in high schools and community colleges. The assumption is clear that unless community-related learning participated in by the student is evaluated by *him* as being socially useful and individually relevant, further changes in the development of his own program must be made. One has but to attend teachers' meetings and committee meetings to sense the objectiveness and the reality of this kind of planning.

While these questions may seem to be very inclusive, it should be recalled that the goal of all study experiences is to involve students at all stages of the process: during planning, during the experience itself, and certainly at the conclusion, when the final and most important step of the learning process is undertaken—learner involvement through creating or inventing ways of interpreting, using, or rearranging the new information learned. Such behaviors must be sufficiently observable so that teachers and pupils *can* evaluate their worth.

Community study is not alone in achieving such results. Nevertheless, when such study situations are employed, great good can be achieved by observing as many as are appropriate of the tried and tested teaching considerations included in this evaluation inventory.

Liability during community study

The community—acting through its school-board representatives—should decide whether community study opportunities are to be provided. School boards and school administrators have the responsibility of establishing policies concerning community study. Similarly, the classroom teacher has the responsibility of planning for the community study situations with the same care he uses in his day-to-day classroom teaching.

FIGURE 6.18

Yet teachers may have questions about their personal liability for accidents or injuries to pupils while participating in community study situations. Some of these questions may be answered if the classroom teacher first understands which responsibilities fall within his own professional bailiwick. The following are the respective responsibilities which school boards, school administrators, and classroom teachers have in connection with community study experiences:

1. The school board should acknowledge community study as a desirable enrichment experience and an integral part of the school's regular program.

2. The principal should make the board's policy known to the teachers.

3. The school board should provide liability insurance for the teaching staff. In Wisconsin, for example, and in many other states, school boards are legally authorized to expend public money for this purpose.

4. The teacher and principal should plan community-resource activities which will help to accomplish goals of existing curriculum plans. Such activities should not be confused with festivals, holiday excursions, and other recreational out-of-class activities.

5. The teacher, with the guidance of the principal, should arrange transportation via school bus or other bonded carriers which are required by law to carry liability insurance.

6. Teachers should never assume responsibility for conducting pupils through a plant or industry themselves, but should arrange to have the management supply a guide. As soon as the tour is ended, the teacher should have the pupils return to school immediately, again by properly insured carriers.

7. The use of the parental permission form (see Figure 6.18) informs the parent that community-resource experiences that take pupils out of the classroom are an ac-

Parental permission form for student participation in community study situations.

knowledged part of the school program. Nevertheless, parents must be given the option, as the form does, to refuse to allow their children to participate in this kind of activity, if they wish. But the granting of parental permission does not absolve the teacher who takes his class out into the community from exercising the same reasonable care he is expected to exercise in the classroom.

The teacher and the school who follow these suggestions will proceed with confidence and enthusiasm toward achieving valuable school and community relationships.

Dear _____ (Parent's name) _____

    Because we wish to make your child's experience in _____ (Subject or Grade) _____ as valuable as possible, we want to give him the opportunity of first-hand acquaintance with things we are studying in the community. We are planning on_____ (Date) _____ to visit_____ (Person or Place) _____as a part of our regular day-to-day study activities.

    We encourage only those students to participate in community study activities who prove themselves trustworthy and responsible.

    Will you kindly sign below to indicate that you want_____ (Pupil's name) _____ to participate, and return this letter to me?

Very truly yours,

_____
(Teacher)

    We wish to have_____ (Pupil's name) _____take part in the community study plans described above. We will discuss with him his responsibilities in this connection.

_____
(Parent signature)

Summary

Of all the means at the disposal of the teacher, investigation of the community and what it contains is a hopeful, imaginative, and amazingly complete way to let students view, objectively and at firsthand, the bewilderingly complex workings of the society they are preparing to enter. Through few other means may a child or young person be brought into contact with the variety of places, processes, and pursuits which represent the alternatives from which he will one day make his own life choices.

The scope of community study is great.

It begins on the one hand with simple walking trips into the neighborhood and, at the other extreme, involves the systematic study of community, industries, professions, governmental agencies, service organizations, and countless other manifestations of human activity. The teacher has but to survey community study possibilities and to relate the most appropriate of these to the objectives identified with his own subject area and grade-level responsibilities to discover countless profitable opportunities. As this is accomplished, students should become continuously involved in

Evaluating community study

IN the first analysis, the worth of community study activities should be judged largely by examining the nature of changes noted in behaviors shown by learners. What skill does the learner perform as he puts into use new-found information? Can changes be noted in his level of interest, in his initiative, or in his involvement in school activities?

Community study should be a carefully planned, carefully conducted, and carefully evaluated learning experience. The teacher and learners together should take the responsibility for evaluating the success of such experiences by systematically judging how and to what extent learners became involved. By helping teachers and learners to discover in a systematic way what changes occurred, questions such as these will also help them evaluate objectively the worth of community study as such:

1
Was the community study learning experience arranged because it not only related closely to planned curriculum objectives, but, more important, because it represented one of the most efficient ways through which to achieve these goals? yes _____ no _____

2
Was the community study learning experience worth the time and effort required because it provided needed and useful learning experiences which could not have been presented as effectively through ordinarily scheduled classroom opportunities? yes _____ no _____

3
Did pupils and teachers work together in undertaking the planning which anticipated the community study learning experience, mainly in developing learning purposes or goals to be achieved? yes _____ no _____

4
Was the community study situation engaged in only after teachers and pupils were reasonably sure of why and how the experience was to be undertaken? yes _____ no _____

5
Did you, as a teacher, observe local school policy regulations concerning community study visits?

a Previsiting the place to be studied. yes _____ no _____

helping with the search and in making the decisions about what are the more appropriate activities, exactly how they should be undertaken, and in what way the results are to be expressed. Under such circumstances involving pupil-teacher planning and pupil-teacher purposes, remarkable outcomes, measurable in terms of visible student responses, can be achieved.

Ordinarily, community study experience falls in one of two broad categories: either members of the community are invited to come into the classroom or the class is given the opportunity of deciding how and why they should leave the school building to examine at firsthand certain specific social or economic manifestations.

As students leave the classroom they learn to assume the ordinary responsibilities of people who seek safe conduct and reasonable communication in the world about them. They may travel to nearby learning opportunity experiences during a given school day or, as the result of more elaborate preparation, share or exchange learning experiences with age-mates who live tens or hundreds of miles away, accomplishing this during a week or more of ex-

b Preparing a statement of goals and purposes and presenting this to the proper school authority (the principal or supervisor) for approval. yes _____ no _____
c Arranging, where possible with pupils' participation, for times of departure, arrival, and

return by school bus or other bonded carrier. yes _____ no _____
d Sending into the homes of pupils study announcements concerning the experiences to be undertaken by the children for the purpose of encouraging family discussion and involvement by all concerned. yes _____ no _____

6
Were opportunities arranged during the community study situation for the documentation of information through one or more of the following?
a Recording by photographic camera. yes _____ no _____
b Recording by portable video or audiotape.

yes _____ no _____
c Drawing sketches, formulating simple charts or diagrams, depicting high-point processes or procedures. yes _____ no _____
d Picking up along the way available pamphlets, explanatory printed information, diagrams, pictures, etc. yes _____ no _____

7
Following return to the classroom, did pupils and teacher spend enough time in questioning and responding in order to clarify and consoli-

date valid interpretations of things learned and conceptualized during the community study experience? yes _____ no _____

8
Were appropriate opportunities given to encourage pupils to demonstrate such behavioral outcomes as the following?
a Selection of the best pictures taken by students during the tour and the best visual reports. yes _____ no _____
b Preparation of descriptive statements for inclusion in the classroom, school, or local newspaper. yes _____ no _____
c Arrangement of specimens, objects, diagrams, and charts accumulated during the trip in two- or three-dimensional displays for the purpose of communicating their new-found information to others. yes _____ no _____

d Review and use of films or filmstrips available about the study situation to consolidate, clarify, and expand useful information. yes _____ no _____
e Extension of invitations to community representatives willing to come to the school to help clarify ideas and develop additional useful ideas with students. yes _____ no _____
f Construction of models of situations best visualized and understood in this way, to consolidate and communicate to others valuable information gained during the community study experience. yes _____ no _____

change learning activity. Beyond this, the nature and scope of community study experiences are limited only by the wisdom of school authorities, the imagination of the teacher, and the carefully organized resourcefulness of the pupils—all oriented toward going farther and staying longer, with the central purpose always to learn realistically about selected social, economic, or ecological phenomena. Thus community study can be a matter of local, state, national, or even international study opportunities.

All kinds of variations in community

study are found throughout the United States during this decade of great unrest and reanalysis of school learning programs. At one extreme, open schools pursue community study with an avidity that is refreshing. In these situations, students are given remarkable latitude in planning, participating, and evaluating. While many schools may not have reached this stage of development, teaching personnel must always consider the potential scope of community study and the many opportunities it has for bringing lifelike learning opportunities to the upcoming generation.

As community study experiences are carefully planned, specific attention should be given to pupil-teacher planning in identifying goals and purposes, arranging the mechanics of travel, recording information, and, finally, in evaluating the experience itself. Evaluation is realistic when learning goals are known to students and when opportunities are provided during which learners can put to use their newfound information and/or skills in visible performances which reflect their knowledge, inventiveness, and creative responses.

Further learner response projects

1

Ask yourself, your fellow teachers, or pupils with whom you work this question: As we try to understand more fully this subject (choose one) which we are investigating during the coming weeks (or months), what opportunities are there in our city, state, or nation which, if we could experience them at firsthand, would help us learn more completely. List as many community study situations as possible which relate to your chosen subject field. List both those that involve bringing representatives of the community to your classroom and those that involve taking your pupils out into the community. Since, as you do this, you will need to know more about your community, consider the following suggestions:

a Consult the Chamber of Commerce.
b Ask experienced teachers for help.
c Study the local business directory.
d Talk with lifelong residents of the community.
e Interview the county agricultural agent (if there is one) and the editor of the local weekly or daily newspaper.

Make a list of the more feasible and promising possibilities and, if possible, visit such people, places, or demonstrations. Report your feelings about worthwhile opportunities.

2

Choose from your list in Project 1, one valued community learning experience and arrange, if possible, for students with whom you work to undertake it as a learning experience. As you plan, follow suggestions made in this chapter. On completion of the experience, evaluate outcomes according to the criteria on pages 264–265. What are your conclusions?

3

Where feasible, ask pupil community study participants to evaluate their experiences.

What are your conclusions?

4

Arrange to preview such films as those listed below under Media References.

5

Arrange to carry on a long-distance speaker- phone interview. Consult your local telephone company to arrange for equipment. Follow the suggestions made on pages 252–253.

References

AVERY, PAUL J. "Students, Architects Team-up To Plan a New High School." *Nation's Schools,* Vol. 85, No. 6, June 1970.

BOCES Field Trip Guide. Board of Cooperative Educational Services, Research and Development Division, 125 Jericho Turnpike, Jericho, N.Y. 11753, September 1971.

Environmental Studies, September 1, 1970. Newsletter published quarterly by Earth Science Educational Program, Box 1559, Boulder, Colo. 80303.

Field Trip Catalog. Garden City Public Schools, Instructional Materials Center, Garden City, N.Y., 1968. Att: Dr. David V. Guerin, Coordinator of Instructional Materials.

"Free Form Learners." *Nation's Schools,* Vol. 84, No. 3, September 1969.

GREENBERG, JAMES D., and ROBERT E. ROUSH. "A Visit to the School Without Walls: Two Impressions." *Phi Delta Kappan,* May 1970.

GUELL, CARL. "Aerospace Field Trips," Chap. 9. In *Introduction to Aerospace Education,* ed. Mervin K. Strickler, Jr. New Horizons Publications, Chicago, 1968.

Local Materials Project: An Evaluation and Description, 1971. Local Materials Office, Madison Public Schools.

RUBIN, HAROLD. "Telephone Network Courses." *Educational Screen and Audio Visual Guide,* March 1964.

Media references

Community Resources in Teaching, 16mm film, sound, b/w, 17 min. State University of Iowa.

Field Trip, 16mm film, sound, color, 11 min. Virginia State Department of Public Instruction.

Field Trips for Discovery, 16mm film, sound, b/w. McGraw-Hill.

Near Home, 16mm film, sound, b/w, 27 min. New York University Film Library.

Passion for Life, 16mm film, sound, b/w, 85 min. Brandon Films.

World in a Schoolroom, 16mm film, sound, b/w, 17 min. (Produced by U. S. Army, National Audio Visual Center.) Universal Education and Visual Arts.

Source references

See source lists in the Appendix; particularly relevant sections are: Free and Inexpensive Materials; Graphic Materials; Photographic Equipment.

See *Student Production Guide,* Chapter 4, "Producing Photo and Sound Materials for Instruction."

SEVEN
Maps and globes

Objectives

Performance responses

1

Given a set of criteria, to select suitable map and globe materials for a unit in your subject area and grade level.

Divide the media class into groups of three or four each of primary, intermediate or middle, and secondary subject-area teachers (social studies, geography, earth science, language, history, etc.). Select a unit or topics in which globes and/or maps would be significant to learning. Using criteria discussed in the text and some representative globes and maps (and/or map and globe catalogs), each committee should select the best materials for purposes of the topic or unit chosen and submit a written or oral rationale for each selection made. Select the best primary-, intermediate-, and secondary-level reports for class discussion and evaluation.

2

To rate world maps based on different projections in terms of their relative accuracy of area representation.

Secure three or more world maps, each based on a different projection (e.g., Van der Grinten, Semi-elliptical, Mercator, Mollweide, sinusoidal, Goode's homolosine, etc.), in wall, transparency, slide, and/or desk outline map form. Apply the grid-comparison test and analysis to three of them, rate them in order of relative accuracy of area representation and write the reasons for each rating.

3

To be able to relate maps of comparable areas which use different methods of showing elevations in terms of suitability for specific grade levels and learning situations.

Using the group of maps in Response 1 and three comparable area maps (state, U.S., Europe, etc.), each employing a different elevation technique (contour lines, hachures, shading, coloration, raised relief, or other), analyze each and prepare a brief written report in terms of the stated objective. Be prepared to justify your rationale in reporting to the class.

4

To identify and describe six different learning or communications situations (in or out of school) in which effective map-reading ability is essential.

Using the text discussion, pertinent references, map catalogs, and other sources, identify and write a brief description of six different kinds of situations or topics in which effective map-reading ability is essential.

ALTHOUGH maps and globes are fundamental to the study of geography and other subjects in school, they are, of course essential in a whole range of human activities. We use them not only in all forms of travel, but also to interpret tomorrow's weather and today's events in far parts of the world. Maps help us to understand the history of the ages, the world we now live in (see Figure 7.1), and the space age we have entered.

As he plans his campaign for a new bond issue, the superintendent of schools makes extensive use of census plot maps to show population trends in the community, what areas have had the highest birthrate during the past five years, and where needed new school buildings should therefore be located. Real estate developers study similar maps in deciding where new housing developments, subdivisions, and shopping centers are most likely to be successful. Maps are essential for interpreting zoning ordinances and determining voting precincts. If you like to hunt or fish or ride snowmobile trails or if you are a boating enthusiast, you have probably become adept at reading detailed maps and navigation charts both to get where you want to go and to stay out of trouble along the way.

Maps, in short, have almost innumerable practical day-to-day uses, as well as being essential to a complete understanding of the world, its people, and the space around us. In fact, map-reading has become so necessary to getting along in today's world that, as teachers, we might well regard it as comparable in importance to verbal and numerical literacy. And as is true of reading and mathematical skills, so it is with map-reading skills—we need to develop them to the point where our students can readily *interpret* the information contained on maps. The difference between simply "reading" maps and being able to interpret them effectively is much like the difference between the mechanical skill involved in reading words and the intellectual skill involved in reading to *learn*. Before a teacher can help his students acquire the ability to learn through maps, however, he must himself become adept in their interpretation and use. This chapter is intended to help teachers to do so.

The new social studies and a new geography

BEFORE considering the specific characteristics of maps and globes, it is important to be aware of the fact that the context in which maps and globes are used is undergoing fundamental changes. A new wave of curriculum reform in the social studies which was initiated by various agencies during the 1960s could have effects on the schools comparable to the effects of the curriculum reform movements in mathematics, science, humanities, and foreign languages (for example, the new math, M.I.T.'s new physics, the PSSC's new biology, and the audiolingual language laboratory approach to foreign language instruction).

FIGURE 7.1

In an analysis of a number of emerging new social studies programs, Lorrin Kennamer, Jr., geographer and dean of the School of Arts and Sciences at Texas Tech University, singles out four elements common to all of them which have significant implications for change in content and also in methods of teaching the social studies and its geography components :[1]

1. Geography and history no longer dominate the elementary social studies curriculum; rather, curriculum builders are drawing concepts from a wide range of the social science disciplines and focusing on topics relating to societal change.

2. Cultural concepts in geography are increasing in importance, whereas physical geography and its environmental influences are of lesser importance than formerly. For example, the University of Minnesota Elementary Social Studies Program is built on a series of themes such as "Earth as the Home of Man," "Families Around the World," "Communities Around the World," "Formation of Society," "Man and Culture," and "Our Political System," with content derived from anthropology, geography, economics, history, sociology, and political science.[2]

3. Students at all grade levels are bringing more sophisticated backgrounds of experience to the study of local, national, and world affairs than was true a generation ago. In consequence, many geographic concepts once reserved for intermediate or upper grades are being taught successfully at earlier levels.

4. In recognition of the great need to

The implications of the jet age world are made clear by the short flying times on great-circle routes between principal cities of the earth.

understand more of the world's peoples, much more attention is being directed to the cultures of non-Western peoples, with increased emphasis on comparative studies of families, cultures, and governments (see Figure 7.2). For this purpose, traditional descriptive regional geography is inadequate. The Providence Social Studies Curriculum, for example, begins with family and community study and later emphasizes the study of cultures, in this case by comparing cultures in major regions of the world, namely, Anglo-American (one culture), Africa and Latin America (two cultures), and Southeast Asia, Western Europe, and the Soviet Union (three cultures)—all as a basis for better understanding of the major contemporary civilizations of the world.[3]

Thus, as Kennamer puts it, we have a "new social studies" and with it a "new

---

[1] Lorrin Kennamer, Jr., "Emerging Social Studies Curricula: Implications for Geography," in *Focus on Geography: Key Concepts and Teaching Strategies*, 40th Yearbook, National Council for the Social Studies, 1970, pp. 388–391.

[2] Progress Report No. 2, University of Minnesota Project Social Studies Curriculum Center, November 1965.

[3] Norris M. Sanders and Marlin L. Tanck, "Providence Social Studies Curriculum Project," *Social Education*, Vol. 34, No. 4, April 1970, pp. 405–406.

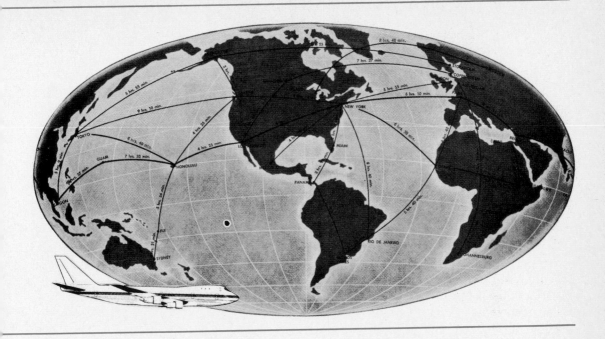

geography'' incorporating changes in content, emphases, and approaches to learning. He continues:

Geography today, which includes the study of culture, spatial distribution, spatial interaction, and functional regions, is quite different from the geography of yesterday, which emphasized the physical environment and the descriptive study of world regions.[4]

The new social studies programs require new and greater amounts and varieties of materials, as well as a multimedia approach. Implications for geography include the development and use of increasing numbers of special-purpose maps, among them local and state maps, and the encouragement of student preparation of map materials for specific purposes (see Figure 7.3). Among additional materials needed for the new programs are booklets on the different skills of mapping, photo interpretation, data collection, and the

preparation of statistical charts. Kennamer also advocates the preparation of new single-concept filmstrips and film loops and the development of additional sets of transparencies. Representative case studies are needed on such problems as industrial location, cultural diffusion, environmental pollution control, and the like.[5]

Does the swing away from emphasis on physical geography in the new social studies programs suggest that there is less need for maps and globe study? Quite the contrary. The new social studies clearly requires that students learn earlier, if anything, than before not only how to ''read'' maps and globes but also how to *use* them readily as primary sources of information in a wide range of societal and cultural topics of local, national, and global significance. Accordingly, as teachers we need to examine the nature and characteristics of globes and maps and how we may select and use them to best advantage.

[4] Kennamer, op. cit., p. 391.

[5] Ibid., p. 390.

FIGURE 7.2

These striking scenes from six of Julien Bryan's films of non-Western cultures reflect three highly significant trends: (1) The new social studies programs emphasize understanding many more of the world's peoples than simply the "standard" Western peoples usually studied in the past. (2) These new programs emphasize the cultural rather than the physical aspects of geography. (3) In an effort to stimulate student observation, inquiry, and discovery, many of the new social studies films include only natural sounds and omit the usual narration entirely. Bryan, who has pioneered in producing nonnarration films, expresses his rationale in the form of this credo:

This I Believe
I believe that children like to be left alone —to make their own discoveries.
I believe that we film-makers have too long preached at children, often with dull narration. We have given all the answers and left nothing for pupils to discover.
How exciting now to make new short films which raise questions instead of answering them and which involve children.

A–F

These stills from Bryan's nonnarrative films give an impression of the knowledge and understanding that can be conveyed by a motion picture camera in sympathetic and expert hands. (a) High above his home village among the cliffs of Mali in former French West Africa, a Dogon tribesman hunts for wild doves. (b) In another part of Mali, people of the Bozo tribe construct a storage house. (c) At an altitude of 10,000 feet in northern Afghanistan, the Tajik people build a bridge. (d) In a Yugoslav rural village, men and sheep return home at sundown. (e) On the coast of Japan, a fishing boat is hauled into the surf. (f) A native woman grinds wheat.

G

In making a film that will communicate successfully, the person behind the camera must have not only technical expertise, but also empathy for his subjects. The rapport that Julien Bryan achieves with the people he films is evident in this photograph of him with a Macedonian shepherd in Yugoslavia.

FIGURE 7.3

The national High School Geography Project emphasizes varied approaches to map understanding. (a) Using stereograms and a topographic map, two girls hypothesize about the characteristics of a New Orleans neighborhood. (b) Students work as a group to build a 3–D map model of a hypothetical American West Coast city, "Portsville." Both activities are part of the "Geography of Cities" unit of the HSGP course, "Geography in an Urban Age."

Nature of globes and maps

A *globe* is a spherical model of the earth. A *map* is a flat representation of some or all of the earth's surface.

Because the earth itself is a sphere, globes obviously have certain unique values. Most globes are too small for detailed study of areas, however, and cannot readily be carried around, anyway; therefore, flat maps are essential for many purposes. Two general aspects of globes and maps should be discussed before we consider them individually. The first concerns their relative accuracy; the second concerns their abstract character.

Relative accuracy

A good globe provides inherently correct information about *areas, distances, direc-*

tions, and *geographical shapes*. With these accurate characteristics—or *properties,* as they are called by cartographers—it is possible to plot courses, determine locations, measure distances, and compare areas with assurance. In short, the globe is the most accurate map we have of the earth's surface.

Even the best of flat maps cannot achieve accuracy comparable to that of a globe. A flat representation of any sizable portion of a spherical surface involves certain unavoidable inaccuracies. This is simply illustrated if you attempt to flatten out the skin of half a grapefruit or half a hollow rubber ball; it can be done only by breaking or compressing the surface. In essence, that is the problem all map-makers face. Because it becomes important in the case of maps of very large areas, such as a hemisphere or the world, we as teachers need to be aware that such maps can create serious erroneous impressions.

It is impossible for a cartographer to make a flat map of the world which *accurately* represents more than one (in rare cases, two) of the four properties of a globe's surface—areas, distances, directions, or shapes. Of these four, the most important one for general school purposes is *correct area*. When area is badly distorted on a world map, the relative positions, as well as the relative sizes, of countries and continents are distorted. Let us see how this happens in the case of one familiar type of world map, the Mercator projection.

If the surface of a globe is "peeled off" along the meridians, sections result which are called *gores* (see Figure 7.4). On most flat maps, either the spaces between these gores are filled in or the gores are stretched out in some manner so as to avoid empty spaces on the map surface. This naturally produces exaggeration in areas where the gores are some distance apart. The farther the distance north or south from the equator on a world map, the greater is the spread between the gores. Hence the farther north or south we go on a flat map of the world, the greater are the inaccuracies (assuming the map is centered on the equator). Thus the Mercator projection shown in Figure 7.5 exaggerates all areas above 50 degrees north latitude— roughly the United States–Canada border.

FIGURE 7.4

When gores are removed from a globe and flattened, they look like this.

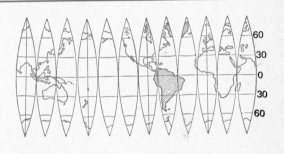

FIGURE 7.5

Note how Greenland compares in size with South America on this Mercator projection. The curved dotted line is the great-circle route between the Philippines and San Francisco, actually the shortest route between those two points.

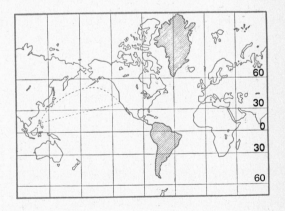

FIGURE 7.6

Here are the Mercator projections of Greenland and South America. To the right, in correct scale, is Greenland. Why is there this amount of distortion?

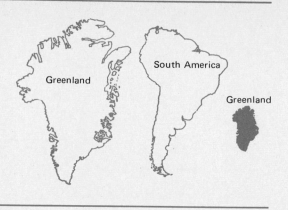

Because any straight line on the Mercator projection can be used as a true compass line, however, the Mercator projection is very valuable for navigators, for whom it was originally intended. For school purposes, on the other hand, such maps are misleading with respect to the actual size of land and water areas. For example, in Figures 7.5 and 7.6, Greenland appears to be larger than South America, when in reality it is only about one-eighth as large.

We will discuss how to select desirable wall maps for school purposes later. First, let us note one other general characteristic of maps and globes which is important to keep in mind as we use them in teaching—their abstract character.

Abstract character

The language of maps and globes is very largely a language of symbols and colors. A dot fixes the location of a city. A line of one type means a highway; another kind of line represents a political boundary; still other lines and symbols designate rivers, railroads, trade routes, elevation contours, natural boundaries between water and land, directions, or other features (see Figure 7.7). Usually these map and globe symbols have little visual resemblance to what they represent. Sometimes—as in the case of parallels (latitude lines), meridians (longi-

FIGURE 7.7

In what ways are map symbols like new words in reading?

tude lines), and contour lines—they represent things that cannot actually be seen anywhere on the earth's surface. Thus before students can begin to ''read'' maps, they have to learn something about map symbols (see Plates 7.1 and 7.2, following page 356). To a degree, the same is true of map colors.

The use of color on globes and maps serves two important purposes. The first and more significant purpose is to aid legibility by distinguishing such features as land and water, lowlands and highlands, and political divisions (see Plates 7.3–7.6,

following page 356). The second purpose is a matter of esthetics; this also is important, because pleasing colors can contribute to the favorable reception of a map or globe. However, the colors used are necessarily different from those found in nature. It is obviously impossible to show the actual colors of land and water surfaces, since these vary with the seasons, vegetation, rainfall, location, and other factors, so the cartographer must assign somewhat arbitrary meanings to the colors he uses. In general, the colors on physical-political globes follow an international color scheme,

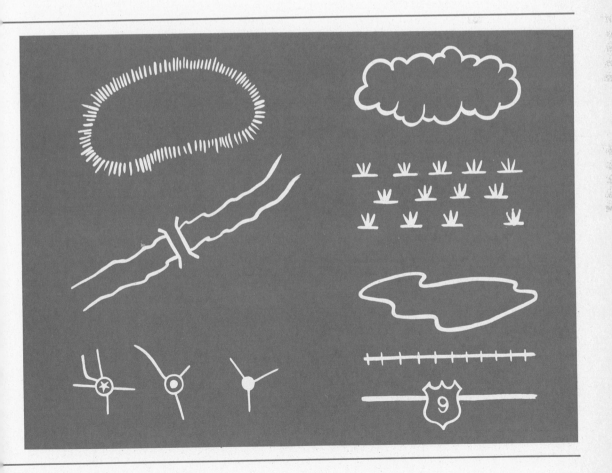

but, aside from that, there is no standard color pattern for map or globes. This means that if students are to read maps and globes successfully, they must be able to interpret a variety of symbols and colors. In other words, they need to learn the language of maps in order to interpret them.

Globes

THE astronauts, of course, are the first men who have actually seen the earth as a sphere (see Plate 7.7, following page 356). Said one: "A beautiful blue and silver ball." Another: "The earth from here is a grand oasis in the big vastness of space." And a third: "Well, we just got our first view of the earth this morning, and can you believe it's getting larger and it's getting smaller. It can be just a very, very thin sliver of a very large round ball."[6]

Globes are necessary to convey the concept of the earth's roundness to those of us who do not yet travel in space. They are also necessary beginning points for students to learn to interpret flat maps:

Understanding the globe is basic to a development of skills and abilities necessary for reading and interpreting maps. The globe must be understood before much can be done with the flat maps. [It is essential] for teaching earth movements, relationships in the solar system, an understanding of rotation . . . of revolution . . . and of such other concepts as time zones, the international date line, and great circle transportation patterns.[7]

The globe is so important, therefore, that the teacher must know something of the nature and types of globes available.

[6] Quoted in a letter from the National Aeronautics and Space Administration, Office of Public Affairs, September 10, 1971.
[7] Lorrin Kennamer, Jr., "Developing a Sense of Place and Space," in *Skill Development in the Social Studies*, 33rd Yearbook, National Council for the Social Studies, 1963, p. 152.

Types of globes

There are three principal types of globes which are valuable for school use: political globes, physical-political globes, and slated outline globes. *Political globes* are designed primarily to show the location and boundaries of countries, principal cities, trade routes, and other features created by man. A simplified political globe with a minimum of details is desirable for use in the primary grades. For some individual uses in both the primary and middle grades, small, inexpensive, machine-made political globes are quite satisfactory, particularly as political globes tend to become outdated through changes in national boundaries or political affiliations.

Physical-political globes show some political features, but, as the name implies, their primary emphasis is on land elevations and ocean depths shown by means of colors. Such globes are practical for use in the middle grades and above because they combine essential physical features with sufficient political information to show relationships between the two. A good physical-political globe will be useful for years with reasonable care, serving effectively both for general observation purposes and for detailed, specific reference. Thus when a physical-political globe is purchased, a good-quality handmade globe is the best buy.

Slated outline globes (see Figure 7.8) are of great value at all grade levels. Teacher and students can write on this type of globe with chalk, indicating such features as locations; air, sea, and land routes; and great circles. One unique advantage of such

FIGURE 7.8

Slated globes have many useful applications, such as the one shown here. Globes provide maximum learning potential when used, as here, with related maps, pictures, and reading materials.

globes is that they permit attention to be focused on one thing at a time. In addition, slated outline globes obviously are particularly well suited for direct pupil activity and experience. Globes of this type are available either with plain surfaces or with the continents outlined and with or without parallels and meridians. (Since slated globes are less costly to manufacture than those with printed surfaces, these globes are relatively inexpensive in proportion to their size.)

There are various other special types of globes, such as raised relief, celestial, moon, and satellite globes. Each has particular values for specific purposes. The celestial globe pictured in Figure 7.9, for example, is used to illustrate the changing locations of stars and planets with reference to the earth's surface. This type of globe and various other materials of several types (discussed in Chapter 15) are valuable for space science studies.

Also available are useful globe sections of major continental areas. Since these sections approximate areas typically included on flat maps of continents, they can facilitate the transition from globes to flat maps. These sections, made of plastic with raised relief surfaces, are strong, light, and easily handled by students. Their utility for various learning activities is suggested in Figure 7.10.

Desirable characteristics of globes

In selecting globes for classroom use, several general considerations should be taken into account. One is that a globe should be an attractive part of the classroom environment. In addition, its size and readability, the amount and level of information on it, and how it is colored are important considerations from the learners' standpoint.

SIZE AND READABILITY Globe size is indicated in terms of diameter, the most common for school use being 12, 16, 20, and 24 inches. The 12-inch globe is excellent for individual or small-group use, while 16-inch or larger globes are best for larger groups of students or classes. Regular globes larger than 16 inches are quite expensive, but slated globes are not; thus slated globes in 20-inch and larger sizes are used in many classrooms in both elementary and secondary schools.

The details on most globes are intended primarily for study at close range. Such broad features as hemispheres, land-water relationships, and the relative locations of continents can be observed by an entire class, however, if a 16-inch or larger globe is used (see Figure 7.11). Another advantage of larger globes is that place names and other printed matter can be made more legible because there is considerably more

FIGURE 7.9

The transparent celestial globe takes on new significance in the Space Age. With such a globe it is possible to demonstrate basic relationships between the earth and the stars, planets, and galaxies which make up the universe.

FIGURE 7.10

Light plastic globe sections with raised relief are especially useful for the transition from globes to flat maps because they cover the same areas as flat maps of continents, and students can handle and work with them in various ways.

FIGURE 7.11

The advantages of a sizable globe and a mounting that permits its removal for improved visibility are illustrated by Dr. Paul Griffin, well-known geographer and educator.

space. For example, a 12-inch globe has only about 56 percent of the surface area of a 16-inch globe—452 square inches as compared with 804 square inches, to be exact. Distance, too, can be estimated somewhat more easily on a 16-inch globe because the scale is a convenient 500 miles to an inch as compared with 670 miles to an inch on a 12-inch globe. In terms of flexibility of use, of course, the types of mountings used for globes are also important (see Figure 7.12).

SUITABILITY TO GRADE LEVEL Related closely in importance to the readability of material on a globe is the level of the information presented. In recognition of the need for graded materials, manufacturers produce political globes and physical-political globes for primary grades, intermediate grades, and more advanced students. Often these are combined with self-instruction booklets, related maps, study prints, audiotapes, and other media into complete programs of study.

EFFECTIVE COLOR The color used on globes is another important feature to consider in selection for classroom use. One important aspect of a globe's coloration is its effect on readability. Dark or vivid colors are more likely than lighter, pastel shades to obscure the words and line symbols printed on a globe. On the other hand, there needs to be sufficient variation in hue and color to provide adequate contrast in such globe features as national areas on political globes and elevations on physical-political and relief-type globes.

An important development of the past decade is the production of globes and flat maps with identical coloration—important because globe study precedes map study, and the transition from globes to flat maps can be made easier for the pupil if the colors used are the same on both. This development, of course, is significant primarily in elementary schools, for it is there that initial globe- and map-reading skills must be taught.

FIGURE 7.12

Mountings influence both the type and the facility of globe use. Shown here are (a) a low cradle, (b) a medium cradle with latitude scale, (c) a medium cradle with horizon ring, (d) a gyro mount with single axis, (e) a gyro mount with dual axes, (f) a gyro mount with horizon ring and removable globe.

Maps

EVEN though, as we have seen, there is some degree of inaccuracy present on any flat map, this should in no sense be taken to mean that there is anything "bad" about flat maps or that their use should be avoided. They are, in fact, invaluable. Indeed, the *only* way to see the whole world at one time is to use a world map. Using a globe, we can see no more than half the world at a time, no matter how we spin or tilt it. Because of their size, wall maps are far more readable than globes; thus they can be used with a group or a class to point out various geographic, economic, political, and other kinds of information. The great number and variety of wall maps available in many subjects is another advantage; this also attests to their wide acceptance as valuable teaching materials. Small project maps are invaluable in helping students develop skills not only in reading maps but also in using them to communicate with others. In short, there is no way we could get along without flat maps in today's schools or today's world. So, as in the case of a married couple, each accepts the other's imperfections and makes the most of the other's good points, thereby benefiting everyone involved. Before you test that analogy too far, we should go back to maps—specifically, to maps of the world—and gain some insights into how we can minimize the effects of the rather important and unavoidable imperfections that are present in all world maps—though on some far more than on others. To do so we need to take a brief look at map projections.

Map projections

The term *map projection* means the method by which the spherical surface of the earth is represented on a flat surface. There are many different map projections, each designed to achieve particular purposes. Some projections represent *areas* with reasonable accuracy. Others are relatively accurate so far as the *shapes* of land and water surfaces are concerned. Some other projections make it possible to read *distances* accurately from

FIGURE 7.13

Three basic types of map projections, cylindrical, azimuthal, and conical, can be demonstrated on this inexpensive map-projection model which shows how a flat map is made from the spherical surface of the globe. The cylindrical and conical maps may be unsnapped to be seen as flat maps.

the center of the map. Still others have the property of showing true *directions*. A ship's navigator can draw a straight line between two points on a Mercator chart and steer this course with confidence, since the Mercator projection was created for this. Unfortunately, no flat map can provide all four of the above properties; actually, few can offer more than one.

It is a help in understanding map projections to know something of how maps are designed (see Figure 7.13). First we should describe the grid lines and their purpose. The term *grid* refers to the par-

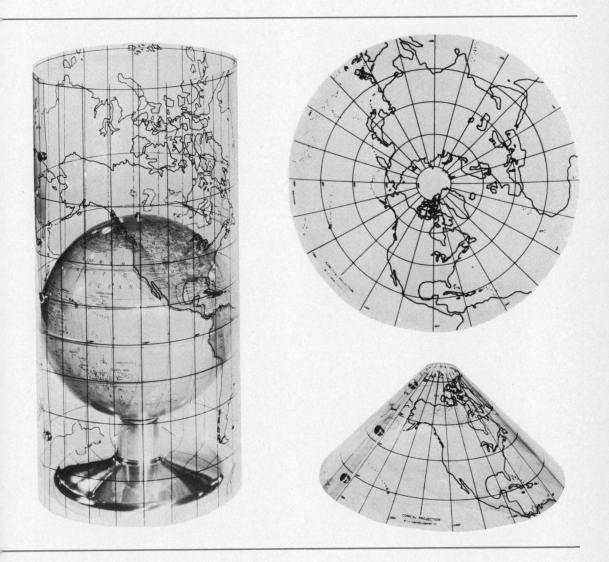

FIGURE 7.14

allels (latitude lines) and meridians (longitude lines) which cartographers universally use as reference lines in plotting their maps and which also are universally used as reference lines in specifying the location of any point on the earth. The parallels are east-west lines extending around the earth, parallel to the equator and numbered in degrees north and south from the equator. The meridians are north-south lines extending from pole to pole and numbered in degrees east and west from the prime meridian, which intersects Greenwich, England. Position on maps is measured in terms of the number of degrees of north or south latitude combined with the number of degrees of east or west longitude.

In essence, therefore, *projection* is the process of transferring the grid system of the globe onto a flat surface and then drawing in the land areas, point by point, according to the position each has in relation to the globe grid. The actual process is largely mathematical, but the principles can be illustrated rather simply. If you place a transparent cylinder around a translucent globe with a light in it, as in Figure 7.13, the grid lines on the globe are "projected" on the surface of the cylinder. With some modification, this is the Mercator projection. If you place a flat or plane surface against the lighted globe, a different pattern of grid lines is projected. With a cone, still another pattern is projected. And each of these projections, of course, is different from the grid on the globe itself.

Since it is quite impossible to transfer the globe grid onto a flat surface without altering it considerably, it is inevitable that land and water areas on the resulting flat map will likewise be considerably altered from how they actually are on the earth's surface. Thus some adjustment or compromise is necessary in terms of which of the four basic properties are to be emphasized.

Dymaxion Water Ocean World Map: Many alternate and equally valid arrangements of the basic set of icosahedron triangles are possible. This configuration shows the three-quarters of our planet covered with water, with all the oceans revolving around Antarctica in the merry-go-round which was the key to the control of the world. Not only is South America greatly isolated from North America, but we also see the historical remoteness of all the world's peoples in separate lands joined only by the oceans.

Several suitable kinds of classroom maps are available in what are called *minimum-error projections*.[8] These projec-

[8] The values of these little-known maps are described in Arthur Robinson, "An Analytical Approach to Map Projections," *Annals of the Association of American Geographers*, December 1949, p. 287. This article by a geographer who is a noted authority in this field is still one of the best discussions of minimum-error maps available.

tions are compromises in which area, shape, direction, and distance properties are balanced so as to present as realistic a map of a segment of the earth's surface as possible. Although no property is completely accurate on a minimum-error projection, the inaccuracies are moderate and inconspicuous even to a skilled observer. For other than technical or scientific purposes, therefore, these projections are quite satisfactory.

There is one quite unusual special-purpose projection which preserves both areas and continental shapes exceptionally well. This is the projection first created by the well-known architect and engineer R. Buckminster Fuller in the 1940s to illustrate some of his dynamic concepts of world geographic relationships and their bearing on man's historical development. Fuller's Dymaxion Projection (see Figures 7.14 and 7.15), is based on a series of triangles

FIGURE 7.15

and, sometimes, squares which can be arranged to form many different maps to illustrate changing world relationships and various historical concepts. The projection is particularly useful for advanced students in today's new social studies programs which are focused on societal and cultural needs. Two examples of this imaginative projection are shown here.

Because areas are particularly important in schoolwork, we should note that projections used for flat maps which give a correct impression of an *area* are called *equal-area projections*. This means that the land and water *areas* are essentially correct, though the *shapes* of these areas must be sacrificed to some extent to achieve good area properties and, in consequence, *direction* and *distance* properties are also distorted. For school purposes, however, direction, distance, and shapes (so long as they remain recognizable) are of minor importance as compared with good area representation in giving correct impressions of the world or of a hemisphere.

On maps of regions *less than* a hemisphere in size, for general school purposes, it makes little difference what projection is used because the errors in areas are very small. It *is* important, however, for the teacher to know how to determine whether a world map has good area representation —a fact that the name or catalog description of the map seldom reveals. Since the globe grid provides the only truly accurate map of the earth's surface, we use it for evaluation by comparing the pattern of grid lines on a globe with that on the flat world map being judged. This is called the *grid-comparison method* of evaluating map projections. It is done by determining how closely the grid of a flat map approaches the following four characteristics of the globe grid, stated as criteria:

1 *Parallels are parallel.*
2 *Parallels are equidistant from equator to poles.*

Dymaxion Airocean World Map: This configuration provides a new north-south world orientation emancipated from the formal cartographic tyranny imposed by the poles. Here the great-circle continuities of the geometrical pieces are assembled around the landmass instead of around the water mass. The earth's skin is unpeeled in such a manner that all the empty spaces occur in the one-world ocean; thus for the first time on a flat map there are no breaks in the world continental contours—and without any visible distortion of their relative sizes or shapes. As this map makes clear, 90 percent of humanity can reach one another on the shortest great-circle air routes without going near the Indian, Atlantic, or Pacific Oceans. Here is the correct relationship of Greenland to Australia. Look at the enormous size of Antarctica, which is completely left out of the Mercator projection. The Airocean map is probably as appropriate to world air travel as the Mercator map was appropriate to travel by square-rigged ships sailing east-west with the trade winds, closely paralleling the equator, around which the Mercator projection is least distorted.

3 *Meridians are equally spaced on the parallels and converge toward the poles.*
4 *The area enclosed by any two parallels and two meridians is the same anywhere between the same two parallels.*

Because only the grid on a globe completely meets all four of these criteria, our evaluation must be based on *how closely* the grid of the map we are examining comes to meeting them (see Figure 7.16). If the four characteristics are reasonably approximated over a major portion of the map's surface, the chances are that the map has good *area* qualities. This means that areas on one part of the map (particularly land areas) are comparable with areas on another part of the map.[9] With a little practice, a teacher can learn to determine quite easily which maps have good area charac-

[9] See Arthur Robinson, *Elements of Cartography*, rev. ed., Wiley, 1960, p. 62.

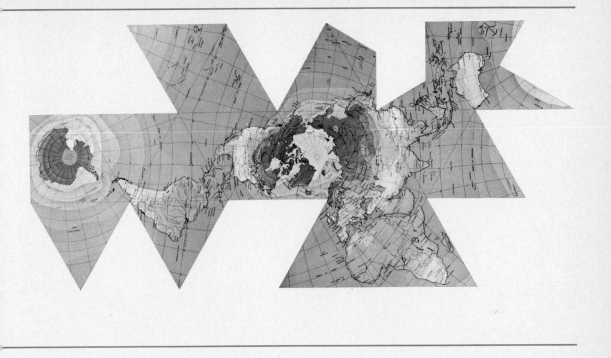

teristics. Try the four tests on the map grids in Figure 7.17 and then on other world maps in your classroom or learning resources center.

Types of maps

Wall maps are available in three principal types: (1) physical relief or terrain maps, which show surface features of the earth; (2) political maps, which show governmental areas; (3) special-purpose maps, which include a wide selection such as those showing land use, population distribution, rainfall, or historical development.

PHYSICAL RELIEF MAPS Physical relief maps emphasize terrain and topographical concepts including elevations and ocean depths. These concepts are necessary for understanding such matters as why people live where they do and some aspects of agricultural production, climate, and routes of transportation. The elementary concepts of mountains, valleys, plains, deserts, rivers, rainfall, and temperature all involve an understanding of topography.

Some flat maps visualize relief effectively by shading one side of mountain ranges, thus giving a three-dimensional appearance (see Figure 7.18). Color tints are also used to show elevation, but shaded relief has been used increasingly in recent years, sometimes combined with color. Still more recently, instead of altitude tints, shaded relief has been used on physical maps along with a natural landscape color scheme such as one might see from a plane at high altitude. Landscape colors of course vary with the seasons, but the colors used, keyed to major vegetation differences, are those that represent landscape colors during good weather in the summer. For example, grass areas are a lighter green than forest regions, and deserts are buff, brownish yellow, or gray. Texture is sometimes used to represent cultivated areas.

Physical maps that show actual relief

FIGURE 7.16

This grid comparison method exercise illustrates the comparisons necessary in determining whether or not a world map is on an equal-area projection. The test for each of the four criteria listed in the text on page 290 is illustrated. (a) *Criterion 1.* Test: Are parallels *MN, KL, IJ,* etc., all parallel to one another? (b) *Criterion 2.* Test: Is distance *X* equal to distance *Y*? Are other parallels relatively equidistant also? (c) *Criterion 3.* Test: Does distance *AB = BC = CD = DE,* etc.? Do meridians *AA, BB, CC, DD,* etc., all converge toward the poles? (d) *Criterion 4.* Test: Does the area in *A = B = C = D,* etc., all across the map between the same two parallels?

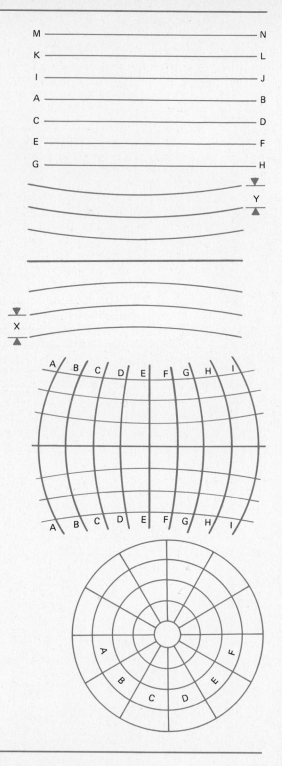

FIGURE 7.17

Apply the tests shown in Figure 7.16 to these two actual maps, *a* and *b*. Check your responses here.

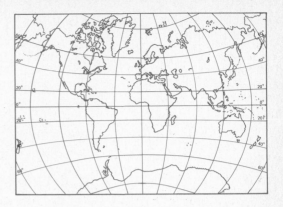

Answers to Map Test: Figure 7.17
Map a.
Criterion 1: *Parallels are parallel near the equator and not seriously off to 60° N or S latitude.* Criterion 2: *Parallels are relatively equidistant only along the equator and through the central vertical section of the map. Beyond 60° N or S the distances between them vary markedly.* Criterion 3: *Meridians are almost equally spaced and do converge toward the poles.* Criterion 4: *Areas between the same two parallels are relatively equal across the center of the map, but become markedly unequal beyond 60° N or S.*

    Summary: Though not an equal-area projection, this map has very good area representation along the equator and reasonably good area characteristics to 60° N or S. Beyond those latitudes distortion of 200 percent or more is evident.

    Map b.
Criterion 1: *Parallels are parallel throughout.* Criterion 2: *Parallels are equidistant throughout.* Criterion 3: *Meridians are equally spaced, but converge only toward the North Pole.* Criterion 4: *Areas between the same two parallels are equal all around the map.*

    Summary: Polar projections such as this one are useful primarily for the perspective provided for the polar regions in relation to the major continents. This projection has very good area characteristics down to the equator. Beyond that point, of course, because the meridians do not converge toward the South Pole, as they do on a globe, distortion becomes obvious.

FIGURE 7.18

An understanding of topography is necessary for many social studies concepts. Some flat maps like this show relief very clearly by shading one side of mountains so as to give the appearance of elevation.

FIGURE 7.19

Three-dimensional relief maps in durable light-weight plastic permit close-up study and feel of the terrain.

in three dimensions and amplify it with color shading are probably the most effective for classroom use. It should be noted that the vertical scale of any relief map is exaggerated in relation to its horizontal distance scale. This difference in scale is essential, of course, if topographical features are to be noticeable; it is therefore standard practice among all map-makers. Excellent three-dimensional relief maps are available in sturdy, lightweight, inexpensive plastic. These enable students to feel as well as to see the surface features of a region (see Figure 7.19). Three-dimensional relief maps of local areas can be made by teachers and pupils for any regions for which U.S. Geological Survey topographical maps are available. Such maps are not difficult to construct and are of significant value in developing map-reading ability among young pupils. The method shown in Figure 7.20 involves enlarging a small section of a topographical map and tracing the contour lines on corrugated cardboard (for a detailed description of this method, see the *Student Pro-*

duction Guide). The contours are then cut out and mounted on top of one another in the correct relationship. Some exaggeration of the vertical scale results, but, as noted, this is desirable. The surface is covered with spackling plaster and painted when dry.[10]

POLITICAL MAPS Political maps emphasize phenomena which are principally manmade, such as national, state, and county boundaries; the location of cities, highways, and railroads; and national and state parks. The familiar road map is a good

[10] For additional suggestions, see Ling Chu Poh, "The Teaching of Contours," *Journal of Geography*, November 1969, pp. 484–490.

example of one type of political map. Another example is a historical world map showing colonial possessions or protectorates, with the mother country in the same color. A political map usually also shows some prominent physical features, such as principal mountain ranges; oceans, lakes, and rivers; islands, shorelines, and, on large-area maps, the continents as well. Even though some physical features are included on political maps, the emphasis on political features is clearly evident (see Plates 7.3 and 7.4, following page 356).

Frequently a good balance of both terrain and political features is achieved on the same map; such a map is known as a *physical-political* map (see Plate 7.5, following page 356). These versatile maps are

FIGURE 7.20

A good terrain map of a local area can be made by teacher and pupils. These pictures show some of the steps involved in one method.

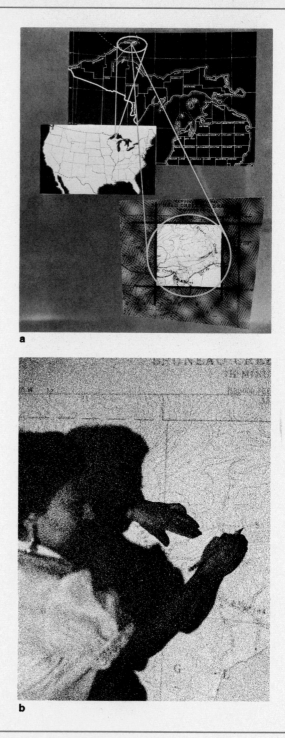

a

b

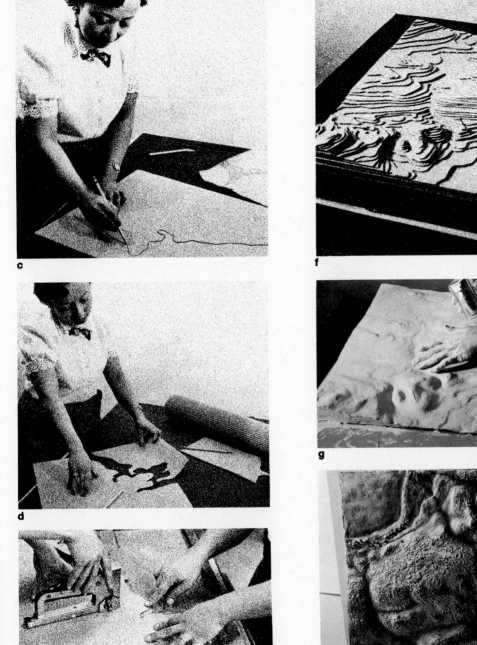

c

d

e

f

g

h

FIGURE 7.21

Distributions of population; climatic distributions
of seasonal temperatures, rainfall, and pressure;
and characteristics of land use in different parts
of the world are representative of one group of
the many special-purpose maps available.

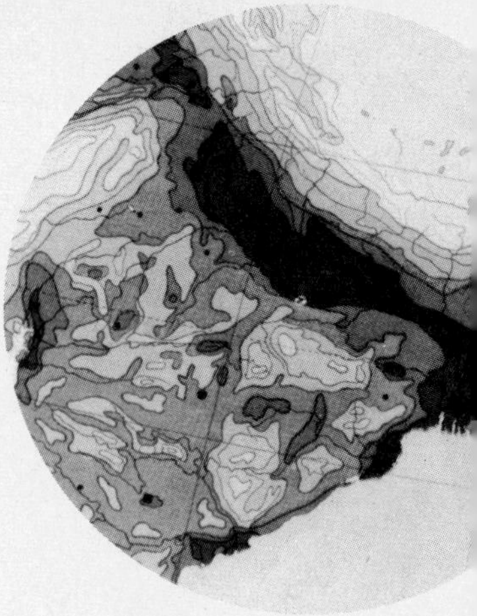

particularly useful in the middle grades
and above in illustrating relationships between the terrain and man's use of the
land. For example, the small number of
larger cities in mountainous regions is readily apparent on a physical-political map.

Small inset maps frequently are
printed on the bottom of a wall map to
provide information on such matters as
rainfall, vegetation, thermal regions, and
population distribution. Such inset maps
are useful for individual or small-group
use in that they can readily be related to
the larger map. The main purpose of such
maps, however, often is to fill up space
when the large map is much wider than it
is high, as is true of some world map projections. Thus, though inset maps are a kind
of information bonus and as such are
doubtless of some benefit, an atlas or textbook special-purpose map is more convenient and practical for detailed individual
map study.

SPECIAL-PURPOSE MAPS Many different types of maps tailored to specialized
teaching purposes are now available. Some

of these maps are closely related to such
basic geographic concepts as climate, rainfall, vegetation, population distribution,
natural resources (see Figure 7.21). Others
relate to commercial, historical, literary,
scientific, and foreign language subjects.
The profusion and quality of special-purpose maps reflect the significant role that
maps and map-reading play in a whole
range of important economic, political, and
cultural concepts. Maps can be vehicles for
the communication of many kinds of information. Once the basic requirements for
globes and for local, state, national, and
world physical and political wall maps have
been met, the teacher will want to explore
the many interesting and stimulating possibilities to be found in special-purpose maps.

DESK MAPS Desk maps have many uses
for individual study and project work and
thus serve a quite different function from
wall maps. Wall maps should be thought of
as "pointer" devices. That is, a wall map is
not intended to serve every purpose for
which maps are needed. Rather, a wall map
is a sharing resource; with it, the teacher

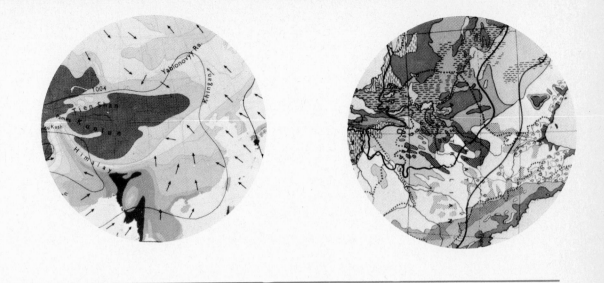

or students can point out to others in the room essential and important aspects of whatever the map emphasizes. Accordingly, wall maps should be used for general observation and discussion of prominent features, while maps in an atlas or text serve better for detailed study and desk maps for individual project activities.

Desk maps are now available in many sizes and types. The most familiar are outline maps, either with or without physical features, of areas ranging from a township or county to the world (see Figure 7.22). Colored maps such as the large-scale ones provided for most regions of the United States by the U.S. Geological Survey are also valuable for individual study. Reusable plastic relief maps on which students can work with marking pencils are now available in sets, along with programed and other self-instruction materials in coordinated multimedia learning packages.

Desirable characteristics of wall maps

Most wall maps are attractive in appearance, and this is certainly to be desired.

Less obvious but of greater importance in teaching and learning are such factors as adequate size and visibility, legibility, suitability to grade level, and effective use of color.

ADEQUATE SIZE AND VISIBILITY Wall maps are visualizations designed to present complete or partial global surface information on a single flat surface. Wall maps of the world make it possible to sense key geographical, physical, or political concepts which would be less visible on a globe.

In order to be useful in classroom situations, wall maps must be so designed and of such size that students seated normally about the room can see and "read" the important relationships revealed by the map. Important symbols, shapes, names of gross land and water masses, and key terrain phenomena must be presented effectively so as to be visible and understandable to all viewers. The amount of information contained on any given map is also closely related to its suitability to grade level. Ordinarily, world maps need to be larger than maps of continents or smaller areas.

FIGURE 7.22

Adequate size is somewhat dependent on the size of the classroom, but world maps 7 feet or more in width are not uncommon, and 5 to 6 feet is probably the minimum for most classrooms.

LEGIBILITY Wall maps that are over-crowded with information may be difficult to read from more than a few feet away. Such maps obviously tend to defeat their purpose as wall maps. On wall maps the names of continents, countries, and oceans should be in large type, suitably spaced so as to make reading them possible anywhere in the seating area. The same is true of the lines representing important boundaries, rivers, and bodies of water and of the symbols representing key cities, mountains, and other permanent topographical features. The comment of a noted cartographer and geographer is as valid today as when he wrote it a half-century ago: "Insofar as any data on a map cannot be grasped by the eye, and easily read, in just that measure is the map encumbered with useless material, and is a failure."[11]

The relative size of printing used on wall maps and charts is accordingly one important criterion for map selection. An authoritative study has shown that 2-inch letters at 30 feet appear the same as letters $\frac{1}{9}$ inch high (about the height of the letter *h* on this line) at a normal reading distance of 18 inches. Letters $\frac{1}{2}$ inch in height require above-average vision to be read at 20 feet.[12] Of course other factors than type size also influence legibility—among them background contrast, variations in type design, and the crowding of elements, as mentioned.

Though a good wall map can be versa-

11 J. Paul Goode, *Goode's School Atlas,* Rand McNally, 1918.

12 Arthur Robinson, "The Size of Lettering for Maps and Charts," *Surveying and Mapping,* January–March 1950, pp. 37–44.

Desk maps of various types are a means of ensuring direct student involvement in meaningful map use. They also are useful for evaluating students' understanding of many concepts in physical geography.

tile enough to serve a number of purposes, there should be enough maps of continents and nations and special-purpose maps available so that no one map has to be used for purposes for which it was not designed. For example, a world map should not be used for the study of Europe or the United States, for if it includes enough information to be useful for that purpose, it is probably too crowded for effective use as a map of the world.

SUITABILITY TO GRADE LEVEL The level of the information presented on a wall map is closely related in importance to its visibility and legibility. As we have noted, globes and maps have a language of

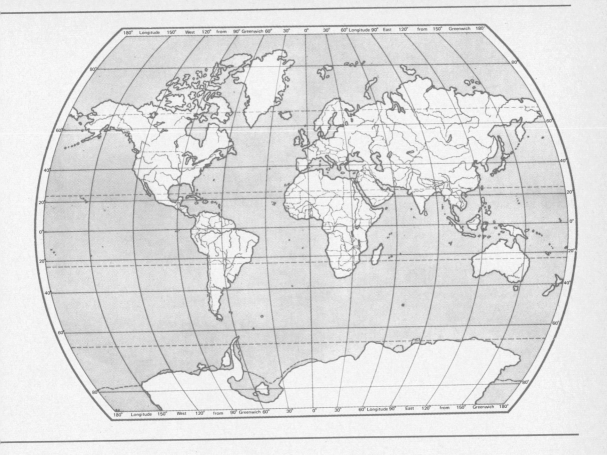

their own which must be learned, just as one must learn how to read words, sentences, and paragraphs. No teacher would think of using an eighth-grade reading book with a second-grade class, yet too often we still find the same or similar map and globe materials being used in both upper and lower grades. Instead, there should be distinct differences in the globes and maps used with beginners and with intermediate and advanced students. Thus we need to be aware of and to examine the many graded map materials now available from map and globe companies for primary, intermediate, and higher grades. The four maps in Plates 7.3–7.6, following page 356, readily show the differences in complexity between maps intended for beginning and intermediate levels.

EFFECTIVE COLOR   As on globes, the use of color is important on wall maps from several standpoints. One of these is esthetic, but more important is the effect of color on readability. On the whole, coloration that provides good legibility as well as pleasing appearance is the objective to be sought. Lighter shades are usually more satisfactory than deep primary colors. Map companies tend to avoid heavy or brilliant coloration, although the colors used on beginners' maps are brighter than on these for higher levels because primary children respond well to bright, cheerful colors.

Color and shading are important, also, in making maps easier to interpret. Historical maps that show the extent of various empires that included a specific area at different times are one example.

Supplementary map materials

Because course opportunities for map applications are so extensive and varied, it would be impracticable for any classroom to have all of the wall and desk maps necessary to fill all requirements. One answer is a stock of supplementary maps in the instructional resources center. Another is ready access to inexpensive and versatile outline and special-project maps which can serve a variety of purposes.

There are three primary types of useful supplementary map materials which combine some of the advantages of both wall and desk maps. That is, they can be viewed by an entire class, but many of them can be traced or filled in by the pupils themselves in the course of discussion or study activities—normally a distinctive advantage of desk maps. These supplementary map materials are projected maps, slated wall outline maps, and chalkboard stencil maps.

PROJECTED MAPS   An important development in projected map materials is the large number of transparencies available for the overhead projector (see Figure 7.23). Many of these transparencies have overlays which permit the teacher more readily to show relationships or to build sequential concepts. (See also Figure 10.15 on page 410). They are available in a wide range of topics in geography, history, earth science, geology, astronomy, meteorology, and mathematics; in format they range from simple outline maps and charts to full-color maps comparable to wall maps.

Such transparencies have two distinct advantages over maps projected from an atlas or reference book by means of an

FIGURE 7.23

These examples of some of the many map transparencies available emphasize size comparisons of the seven continents and the United States; all are drawn to the same scale.

opaque projector or from homemade photographic slides. The first and most important is that the lettering on such maps has been designed for projection; the lettering on book maps is too small for projection purposes because different-size ratios are necessary for lettering that is to be projected. The second advantage is that any room-darkening problem is minimized.

Projected maps have these advantages: they make a considerable number and variety of maps available at low cost; they provide whatever enlargement may be needed for class use; with transparent overlays, they have versatility in use by the instructor or student.

SLATED WALL OUTLINE MAPS   Teachers know that pupils learn by doing, that directed pupil activity is necessary for

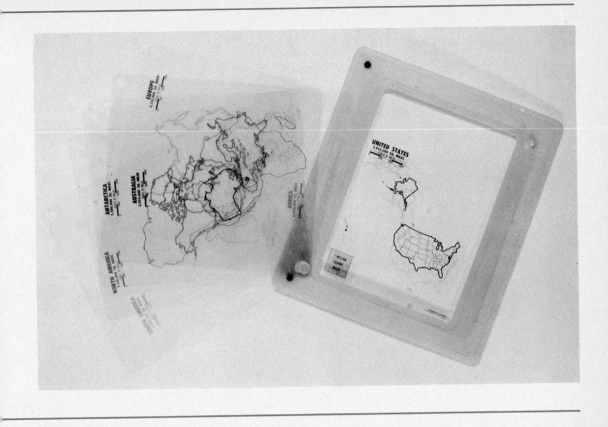

"fixing" concepts in their minds. Teachers also know that complex ideas must be built up step by step, with each step simply and clearly defined. The slated wall outline map is helpful in applying both of these teaching principles. The instructor can draw one thing at a time on a slated map without the class being distracted by extraneous details. Further, as teachers well know, group interest is greatly heightened when one member of the class goes to the wall map and chalks in a name, outlines an area, or traces an important parallel or trade route under the watchful eye of the rest of the class. Like the modern chalkboard, slated maps are made attractive by the use of color. A slated outline world map and a slated globe on the same scale provide an excellent combination for teaching important area and location concepts.

CHALKBOARD STENCIL MAPS An interesting and inexpensive addition to a school's map materials is a chalkboard stencil map. This is a wall map that has perforation along local, state, and/or national boundaries (see Figure 7.24). Chalkboard stencil maps can be used in much the same way as slated wall maps. The stencil map is particularly useful when the classroom teacher feels it is desirable to have a number of pupils at the board at the same time, because as many maps can be stenciled on the chalkboard as space permits. It also is convenient when the instructor wishes to present an additional illustration or two without disturbing work already on a slated map. Chalkboard stencil maps can be made rather easily from inexpensive window shades; a few stencil maps are available commercially.

FIGURE 7.24

To make and use a stencil map from a window shade or heavy paper, first trace or draw the outline of the map on the material. Then (a) punch holes with a leather punch about 1 inch apart along the outline; (b) hold the stencil firmly against the chalkboard and rub a dusty eraser over the perforations (c) check the outline before removing the stencil; (d) connect the outline of dots with a solid chalk line.

Effective teaching with maps and globes

BECAUSE the world is becoming increasingly complex in its political, cultural, and technological relationships, it is increasingly important that today's pupils fully grasp the concepts involved in map and globe use. As the geographer and educator Lorrin Kennamer, Jr., has put it:

Speed of travel, mass communication, mobility of people—all are aspects of the modern world which are continually expanding our personal horizons. In one sense, the world is not shrinking; it is getting larger and larger in terms of each individual's contact with other peoples, other cultures, other areas. It is this enlarging personal world that necessitates the development of a sense of place and space. It is to the social studies that we must turn for the development of the skills necessary to equip each citizen with a global framework and with the ability to use this framework. Maps and globes are the vehicles whereby we travel with our students into realms beyond our immediate horizons.[13]

Thus, assuming an adequate supply of good globes and maps, we must proceed to the next, even more important, step: we must consider seriously how to *use* them to best advantage so that our pupils can learn both to read and interpret them properly. One important teaching principle is: start with the pupil where he *is*. Closely related principles were emphasized earlier in connection with teaching students to read graphs and diagrams and other symbolic materials—that is, before symbols of any kind can be internalized, pupils must have *a background of experience which can give these symbols meaning*. In the rest of this chapter, we deal with suggestions for developing initial map-reading readiness and some materials and techniques which teachers have found effective at the primary, intermediate and upper elementary levels and at the secondary levels.

Developing map-reading readiness in the primary grades

Where *is* the child so far as globes and maps are concerned? What is he familiar with that the teacher can use as a basis for beginning to teach him globes and maps? In developing map skills in the primary grades, it is important to base the geographical-readiness program on the immediate environment:

Geographers agree that children should not be faced with a symbol on a map which does not bring to mind an image of the reality for which it stands. Elementary pupils need carefully graded and appropriately sampled experiences in observing real landscapes in the immediate world around them. They must be given opportunity to think over, discuss, and relate what they have seen. They must be allowed to map what they themselves have seen and discussed, and to read simple maps made by others for which they now have adequate images.[14]

The pupil's home and yard, his immediate neighborhood, the way to school, his schoolroom, the school yard, and perhaps other parts of the community where his class has gone on a field trip—all provide solid bases for building an initial conceptual framework for understanding geography generally. For example, in a successful experiment some years ago, which has been replicated many times since then, one class of very young children were

[13] Lorrin Kennamer, Jr., "Developing a Sense of Place and Space," op. cit., p. 169.

[14] Rose Sabaroff, "Firsthand Experiences in Geography for Second-Graders," *Journal of Geography*, September 1958, p. 306.

started out with a sound learning experience of this nature:

Children begin early and without direction to represent places they have seen by representing them with blocks or other materials. After a Buffalo kindergarten class had visited the Peace Bridge, the children built a model of the bridge across the classroom. They were able to tell which end of their bridge represented the Canada end and which represented the end near their school. They pointed out where the river flowed beneath the bridge.[15]

The importance of observation and field trips to nearby areas for young children is universally stressed as a basis for building initial geographical concepts. In other words, true geography can neither be taught to nor learned by young children

[15] Kathryn Whittemore, ''Maps,'' in *Geographic Approaches to a Social Education,* 19th Yearbook, National Council for the Social Studies, 1948, p. 120.

without constant reference to their own completely understood home area.

By the time they are in the third grade, most children are ready to participate in making pictorial maps of familiar sections. The harbor as they saw it will be faithfully reproduced, with ships, docks, and lighthouse likely to be drawn realistically (see Figure 7.25). Perspective and scale may be crude or absent, but, nonetheless, such maps show the beginning of a feeling for relative size, location, and distance. Providing experiences that naturally give rise to pictorial murals and maps is a good way to begin formal map work. Before long, symbols can be introduced to represent streets, buildings, important landmarks, and topographical features. The new meanings will take shape through appropriate application of standard geographical terms. Figure 7.26 shows a three-dimensional labeled representation of topographical features that helps the student in comprehending such terms as *plateau, desert,* and *piedmont.*

FIGURE 7.25

This map of Los Angeles Harbor was made by primary pupils after a field trip. What educational benefits do you see in this kind of map activity?

FIGURE 7.26

The language of maps involves learning many geographical terms, such as those painted on this three-dimensional representation of topographical features.

Pictures also play a vital part in map-reading readiness. They can help interpret and generalize concepts acquired from field trips and they can open large areas of the earth to observation which would otherwise be impractical to observe. Early concepts of land surfaces and climate can be developed and generalized through pictures and films. Charts are available which combine pictures with large-scale maps of small areas to illustrate the meaning of various map symbols (see Plates 7.1 and 7.2, following page 356). There are many specific ways of using pictures to teach map concepts and to lead directly into the use of globes and maps. The use of pictures with maps can help children to "see" the relationships on the maps.

A globe is also an essential part of the map-reading readiness program. Not only are all flat maps derived originally from the globe, but it is by all odds the best medium for developing a true idea of the earth's sphericity. The importance of having a globe constantly at hand is obvious, for a globe is essential in acquiring such concepts as the earth's rotation, the explanation for day and night, the poles, the meaning of direction, and the large proportion of the earth's surface which is covered by water.

A noted geographer, Henry Warman, makes a strong case for the development of world and universe concepts at the same time as we are developing the relationships of the near, the small, and the local community to larger areas and to the world as a whole. He points to the need for the development of a "one-worldism, a globalism, even a multi-globalism" conceptual framework as a major need for the solution of man's problems now and in the future. He concurs with the merit and logic of starting to build young children's geographic concepts from where they are, but he also observes that through the communications media, young children, youth, and adults alike are also being made aware of significant events throughout the world. He continues:

Global happenings as well as local events are not only heard about soon after their occurrence but frequently are also seen as they are occurring. The global probings, the space experiments, the preparations and actual performances in recent and coming months are cases in point. To this writer there seems to be strong evidence to support and vital reasons for introducing the far along with the near in relating the big more closely to the small. . . . *And why can we not keep head, eyes, and ears attuned to the universe, while we keep hands and heart attuned to the immediate?*[16]

Among a number of helpful suggestions on how globalism and related ideas can be dealt with effectively at various grade levels, Warman points to the fact that it

is not too soon in the primary grades to stress cleanliness in all its facets and also its opposite—pollution :

On trips to high vantage points as well as on photographs, man's smogging of the air his clogging of the water with germs and filth may be pointed out. To-day's pupils will not escape these pollution problems. Increasingly the disposal of waste materials of the globe's inhabitants looms larger as a major problem. Into which sphere is the waste to be cast —air, water, or land? Here is an opportunity to blend a topic in a local small area, single "habitat" studies, with the same topic in the global region of earth inhabitants.[17]

For primary rooms, the globes used should be simple ones—one a slated globe

[16] Henry J. Warman, "Globalism: A Concept and Its Development," *Journal of Geography*, January 1970, p. 10.

[17] Ibid., p. 12.

FIGURE 7.27

Two students examine a planetarium model that helps explain day and night, phases of the moon, and various other astronomical phenomena.

on which the teacher can write and which shows primarily the land and water areas, and another a simplified cradled globe which can be lifted out and handled by the pupils. One use of the cradled globe suggested by Warman is to take it outside in the morning, at noon, and in the afternoon and position it so that the local area is facing the sun. Then pose the questions, "Did the sun really rise in the east, cross the sky, and then set in the west?" "Or could it be that the sun is 'fixed' in its position and the earth, especially that part where the class is standing, went around to meet the sun?"[18] The rotation and revolution concepts can also be introduced by shadow casting, as illustrated in Figure 7.27.

The colors on beginners' globes are used to differentiate major regional, national, and surface features rather than subtle gradations in elevation, sea depths, and the like. Such globes are often paired with simplified flat maps of identical coloration so as to facilitate the transition from reading globes to initial reading of flat maps. School map companies are applying these principles in special multimedia kits of materials including special globes, maps, study prints, and desk maps of various types. There are special programs for map-reading readiness, the teaching of geographical terms and concepts, space science programs, earth science programs, history projects, and others. Some of these programs are self-contained, and most of them have been designed to meet specific learning objectives. The materials and suggested activities typically provide for substantial student involvement. The extent to which such programs have been validated in Instructional Development terms is probably limited, but there is little question that such programs are an improvement over what teachers and pupils have previously had to work with.

Developing skills and applications in the intermediate grades

In the fourth, fifth, and sixth grades, globe- and map-reading skills are developed at a more advanced level. Systematic instruction includes regular *use* of globes and maps, plus increased development of skill in reading them. History and geography are brought together in meaningful contexts, each reinforcing the other and establishing an initial basis for a better understanding of why people live where and how they do today.

It is in these middle grades that physical-political globes and maps are introduced. When North and South America and the other areas of the earth are studied in the fifth and sixth grades, the globe should be used regularly to establish and to maintain correct concepts of relative location, size, and climatic influences. Continuous cross-reference between maps and globes is emphasized at this level and should become habitual. During this period, the student also needs to learn the use of legends and color keys in order to interpret maps and globes which may not have matching coloration, since most maps he sees after this time are apt to vary in the colors used.

As still more maps are used, the *scale* assumes significance, and its meanings must also be taught in order to avoid misconceptions. The ability to approximate locations in terms of latitude and longitude, plus a comprehension of scale applications at different latitudes, enables the pupil to begin to make meaningful comparisons among different countries and to assimilate related concepts. He may discover such fundamental facts as, for example, that Japan, which has more than six times as many people as California, has about the same area. Such discoveries stimulate questions and set the stage for further meaningful learning.

Although both subject content and map-reading skills are more complex in the

[18] Ibid., p. 11.

middle grades than they are in the earlier grades, the teacher should not overlook the importance of providing *motivation* and *opportunities* to learn by doing. One fifth-grade teacher utilized both these principles when he asked his class, "Have you made your vacation plans?" A flurry of hands shot up.

"I'm going to camp in Maine!" exclaimed one pupil.

"We're driving to Yellowstone Park," volunteered another.

"My dad wants to go to the Lake of the Woods and fish, but Mother wants to go to the Gaspé Peninsula instead, so I think we're going there!" said a third, grinning.

Out of the enthusiasm of anticipation, a series of useful writing, reading, and story-telling activities were developed. The location of destinations and routes of travel brought into use maps of the state, the United States, and numerous road and historical maps as the students became involved in their families' vacation plans.

One valuable application of "learning by doing" is to have pupils make maps of their own. This is excellent for developing both map-reading ability and the power to interpret the data on maps. When a child makes his own map by plotting data on a base map, he not only receives training in observation, but he also begins to acquire a fuller understanding of maps as a medium of communication. A simple example would be to trace one's route from home to school on an outline map of the immediate area; another would be to locate polluting drainage outlets that empty into a stream on a map of the local area. There are many useful applications of this technique, but it is important here to distinguish between mere copying exercises and creative map construction. While there may be certain values in transferring the 13 colonies from a textbook map to a desk outline map, this should not be confused

with actual map construction or the learning values that come from it.

Relief maps of a local area provide an excellent basis for understanding surface features of the area and the physical and elevation symbols used on physical maps. These three-dimensional maps can easily be made by the teacher and pupils. U.S. Geological Survey topographical maps, which are available for most local areas, should be used, along with firsthand observation, for accurate construction. One method of construction is illustrated and briefly described in Figure 7.20 and on page 297. Several others give satisfactory results.[19] The great value of this type of map is that it is considerably more realistic than any flat map and, accordingly, can be very valuable in giving meaning to the physical symbols on flat maps. When students make a relief map of their own locality or country that is big enough for them to walk on and around, there are particular advantages in group cooperation while the map is being made and group learning afterwards (see Figure 7.28).

We should emphasize again that the pupil's creative and inventive use of maps and globes is of great importance. Once he understands these instruments, he should be encouraged to use them and even to create needed adaptations of them as he becomes more adept in communicating geographical ideas and concepts to teachers and classmates.

Developing interpretive abilities in the secondary school

A wide variety of maps and globes is essential at the secondary level where na-

[19] For details of a simple method of constructing a plastic relief map, see Ralph C. Preston, *Teaching Social Studies in the Elementary School*, Holt, Rinehart and Winston, 2nd ed., 1968, pp. 284–288, 349–351. See also the *Student Production Guide*.

FIGURE 7.28

What learning opportunities are possible as these Indian pupils study and work with and on this relief map of their country? Could you adapt this project to help pupils understand their own locality?

tional and world concepts are developed on a broad scale. By this time, though the student should have learned to interpret maps as well as to "read" them, this ability cannot be taken for granted. All too frequently he will have missed something along the line, perhaps because one of his earlier teachers was not well enough trained. As an example, students and teachers alike are frequently unfamiliar with how to read directions on maps that have curved meridians or parallels, as many maps now do. The relationship between the grid and directions on maps is implied, but is often not presented clearly in textbooks for any level from elementary to college.[20] In any case, map-reading—like English and spelling—is the responsibility of teachers at all levels. If the secondary school pupil lacks basic map-reading skills, he must

be taught them before he can proceed successfully.

In the junior high school, new concepts must be learned, such as the equinoxes and solstices, time zones (see Figure 7.29), the international date line, and great-circle routes. Globes are essential for teaching such concepts, and slated globes are particularly helpful for related pupil exercises. At the junior and senior high school levels numerous special-purpose maps containing economic, historical, and literary data are used regularly, in addition to physical-political maps and globes. Before completing senior high school, a student should have become adept at both reading and interpreting a variety of maps and globes. If he is fortunate, his teachers in various subjects will use maps effectively themselves and will recognize the continuing need to help him improve his ability to the point where he is as much at home with maps as he is with books.

As with all other forms of media and materials, the good teacher selects and uses

[20] See Joseph A. Hazel, "Most 'Good' Maps Do Not Have a Directional Symbol," *Journal of Geography,* February 1965, p. 83.

FIGURE 7.29

The sophisticated concepts of time and space become enormously important in the Space Age. The students' understanding of them begins with comprehension of day and night, the time zones on earth, and why we measure time as we do.

the globes and maps that achieve his purposes better than any others available to him. He uses them in combination with such other materials as textbooks, reference books, atlases, flat pictures, slides, films, film loops, filmstrips, field trips, study displays, and desk outline maps—according to the needs of his class. He recognizes that these materials are means rather than ends in themselves—means to gaining a clear and vital understanding of the geographical, social, and cultural concepts that give meaning to the world we live in.

Summary

Globes and maps are a vital part of the school's instructional materials because they are the only means by which large areas of the earth, or the earth itself, can be effectively represented. Although globes are the only true maps of the earth, flat projections are necessary for detailed study, for ease of viewing, and for seeing the whole earth at one time.

Appropriate globes for teaching purposes include simplified political globes for beginners, slated globes, and physical-political globes. Simplicity, size, visibility, and color considerations are important in selecting globes. Several sizes and mountings are available. Although most globes cannot be read from a distance of more than a few feet, there are advantages in using globes 16 inches in diameter or larger rather than smaller ones.

Flat maps of the world are unavoidably inaccurate in two or more of the following properties of the globe: areas, shapes, directions, and distances. For most school purposes, good area representation is of primary importance in preventing basic misconceptions. It is necessary, therefore, that the teacher be able to determine whether small-scale maps of large areas have good area representation. He can do this visually by comparing the map grid with the grid on a globe in terms of four characteristics of the globe grid.

Additional factors in evaluating flat maps are adequate size, legibility, and color. Maps for beginners should be simplified, larger than is commonly the case, and colored so as to enhance both legibility and attractiveness.

In summary, the primary considerations in the selection of wall maps are:

1   *Equal-area projection is important for avoiding gross misconceptions on world maps or maps of a hemisphere; the type of projection is relatively unimportant for maps of smaller areas.*
2   *Maps should be suited to grade levels in terms of complexity and amount of information contained.*
3   *Larger wall maps should be preferred to smaller ones in any instance.*
4   *Coloration should contribute to map legibility; its use for esthetic reasons is a secondary consideration.*

Valuable supplementary map and globe materials for group and individual instruction include commerical map slides and transparencies, slated wall outline maps, and chalkboard stencil outline maps. Plastic relief maps and pupil-made large-scale relief maps of local areas are of much value in teaching map-reading, as are a number of the special multimedia programs now available from map companies.

Effective use of maps and globes is based on map-reading readiness; this is developed in the primary grades through extensive observation of the local environment and early experience with globes and global concepts. The use of pictures and, later, of motion pictures and other instructional materials gives important meaning and visual imagery to maps and globes.

Systematic instruction in geographical concepts and in reading globes and maps begins in the third or fourth grade and continues thereafter. Geography instruction today incorporates history and cultural concepts to the end of promoting better understanding of the peoples of the earth. The ability to *interpret* maps, above and beyond the essential ability to read them, is vital to the development of this understanding.

Further learner response projects

1

Prepare a simple test on map-reading and give it to the media class. Include such items as the following:
a   *Alaska is nearly as large as the United States. (True or false?)*
b   *Greenland is larger than Mexico. (True or false?)*
c   *Name six countries that the 40th parallel runs through.*
d   *In what general direction is Moscow from Chicago?*
e   *Which of the following is the most di-* *rect route from San Francisco to Japan?*
   (1)   Westward via the Hawaiian Islands
   (2)   Westward, but slightly north of the Hawaiian Islands
   (3)   Northwestward along the Alaskan coast and the Aleutian Islands
   (4)   Northward and nearly over the North Pole
Have the students check their own papers and discuss the implications of the errors that were made.

2

Examine catalogs from several map and globe companies and select specific globes and wall maps for use in one of the following:
a   A primary room
b   An intermediate or middle-grade classroom

c   A social studies room in senior high school
d   An adult class in world affairs
Be ready to state the reasons for your selections.

3

Examine your local newspapers, magazines, and even the books you are using to see how widely maps and globes actually are

used in our daily lives. Be alert for ideas and materials that you can use in teaching.

4

Send for some or all of the following materials to add to your media library:
Map Projection Studies (free); *Toward Better Understanding of Maps, Globes, and Charts* (free); *The Place of Maps in Current Events* (free); all from Denoyer-Geppert, 5235 Ravenswood Avenue, Chicago, Illinois 60640.
Guide to Effective Globe Usage ($2.95); *Learning To Use a Map* ($1.95); both from A. J. Nystrom & Company, 3333 Elston Avenue, Chicago, Illinois 60618.

Handbook of Map and Globe Usage ($2.96), Rand McNally & Company, School Department, Box 7600, Chicago, Illinois 60680.
The Use of an Atlas by Harold Fullard (free), Aldine Publishing Company, 529 South Wabash, Chicago, Illinois 60605.
Exploring Space with a Camera ($4.25), Superintendent of Documents, Government Printing Office, Washington, D.C. 20402.

References

BACON, PHILLIP. "A Way To Teach Children To Use the Globe." *Grade Teacher,* October 1964, pp. 66–67.

BACON, PHILLIP, ed. *Focus on Geography: Key Concepts and Teaching Strategies,* 40th Yearbook. National Council for the Social Studies, 1970.

BARTZ, BARBARA S. "Maps in the Classroom." *Journal of Geography,* January 1970, pp. 18–24.

CARPENTER, HELEN MCCRACKEN, ed. *Skill Development in Social Studies,* 33rd Yearbook. National Council for the Social Studies, 1963.

DAHLBERG, RICHARD E. "The Elements of a Map." *Journal of Geography,* December 1969, pp. 527–534.

DANDO, WILLIAM A., *et al.* "New Developments

in Educational Cartography." *Journal of Geography,* April 1970, pp. 204–212.

EdCom Systems, Inc. *The 30-Inch Contoured Relief Globe—An Educational Innovation.* Princeton, N.J.: EdCom Systems, Inc., 1969. (Contact also for information on Global Learning Systems.)

EDIGER, MARLOW. "Locating Places on Maps and Globes." *Journal of Geography,* March 1969, p. 161.

ERHART, RAINER R., and DAVID S. MELLANDEG. "Experiences with an Audio-Visual-Tutorial Laboratory." *Journal of Geography,* February 1961, pp. 88–92.

GRITZNER, CHARLES F. "Sources of Map Information." *Journal of Geography,* March 1970, pp. 141–146.

HARTOCH, SISTER DONNA. "Social Studies Is a

Tribal Affair." *Grade Teacher,* September 1969, pp. 103–107.

HAZEL, JOSEPH A. "Most 'Good' Maps Do Not Have a Directional Symbol." *Journal of Geography,* February 1965, pp. 81–83.

HUNTER, JOHN M., and MELINDA S. MEADE. "Population Models in the High School." *Journal of Geography,* February 1971, pp. 95–105.

JAMES, PRESTON E. "The Significance of Geography in American Education." *Journal of Geography,* November 1969, pp. 473–483.

KELMAN, HERBERT C. "Education for the Concept of a Global Society." *Social Education,* 32:7 (November 1968).

KENNAMER, LORRIN, JR. "Developing a Sense of Place and Space." in Skill Development in the Social Studies, 33rd Yearbook. National Council for the Social Studies, 1963, pp. 148–169.

KENNAMER, LORRIN, JR. "Emerging Social Studies Curricula: Implications for Geography." In *Focus on Geography: Key Concepts and Teaching Strategies,* 40th Yearbook. National Council for the Social Studies, 1970, pp. 388–391.

KINGSBURY, ROBERT C. "Comparing Maps and Aerial Photographs." *Journal of Geography,* October 1969, pp. 426–429.

LAWRENCE, MARGARET. "Making a Reusable Wall Map." *Instructor,* October 1970, pp. 135–136.

MARINE, HELEN. "Using Audiovisuals in Map Reading Readiness Instruction." *Audiovisual Instruction,* January 1968, pp. 48–50.

MCCUNE, SHANO. "Geography: Where? Why? So What?" *Journal of Geography,* November 1970, pp. 454–457.

MCDERMOTT, PAUL D. "What Is a Map?" *Journal of Geography,* November 1969, pp. 465–472.

MCKINNEY, WILLIAM M. "The Globe." *Journal of Geography,* October 1969, pp. 406–410.

MONK, JAMES. "Our Giant Map." *Instructor,* August 1970, p. 98.

MORRIS, DONALD N., and EDITH W. KING. "Bringing Spaceship Earth into Elementary Classrooms." *Social Education,* Vol. 7, November 1968, pp. 675–680.

POH, LING CHU. "The Teaching of Contours." *Journal of Geography,* November 1969, pp. 484–490.

RIFFEL, PAUL A. "A New Approach to Teaching Map Reading." *Journal of Geography,* December 1969, pp. 554–556.

SAVAGE, TOM V., and PHILLIP BACON. "Teaching Symbolic Map Skills with Primary Grade Children." *Journal of Geography,* November 1969, pp. 491–497.

STEWARD, H. J. "Map Projections: Approaches and Themes." *Journal of Geography,* October 1970, pp. 390–400.

WARMAN, HENRY J. "Globalism: A Concept and Its Development." *Journal of Geography,* January 1970, pp. 6–17.

WINTERS, HAROLD A., and VON DEL CHAMBERLAIN. "The Planetarium in Teaching Physical Geography." *Journal of Geography,* February 1970, pp. 77–82.

Media references

Continents of the World, 16mm film, color, 11 min. Coronet Films, 1969.

Earth: Man's Home, 16mm film, color, 10 min. WBEC, 1970.

Globes, Their Function in the Classroom, 16mm film, color, 14 min. Bailey Film Associates, 1961.

Map Reading: Its Development in Cartovues, transparency series, Denoyer-Geppert, 1969.

Map Skills: Recognizing Physical Features, 16mm film, color, 11 min. Coronet Films, 1969.

Mapping the Earth's Surface, 16mm film, color, 16 min. Coronet Films, 1969.

Maps Add Meaning to History, 16mm film, color, 11 min. Coronet Films, 1969.

Maps and How To Use Them, 35mm filmstrips. Eye Gate House, 1958. Series includes:
    Elements of Maps, 28 frames.
    Flat Maps of a Round World, 31 frames.
    Maps for Air Age, 39 frames.
    Maps for Special Purposes, 36 frames.
    Maps of Physical Features, 37 frames.
    Maps Through the Ages, 39 frames.
    The Globe, 31 frames.

Using Common Maps, 29 frames.
Using the Globe, 36 frames.
What a Map Is, 25 frames.
Maps—Land Symbols and Terms, 16mm film, color, 14 min. Academy, 1967.

Plains and Plateaus, 16mm film, color, 10 min. NET, 1968.
World Population: 1000 B.C. *to 1965* A.D., 16mm film, color, 4 min. Film Productions, Southern Illinois University, 1965.

Source references

See source lists in the Appendix; particularly relevant sections are: Free and Inexpensive Materials; Maps, Globes, and Supplies; Planetariums.

See *Student Production Guide,* Chapter 3, "Graphics Techniques for Instructional Materials Production" and Chapter 4, "Producing Photo and Sound Materials for Instruction," for pertinent sections, including suggestions on making 3-D maps of local areas.

EIGHT
Audio recording and playback

Objectives

Performance responses

1

To identify several types of audiotape recording devices and demonstrate one's ability to use them by recording and playing back audio information or a performance.

Demonstrate your ability to record and play back situations produced in small groups, taking into account environmental sounds, pickup conditions, and individual audio situations. Evaluate by referring to the criteria on pages 333–336.

2

To acquire understandings about the instructional usefulness of such audio playback and retrieval systems as open-reel, cassette, card-type, and special-use recording and playback equipment.

Demonstrate your grasp of the instructional uses of audio recording and playback situations by originating teaching examples with one or more of the following: open-reel, cassette, or card-type recordings and playback. Use the criteria on pages 333–336.

3

To gain insights and understandings about the interrelationship between audio learning instructional materials and the six learning tenets described in Chapter 2, pages 46–74.

Demonstrate how audio instructional learning experiences may be employed most profitably as one creates and uses such audio experiences as the following: open-reel, cassette, or card-type recordings and playback. Evaluate your outcomes by measuring them in terms of the six learning tenets described in Chapter 2, pages 46–74.

HISTORIANS, scientists, musicians, teachers, lawyers, and countless others for years dreamed about and longed for the ability to capture and re-examine words, music, and other auditory manifestations of human or natural activity. Today, of course, this ability is a reality. For example, each word of direction spoken by control tower personnel and each audible response of men or machines during the flight of any commercial jet aircraft is recorded, stored, and made available for later replay and study. Space engineers rely on total recording and playback for study and evaluation of every audible phase of human response during space flights. Engineers and scientists use similar procedures to reconstruct and evaluate the nature of past actions or performances of human beings and machines and from such analyses they are able to formulate better plans and procedures for the future.

Now such machinery is available to every teacher who undertakes to understand its functions and possibilities sufficiently to use it in his own classroom, that is, to use tape-recording equipment and related playback techniques or equipment. In this chapter we investigate the nature and uses of audiotape recording and playback, both tape and disc techniques.

The audiotape recorder is a kind of mechanical memory which, when used skillfully, is capable of capturing and recording every sound wave that strikes the face of its sensitive mechanical "ear," the microphone. It is a complete "listening post"

—it does not delete or screen out anything during the recording process This last quality sometimes surprises teachers who use a tape recorder: often the mechanical "ear" picks up and records sounds—street noises, hallway disturbances, or even whisperings—of which the teacher was quite unaware. How this can be avoided is described later.

Used wisely, audio recording and playback can virtually create an "assistant teacher" which will communicate information tirelessly and dependably while the human teacher is busy humanizing and personalizing instruction. Many learning information situations can be recorded, for example, suggestions made by community resource visitors to the classroom and the responses of individuals or small groups of pupils. The tape recorder is useful in organizing and reporting important information or in developing how-to-do-it procedures for use by fellow students. Evaluations by students of fellow students' performances of oral reading of poetry or prose, speaking a foreign language, extemporaneous speaking, singing, instrumental music, and dramatic interpretations represent unique recording, playback, and evaluating learning experiences provided by means of tape recorders.

To make possible the effective use by learners and teachers of such audio recording and playback experiences, suitable equipment must be carefully selected and certain skills must be acquired, as now described.

Types of audio recorders

RECORDING equipment is designed to accomplish tasks that vary in complexity. A moderately priced medium fidelity audio recorder fills most of the needs in a small classroom where individuals or small groups use the equipment. However, a small-group recorder and its inexpensive microphone could not be expected to record with the degree of fidelity—the quality of reproducing sounds which are identical to, or at least comparable to, the original—needed to record and play back the performance of a choral speaking group, a chorus, or a band.

The intricacies of audiorecording performance as measured in terms of the electronic engineer's standards—frequency response (hertz), output (decibels), and wave form (fidelity)—are not discussed here, as most teachers do not need this technical knowledge. What the teacher does need to do is decide exactly why, how, and where the equipment is to be used and the nature of the learning goals it is to be used to accomplish. Equipped with such a list of conditions and desired functions, he should then seek the advice and counsel of the media specialist or a local tape-recorder dealer about the best kind of recorder to use. Simplicity should be the rule —simplicity of controls, ease of setting up and taking down equipment, simplicity of operation, and so forth.

At least three useful types of audiorecording equipment are available—general classroom recorders, large-group high-fidelity recorders, and special-purpose "card-reader" recorders developed for individualized instruction. These are now discussed.

Classroom recorders and playbacks

Classroom audio recorders use either open reels of ¼-inch magnetic tape or cassettes (closed plastic containers) which hold either ¼-inch or ⅛-inch tape (see Figure 8.1). Some readers will be able to recall recorders which cut a variable-depth groove into the surface of a plastic coated "blank," a disc or record, or the intermediate development, the wire recorder, which first used the magnetic sound-recording principle to capture electronic counterparts of sound waves and then to reproduce them.

FIGURE 8.1

Audio recordings are available in a variety of forms. Shown are: (upper left) 1/4-inch tape on 7-inch and 5-inch open reels; (middle left) 1/8-inch tape cassettes; (lower left) 1/4-inch tape cartridges, gradually being superseded by cassettes, but still in use; also (upper and lower right) 12-inch and 8-inch traditional records.

FIGURE 8.2

How sounds are recorded on magnetic tape.

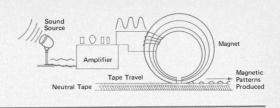

Since very little such equipment remains in use today, neither the disc nor the wire recorder is considered further here.

All forms of tape recording and playback—open reel and cassette—employ the same principle: Sound waves are picked up by a microphone and instantaneously converted into a series of varying electrical impulses. These impulses travel to a small magnet which touches the moving tape which is coated with a magnetic substance, usually iron oxide. The coating receives and retains magnetic impressions of varying strengths which correspond directly to the original impulses set up by the sound waves of voice or music (see Figure 8.2). The tape can be rewound and played back at once. In this reverse process, the invisible magnetic impressions excite a magnetic head and create electrical impulses which, after being suitably amplified, activate the loudspeaker diaphragm to produce sound waves identical to those originally recorded on the tape.

Tape recordings can be used again and again. A reel of mylar plastic tape may be run thousands of times without any visible evidence of wear or any decrease in the fidelity of the sound. If, on the other hand, an error has been made or the recording is no longer needed, the magnetic image can be erased in a matter of seconds. Erasing makes the tape magnetically neutral, and the tape is then ready for immediate reuse for other recordings. Many models and types of open-reel and cassette tape recorders are available, ranging in price from $15 up to hundreds of dollars (see Figure 8.3).

Open-reel recorders offer a significant advantage: the material can easily be edited; that is, it is possible to delete material and rearrange sections of material which are worth saving and thus warrant the effort of organizing such material in a more permanent form. Cassette recorders offer other advantages: the tape is permanently enclosed in a plastic container, but the forward or rewind movement of the tape is controlled easily by pushing a button or turning a knob. Cassette tapes may be "loaded" or unloaded" in a matter of seconds. Prerecorded or blank cassettes drop easily into place and are immediately ready for use, either to record new audio information or to play back what has already been recorded. By breaking out a small plastic spur on the back of a newly recorded cassette tape, one can make it impossible to erase the material on a tape or on the instruction track of a dual-track tape. The usual cassette recorder is simplicity itself to operate, either in recording material or playing it back. (In addition to hundreds of open-reel models, more than 8,000 cassette recorders are being used by teachers in the public schools of Hawaii.)

These are among the many questions a teacher should ask about the functions of audio recording-playback equipment:

1. Is the recorder-playback suitable for use by individuals or small groups of learners who wish to evaluate their spoken communication—reading, giving directions, describing experiences, reporting information, and so forth? If it is light in weight and easily operated, either an open-reel or a cassette recorder-playback is suitable.

However, for the most effective self-evaluation or peer evaluation, the sounds being played back must match faithfully the original quality of the sounds recorded. Such fidelity is needed if judgments are to be made on the basis of human performance rather than on some "trick" of recording quality. Pronunciation, enunciation, expression, enthusiasm, and so forth, may be judged effectively only when the played-back sounds truly reflect or "mirror" the the original ones. The use of an inexpensive but reasonably good-quality microphone does much to ensure such fidelity. The proper use of the microphone and recording level controls is described on pages 332–334.

2. Is the recorder-playback suitable for individual use and study? For this purpose, equipment must be almost indestructible and yet lightweight. Many recorders constructed for long use under a warranty do, in fact, weigh five pounds or less. To use recorders properly as communications tools, pupils should take them home, to the library, to study carrels, and to small-group study meetings. Thus they must be equipped with earphones as well as adjustable-volume speakers. The use of microphones and earphones, single or multiple, should be simple enough so that primary-grade pupils as well as older students can use them effectively (see Figure 8.4).

3. Will the recorder-playback permit the learner to listen to information, respond on the same tape as he evaluates his efforts, and/or listen to the teacher's or fellow pupil's evaluations? To do any or all of these things, a multiple-track machine is needed. In such a machine, preferably a cassette type, parallel tracks or areas of the same tape are used to record and play back prerecorded information and carry the voice responses of the pupil and evaluations or comments by the pupil himself, the teacher, or other pupils (see Figure 8.5). The recording instrument should be capable of high-fidelity reproduction, which is

particularly essential in vocabulary and language development.

For example, in helping pupils gain skill in more accurately pronouncing words, phrases, or sentences, a teacher may prepare as a drill a tape-recorded series of suggestions. Following the directions he may record words or sentences as models for each listener to heed and imitate. (Once recorded, such an experience should be re-

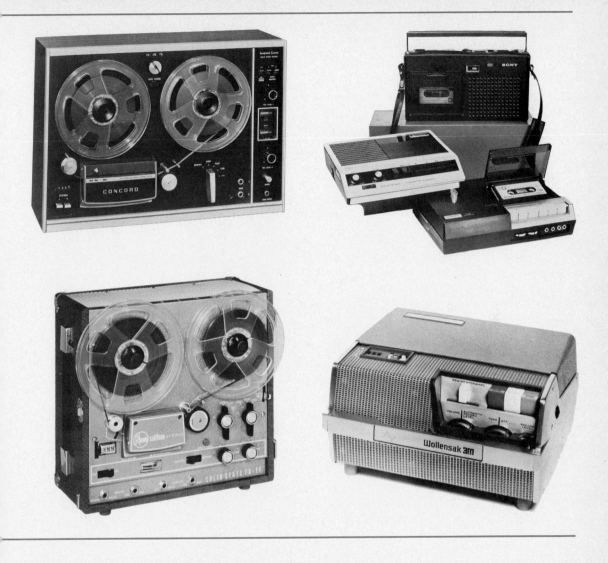

played and checked for accuracy and quality by the teacher.) Later, as the student listens, he should be able to record his own attempts to speak with the desired pronunciation or inflection indicated in the model. More important, he should be able to compare his performance with the model. This enables the learner to perform, compare, and evaluate; it also motivates him to practice further because he can instantly hear the results of such practice. He should be able to erase his own responses and try again repeatedly. A multiple-track recorder makes all this possible.

4. *Is the recorder-playback flexible enough to make it possible to copy or "dub" from original tapes?* For example, sometimes it is desirable to make copies of the creative work of individuals or groups of pupils which would be useful to age-

FIGURE 8.4

This student is about to insert a 1/8-inch tape cassette into the recorder-playback. He may listen, record, move rapidly ahead, or relisten by operating one of four push-button controls. The tape is permanently enclosed in the cassette. What advantages or disadvantages do you associate with such a system?

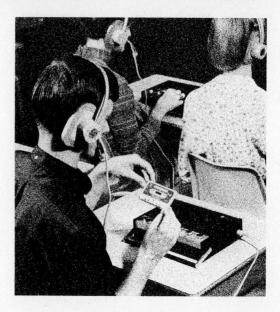

FIGURE 8.5

This diagram shows how multiple-track tape works. Track 4 contains the teacher's pre-recorded "model," while tracks 1 and 2 (combined for monaural use) are used by the learner to record his responses. (The "safety zone," which includes track 3 in this case, is not used for recording; its function is to prevent deterioration of the teacher's instructions and examples while the student is recording and erasing on the response track.) Thus the learner is able to listen, learn, respond, evaluate by immediately comparing his attempts with the model. How can you use such a procedure in your teaching?

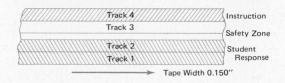

Track 4 — Instruction
Track 3 — Safety Zone
Track 2 — Student Response
Track 1
Tape Width 0.150"

mates in other classes. To do this a second or companion recorder is needed which when interconnected with the first by means of a special set of wires and plugs will copy or dub a duplicate *electronically*. Copies thus produced are superior in quality to those produced by setting the microphone of the copying recorder in front of the speaker of the playback machine.

5. *May the recorder-playback be adapted to use in a wireless transmitting system?* It is often very advantageous to be able to use playback via limited broad-casting within a school building. Under such a system, it is possible to distribute as many as from four to a dozen or more informational or instructional programs or experiences simultaneously. In a few minutes teachers or students can select needed cassette tapes of audio information and place them in the transmitter playback, thus making the information available to listeners anywhere in the school. The pupils are equipped with headsets attached to a selector box. By manipulating a dial on the box the program may be selected.

6. May the recorder-playback be used to record community study experiences? Often an interview with a local business-man, farmer, or engineer may produce information or suggestions of such importance as to warrant recording the experience for later reference and study. To do this the recorder must be powered by a battery so it can be used in places where electrical wall sockets are not available. Most classroom cassette recorders and some open-reel types are available in dual battery-AC current models.

Almost any audio recording situation which the creative mind of the teacher can envision can be accomplished easily and effectively if the right kind of lightweight and easily operated classroom recorder-playback is used. As noted, because of the number and types of equipment available, the teacher should seek the advice and counsel of the professional audiovisual media specialist or dealer. Fortunately, much tape-recording equipment is now designed so that primary-grade children can handle recording and playback. Teachers who remember some of the complicated "pioneer" equipment will be glad to discover that it has been replaced by simplified models. It is now easy to set up and use audiotape in either open-reel or cassette units.

Large-group recorders

The essential difference between the class-room audio recorders just described and those suitable for recording large groups is often only a matter of degree. Large-group recording situations usually demand higher-quality microphones; a greater degree of recorder sensitivity in order to capture and reproduce very low and extremely high sounds; and the reproduction of these sounds with lifelike fidelity, as well as sufficient volume so that large audiences will hear comfortably. Equipment that can achieve these qualities may be expected to be larger, heavier, and more costly. Also, more expertise is required of the operator. Nevertheless, many such audio machines are marvels of compactness, efficiency, and reasonable ease of operation.

As in selecting classroom audio recorder-playback equipment, one must select large-group recording equipment only after determining the uses to which it will be put. Selecting and using microphones are important; one or all of the three basic types of microphones should be available for the varying uses to which such recorders are put. The one-direction pickup or *unidirectional* microphone is best suited for use by a single student as he faces an audience. His voice alone will be picked up and such audience noises as shuffling of feet, whispering, and coughing will be minimized. Where two persons or small groups speak or perform from opposite sides of the microphone, a *bidirectional* microphone is needed. All-directional or *omnidirectional* microphones are widely used, but unless they are used carefully they easily become "overloaded" by excessive sounds and produce annoying "squeals" called feedback. This brief explanation is intended merely to inform the teacher that there are three basic types of microphones; it is best to seek the assistance of the media specialist or qualified local dealer when actually selecting and using microphones (see Figure 8.6).

Stereophonic audio recorder-playback equipment is used in many schools to record, play back, and evaluate choral speaking and dramatic, vocal, and instrumental performances of individuals and groups. Stereophonic audio recording uses two or more microphones. The sounds picked up by each are recorded separately and then played back separately through two or more speakers or both sides of a headset. Lifelike sound fidelity is the result—the listener hears the reproduced sounds as he naturally hears sounds, coming from two or more directions at the same time, but in

FIGURE 8.6

This diagram shows the pickup pattern of three general types of microphones that are useful to the teacher. Which do you consider best for your various audio recording activities, classroom as well as large group?

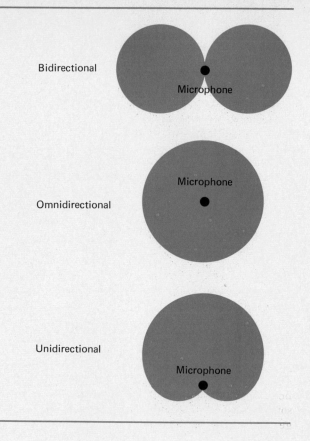

Bidirectional

Microphone

Omnidirectional

Microphone

Unidirectional

Microphone

intensities that vary according to distance and direction, as they do in "natural" hearing. For example, in recording a school orchestra, two microphones may be used, each one recording only one important section of the entire group. Thus, as shown in Figure 8.7, M1 (microphone 1) will pick up primarily the sound of the strings and part of the percussion and the brasses; M2 will pick up primarily the sound of the woodwinds, and so forth. The recording will be played back over a stereophonic tape

FIGURE 8.7

Stereophonic microphone placement depends on the size and characteristics of the room and the sound qualities to be recorded. The teacher should experiment until he finds the placement that produces the best results.

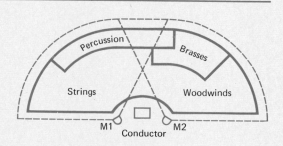

Percussion

Brasses

Strings

Woodwinds

M1   M2
Conductor

playback in which the sounds picked up by M1 are reproduced by one corresponding loudspeaker and those picked up by M2 are reproduced by a second loudspeaker placed some distance from the first. In the playback, the relationship and emphasis of the sounds are reproduced so that the actual physical positions, quality, and volume in the original performance are closely duplicated.

The listener is usually impressed by stereophonic recording because of the great "presence" or lifelike quality in the sound reproduction it achieves. He can close his eyes and solely by listening identify sounds as to their type and location—and even change of location, if this has occurred. Listening to stereo recording is not only a remarkably esthetic experience, but one that enhances audiolearning, particularly in cases where identification of location, emphasis, and relationship of sounds is important. Sound reproduction by tape is efficient in that it eliminates both surface noises and the noises due to mechanical sound reproduction techniques. Like tapes generally, stereo tapes are not subject to rapid deterioration and hence can be used over a long period of time.

Card-type audio recorder-playbacks

In the usual audio recording and playback learning experiences we have described, the student records and listens for a number of minutes or longer at a time. The use of very short audio messages—3 to 5 seconds long—in connection with cards is an exciting new development. This variation is described by those who have developed it as audio flashcard systems, audio card readers, or Language Master programs. Regardless of the name used, all these terms refer to a means of recording on one 9- to 15-inch length of audiotape that is attached permanently to a card. The cards vary in size: 3½ × 9 inches, 4 × 15 inches or similar dimensions. Words, sentences, ques-

tions, symbols, or pictures may be written or printed on these cards; to the lower portion of each card the short strip of recording tape is attached, providing a "sound track" to describe the printed material on the card. The student inserts a selected card into a slot on top of the recorder and the card automatically moves across a magnetic head or vice versa. As this occurs, the user hears his own or the instructor's voice reading or describing the visual material printed or pictured on the face of the card (see Figure 8.8). The learning effect thus combines the visual with the aural.

The recording phase motivates the student to engage in active participation, which helps to sustain interest. To reinforce the "seeing" and "hearing" steps in this learning process, the student turns a "record" switch and repeats the materials he has just seen and heard. The student's voice may be rerecorded in such a way (dual-track tape) that he can replay his own response and then that of the "model" for comparison. If the student's performance is faulty, he can erase and record again—as in traditional tape-recording experiences—as many times as he wishes.

Preprinted and precoded card sets are now available in vocabulary building, words and pictures, language stimulation, English grammar development, pronunciation and phonics, and many other areas. Blank cards are also available, making the device readily adaptable to many uses. Applications in teaching the meanings of symbols and vocabulary, modern math, chemistry, spelling, etc., should be explored by imaginative teachers. It is conceivable that the use of this device in the teaching of reading may reveal new pathways to skill mastery and comprehension. A teacher can write, draw, or even paste pictures on a blank card. By inserting the card in the machine, he can then record on the magnetic track the word or phrase describing the image, symbol, or word. His recording

FIGURE 8.8

These are three widely used audio card-reader models: (upper left) TTC—Teaching Technology Corporation; (upper right) Language Master— Bell & Howell; (lower right) EFI—Electronic Futures, Inc. All of these accomplish similar basic recording and playback functions. The sample tape cards shown give an idea of the variety of subject content presented as visual-audio experiences. Can you identify some that would be useful in your teaching? On blank cards, also shown, teachers or pupils can attach cutout pictures, draw, or print words or phrases. What opportunities do blank cards present to you or to your pupils?

can't be erased unless he himself decides to change it. Pupils then play the "sound card" and are free to imitate and learn at their own pace (see Figure 8.9).

The card reader has a unique capacity to make possible rapid and efficient individualized special vocabulary study. Consider this example described by a professor at a school of nursing:

"I have spent months with the members of incoming classes of student nurses helping them master the meaning of the special vocabulary which they must know in order to carry out the instructions of supervisors and doctors. The process was always the same. Many of the group completed the 300-word vocabulary in a few weeks. Others needed much more time and endless hours of my attention in evaluating and helping. We realized there must be a better way—so we decided to try this." The professor picked up a 2-inch-thick packet of tape cards. On each of the several hundred cards was neatly printed a vocabulary word or phrase. The tape carried the correct pronunciation of the word or phrase, and on the back of each card the definition was typed.

"The student nurses now come to one of these machines," the professor continued. She paused to indicate three card readers, each located in its own carrel and equipped with earphones. "The student reads the directions, turns on the machine, and teaches herself by looking, listening, recording, and evaluating her own efforts. Last term we had one girl complete the assignment during the first week—others took longer. But all were willing to stick with it until they knew the basic vocabulary. You have no idea how this has helped their work in the wards—fewer mistakes than ever before."

Other basic vocabulary problem areas —foreign languages, mathematics, science —can be approached in this way and at any grade level.

The card-reader audio system is particularly well adapted to providing for the wide variations among pupils in learning facility, as well as in individual interests. In all aspects of education, this variation is reflected in a great range in span of attention, amount of repetition that is necessary, and degree of individualization that is necessary in the pace at which learning ex-

FIGURE 8.9

Card readers present, both visually and aurally, words, numbers, pictures, or symbols. The learner sees the information shown on the card and simultaneously hears the word, phrase, or sound which relates to it. (a) This girl is working on operations with fractions. (b) This boy is reporting his progress in vocabulary development. (c) These children have cut out pictures, pasted them on cards, and recorded the words that describe the pictures. They have created, for one another's use, an original and very personal learning experience. What uses can you envision for your own teaching situation?

periences are presented. For example, one child can hear a concept explained just once and retain it for a lifetime. Another learner, however, must hear the same concept repeated dozens of times, often in different ways, before he grasps or absorbs it.

Recently, card-reader audio systems have been extended to special education. The handicapped child, even more than the normal child, needs dependable and understandable experiences which can be presented to him at his own pace (the hard-of-hearing child, for example). It is not surprising to find that handicapped children often profit greatly from card-reader learning materials.

As card-reader tape recorders continue to capture the imagination and enthusiasm of teacher, pupil, and manufacturer, the teacher may wonder which type of recorder will be the most useful and economical for his teaching purposes. One answer that applies to most electronic equipment is that quality merchandise must command a reasonable price. A current model, though it may seem simple to operate, rugged, and attractive, should be purchased only after

a careful classroom tryout is arranged through a reputable audiovisual dealer. The teacher should ask for a demonstration in order to determine which recorder will be best for the type of use that is anticipated. Further, because even the best equipment needs servicing at times, the availability of service and repair arrangements should be thoroughly explored before purchase.

Recording *environmental sound* is another exciting type of audio recording that we should mention here. This kind of recording is made possible by the use of a special microphone—the parabolic microphone. Those who are interested in the technical aspects of recording environmental sound should refer to the *Student Production Guide,* which includes instructions on using this type of microphone. Also, the media supervisor or local dealer can be helpful. The construction of the parabolic microphone enables it to be accurately focused on either near or distant sound sources (bird calls, industrial machinery in operation, the sounds of barnyard animals, and so forth).

Recording: how to do it

FOR many teachers, the thought of taking a microphone in hand and showing learners how to use it efficiently is a step toward "the mysterious unknown." If this is the case for you, why not invite several of the more interested pupils to explore *with* you the ways to get the very best results from the equipment available to you? One must recognize that even the best equipment will not guarantee excellent recording unless reasonable skills are developed by those who select where the recording is to be done, how the microphone is to be placed and spoken into, and how the simple controls must be adjusted during recording and playback. Too often one sees

perfectly good recording equipment lying idle because past hurried attempts to use it have produced poor results.

Another good way to become familiar with effective recording techniques is to seek the assistance of someone who has already planned and produced good recordings: a fellow teacher, an experienced student, or the media specialist. Usually the dealer from whom the equipment has been purchased will volunteer to offer instructions to those who wish to use it. In any case, if the simple suggestions that are now discussed are followed, recordings of fidelity and satisfactory playback volume can usually be assured.

Acoustics and microphone placement

The acoustics of the room or recording area should be studied. Unfortunately, most teachers have to contend with classrooms that have poor acoustics. You can soon distinguish between a "live" room and a "dead" room: A "live" room is one in which the sound is *underabsorbed,* allowing sound waves to echo and reverberate; a "dead" room is one in which the sound is *overabsorbed,* preventing the sound waves from carrying far enough. The usual classroom is "live," characterized by hard plaster wall and ceiling surfaces. A "live" room is likely to be filled with reverberated or echoed sound waves which cause confusion as they enter the microphone. Such a classroom can be made less "live" by drawing the shades or, if there are draperies, by spreading these out over as large an area as possible. Wall hangings, cloth-covered screens, and surfaces which can be hung temporarily with sound-absorbing material also help remarkably.

In contrast to the "live" room is the "dead" room. Though the ceiling of such a room may have good acoustic properties, the room may be crowded with rugs, draperies, overstuffed furniture, or other sound absorbers. Here there is an undesirable amount of sound absorption which results in "hollow-barrel" recordings. Once simple trial and error has revealed the sound-absorbing surfaces, the hollow recordings can be avoided by placing the microphone properly.

After the acoustic properties of the classroom are known, recommendations may be made concerning the betterment of poor acoustics. If the room is too "live," thick acoustic tile may be installed on the ceiling. Usually this is sufficient, but sometimes additional panels are needed on one or more walls. In rooms that are too "dead" (the exception), drapery materials or some acoustic tiles may be removed. (Those who are planning on remodeling present schools or building new ones should consider the use of acoustic plaster for the ceiling surfaces.)

In placing the microphone, the teacher is at first likely to depend on his own hearing. He does not realize that sound heard by two ears is entirely different from that "heard" by a microphone. Our ears and minds possess the ability to concentrate our attention on the one person who is talking to us, even though the room is filled with chatting people; that is, if we have so trained ourselves, we may disregard extraneous sounds. The microphone, on the other hand, is monaural—one eared—and that one ear can make no discrimination. Every sound that reaches it is picked up.

The microphone—either unidirectional or bidirectional (see page 326)—should be 4 to 6 feet away from any hard, flat, reverberating surfaces that reflect sound; also, the corners of the room should be avoided. The microphone should be head-high on a small microphone stand or similar support. Visualize the area or areas in front of the open face or faces of the microphone as a zone or zones of reception, and within this zone experiment with recording and playback to acquire a feeling of the range of pickup and the quality of reproduction characteristic of the microphone. Too low or too high a recording level will actually change the identifying qualities of the voice; a low recording level for a speaker who is only inches from the microphone will eliminate almost all extraneous noises; a gusty voice will be recorded better if the person speaks slightly across the face of the microphone, and so forth. (Fortunately for both teacher and student users, more and more recorders are being equipped with self-regulating sound-level controls which automatically prevent overloading microphone capacity. For further information, see the *Student Production Guide.*) Classrooms vary, of course, but the two schematic layouts shown in Figure 8.10 embody general suggestions for group tape recording in the classroom. Experiment

FIGURE 8.10

Two schematic plans for effective classroom audio recording. (a) Pupils position themselves in front of a unidirectional microphone. Pupils with weaker voices should stand within 12 to 15 inches of the "mike," those with stronger voices close behind them. (b) Pupils position themselves on opposite sides of a bidirectional microphone. Which arrangement will better suit your purposes? Why?

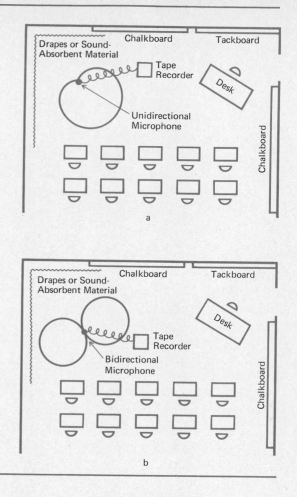

—that is, record, play back, reposition pupils, and so on—until you discover the locations of both microphone and pupils that give maximum results.

Some microphone techniques for teachers and pupils

In using a recorder in the classroom, the teacher of course wishes to produce playbacks that sound "real" or "natural." When the recorder is used for self-evaluation, the recorded sounds must duplicate the original ones as completely as possible; in other words, the recorder must achieve *fidelity* and *presence*. "Fidelity" refers to the reproduction of musical, speech, or environmental sounds in such a way as to approximate or come very close to the original. "Presence" refers to sound reproduction of such fidelity that the listener feels he is listening to the original music, voice, or sound; that is, he feels he is in the "presence" of the original. Stereo sound recording and reproduction, if it has high fidelity, can usually be relied on, by its very nature, to produce believable feelings of "being there live."

The teacher soon discovers that there is more to using a recorder than merely putting a microphone in front of an individual or group. *To attain fidelity and presence, he must know how to use the microphone and its controls.*

Even though the microphone is an inanimate object, it is helpful to think "beyond" it. The ultimate aim in using a microphone is to communicate ideas, a series of directions, or how-to-do-it information to a learner. The central point is the *communication* with fellow human beings; in other words, the microphone should be accepted as a mere means to this overall goal. If possible, anyone using a microphone should imagine that he is conversing with or performing for another human being.

1. BE PREPARED Usually the thought of recording information motivates one to spend a reasonable amount of time in preparing the information. Time spent in preparation invariably results in a recorded message that is better organized and more understandable than casually given "spur-of-the-moment" directions, suggestions, or information.

It is best to use a single-page outline or a series of cards. Avoid shuffling papers noisily, handling or fussing with the microphone, or brushing against it—all of which produce sounds that become recorded with unwanted clarity.

2. BE COMFORTABLE Continuing practice in making recordings should allow one to relax and actually enjoy the experience. As one teacher expressed it, "I wouldn't believe the first recording I made. When I played it back I could hear and almost feel the 'uptight' quality of the recording. How excited I'd been! But, no more of this! After working with the students for less than a week we learned to relax and have fun expressing ourselves in this new way—other than by paper and pencil and poorly-thought-out oral reporting."

Even a little practice in facing the

microphone usually results in gaining assurance in speaking in the same conversational, friendly manner one employs in day-to-day teaching.

3. FACE THE MICROPHONE The most frequent cause of uneven volume in recording is that the teacher or pupil forgets where the microphone is. Every time one turns his head, he usually increases the distance to the recording surface of the microphone. This can be avoided by remembering a simple rule and practicing it: Keep the microphone at a uniform distance from you and in a line between you and the imagined or real audience. Learn to face the microphone constantly by stepping a little to the left if you wish to turn your head right and vice versa.

4. ELIMINATE HUMAN STATIC Remember that the microphone is a mechanical ear that records everything it hears. If you are too close to the microphone, hissing or sibilants will be picked up (S-S-S-S-S or Sh-Sh-Sh-Sh-Sh). Weaving forward and backward before the microphone may produce annoying breathing sounds or booming sounds. Care should be taken to eliminate one's own carelessness in oral communication—the use of superfluous Ahs, throat clearings, U-m-m-ms, and so forth.

5. LET THE CONTROLS HELP YOU Two very important controls, the volume and tone controls, should be used knowledgeably in order to achieve lifelike recording and playback.

The volume control determines the volume at which a recording is made. The higher the volume control is set, the greater the pickup range of the microphone. One teacher complained that playground noises outside the building were being recorded along with the songs two children in the classroom were performing before the microphone. Obviously, the volume control was set at "high" or maximum, with the result that the mechanical ear, the microphone, was reaching out far beyond the walls of the classroom to gather in every sound. To help here, most machines have visual signals which wink or glow to indicate that the recording level is correct. But the best procedure is to experiment with volume settings until good results are achieved. Record—play back—evaluate, then try again—this is the rule.

The tone control determines the degree of treble or bass quality of the voice, music, or other sounds picked up by the microphone and recorded. Short test recordings and a little experimenting—perhaps more or less treble or bass—will reveal when the tone setting is correct and reproduces sounds that are true and lifelike.

One of the most frequent causes of poor recording quality is small deposits of magnetic material that brush off the surface of the tape and accumulate on the sound recording head. It is extremely simple to keep the recording head clean by merely running over its surface a cotton swab saturated with any one of a number of special cleaning fluids intended for magnetic heads. After such a cleaning has removed accumulations of dirt and magnetic material, recording quality is vastly improved. For further information, see the *Student Production Guide.*

Duplicating or "dubbing"

Frequently a teacher will secure for use a tape recording which is of such value that it is desirable to make a copy for inclusion in the school tape collection. The procedures involved in duplicating or copying or "dubbing" are relatively simple. Ordinarily, two recorders are used: one to play the recorded tape, the other to duplicate on blank tape the recorded material. Special connecting wires with plugs at one end and "alligator" clips at the other should be employed to pick up the sounds

electronically from the playing machine. The magnetic sound signals from the recorded tape are transferred to the blank tape by placing the alligator clips on the speaker posts of the playing recorder and plugging the other ends of the wires into the dubbing or copying recorder. The sounds from the original recording should not be allowed to travel through the air from the playing recorder to the microphone of the dubbing recorder, as this lessens the fidelity of the dubbed recording and perhaps adds secondary or background noise to the duplicate. The media specialist or the local dealer can provide further help. Also see the *Student Production Guide.*

Evaluating recording

Just as the proof of any pudding is in the eating, the quality of a recording is measured best when it is played back as a learning experience and its qualities noted. As one attempts to judge the quality and usefulness of a recorded message, it should be possible to answer such questions as the following in the affirmative:

1. Is the volume of the played-back recording high enough so that all can hear and understand?

2. Does the played-back recording possess good tone quality so as to produce the feeling of naturalness associated with fidelity—the reproduction of sounds similar to those recorded?

3. Is the played-back recording clear and distinct and free of unwanted background noises, interruptions, scratchiness, or other annoying sounds which indicate poor microphone placement or unsatisfactory manipulation of tone or volume controls?

The pupils who participate in recording activities usually find profitable the opportunity to evaluate their efforts (see Figure 8.11). It is not uncommon to discover that learners are often more critical of their own efforts than the teacher. For example,

FIGURE 8.11

These photographs capture three pupils' candid reactions to the use of the tape recorder during their own creative efforts to record and play back a short dramatization they have written. What desirable learning outcomes seem to be present?

midway during a unit on Hawaii, one group of fifth-graders wrote to a former exchange teacher who had returned to Hawaii asking whether they might initiate a tape-recorded cultural exchange with their Hawaiian age-mates. The answering letter promised to send a tape recording made by Hawaiian fifth-graders in response to one prepared by the mainland class. The initial excitement of the mainland pupils was followed by a more controlled planning period. Questions about school, home life, pets, dress, climate, and local customs were quickly formulated and then recorded on tape. The playback of this first effort came as a shock to the pupils.

"We can't send this!" exclaimed one student. "They'll get a bad impression of us!"

"We can do better—if we can't, we shouldn't send it," suggested another pupil with disappointment.

The pupils' discouragement was brief, however—soon their enthusiasm mounted again as further discussion involved opinions on how ideas should be more clearly stated. Finally, several groups were formed to put on paper the key ideas they wanted to communicate to the Hawaiian class. These groups agreed that some tape time should be left for extemporaneous comment at the end. Three days elapsed during which writing, recording, and rerecording took place. Finally, when the pupils were satisfied, they mailed the tape reel.

"The students were very critical of their efforts," the teacher reported. "They set standards for themselves which they might not have accepted as reasonable had I suggested them" (see Figure 8.11). Here was an experience in self-criticism and improvement which had taken place through the trial and error made possible by the tape recorder's flexibility.

Playback and retrieval

T HE two most frequently used means of creating audio playback are tape recorders *and* record players. The same piece of equipment used to record sound on magnetic tape serves also to play back these same sounds. Older and more traditionally used record players serve widely as the means for playing back records or, as they are often called, discs or transcriptions. In many sophisticated learning centers, combinations of magnetic audiotape recorders *and* record playback machinery are built into retrieval systems to which learners can come to listen to desired audio experiences. They do this by reporting to a listening carrel, consulting a list of the currently available audio program titles, noting the assigned "telephone number" of from one to four digits, "dialing" the selected number, and listening. The way all this is currently being done is now discussed to illustrate the range of audio play-

back or retrieval possibilities in individualizing, enriching, and increasing learning opportunities, whether in the classroom, learning resources center, dial access center, language laboratory, or audio information center.

Classroom audio playback
It should have become apparent that open-reel or cassette audio magnetic tape offers a very flexible means for not only recording, but also for playing back audio-learning experiences in the classroom. Tape-recorded materials can be played back an indefinite number of times with very little decrease in the quality of the audio message. Occasionally, one who is not familiar with the open-reel recorder may accidentally erase the prerecorded information, but when audio information is "packaged" in cassette form, it very

seldom is accidentally erased or damaged. Cassettes which hold ⅛-inch-wide tape are very small and can easily be stored in the classroom or the teacher's desk, since the cassettes measure only 2½″ × 4″ × ½″ overall. Cassette tapes "play" at a standard speed of 1⅞ inches per second and can record *and* play back programs of from 15 minutes to *one hour* in length. The larger cartridges or magazines which use ¼-inch tape play at a standard 3¾ inches per second and carry programs of 15 or 30 minutes in length.

An advantage of open-reel or cassette magnetic audio recording and playback equipment is that one piece of machinery can be used for both processes. Thus a single inexpensive and lightweight tape recorder can be used to record original work by the teacher or students and play back such material or play back prerecorded audiolearning experiences commercially published for school use (see Figure 8.12).

An alternative way of playing back audiolearning experiences in classrooms is through the use of record players. Those who are responsible for organizing new audiolearning programs favor the use of tape recording and playback equipment; nevertheless, hundreds of thousands of record players are still in use (see Figure

FIGURE 8.12

Easy access to audiotapes and playback equipment expands learning opportunities and strategies. (a) Two first-grade children use a prerecorded cassette audio playback book-reading experience which they selected.
(b) Four fifth-grade children form a homogeneous small group to pursue an audio-cued language arts drill. What teaching strategies can you envision as accessible individualized audio playback materials become easily available in your school?

8.13), and educational record sales still represent expenditures of great sums of money.

Long-playing records—or LPs, as they are commonly called—are particularly well suited for relatively short pieces of educational content, such as poetry readings; essays and short stories; brief dramatized historical episodes; songs; and the like. To record such brief pieces on individual tapes would be to use magnetic tape uneconomically, and to record several such items on a single tape poses difficulties in locating individual selections. LPs that rotate at the

FIGURE 8.13

Schools everywhere are equipped with such record players as these which are well suited for classroom use, since they can be played at varying speeds; thus they can play back older high-speed records as well as slower long-playing 45-, 33 1/3-, and 16-rpm discs.

rate of 45 revolutions per minute (rpm) usually hold anywhere from 5 to 8 minutes of recorded material on a single side, depending on the number of microgrooves engraved on the disc. LPs of 33⅓ rpm contain from 10 to 15 minutes of recorded information per side, depending on the number and spacing of the microgrooves. These latter discs are particularly useful in some situations, as several selections can be inscribed on one disc. The location of any one piece can be identified by its "band"—that is, the ring of microgrooves it occupies—in relation to the other bands on the side. Thus, "Side 1, Band 4" indicates that the particular selection can be played by moving the phonograph needle to the fourth band of microgrooves in from the circumference of the first side of the record.

Transcription is the technical term used to refer to professionally recorded discs that are not commercially available to the general consumer. Originally, transcriptions came into use for radio rebroadcasting, before wire and magnetic tape recording processes had been sufficiently developed for these purposes. Transcriptions are generally larger—from 14 to 18 inches in diameter—than the 10- and 12-inch "platters" available commercially; they also are recorded at speeds of 16, 33⅓, and 45 rpm. Transcriptions of 16 rpm are particularly widely used in schools today for "talking books." These are discs on which some of the current and classic titles in children's literature are recorded in their entirety.

A variety of audiolearning materials and strategies, including individualized, small-group, and entire class group use, should be studied. Alternatives and examples are discussed in Chapter 9.

Audiotape playback for self-evaluation

Most audiotape recorder and playback equipment is easily operated and cared for. Under the guidance of the teacher, the pupils themselves can learn effectively to set up the equipment, use the microphone, rewind and play back recorded materials, and proceed to experience the thrill of self-realization that comes with evaluating one's own communication efforts. By mastering the suggestions given on pages 332–334, the teacher can pass on to pupils his newfound tape-recording skills. So important is the use of recorded pupil performance in encouraging self-evaluation that specific activities related to five general subject areas and guidance are now described.

THE LANGUAGE ARTS The value of hearing oneself as others do by means of tape recordings has already been suggested. This objective opportunity for self-criticism is valuable during the entire span of school experience. Its value first becomes apparent in the primary grades when the youngsters attempt to read aloud; when they engage in "Monday morning reports" of the weather, weekend activities, and events at home; and also when telephone-answering techniques are recorded and listened to.

In the upper grades, panel discussions, reports of books read, discussions of the news, explanations of processes, and how-to-do-it accounts continue to demonstrate the true importance of *being able to get up on one's feet and express one's ideas verbally in a clear and well-organized manner.*

Children too often become so accustomed to a teacher's admonitions about improving speech or grammar that such remarks are no longer incentives to improvement. But the tape-recorded "voice" played back frequently serves as a fresh new incentive. Errors of grammar and sentence structure and needless repetitions become painfully apparent when the child hears them committed in his own played-back voice.

"Do I sound like that? How can I have a better voice?"

"Do I talk that *fast*," "that *slowly*," or "with all those 'ah's,' 'er's,' and 'and-ah's'?"

When the students have these reactions to themselves and to each other, the teacher no longer needs to wear his own voice and his patience thin trying to drill suggestions for improvement into his pupils. The child is usually his own critic, and this role is also played by his classmates.

SOCIAL STUDIES A primary goal of the social studies is to provide experiences which are so lifelike that they give the learner true understandings of people, places, and things throughout the world. The tape recorder makes possible the experience of listening to others as they express their ideas and that of exchanging spoken ideas with others. For example, in one civics class, students were assigned to one of several committees, each committee being responsible for gathering information on one aspect of governmental control—public school and adult education, fire and police protection, traffic control, recreation provisions and maintenance, sanitation and public health, and taxation and finance. In their planning sessions, each committee reviewed and decided upon the offices and personnel they would visit to gather their facts. Some members of the committee decided that by tape-recording their interviews—later editing the tape to eliminate secondary information—they could, in effect, bring the government officials right into the classroom. The carrying out of these plans resulted in levels of effort and learning accomplishment seldom experienced through more traditional methods of teaching the same types of units.

The tape recorder also presents a challenge to those who are willing to undertake the research, writing, editing, rehearsal, and final production of "reports from history." It is one thing to read passively history book descriptions of the Norman Invasion or the Battle of the Coral Sea or magazine accounts of our astronauts' first landing on the moon. It is a more exciting project to reconstruct factual occurrences into dramatic, "on-the-spot" news accounts with background "color" narration of such quality as will hold the attention of the class group. The tape recorder is well suited to such projects, for it enables the students to test themselves and arrange for tryouts before presenting the finished product to the class. Pupil and teacher interest runs high in such projects.

MUSIC In beginning band and orchestra work, the thrill of listening to themselves perform through tape-recording playback can be a great incentive to the pupils to listen, evaluate, and practice—all to the end of better performance. Recordings of individual vocal and instrumental performances and quartet and choral singing all allow the individual or group to listen, learn, and improve. Older pupils can carry on recording and playback activities independently. Today many school music departments have tape recorders set up on which soloists can record their work, then listen and practice. This procedure places the responsibility on the learner, giving him the opportunity to advance as rapidly as he wishes.

The tape recorder can also be used advantageously in music to individualize help for pupils who experience difficulty in note reading and tone accuracy. By listening to prerecorded new songs pupils develop an ear for the tunes and thus learn them more rapidly. The prize-winning performance of a group at a music festival may serve as a goal and an incentive to strive continuously for quality achievement in either instrumental or choral music.

BUSINESS EDUCATION Speed tests and vocabulary and spelling drills all lend themselves admirably to prerecording on tape. In typing and shorthand classes, a tape recording that has been carefully worked out in advance by the teacher can be used repeatedly to measure the speed and accuracy of various classes.

In order to give his pupils experience in doing typing and shorthand in actual business situations, one commercial teacher arranged for each of 15 local businessmen to dictate on tape three letters of varying length and difficulty selected from his files. The resulting 45 letters were a challenging and exciting variation from the regular class routine and gave the class a realistic idea of the requirements of actual business firms. Similar tapes for use in business education have also been commercially recorded.

Other uses of tape recording in business education include taping business telephone conversations, employer interviews at local business firms, and both imaginary and genuine sales talks—the latter recorded by local sales people.

DRAMATICS AND SPEECH Unusual examples of speech, debates, reporting, or dramatics are frequently heard on radio or television, and these can be useful in teaching speech or dramatics. Most tape recorders are equipped with a radio or television takeoff line, a length of wire with a plug-in device at one end and twin metal clips at the other. By attaching the clips to the "voice coils" of the radio or television set (ask your audiovisual supervisor or physics teacher for help) and then plugging in the tape recorder, the teacher can tape an address by the President of the United States, the audio part of a television drama, a panel discussion, or a well-delivered commercial.

Any of these may become teaching materials at the right time and under the right circumstances. Used as models, such tapes can help pupils make judgments about good speaking, clear enunciation, pleasing phrasing and voice intonation, vocabulary choice, and sentence structure.

When a tape recorder is used during a rehearsal of a play, the members of the cast can gain a vivid idea of their strengths and weaknesses from the playback.

Once the teacher has experienced the unique characteristic of the tape recorder to improve student audiolearning, listening-skill development, and oral criticism, other values and uses of the tape recorder become apparent.

GUIDANCE ACTIVITIES Periodic and cumulative recording of pupils' progress by means of tape recording can become a valued and very lifelike counseling experience for both teachers and students.

"At one-year intervals," a guidance director reports, "I arrange for teachers to record brief and direct observations about given students. This is done on cassette tapes—at least one tape per student is needed to 'hold' the accumulating information. When it seems desirable, I invite the student to record, right on the same tape, his own value judgments about his experiences or progress. In some cases I add interpretive comments." The guidance director pulled one cumulative folder out of a filing cabinet, opened it, and displayed the included cassette, which fitted easily into the folder.

"Teachers," this director says, "are very willing to stop by my office and, as if they were chatting with me, record their comments on tape, knowing that I will add their taped report to the progressively growing information record on a given student. At the time of graduation or on any occasion for listening, the tape record can be played back for parents, teachers, or pupil."

We are only beginning to realize the many important guidance uses that can be devised for the tape recorder. Suppose that when Johnny comes to kindergarten, a simple conversation with him is recorded. As he goes from grade to grade, his oral speech habits, oral reading, and conversations revealing his interests, likes and dislikes, ambitions, and relationships with home, school, and friends could be captured on tape, placed in his record folder, and on graduation be spliced together as an aural document of his school life and progress. Imagine the interest of his parents, and possibly an employer, in such a document.

For students who plan to start working after high school, the tape recorder is also valuable. After the guidance director determines what kind of employment offers the best opportunities for the student, both the student and his instructor may engage in role playing, the instructor taking the part of an employer interviewing the student about a job. The taped interview is then played back for criticism.

Audiolingual playback

The use of audiolingual models as an effective means of improving oral communication and learning foreign languages has been described briefly. This process is so important, however, that it warrants further discussion here.

Audiolingual learning refers to the use of recorded "models" of phrases, sentences, conversations, or descriptive passages as experiences to be imitated and learned by the student. When such a recording is played back by the learner, he hears the "model," is directed to imitate it as best he can, record himself saying his own version of the model, and evaluate his own response himself or heed the judgment of the teacher. Following his own or the teacher's evaluation, he can repeat the given learning experience for further mastery or continue to study additional audiolingual models.

The mechanics by which such experiences are arranged take many forms within two basic types of arrangement. At one level, programs are made available to learners through the means of "packages" of materials and equipment which may be sent around from classroom to classroom.

The teachers who receive such materials then schedule the programs into their own instructional plans. In more highly developed cases, audiolingual experiences are made available by means of permanent language laboratory installations to which both teachers and pupils come as they engage in language study. No matter what specific arrangement is used, however, the basic learning strategies employed are likely to be very similar. Some examples follow.

In order to bring the advantages of audiolingual language experiences to a widely scattered group of elementary-grade pupils and their teachers, the Hawaii Japanese Language Program has been de-

FIGURE 8.14

This multimedia audiolingual language program in Japanese is sent to teachers as a "package" which includes audiotaped "models," charts, pictures, slides, and film loops. Cassette or open-reel playback units are provided by the local schools. (a) A teacher makes some beginning explanations and displays visual "cue" posters to a team. (b) The team listens to instructions and language models. (c) Peer evaluation is based on cue cards which help the pupils recall key words and phrases. (d) The taped language models are reviewed so that further mastery can be gained. What are your judgments about the audiolingual process, specifically about the learning elements that comprise the experiences shown here?

veloped. (The program is currently in use by children on the islands of Hawaii, Maui, and Oahu.) The heart of the program is a sequence of audio-recorded lessons or language "models" which are listened to and imitated; these pupil responses are then evaluated by the pupils themselves and their teachers. The audiolingual tapes carry recorded conversation and directions spoken by native Japanese persons. The voice quality, purity of enunciation, and pronunciation provided in the models become experiences with the Japanese language from which both pupils and teachers can profit.

To assure ease of handling and use, lightweight cassette or open-reel playback machines are used. Since the ⅛-inch-wide tape used in the cassettes does not ordinarily provide a channel for pupil responses, evaluation must be based on peer or teacher judgments of how well listeners "say" their responses. This situation actually encourages unusual learner involvement. As teams of two pupils listen and respond, the pupil who is to evaluate his partner must listen intently to the model in order to arrive at a judgment that will be convincing to his teammate (see Figure 8.14).

As the result of several years of study and refinement, the Hawaii Project has become multimedia—more and more related experiences have been added to the audio-

lingual language models. Language describes social experiences. It is logical that visualizations of spoken conversations will produce "cues" useful in judging the meaning of the words used on the tapes to describe these experiences. A student of a foreign language profits by being able to study visualizations of these episodes which are later to be discussed in the aural language lessons. Because of this, many of the Japanese lessons are introduced and later summarized by using pictures, charts, projectuals, slides, or 8mm motion picture film loops.[1]

An alternate way of making audio-language models easily available to students is to place them in uniform cassettes or cartridges and organize these into a library of materials. Teachers then assign lessons to students by topics, lesson numbers, or titles. Students locate the material in the school in much the same way as they locate books.

For example, at the Punahou School in Hawaii, teachers and administrators became increasingly interested, over a 10-year period, in the use of audio-recorded learning materials as the means for studying foreign languages as well as for acquiring source information in the social studies, science, language arts, and so forth. It was noted that even the best materials were widely used only when they were easily accessible to students and faculty. A variety of storage information retrieval systems had been tried, but the most efficient access for students in this case was provided by recording materials on ¼-inch tape packaged in special cartridges and arranging them on shelves so that an attendant could, on request, hand a cartridge to a student. The student could then take the audiolearning material to

any one of 50 carrels, all of which were equipped with playback units, drop the cartridge into the recess, turn on the machine, and listen through earphones (see Figure 8.15). Cartridges are plastic containers large enough to hold ¼-inch tape but used in the same way as cassettes. Cartridges are preferred by those who feel that the wider tape is more durable, longer lasting, and capable of reproduction of higher fidelity and that the container itself can withstand more handling.

AUDIO LANGUAGE LABORATORIES In most audio language laboratories, a combination of the audiolingual and traditional aproaches to language instruction is used. In the language laboratory itself, tape-recording materials are provided for the pupil's audiolingual learning, while points of grammar, background, and explanatory information are learned during regular class periods. Language laboratory activities generally comprise about 50 percent of course time or more, although this proportion varies fom school to school.

As a general rule, the pupils hear introductory explanations provided on the master tape and then the core of the lesson itself—the language words and phrases. There is then a short pause during which the pupil imitates what he has heard, his own voice being automatically recorded. At this point the teacher, who is at the control center, may have each student listen immediately to the model tape and then to the pupil's own version, thus allowing the pupil to judge his own pronunciation immediately and to correct it. Usually these corrections require the student to repeat the model-imitation-playback-compare procedure several times, and sufficient time should be built into the program for him to do so.

While at first pupils in a language laboratory usually work as a group, with all pupils using the same taped lessons, the

---

[1] Esther Sato and John Young, *Development of Instructional Materials in Japanese*, University of Hawaii, Department of Education, Honolulu, 1969.

FIGURE 8.15

Audio playback materials must be easily available to learners or teachers if they are to be put to use in the classroom. (a) The children are selecting cartridges from an open-access holder in the school media center. (b) The media librarian, a student helper, and a supervisor review the school's tape inventory, which is completely available to students and faculty for use in central carrels or classrooms. Do these procedures have meaning for you in your teaching situation? If so, can they be adapted to your specific needs and uses?

audiolingual method ideally encourages individual pupils to proceed as rapidly as they can. Since most language laboratory systems make it possible for the teacher to tune in on any individual pupil, learners who are having special difficulties may be given special attention and drill. Thus the programing should be flexible enough to accommodate the learning rates of both slow and fast learners. If such flexibility is built into audiolingual programs, the class may soon be strung out into various groups, each of which is proceeding at its own rate of learning, with some slow and fast learners working individually. Indeed, perhaps the greatest advantage of the audiolingual method is that it permits each pupil to proceed at his own pace (see Figure 8.16).

The audiolingual program must also provide for class measurement and evaluation and for supplementary and follow-up activities. During laboratory sessions, the teacher makes sure that the pupils are making the most of the taped lessons by tuning in on any of the pupils to check the progress and quality of the work being done (see Figure 8.17). The teacher also determines, by means of periodic tests, how well the pupils know the meanings of the words, phrases, and sentences they have been listening to. But interesting follow-up activities also should take place after the

FIGURE 8.16

These playback carrels provide instant access to any of hundreds of audiolingual lessons. Each learner is involved in continually listening and responding. Contrast this with the traditional situation when each pupil is one of a classroom group of 30 or more students and thus can recite or respond only a few times or not at all during a class period. What judgments do you have about the arrangement shown here?

FIGURE 8.17

(a) The control center of the language laboratory permits the teacher to monitor the quality of the lesson materials, listen in on the responses made by individual pupils, and interrupt to give instructions or corrections. (b) In her own individual carrel, a student listens to the teaching tape and records her own responses, then adjusts the dial to play back the model *and* her responses. What is the worth of such evaluation?

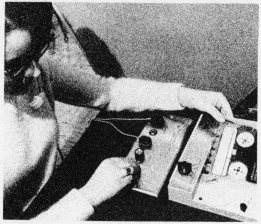

FIGURE 8.18

Projected visual materials are used in this language lab to provide background cues that assist in language comprehension. Do you agree that such visual experiences help place language learning in the context of the society that developed the language?

language laboratory period. These may include conversational situations, games, and cultural drills that enable the students to try out their newly acquired language skills as a group.

There is more to learning than being able to speak, read, and write it, however, and understanding the sociocultural backgrounds of the language itself is an important part of language instruction. In providing for this aspect of foreign-language instruction, the role of related audio-visual materials should be considered. Films are available that depict sociocultural scenes in France, Spain, Germany, and other countries. These films have foreign-language sound tracks that give most learners ample time to understand the language as it takes on concrete meaning from the visual presentation itself. Series of photographic slides and filmstrips with corresponding taped language narrations, also available from commercial sources, are widely used. These tapes carry words and simple dialogues between the characters shown on the filmstrips. This combination of prerecorded tapes and filmstrips offers great promise for efficient foreign-language instruction (see Figure 8.18). Many

teachers provide a visual environment by using travel posters and pictures of cities, people, and costumes in the country whose language is being studied. Typical folk songs can be brought into the foreign-language laboratory through prerecorded tapes as well as through transcriptions and records. Similar aural materials give students a chance to hear the works of well-known native composers. This use of recorded music makes a learner's interest in good music a powerful motivational device in foreign-language study.

The language laboratory, with its audiolingual and related visual materials, should not be thought of as a replacement for the teacher, but as a powerful tool that allows the pupil to hear language as it is spoken by native speakers and to engage in carefully controlled and recorded drills. When a person is learning to speak a language, he must practice speaking it correctly and, as has already been noted, the language laboratory encourages trial, evaluation by means of self-appraisal, and improvement through practice with a model tape.

Nevertheless, the teacher-pupil relationship of traditional language instruction has changed. In traditional language-class situations, one pupil may recite about once in 30 times, whereas a pupil in a language laboratory is listening about half the time and "reciting" the other half. Instead of 30 children listening to one teacher, the language laboratory teacher can listen to any one of the 30 pupils, each of whom is making individual judgments and responses.

Dial access playback

As more and more teachers and students discover the worth of audiolearning experiences, more and more such materials are accumulated. The problem of managing accumulating inventories of open-reel tapes, magazines, cassettes, cartridges, and disc records becomes increasingly formidable. Ordinarily, the more audiomaterials the school owns, the more difficult becomes the learner's access to the experiences they can provide. In many cases, audio dial access systems have proved to be the solution.

"Dial access system" refers to a method of storing recorded audio information in such a way that specific needed lessons or programs can be retrieved instantaneously through electronic means. Usually, several hundred or more lessons recorded on tape in open-reel, cassette, or cartridge form are arranged in "tape decks" connected through sophisticated switching equipment to many dials or sets of push-buttons very similar to those used on telephones. By dialing a call number as he would dial a telephone number, the student who is seated in one of numerous carrels, is instantaneously interconnected with the program he has selected. Because he listens through earphones, his program does not disturb those seated in nearby carrels or work areas (see Figure 8.19).

The end result of dial access systems, complicated though they are in some ways, is to simplify accessibility procedures. The following is a typical example of the use of

FIGURE 8.19

(a) Audiotape banks hold in readiness hundreds of audio lessons and other sources of information which are used by thousands of students at work in (b) audio retrieval carrels located in nearby buildings. (c and d) Needed information is secured by "dialing" the appropriate call number. How does this type of learning resource affect the roles of both teacher and pupil? What is the logical next step?

such a system to overcome accessibility problems:

The school's book librarian had asked for the opportunity to report on the constantly increasing demands for library services. "Our library is growing like 'Topsy,'" he began. "It seems the more instructional materials the students use— films, filmstrips, tapes, and so on, the more books they read. My helper and I just can't keep up. I'd like to tell you about the tape situation. Five years ago we regarded a reel of tape as a curiosity. Today look what we have. In addition to 414 disc record-

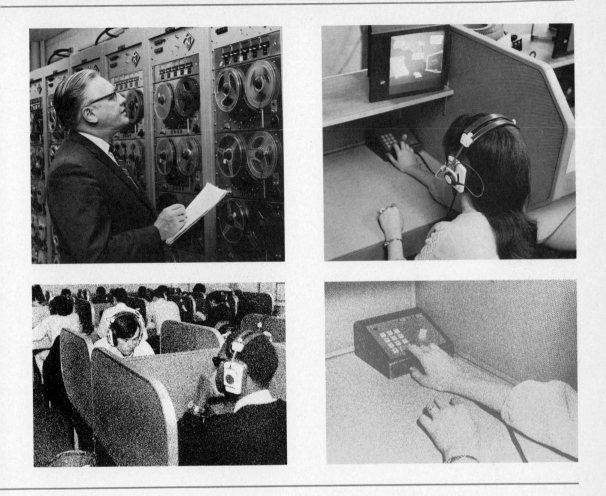

ings—some very old—we have 260 open-reel tapes, 124 ¼-inch cartridge tapes—mostly for the new foreign language program—and 540 cassettes. Can you wonder why many students simply can't locate what we all know is there? Often a month or more passes before we can get the subject and title cards made up. I need help!"

Help came in the form of a recommendations committee which included teachers, the principal, the media specialist, *and* the librarian. The school is small, and funds are limited; therefore, the dealer audio specialist who worked with the committee matched the most pressing needs with the available budget by installing a cassette wireless system which meets about 80 percent of the demands. The less frequently called for materials are still "shelved" in the school library.

There are many types of dial access installations; the type used depends on the nature of the specific problems to be solved. For example, certain systems very efficiently make available the typical inter-mixture of old and new forms of recorded information. For instance, at the Sinclair audiolearning center in Hawaii, as shifts in technology occurred, the library had first purchased records of varying speeds (78, 33⅓, 45, and 16 rpm) ; next, cartridges and magazines containing materials used in the language laboratories had been acquired; finally cassette audio materials had been added. During this time, the use of audio resource learning materials had been increasing steadily. The problems involved in reconciling the ''technical'' with the ''academic'' have been solved through the installation of one of the nation's most sophisticated and flexible dial access systems (see Figure 8.20). No matter what form the audio information was originally supplied in, the system converts it easily into tapes that can be instantly available to students. During a process like this one, a subtle evaluation procedure is at work. Materials that students do not think are useful are not called for and thus are not converted to currently usable form. On the other hand, materials that are in great demand are quickly converted to easily

available form as a result of student demand.

The teacher is at work in an environment of change. While he is awaiting the time when the best of currently available technological innovations are available to him, he should remember that there is much that can be done in the meantime. The tape recorder as an instrument of self-evaluation should be intensively explored. By using inexpensive cassette recorders and blank cassettes, the teacher and interested pupils can rerecord the best of existing traditional audio information— from records, and so forth—and thereby create a beginning collection of source information which might be kept right in the classroom for easy access. Most publishers of audiolearning materials make the materials available in record, cartridge, open-reel, or cassette form. Perhaps each school should begin now to standardize the form in which new materials are acquired. The advantages of cassette audio systems should

FIGURE 8.20

This is the heart of one dial access system. On the table are recording and playback units for long-playing discs, 78 rpm records, magazines, cassettes, cartridges, and live voice; no matter what its original form, audio information can be converted to uniform-speed monaural or stereo playback tapes mounted in a 400-channel tape deck. Students seated in carrels consult a directory and dial the audio resources. The system is open-ended; that is, later it can accommodate video cartridges in any form— film, tape, or magnetic disc—or be expanded for more audio input. What does this mean in terms of teaching strategies and learner involvement?

be carefully evaluated when standardization is planned.

Because the ways that audioinstructional strategies and materials can be used to affect the *learner* are the central concern of the teacher, additional examples of audiolearning plans and opportunities are set forth in the next chapter, on audio-cued learning.

Summary

Audio recording and playback equipment is available in various forms and for various uses. Though the teacher should be able to operate recording and playback devices, the reasons for acquiring such skills should always be kept in mind—to create effective learning opportunities for students.

Open-reel and cassette types of tape recording and playback equipment differ in significant ways. Understanding and achieving high-fidelity recording and playback should always be the aim.

Audio recording and playback may be used to carry on highly effective learner-centered experiences in self-evaluation. To play well and then to speak one's own efforts and thoughts, to be able to record such efforts and play back the results immediately can become a never-to-be-forgotten experience for the one involved.

Various types of card-reader recording-playback units are available which can be used in effective ways to accomplish individualized instruction, drill, and self-evaluation.

Whether tape or record playback equipment is used, the emphasis should be on how and why such playback experiences can be used to benefit both learner and teacher. Audio playback experiences are the central core of such teaching strategies as audiolingual instruction, language laboratory learning, and sophisticated audio dial access questioning. Each has specific advantages. In each case, many types of activities can be carried on by teachers and learners. Such innovations profoundly influence the roles they assume.

Audiolearning experiences can be related effectively to other appropriate media: films, still pictures, posters, and books.

Chapter 8 is organized as an introduction and companion to Chapter 9, "Audio-Cued Learning."

Further learner response projects

1

Locate and set up an open-reel tape recorder and demonstrate to your own satisfaction that you can operate it effectively. Judge your success by applying the evaluation criteria on page 334. If needed, seek the assistance of someone who has mastered the techniques of recording and playback—a friend, the media specialist, or the local dealer.

2

Repeat Project 1 with a cassette recorder-playback, a record player, a magnetic card reader. You may find it economical to share these activities as a member of a small group. You may arrange to master the equipment and then demonstrate your accomplishments in an interesting way to others.

3

As a practice teacher or a teacher in service, plan for the actual use of the tape recorder in enriching learning opportunities in your subject area. Include a statement of objectives and a description of the recording activity you will use. Also describe the physical and mechanical arrangements for using the tape recorder.

4

Set up a tape recorder in any normal classroom situation. Later, in private, listen to the playback and ask yourself such questions as these: Is my speech pleasant? Is my enunciation clear and understandable? Is my manner toward children pleasing? Can I learn anything from the children's responses to my questions and leadership?

5

As a teacher, anticipate the problems in language arts, music, or general learning that will arise and plan to use a tape recorder for handling them.

References

Creative Teaching with Tape. 3M Company, St. Paul, Minn.

DAVIDSON, RAYMOND L. *Audiovisual Machines.* 2d ed. International Textbook Co., Scranton, 1969, pp. 12–21; Chap. 2 "The Technology of Recording and Reproducing Sound."

KEMP, JERROLD E. *Planning and Producing Audiovisual Materials.* 2d ed. Chandler, San Francisco, 1968, pp. 129–134, Chap. 17 "Recording Sound."

SIMMONS, WARREN. "What To Look for When Selecting Blank Cassettes." *Stereo Review's Tape Recorder Annual 1971,* pp. 38–40.

WYMAN, RAYMOND. *Mediaware: Selection, Operation and Maintenance.* Wm. C. Brown, Dubuque, 1969. TS 2301. A7W9. Chap. 13 "Tape Recorders," pp. 117–128.

Media references

Audiovisual Language Laboratory, 16mm film, sound, 13 min. Purdue University.

Basic Language Laboratory Equipment and Its Use, 16mm film, sound, b/w, 14 min. Pennsylvania Department of Public Instruction, Harrisburg, Pa.

Microphone Speaking, 16mm film, sound, color, 14 min. Centron, Kansas City.

Planning for the Language Laboratory, 16mm film, sound, b/w, 13 min. Pennsylvania Department of Public Instruction, Harrisburg, Pa.

Speak, Listen, Learn, 16mm film, sound, color, 11 min. Rheem Califone, Los Angeles.

The Tape Recorder, 16mm film, sound, b/w, 6 min. Iowa University.

Source references

See source lists in the Appendix; particularly relevant sections are: Audio Equipment and Materials; Free and Inexpensive Materials; Furniture and Facilities.

See *Student Production Guide,* Chapter 4, "Producing Photo and Sound Materials for Instruction," Audiotape Production.

Objectives	Performance responses

1

To understand the nature and use of audio-cued individualized learning activities and test one's understanding by selecting, using, and evaluating available or created audio-cued individualized learning materials useful in group or individualized learning-response situations.

Plan, create, use with a group, and evaluate an original audio-cued learning experience. If possible, use this experience with an individual or small group and report the responses. Evaluate your attempt by using the Evaluation Criteria on pages 382–385.

2

To learn about and evaluate a variety of techniques through which pupil participation and involvement may grow out of audio-cued learning activities arranged for one or more teaching strategies: individualized, small-group, and large-group instruction.

Arrange to help one or two learners who wish to and are able to plan and create an original audio-cued learning experience suitable either in an individual or group situation. Evaluate the experience by using the Evaluation Criteria on pages 382–385, as well as the learning tenets described in Chapter 2, pages 46–74.

3

To formulate working plans for the utilization of audio-cued learning that relates to your teaching responsibilities.

Arrange to examine and evaluate audio-cued learning materials (see pages 382–385) available in your subject area and grade level. Locate materials in your school library, in the inventories or your local audiovisual dealer, or through other sources.

4

To understanding the physiological and psychological nature of learner attention to and response to audio-cued learning experiences.

Arrange to test suggestions made about the nature of the efficiency of listening and possible ways to improve it; evaluate and report outcomes by applying as criteria the learning tenets described in Chapter 2, pages 46–74.

LEARNER responses to directions, explanations, or descriptions given audibly by the teacher or by fellow students have for decades made up a great part of normal classroom procedures. As long as teachers have taught and pupils have been at work, listening has been a primary means of receiving instruction and thus of responding. Research studies have established that nearly 50 percent of the typical classroom day is spent in listening activities. Also, the higher the grade level, the more time is usually spent in listening —at the college level, for some students, nearly 90 percent of the student's time may be spent in listening to discussions and lectures.

So usual is the practice of communication through the spoken word or message that its inefficiencies, though widely acknowledged, are still widely accepted as "occupational hazards." These hazards include individual variations in ability to comprehend audio messages, the incomprehensiveness or inaccuracies of the messages themselves, and the reality that though some listeners can achieve understanding immediately in response to audio messages, many others must have repeated opportunities to listen before they can fully comprehend. A final and all too often insurmountable hazard is the fact that for many learners who need to refer to or restudy an audio message to gain understanding, the original message itself—because of its transient nature or dependence on the sender's memory—is unavailable. The child who asks sincerely for a "repeat" all too often gets one that is quite unlike the original or a too hastily repeated and incomplete form of the original.

Now with the development of mechanical recording devices, including open-reel and cassette tape recorders and playbacks (described in Chapter 8), audio-cued learning materials have moved ahead into new areas of precision and usefulness. It is these new areas that teachers should understand. Thus they should acquire knowledge of these new devices and of techniques for using them in their day-to-day classroom procedures. This chapter is intended to help teachers acquire such knowledge.

Audio-cued learning defined

AUDIO-CUED learning refers to the preparation of magnetically recorded explanations, descriptions, directions, and the like, and their use by individuals or groups of learners as they seek knowledge or develop skills. The materials may be recorded on open-reel tape, audio cassettes, audio cartridges, cards, or records. It is the nature of audiolearning experiences themselves, however, that is considered in this chapter, rather than the various specific mechanical means that can be employed in making them available to learners.

In the last 10-year period, audiolearning materials have undergone a dramatic metamorphosis. Initially, almost all recordings (disc and tape) and educational radio broadcasts consisted of descriptions, readings of stories, poems, and great literary works, dramatizations of historical events, foreign-language instruction, and so forth. Currently, however, a greater amount of imagination is employed in the use of the audio channel. It has become the central and connecting thread used to bind together other media. Thus audio materials are used to achieve the necessary interrelated simultaneous use of pictures (projected or opaque), charts, maps, specimens, films, and so on. Nevertheless, whether a form of audiolearning is older or newer, as long as it is pertinent to the improvement of learning and encourages constructive development of effective learning strategies (individualized, small groups, etc.), it is considered here. In other words, the *learning* aspects of all audio-cued instructional experiences are the basic point of concern in this chapter.

We begin by describing examples of the newer forms of audiolearning, that is, the use of comprehensive recorded instructions, explanations, descriptions, or directions that refer to related essential materials which the learner turns to and learns from while he simultaneously follows the basic strategy and further explanations outlined to him. This reciprocal process is audio-cued instructional experience in its pure form. Though many specific names are used—audiotutorial instruction, tape-directed instruction, audio-directed learning—to describe such learning systems, any of these which rely on prerecorded directions or explanations to guide the process are usually called audio-cued learning in this book.

The first example is vividly described by S. N. Postlethwait, professor of biology at Purdue University, as he recounts his experiences in developing what he calls audiotutorial learning materials as a result of his increasing dissatisfaction with the traditional lecture method of teaching (see Figure 9.1):

I had become very much concerned about the diversity of backgrounds represented among students who were enrolled in a freshman botany course. Of 390 students, some came from high schools where they had received very good instruction, and others from schools where they had received poor instruction. Yet I was trying to teach all of these in one lecture. In order to help those who had poor backgrounds in botany, I asked the people in audiovisual for ideas. They suggested that each week I make up a special tape explanation of the essential information I had covered and make it available at a central place for those who wished to come and listen to it. So I began to prepare such a special lesson each week.

As I prepared more and more of these lectures, I reasoned, "Why don't I ask the students to bring along their textbooks so I can direct them to open the book to page so and so, so they can see how the subject matter in the text is related to the things I'm lecturing about?" Then I soon reasoned that I would like to have them bring a laboratory manual, too, so they could open the manual to where they could see how the text and the lecture related to what the lab manual asked them to do. And this worked out all right. Next, I reasoned, "Why not, when I refer to a plant, let them see the plant? Why not send a plant over so they can see how

FIGURE 9.1

(a) Botany students at Purdue listen to and respond to audiotutorial directions and explanations that refer to related experiences with objects, specimens, pictures, diagrams, and so on, as shown in (b) a carrel prepared for a specific audiotutorial botany demonstration. Where in this range does your own classroom practice fall?

PLATE 7.1

Pictures add significant meaning to maps and map symbols. Here actual photographs of an island and lakes are compared with the map symbols that represent them.

How an Island is Shown on a Map

How Lakes are Shown on a Map

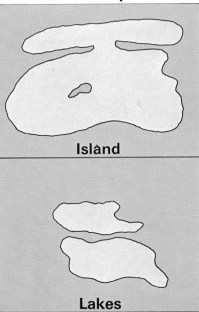

Island

Lakes

PLATE 7.2

Map symbols for cities and roads are particularly
abstract. Thus concrete visual experiences in
the form of color photographs should accompany
early learning of such symbols.

Small City Map Symbols

Capital City Map Symbols

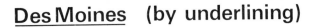 <u>Des Moines</u>   (by underlining)

 Springfield   (by using a special symbol)

How Pipelines are Shown on a Map

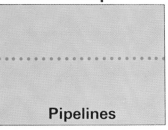

Pipelines

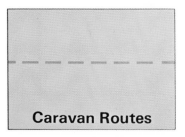

Caravan Routes

How Caravan Routes are Shown on a Map

PLATE 7.3

PLATE 7.4

This is a section from a primarily political map for beginners, with few place names and only major relief indicated.

This section is from another elementary map, which includes altitude tints for land and water areas.

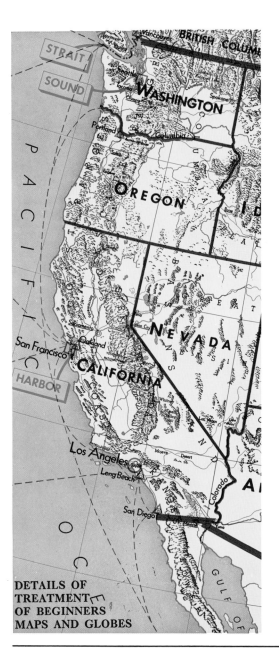

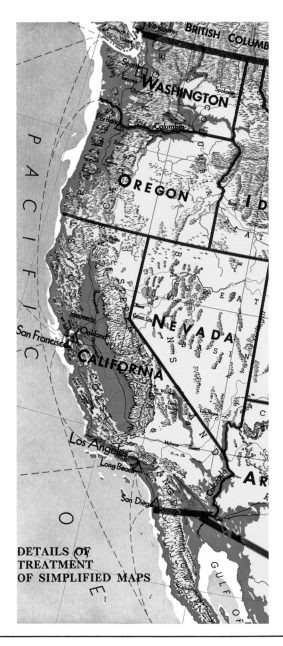

PLATE 7.5　　　　　　　　　　　　　**PLATE 7.6**

The same region is shown on an intermediate physical-political map, which includes more place names and other details than the two elementary maps.

This map uses both color and shading to show relief. The shading is shown on the east and southeast slopes of hills and mountains as if the summer sun were casting shadows in the late afternoon.

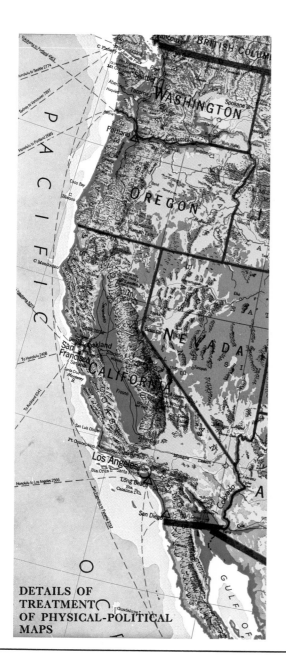

DETAILS OF TREATMENT OF PHYSICAL-POLITICAL MAPS

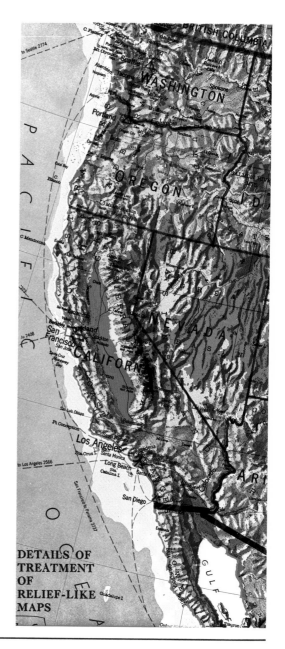

DETAILS OF TREATMENT OF RELIEF-LIKE MAPS

PLATE 7.7

This view of the rising earth greeted the Apollo 11 astronauts as they came from behind the moon shortly after entering lunar orbit. The astronauts were then on their way down to the moon's surface. The surface features of the moon in the foreground are near the eastern side of the moon as seen from earth. Our earth, 240,000 miles away, hangs above the lunar horizon.

PLATE 11.1

The Artificial Kidney is a teaching film that combines direct photography with animation. These frames are taken from an animated sequence that shows how the normal kidney functions.

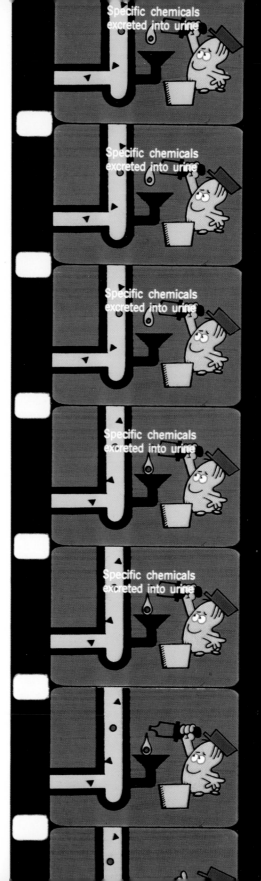

the plant is related to the laboratory manual—is related to the text—is related to the subject matter on the tape?"

It turned out that the whole thing was not a lecture on tape at all, but quite a different kind of thing. It was a matter of placing before the students all of the different kinds of items, regardless of what they might be, which contribute to their learning—experimental devices or whatever—and then talking into a tape recorder as if I were talking to one student or a friend—trying to help that friend learn botany—in other words, tutoring a student via tape recorder to go through a sequence of carefully planned related learning events.[1]

During the first semester, more and more students began to use the facility. Some students asked Dr. Postlethwait if he would mind if they didn't come to the

[1] This and the other direct quotations are taken, with his permission, from a lecture-demonstration presentation made by Dr. Postlethwait to the faculty of the University of Hawaii and members of the Department of Educational Communications Experienced Teacher Media Fellowship group, spring, 1967. (In his full presentation, Dr. Postlethwait also described the further refinements to his audiotutorial method and the significant gains in learned achievement which resulted.)

regular lectures. "Sure," he replied "go ahead and fail the course if you want." As he summed up the results in his account, however, "So they stopped coming to the regular lectures *but* they didn't fail!"

Student responses to this "audiotutorial" experience were significant. Several young people volunteered that never before had they gained such a feeling of confidence and rapport with an instructor. Many responses were phrased like this one: "We felt that you were speaking to us as friends more than students." Another reported: "I no longer felt embarrassed about 'seeking assistance.' Now all I had to do was rewind the tape and listen again or as often as necessary, with the result that I could successfully complete anything to which I was willing to give the time." This was the reaction of still another: "It is wonderful to know that such carefully worked-out instructions and explanations are available to use not just once, but as often as I find it necessary to refer, to rethink, and to check myself."

A final observation is germane. Contrary to popular belief, the poor students, those who frequently receive excessive sympathy, spent only 25 percent of the time on the audio lessons as the "A" students. Through such means as these, therefore, complete opportunities are *uniformly* avail-

able to those who wish to learn; they need only be willing to spend the necessary time.

Another example comes from the Hawaii English program (described in detail in Chapter 15):

In a primary-level classroom, one of many such classrooms, nearly 60 children ages 5 through 8 are engaged in an exciting program of individualized instruction. Continued observation reveals that even the youngest children are, at their own instigation and pace, engaging in independent activities. Around one table, three children have donned earphones; while listening intently, each is following the words of a recorded story in his own copy of an illustrated book. These prereaders have selected listening-looking stories. "The goal is enjoyment," the teacher comments, adding, "But some of the children learn to recognize the relationship between the audio and visual word—and—learn to read. They can't help it!"

At another table, two children work as a peer team. One checks the other's responses to vocabulary cards which they run through a card reader. As they listen to the prerecorded words which describe colors or geometric shapes, they learn to associate each audio cue correctly with the pictured color, shape, or word. They continue until either wishes to select additional cards or pursue another kind of audio-cued learning experience, perhaps one that involves listening to and following directions.

During this time the three teachers assigned to each 60 pupils monitor the work of those who are self-occupied, evaluate the quality of responses students are making, help pupils select and use individualized learning activities, and encourage learners as they plan how to use their new-found information—drawing a picture, writing a sentence or two, or telling other students about some of their discoveries.[2]

[2] *Evaluation Report of the English Skills and Literature Program,* Hawaii Curriculum Center, Honolulu, November 1971.

Audio-cued learning serves well in the area of skill development. For example, an industrial arts teacher had long been concerned over the countless hours he was devoting to repeating directions related to some of the beginning skills which must be mastered by those seeking to accomplish even the most rudimentary woodworking projects. He explained his solution as follows:

I got the idea when I visited an electrical appliance manufacturer and watched a new worker being introduced to her job— soldering wires onto a circuit. The supervisor himself showed her how to manipulate an automatic soldering iron. Then he directed her to put on earphones and indicated a switch which activated an audio tape. In response to audio-cued instructions, the new worker selected from a tray of wires two which were identically color-coded. She placed the wire ends onto a terminal of the same color, deftly touched the tip of the soldering iron to the terminal, withdrew the iron, and tested the strength of the connection by touching it with a voltmeter terminal. The needle jumped to indicate that the first step of the new task sequence had been mastered. I reasoned that if they could teach skills this surely in industry, I could do the same in my classes.

He then displayed a half dozen audio "talk-throughs" which he had prepared: identification and use of basic drawing instruments, vocabulary terms used in woodworking, identifying 10 kinds of wood used in cabinetmaking, steps in making a molded plastic saucer, and so forth. In each case, the audio instructions were related to trays filled with appropriate objects, tools, and specimens (see Figure 9.2). "Now," he continued, "I spend most of the time in class helping answer questions growing out of the individualized audio lessons; more important, I supervise the students as they plan and produce the projects they want

FIGURE 9.2

This industrial arts student is responding to audio cues as he is being "talked-through" the steps involved in making a molded plastic object. He responds to the audio suggestions by manipulating tools and identifying chemicals and other equipment used in plastic casting. What advantages do you see in this kind of procedure?

to make. When I notice that skill information still is lacking, I suggest they go back to the appropriate 'talk-through.'"

At another school, the audiovisual coordinator has, as have many of his counterparts elsewhere, solved the fall-of-the-year "I've forgotten how to use the ——— equipment" questions from teachers by preparing audiotaped instructions on the use of projection devices and various copying machines. He described the procedure thus:

During the summer a good deal of forgetting occurs. To avoid possible embarrassment about this and to make sure that any teacher at any time can review any procedure he wishes, I recorded directions in the same friendly conversational manner I would if the teacher were standing with me in front of the machine. I describe a step, wait for the teacher to respond, go on to the next step, wait again, and so on. I suggest at the end that if the finished result was not entirely satisfactory the teacher should ask me for more help. I have had very few such requests but many congratulations.

The uses to which audio-cued learning procedures may be put are limited only by the availability of materials or a teacher's willingness to contrive descriptions or "talk-throughs" of his own invention.

Some advantages of audio-cued learning materials

IT may be assumed that among a group of 25 young learners there are 25 levels of comprehension and 25 variations in attention span and interest. Audio-cued learning materials are, by their very nature, a most effective means of providing for these inevitable differences.

Audio-cued learning opportunities can enable any learner, regardless of his individual levels of ability, to become more involved in instructional learning experiences. The learner chooses what he wants to do and the pace at which he wants to do it. Through this procedure, increased learner involvement is developed that overcomes two of the long-acknowledged limitations of large-group instruction: the inertia that results for some and the discouragement that results for others from moving forward at the pace set by the entire group rather than that set by the individual.

A record based on observation of group interaction between the teacher and the members of an actual class of 25 pupils visualizes the explanation-question-answer interrelationships during a 20-minute session (see Figure 9.3). What might have happened if pupils 4, 23, and 25 had had the opportunity of pursuing audio-cued learning experiences in addition to participating in the group lesson? What might have happened if pupils 1, 2, and 15 had had such an opportunity? If these three were "slow learners" who needed more time to listen or even relisten to information and suggestions, audio-cued materials could have provided this flexibility. These children then might have had creative ideas which they could have effectively contributed during the next large-group discus-

sion. On the other hand, if pupils 1, 2, and 15 were so far ahead of their age-mates that they were bored with the slower-paced group discussion, then the alternative learning experiences provided by audio-cued materials might have allowed them to quest independently for further information. Thus they might have been temporarily separated from the rest of the group, later acting as informed "reporters" to the group or even as "peer teachers."

There are presently available at least 20,000 well-planned and carefully produced audioinstructional programs or learning materials, most of which are readily available to the classroom teacher in either tape, record, or cassette form.[3] The majority of existing audio programs are useful for individualized listening and response. For example, many more fifth-graders (Figure 9.3) would surely have participated if all had been permitted to select, in terms of their personal interests, individualized advance listening experiences about the Panama Canal.

[3] The National Center for Audio Tapes (described on pages 366–367 of this chapter) issues regular biannual catalogs. The 1970–1972 edition lists more than 12,000 taped programs.

FIGURE 9.3

The nature of the responses of the 25 members of a fifth-grade class following their listening, as a group, to a 15-minute audiotape playback entitled "The Building of the Panama Canal." The diagrammatic sociogram shows the origin and direction of responses during a 20-minute discussion period. Discussion centered around prelistening questions developed by pupils and teacher in anticipation of the group listening experience. The questions had been summarized on the chalkboard in short statement form. Thirteen pupils entered into the discussion—what is your reaction? What is the effect on the class of the participation of pupils 4, 23, and 25? What comments do you have about this group instructional technique? What alternatives are now available?

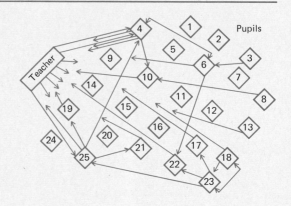

The benefits of expanding the number of learners who become involved are most effectively achieved when classroom procedures are arranged so as to encourage small groups or peer teams of two and three pupils to work together in planning activities, selecting audiotapes, records, or cassettes, and using them. Usually it takes some reasonable time to build such new ways of organizing for learning into the habit patterns of students. For those who have spent years accommodating themselves to active or passive participation in large-group instruction, the freedom of individualized activity must be explored and its benefits learned. At first such freedom may be used carelessly, and if so, the teacher must guide the learners' energy toward realizing that profitable involvements will yield rich rewards.

The teacher may delegate to well-planned and well-produced audio-cued instructional materials the endless and often repetitious task of "information giving." "How wonderful it is," a teacher reports, "to find that audio-cued instructions and informational descriptions are reliable in that they can be referred to endlessly to 'tell' the same explanation or describe the same sequence of instructions and be available immediately when it becomes desirable to ask a student to review a procedure before coming to the teacher for help in planning and doing creative work." More and more, the truth of this axiom is being demonstrated: Use media to communicate cognitive and skill information and *free the teacher to teach.*

Just as an airport traffic control officer can "talk down" an approaching pilot who seeks his way in through a fog, a teacher may explain, on tape, how to choose relevant information from an arithmetic work problem and make such explanatory information reliably and endlessly available for those who need it. The enunciation and pronunciation of new vocabulary items, which must be learned before reading with comprehension, may also be done effectively through taped directions and explanations. Drill information lends itself well to this kind of specific communication—to give another example, explanations of maps and charts relating to locations of rivers, mountain ranges, capitals, principal cities, ports, and so forth.

Ordinarily, when a teacher has completed some tape-recorded informational material, he automatically replays it to evaluate the manner in which the explanation has been accomplished—its completeness, the understandability of the words used to describe the thing or idea, and the pace at which the information is presented. This kind of almost automatic evaluation of tape-recorded audiolearning material is seldom practiced by the teacher who explains and describes things during the "catch-as-you-can" pace of ordinary classroom verbal instruction. One teacher described his experiences this way:

I admire my pupils' willingness to accept my explanations in answer to their questions. The first, second, or third time the same question was asked, I usually managed to maintain my patience and "temperament." By the time the same problem had to be explained the sixth or seventh time, I'm afraid that I got quite "short" in my answers and possibly on some occasions even a little "angered." This, of course, affected my whole attitude toward the learners and teaching—this should not be. Now, I tape record much of the mechanical explanations, drill materials, and descriptions of assignments. Then I listen to a playback. As I do this, I attempt to judge the material as a child would, anticipating their need for explanations and directions which are well paced, concise, complete, and understandable. Often, I rerecord my explanations—sometimes three or four times— before being satisfied. Then, to be sure that my "talk-throughs," explanations, or descriptions are meaningful to the learners, we try them out together.

FIGURE 9.4

(a) The children participating in this small-group activity are seeking information. They respond to cues given in the audiotape accompanying the filmstrip. (b) They follow other tutorial suggestions as they evaluate their new-found information. (c) This group member is pursuing a highly individualized goal as she responds to new insights gained by using a low-powered microscope. How does such classroom organization affect the traditional attitudes and feelings about teaching responsibilities? What effect does all of this have on the involvement, participation, and creative outcomes experienced by pupils?

"But how," one conscientious teacher asks, "can I be sure that the child will accept a tape-recorded explanation with the same interest and enthusiasm as he accepts me?" (See Figure 9.4.) This question has ego overtones. Quite naturally, the teacher who is used to being surrounded by a bevy of youngsters seeking his attention thinks he will miss a little of this. But will he? With reasonable practice, the teacher is able not only to feel "personal identification" with each child, but also to convey these feelings of personal interest by his recorded voice to each child who listens. True, a certain amount of conditioning, particularly of learner expectations and attitudes, is necessary when audiolearning materials are introduced. Some children may not accept the idea at once. However, after explanations have been made and use of the materials begun, most learners realize they may have *more* of a teacher's attention through these means. Audio recordings which present careful explanations through the voice of the teacher (or able fellow pupils) are advantageous ways to learn at one's own pace, with the built-in opportunity to review or "restudy."

Thus much dependable information, on which the teacher may now spend countless hours in initial and repeated explanations, can be presented in tape-recorded form for the benefit of the child who will listen and who has the opportunity to re-listen and, on occasion, ask the teacher to answer his own questions before he returns to the playback for his final opportunities to restudy and to learn. The great advantage is that when recorded materials are used, learners soon realize that they have even more "living" contacts with their teacher simply because the teacher spends time counseling them, and advising them.

Audio-cued learning materials are highly valid. Most audiolearning materials currently available through educational or commercial sources are the result of careful planning by professional educators and subject content experts. Audio recorded information is usually offered with related and needed learning materials. For example, an audio explanation of the metamorphosis of honey wasps may refer to actual objects and specimens in the learning kit available to the learner while he listens. Tape-recorded directions refer the listener to areas of an exhibit—the wings of the honey wasp, a portion of the wasp's nest, the cells within it—all as supplementary interacting learning opportunities which, when brought together by the audio "talk-through," are bound to produce an effective total learning opportunity.

As noted earlier, the initial use of audio recorded materials was for informational purposes alone; therefore, it has been only recently that increasing numbers of cues, directions, or suggestions to learners have been incorporated into the stream of the audio experience. Thus it is that from content tape-recorded materials—characteristic of what was available a decade ago—the current trend is toward the development of audio-cued materials which, in addition to imparting information, actually assist the learner by referring him to interrelated experiences out of which he may ultimately grasp larger and larger amounts of understandable information or attain the development of skills, or both.

Some sources of audio-cued learning materials

DURING the last decade, one of the most rapidly expanding areas of educational communication technology has related to the production, distribution, and utilization of records, open-reel tapes, tape cassettes, and language master types of playbacks developed with commercial, governmental, and local school district impetus.

Though this discussion of the sources of audio-cued learning materials includes references to format (materials in record, tape, or tape plus related media form, etc.), the emphasis is on the manner in which various audio-cued learning materials direct the student through *experiences* with interrelated materials such as flat pictures, models or specimens, 8mm continuous film loops, projected still images, workbooks, laboratory manuals, study sheets, and so forth.

School radio broadcasts

Today vast areas of the United States are within reach of the 450 educational radio stations which provide systematic instructional audio programing for school use. Educational radio began in 1919 when the University of Wisconsin's state-owned station WHA began broadcasting. From this beginning, local, state, and regional educational broadcasting systems have come into existence: the New York State Empire School Broadcasting Service, the Wisconsin School of the Air (a network of 12 satellite stations), the Indiana State School of the Air, the Minnesota School Broadcast Service, the Texas School of the Air, and others. In addition, many city school districts use radio to distribute audiolearning programs: Phoenix, Arizona; Los Angeles and San Francisco, California; Carbondale, De Kalb, and Urbana, Illinois; Iowa City, Iowa; Louisville, Richmond, and Lexington, Kentucky; Boston, Massachusetts; Detroit, East Lansing, Grand Rapids, Kalamazoo, and Marquette, Michigan; Portland, Corvallis, and Eugene, Oregon; Philadelphia and Pittsburgh, Pennsylvania; Knoxville, Murfreesboro, and Nashville, Tennessee; Seattle and Pullman, Washington; Provo and Salt Lake City, Utah; and others.

Currently, the National Education Radio Network, a division of the National Association of Educational Broadcasters, has become the means of interchanging among their membership of 200 educational radio stations a minimum of five hours per week of high-quality audioinstructional programming including the physical sciences, social sciences, arts and literature, current news and events, and enrichment programs for disadvantaged children. Such programs are produced by individual network affiliates and made available to association members by interchange for rebroadcast. Through such programing, the teacher has available to him a continuing resource from which to choose those learning experiences which apply.

NATURE AND ADVANTAGES OF SCHOOL BROADCASTS   School broadcasts are carefully planned audiolearning experiences which represent resources ordinarily beyond those available to local classrooms. Lessons are prepared under the supervision of excellent teachers, radio program specialists, and subject authorities who work directly with professional radio writers. Such cooperation results in a learning resource which effectively anticipates the needs of the pupil and makes the most of the strength of the characteristics of the medium.

1. School broadcasts are actually team-teaching demonstrations   Because the production of a broadcast audio series grows out of months of planning and consultation with local classroom teachers and other specialists, the educational program represents the combined effort of subject supervisors, classroom teachers, and subject-matter experts who plan and work together to determine what learning experiences can be accomplished through an aural presentation. An example is a series entitled *Sense of the World*.[4] This series aims to make listeners more acutely aware of the world around them through the use of their own senses and encourages creative behavioral

[4] *National Audio Tape Catalog,* 1970–1972.

responses through such means as writing stories or poems, dancing, drawing, and composing. The teacher may choose to record experiences from such a series for use by those few learners in the classroom who are, because of their temperament and ability, capable of responding to such enrichment experiences more extensively than some of their classmates.

2. School broadcasts provide documentations of current history Radio broadcasting can provide the means of recording special events as audio documentations of reality. High-point historical episodes of the events leading up to World War II, the World War II peace ceremonies, and the establishment of the United Nations, key episodes in the 10 years of developments that preceded landing a man on the moon—these events and many others have been made the subjects of documentation and explanation through the facilities of school broadcast stations.

3. School broadcasts effectively present music for study and appreciation Educational school broadcasters have arranged for skilled performers to participate in programs that are planned around musical themes: music of other times, music of other lands, folk music, and so forth. The Civic Orchestra concert sponsored by the New York State Empire Network, "Music Time and Rhythms and Games," and others sponsored by the Wisconsin School of the Air are examples. One such program sequence, "Let's Sing," during which representatives from local schools assemble annually to conduct a song festival, attracts an audience of thousands of students each year (see Figure 9.5).

4. School broadcasts often are planned to engage the active participation of local teachers and pupils Radio lesson manuals or handbooks describe the program content, outline local classroom pupil responsibilities, and list the materials that should be on hand when the broadcast begins. Such materials are usually prepared and distributed to participating teachers well before the broadcast. Preliminary study and discussion by the class are encouraged, and suggestions for these activities are also included in the manuals. Whenever possible,

FIGURE 9.5

Educational radio broadcasts are produced in many countries. In Japan, a pioneer in instruction by radio, the schools rely heavily on broadcasting in all subject areas. For example, these kindergarten children are listening to "The Piano That Fell into the Sea," one of the many radio programs that form a large part of the general educational experience in Japan.

the programs include audio instructions or cues relating to experiments or activities which necessitate pupil participation during the broadcast or immediately after it. The class is also encouraged through broadcast suggestions to carry on a follow-up discussion, projects, or creative activities.

For example, in St. Louis, radio broadcast lessons in science are coordinated with local classroom use of related media. The science lessons are prepared by expert script writers in consultation with teachers and subject experts. As a program proceeds, the teacher in each classroom assembles the simple science paraphernalia referred to during the broadcast. The lessons anticipate classroom pupil participation (see Figure 9.6).

This method can easily be adapted for other subjects. Before a social studies broadcast on the southwestern states, for example, photographs of the area are assembled and arranged as a learning display. Specimens, manufactured objects, or agricultural items may be included, and maps of the area may be displayed for reference during the broadcast. Similarly, in anticipation of a broadcast on soil erosion, specimens of sandy loam, clay, or alluvial silt are gathered and arranged in a tray, so that the students can examine the specimens during or after the broadcast, or both.

5. School broadcasts are available on tape Teachers may procure "the best of educational radio broadcasts" in tape-recorded form through the National Center for Audio Tapes (see below). This service has overcome one of the dilemmas of radio broadcasting, that is, the inevitable inconsistencies between local planning for learning purposes and central planning for broadcast purposes. Obviously, audiolearning materials should be available at the time that they should be used within a specific classroom context. In other words, for the most effective use of audiolearning experiences, the teacher should be able to order in advance specific materials for the use of his own group. The NCAT makes this possible.

National Center for Audio Tapes

The National Center for Audio Tapes is a department of the University of Colorado which assumes the responsibility of selecting the best of the available audiolearning programs and makes them available through a tape dubbing service to any school district or educational agency.[5]

[5] Teachers and administrators who are interested should address inquiries to Director, National Center for Audio Tapes, Room 320 Stadium Building, University of Colorado, Boulder, Colorado 80302.

FIGURE 9.6

After a science broadcast, these pupils are doing one of the experiments described. What opportunity does this procedure provide for integrating audio information—received by radio in this case—into the stream of ongoing classroom instruction? How does this procedure encourage creative follow-up activity?

Many of these programs are chosen from educational radio broadcasts, and all may be obtained by the individual classroom teacher. Thus a tremendous reservoir of audiolearning experiences is accessible to all school districts of the United States, including the remote districts which are outside the reception areas of any current educational radio facilities.

The 1970–1972 catalog of the Center lists more than 12,000 audiolearning tapes which represent selections from 34 educational broadcasters and schools of the air; 12 government agencies; commercial broadcasting networks, including NBC, ABC, and CBS; 44 American colleges and universities; 35 national leagues and foundations; 6 foreign educational broadcasting services, including the Canadian Broadcasting Service, French Broadcasting Service, and British Information Service; selected industrial groups; the Voice of America; the United Nations; the National Education Association; the U.S. Office of Education, and so forth (see Figure 9.7).

Government sources
The efficiency of audio communications, at first by radio, then supplemented by distributing actual tapes and recordings to schools, has for years been recognized by many government agencies that need to distribute information at a low cost to mass audiences. A large number of such information materials are now available which may be useful for instructional purposes. Audio materials obtainable from the National Aeronautics and Space Administration are examples. During the course of NASA activities, periodic reports are made about activities at space centers (Houston, etc.). These reports usually consist of actual interviews—astronauts describing the Apollo space voyages, scientists discussing the reasons for space probing, and the like. Available first as radio broadcast materials, they almost immediately become available

also in tape-recorded form for use in schools.

The Department of State produces weekly radio reports which are later taped and distributed to schools requesting such materials. Department of State reports include accounts of current problems in world affairs, special reports on developing countries, and other authoritative reports of use to students as they study problems of government, United States history, and current affairs. Similarly, the Departments of the Interior, Agriculture, and Health, Education, and Welfare, the Bureau of Fisheries, and many other departments and agencies use radio and simultaneously recorded or taped versions of the information.

Fortunately, all of these government agencies now distribute appropriate taped materials to the audiovisual directors or media specialists assigned to such work in the various state education departments of the 50 states. Inquiries sent to one's state department of education media or audiovisual officer will provide the teacher with local information about which are available and under what circumstances.[6]

Commercial sources
Virtually all school subjects are now enriched by audio-cued learning materials produced under careful supervision by newly organized media learning materials companies, as well as by textbook publishers. It is fascinating to observe how book publishers, for decades engaged in the production of printed materials alone, have engaged in creative leadership in bridging the old and the new by producing new media materials—including many audio-cued learning experiences. Originally, audioin-

[6] Additional sources of government audio materials are listed in *Educator's Guide to Free Tapes, Scripts, and Transcriptions*, Educator's Progress Service.

FIGURE 9.7

In a world where information sources of many
types are distributed through radio and recorded
channels, almost every classroom should be so
equipped as to allow students ready access to
these sources. Provisions for (a) large-group
listening and (b and c) small-group listening
encourage involvement and learner interest.

structional materials were produced only by companies that were involved only in the manufacture and distribution of informational records and recordings.

For example, social studies for years has been well served by such materials as Landmark Records, the Enrichment Records series,[7] and the "You Are There" series and "I Can Hear It Now" series (1919–1949, 1960–1969), both by Columbia.[8] The last series brings to the classroom the actual voices of famous people recorded originally during the actual rush of events that inspired what they were saying. Roosevelt, MacArthur, Eisenhower, Kennedy, and many others have been immortalized in this way. The Enrichment Records and "You Are There" series present dramatized events in American history, including recordings such as "Voyages of Columbus," "Landing of the Pilgrims," "California Gold Rush," "Lee and Grant at Appomattox," etc. Most teachers have discovered how effective such materials are in the teaching of history and current history.

The work of the National Council of Teachers of English is well known. Over the years, the Council's collection of recorded readings, interpretations, and dramatizations has grown to include the plays of Shakespeare, the prose of American authors, ballads and verses of the American frontier, and many other types of literature; all offer excitement and thrilling rewards for both teachers and pupils who incorporate them into the stream of instruction in literature.[9] Readings by contemporary English-speaking authors virtually bring the author into the classroom to read his own works and, in some cases, have

them interpreted by professionals, as in the "Modern Poets Anthology of 98 American and British Poets (Caucasian and Black)."[10]

Audioinstruction in foreign languages represents a particularly widespread use of recorded materials. The audiolingual approach to modern language education was developed during World War II. Originally, records and transcriptions were used to record lessons given by a native of the language or by an instructor whose pronunciation of the language was representative of native speakers. Today, however, most of the audiolearning materials bridge across a decade of progress and thus appear in the form of audio-cued materials. Such materials, which are commercially produced, may be used by groups or by individuals. Most of these audio materials are cued in such a manner as to allow learners to refer to related materials: 8mm continuous-loop films, maps, diagrams, or charts, printed books to accompany spoken stories, filmstrips, slides, and selected specimens or objects to manipulate as the audio suggestions or cues indicate. Usually, suggestions cue both teacher and pupil concerning the nature of learner-oriented creative and inventive utilization opportunities.[11] Such responses reveal the nature of any behavioral changes taking place in learners and become a most valid basis for evaluation.

The following are representative of a vast number of currently available commercially produced audio-cued materials:

The audio-cued lesson entitled "Simple Geography Terms"[12] is used in the social

[7] *Enrichment Teaching Materials and Landmark Records,* Enrichment Records.

[8] Columbia Records, Educational Services.

[9] See *Resources for the Teaching of English,* National Council of Teachers of English (published annually).

[10] McGraw-Hill Book Company.

[11] Encyclopaedia Britannica Educational Materials including Spoken Arts recording series, Afro-American History series, Communication Skill Records, and the Audio Cued Social Studies filmstrip series.

[12] Wollensak Teaching Tapes, Minnesota Mining & Manufacturing Co.

studies to impart factual information to the learner. By means of an audio talk-through, suggestions and directions are given which refer the student to the examination of maps, diagrams, and a worksheet of terms, all of which are interrelated. Evaluation is a part of the activity, relying on the individual learner's participation. Final suggestions refer the learner to the study of classroom maps or globes. At the high school level, "The Changing Face of the Soviet Union,"[13] a combination of experiences in listening to descriptions and heeding instructions, refers the learner to pictures, diagrams, maps—all in filmstrip form—newspaper reprints, and a bibliography of readings which relate to contemporary Russian history. The series "Asian Folk Tales"[14] uses records to bring environmental sounds, music, and narration to the listener as he is referred to related pictures projected from filmstrips. Materials of this nature are paralleled by currently produced audiolearning experiences which describe Negro cultural accomplishments.

The audio-cued lesson entitled "The Story of Milk"[15] employs interrelated audioinstructions with records; an accompanying 8mm silent film loop helps learners hear and see how dairy cows are milked and how milk is processed and taken to the consumer. The records tell the learner what to expect when, following the audio experience, he is told to turn on the 8mm film loop. Following this, he is instructed to listen for further instructions and activities which test his mastery of information presented in the film. Since the film is silent, the learner is expected to rely greatly on the cues given in the audio portions of the lesson.

In the area of science, the "Sound of

Nature"[16] represents an intermingling of environmental sounds and the calls of elusive birds, with identifying explanations by an ornithologist. Instructions refer the listener to activities involved in conducting simple inquiry research in identifying birds through pictorial and verbal descriptions. The learning packet "Man on the Moon"[17] uses tape cassettes and recorded information to lead the student through the examination of interrelated discovery source materials, including flat maps, actual newspaper accounts, and a filmstrip sequence of pictures, all of which comprise source information for the learner to use as he engages in the series of individualized, creative, and inventive activities presented in a well-worked-out teacher's manual. Drill aspects of science are well exemplified in "Animal Classification: Vertebrates."[18] Basic information and explanations are presented through an audiotape. Further instructions are given which lead the learner through a series of discoveries that help him to understand the reason for and nature of classification.

In the area of language arts drill experiences, exemplary materials include "Our Daily Words,"[19] "Listening and Doing,"[20] "Developing Reading Skills,"[21] "Spelling for the High School Student,"[22] "Practice in Accomplishing the Pronunciation of Short Vowel Sounds."[23] Countless audio experiences are available which make use of readings from printed books ordinarily used in school library and class-

[13] EMC Corporation.

[14] International Book Corporation.

[15] Society for Visual Education.

[16] Houghton Mifflin Company, 777 California Avenue, Palo Alto, California.

[17] New York Times, Book & Educational Division.

[18] Wollensak Teaching Tapes, Minnesota Mining & Manufacturing Co.

[19] Imperial International Learning.

[20] Houghton Mifflin Company.

[21] EMC Corporation.

[22] EMC Corporation.

[23] Classroom Materials Company.

room situations. The basic strategy is quite uniform: the student is asked to respond to a sequence of instructions, listen to a passage read aloud and then to explanations, and perform activities as a response. The learner's responses are then evaluated immediately by the tape "voice." When successful, the learner is told to proceed. If the student is not correct or unsure, he is advised to go back, relisten, and learn.

Still other materials that use an audio channel to direct learners through well-organized cognitive information-getting kinds of activities and free the teacher to pursue work which he alone can accomplish with the children are: "Understanding Decimals,"[24] "Art in Africa,"[25] "19th-Century Development in Art,"[26] "American Folk Art,"[27] and "We Learn the Sounds of Instruments."[28] The reliability and validity of the materials are above and beyond anything that most teachers can hope to accomplish within the limitations of the time and energy they are able to expend. In any case, the intelligent use of such materials exercises a multiplier effect. It deploys the time of the teacher wisely and efficiently and makes available, through his planning function, a rapidly expanding variety of needed and desired learning experiences from which individuals or small groups of learners can profit immeasurably (see Figure 9.8).

[24] Wollensak Teaching Tapes.

[25] Society for Visual Education.

[26] Society for Visual Education.

[27] McGraw-Hill Book Company.

[28] Imperial International Learning.

FIGURE 9.8

Giving students free access to audiolearning materials assures learner involvement in following activities of their own choice. The members of the small group in the background pursue their specific interest. The teacher and another student are in the foreground. What does this picture reveal about the role of the teacher when audio materials are used? What applications can you make?

Teacher- and pupil-created audio-cued learning

MANY situations arise which make it highly profitable for the teacher to create audio-cued learning activities with the pupils' participation. For example, in an arithmetic class, the teacher had spent much time, following his group demonstration, in explaining and reexplaining how to develop and use simple formulas for finding areas and volumes of simple figures. Some pupils understood the process immediately, others were slower. Sensing the situation, the teacher called together several of the students who grasped the concepts. "Why not," he suggested, "explain all this on tape—and perhaps refer to some actual 'cutouts' or solid figures?"

Smiles of recognition and understanding lit up the faces of his helpers. Using a tray which included small models of squares, rectangles, and triangles, both two- and three-dimensional, the teacher helped the trio write, correct, and explain in tape-recorded form the relationship of the sides of plane and solid figures and how these sides or edges are used in finding the area or volume of a figure. Those who still encountered difficulty with this kind of problem were helped to listen to the tape. Some of the slower youngsters needed to listen several times to the tape, which referred to the cutouts or models, explaining how simple formulas are developed and how one can then substitute quantities into a formula and complete the computational process with success. During all this, the more "gifted" pupils helped those who needed it, interpreting the taped reference materials and checking out answers. This kind of peer "teaching" makes use of the desire of all human beings to teach.

One of the problems that immediately confronts the teacher who wishes to create teacher-pupil audio-cued learning materials is time. In some situations, this can be provided through in-service meeting times before or after school hours or, as some schools are doing, announcing to the community that Wednesday afternoons are faculty planning and producing times. Knowledgeable teachers, local audiovisual coordinators, supervisors, and principals who see the value of such activities are currently organizing such scheduled activities.

Over a one-year period, a number of audio-cued learning materials were created by teachers who had received instruction on how to proceed (see Figure 9.9).[29] The following are examples:

The audiolearning module entitled "Root System" is a learning experience with actual mounted specimens of roots and accompanying audio talk-through. The child is referred to a series of diagrams and laminated dry-mount specimens of various types of roots. He learns from the explanations and the mounted specimens. At the end of the lesson, he is asked to identify the various types of roots, is evaluated, and relistens where this is suggested.

In an audiotutorial lesson entitled "Sharks," the learner is instructed to refer to numbered photographs, flat pictures, and diagrams (which are mounted on 7-by-10 cards for easy manipulation by the student); he listens to explanations of each of these. In the process, he learns about the nature, habits, reproductive cycles, and so forth, of several kinds of sharks found in Pacific waters. Finally, he is given an oral quiz, is evaluated, and receives suggestions about creative follow-up activities.

In another audiotutorial lesson, "Oceanography," the learner is referred

[29] The described audio-cued learning experiences were planned, produced, and evaluated in learning situations by the following people who were participating in in-service media experiences at the University of Hawaiii in 1969: M. Mesaku, W. Yamamoto, N. Harney, A. Yamada, J. Hightower, C. Young, B. Kashiwahara, and A. Allan.

FIGURE 9.9

This teacher is explaining how to proceed into an audio-cued lesson, "Humorous Poetry," which she created. She capitalized on the opportunity to lead students from such a beginning toward further questing and discovery on the subject of poetry in general. Do similar opportunities occur to you?

to opaque pictures and coded illustrations, diagrams, and charts which give a beginning understanding of the nature of activities involved in oceanography. The learner listens to explanations and examines pictures, diagrams, and exploded drawings of clam buckets, seines, and underwater cameras; he identifies photographs of living creatures which swim in or crawl over the bottom of the Pacific Ocean. Final suggestions to listeners describe how they may carry on further simple research on selected areas of oceanography and report this information to classmates.

An audio-cued learning experience entitled "Knowing About Investments" uses actual specimens of investment documents and tape-recorded explanations to lead the learner through a beginning experience in understanding a variety of investment possibilities. The learner is given explanations, referred to specific forms, and asked to identify these forms; he is then asked to make some beginning judgments about the strengths and weaknesses of the forms.

An audio-cued description, "Conestoga Wagons," was an outgrowth of two students' curiosity about these wagons used during the westward expansion. During the audio-recorded lesson, the learner listens to explanations and is referred to accompanying slides which are photographic

copies from history source books, wood engravings, and transient sources which the librarian helped locate in his picture files. The learner is asked to move from slide to slide, listen to identifying explanations, and, finally, is evaluated by making judgments about the nature of this means of transportation.

One of the great rewards of teaching is the discovery of surprising talent and ingenuity among the pupils with whom one works. This was the experience of an elementary teacher who found that a very superficial explanation of lasers led a fifth-grade boy into an exhaustive study of not only lasers, but masers as well and that he wished to share with his classmates his new-found information. He took upon himself the original task of rewriting the explanations which accompanied a commercially available filmstrip. He searched for additional information and located it himself in the library. Finally, he put all of these together in audio-cued form, and the presentation was made available to his classmates who were interested in sharing his new discoveries with him (see Figure 9.10). How many such creative activities currently lie fallow among the pupils in any typical classroom—perhaps your own?

A final example shows how highly motivated and interested students can come

FIGURE 9.10

This fifth-grade boy has chosen to express his inventive ideas by creating for his classmates an audio-cued explanation of masers and lasers. Do you agree that in any normal classroom situation such unique possibilities actually exist?

FIGURE 9.11

This teacher is checking the progress of a small group as they follow directions and make responses to an audio-cued learning experience she created. The idea was picked up by several of her colleagues. The result: a growing inventory of locally produced and highly useful audio "minipacs," as these teachers chose to call them. What opportunities are there for this kind of activity in your situation?

to the assistance of a teacher, in this case a teacher who was planning the production of a series of audio-cued learning experiences to describe animals around the world. The group's study of the animals of North America became the beginning point of activity. As the students responded to the initial teacher-made audio lesson, several became sufficiently enthusiastic to volunteer to continue the search about the animals of other continents; these highly motivated students set about locating flat pictures from transient sources (magazines, etc.) and mounting them in suitable forms so that classmates could manipulate them as they listened to an original tape-recorded narration prepared by members of student committees.

There is no reason why the creative responses of learners cannot include audio recording. Rather than relying solely on traditional communication means (writing, speaking, etc.), using tape-recorded messages which relate to objects, specimens, selected pictures, original drawings, diagrams, and so forth, can become the avenue through which students can respond by interpreting new-found information to their fellow learners. For example, at the Kaahumanu School in Honolulu, cooperating teachers and selected students created an inventory from audio-cued learning resources which, while originated for use in specific classes, when placed in the library for general circulation, became available as interesting and exciting audio-cued learning materials for use by all (see Figure 9.11).

The extent to which audio-cued learning devices can interrelate the use of flat pictures, diagrams, specimens, objects, models, and so forth, is limited only by the imagination of the teacher. When the teacher is successful in explaining the possibilities to able and interested students, the nature of the learners' creative response activities becomes limitless.

Developing audiolearning skills

As more and more opportunities become available in the classroom for learners to use selected audio-cued learning experiences, it will become apparent to the teacher that some formal attention must be given to listening skills per se. *Just as years are spent in the development of reading skills, more time and attention must be given to the development of those listening and response skills which will increase the efficiency of the learner's search for information and acquisition of it through audio-cued instruction* (see Figure 9.12). Methods that both teachers and learners can use to improve listening skills are now discussed.

The teacher who wishes to improve audiolearning skills should first understand the nature of the hearing-listening-understanding sequence that is involved in audio-cued learning. Learning from auditory experience is actually more complex than one would think. The mere presentation of audible words and sounds to a pupil is no guarantee that he will achieve the desired learning goals—nor even that he will hear the material presented. Our ears take in much audible information from our environment at every moment, yet we do not "hear" all of these sensory impressions. Indeed, if we were aware of every sound that our ears sense, our world would be an incomprehensible hodgepodge of noise. Thus, those sounds of which we are *aware* at any given moment are the result of auditory discrimination. This is accomplished quite without our knowing it as the result of autonomic response mechanisms in our brains which have been trained in selection of information by our learning to discriminate from among the various sounds taken in from the environment. For example, most people are familiar with the experience of concentrating so intently on something that they did not "hear" someone speaking to them. Perhaps an even more familiar experience is that of being annoyed by, and therefore consciously disregarding, an unpleasant or tedious sound which we wish not to hear. Both types of experience are indicative of the complexities involved in audition, a basic factor which affects listening and thus also the efficiency of audiolearning.

The audiolearning sequence

Though the scope of audition is too broad and too deep for comprehensive treatment in this chapter, we will describe briefly here the basic sequence through which the learner must pass if he is to achieve audio-

FIGURE 9.12

Together this teacher and her pupils have worked out techniques for developing audio-cued learning materials. (a) Students learn how to produce their own display materials to accompany their audio report. (b) Later, the members of the small group listen to their own efforts, follow the cues, and evaluate their own effectiveness in terms of the visuals they have prepared —all before making their presentation available to their classmates. What learner goals are achieved in such a situation?

learning. First, if the pupil is to hear the instructional message, the message itself must be audible to the normal ear. Also necessary, of course, is that the learner be able to *hear* the message; that is, his own hearing mechanism must be capable of responding to vibrations that fall within the normal human range of audibility. The sensory impressions taken in through this mechanism must then be transmitted to the pupil's cognitive awareness.

Next, the learner must *listen* to the message. It is possible to hear—that is, to be aware of—a sound without *attending* to that sound. This is particularly true in the case of word sounds which require attention if the subtle syllabic differences are to be distinguished and the intended message is to be received. Finally, if the communication is to be complete, the learner must become involved—must be able to *respond* as a direct result of the audiolearning; that is, the learned information must create in the learner an ability to demonstrate that

FIGURE 9.13

The listening-learning process.

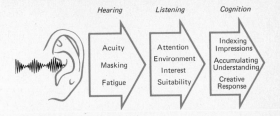

FIGURE 9.14

Audiometer tests are usually given to school-children periodically by the school's speech and hearing specialists.

he has fully grasped the learned information (see Figure 9.13).

THE LEARNER MUST HEAR Basically, hearing may be thought of as the physical response of the ear to sound vibrations. In this sense, not all learners hear with normal acuity; it is estimated that 5 percent or more of the school population suffers hearing losses which may interfere with audiolearning. Obviously, a pupil whose auditory mechanism is impaired cannot be expected to profit completely from audioinstructional materials. Thus the teacher's first responsibility is to determine whether all of his pupils can actually hear sounds which are within the normal ranges of volume and pitch, and which, if any, pupils exhibit difficulty in this area. Auditory sensitivity can be measured objectively by the speech and hearing specialists who are employed in most school systems (see Figure 9.14). If the behavior or performance of a pupil creates doubt that his hearing is physiologically normal, the teacher should refer the child for appropriate therapy or remedial measures.

Even when the physiological aspects of hearing are normal, however, some pupils may seem to exhibit a pathological hearing defect for psychological or psychoneurological reasons. A pupil may have become so accustomed to "tuning out" unwanted noise, for example, that he virtually doesn't hear otherwise audible information. Often this tuning out is so habitual that the pupil himself is unaware of doing it, and though he may want to please by listening and remembering the audioinstructional message, he is unable to control his listening activities. To illustrate by a somewhat extreme, but all too frequent, situation, if a child has been raised in a noisy home—perhaps one in which the parents are prone to raising their voices in anger at him or at each other—he may have adapted at an early age to this environment by shutting out this noise. Of course, a disinterested pupil may deliberately or semideliberately tune out unwanted hearing experiences. This may be a temporary adaptation to content that is tedious or seemingly irrelevant from the pupil's point of view or perhaps the result of distraction by some competing sound. As pointed out in Chapter 1, a pupil who does not seem to hear may be attending to introspective thoughts or fantasy and thus shutting out the learning message. Rather than view such pupils with negativism, the teacher should give some thought to specific development of their listening skills. Of primary importance to such training is the nature of the subject matter itself—which should be both interesting and relevant to the pupils—as well as its method of presentation.

In classroom situations where audioinstructional techniques are relied upon excessively, fatigue may interfere with the pupils' hearing. Here again, the pupils may tune out the educational communication.

Fatigue is apt to occur when teachers rely endlessly on spoken directions, lecturing, prolonged or tedious class discussion, or oral reading of lengthy passages or sequences which could better be left for the students to read individually. Such excessive reliance on the student's hearing faculty will exhaust even the most conscientious student, a factor that should be recognized by teachers to the same extent that it is recognized with respect to excessive *physical* exercise. *The alternative is to arrange a classroom schedule which utilizes various audiovisual techniques and thus permits multisensory learning, as is the case with many audio-cued learning materials which have been described earlier.*

There are many other factors that can obstruct pupil hearing. Extraneous environmental noises, for example, can strongly interfere with the audibility of the instructional message. Noises which emanate into the classroom from out-of-doors can be disruptive. Drilling and other building-construction sounds, heavy traffic noises, the noise from school playground activities, and so forth often can interfere with audiolearning. Similarly, sounds generated within the classroom itself—perhaps due to poor discipline habits among the class members—can provide highly effective competition to audioinstruction.

Such noises need not be extreme to affect at least some of the pupils' auditory faculties, and the teacher should not ignore extraneous noises of seemingly low volume as potential learning interference merely because he himself is not disturbed by them. It may be that the teacher has become so used to such noises that he has learned automatically to sift them from his awareness, or it may be that his powers of concentration are such as to screen out extraneous sounds. The same may not be true of his pupils.

The degree to which pupils are affected by extraneous noise varies, not only according to the volume of the noise itself, but also according to the pupils' individual *sensitivity* to the nature and volume levels of the noise and according to the individual concentration and auditory-discrimination habits of the pupils. Some children may find it easier to shut out the lesson in favor of attending to the interfering noise. Significantly, even annoying or bothersome noises may enable the student to discriminate *against* the audioinstruction.

Another important deterrent to some forms of audio-cued learning derives from the acoustical situation in the classroom. If the acoustics in the room are such as to create an echo or reverberation of the sounds being communicated or if the sound is overabsorbed so that it does not reach the student's ear with full impact, audiolearning will be impaired. Thus, even when extraneous noises are not present, audioinstruction will be ineffective in an acoustically inadequate classroom.

To overcome these physical barriers to hearing, the teacher should see to it that the classroom effectively keeps out annoying extraneous noises and, at the same time, provides a good acoustical environment. Excessive reverberating noise within one's own classroom may be overcome by tacking monkscloth or colored burlap display panels neatly across the offending surface, for example, the back wall. This not only traps sounds but offers more pin-up display area for student work. With the principal's consent, the janitor and a few competent students can install "do-it-yourself" acoustical tile on the wall surfaces above the chalkboards, an area most frequently the cause of annoying classroom acoustics. In new buildings specified to provide good acoustics, a polite complaint to the principal may secure corrective measures by the contractor. The key idea is to be aware of such problem acoustics and call attention to the fact that instruction can be improved by corrective measures.

THE LEARNER MUST LISTEN   Just as it is possible to screen out from one's awareness all of the sounds picked up by his auditory sense, it is possible to *hear* sounds without heeding or responding to them. Teachers are familiar with students who look alert and attentive during class discussion and who respond when called upon, yet whose quickly ad-libbed responses indicate all too clearly that they have not paid attention, or *listened* to, the substance of the discussion itself.

For true audiolearning to be achieved, it is important for the pupil to do more than just follow the thread of the information being communicated; he must become *actively* involved in the information itself —he must think about it, analyze its meaning, organize and reorganize its content elements into his existing frame of reference, and, where appropriate, respond. If this degree of listening participation in audioinstruction is to be attained, several conditions must coexist: The audioinstructional content must be interesting, provocative, and suitable to the pupils' level of background experience, and the audible messages must be clear and distinct so as to make full impact on each pupil's auditory faculty.

There are many ways by which the teacher can create favorable listening conditions. First, the teacher should arrange the classroom itself so that it is conducive to listening.

Next, if attentive listening is to be accomplished, the nature of the aural message must be such that the learner will be interested enough to become involved with, and to react to, the material spoken or played. Of primary importance here is that the audioinstructional material be selected in terms of the maturity of the learners, their interests and vocabulary level, and their *need for the audioexperience itself.*

It is futile for the teacher constantly to enjoin pupils to "be alert," "listen carefully," and "pay attention" to listening exercises. Unless previous teacher-pupil planning has encouraged in the pupils a *desire* to listen and a willingness to investigate audiolearning experiences, no amount of telling them to listen will be effective. This desire is created by arranging experiences that answer questions relating to teacher-pupil planning. When such readiness occurs and audiolearning materials are appropriately selected, the chances that pupils will want to listen and to react to listening experiences are enhanced. On the other hand, epitomizing the consequences of failing to provide interesting, suitable, and clearly presented material is the student who advised another, "In that lecture room you can't hear Professor X beyond the fifth row. So don't sit any closer than the sixth."[30]

Of considerable value in motivating students to listen, then, is to involve them in activities which are preliminary to the audiolearning experience itself. This may be achieved through pupil-teacher planning carried on before the beginning of the audioinstruction. It is of little use to ask a pupil to pursue a learning activity until he realizes what he is expected to accomplish. The pupil must know in advance why he is to listen, that is, what purposes or goals he wishes to or is instructed to achieve—in short, what objectives he hopes to reach as a result of a given audio-cued learning experience. If possible, the pupils should have a voice in the selection of the materials; this will provide them with the opportunity to realize their own responsibilities with respect to audiolearning generally and to understand thoroughly the purposes of the specific audio-cued learning experience. Also helpful are the positive experiences gained from past audiolearning experiences. From such past experiences, students are more likely to know that the dramatic recording or audio-

cued demonstration is apt to be interesting and helpful to them.

THE LEARNER MUST RESPOND If audiolearning is to be complete, the pupils must not only be able to hear the message and be willing to listen attentively; they must also be capable of demonstrating or applying their newly acquired knowledge. Typically, the avenues by which the pupil is asked to demonstrate this learning are tests and examinations, pupil reports and essays, classroom discussion "feedback," and similar situations. However, these avenues provide the pupil with little opportunity to exhibit creative involvement with, and expressive use of, his learning and, as stressed earlier, creativity is a most important outcome of any learning. Thus, creative response is the goal of listening-learning activities just as it is of other classroom learning activities. Effective teachers will complete the successful audiolearning situation by encouraging this creativity. A few suggestions from the teacher may stimulate the pupils to carry out one or more of these suggestions or, better, to invent creative projects on their own.

The learners' achievement gained through audio-cued instruction may be gauged best by examining the nature of the responses students evolve after such experiences. Creative responses may include dramatic improvisations, participation in a debate, a demonstration of a newly learned skill, writing a report, new account, or poem, or individually creating a new audio-cued learning experience. There are many ways in which a pupil can express himself by producing his own version of an audio-cued learning experience and, wherever possible, he should be encouraged to do so.

Improving listening skills

Listening is a skill which responds well to developmental guidance. Thus it is pos-

[30] Edgar Dale, "Why Don't We Listen?" *The Newsletter*, February 1957.

sible to provide specific training by which pupils may improve their skills in listening for central ideas, details, and inferences, in following directions, and so forth. This training can be carried out within the context of many subject areas, for example, in foreign languages, English, literature, and the social studies. The degree to which a teacher can instill among pupils the motivation to become better listeners is of real importance in improving these skills, assuming that, as indicated earlier in the chapter, the physiological hearing ability of each pupil is known. Mechanical hearing aids should be provided in extreme cases of hearing pathology, but for those with lesser degrees of impaired hearing and for those whose inability to hear instructional content seems to be due primarily to psychological adaptation, pupils may be grouped for special instruction. In many cases, conditions may be improved simply by changes in seating.

PRESENTING SKILL-TRAINING SITUATIONS Skill in listening is usually the result of the pupil's own interest in developing better listening habits and of his understanding of effective listening methods. The manner in which the teacher may assist in providing the physical setting for better listening has already been discussed, but if the pupil himself is going to take part in listening development, the teacher must begin by awakening the individual's awareness of his own listening process. The pupil's concentration on sounds and his *willingness* to concentrate may be developed and strengthened if the teacher describes the listening habits of such "expert" listeners as the court reporter, the news editor at the city desk, the telephone-order clerk in a large department store, and others. From this foundation of pupil awareness, concentration, and willingness, listening skills can be developed through continued classroom practice.

Through pupil-teacher planning sessions, appropriate and interesting audio-cued learning materials should be selected for listening practice. While the subject matter chosen for the listening experience may relate to classroom study units, the teacher should bear in mind that the goal of these practice periods is *listening skill*, rather than subject-matter learning, and thus the materials chosen should be especially geared to pupil interests. In other words, if inefficient learning of regular instructional content is in part due to poor listening skills, it may be wise at first to choose listening-training materials that do not focus on content. Later, when the pupils have achieved better coordination of the auditory and mental processes, listening practice and content learning may be achieved simultaneously.

In providing listening-skill instruction, the teacher should encourage pupils to record and index—either mentally or in written form—every fact or impression they think is important. It should be made clear to the listeners that they can think much faster than a speaker can talk, and thus they have ample time to consider what they hear and to reject, rearrange, or select the information according to what seems meaningful and useful to them. Before the actual listening experience begins, the teacher may demonstrate how to record and index useful points of information and provide some initial guidance to the kinds of information to be listened for. For example, the home economics teacher may ask her listeners to organize and to record in number and word form the important points in her oral description of the nature and quantity of cooking ingredients. The English literature teacher may instruct pupils to record the names of key characters in a short story or dramatic reading as it is read aloud or presented on tape and to classify these characters according to their relationship to one another and to the action sequence. The algebra teacher may read several equations or problems aloud, asking his students to record them on paper in symbolic form.

Depending on the subject matter involved, meaningful ''doodling''—sketching symbols and diagrams, and so forth—can help the pupil to visualize the concepts he hears explained. The teacher may need to encourage pupils to do just that, since ''doodling'' is a form of behavior students have been taught to believe is nonconforming. To illustrate, the social studies teacher may demonstrate how one can create a flow chart or a diagrammatic graphic, the elements of which include brief phrases or single words which describe causes or events leading up to other events. The entire thread of information received from listening to and witnessing an audio-cued

lesson may be summarized briefly in an appropriate diagram, expanded chart, or graphic. Similarly, the history teacher may narrate a historical episode, asking that the listeners record along a time line the major events and the principal personalities connected with them as they listen. The science teacher may instruct his pupils to diagram a physical process as he describes it orally. Other examples could be cited in virtually every subject area. Such sketches and diagrams should be kept simple, however, and the ''doodling'' should not be permitted to interfere with listening attention.

EVALUATING SKILL-TRAINING SITUATIONS Listening outcomes should be

---

Selecting and evaluating audiolearning experiences

THE teacher is continually confronted by many demands to consider and try out ways to extend class time and effort. When the decision has been made, in response to such demands, to use audio-cued learning materials, the teacher should assume the core responsibility for selecting or creating

the best of such experiences.

In order to make sure that the most appropriate and useful of existing available or created audio-cued materials are brought into the classroom, it is suggested that the following criteria be used by the teacher:

Audio-cued learning: selection criteria

Description

Title of ACL lesson, packet, or device _____

The nature of ACL: Subject content area _____

    Grade level _____ Source _____

Channels employed: Audio _____ Visual diagrams _____ Pictures _____

    Motion films _____ Specimens and objects _____

    Other _____

Preuse Evaluation Criteria

1   The ACL seems to be best suited for use in developing in the learner:

    a   Understandings about _____

evaluated in terms of both quantity and quality—that is, the sheer *number* of specific points accurately remembered from the listening experience and the *nature, properties,* and *interrelationships* of these points as they occur in the content that was presented. For example, the child who recorded all or most of the names in a multicharacter story or drama, but who had not properly indexed the roles these characters play in relationship to one another and to the story plot needs further skill development in the *qualitative* aspects of listening. Conversely, the child who recorded accurately the roles and relationships of only one or two characters needs further skill development in listening for *quantities* of information.

In providing listening-skill training, it is most important for the teacher to bear in mind that the primary purpose of the audiolearning activity is to improve pupil *listening,* rather than to impart subject matter per se. Learning the content of the audiolearning experience is thus secondary to listening-skill development. Although both may be achieved at the same time, if emphasis is placed initially on the subject matter at the expense of the listening activity, the child will not devote enough attention to his listening habits and to improving his listening ability. On the other hand, the teacher who begins the class by emphasizing to the children the *listening* aspects of the learning situation, but who then terminates the period by

		No, or Low	Average	Yes, or High
b	Skills in _____			
c	Other _____			
2	**The nature of the ACL:**			
a	Aural explanations are clear and feasible	_____	_____	_____
b	Presents a dependable message	_____	_____	_____
c	Manipulative tasks are feasible	_____	_____	_____
d	Permits learner to control time, pace of use, and repetitious reference at will	_____	_____	_____
e	Provides cues for learner involvement and response	_____	_____	_____
f	Provides learner with self-evaluation of his efforts	_____	_____	_____
g	Provides cues toward further questing by learner	_____	_____	_____
h	Encourages learner to use new-found information or skills in creative manner	_____	_____	_____
i	Encourages deployment of teacher time to teaching per se	_____	_____	_____
j	General evaluative comment:	_____	_____	_____

testing subject-matter learning only fails in his purpose and confuses the pupils as well. In addition, the teacher should be sure that listening evaluation occurs immediately after the listening activity and that its results, especially if obtained by means of written tests or essays, are presented to the pupils before the end of the same period. These results should make explicit to each pupil what *kinds* of information he failed to notice and what kinds of details he should attend to in further aural experiences. The final goal is to improve listening as one means of achieving greater cognition.

The use of audio-cued learning materials in teaching is justified only when greater reality, interest, vividness, and authenticity and thus better *learning* result because of them. In each area of schoolwork, therefore, aural materials must be evaluated in terms of what they are, after all, intended to achieve—learning outcomes. In evaluating learning outcomes, however, the teacher should bear in mind the many factors that can affect learning.

For example, the child who is working as a member of a committee to reconstruct a model of the Conestoga wagon used during the westward expansion may need to supplement his listening experiences with visual study of plans and diagrams of various means of transportation used during this period. Similarly, the pupil who wishes to write a short story cannot be expected to be very creative unless he first has the opportunity of listening to many short stories from which he can develop a sense of word rhythm, sentence patterns, and so forth, that will guide his own craftsmanship in word selection, description, plot development, and so on. In short, a child cannot be expected to be creative out of nothing, and the avenues of aural experience should not be overlooked as providing foundations for *creative* response. Thus it is desirable that—following a broadcast or recorded learning experience—both the teacher and pupil evaluate how effectively these foundations have been acquired through the audiolearning situation by using the *evaluation criteria* on the following page.

Summary

Too little attention has been paid to the nature of classroom use of audio-cued learning experiences. Perhaps even less attention has been given to ways of improving listening skills which are needed as one witnesses and responds to such instructional experiences. There are, however, many types of learning opportunities inherent in audio-cued experiences. There also are many feasible approaches to the improvement of learner listening skills as such.

Audio-cued learning experiences utilize recorded explanations, descriptions, directions, and the like to communicate successfully dependable cognitive drill and skill information to learners. Initial audio-learning experiences were characterized by readings, recitations, dramatizations of historical events, foreign language models, and so forth. To these beginning informational presentations systematic suggestions or cues have been added as connecting threads used to bind together interrelated and needed experiences provided by selected and appropriate pictures, charts, maps, specimens, films, objects, and so on.

As shown in a number of examples, audio-cued materials can be devised for individualized learning opportunities which give the learner self-directed and self-paced options of time, place, repetition, and reference. Further illustrations reveal how audio-cued learning consistently, re-

Audio-cued learning: evaluation criteria

For the Teacher

1
Did the audio material provide learning experiences which could not have been provided more easily with traditional materials?

2
Am I acquainted with all the sources of audio materials in my subject area?

3
Did I carefully preaudit the material I used?

4
Did I give attention to such factors as acoustics, seating arrangement, location of the speaker, and volume while the class was listening?

5
Did I adequately prepare students for this listening activity by:

a outlining vocabulary problems?

b helping them to know what they were to accomplish?

c encouraging discussion in which they could show their interest?

6
Did I encourage creative follow-up activities such as discussion and self-evaluation through testing?

7
Did I encourage creative follow-up activities such as creative simple research, art expression, dramatic expression, etc?

For the Student

1
Could I hear well enough to understand the material?

2
Did I know what I was to do before I began to listen?

3
Did I contribute any ideas during the discussion?

4
Did I help plan follow-up activities?

5
Did I initiate original reports, dialogues, dramatizations, or other creative projects that incorporated my new-found information?

liably, and validly presents dependable messages, how the learner receives immediate evaluation, and how the teacher proceeds to evaluate the activities of the learner by observing his responses—the creative or inventive uses to which he puts his new understandings or skills.

There are many sources of audio-cued experiences, including radio, commercial and governmental sources, and teacher-pupil-planned and -created materials. The National Center for Audio Tapes is a particularly rich source of such audiolearning information and skill developmental materials. Teacher and pupils should be involved in the production of audio-cued learning activities of their own design.

As with any learning-skill development, pupils can be helped to sharpen their abilities to listen to, select, and organize audiolearning experiences for use and response. The learner is greatly assisted when he understands that he can listen much more rapidly than he can speak. Thus he understands that while listening he should have time to organize and discard—even decide how to use the information gained through listening or "auding." A number of specific listening-skill development techniques are included in the chapter.

Certain evaluation criteria-suggestions, which are listed, should be followed when teacher and pupils select or create audio-cued learning experiences constructively in pursuit of the acquisition of understandings and/or the development of skills. Other criteria, also listed, should be followed when teacher and pupils evaluate the outcomes of audio-cued experiences.

Further learner response projects

1

In order to become familiar with sources of audio materials and audio-cued materials, contact such agencies as the following to discover what is available and under what circumstances:

a   Your state department of education audiovisual or media officer.

b   Your local school district or area school radio broadcasting service.

c   Your local instructional materials center, local audiovisual supervisor, or media specialist.

d   Your local audiovisual dealer.

2

Obtain for evaluation several audio-cued learning programs. Listen to them and evaluate them by using the form on page 385. When you have found one that you think is particularly worthwhile, plan for its use and then use it:

a   Describe the preplanning activities, that is, setting of purposes and goals, etc., which should take place before the ACL material is used.

b   Describe the manner in which the room environment and location of audio and related media equipment should be arranged.

c   Describe the actual responses of an individual pupil or members of a small group to the ACL experience.

d   Describe how one specific learner became involved during the ACL use and the nature of his responses.

e   Describe the learner's motivation and whether or not it was strong enough to lead him to continue his questing.

f   Describe your general evaluation of the worth of this experience.

3

Visit the nearest educational broadcast facility or instructional materials center to learn what broadcast or recorded audio- learning experiences are available and in use. Report findings that you consider significant.

4

Arrange to use and evaluate one or more listening-skill activities. For example, imagine that the following passage is being read aloud to you; better still, ask a fellow student to read it to you. As you read or listen, use a device of your own choice to record key information—listing facts, sketching, or diagraming:

Battle of Waterloo

In order to get a clear idea of the Battle of Waterloo, we should imagine in our mind's eye a large capital letter A. *The left leg of the* A *is the road from a town called X. The right leg of the* A *is the road from a town called G. The crossbar of the* A *is known as the "sunken road." At the top of the* A *is Mont St. Jean. Wellington is there. General Jerome Bonaparte is located at the lower left leg of the* A. *The right lower leg is where Napoleon Bonaparte is located. A little below the point where the crossbar of the* A *cuts the right leg is a town called Q. At this point the final battle word was spoken. Here the lion was placed, the symbol of the supreme heroism of the Imperial Guard.*

The triangle formed at the top of the A *by the two legs and the crossbar is the Plateau of Mont St. Jean. The struggle for this plateau was the whole of the battle. The wings of the two armies extended to the right and left of the two towns called X and G. Beyond the point of the* A, *beyond the Plateau of Mont St. Jean, is a large forest. As to the plain itself, we must imagine a vast, rolling country; each rolling hill commands the next; and these hills, rising toward Mont St. Jean, are bounded by a forest. In order to visualize the various relationships presented in the narration and to keep separate in your mind all of the positions mentioned, you had to make a series of notes; perhaps you sketched a diagram. To what extent did your diagram, if you made one, compare with that shown in Figure 9.15? Try this passage out on friends or pupils, instructing each to make a diagram, and see how closely their sketches match Figure 9.15.*

Listening efficiency should be evaluated immediately after the aural experience. This evaluation may be made by means of a brief quiz composed of multiple-choice questions such as these that were made up for the passage quoted:

1   *What was the Battle of Waterloo a struggle for? (a) Mont St. Jean itself. (b) The forest of Mont St. Jean. (c) The Plateau of Mont St. Jean. (d) The town called Q. (e) The sunken road.*

2   *Which of the following words will not help your understanding of the battle? (a) Plateau. (b) Plain. (c) Square. (d) Triangle.*

3 What is the most direct route between Mont St. Jean and the town called Q? (a) Along the sunken road. (b) Across the plateau. (c) Along the right leg of the Λ. (d) Along the left leg of the Λ. (e) None of the preceding.

4 What natural advantage did Wellington hold over Napoleon at the Battle of Waterloo? (a) Superior heroism. (b) Superior concealment. (c) Superior know-how. (d) Superior altitude. (e) Superior initiative.

5 Whom did the author of the passage sympathize with? (a) Wellington. (b) Napoleon Bonaparte. (c) Jerome Bonaparte. (d) The Imperial Guard. (e) None of the above.

6 Which of the following phrases contributes nothing to your understanding of the battlefield of Waterloo? (a) The town called X. (b) The sunken road. (c) The Plateau of Mont St. Jean. (d) Supreme heroism. (e) The town called Q.

7 Where was Jerome Bonaparte? (a) At the point of the Λ. (b) In the closed triangle of the Λ. (c) Near the crossbar of the Λ. (d) At the left lower leg of the Λ. (e) At the right lower leg of the Λ.

8 Where is the town called Q? (a) At the point of the Λ. (b) In the closed triangle of the Λ. (c) Near the crossbar of the Λ. (d) At the left lower leg of the Λ. (e) At the right lower leg of the Λ.

9 Where is the "sunken road"? (a) At the points of the Λ. (b) In the closed triangle of the Λ. (c) On the crossbar of the Λ. (d) At the left lower leg of the Λ. (e) At the right lower leg of the Λ.

10 Where is the Plateau of Mont St. Jean? (a) At the point of the Λ. (b) In the closed triangle of the Λ. (c) Near the crossbar of the Λ. (d) At the left lower leg of the Λ. (e) At the right lower leg of the Λ.

Answers: 1–c; 2–c; 3–c; 4–d; 5–e; 6–d; 7–d; 8–c; 9–c; 10–b

FIGURE 9.15

One way to increase learner efficiency is to visualize key ideas through sketches or "doodles" like this one. Such efforts should be kept as simple as possible so as not to interfere with listening as such.

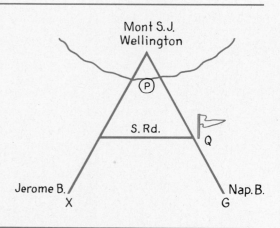

culating sets of these lantern slides to schools. However, with advances in photographic techniques, the less expensive and more convenient 2 × 2 slide came into general use and replaced the larger slides for most purposes. Since the development of inexpensive 35mm cameras and color film, the 2 × 2 slide made from 35mm film has become a valuable and popular teaching tool.

An important advantage of 2 × 2 slides is the fact that excellent color quality is possible at low cost. Factors influencing the educational value of color and the selection of colored slides and filmstrips are the same as those discussed in connection with flat pictures (Chapter 3), study displays (Chapter 5), and motion pictures (Chapter 11). Convenience of use, quality, low cost, and ease of procurement are among the many other reasons for the wide popularity of 2 × 2 slides. The particular convenience provided when these slides are stored and

used in drums is suggested in Figure 10.2.

The commercial sets of 2 × 2 slides are usually of excellent quality. Commercial slide sets are available in numerous subject areas such as foreign and domestic geography, travel, architecture and fine arts, all the sciences, medicine, agriculture, ecology, nature study, and sports.[1]

A teacher also can readily make his own slides because 35mm color film normally is mounted by the processor in 2 × 2 cardboard slide mounts ready for projection. Thus a teacher can take pictures of field trips, laboratory experiments, class activities, travel scenes, or any subject lending itself to photographic treatment and

[1] *Some Sources of 2 × 2-Inch Color Slides,* Kodak Pamphlet No. S–2, Motion Picture and Education Markets Division, Eastman Kodak Company, 1967. See also magazines such as *AV Instruction* and *Educational Screen and AV Guide* for information about new slide sources and slides on additional subjects.

FIGURE 10.2

---

2 × 2 slides can easily be stored in drums and then projected with a drum-type slide projector such as this one. The Ektalite screen shown is a special aluminum-surfaced one specifically designed for use in lighted rooms.

then project them (see Figure 10.3). Some media centers provide specialized illustrated listings of locally assembled 2 × 2 slide sets available for distribution.[2]

SPECIALIZED SLIDE APPLICATIONS
Slides are readily adaptable to a variety of uses. Slide-tape visual-audio presentations, for example, can be highly effective on an almost limitless range of topics—for large and small groups as well as for individualized instruction. Although such presentations can be operated manually, many are automated by means of inaudible signals or sync pulses recorded on the tape which activate the advance mechanism of the slide projector to provide a synchronized presentation. This combination is known as *sync-tape slides*. This system is particularly useful in individualized instruction—car-

[2] For example, "Italian and Spanish Paintings, Renaissance and Post-Renaissance Periods," Art History Series, Department of Education, San Diego County, California, April 1965.

tridged tapes and simple mechanisms make it unnecessary for an instructor to be present. Some fairly sophisticated systems such as the one in the Learning Laboratory in the College of Education at Illinois State University are making use of random-access slide systems. At Illinois State, a computer is used to make about 1,000 slides and sound tapes available to individual study carrels on an individually selected basis. Some of these are sync-tape slide combinations; others are separate slides or tapes—any of which can be retrieved at will. For the most part, such systems are still in experimental and developmental stages, but they are likely to come into common use during the next few years.

Another slide development for specialized uses is *animated slides*. These slides are made of a material that reacts to polarized light in such a way as to give the impression of animation. A polarizing spinner is attached to the projector, and the slide is projected through the spinner to the screen. Sets of such slides are becoming available;

FIGURE 10.3

Teachers who use many 2 × 2 slides frequently store them in convenient plastic holders which fit in any standard three-ring notebook. Here two students are putting together a special presentation. The individual slides chosen will be loaded in sequence into the drum on the table for projecting.

FIGURE 10.4

This is a popular type of stereoviewer containing a disk with seven matched pairs of scenes taken with a stereo camera. When looked at through the viewer, the scenes appear strikingly three-dimensional.

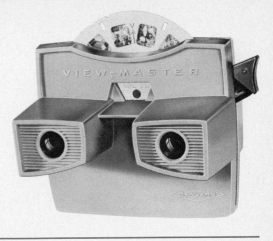

for example, there is one set called *Science in Motion* that is designed for kindergarten through grade 6 in such areas as "Exploring the Earth," "Biological Sciences," "The Solar System," and "Exploring Space."[3]

Another mechanism that is widely used in slide presentations before groups is the *dissolve unit*. This unit is normally used with two projectors; it alternates the images projected with a soft fade-in from one to another rather than an abrupt switch from one scene to the next. The unit can be operated automatically with a predetermined number of seconds for each slide or manually at any speed desired. Although this dissolve technique is not necessary in normal classroom use, it is a good thing to know about, especially for presentations for public audiences or auditorium programs. (For such auditorium uses or for any large-group presentations, a Xenon high-intensity lamp usually is necessary in the projector; see the *Student Production Guide*.)

STEREOSLIDES Another type of slide that deserves mention is the double-image slide known as a stereoslide. Such slides are

[3] American Book Company.

prepared in pairs from photographs taken with a stereographic camera. This type of camera takes two pictures simultaneously through two lenses that are a few inches apart, as are human eyes. Each picture thus is taken from a slightly different angle, just as our eyes see from slightly different angles. The human brain gives us depth perception of actual scenes by combining the two images perceived. Thus when two stereographic photographs are viewed through a stereoscope or stereoviewer, the left eye sees one image and the right eye the other. The brain combines these into one image that has depth, just as the brain combines actual images. The result is a highly realistic and vivid three-dimensional effect.

A convenient form of the stereographic slide is the stereodisk. Seven pairs of 16mm transparencies taken with a stereographic camera are mounted in a disk and viewed in a compact and inexpensive viewer (see Figure 10.4); the viewer enables the left eye to see one picture of each pair and the right eye to see the other.

Initially, these stereodisks, or reels, were devoted largely to popular entertainment and scenes of general interest; commercial stereodisks sold to the general public are still mostly of these types, showing

FIGURE 10.5

These filmstrips shown in actual size are (a) the single-frame type and (b) the double-frame type. Commercial strips are almost all single-frame strips. Double-frame strips have frames that are the same size as 35mm slides; thus such strips can be made by anyone with a 35mm camera. See the *Student Production Guide* for details.

such subjects as scenic wonders, world travel highlights, nature, and world events. Children's stories also are included in commercial stereodisks. The success of the device, however, has led to several more serious applications, especially in the fields of science and technology. For example, stereodisk materials have been prepared on human anatomy, oral surgery, and air contamination. A number of scientific books have been published with illustrations on stereodisks; a folding plastic viewer is provided in each book along with the disks.

Filmstrips

A filmstrip is a sequence of related still pictures imprinted on a strip of transparent 35mm film. Typically, a commercial filmstrip contains from 20 to 50 frames about ¾″ × 1″ in size (see Figure 10.5). A complete filmstrip usually several feet long, is rolled up to fit into a small container for easy storage (see Figure 10.6). Filmstrips are relatively inexpensive (from $6 up) so it is feasible to provide sets of filmstrips

in each classroom for use when needed. In addition filmstrips are simple to use—the projectors are inexpensive, simple to operate, and relatively trouble-free. Good pictures of almost anything can be projected on a screen, since a great many filmstrips are available on a wide variety of topics in most subjects.

Such operational advantages of filmstrips help account for their general popularity with teachers, but filmstrips also have some distinctive learning advantages for the pupil. One such advantage is the sequential order of frames. Topics are treated in a step-to-step sequence that stays the same, since there is no way for the pictures to get out of order, as slides occasionally do. On the other hand, since the order of scenes on the filmstrip *is* fixed, it is not convenient to show scenes in another order; for that purpose, slides, of course, are better. Nonetheless, when a particular filmstrip fits your teaching purposes, you have a ready-made, efficient, and convenient teaching tool.

Another advantage of the filmstrip from a teaching-learning standpoint is that

FIGURE 10.6

The large number of filmstrips currently used in school systems and their small size necessitate a rapid, convenient system of storage and retrieval like this one.

FIGURE 10.7

Selected frames from 9 filmstrips, made by
three different producers, that indicate something
of the variety of available filmstrips. Except for
flat pictures, no other form of visual material is
so readily available to the teacher.

Therefore, each house is divided
committees to which bills are ser

it can be used at any desired pace. This is obviously a particular advantage for individualized instruction, but it is a feature that a teacher can also employ with a group. For introductory or review purposes, the teacher can rather quickly run through a filmstrip to provide a general overview. Then if detailed analysis is needed later, each frame can be held on the screen as long as necessary.

A third practical advantage of filmstrips is the wide range and number of titles available. Because of the popularity of filmstrips, combined with their relatively low production costs, great numbers of new filmstrips are constantly produced. The range of subject matter goes well beyond the elementary school curriculum into many areas at the secondary school, college, and adult education levels. A few examples of the variety of the types of filmstrips available are shown in Figure 10.7. This selection would have to be multiplied hundreds of times even to suggest the number of new filmstrips currently produced in the United States each year.

The trend toward "packaged" materials for individualized instruction and independent instructional modules is having marked effects on filmstrip production for educational and training purposes. This trend is evident in the increasing proportion of sound filmstrips being produced for the school market. Instead of using printed captions, sound filmstrips typically present verbal information on an accompanying record or audiotape (see Figure 10.8). In many cases, a cassette tape can be ordered in place of the record at a slight additional cost. Special projectors are available which, in addition to projecting the filmstrip, play the record or cassette tape and advance the filmstrip at the proper times by reacting to inaudible recorded pulses (these are similar to the sync-tape slide projectors discussed earlier).

The recorded sound normally carries a narration and may also include appropriate music or sound effects. Sound filmstrips are valuable in a variety of subjects such as music, reading readiness, industrial arts, guidance, and social studies. Although they cost usually 50 to 100 percent more than silent filmstrips, the potentials of quality sound filmstrips are sufficiently high to warrant their use.

When a synchronized recording and filmstrip are played together, the pace of the filmstrip is, of course, fixed by the recording. Although this combination is effective for many teaching purposes, it may be desirable at times to turn off the sound, operate the projector manually, and provide the commentary directly (or have a student do it) at whatever pace is appro-

FIGURE 10.8

In addition to large-group use, filmstrips are effective also with small groups and individuals. (a) Prerecorded tapes and headsets facilitate self-instruction and avoid disturbance to others. (b) This is a self-contained, projection-tape unit with cartridge-load tape and rear-vision screen. (c) This teacher is recording a narration to accompany a filmstrip.

priate for the situation. This procedure permits a more detailed study of the concepts involved or a more rapid overview than that provided by the record or tape.

There is also a combined still and motion picture projection and sound system designed particularly for use in individual study carrels. This consists of an 8mm motion picture projector that can be operated manually or programed to start and stop and to project individual frames or motion sequences (see Figure 10.9). As is the case with the sync-tape slide and filmstrip projectors already mentioned, this motion picture projector can be synchronized with a separate audiotape that provides pertinent narration or directions to the student. Inaudible pulses on the tape vary the speed

of the projector from single frames to specified speeds as required. The value of such a system in compactness, convenience, and versatility is evident. For its most effective use in schools, however, sufficient amounts of relevant, high-quality materials must be made available. Actually, much material of this kind can be developed by teachers, students, or school media staffs with the relatively inexpensive and foolproof super 8mm cameras now available (see Chapter 11), plus standard tape-recording sound equipment.

The adaptability of the filmstrip medium to many different kinds of subject matter can be further illustrated by brief discussions of four distinctive series by different producers. The series *American*

FIGURE 10.9

This is a super 8mm motion picture projector which can be programed for frame-by-frame use like a filmstrip projector as well as for motion sequences at standard, slow, or fast speeds.

Patriots contains filmstrips on Nathan Hale, Francis Scott Key, Betsy Ross, Patrick Henry, Commodore Oliver Hazard Perry, and George Rogers Clark.[4] Appropriate for upper elementary and middle grades, these silent filmstrips are particularly well suited for independent study or as motivators for class discussion.

Science classes studying ecology at the intermediate, middle school, or high school level will find much of value in a series called *Ecological Systems, Group I.*[5] These four sound filmstrips, beautifully illustrated, treat the ecologies of a seashore, a desert, a pond, and a forest (see Figure 10.10).

In language arts or social studies, primary-grade children can enjoy and learn from a delightful sound filmstrip series on folk tales. Two representative stories are *The Wave: A Japanese Folk Tale* and *My Mother Is the Most Beautiful Woman in the World: A Ukrainian Folk Tale.*[6] Each

complete with a teacher's guide including a synopsis, narration, concept definitions, and questions for discussion, sound filmstrips of this nature and quality are of particular value for teachers and learners alike.

Filmstrip producers quickly respond to changing curriculum needs. One example is a sound filmstrip program entitled *Me, Myself . . . and Drugs,*[7] which includes three filmstrips: *What Are Drugs?, Feeling Bad—Feeling Good,* and *Outside Influences* (see Figure 10.11). This current material also includes a carefully prepared teacher's guide.

Other distinctive and significant filmstrips include *Life*'s pictorial features on the history of man and the world and *The New York Times Current Affairs* filmstrips, which are published monthly. Several filmstrip services send out information on new releases—on such topics as current events and new developments in science—at regular intervals during the school year (see the source lists in the Appendix)..

A fourth characteristic of filmstrips

[4] Encyclopaedia Britannica Educational Corporation, Filmstrip Series No. 8000.

[5] Imperial Film Co., Inc., Series No. 434–M (with records).

[6] BFA Educational Media, Sound Filmstrips No. 304001 and 304002.

[7] Guidance Associates, Sound Filmstrips, Set No. 300 606.

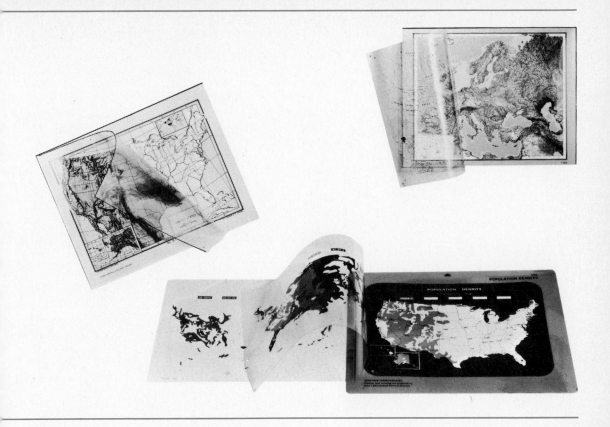

tical importance—has established the fact that letters of primary typewriter size—about ³⁄₁₆ inch—are the smallest that can be used on transparencies if they are to be readable from 20 to 40 feet away and that ¼-inch lettering is best for projectuals that may be used with either small or large groups.[9] This point is particularly worth noting because many teachers do not realize that copy prepared with elite or pica size typewriters is too small for satisfactory legibility on overhead transparencies except at very close range. (This subject is discussed in detail in the *Student Produc-*

[9] Sarah Adams, Robert Rosemier, and Phillip Sleemen, "Readability Letter Size and Visibility for Overhead Projection Transparency," *AV Communications Review,* Vol. 13, No. 4, Winter 1965, pp. 412–417.

tion Guide in connection with various methods of preparing transparencies.)

Opaque projection

As we have noted, still projection is usually accomplished by passing light through transparent materials. Slides, filmstrips, and transparencies, which we have discussed so far, are the most common of these types of materials in use. The exception, opaque projection, is the type of still projection that uses nontransparent materials, projecting them by means of reflected light. Opaque projectors are familiar and very useful projectors. We therefore discuss opaque projection before some relatively less common types of projection that use transparent materials.

FIGURE 10.16

The opaque projector has the attention-focusing power of any projector plus the unique capability of projecting virtually any nontransparent material that will fit into the opening of about 10 × 10 inches, including students' work in its original form.

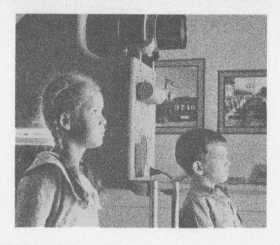

Opaque projection permits nontransparent materials—such as flat pictures, book illustrations, tables, drawings, photographs, students' work, and even certain specimens and objects—to be shown on a screen for group observation (see Figure 10.16). The instructor with access to an opaque projector thus automatically has available an almost unlimited amount of illustrative material that he can use with it at little or no cost. Furthermore, much of this material can be used just as is without mounting or other preparation. A theme, a mathematics paper, a sheet of typing, a page or diagram in a book, a picture in a magazine, a culture dish, a watch, coins, stamps, flowers, or leaves—in fact, nearly anything that is within about 10 × 10 inches in size can be projected on an opaque projector (see Figure 10.17).

Obviously, an important and unique advantage of opaque projection in instruction is the great mass of readily available and cost-free materials that can be projected. Another distinct advantage is that illustrative material of various kinds can be enlarged and then transferred. Small news maps, tables, diagrams, graphs, and similar materials can readily be projected in enlarged form for discussion purposes; those having more than transitory value can then be traced on the chalkboard or on a large piece of paper for further use.

The many practical and effective uses opaque projection can have in the classroom have been explored over a period of years. The following list is representative of the usefulness and versatility of this particular medium:

Elementary Grades

1 *Language arts: story sharing, animated word games*
2 *Arithmetic drill: pull strips that reveal numbers of objects*
3 *Science: the enlarging of pictures to show size; the showing of collections of shells*
4 *Social studies: maps locating school and homes*
5 *Enlarging figures and diagrams for bulletin boards*
6 *Science specimens; weather map symbols*
7 *Test reviews*
8 *Book illustrations*
9 *Music: sharing a song*
10 *Mathematics: diagrams, problems, exercises*

Secondary Grades

1 *Social studies: map projection*
2 *English: creative writing, correction of grammar on written work; letter forms*
3 *Civics: current maps and pictures*
4 *Art: drawing techniques, illustrations*
5 *Science: specimens*
6 *History: reference pictures, artifacts*

College

1 *Business education: business and accounting forms*
2 *Journalism: creative writing, advertising layouts*

3 *Home economics: textiles*
4 *Fine arts: photographs, graphs, charts, instruments, drawings; illustrations for various subject areas*[10]

[10] Ray Denno, *Using the Opaque Projector,* Squibb-Taylor, 1958, pp. 12–25. See also Kenneth L. Bowers, *The Opaque Projector, Bridges for Ideas #10,* Visual Instruction Bureau, The University of Texas, 1960, pp. 14–25; and the booklet, *Digest of Educational Opaque Projection Practices,* published by Charles Beseler Company, East Orange, N.J., 07018, 1970, for additional ideas and suggestions.

FIGURE 10.17

Specimens as well as flat materials can be shown readily in the opaque projector.

Microprojection

The terms "microprojection" and "microfilm projection" are sometimes confused by the uninitiated, but they should be carefully distinguished. In *microprojection*, microscope slides are used, as discussed in this section. Microfilm projection, which uses film, is described in the next section.

The microprojector is designed to project microscope slides or microslides, as they are called, so that an entire class may see what would be visible to only one pupil at a time if seen through a microscope (see Figure 10.18). Both wet and dry slides may be projected with this instrument.

The microprojector not only reduces the need for expensive microscopes, but also helps assure the instructor that his students are seeing precisely what he wants them to see. The proper and effective use of microscopes is often a difficult skill to learn in itself, and training in this skill often retards instruction in the subject under study. Furthermore, even when instruction in the use of the microscope has been given, the instructor cannot be sure

FIGURE 10.18

Two types of microprojectors are shown in use. (a) This microprojector can be used with a screen, as here, or it can be tilted to project an image onto a table. (b) A microscope slide is projected into a shadowbox screen. A microprojector can be used effectively for an entire class in a darkened room. Three levels of magnification usually are available. For what purposes is a microprojector superior to individual microscopes?

that each of the pupils has properly adjusted the microscope lenses or that he is seeing what the instructor wishes him to see. With the microprojector, on the other hand, microslides can be projected on the screen so that the proper view is assured for all and attention can be directed to specific points as desired.

Many phenomena suited for presentation on microscope slides can be shown with marked effectiveness on a microprojector. Such uses as the following are representative:

1   *Illustration of stresses and strains on fibers, filaments, and surfaces*
2   *Physical examination of wood, cotton, silk, rayon, linen, and other textile fibers*
3   *Gross projection of prepared slides showing fingerprints or other semitransparent print materials such as blood smears*
4   *Visualization of interference patterns of light and optical principles of refracted light*
5   *Gross examination of properties of crystals and other common compounds such as minerals, salt, sugar, other food materials, rubber, and petroleum by means of white and polarized light*
6   *Projection of crystal growth in various solutions; further, since removal of the projector cooling cell causes melting, replacement of this cell results in crystallization that can be shown without changing the field of projection*
7   *Projection of one-celled animals and plants on wet slides, cell division, plant and animal tissues, bacteria, mold spores, and the like*[11]

Most prepared microscope slides now available can be projected with the microprojector, but those requiring high resolution are better examined directly with a microscope. It should also be kept in mind, when projecting live specimens, that the light beam must be cooled sufficiently to prevent damaging the specimens on the slide. Thus it is best to project such materials only a minute or two at a time; if you want to come back to them, simply turn off the lamp and leave the fan running.

[11] Theodore Sargent, ''Using the Microprojector in Physics and Chemistry,'' in Harry C. McKown and Alvin B. Roberts, eds., *Audio Visual Aids to Instruction* (rev. ed.), McGraw-Hill, 1949, pp. 512–513. For additional suggestions, see *Teachers Manual for the Bioscope Microprojectors*, Bioscope Manufacturing Co., 1970.

Microfilm and microfiche

ALTHOUGH their functions of information storage and retrieval are quite different from the functions of other still-projection media, microfilm and microfiche (pronounced ''microfeesh'') are of sufficient importance to both students and teachers to be included here. As the volume of human knowledge multiplies, the problem of storing and retrieving information in normal printed forms has become massive and increasingly unmanageable. School, college, and public libraries have long since run short of adequate storage space for books and periodical files. To accommodate such pressures, some years ago microfilming was introduced, and various publications such as rare books, theses, newspaper files, periodicals, and important documents were photographed on 35mm microfilm, each frame of the film containing a greatly reduced separate page. The resulting rolls of film, which look very much like filmstrips, are placed in special projectors called *microfilm read-*

FIGURE 10.19

The capability of microfilm readers is well illustrated here. A large screen, good definition, and adequate light actually improve on the readability of the original front page of *The New York Times.*

ers which project each page on a rear-vision screen (see Figure 10.19).

Microfilm was the first step in what now promises to be a revolution in libraries, perhaps in reading habits, and even in publishing itself. As the technology of miniaturization has advanced, microfiche has become the other widely used form of film reduction of information for the purposes of storage and retrieval.[12] Microfiche is a sheet of film carrying many rows of images of printed or other matter that are much more greatly reduced than the images on microfilm. Microfiche is usually used in the form of cards of some standard size that can easily be stored. The technological advances in information storage and retrieval have come rapidly in many areas, but in none more strikingly than in this miniaturization:

What the transistor is to radio and television, high-reduction photography is to the printed page. By photographing materials at very great reductions onto a small, transparent film card called a microfiche, this process at first was able to transfer a whole book onto a single card. With advanced technology, however, it is now possible to print six books on a single 3″ × 5″ card.[13]

Microfilm remains in extensive use, for a great deal of material has already been microfilmed, there are a number of well-

[12] Microfiche should not be confused with microcards, which were an intermediate step in miniaturization. A microcard is an opaque sensitized card on which rows of reduced matter are reproduced photographically. Microcards are passing out of use as microfiche rapidly becomes the predominant microform.

[13] John Tebbel, *Saturday Review*, January 9, 1971, p. 41.

established continuing microfilming programs, and microfilm readers are widely available in schools, colleges, libraries, and research centers. The many recent noteworthy developments in information storage and retrieval, however, almost invariably utilize the high-reduction capabilities of microfiche. Among these is what Encyclopaedia Britannica calls a "Microbook Library," which will cost libraries far less than the normal price of books and which can be stored in a minute fraction of the space (some 250 Microbook cards fit into a space normally occupied by one regular book). This process is known as Super-Microfiche. Both a desk model reader and a lap reader that can be used at home are already available. These readers automatically center each image on a card and project it clearly on the screen. Further, a

FIGURE 10.20

The progress of miniaturization is exemplified in this 4″ × 6″ PCMI transparent microfiche card which has a capacity of 48 × 35 or 1,680 pairs of photographed printed pages—3,360 pages on a single card.

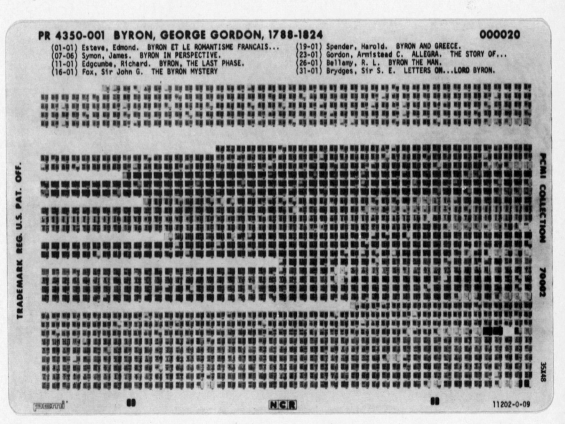

reader-printer is under development which will make print-out copies of any page desired.

A similar development called Ultramicrofiche is National Cash Register's new process that enables each card to carry about 3,300 book pages (see Figure 10.20). These cards are being assembled into the PCMI Library Information System, which will eventually provide whole libraries-full of information in a manageable space. The initial collections are grouped in five principal areas. American civilization, literature-humanities, social sciences, science and technology, and government documents. This system is to be sold to libraries at a reported cost of about $1.50 per volume. Some 50,000 volumes are expected to be available by the mid-1970s. NCR also markets a PCMI reader that provides an excellent image (see Figure 10.21) and a reader-printer.

Another significant milestone in the rapidly developing field of information storage and retrieval is the New York

Times Information Bank, which began operations in 1972. This is a computerized, fully automated system designed to retrieve general information of the type included in the *Times* itself as well as selected material from more than 60 other newspapers and periodicals. Abstracts of the material are carried in computers, and the full texts are carried on microfiche. Initially limited to printed material from periodicals, the system will ultimately be expanded to include printed reference materials and nonprinted sources such as photographs and other graphic materials.

A similar information bank is being developed for some 35 periodicals by University Microfilms, a subsidiary of the Xerox Corporation. The information will be fed into and stored in a data bank; the company plans to issue index printouts at regular intervals that will be keys to the information stored in the data bank. It is anticipated that eventually from 100 to 150 periodicals will be stored in the data bank. The plan is to make the index avail-

FIGURE 10.21

This reader quickly locates and focuses on any one of the approximately 3,300 pages which an NCR microfiche card can accommodate and projects it on the rear-vision screen in a readily readable size.

able to users at the low price of about $100 per year so as to achieve the widest possible market.

The enormous educational potentials of these developments just discussed and other similar ones excite our imaginations today. In a few short years, however, such information storage and retrieval systems will be commonplace in thousands of schools and colleges and will be used by millions of students and laymen. Such is the promise of technology—and also the challenge. At the moment, we can only marvel; nevertheless, our experience with other technological innovations leads us also to wonder about the vast changes that must take place before we can learn to use these potentially powerful resources *effectively* in our educational programs. At worst, they can simply facilitate what we are now doing in our schools and colleges. At best, used with sufficient imagination and energy, the new information-handling systems can readily update old programs and bring new and exciting programs of education into being.

Holography

There is some question that a discussion of holography properly belongs in a chapter on still projection. Although holography can be and is being used successfully in connection with still images, it also has many applications in motion pictures, television, and computers, as well as a great variety of uses in science and industry. But holography does relate basically to photography, which is the basis of most types of projection. Therefore, this seems as good a place as any to describe it briefly. In any case, we certainly should describe it—holography's potentials for instruction in the future are great.

The following quotation from an article by a photography scientist eloquently conveys some of the significance and excitement of this new development.

Can you envision 3–D color TV, art treasures of the ages seemingly reincarnated in your living room on command, full-color images from black and white film without cameras and lenses? All these may lie on photography's horizon, for there is a quiet revolution going on, much of it still behind closed doors. The revolution is holography—the most exciting advance in imagery since photography itself.[14]

In 1971, as this is written, motion picture holography has already been successfully achieved in research laboratories, and a holographic video-playback system is being developed for home use. Holograms are beginning to come out of the laboratory to be put to a variety of practical uses. These relate to such varied areas as microscopy, information storage for computers, aerial mapping of greatly increased speed and precision, nondestructive testing of aircraft tires and other products, and medical examination of internal organs—the latter done with sound waves from which 3–D pictures can be reconstructed![15]

Holography is sometimes called "lensless photography" because images are created on a holographic plate without a camera. Instead, a laser light beam is split into two parts, one of which is reflected off the subject onto a photographic plate.[16] The other part of the beam, known as the reference beam, is reflected off a mirror and onto the same photographic plate (see Figure 10.22).

[14] James Forney, "New Wave in Image Making—Holograms Tell It Like It Really Was," *Popular Photography,* January 1967, p. 120.

[15] Richard Straube, "Three-Dimensional Future?" *Industrial Photography,* October 1969, pp. 34 ff.

[16] The word "holography" comes from the Greek words for "whole" and "to write." The word "laser" is an acronym for "light amplification by stimulated emission of radiation."

FIGURE 10.22

A light beam emanating from the laser as a pencil-thin ray is separated into two beams by the beamsplitter. The brighter beam is deflected off a mirror, passes through a diverging lens, and then reaches the subject, from which it is reflected to a photographic plate. The other beam, called the reference beam, passes through the beamsplitter and a diverging lens and is then reflected off a mirror directly to the photographic plate. The light reflected off the subject and the reference light combine to set up wavefront interference patterns that are recorded on the plate in the form of a three-dimensional image of the subject—a hologram.

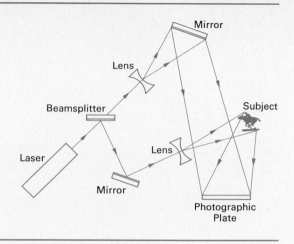

Although the scientific explanation of holography is somewhat complex, the basic principles involved are relatively simple. The first essential is a laser light beam, which is used to illuminate the subject because the light produced by a laser has two essential properties. First, laser light is very pure, having only one frequency or wavelength, rather than the many that typically make up colored (or white) light; it is thus *monochromatic*. Second, laser light is *coherent,* which means that the light rays are parallel, appearing to come from a source infinitely distant, as from a star. Ordinary types of light, such as incandescent, fluorescent, or mercury vapor light, have neither of these qualities, since they usually contain a full spectrum of colors and diffuse them in all directions. Thus, with laser light, we have the precision necessary to set up controlled *wave interference,* a second necessary condition for creating holograms.

The wave interference concept is much like the wave patterns caused by tossing two rocks into a quiet pool. The wave patterns created radiate outward in two sets of concentric circles and, as they meet, wave interference takes place. If the waves peak together, they reinforce or amplify one another. If they are out of phase, they

tend to minimize or cancel one another. Light waves (and sound waves) from separate sources react in much the same manner except that they do so in all planes rather than just the horizontal.

These light wave interference patterns completely envelop any object in their path, just as water waves constantly lap on all sides of a boat or other object on the surface. There is a difference, however, in the wave action on one side of the boat as compared with that on the opposite side—and, of course, at any given instant there are graduated differences in the wave action from point to point around the entire hull. When wave interference patterns are set up—as by the wash from a passing power boat—many of these differences are accentuated, made more visible.

The analogy ends there because waves of light do not have an effect on a physical object comparable to the effect of waves of water. The visual "pond," in other words, remains totally unruffled—flat—until wave interference patterns are set up by the split laser beam technique. What happens then is that the photographic plate records an instant cross section of these wave interference patterns caused by the meeting of the two light beams on the plate. These interference patterns literally produce a three-dimensional image of startling reality. Because the holographic plate simultaneously records in all planes, it records a different image from every angle and combines them, just as the eyes record different images from different angles and combine them when viewing a real object.

The plate is then developed by fairly conventional procedures. The resulting hologram can be viewed from the front with an almost monochromatic light source such as a sodium vapor lamp; it can also be backlighted or projected with a similar light source. Backlighted scenes in full color are also possible by using one exposure for each of the three primary colors.[17]

[17] Those interested in pursuing the technical side of holography will find several articles listed in the References at the end of this chapter. Relevant articles also appear frequently in current issues of *Industrial Photography* and other technical photography journals.

Experimentation with holography is going on at a steadily increasing pace. One company has devised a system whereby any motion picture film, no matter when it was originally made, can be shown in three-dimensional stereo to audiences using polarized viewing spectacles. However, the CBS Laboratories have developed a new method of using holographic techniques to project motion pictures in three dimensions that can be viewed without special glasses. The implications of such developments and techniques for the motion picture industry are fairly clear. The implications for schools are less obvious at the moment.

In any case, instructional holograms of various sizes can already be purchased at prices from $5 to $10, and new developments may be expected to make these and other holographic applications increasingly practical and functional in education as well as in many other areas.

Effective selection and use of still-projection materials

THE value of still-projection media in a variety of subjects and grade levels has been studied here and abroad primarily with filmstrips and slides,[18] but the principal conclusions are probably applicable to still projection generally, since the learning achieved from such materials has been demonstrated to be more dependent on the nature and quality of the message presented than on the type of medium employed. Effective instructional materials are carefully designed (or selected) to achieve clearly identified and specific objectives—as is done in Instructional De-

[18] William H. Allen, "Audiovisual Materials," in *Encyclopedia of Educational Research*, Macmillan, 1960, pp. 120–121, provides a very good summary of research on the effectiveness of filmstrips and slides.

velopment (see Chapters 3 and 15). Ineffective instructional materials contain little information to be learned, have unclear goals, or are of an incidental nature.[19] Within this general frame of reference, research has demonstrated the following:

1. Still projection is an effective means of communicating factual information and certain skills.

2. Combining still-projection media with other types of teaching materials and methods in terms of a careful analysis of the needs of the learning situation is likely to produce the most efficient learning outcomes.

[19] Loran Twyford, "Educational Communications Media," in *Encyclopedia of Educational Research*, Macmillan, 1969, p. 371.

3. The extent to which still-projection materials embody unique pictorial or graphic content of good quality has a direct bearing on their effectiveness in teaching. In other words, as is true of other teaching materials, still-projection materials must be selected and used effectively if they are to provide the maximum benefits.

Selection of still-projection materials

The first step in efficiently selecting materials is to decide whether or not a particular material can serve the specific teaching purpose better than another learning device or medium. This decision must be made partly in terms of what the projected material itself can and cannot do; that is, in terms of its inherent characteristics. Five basic questions the classroom teacher might well ask himself are the following:

1. *Does my teaching purpose require motion to accomplish full pupil understanding?* If it does, a still-projection device obviously is not the best learning medium. At best, still projection can only imply motion, and therefore should not be used to teach concepts of motion. On the other hand, projected diagrams, schemata, and the like can be effective means of analyzing the component *parts* of motion in detail if the motion itself is visualized before or after the still-projection presentation by a motion picture film or a working model, and so forth.

2. *Are suitable materials available for my particular teaching purpose?* This is a question of practical import to most teachers, because keeping track of the large number of slide sets, filmstrips, transparencies, and other educational materials put out each year in a given field is a considerable task. Professional journals frequently contain sections that review new educational materials, and several publications are specifically devoted to the task of pro-

viding periodic evaluations of such materials.[20]

3. *Does my teaching purpose involve a series of step-by-step developments according to a fixed logical progression?* If so, the teacher must decide if a filmstrip can best provide this sequence or if the job can best be done by using a series of transparent overlays and an overhead projector. Overlays are particularly appropriate if the teacher himself wishes to provide sequential analytic markings on the material during the class discussion. If the overlay technique is not necessary, a filmstrip may present the material most effectively. Drum-type slide projectors permit the same control over fixed sequence as do filmstrips, but can also be rearranged as desired. In general, slides are most suited to learning situations that demand no particular sequence or situations that make it desirable to change the sequence to show different aspects of the content under study.

4. *Does my teaching purpose require materials that tell their story primarily through pictures rather than words?* Because still projection is essentially a visual medium, it should be relied on to communicate visual ideas—pictures, graphs, diagrams, and the like. Projection materials should emphasize that which is visual; verbal materials, while useful and often essential for complete understanding of visual media, should not dominate the use of still projection. (An exception is

[20] The Educator's Progress Service compiles annually revised listings of free films and filmstrips and their accompanying instructional materials in both general and special subject areas. The National Information Center for Educational Media (NICEM), University of Southern California, provides separate catalogs for each kind of medium. The Westinghouse Learning Corporation publishes the *Learning Directory*, a regularly revised source index that includes all types of media. Film evaluation services are available from the Educational Film Library Association and Landers Film Review.

in remedial reading and arithmetic, where visual images of word and number symbols are used extensively.)

It should also be borne in mind that the visual materials for which still projection is an excellent teaching tool include many that are primarily symbolic; for example, graphics, diagrams and schemata, maps, and so forth, are largely symbolic rather than pictorial. Thus the teacher should decide on the kind of material—pictorial, diagrammatic, and so forth—which will be the most useful means of presenting the concept at hand. It may be best to use a particularly good picture in a recent magazine projected on the opaque projector, or a series of intricate map or diagram overlays projected on the overhead projector may be more appropriate, or a combination of several different media and materials may be the best answer.

An educational psychologist who studied the effectiveness of filmstrips in learning has stressed that the pictures on a filmstrip (or, by implication, on other projected material) must contribute something unique if the filmstrip is to be any more effective than words in a learning situation. He compared results achieved, in terms of immediate factual learning and recall of information over a three-week period, from using a particular American history filmstrip with one group and using only the reading material from that filmstrip with another group. He found no significant advantage for either group, but in assessing his findings he questioned the pictorial quality of the material used: "When the pictorial element of the filmstrip is deficient in detail, definition, or clarity, it not only fails to contribute to the students' knowledge but may actually serve to inhibit learning."[21]

5. *Are speed or other aspects of timing important considerations to my teaching purpose?* Although all still-projection devices permit detailed analysis of each image by holding it on the viewing screen for as long as necessary, it may occasionally be desirable to show several images in rapid succession to provide an overview or review. Further, such subjects as remedial reading and arithmetic can employ flash views of single images to advantage. If speed of presentation is desirable for the instructor's purpose, a filmstrip may be the wisest choice, provided that it fulfills the other criteria demanded by the learning situation. Also, some overhead projectors are equipped with a *tachistoscope* that enables the teacher to flash images onto the screen at speeds up to $\frac{1}{100}$ of a second. Certain slide projectors are designed for tachistoscopic use, as are some filmstrip projectors (see Figure 10.23).

The tachistoscope technique was used extensively during World War II for aircraft recognition training; it replaced the earlier WEFT system in which *w*ings, *e*ngine, *f*uselage, and *t*ail were analyzed separately in identification. The new system, developed by psychologist Samuel Renshaw of Ohio State University, was based on *total perception* of visual elements rather than *step-to-step perception*. Thus the aircraft is seen as a whole rather than in terms of wings, an engine, a fuselage, and a tail. In other words, the whole is something more than the sum of its parts and is seen as such. This is a basic concept of such Gestalt psychologists as Wertheimer, Kohler, and Koffka.[22]

The Renshaw system employed thousands of photographs of airplanes on 2 × 2 slides. The planes were pictured in as

[21] A. W. Vandermeer, "Relative Contributions to Factual Learning of the Pictorial and Verbal Elements of a Filmstrip," *School Review*, February 1950, pp. 84–89.

[22] For an interesting summary of the principles of Gestalt psychology in relation to perception and insight, see James B. Stroud, *Psychology in Education*, 2d ed., Longmans, Green, 1956, pp. 359–369.

many different positions, angles, distances, and conditions of visibility as could be secured. The slides were projected slowly at first and then for progressively smaller fractions of a second. Pilots, gunners, and other military personnel became adept at recognizing aircraft almost instantaneously after sufficient practice with the tachistoscope technique for flash recognition to become habitual. The latter point appears to be significant in achieving initial increases in reading speed and perceptual span with a tachistoscope or other accelerating devices, such as the Iowa Reading Training Film and the Harvard Reading Films.[23] If the increases are maintained in practice, they can become permanent; if not, they are soon lost.

Aside from the motivational effect of these devices, their proper use appears to result in a signficant improvement in speed of reading and number recognition. Expert use by the instructor is essential, however, including short, follow-up practice sessions for students; also, students must be highly motivated to maintain increased speeds. For, as has been pointed out in connection with the Iowa Reading Training Films,

If the student tires, as he must in longer periods, he will have a tendency to revert to a slower and more comfortable rate. After the faster rate becomes habitual, it is no more tiring than a slower rate. Effort requires motivation. Here the attempt is made to arrange conditions so the student will practice reading in a different way. Mere practice, reading in the accustomed way, will only maintain the status quo. One learns by practice what he practices.[24]

To summarize, the teacher must first evaluate the specific purposes for which

---

[23] University of Iowa, Iowa City, Iowa 52240; Harvard University Press, Cambridge, Massachusetts 02138.

[24] Stroud, op. cit., p. 383.

FIGURE 10.23

Group use of tachistoscopic techniques with a 3 1/4 × 4 overhead slide projector. A portion of a representative slide used for speed drill on phrase recognition is also shown.

the learning materials are to be used and then judge which types of material and means of projection will be most efficiently geared to accomplishing these purposes. Finally, the visuals he chooses must be of such a nature and quality as to contribute something at once significant and unique to the learning situation. Preview of the materials is clearly indicated if the teacher is to make good judgments on these points (see Figure 10.24). Not only is he guided in his final selection, but preview also serves to prepare him for the specific teaching situation. The teacher must know the content contained if he is to plan and to execute the learning situation efficiently— what points to emphasize, what points will need additional clarification, and, unless he is using a filmstrip, the order and sequence in which the slides, transparencies, or opaque materials are to be presented.

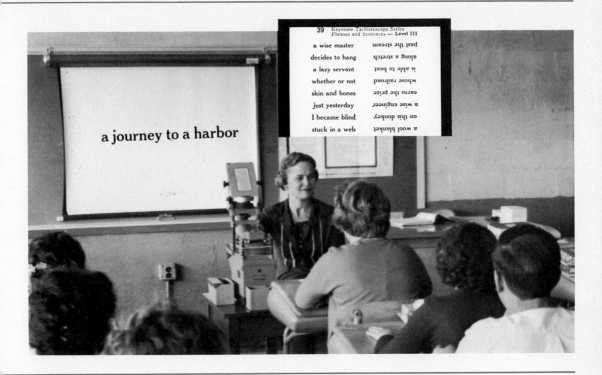

Use of still-projection materials

Once the teacher has decided which projected and other materials he will use with his class, he must know how to present them in such a way as to impart their content effectively to the pupils. In planning and executing the teaching situation, the teacher should bear in mind that the pupils should not only learn the information and concepts involved, but should also be able to *apply them accurately and creatively as a result of the experience*. If use of the still-projection materials is to achieve these goals, the teacher must consider not only the presentation or the actual showing itself, but also preparation for the experience and follow-up activities as well.

PREPARATION   As suggested previously, the first step in preparation is the one during which the teacher himself becomes fully acquainted with the points to be highlighted or clarified in the learning situation. In previewing the filmstrips, sets of slides, or transparencies, the teacher should outline the salient features in order and note any comments or questions he may wish to raise in classroom discussion. It may be desirable to record his presentation or his comments on sound tape in the form of a narration. Such a prerecorded narration not only establishes beforehand the ideas to be covered and the pace at which they will be presented, but also prevents the ideas from getting lost because of pupil questions or spontaneous digressions. The tape—like the projection—can be stopped at any point for discussion and can later be replayed for review so that the pupils are presented with the ideas in a consistent fashion.

FIGURE 10.24

Evaluating a filmstrip means assessing its quality in terms of general curriculum requirements. Selecting one for a particular lesson and specific objectives is a much more exacting task requiring careful examination and considered judgment.

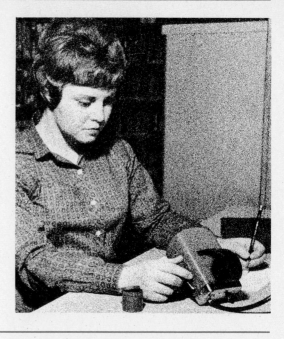

Having planned the overall presentation, the teacher must prepare the class to see it. Just how he goes about this will depend on the pupils' readiness and initial interest, but the important point to bear in mind is that the students should *want* to see it for reasons of their own. Thus, though the teacher may feel that he should give an introductory explanation of why the pupils are being shown this particular material at this particular time, the purpose of the experience, and so on, he should at the same time be sure not to overlook the necessity to inspire pupil motivation. As is true in most teaching situations, active pupil involvement is an essential element in effective learning during this preparation stage.

In preparing the pupils for what they are to see, the teacher must provide ways by which they will understand clearly what to look for. How a teacher uses a filmstrip or any other kind of teaching material naturally depends on *why* he is using it—in other words, on his specific ob-

jectives. Should his purpose be to provide a general overview and to arouse interest, he may indicate general rather than specific points to be looked for. On the other hand, if he wishes to clarify certain definite concepts, he will wish his students to be alert for the answers to specific questions. For example, in using the filmstrip *The Slide Rule—Multiplication and Division*,[25] the mathematics instructor might well ask in advance such questions as the following:

1   *Which two scales on the slide rule are used for multiplication and division?*
2   *How should the scales be lined up to multiply? To divide?*
3   *How and where is the result found?*

The teacher should also anticipate new or difficult words, phrases, and symbols. For example, one teacher of a pri-

[25] U.S. Office of Education; available from United World Films.

mary reading class was using a book called *My Mother Is the Most Beautiful Woman in the World* and the sound filmstrip adapted from the book.[26] Together, the teacher and the children read part of the book one day. The next day, the teacher asked the children—before she wrote new words on the chalkboard—"Now, children, where was Varya when we finished our reading lesson yesterday?"

"She was in the village," said one child. "And why was she in the village?" asked the teacher. A flurry of hands shot up and the excited responses to these and similar review questions elicited the fact that little Varya and her mother were in the village for the annual harvest festival.

The teacher was setting the stage for the filmstrip illustrating the story as read by a professional storyteller on the accompanying record. The story is a delightful Ukranian folk tale about a little girl who becomes separated from her mother during the harvest celebration. When asked by others what her mother looks like, she responds, "My mother is the most beautiful woman in the world." With only that clue to go on, the tale unfolds—charmingly—and, of course, with a happy ending (see Figure 10.11).

But the teacher had more than entertainment in mind. In addition to asking such questions as "What do we mean when we say that a person is beautiful?" she wrote certain new vocabulary words on the board, such as *scythe, village, streamers, celebration, clearing, stranger, leader*—words the children had to understand to appreciate the story. In the process, the children's vocabulary was increased.

"Now, let's go back to Varya and find out whether she finds her mother. Maybe

we'll discover some other things too. Let's listen and watch closely." Thus one primary teacher prepared her pupils for an exciting sound filmstrip adventure which gave pleasure to the children and helped develop several new concepts with them.

When the main purpose of using a filmstrip is to teach new concepts and new words, as in this reading lesson, it is essential to remove in advance such barriers to learning as unknown words or unrecognized symbols. This can be done, as in this case, through discussion; it can also be done by using the dictionary and/or illustrations. The new concepts are then more likely to be applied promptly as the filmstrip is shown and, in consequence, to be well learned. In the process, also, removal of vocabulary barriers facilitates comprehension of the filmstrip content and enhances the whole learning experience.

Mechanical as well as instructional preparation is necessary in using filmstrips, slides, and transparencies effectively. Most teachers quickly realize that it is much more convenient, as well as more effective, to have all their teaching materials ready for use at the beginning of a class period. It takes only a few minutes to set up the projector and test it so that at the proper moment a flick of the switch will bring the first picture to the screen without delay and confusion. More important is the fact that when everything is in readiness, lesson interruptions are held to a minimum. The filmstrip, slide, or other projected medium fits smoothly and naturally into the learning experience. It assumes its proper role in helping to put across certain ideas without attracting undue and unwanted attention to the projection operation itself.

PRESENTATION   The particular modes of presentation of projected materials—for example, the pace at which they are presented, the kind of narration or accompanying sound effects used, the way

---

[26] The authors of the book are Becky Reyher and Ruth Gannett; it was published by Lothrop, Lee and Shepard Co., Inc. The filmstrip of the same title, adapted from the book, is a BFA Educational Media Film, produced by Stephen Bosustow.

FIGURE 10.25

This frame from the filmstrip *Teaching with the Filmstrip* suggests several ways in which filmstrips can be used.

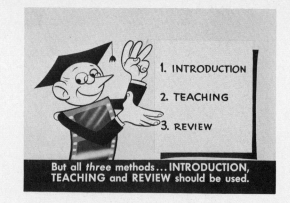

captions are handled, and whether or not other learning media are used in conjunction with the still projection—are contingent on the specific objectives the teacher hopes to achieve in the particular learning situation (see Figure 10.25). For example, if the initial showing of the material is to provide an introductory overview of a new unit of study, the instructor may wish to show a complete filmstrip in one showing and save class questions, comments, and detailed analysis of any one frame or idea for later when detailed study of individual frames may be appropriate. For such an overview, a filmstrip may be run through at a fairly rapid pace to emphasize only the highlights to be assimilated by the pupils. In this case, if it is a silent filmstrip, the captions might be read aloud by the instructor as the filmstrip proceeds in order to save time, keep things moving, and assure that everyone is following the basic story as it unfolds on the screen.

When still-projection materials are to be used as a basis for class discussion—perhaps in a detailed study of materials the students have already seen—there is no reason to hurry, and flexibility in timing and discussion should be built into the presentation. It may be that the entire class period is to be devoted to the showing of just a few frames of a filmstrip or a few individual slides. In this case, the captions on the filmstrip or slides need not be read aloud, as the concepts verbalized in these captions undoubtedly will be covered in the class discussion. With a sound filmstrip, of course, this is a time when only short segments of the recording would be used or, more likely, the sound would be turned off entirely.

Still projection can also be used spontaneously, to clarify or to communicate ideas that have arisen unexpectedly in a class discussion or unit of study. This is particularly true with opaque projectors. For example, as one social studies class assembled, there was a buzz of excitement over the successful rendezvous of the Apollo 15 lunar module and its command module the day before. Many students had watched the simulation of the rendezvous on one of the school's television sets, and they were particularly eager to discuss the space flight. The teacher had naturally anticipated this opportunity. Producing a spectacular news photograph clipped from the morning paper (see Figure 10.26), he projected it on the opaque projector, commenting, "Some of you may have seen this in today's paper, but I thought you might like to look at it again." The discussion that followed resulted in a planned investigation of the national space program during which the pupils, arranging themselves in committees, read about and reported on the moon-landing program, the Skylab missions, the space shuttle program, and other space projects planned for the future. One committee located and used in its report a filmstrip that showed photographs of satellites, missile launchings, and moon landings.

There is also the possibility that the filmstrip, slides, or transparencies are to be used for a quick review to "clinch" ideas that have been developed in detail previously. Here, too, the pace of the show-

ing may be fairly rapid, and it might be a good idea to read the titles or captions again. The teacher is the best judge of whether or not the ideas contained in the captions should be read aloud for reinforcement learning of these ideas. But, if so, why not let some of the students do the reading? The teacher can tell something about how well the pupils understand the subject by the way they read the captions; this also, of course, provides an opportunity for pupil participation.

A further consideration is that students may be using the projection materials by themselves. This is definitely an-

FIGURE 10.26

Illustrations relating to current topics become immediately available for use in class discussions via opaque projection.

other way that still projection can aid learning (see Figure 10.27). In this case, the students can help one another read the captions and titles as necessary.

A fundamental principle in media use is that where feasible we should employ variety. For example, several still-projection techniques and materials can be used together in multiscreen presentations. In geography, for instance, a map of a large area may be projected onto one screen on an overhead projector, and a small section of the map may be projected in enlarged form next to it on another projector. Perhaps a small mountainous area that is represented symbolically on the map can be visualized concretely by projecting slides of the same area. The climatic or cultural effects of geography might be visualized by slides, transparencies, or filmstrips that show schematic diagrams of airflows, rainfall, and so forth, or cultural scenes depicting clothing worn by inhabitants of the area, dwelling structures, and so forth. Likewise, in mathematics, a problem projected on one screen on an overhead projector can be retained while the solution is worked out by using a series of transparent overlays on a second projector or by writing on the surface of a continuous plastic roll on the second projector.

By the same token, the learning situation may call for several different media to be used in a single lesson. A few slides, a short film, a section of sound tape, and perhaps a summary of points on the overhead might be an appropriate combination to use within a class period. Should it be—and the answer must lie in the specific learning needs of the particular lesson—a second screen will frequently facilitate the operation and placement of equipment.

If multimedia use seems visionary to the teacher who is still having difficulty getting even a single projector when needed, let two things be noted: First, multimedia applications are already common in many schools and in industrial and military training programs, where they have effectively demonstrated their value. They are also found in increasing num-

FIGURE 10.27

This is another type of viewer well suited for either individual student use or teacher preview.

bers of colleges and universities where serious and often highly imaginative efforts are being made to improve the quality of undergraduate instruction (see Chapter 15). Second, federal support programs are making it increasingly practicable for many schools and some higher institutions of learning to have the instructional equipment and materials they need to strengthen their instructional programs. In view of the essential importance of education to national progress, there is little doubt that federal support to all levels of education will increase in the future.

The key questions now are the extent to which teachers and administrators will avail themselves of these opportunities and then translate them intelligently into educational programs that are significantly better than those of the past. Clearly, media have an important role to play in instructional developments of the future. But, just as clearly, the quality of new educational planning which educators can bring to bear on the problems of learning, teaching, and curriculum will provide the real measure of whether or not we are equal to the task. This is another reason for giving serious attention to the Instructional Development principles referred to frequently in this book. The I.D. training program was specifically designed to assist teachers, administrators, and other educators in doing effective educational planning and putting it into operation.

FOLLOW-UP ACTIVITIES As stressed repeatedly in our discussions of learning with media, no learning situation is complete without ample provision for follow-up activities that will permit the pupils to reinforce their learning through self-evaluation, demonstrations of the concepts learned, and application of the learning in new situations. Such follow-up activities permit the teacher to evaluate both pupil learning and the relative effectiveness of the media and methods used.

Thus, after the filmstrip, slides, or other still-projection presentation has been given in full, the teacher may wish to give a brief written or oral test on the material covered. Wherever possible, however, the teacher should call for a practical demonstration of the concepts learned. Suppose that a filmstrip on how to read a micrometer was shown. The real test of pupil learning in this case is how well each pupil can handle and actually read a real micrometer. From such evaluative activities, the teacher may judge the pupils' weak areas and those points that thus need to be reviewed or taught again, individual pupil difficulties, and, particularly, pupil interest in further learning. The teacher may also judge from the results of the evaluation whether the particular still-projection medium, or the teacher's presentation of it, has efficiently accomplished its purpose. If the class generally seems to exhibit less understanding than hoped for —if a fairly sizable number of pupils seem to be having some difficulty—the teacher should review in his own mind the adequacy of the materials he chose and the methods he used in presenting them. Perhaps the teacher failed to prepare the pupils sufficiently for the learning experience or failed to elicit their interest in the experience.

Aside from evaluation, the follow-up period provides the students with avenues for applying their new learning in areas and ways of their own choice that interest them. When pupils choose their own ways to use new knowledge, the new learning is much more likely to become permanent.

The learner normally proceeds from concrete observation to an initial understanding of ideas, to application of these ideas in new situations, to generalizations drawn from a number of such applications, and finally to assimilation of these generalizations as a part of his permanent store of knowledge. Thus the viewing or reading of materials is only a small part

FIGURE 10.28

Individual inquiry or individualized self-instruction is frequently carried on in study carrels equipped with a variety of equipment and materials. This student at Carroll College is pursuing a systematic self-instruction sequence as part of a programed course in geography.

of this process. A variety of further activities should develop from the new learning gained. Class discussions can lead to the initiating of projects that truly interest the pupils and that will enable them to acquire greater depth of understanding. Some students may wish to work on small-group projects, others to pursue projects individually on topics of particular interest to them (see Figure 10.28).

As the students report on the progress or completion of their respective projects, they have an opportunity to make comparisons with similar experiences they have had. Out of such comparisons, some generalized conclusions may come. When these generalizations provide the basis for further related learning, we say that the learner has *assimilated* his knowledge.

Still-projection equipment and screens

THE operation and use of still-projection equipment are discussed in some detail in the *Student Production Guide*. There are a few general aspects of still projection, however, that all teachers should be familiar with, including the various types of equipment and some of their advantages and limitations for particular uses in schools.

Filmstrip and 2 × 2 slide projectors

A filmstrip projector is essentially a simple mechanism (see Figure 10.29). It consists primarily of a lamp, a reflector, a series of lenses, and a smooth channel for the film. Near the base of this channel is a knob that is turned by hand to pull the filmstrip through the projector. The knob turns a sprocket wheel whose teeth fit into

FIGURE 10.29

These are three of the many models of filmstrip
projectors that are available, some of which also
accommodate 2 × 2 slides. (a) Viewlex;
(b) Standard (c) Graflex.

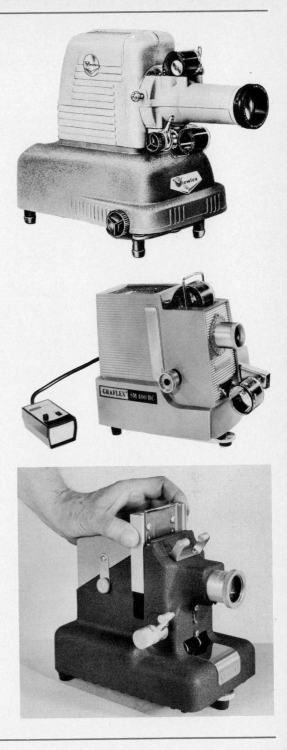

sprocket holes on the filmstrip. The projector is easy to set up and operate, inexpensive, and light in weight—all points of practical importance. A filmstrip viewer is similar except for its self-contained screen (see Figure 10.30).

A slide projector is also a simple mechanism, incorporating essentially the same elements as a filmstrip projector, except that individual slides are used. Some filmstrip projectors can also be used for slides by inserting a slide carriage. Most 2×2 slide projectors today, however, use drums or cartridges in which a large number of slides can be loaded in advance. Both types of projectors usually can be operated and even focused by remote controls. Thus an operator is unnecessary, since the teacher can change slides or reverse them at will from the front of the room. The particular convenience and flexibility of drum-type slide projectors has led to almost universal use of this type (see Figure 10.31). Such projectors normally also include an automatic change device that changes slides at predetermined intervals. This makes them particularly useful for display purposes of various kinds. It is also quite possible and feasible to hook up a tape recorder to such a projector and record the narration to fit automatically changed slides. As mentioned earlier, an inaudible pulse can likewise be recorded on the tape which changes the slides at varying appropriate intervals. There are many sound-slide and sound-filmstrip projectors, which are currently available, that facilitate such automated presentations.

THREADING Most filmstrip projectors are threaded by inserting the film into the film channel from above and pushing it down to engage the sprocket teeth. This method has the advantage of insuring correct alignment in the film channel and proper engagement with the sprocket teeth.

FIGURE 10.30

These are three of the many filmstrip viewers that are available. (a) Viewlex with cassette sound tape; (b) Standard; (c) Graflex.

Ease of threading is important because the sprocket holes on filmstrips are easily damaged. Since sprocket-hole damage ordinarily occurs on the leader strip while the projector is being threaded, however, it can usually be detected before the picture section itself is damaged. Rubberized pressure rollers and self-threading cartridge arrangements are also available; these provide a solution to the problem of filmstrip damage. With any type of filmstrip

projector, reasonable care in its use will hold such damage to a minimum. In any case, new models of filmstrip projectors are making the threading operation easier and more foolproof.

Overhead projectors

The overhead projector transmits a strong beam of light through a transparency and onto a screen behind the instructor, who is at the front of the room facing his class (see Figures 10.13 and 10.14). In most overhead projectors, the light is reflected through a large plastic lens (Fresnel lens), which directs the light through the transparency into a second reflector above and on out to the screen (see Figure 10.32). The light is sufficiently brilliant so that little room darkening is required. (One lightweight portable overhead projector provides the light source in the head, directs

FIGURE 10.31

Drum-type 2 × 2 slide projectors are more widely used than any other types because they can accommodate large numbers of slides, usually have remote control and focus, and are highly reliable. Shown here are: (a) Kodak Carousel; (b) Sawyer's Rotomatic; (c) Spindler & Sauppé Selectroslide 900 with a flexible magazine and interlocking trays, loaded with 200 slides and (d) loaded with 500 slides.

it downward to a reflector in the base, and then back through the transparency to a reflector in the head and on out to the screen. The principle is the same as that described, though the mechanics are different.)

The operation of the overhead projector is very simple; little more is involved than placing the transparency on the projector stage. The material is focused by raising or lowering the upper reflector unit by turning a knob. The projection area is usually 10 × 10 inches in the numerous models available. Most overhead projectors contain a 100-foot strip of clear plastic which passes over the projector stage between two rollers located inside the projector. The instructor can write on the clear plastic as he would on the chalkboard, or he can prepare panels ahead of time and roll them into position by turning a small crank. Diagrams, lesson assignments, tests, and similar material can effectively be presented in this way with a minimum of time and effort.

One useful accessory for the overhead projector has already been mentioned in connection with slides, but it can also be used with transparencies. This provides for the use of polarized light to create an

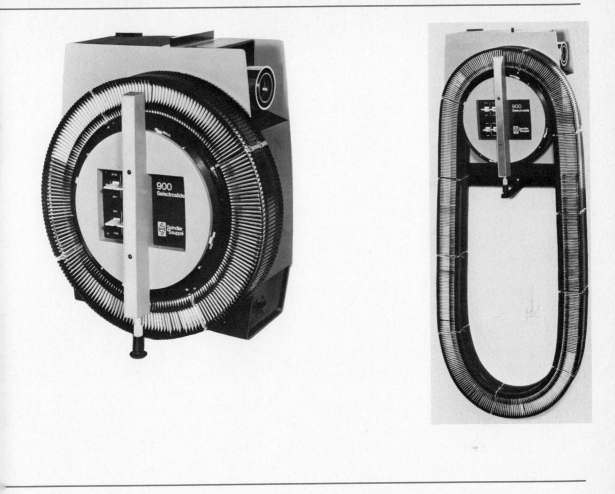

effect of animation on projected transparencies. It involves a motor-driven polarized disk beneath the projector head and polarized strips on the transparencies themselves. The disk revolves, causing the light and color patterns to change rapidly, giving the effect of animation. This device is useful for providing animated diagrams, graphs, lettering, or other display material.

Another device which can be attached to some overhead projectors, and to some 2 × 2 slide projectors, is the tachistoscope. This attachment enables the instructor to flash scenes onto the viewing screen at speeds up to 1/100 of a second. The uses of tachistoscopic techniques for improving reading speed and other recognition skills have already been discussed in this chapter.

Opaque projectors

Opaque materials are projected by means of *reflected* light. A strong light from the projector lamp is thrown onto a book page or other opaque material and is reflected by a tilted mirror through a lens onto a screen (see Figure 10.33). Although the screen image is less brilliant than in the

FIGURE 10.32

(a) This diagram shows how an overhead projector works. Two typical overhead projectors are also shown: (b) Beseler; (c) American Optical.

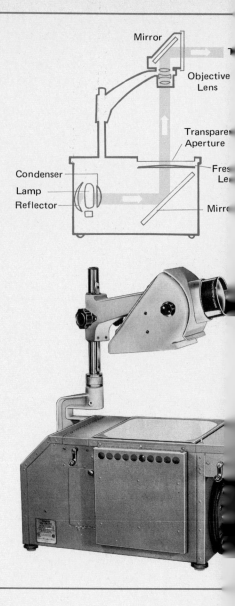

Mirror

Objective Lens

Transparen Aperture

Fres Le

Condenser

Lamp

Reflector

Mirr

case of a slide or transparency, highly satisfactory images can be obtained if the room is reasonably well darkened. Further, the lighting efficiency of the newer projectors has been improved to the point where effective projection is possible even in moderately darkened rooms. These improved projectors have a 1000-watt lamp, an opening large enough to accommodate 8 × 10-inch materials, and an efficient cooling system. Down-draft ventilation holds loose or unmounted material in place without fluttering or loss of focus. A loose postage stamp, for example, can be projected without difficulty with this type of projector. When projecting a page in a

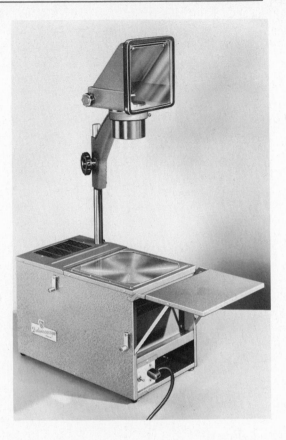

need not be an expert to know enough to select among several screens available the one that will do the best job for you. There are two major considerations: size of screen and type of screen.

SIZE OF SCREEN The most useful and versatile screens for classroom use are *square* rather than rectangular. For most purposes in the usual classroom the screen should be at least 60 × 60 inches; in larger classrooms a minimum of 70 × 70 inches should be used. The square shape is necessary to accommodate vertical slides, transparencies, or opaque projected materials without cutting down the size of the image; it is readily adaptable, as well, for motion picture projection.

TYPE OF SCREEN There are, essentially, four types of projection screens. The first two are the most common: (1) beaded screens and (2) matte-surfaced screens. (3) Lenticular screens are especially designed for color projection. A subtype is a similar screen, the Ektalite screen. (4) Rear-projection screens, which are translucent, are used for a variety of specialized applications. We limit our discussion here to the first two types, those commonly found in schools. The other types are described, and additional information on screens is provided in the *Student Production Guide*.

Beaded screens Beaded screens are the type most often found in classrooms. Such screens provide a very good image on a line directly between the projector and screen and to an angle of approximately 30 degrees on either side. (A new type of chemical coating on some beaded screens may help improve the quality of the image and increase the viewing angle.) Beyond that point, the brilliance of the image drops off rapidly; thus beaded screens are best used in long, narrow rooms.

book, a piece of heat-resistant glass holds the page flat so that all parts of it can be focused sharply.

Projection screens

In all types of projection, the screen is an important element in the effectiveness of the results obtained. As a teacher you

FIGURE 10.33

(a) This diagram shows how an opaque projector works. Two good 1000-watt projectors are also shown: (b) Beseler; (c) Projection Optics. (d) This picture vividly illustrates a unique value of opaque projection—immediate projection of student work in its original form.

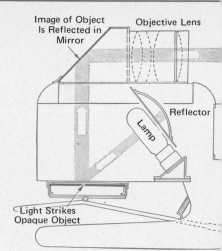

Image of Object Is Reflected in Mirror

Objective Lens

Reflector

Lamp

Light Strikes Opaque Object

FIGURE 10.34

For group showings, the best screen position may well be in the front corner of the room next to the windows at an angle so as to minimize unwanted light on the screen surface. Another hint: for best sound results locate the speaker at ear level or above—*never* on the floor!

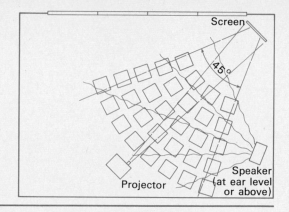

Matte, or flat-surfaced, screens Matte screens, on the other hand, provide less initial brilliance, but diffuse the available light more evenly than beaded screens and over a wider area. Thus, in rooms that are square or as wide as or wider than they are deep, matte screens are the more satisfactory type for all-purpose use.

Research and development on all types of screens may be expected to continue producing improvements as time goes on. For the present, however, as we have said, the average classroom teacher needs to be concerned primarily with beaded or matte screens and their placement for normal classroom use.

Screen placement is a variable the teacher can control. Instead of automatically placing a screen in the center of the front wall—theater style—a teacher should try for screen positions that reduce the surrounding light on the screen's surface to a minimum; obviously, such positions provide the brightest and most visible projected image. Normally, the best position is in the front corner of the room with the screen surface angled away from such light as may be getting in around blinds or shades (see Figure 10.34). Often this corner position also provides a better viewing angle for most of the students. The main thing to remember is that direct light on the screen surface, whether a front- or rear-projection surface, drastically cuts down the brilliance of the projected image. Knowing this, you should be in a position to place the screens in your classroom so as to achieve optimum viewing for your students.

Summary

One of the definite advantages of still projection is that it makes possible individual or group examination of projected still pictures and other illustrative materials for whatever length of time is necessary. Other advantages include the wide variety of means by which still projection can be accomplished, the ready availability and low cost of materials for still projection in most instances, and the convenience and ease of operation of most still-projection equipment.

There are various types of still projection, including 2×2 and other sized slides, filmstrips, transparencies, opaque projection, microprojection—the projection of microscope slides—and microfilm and microfiche. In addition to the general advantages indicated, each of these types of still projection has its own unique advantages and applications—that command its use for particular purposes; and, of course, each has certain limitations as well that must be considered in selecting them for use.

Two kinds of considerations are important in getting effective results with still projection. First, as with other kinds of instructional media, the effectiveness of still-projection applications depends to a large extent on *how* they are carried out. In general, the principles of all good teaching and learning apply: thoroughness and quality of initial planning; preview and selection of the most appropriate materials; class preparation, including motivating pupils and telling them what to look for; good projection conditions; follow-up activities, including testing, application, and reteaching as needed. Effective methods are flexible rather than rigid and are adapted both to the requirements of the learning situation and the needs of individual learners.

It is important also for the teacher to know something about still projectors so as to facilitate the selection of the most suitable types for situations in which they are to be used and to feel confidence in their use. In addition, the teacher should be generally familiar with the proper types and sizes of screens to use for various situations and where to place them so as to get the best possible image. Knowledge of this kind is essential for achieving the best physical results that available still-projection equipment can provide.

Further learner response projects

1

As a committee or individual project, have units of work in a given subject and grade area analyzed as to—
a   Where still-projection materials could

make significant contributions to learning.
b   What specific materials could do the job.

2

Survey the still-projection equipment and facilities of your school and prepare a report for your principal or superintendent that includes—
a   Present status

b   Recommended additions and changes for next year.
c   Recommended changes and additions for the next five years.
Draw up supporting statements for your recommendations.

3

As a building director of audiovisual instruction, you have been concerned for several years about the tendency of most of your teachers to use motion picture films rather than available still-projection materials, regardless of the superiority of the latter in many teaching situations.

You get permission from your principal to call a faculty meeting for the purpose of "educating" your teachers in the potentialities of one or two types of still projection. Prepare a demonstration for your instructional technology class showing how you might do this.

4

Divide the class into committees and have each one prepare a demonstration showing interesting applications of one of the following:
a   Opaque projection
b   Filmstrips

c   2 × 2 slides
d   Microfiche
e   Microprojection
f   Overhead transparencies
g   A stereoviewer

5

In order to give class members information about various types of still-projection equipment, ask an interested group to write for literature in sufficient quantities so that each member will have individual copies. If feasible, arrange with your local dealer to demonstrate several makes of equipment during a laboratory period or outside of class. Report to the class your reactions concerning new ideas and the strong and weak points of the equipment demonstrated.

References

BABITS, VICTOR A. "Holography, the Lensless 3D Photography." *Technical Photography,* January 1971, pp. 12–13 ff.

BARSON, JOHN, and GERRY B. MENDELSON. "Holography, a New Dimension for Media." *Audiovisual Instruction,* October 1969, pp. 40–42.

CARPENTER, R. L., and K. I. CLIFFORD. "Simple Inexpensive Hologram Viewer." *Journal of the Optical Society of America,* June 1967, p. 276.

CRAIG, DWINN R. "Invision: Three-dimensional Movies." *Industrial Photography,* March 1970, pp. 26–28 ff.

FORNEY, JAMES. "New Wave in Image-Making: Holograms Tell It Like It Really Was." *Popular Photography,* November 1967, pp. 120–123 ff.

GORVINE, GEORGE. "Using the Overhead To Train Perception." *The Instructor,* January 1970, p. 146.

GREESHABER, EMIL W. "Overhead Projection— How to Make the Most of It." *Audiovisual Instruction,* April 1962, pp. 236–237. (Entire issue devoted to overhead projection. Note also articles by Arthur Lalime, Neville Pearson, and Emma Starstream.)

HARTSELL, H. C., and WILFRED VEENENDAAL. *Overhead Projection.* Henry Stewart, 1960.

"Holograms Produced in Ordinary Light." *Aviation World,* January 1967, pp. 86–87.

"Holographic." *Industrial Photography,* April 1970, pp. 26–27 ff.

MAY, LOLA J. "Teaching Tools: How To Use Them in Math." *Grade Teacher,* February 1970, pp. 126–130.

RICHASON, BENJAMIN F., JR. "Teaching Geography by the Audio-Visual-Tutorial Method." *Audiovisual Instruction,* Vol. 15, February 1970, pp. 41–44.

RICHASON, BENJAMIN F., JR. "The Audio-Visual-Tutorial Method in Geography Instruction." Chap. 27, pp. 326–331. In *Developmental Efforts in Individualized Learning,* ed. R. A. Weisgerber. Peacock Publishers, Itasca, Ill., 1971.

ROCCO, JOHN A. "Developing a Transparency File for Elementary Schools." *Audiovisual Instruction,* September 1967, pp. 716–717.

SCUORZO, HERBERT E. "The Overhead Comes of Age." *Grade Teacher,* April 1963, pp. 15 ff.

Some Sources of 2 × 2 Inch Color Slides. Eastman Kodak Company, 1967.

STRAUBE, RICHARD. "Three-Dimensional Future?" *Industrial Photography,* October 1969, pp. 34–42.

Teachers' Manual for the Bioscope Microprojector. Bioscope Manufacturing Company.

ONE of man's persistent quests—to record in lifelike exactness everything in his world that moves—was first attained by Thomas A. Edison in 1894. His invention of the motion picture brought a new dimension to the communication of information—the photographic documentation of natural and social phenomena as visual happenings and their reenactment anywhere, anytime.

Today, motion picture films and their related sound images are used to document everything, everywhere—around the world and in space. Such films, supported by sound tracks that play back environmental sounds or carry the word of man in any language, are remarkably effective means of communication for their viewers-listeners. Motion pictures are universally used for both education and entertainment. Their impact has been heightened in recent years as they have come to occupy an increasingly important place in television communication and thus hold the attention of added millions. Televised motion picture reports are flung instantaneously to the outposts of the world over networks of communication satellites (see Figure 12.1, page 506).

Motion picture films play a part in many other aspects of modern life. For example, the United States Department of Agriculture uses films to describe innovations in agriculture to millions of farmers. Sound films are given to county agents across the country so that they can show farmers the latest methods for improving crop yields, preventing erosion, and so forth. To cite another type of use, service and manufacturing industries make motion picture reports that describe their methods,

achievements, and progress, not only for their stockholders, but also for interested citizens and students in many countries.

Today the governments of the world produce countless motion picture films for many purposes—to report their progress, services, problems, and attempted solutions to problems to the public everywhere (see Figure 11.1). The American armed forces discovered during World War II how effective films can be, and they have used them extensively ever since in training servicemen and in reporting military events to the public.

As motion picture films have come into use for almost innumerable purposes and in almost innumerable ways over the years, they have brought about a revolution in classroom learning procedures. As a result of the acceptance of the motion picture film as a reliable teaching and learning technique in education, there are now more than 500 producers of educational film materials.[1] More than 1,000 new 16mm films and still more 8mm films are produced for educational purposes each year. Among all the film producers are a number of successful pioneers that are still ably producing consistently reliable and validated learning materials; some of these are Encyclopaedia Britannica Educational Corporation, Coronet, McGraw-Hill Film Division, Universal Education and Visual Arts, Academy, International Film Bureau, Films Incorporated, Churchill Films.

The worth of motion picture learning is today so widely accepted that films no longer are thought of as supplements to in-

[1] Bertha Landers, *Film Reviews 1972 Source Directory*, Landers Associates.

449

FIGURE 11.1

The governments of the world make extensive use of 16mm sound motion pictures. (a) This still is from an Atomic Energy Commission film, *Project Warm Coat,* which describes efforts to move sea otters from an ocean area with a depleted food supply to an area with a rich supply. (b) In another film, *Project Salt Vault,* the AEC displays a special transporter designed to carry radioactive wastes to mined-out underground storage areas. (c) *Wheeler Dam,* a Tennessee Valley Authority film, shows this huge dam functioning in power production, flood control, and navigation. (d) *Electronics Industry of Japan;* distributed by the Consulate General of Japan, shows the transistor assembly-inspection lines at a Sony plant.

struction, but, rather, as primary and highly effective sources. Furthermore, the production of original motion picture films by students themselves has recently come to be a rapidly expanding creative activity. The photography, editing, and narrating of such films are now accepted as integral parts of language arts programs. (Such activities are supported by most of the primary learning tenets described in Chapter 2 and the visual literacy experiences described in Chapter 3.)

Sound motion picture communication enables teachers to fulfill better their demanding roles. For example, by means of carefully selected and wisely used motion pictures, the social studies teacher can provide his students with learning opportunities that help them understand the farthest reaches of earth and space. The science teacher can provide visual explanations to help students understand the nature of natural phenomena. The history teacher, by using films that reenact important historic episodes, can bring to his pupils virtually firsthand experiences as witnesses to events of the past. The foreign language teacher can use motion pictures advantageously to create visual meaning and to encourage language use in interpreting visualized concepts. The language arts teacher may use motion picture communication to help his students to express their understandings and interpretations by encouraging them to write, film, edit, and produce their own original films.

A brief history of motion picture films

A MOTION picture film is simply a long strip of film that consists of a sequence of still photographs, each of which is called a frame. Nothing moves on a motion picture film except the film itself as it runs through the projector. (The mechanics of this process are explained in the *Student Production Guide* that accompanies this book.)

As is the case with many seemingly simple devices or processes, the thought that led to the invention of the motion picture film was far from simple. Edison understood that any *image* that is comprehended by the human eye persists as a mental impression for a small fraction of a second even after the source—the actual light—has been removed or has disappeared. What he invented on the basis of this knowledge was a mechanical device for taking a succession of pictures very rapidly (16 per second) and another for projecting these same images on a screen at the same rate of speed. The human eye and mind do the rest. As 16 separate images or frames flash in sequence onto the screen each second, the eye is unable to keep pace, but instead sees a flow of images; because each image persists into the next, the eye and mind receive an impression of continuous motion.

Among the first films that Edison produced were *The House Fly* and *The Frog.* These were on film 35 millimeters wide and were, of course, silent. They moved through a primitive projector at 16 frames per second. Crude and short though these first films were, they quickly caught the imagination of educators who saw them. Thus was born the idea of films for education.

In the early 1920s came a dual development that brought the use of films in education to the point of practical reality. The old 35mm cameras and projectors were rather cumbersome; also, the film they used was explosive. George Eastman evolved a nonexplosive "safety" film, and he decided to market it in a smaller size that would make possible the use of smaller and simpler cameras and projectors. He chose 16mm as the size so that the unsafe flammable 35mm film of the time could not be sliced in two and used. At the same time he also designed and developed the 16mm silent projector which was necessary for the new size of film. This 16mm size became the standard for large-group educational use, supplemented later by the 8mm size, which is now widely used for small-group and individual educational applications. (The 35mm size has continued to be the standard for theatrical feature motion pictures; in addition, many feature films are now made with 70mm film.)

Soon afterwards, in 1922, Yale University began to produce *The Chronicles of America Photoplays,* a series of 15 16mm silent motion picture films with explanatory titles and accompanying historical publications. A board of editors which included historians and teachers supervised every step in the writing of the scripts and the production of each film. Great care was taken to re-create costumes and properties accurately, and historic sites were actually rebuilt. Everything was done to recapture realistically and correctly the essence of the 15 historical episodes presented by this series.

The release of these films, beginning in 1924, led to the undertaking of the first carefully controlled research which attempted to answer the question, "Is the motion picture film a serious and worthwhile means of contributing to classroom learning experiences?" The results of this research established that the use of *The Chronicles of America Photoplays* series increased pupils' knowledge of places, personages, and events from 19 to 35 percent. More important, the films stimulated 40 percent more free reading by pupils who had seen and studied them.[2]

Shortly after the completion of this study, the National Education Association and the Eastman Kodak Company cooperatively produced the materials for a second research experiment. Several 16mm silent films in science and the social studies were tried out in classroom situations, with the result that more than 60 percent of the pupils who saw and studied the films achieved a level of proficiency attained by only 50 percent of the pupils who did not see the films. Once again it was established that there was greater interest in voluntary reading among the film-using pupils.[3]

These early experiments heightened the interest of educators everywhere. The addition of sound to the motion picture film during 1929 and 1930 brought in the era of the educational sound motion picture film. Since that time the production of educational sound films has advanced steadily in both quality and quantity.

Today the most recent innovation in motion pictures plays a part in education that is almost more important than the part played by 16mm films. This newer development is 8mm film, which is available not only in the familiar open-reel form, but also as continuous film loops in cartridges. These films usually are silent, but an increasing number now carry sound tracks. The 8mm film is, of course, half the width of 16mm film, but because two 8mm frames fit into the length of film taken by one 16mm frame, the result is, in effect, four 8mm frames in the space of one entire 16mm frame. In other words, an 8mm frame is about one quarter the size of a 16mm frame. Accordingly, 8mm film usually is projected onto a smaller screen or onto a rear-view screen to produce a highly visual and well-defined image.

Super 8 film, introduced by Eastman Kodak in 1966, produces better motion

[2] D. C. Knowlton and J. W. Tilton, *Motion Pictures in History Teaching,* Yale University Press, 1929.

[3] Ben D. Wood and Frank N. Freeman, *Motion Pictures in the Classroom,* Houghton Mifflin, 1929.

pictures by using a considerably larger percentage of the film area for each frame than standard 8mm. Super 8 films have rapidly overtaken standard 8mm for educational uses; in fact, this size is now the predominant one in use in schools. Because of the difference in frame size and other differences, only super 8 cameras and projectors can be used with this film—much simplified equipment is now available (see Figure 11.2). The use of super 8 is now so general that when the term "8mm" is used in this chapter it can usually be assumed to mean super 8.

Most 8mm silent films are 3 to 4 minutes long, mounted in continuous-loop cartridges which may be pushed into the projector, shown, and removed for reuse or storage with great simplicity. Sound 8mm films are becoming increasingly available in lengths of 10 to 20 minutes, either in standard reels for manual or automatic thread-

FIGURE 11.2

Various types of simplified and miniaturized 8mm projection equipment are now available to schools. All this equipment features automatic film-loading or film-threading. Therefore, in today's schools, children from 4 years of age and up easily learn to operate these projectors and see the surprising, interesting, and gripping results—the world as it actually exists brought to them when they want. Are such facilities available to your pupils as they carry on their questing and discovering activities? (a) A child is about to insert one of the cartridge film loops on the table into a super 8 silent projector, which she is moving into position. When the cartridge is inserted, the projector instantly starts, showing the film on the rear-projection screen at right. (b) This super 8 silent open-reel projector automatically threads the film onto the take-up reel.

ing or in larger continuous-loop cartridges. In most cases, the sound is carried by a thin strip of magnetic material on the surface of the film.

The production record of 8mm silent and sound teaching films is the clearest indication of the status of this size. More than 100 film producers throughout the world, most of them long experienced in the production of 16mm silent and sound films, are now engaged in producing silent 8mm film cartridges on various subjects, most of them 3 to 4 minutes long. A composite listing of available 8mm films includes more than 8,000 titles.[4]

The subject of 8mm films parallel closely those available in 16mm film. Silent film cartridges, or single-concept films, are available in physical education, oceanography, vocational arts, the social studies, and many other subjects. Entire series of 8mm sound films are available for teaching

[4] *Silent Film Loop Source Directory*, 6th ed., 1970–71, University of Southern California, Technicolor Corporation.

foreign languages. Since most 8mm films are silent, eliminating the need for costly dubbing of sound-track translations, there is a free interchange of these films thoughout the world. Consequently, the 8mm silent film is a dramatic force in bringing large amounts of American "know-how" to the schools of the rest of the world. International developments in the audiovisual field are being pushed forward rapidly for this reason. Also, foreign producers in Europe, Africa, South America, Asia, and even Iceland are now producing 8mm cartridge films for their own use and for export.

In the short space of the last 10 years, the production of 8mm instructional concept loop films has overshadowed the production of the traditional 16mm film. This development, together with the fact that the initiative for film communications is being placed in the hands of students (as will be described later), makes motion picture learning one of the most exciting and understandable pupil-teacher learning experiences available in today's society.

The nature of film communication

THE most accurate way that man has yet devised to record his environment is the sound motion picture film recording technique. The result is a living document of what the camera sees, what the sound recording mechanism hears, and what man later, through his editorial techniques, accomplishes as he coordinates motion pictures with sounds and words to produce a living record of the people and places and things of this earth and space environment.

The products of this process are countless effective films that allow pupils to respond to learning experiences they see and hear revealed in highly interesting and understandable form. In making such films, four important basic techniques are used: (1) direct photography; (2) changed-speed

photography; (3) photomicrography; (4) animation. After describing these briefly, we discuss each in detail, and then some other special techniques.

Direct photography is used, for example, in filming historical episodes. When they are part of current history, they often are shot and recorded as they actually happen. Obviously, historical episodes that occurred before the twentieth century are reenacted. Various natural processes are so slow or so rapid as to be incomprehensible, but *changed-speed photography* can overcome such obstacles. For example, the growth of a plant can be "speeded up," and the flight of a hummingbird can be "slowed down." Through the use of *photomicrography*, things that are too small for the naked eye to see can be filmed through microscopic techniques and thus enlarged when projected on a screen. Things that are staggeringly large in actuality or hypothetical or theoretical or very complex can be visualized by means of *animation* using diagrams, models, or mockups, so that explanations can be seen in moving form.

Motion picture photographic techniques enable the human eye and mind to witness visual and sound explanations which, as they actually exist, are beyond the limits of normal human sensory capacities.

Direct photography

Direct or documentary photography refers to the technique of setting up the camera, opening up the lens, and recording on film what occurs before it. Thus a "document" of an experience, a process, or event is secured for later viewing and study. The importance of direct photography is evident when it captures events which occur at a political convention, at the bottom of the gorge of the Grand Canyon, as a space satellite approaches the landing area of the moon, or during the life cycles of plants or animals in their natural habitats.

Direct photography is used effectively to "replay history." Castles are restored or duplicated; museums supply authentic costumes, utensils, and other paraphernalia required for authentic reenactments of historical episodes. When, in addition, historically accurate patterns of speech and pronunciation are used by those who speak in the sound track, a close approximation of actual historical events is produced for use in social studies and history classrooms.

Through such films as *Let's Look at Castles*,[5] *Westward Movement—The Gold*

Rush,[6] *Kentucky Pioneers*,[7] and *Black Men or Iron Horses*,[8] useful historical episodes can be presented for study. Such films are possible when historians, teachers, and motion picture producers work together. Thus one may observe the lives and accomplishments of great men of history, for example, Horace Mann, Thomas Jefferson, John Marshall, Abraham Lincoln, George Washington, and many others. Direct photography lets the student witness the life and times of man of the past and man of the present (see Figure 11.3).

The production of contemporary social studies films is an international pursuit. In Germany, the Institut für Film und Bild (Institute for Films and Pictures), which receives government financial support to carry on curriculum research and film production, produces from three to five sound motion picture films per month. These films are interesting and understandable picture sequences in themselves; more important, they report on economic and political problems and current social progress. Examples are *Tokyo Industrial Worker*, *New Life for a Spanish Farmer*, *Miners of Bolivia*, *Bedouins of Arabia*, and *River Journey on the Upper Nile*,[9] which show how man seeks to improve his life through constructive activity. (Sound tracks in several languages, including English, are prepared and recorded for these films at the time of production. When prints are made of a film for a particular market, the sound track in the appropriate language is put onto them. The U. S. Department of State and many other organizations and agencies produce films

[6] 16mm film, b/w, 23 min., Encyclopaedia Britannica Films.

[7] 16mm film, color, 26 min., 2d ed., Encyclopaedia Britannica Films.

[8] 16mm film, sound, color, 18 min., New York Times and Arnold Press.

[9] Each: 16mm film, sound, color, 18 min., Institut für Film und Bild (U.S. distributor: Films Incorporated).

[5] 16mm film, sound, color, 20 min., International Film Bureau.

FIGURE 11.3

Direct photography brings man in his world into the classroom, man of the past and man of the present. (a) *First Year in the New World* reconstructs the past. (b) *Bedouins of Arabia* shows how ancient ways of life still exist in a technological world. (c) *The Dolphin Hunters* takes the viewer to the South Sea Islands.

that are available in a choice of language sound tracks.)

The direct photography of natural phenomena makes an outstanding contribution to the field of nature study and biological science (see Figure 11.4). Direct photography and high fidelity sound recording are used to produce, for example, these living documents: *Birds of the Woodlands*,[10] *The African Lion and His Realm*,[11]

and *Miss Goodall and the Wild Chimpanzees*.[12] The last film allows the viewer to witness Miss Goodall's life and adventures over a five-year period as she befriends and makes unbelievable discoveries about chimpanzees. Direct photographic records may be used successfully as large-group learn-

[11] 16mm film, sound, color, 19 min., Walt Disney Productions.

[12] 16mm film, sound, color, 25 min., National Geographic Society.

[10] 16mm film, sound, color, 11 min., 2d ed., Coronet Films.

FIGURE 11.4

Two very different types of life cycles that constantly repeat themselves in nature are shown in (a) *Animals Hatched from Eggs* and (b) *Seed Dispersal*. What specific values do you think are gained from studying films such as these?

ing experiences and even more significantly as individualized or small-group questing and discovery experiences, as described on pages 486–489.

Changed-speed photography

Changed-speed photography refers to camera techniques that permit the taking of pictures at an extremely rapid pace, or, on the other hand, at a very leisurely pace, so that when the result is projected on a screen, motion is either slowed down or speeded up. Many of the things we study, particularly in the sciences, occur too rapidly for the eye to witness or very slowly. In slow-motion photography, high-speed cameras that take as many as 4,000 individual frames per second are used; the actual motion of, for instance, the human larynx is photographed at this high speed, but when projected at the normal 24 frames per second, the motion is greatly slowed down and thus becomes understandable.[13]

In the reverse process, the camera eye is opened at intervals (1 second or 1 minute or 1 hour or 1 week apart—whatever is appropriate) to observe the leisurely blossoming of a flower, the winding tendrils of the pea vine, the metamorphosis of a pupa into an adult insect, and so forth.[14] Through such time-lapse photography, developmental phenomena that actually take hours, days, weeks, or months to accomplish can be speeded up, at least for the purposes of human vision, when projected at the normal 24 frames per second; such phenomena thus become readily understandable (see Figure 11.5).

Not too long ago, one could cite only occasional films that capitalized on changed-speed photography. Today, teachers have available to them hundreds of these films, all with sound tracks and carefully produced. Among them is *Dr. Heidegger's Experiment*,[15] a film that allows the viewer to witness the changes undergone by four aged characters who drink water allegedly from the Fountain of Youth; as they become restored to youth, their bodies change, their wrinkles disappear, and so forth. Another is *Egg into Animal*,[16] which shows step by step, the actual life cycle, from egg to adult, of the roundel skate, a sea creature. Still another is *Wood Bending: A New Twist*,[17] a film that employs time-lapse photography to allow the viewer to understand exactly what occurs as wood is bent and twisted during industrial processes—a film of particular interest to industrial arts students.

The effects of witnessing one such changed-speed film were vividly described by a noted educator, the late Glenn Frank, when he wrote down his reactions after seeing *Plant Growth,* a pioneering film of this type:

Yesterday within the space of 10 minutes, I saw a plant grow to full maturity, bear fruit, and die. As a child I often stood with awe before the mystery of plant growth and wondered what it would be like to see the actual processes of growth as I saw my playmates run back and forth across the village lawn. I had to wait 40 years, but yesterday, the thing I wondered about as a child happened. I saw the processes of growth as clearly and as plainly as this morning I saw cars streaming by in the

[13] *Your Voice*, 16mm film, b/w, 11 min., Encyclopaedia Britannica Educational Corporation.

[14] *The Honeybee*, 2d ed., 16mm film, sound, color, 10 min., Encyclopaedia Britannica Educational Corporation; *Flowers and Bees: A Springtime Story*, 16mm film, sound, color, 11 min., Encyclopaedia Britannica Educational Corporation.

[15] 16mm film, sound, color, 22 min., Encyclopaedia Britannica Educational Corporation.

[16] 16mm film, sound, color, 13 min., Sterling Communications.

[17] 16mm film, sound, color, 13 min., International Film Bureau.

FIGURE 11.5

Changed-speed photography works in two ways. (a) This kind of photography can stop actions that are too rapid for the human eye to follow, as are these splashes formed by drops of milk falling into shallow water. The still is from *Fluid Mechanics.* (b) The reverse, time-lapse photography, can summarize the life cycle of a bee, from egg to adult, in 10 minutes. This still, showing a bee bringing pollen to its hive on its hind legs, is from *Biography of a Bee.* Why should changed-speed photography be explained carefully to young learners before they are expected to study and understand such films?

street below my hotel window.

Conan Doyle had not come back to show me the marvels in a séance. I was not under the delusive spell of a magician. I was simply watching an educational film on plant growth.

A pea was dropped on the ground. Soon its sides burst open and a white sprout, or whatever the experts call it, came peering with manifest curiosity out into the open. The white sprout turned downward and began nosing about for a way to burrow downward into the soil. It nosed about with an appearance of almost animal sense. Soon it began its downward journey into the soil which had been cut away so that the camera could catch the downward journey of the roots.

459

Photomicrography

Photomicrography, or microphotography, is the camera technique that permits the viewer to enter the immense world that is too small to be seen with the naked eye. To do this, the camera "looks through" the eye of the microscope and records what it sees. Films that introduce the viewer to the worlds of molds, spores, and cell life use microphotography. Examples include *Molds and How They Grow*,[18] *Cells of Plants and Animals*,[19] *How Green Plants Make Food*,[20] and *The Roots of Plants*[21] (see Figure 11.6).

[18] 16mm film, sound color, 11 min., Coronet Films.

[19] 16mm film, sound, color, 11 min., Coronet Films.

[20] 16mm film, color, 13½ min., Universal Education and Visual Arts.

[21] 16mm film, b/w, 11 min., Encyclopaedia Britannica Films.

The extremely powerful electron microscope still farther expands the visual field of man. For example, by photographing what the electron microscope sees, it is possible to visualize realistically the fibers, fibrils, and filaments of muscles and the regular arrangement of molecules of miocin and actin within individual fibers.[22]

A variation of this photographic technique is X-ray photography, by which the internal mechanisms of the human body can be photographed as normal activities occur. Thus a person may be shown eating, swallowing, and actually digesting food.[23]

[22] *Muscle: The Dynamics of Contraction* and *Muscle: The Chemistry of Contraction*, both 16mm films, sound, color, 21 min., Encyclopaedia Britannica Corporation.

[23] *The Human Body*, 16mm film, sound, color, 16 min., Coronet Films.

FIGURE 11.6

Motion picture photomicrography allows an entire group or an individual to see what is beyond the limits of human vision. Through this technique, one may witness microscopic life in all its color and motion, such as (a) this colony of volvox in *Microscopic Life: The World of the Invisible*. (b) In *Molds and How They Grow*, the development and growth of these minute organisms are shown by combining photomicrography with changed-speed photography.

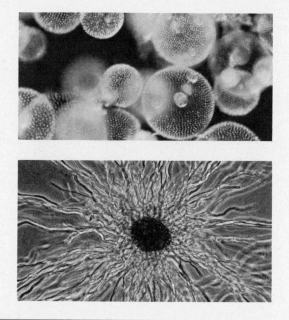

FIGURE 11.7

X-ray motion photography is the means for visualizing processes as they occur within the ordinarily invisible interiors of plants, animals, and human beings. These are frames from a film showing a human being in the act of swallowing, with the radio-opaque bolus (dark object, fish-shaped in the first frame) passing down the esophagus. Since this sequence was filmed at 16 frames per second, these six frames represent an actual elapsed time period of less than ½ second. Does the teacher have any specific responsibilities in introducing such a concept as X-ray photography?

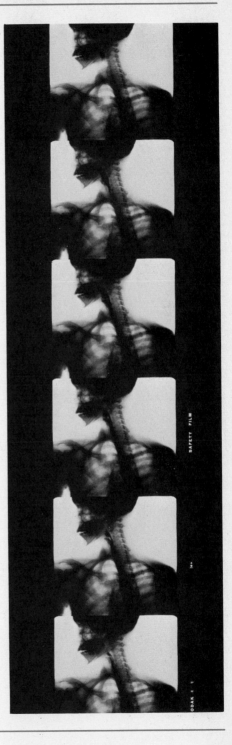

Through these fascinating combinations of techniques the world of the previously unknown is now visualized and understandable (see Figure 11.7).

Animation

In solving the problem of how to show visually how mountains, valleys, and seas have been formed, the film producer may rely on a series of carefully drawn visualizations made to move progressively and thus reveal their meaning.[24] In some cases, the visualizations consist of photographs of a model; the parts of the model are moved a tiny amount between photographs, and when the pictures are rapidly projected, the model moves. This is animation, a process used to visualize what is inaccessible, hypothetical, or theoretical. Ordinarily, the teacher selects such animated film learning experiences when pupils encounter learning problems or concepts which require explanations which are beyond their ability to observe directly. Just as motion and sound are effective in explaining tangible, observable things, so animated visualization can be employed with great effectiveness in explaining theories, future hypothetical possibilities, and so forth.

Animation is therefore extremely useful in demonstrating, with motion, molecular structures, chemical reactions, and the complicated processes involved in photosynthesis in plants or the change of plant life to coal and fossil structures.[25] Animation is used effectively in visualizing complex problems in space travel and communication,[26] how water desalination is achieved,[27] or how television recording and signal transmission are accomplished with cameras and sending and receiving stations.[28]

In today's schools, animation is increasingly used as an effective way of explaining difficult science concepts. When the teacher wishes to clarify the nature of the molecular structure and action of DNA or the logistics of space probes and lunar landings or human reproduction, animated films are available which present information in forthright, simplified, and understandable manner (see Plate 11.1, following page 356). The animated film can explain virtually anything that exists in man's mind. To sum up, so many animation techniques are available that there are few areas of human thought and experience that cannot be well and efficiently taught through animated motion picture film presentations.

Some special motion picture techniques

Recent experiments in the language arts have demonstrated that films without narration are highly successful in enticing learners into response situations. For example, *without benefit of narration,* visuals alone are used to develop completely the life cycle of the carp.[29] The producers of *Snow* use musical accompaniment without narration to interpret the visual intensity of a whirling snowstorm and the gigantic roar of an avalanche.[30] The story of how

[24] *Diastrophism: What Moved the Mountains? What Shaped the Seas?* 16mm film, sound, color, 19½ min., Universal Education and Visual Arts.

[25] *Energy and Man,* 16mm film, sound, color, 10 min., McGraw-Hill.

[26] *Interplanetary Space,* 16mm film, sound, color, 23 min., McGraw-Hill.

[27] *Problems of Conservation: Water,* 16mm film, sound, color, 16 min., Encyclopaedia Britannica Educational Corporation.

[28] *Television Line-by-Line,* 16mm film, sound, color, 11 min., International Film Bureau.

[29] *Carp in a Marsh,* 16mm film, sound, color, 7 min., Institut für Film und Bild (U.S. distributor Films Incorporated).

[30] *Snow,* 16mm film, sound, color, 8 min., King Screens Productions.

significant the wheel has become in our civilization is revealed through visuals without narrative comment, but with an excellent musical score.[31] A series of such films has been developed by the Encyclopaedia Britannica Educational Corporation to encourage pupils to react through creative verbal or oral responses. Experi-

ence in the use of such films has shown that learners invariably are moved to express their own reactions. A learner may be inspired to try his hand at producing a narration. Often, the film story is so "strong" that he cannot resist the temptation to supplement it, interpret it, or describe to others the meanings he finds in it.

The case study film is a unique type of presentation. One series of such films by Doubleday is entitled *The Unfinished Stories Series.* For example, in one of these

[31] *Wheels, Wheels, Wheels,* 16mm film, sound, color, 11 min., King Screens Productions.

FIGURE 11.8

Case study films enable teacher and students to view the actions of other people and to discuss them objectively, without the consequences of direct involvement. What unique advantages do these opportunities give in these films for high school use? (a) *VD—Name Your Contacts.* (b) *The High: Drugs and You.* What behavioral problems do you experience in your teaching which might be met successfully through viewing and discussing such films?

films[32] a student is shown discovering that she has somehow badly scratched a record she is about to return to the library. A friend suggests that since the librarian will not have the time to trace the record to her as the cause of the scratch, she might just as well forget it and use the money she would spend paying the fine to buy something she wants. The viewer is left to answer the question of responsibility and alternative actions. Other "case films" deal in a frank, forthright way with social problems and their impact on high school age youth; for example the personal penalties likely to result from sexual promiscuity,[33] the circumstances which may lead to drug abuse and its consequences,[34] the dangers of too early engagement and marriage[35]— these are among the topics presented in simulated direct experiences *without* the pain and suffering associated with such actual experiences (see Figure 11.8).

Such case studies are believable because of their own relevance to teenage preoccupations. The "film case" involves detached third parties. Because they are neither teacher nor pupils, both can argue and learn from the "case," from their positions as observers. Because the case is not identified or associated directly with classroom personalities, the discussion usually results in free and open opinions leading to rather objective generalizations.

The iconographic technique is a film form used to present visually the high-point conceptualizations found within books. The methods and purposes of this technique are well described as follows:

Unlike animation, where hundreds of pictures are drawn to impart motion to an illustration, it is only the camera that moves in iconographic photography. Hovering over the enlarged projection of the page much as the child would examine it, concentrating always on the picture as it was originally drawn, the camera probes for the essence of each idea that went into the total composition of each picture. By varying light intensity and perspective, by emphasizing one detail and then another, by moving in a deliberate direction at a controlled speed, the camera is made to release the mood and action that the illustrator captured in the pages of his book.

When the pictures are completed, a recorded sound track comprised of the telling of the story, as original musical score, and sound effects is placed in careful juxtaposition to the pictures.[36]

The iconographic technique has been used extensively to make picture-story books "come alive" for younger children. Two such films are *Over in the Meadow*[37] and *The Fox Went Out on a Chilly Night*[38] (see Figure 11.9).

To sum up, the four basic film techniques and the special techniques just described make it possible to bring a degree of reality to today's instructional environment which heretofore could not be achieved. Through such techniques, the motion picture film makes possible the following kinds of enrichment:

1. Things that exist in understandable but inaccessible forms can be photographed from life by means of direct photography and made available in the classroom.

[32] *What Will Ramona Do?*, 16mm film, sound, color, 7 min., Doubleday.

[33] *VD—Name Your Contacts*, 16mm film, sound, color, 15 min., Coronet Films.

[34] *The High: Drugs and You*, 16mm film, sound, color, 15 min., Coronet Films.

[35] *Anatomy of a Teen-Age Engagement*, 16mm film, sound, color, 15 min., Coronet Films.

[36] Morton Schindel, "The Picture Book Projected," *School Library Journal*, February 1968.

[37] 16mm film, sound, color, 10 min., Weston Woods Studios.

[38] 16mm film, sound, color, 9 min., Weston Woods Studios.

FIGURE 11.9

Interesting and widely used trade books for children are now portrayed through motion, color, and sound by means of iconographic photography. What advantages in developing better attitudes toward reading do you see through the use of such films? (a) *Over in the Meadow.* (b) *The Fox Went Out on a Chilly Night.*

2. Things that happen too rapidly or too slowly for normal observation can be slowed or accelerated to comprehensible speeds by changed-speed photography.

3. Things that are too small to be seen can be made visible in motion by photomicrography.

4. Things that are too abstract, too large, too hidden, or too theoretical for effective comprehension by the average learner can be visualized by animation.

5. Things that are better not experienced directly because of their harsh consequences may be presented realistically for discussion and behavioral decisions through the use of case study films.

Research in motion picture learning

MOTION picture learning experiences make it possible to bring into the classroom living, moving portrayals of the activities of people, animals, places, and things regardless of where they took place. Although it should be obvious, even on casually considering the matter, that this form of communication is superior in countless situations, we will add that research evidence clearly shows that "where motion is a defining attribute of a concept, it is better to present that concept using

465

motion picture film than by nonmotion media."[39] Consider the futility of attempting to portray the activities of man in the remote outlying reaches of this world through a means that is incapable of documenting motion and sound. Yet this is what teachers have been attempting to do for decades with less valid communication tools —the printed word, still pictures, and verbal descriptions.

Silent and sound motion picture films have now been used long enough in learning situations so that four general cycles of research activity have been undertaken: (1) studies that probe the usefulness of films in helping achieve the learning of increased amounts of useful and needed cognitive information; (2) studies of the retention quality of film-learned cognitive information; (3) studies of the attitude relationships that learners develop as a result of film experience—the feelings that students evolve as the result of film viewing; (4) controlled studies of the effects of certain innovations included in second editions (revised versions) of films that have survived the test of usefulness over periods varying from 5 to 20 years. This last area of investigation has become necessary and desirable because film learning has now matured and attained the status of an accepted and ongoing utilization experience of value (an example of this type of research is cited and briefly described on page 477 of this chapter). The first three of these types of research are now discussed, followed by a brief section on films and learner interest.

Film use and cognitive learning
Two significant early research studies in cognitive learning were described at the be-

ginning of this chapter—those involving the Yale *Chronicles of America Photoplays* series and the NEA-Kodak films, all silent films.

After sound had been added to films in the early 1930s there came the most intensive attempts to discover the worth of motion picture films in the cognitive area. Three of these research studies, those by Philip J. Rulon, Varney C. Arnspiger, and Wesley C. Mierhenry, are particularly significant because they represent historical milestones in defining the advantages of instruction through the careful selection and wise use of sound motion picture films. These studies showed conclusively that the advantages of learning through sound films over the use of traditional materials varied from 12 to 50 percent in the areas of science, the social studies, and music.[40]

Film use and retention of cognitive information
Parallel research studies were carried on by the same researchers on the retention of information. The question was: Is there any measurable long-term advantage in film-learned cognitive information? The studies produced conclusive evidence that film-learned information is remembered longer than is cognitive knowledge assimilated through exposure to traditional verbal materials. Advantages, as expressed in percentages, varied from 9 to 39 percent in fifth-grade and junior high science and seventh-grade music.[41]

It seems very obvious that the vivid manner in which motion picture films portray lifelike situations and natural phenomena enhances learning and retention.

[39] Ronald L. Houser, Eileen J. Houser, and Adrian P. Van Mondfrans, ''Learning a Motion and a Nonmotion Concept by Motion Picture versus Slide Presentation,'' *AV Communication Review*, Vol. 18, No. 4, Winter 1970, p. 425.

[40] Philip J. Rulon, *The Sound Motion Picture in Science Teaching*, Harvard University Press, 1933, p. 98; Varney C. Arnspiger, *Measuring the Effectiveness of Sound Pictures as Teaching Aids*, Teachers College, Columbia University, 1933, p. 83; Wesley C. Mierhenry, *Enriching the Curriculum Through Motion Pictures*, University of Nebraska Press, 1962.

[41] Rulon, op. cit.; Arnspiger, op. cit.

Nevertheless, more formal research is needed to identify the precise amounts of original positive learning outcomes and the specific degree to which retention of such film-learned information may be achieved.

Film use and attitudes

The original research just described was concerned largely with cognitive learning from films. However, the more elusive area of the relationship between the use of instructional film-learning experiences and the general feelings or attitudes produced by exposure to such experiences only recently became the subject of controlled experimentation. On the basis of research studies conducted between 1962 and the present, there is strong evidence to support the idea that film-learning experiences, because of their identification with the realities of life and natural phenomena, exert a measurable positive influence on the feelings or attitudes of learners.

For example, one researcher demonstrated that he could use films to help first-year algebra students develop within themselves the desire to pursue the learning of algebra with increased enthusiasm and greater achievement.[42] When films were used with junior high school and sixth-grade pupils either before or after reading stories from which the content of the films was drawn, learners demonstrated enthusiasm and heightened verbal responses to the stories as such.[43] In an urban school attended by white and black students, films were used to show successful achievements by members of both races. Although a variety of strengthened attitudinal re-

actions occurred, the investigator concluded that the films had one particularly important result: they caused lower-class black children to raise their vocational aspiration levels—their self-images—materially.[44]

On the basis of the three types of research cited, films are becoming increasingly widely accepted and used in the schools of the United States and Europe. During the first stages of use, the film was usually thought of as a teaching example to be presented most economically to large groups of students. Filmed materials currently, however, are made the subject of individual and small-group study as questing activities in the social studies; discovery activities in the field of science are being pursued.

As is the case with all teaching efforts to develop useful learning environments, the teacher is responsible for selecting the materials and the strategy through which learners may utilize film resources as they seek the fulfillment of their individual goals. This topic is discussed later in this chapter.

Film use and learner interest

The question addressed to pupils, "What do you 'feel' about the films we have been studying?" brings responses which need no formal research to verify. When this question is put to learners who are familiar with the processes of questing for answers through film experiences, there are such responses as:

"It's so easy to understand when you see it happen."

"Films explain things that words can't."

"Movies tell things so quickly and the way they are."

[42] Robert K. Tiemans, *The Comparative Effectiveness of Sound Motion Pictures and Printed Communications for the Motivation of High School Students in Mathematics*, University of Iowa, 1962. ERIC ED 003 573.

[43] Elias Levinson, *Effects of Motion Pictures on the Response to Narrative*. New York University, 1962. ERIC ED 003 567.

[44] John E. Teahan, *Some Effects of Audio Visual Techniques on Aspirational Level and Ethnocentric Shift*. University of Wisconsin (Milwaukee), 1964. ERIC ED 013 862.

"I can go places I'd never get to any other way."

"I can hear people talk and watch them do things—then I 'know'!"

This generalization can now be made: The interest that is produced when two of man's primary sensing mechanisms are simultaneously challenged and activated creates a sense of involvement and response which fulfills most of the conditions necessary for learning to take place (see Chapter 2).

A recent investigation into the universality of this generalization is Project Discovery, which sought to measure the extent of pupil responses to a learning environment that makes it very easy for students to gain access to films and related learning experiences. Teachers and students in four widely separated school districts were given the opportunity to conduct film questing and discovery activities by working independently or as members of small groups;

the results were evaluated and conclusions were reported.[45] Some of the strongest generalizations made include the following about learner response to consistent and easy access to film learning:

1. Films made available for individual study encourage both the gifted and the less mature student—the former to range farther and more intensively into the areas of his interests, the latter to discover that there are few barriers in the way of his pursuing his interests and increasing his basic learnings.

2. Films are a natural way of rounding out the relatonships between the more traditional school library and the current learning resource center. In one of the participating schools, pupils increased their calls for free reading opportunities (use of library books) from 14,000 volumes to

[45] Project Discovery, Progress Report 2, Encyclopaedia Britannica Educational Corporation, 1970.

FIGURE 11.10

Research indicates that there are specific values gained from film study in the areas of interest, identification, and understanding. Films affect attitudes too. What kinds of feelings do you see in these children's faces?

68,000 volumes. This statistic should be pondered by those who at one time may have questioned the effect of media use on free or creative reading habits.

3. The sensory impact of motion, sounds, and color increases the participation of slow learners and broadens the horizons of the more able students.

This project has affirmed most of the conclusions of 25 or more years of formal research. This research establishes that appropriately selected and wisely used films bring about constructive and positive changes: *increased student interest, improvement in cognitive and skill learning both initially and in terms of retention, increased interest in reading,* and, finally, a positive direction given to learner involvement as expressed through observable learner behavior (see Figure 11.10).

Film sources—16mm and 8mm

T EACHERS should certainly be encouraged to think of optimum learning resources as including all kinds of 16mm and 8mm continuous films, film loops, concept films, and so forth. But teachers also must consider the realities: in actually securing and using films, both planning and effort are necessary for teacher *and* pupils, since pupils should be encouraged to take an active part.

The primary source of basic teaching film resources produced primarily for school use is the commercial producers of 16mm and 8mm materials. The production procedures followed by recognized companies (those whose films have been cited earlier in this chapter and others) include careful studies of learner needs for sound-visual-motion experiences and the manner in which film communication techniques can most usefully fulfill such needs. Whether lifelike historical reenactment, changes in speed, photomicrography, documentary photography, or any of the other techniques are needed, singly or in combination, a carefully produced film, film loop, or cartridge film is made that uses the most effective of these techniques. Today, the motion picture as such is available in a variety of formats, each with its own special learning uses. At the same time, all of these owe their fundamental strength to the fact that each offers to its users basic film learning communication.

16mm film sources

Because of the high light and sound output of the projectors used with 16mm films, these films remain the most effective way to present film experiences to groups of 20 or more students at work in a reasonably well light-controlled situation through the use of a standard classroom projector and a 40- to 60-inch-wide screen.

Reliable sources of information about 16mm films are the school or public reference library staff member or the local audiovisual director or media specialist. One or more of the local audiovisual dealers can supply descriptive annotated film lists. Collect your own current catalogs (ask interested students to help by writing to the established film producers for information). The addresses of film producers are listed in a variety of places. Key references are the Landers Film Bibliography,[46] McGraw-Hill's every encyclopedic film list,[47] and Teaching Film Custodians' master list of special teaching films[48] prepared by "edit-

[46] Landers Associates, *Landers Film Review: A Guide to Current 16mm Films,* published monthly.

[47] NICEM, *Index to 16mm Educational Films,* McGraw-Hill, 1967.

[48] Teaching Film Custodians, *Films for Classroom Use.*

ing down'' or abridging original feature entertainment films to produce segments that have high utility in learning and reference sitSutions (see Figure 11.11).

GOVERNMENT FILM SOURCES Another rich source of teaching films, although they may have been produced originally for another but usually quite closely related purpose, is the various departments of the federal government. The role of the Department of Agriculture has already been mentioned. In addition, the Departments of Justice and Health, Education, and Welfare and the Bureaus of Fish and Wildlife, Forestry, and others have for years created and used films to report activities to the public. Many of these films are not only highly useful but also are available without charge (except for library-rate postage one way). The opportunity to search out, secure, and evaluate such films can become a search-and-find activity that interested

students may pursue as a first step in their questing activities.[49]

The production of government films used to be largely a United States Government activity. Most of the governments of the world, however, now use films to carry on an intensive program of information reporting, not only domestically, but worldwide. The Japanese, for example, are best able to describe unique events in and the progress of their country. The people of India similarly are best at making film reports about their social progress, public works, and successes in identifying national problems and attacking their solution. Literally thousands of such government films are available to teachers and pupils around the world. All of these film

[49] *Educator's Guide to Free 16mm Films*, Educator's Progress Service, 1972. *U.S. Government Films*, National Audiovisual Center, Washington, D.C., 1969; *Guide to Government Loan Films*, Service Press, Alexandria, Va., 1971–1972.

FIGURE 11.11

Through the cooperative work of specially selected teacher committees, Teaching Film Custodians makes available to schools everywhere some outstanding "edited-down" versions of original entertainment films. A case in point is this scene from *Henry V* in TFC's film, *Shakespeare's Theater*. What advantages are there when the best and most appropriate portions of entertainment films are made available to learners?

FIGURE 11.12

Compare the understanding gained from these stills from three films produced by the Australian government with your own information (or lack of it) about that subcontinent. (a) *Marsupials— Naturally, the Numbat* features this little-known small termite-eater found only in Australia; here a baby clings to his mother's back. (b) In *Desert People,* an aborigine, watched by his sons, cuts out a new spear-thrower. (c) *The Australian Way* gives a glimpse of modern technology—a giant radio telescope. What contributions would such films make to your own social studies or other teaching tasks? What role might your students play in securing, evaluating, and using such films?

learning experiences are the result of documentary film-making by authorities and professionals who actually live within the environments they record. Thus, through such government activities as these, documentary film information is now made available internationally. Similar film services are supported by the governments of Canada, Finland, Germany, France, Great Britain, and New Zealand, to name only a few. Merely contact the nearest embassy, consulate, or information office for information. (All the countries of the world maintain such offices in the large cities of the United States; one or more may be very near your school.)

A government film-making service that is particularly worthy of note is the Commonwealth Film Unit, part of the News and Information Bureau of Australia, which produces in film form authorized reports on Australia's natural and social phenomena and events.[50] Through films the Australians thus tell their "stories" to the world. The remarkable animals of that country—wombats, numbats, platypuses, koala bears, kangaroos—are subjects of several films that show them in their natural habitats, with environmental sounds and explanations carried on the sound tracks. Through films, one may travel alongside a family of aborigines and develop an insight into how these primitive people win a livelihood from the vast, arid, and hostile environment of the central Australian Desert. Other well-planned and beautifully photographed and edited films report current governmental, urban, and rural developments in Australia (see Figure 11.12). Through the realities that such motion, color, and sound can create, the student gains understandings.

Many agencies of state and local governments also make extensive use of the motion picture film for reporting to the public. The teacher should investigate film municipal offices such as those concerned with tourism, land management and development, conservation and recreation, and health, welfare, and safety. Almost every state maintains offices that make it their express business to make available educational materials—largely 16mm sound motion picture films—for the asking.

Many state universities and larger colleges now maintain film units in connection with the documentation of increasing numbers of ongoing research and development projects. Many universities take seriously the responsibility for reporting their research findings to their citizens. Through these means, they hope to communicate immediately, through 16mm sound films, practical applications of research through which the life and welfare of the state may be enhanced. Teachers and students should share the responsibility of locating such sources through directories, bibliographies, and so forth. Ordinarily, such films are available for the asking.

COMMERCIALLY SPONSORED FILMS American manufacturers, distributors, and merchandisers successfully use 16mm sound motion picture films as a way to communicate with the public. Films produced by business sponsors have been evaluated for their use in learning situations since 1945. Those judged useful in teaching are listed in the annual *Educator's Guide to Free 16mm Films;* in 1951 about 2,000 business-sponsored film titles were included; in 1955, this number had increased to 4,000. The current issue lists and describes 9,000 such films available to school personnel without charge (except postage, usually at the library rate).[51] Originally, many commercial film sponsors tended to take advantage of captive school audiences by "loading" their films with sales propaganda. Recently, however, sponsor producers have met in national conferences devoted to the best ways to report methods, services, and procedures objectively, so as to produce film materials that are highly suitable or adaptable to school use. Hence the increasing number of sponsored films useful in helping meet educational objectives. Teachers and students, however, must assume the responsibility for previewing and selecting from these in terms of their own learning needs.

As has been described in Chapter 6, curriculum planners, teachers, students, and parents are increasingly insisting that teaching and learning take account of the

[50] Commonwealth Film Unit, P.O. Box 46, Lindfield, N.S.W., Australia.

[51] *Educator's Guide to Free 16mm Films,* Educator's Progress Service, 1972.

community—its strengths, weaknesses, and opportunities for future vocational involvement. One very effective way to discover the resources of the community is by selecting and viewing appropriate commercial films. The sponsor often is best able to describe techniques and opportunities because of his immediate involvement with them. This applies to films about, for example, air, sea, or land transportation facilities and the recovery and marketing of natural resources—minerals, oil, and timber.

Super 8mm film sources

The fact that 8mm film production each year during the past several years has outstripped 16mm titles produced is evidence of the tremendous swing toward 8mm motion picture learning opportunities. (As noted earlier, 8mm films in educational use are now, for all practical purposes, super 8 films.) In almost all respects, 8mm films parallel 16mm films in communication strengths. The exception is apparent, however, in the tremendous flexibility in format that 8mm films now have. As continuous loops in cartridges, they present individual concepts in such a way that small groups or individuals can use the materials for independent or continuous learning activities. (The nature of these particular advantages is described on pages 455–465.)

While this book was being written, the authors analyzed more than 75 current articles on the 8mm film in education. On the basis of this analysis, such generalizations as the following can be made. Time will tell how far they are completely or partially accurate, but they now seem very appropriate.

1. With the exception of the cassette tape recorder, the 8mm silent loop cartridge projector is the piece of audiovisual equipment most frequently added to the equipment of schools. Furthermore, 8mm continuous loop silent film subjects or titles are being acquired more rapidly and in greater numbers than any other item of instructional software.[52]

2. The 8mm silent and longer length sound film learning materials have so challenged the imaginations of school people as to have encouraged exciting variations of the traditional learning organization of 30 pupils and one teacher. That is, cartridges of continuous loop silent film learning materials,[53] as well as other 8mm variations, including the new sound cartridges, projection cartridges,[54] open-reel sound and silent films, and the longer length sound cartridges—all have encouraged organizing learning in stimulating new ways. These new techniques involve such learning strategies as self-tutorial, individualized instruction, and small groups —diads or triads of students who learn together and evaluate each other. (These and other strategies are described on pages 486–489.)

3. The simplicity of setting up and projecting 8mm silent and sound films is such that the teacher or pupils consider using these films comparable to readying paper and pencils, handing around workbooks, and so forth. Pupils as young as 4 years use 8mm equipment and materials confidently and skillfully, as in the Hawaiian English Project, where such

[52] "The Changing Software/Hardware Market," *Audiovisual Instruction,* November 1969. In instructional technology and media contexts, whatever is essential to carry information is "software" —films, slides, tapes, cards, etc. The term "hardware" refers to the equipment that is essential to complete the act of communication by making the information carried by the software visible and/or audible and understandable—projection equipment, tape playbacks, card readers, etc.

[53] Technicolor Magicartridges, Technicolor Corporation, Commercial Educational Division.

[54] Kodak Projection Cartridges, Eastman Kodak Company.

FIGURE 11.13

learning materials have been used routinely for more than six years (see Figure 11.13).

4. Of all the types of audovisual equipment in use, the simple and lightweight 8mm projection units hold up exceedingly well when subjected to daily demands throughout the school year; furthermore, the per-pupil cost is within rather universal budget expectations. Without doubt, the simplicity of the 8mm projector has influenced engineering simplification of 16mm projectors, which now incorporate self-threading features and thus are even more universally used.

During the short life history of the 8mm film, its growth has caused the appearance of at least two internationally circulated source directories. One of these, the *Silent Film Loop Source Directory*,[55] which has been published annually since 1964, is in itself a growth chart. The first list included fewer than 1,000 titles, but the current list contains more than 9,000 selected titles considered to be of use in instructional situations. Films are listed in this directory by subjects and, in addition, are coded by approximate grade levels for which the experiences are appropriate.

A second and even more comprehensive directory is entitled *The National Information Center for Educational Media, Index to 8mm Motion Cartridges*.[56] This volume is a compendium of information organized first in a computer data bank which serves as a primary source of individualized instructional motion picture learning experiences. The advantage to teachers of the NICEM index is that it contains brief but inclusive annotations, in addition to grade-level and subject information.

In almost all cases, 8mm films were

[55] Technicolor Corporation, Commercial and Educational Division, 1970–1971.

[56] NICEM, *Index to 8mm Motion Cartridges*, University of Southern California, 1969.

No one has told these children they cannot teach themselves a skill. No one has told them they should be afraid to manipulate an 8mm automatic silent projector. (a) A 5-year-old practices writing groups of letters she has taught herself to understand and form. (b) A classmate patiently waits while she sponges off her work, readying the materials for him. (c) Setting about his own work, he selects the letter "M"—actually, an 8mm silent film loop. (d) He easily places it in the projector and then turns the switch. (e) He proceeds with his self-appointed task. Naturally, the teacher is always there to help with evaluation and encouragement. What are your responses to this kind of learning?

first produced as selected portions of 16mm films. Most 16mm films are organized as a comprehensive and developing body of concepts—bundles of closely related information—which tell a rather complete story. The breaking apart of any well-planned 16mm film usually yields a series of subconcepts, each of which may be expressed as a 2-, 3-, or 4-minute visual explanation, that is, a complete and limited single concept. To be sure, not all single-concept films completely meet this definition—one concept, fully and understandably developed through visual presentation—but many do.

Although 8mm continuous loops began as selected portions of complete 16mm films, the increasingly prevalent method of production now is to plan 8mm loops carefully as original scripts which are then interpreted visually, in many cases with sound. As this method continues, the single-concept 8mm motion picture learning experience will more and more often fulfill its complete role. In any case, imperfect though many still are, the single-concept film is making a unique contribution to the development of alternative learning strategies—particularly in small-group and individualized learning.

Selecting film learning experiences

OBVIOUSLY, the task of selecting useful films from among the thousands available is considerable. The goal, of course, is for teacher or students or both to identify their learning objectives and to locate films that will meet these objectives in a manner that produces more effective learning than can be accomplished by using other types of learning experiences. In attaining this goal, a teacher may seek a film to use in a large-group study situation, while his students may seek films that will help them in their individual or group questing and discovering. An important corollary goal is to systematize film selection and record the results for future reference. A growing and "tested" file of film learning resources can be very valuable to future students in a school as they pursue their searches.

Experienced producers of 16mm and 8mm films systematically study course outlines, textbooks, and curriculum plans as they seek to identify learner needs. The decision to produce a given film is made after judging the extent to which the planned film learning experience is likely to contribute more to learners than already available instructional materials. If the judg-ment is favorable, production begins. Such decisions are not made lightly, for the production of a film often involves an expenditure of from $20,000 to $50,000. The fate of a film once on the market is determined by the thousands of teachers (and students) who decide whether or not to use it. If the producer's research and judgments prove to be correct, the film will be widely used, and he profits.

In carrying out their responsibility to select films carefully and thoughtfully, teachers and/or students should preview them, when possible; if this is not possible, they should base their decisions on meticulous examinations of descriptions in catalogs and other sources.

As the teacher pursues the continuing task of film selection, he—and also his pupils—may find an evaluation reference guide useful; one such guide is shown in Figure 11.14. The first step in film selection is to review the reasons for seeking a given film learning experience. By relating these reasons to items included in the evaluation guide, a record of information is created that can be kept available either in the classroom or in the school library. The following discussion refers to specific items in the record shown in Figure 11.14:

Item 1. This item takes account of the fact that films appear in a variety of formats. Usually, 16mm films are more comprehensive, while 8mm silent loops are shorter and limited to explaining "single concepts." Nevertheless, many 8mm films of longer length, with magnetic or optical soundtracks, are now available (see the explanation of sound-recording techniques in the *Student Production Guide*).

Item 2. The reputation of the film producer is important. Films produced by such experienced and successful publishers as Encyclopaedia Britannica Educational Corporation, Coronet Films, McGraw-Hill, and others cited earlier are almost invariably reliable and valid. The date of a film is important. Dates are not included for many older films, but the production dates of more recent films are given in the title or catalog description.

The teacher should be on the alert for *second editions* (revised versions). The fact that a film has been produced in a second edition is usually an automatic signal to the teacher that the content, organization, and communication strength of the film not only have survived the initial tests of usefulness, but also have been further improved by revising, amending, and refining the quality of the film communication techniques employed. A research study of the learning effectiveness of second-edition films indicates that systematic modifications—including added environmental sound, color photography, improved animation, use of changed speed, and microphotography (when any of these specifically improved understanding)—all improved learner performance.[57]

[57] A. W. VanderMeer, Jack Morrison, and Philip Smith. *An Investigation of the Improvement of Educational Motion Pictures and a Derivation of Principles Relating to the Effectiveness of These Media*, College of Education, Pennsylvania State University, April 1965.

The cost of securing films is important. In most school districts, rental cost budgets are announced, so that teachers know in advance approximately what they may spend (rental cost allowances per teacher vary from $10 to $50 per school year). However, free films are available which are, as a whole or in selected sequences, highly useful for instructional purposes. Writing for and evaluating quantities of free films can be undertaken in large part by interested and qualified students.

Item 3. The target curriculum—the subject for which the film is intended—is important. Films produced after careful analysis of the communication and learning needs created by the study of various subject areas can make unique contributions. Social studies films "carry" learners into areas of the world which they ordinarily cannot visit. Science films, by making possible the reenactment of costly and sometimes difficult experiments, enable the teacher to bring ordinarily elusive evidence into the classroom. In the language arts, there now are many "no-narration" films that offer remarkable stimuli to students to express themselves, "triggered" information presented or by the film experiences themselves.

Item 4. The target age—the age level at which the film is directed—is important: the teacher must know how many of the students in his class are likely to find the film intelligible. A film aimed at the center of the age group is useful as a large-group learning experience, while a film that deals with more sophisticated concepts and vocabulary may be used efficiently by the more advanced students and vice versa. The speed with which the film moves from scene to scene, the pace of the dialogue or narration, the numbers of concepts presented—all must be evaluated in terms of the readiness or maturation of the learners who are to use the film (as members of a group or independently).

Item 5. A brief description of the con-

FIGURE 11.14

Suggested film evaluation record (see text for discussion).

tent of the film, stated in the teacher's or learner's own words, will be a valuable cue in making future decisions on the use of the film. The central concept of a continuous film loop, a series of central concepts of a more comprehensive 16mm film, or the concepts of one of the new 8mm sound continuous film loops should be briefly described so that in the future a quick perusal will give a reasonable understanding of "what the film is all about."

Format Item 1. The manner in which a film contributes to understandability often depends on the unique communication techniques used. If changed-speed photography, animation, diagrammatic presentation, documentary photography, photomicrography, or other modes are used, the entire film presentation is apt to be superior. A film that explains the interior action of a rotary internal combustion engine may employ slow motion, animation, and direct photography to present its information. An alternative film that does less than that is likely to be inferior. The teacher should know which of the various kinds of techniques are best used to present certain types of information. Variety and clarity in techniques used usually reinforce the possibility that understanding will result in the minds of the learners.

Format Item 2. Though most films employ sound to reinforce the visual presentation, there are many films that eliminate narration (many films employ music alone) and tell their story entirely through visual communication. These circumstances should be noted. Though narration is useful in supporting and explaining what the visual portion of the film portrays, the presence of desired environmental sounds may make a film even more understandable. Today, clear, natural, and easily recognized environmental sounds—machinery in motion, birds in song, or animals rustling through camouflaged environments—make a teaching film a more realistic and believable learning experience.

FILM EVALUATION RECORD

1. Title of film _____ 16mm ___ 8mm ___ Sd ___ Silent _____

   Color _____ B/W _____

2. Producer _____ Date produced _____

   Length _____ Minutes _____ Rental cost _____ Postage _____

3. Target curriculum : Social studies _____ Science _____ Language arts _____

   Other areas of suitability: _____

4. Target age: _____

5. What is the film about? _____ (major concepts) _____

   _____

   _____

Format

1. Film techniques used: (changed speed, animation, etc.) _____

   _____

2. Sound: Narration quality _____ Environmental sound _____

   No narration _____ Music _____

3. Use of color: _____

4. Pace and organization : _____

5. Photographic quality : _____

Recommended for future use: Yes ____ No ____ If yes, how and by whom? _____

_____

Suggested uses: Large group _____ Small group _____

Individual questing _____ Skill mastery _____

Format Item 3. When should a sound or silent motion picture film in color be used in the classroom? Often asked by teachers, this question is even more often asked by others who are responsible for buying films when they become aware of the wide difference between the prices of a film that is released both in color and in black and white.

The effective teaching film records what actually exists. If color will assist in imparting understanding, comprehension, and esthetic appreciation, then color obviously is desirable. Color films should be used when the color enables the viewer to gain a more accurate, realistic, and vivid understanding of what is being shown. Many subjects—such as animals, mechanisms, objects in nature—are identified through color (see Plate 11.2, following page 000); thus, films on such subjects will provide far more valuable learning experiences if they are in color. Although these sound like simple rules of thumb, they are not, for they assume that one does not consider the interest and enthusiasm produced by color merely because it *is* color. Such slogans as television's "in living color" are not easily dismissed from the minds of TV- and movie-conditioned teachers and young people. Nevertheless, in assessing the role of color in the selection and use of classroom teaching films, it should be remembered that the single most important consideration should be whether the color actually *contributes to learning.*

In the realm of nature, color and meaning are virtually synonymous. Color in nature attracts and, in other cases, camouflages or distracts. Thus, a film that shows how color helps camouflage desert animals must be shown in color. Color films are equally important in showing the coloration of plants, birds, and animals. For esthetic appreciation of certain types of art and accurate understanding of some styles of decorations used in architecture and of the costumes of other social groups, particularly those that are remote in time or distance, color films are necessary.

When color is used, it should be as close to the real color as possible. Color film that is heavily overcast with bluish or greenish hues is not desirable because it does not portray the true natural colors. Poor color, in fact, is often worse than no color at all.

Although it is said that the average learner can "read" color into black-and-white pictures, this is not usually the case. When situations are too far removed from his firsthand experiencing of color, the learner probably will not have had the opportunity for enough color experiencing to enable him to impose his own sense of color on the black-and-white pictures.

You can investigate the role and value of color in Plate 11.3, following page 580. This plate shows several frames from current color sound motion picture teaching films in black-and-white form. Examine these frames carefully and at length and list mentally or in writing what you see in each one. Now look at these same frames in their original color (the black-and-white pictures were made from these). Examine the color frames carefully. Then check your notes on each black-and-white picture. What additional information and, just as important, esthetic impressions did you gain from the color frame? Then answer these questions:

1. What specific additional information was supplied through the color alone?

2. What relationships depended solely on color for meaning? (This is brought out particularly well in the frame showing the nymph and the mature grasshopper.)

3. What esthetic feelings did you have after viewing the color frames which the black-and-white frames did not give you?

You are now as well prepared as anyone to assess the role of color in the sound motion picture teaching film.

With the communication of facts as important as it is in the learning situation, the use of color in its more general functions—

as a means of centering attention, inciting interest, and creating sheer esthetic appreciation—should not be overlooked. Indeed, many educational film producers are convinced that if the economics of film production permitted the production of low-cost color films, teachers would use only color films.

Format Item 4. Pace and organization refer to the smooth flowing together of the photographic scenes and the accompanying narration or environmental sounds. In a well-organized film, the learner is hardly aware that one scene moves into another because it is so smoothly and logically done. The film often includes "punctuation"—accomplished through such mechanical devices as fades (the slow disappearance of one scene before the next one appears), quick cuts (abrupt shifts from one scene to another), and dissolves (the merging of the end of one scene into the beginning of the next). A film that is jerky, meanders, or has confusing sequences interferes with the meaning it attempts to create.

Format Item 5. Since to communicate, instructional film depends on vivid, clear-cut, and understandable visual portrayal, it is obvious that the photography must be as perfect as possible. Just as important is the manner in which the camera angles are chosen. The viewer must have the opportunity to *see* what he needs to understand. The camera must also be placed in such a position that the viewer can comprehend what he sees. Only through logical camera placement and reasonably edited length of

scenes can the finished product represent a complete and understandable learning experience.

The final question the teacher should answer is whether or not the film should be used again. The answer depends on the responses shown by the student who viewed it. If the information learned from the experience was understandable, the chances are that many learners will give some evidence of having acquired the information as they attempt to respond in their own creative and inventive ways. Were any moved to discuss their new-found information? write about it? search for further information? build a model or mock-up?

Frequently, teachers report difficulty in securing films for use in their classrooms. While waiting for prescheduled school-owned films or films already ordered by the school administration, the other sources that do exist should be investigated. By referring to the variety of film sources, catalogs, organizations, and distribution outlets described earlier, many highly usable films may be secured. If the teacher is willing to put forth the effort and encourage similar efforts among students who are interested, the process of locating, ordering, previewing, and evaluating can become an integral and rewarding part of the teaching day. The teacher should constantly consider the appropriateness and the effectiveness of enlisting the participation of able and interested students. Too often he tries to do it all himself.

Teaching and learning with motion pictures

T HE ultimate effectiveness of film learning experiences is determined largely by the way the teacher arranges for students to pursue their orderly study of films. A 16mm film may be considered a "package of information"; a shorter 8mm film loop

usually presents a brief and streamlined single-concept experience. The use of such materials is very similar to studying from books and other traditional materials of varying lengths and types—encyclopedias, source books, and periodicals. The "key" is to *study seriously* the messages included in film learning experiences.

Unless careful film study plans are made in advance, only a part of a film's message— from ¼ to ⅓—will actually be perceived and understood by learners. Film experiences are organized—partly because of the high production costs involved—in a highly concentrated series of episodes which are revealed quite rapidly and intensively to the learner. For this reason, he should approach the study of film for what it is—a series of rapidly moving and interrelated sound and visual experiences.

The student who studies continuous loop film subjects is at an advantage because he can review what he "misses the first time" simply by "staying with it" a little longer—going through it again and again. When films are used in large-group situations, opportunities to meet individual needs are not quite so easily achieved. Nevertheless, any film experience should be available for reference and restudy.

Maximum effectiveness is achieved through films if there is total involvement of learners—during prefilm preparation, during viewing, and during follow-up responses. An early study of fourth-, fifth-, and sixth-graders demonstrated that learning through motion picture films in large-group situations is most efficient if pupil

purposing goes on before viewing a film and pupil reviewing follows the film[58] (see Figure 11.15). Nevertheless, Figure 11.15 indicates that even without any kind of prefilm preparation, pupils learn substantially more from film experiences than from traditional no-film ones. The children who engaged in prefilm readiness planning and became more involved in the film learning process gained nearly twice the information from subsequently viewing a given film as those who approached film viewing "cold."

The prefilm involvement activities of the groups who participated in this study (Figure 11.15) included such activities as:

1. Reading a brief, storylike description that conveyed a general impression or mood about the film.

2. Studying difficult words or phrases that would be encountered while listening to the sound track.

3. Anticipating the content of the film by studying questions the teacher had prepared in advance indicating the nature of large areas of information presented in the film.

4. Identifying questions offered by the members of the viewing group. These ex-

[58] W. A. Wittich and John Guy Fowlkes, *Audiovisual Paths to Learning*, Harper & Row, 1946.

FIGURE 11.15

The importance of learner involvement. This graph shows the effects of three types of film instruction on information learned by elementary pupils. (Though this study was done some years ago, this kind of research has been replicated at least three times since then with virtually identical findings.) The percentages show gains over pupils who had no film use.

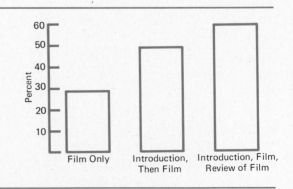

pressed learner interest in the general subject covered by the film.

After viewing the film, the students were given a test on cognitive information included. Figure 11.15 shows the achievement of the students. Also shown are the further substantial gains of other groups after discussion of the film, identification of yet unanswered and additional questions, and seeing the film a second time.

Additional studies on the subject of efficient film study procedures indicate that instructional films are likely to result in more effective learning under these conditions:

1. Students know how the content of the film is related to their instructional problem and thus realize why they should study it.

2. Students know clearly their specific purposes in seeing the film and understand its relationship to their larger area of study.

3. Students know in advance what they are specifically expected to learn from the film.

4. Students understand that the film is a learning experience and not just an entertainment or diversion from ordinary study activities.

5. Students understand that the film is available for a second showing or "reference" learning experience if the factual content warrants this and if they have unanswered questions that need further investigation.[59]

All of the foregoing seem to indicate that if the teaching film experience, either 16mm or 8mm, is to become the powerful and useful instructional tool that it can be, both teachers and learners should expect to become deeply involved in selection,

planning for use, using, and engaging in various response activities which allow the participating learners to employ their newfound information as they plan and wish.

Several specific teacher and learner responsibilities apply as surely to the effective use of films as to the intelligent use of books, reference books, maps, models, charts, community study experiences, and so forth. As in book study, special vocabulary used in the film may cause the stream of film learning to be interrupted. By identifying such vocabulary in advance, by learning the meanings and applying them during film study, the process of learning may proceed uninterruptedly.

Pupil-teacher planning

No matter whether the questing through film study is done as a large-group, a small-group, or an individual activity, the teacher may exert positive influences by guiding learners toward film experiences that are appropriate and enticing.

For example, in the study of history the teacher can help by suggesting specific titles of films about the Middle Ages, the Renaissance, or current history to members of groups or individuals. The teacher should at least help the learner locate among reference materials the sources of films he needs. Once materials are located, the teacher can help pupils formulate key questions to be answered through film study. By engaging in preliminary planning and discussion, both teacher and pupils will heighten their anticipation for seeing, listening to, and studying the approaching film experiences.

Preparation and planning may reveal possible barriers to film study. Specific vocabulary problems have been mentioned. Similar barriers are encountered when new or strange concepts are introduced during a film presentation. Fortunately, most well-produced films explain most of their own vocabulary and concepts through the simultaneous presentation of visualization and

[59] *Instructional Film Research Reports*, Vol. 2, United States Naval Training Device Center, Port Washington, Long Island, N.Y., 1957; C. L. McTavish, Instructional Film Research Program, Pennsylvania State University, 1958.

narration. In the case of the silent film loop, special emphasis is placed on carefully paced and sequentially presented visualizations.

Creating good viewing conditions

Because pupils work on day-to-day school projects in their classrooms, it is here that teaching films should be shown and studied when viewed by groups. A classroom should be so arranged and equipped that every pupil can see well-defined images on the screen and hear the sound track without distortion or strain (see Figure 11.16). When small-group viewing experiences are planned, areas free from distraction should be set aside that permit maximum viewing and listening. In recent years, of course, special projectors for individualized viewing have become available. Thus many learning resource centers or school libraries are now equipped with specialized machinery and spaces that encourage individualized questing and discovery through film learning experiences.

Before a film is shown, the projection equipment should be placed in mechanical readiness. Projectors with automatic film threading have eliminated one major problem, but there are other important details, such as keeping apertures and lens free from smudges or dirt. Nothing is so distracting as a large "blob" on the screen caused by dirt lodged in one corner of the projector aperture. Projectors and their operation are described in detail in the accompanying *Student Production Guide*.

Room ventilation should follow the general air change and circulation specifications recommended by school building authorities for regular classroom use—15 cubic feet per person per minute. When sound films are shown, acoustical arrangements should be such as to allow every pupil to hear lifelike, understandable tones from the speaker or speakers.

When using films in large-group situa-

FIGURE 11.16

The arrangement of projector, screen, and speakers is very important for classroom viewing. The diagram gives suggestions for two types of classroom. The space directly between screen and projector is the most efficient viewing area. Thus when students sit at a wide angle from the screen, they may experience very little visual identification with the film because of reflected light "falloff." How may you arrange your classroom to provide spaces for large-group or small-group film study? Consider the possibility of using earphones for small-group study. (The principles of placement illustrated here also apply to small-group viewing.)

tions, control of light in the room is essential. The distance from the projector to the screen and the power of the light source in the projector determine whether more or less light should be kept out of the room. Shades, drapes, louvers, or blinds should be standard equipment in every classroom in which day-to-day teaching incorporates the use of projected instructional materials for large groups. In the case of individualized film instruction, however, lighting presents very few problems. The equipment used for

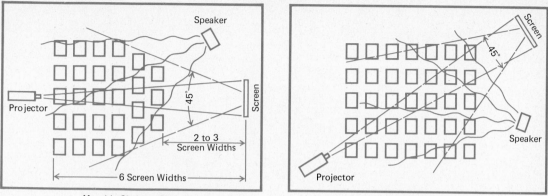

Movable Chairs or Desks   Fixed Desks

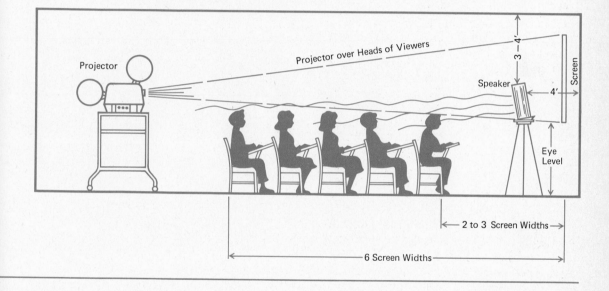

this purpose encourages individualized or small-group viewing by presenting to the learners clear, definable images under normal room lighting conditions (see Figure 11.17).

Arranging creative film learning activities

Instruction is never complete until the learner has given visible or tangible evidence of using his new-found information in observable ways. The traditional means

of accomplishing this should certainly not be overlooked as a wholesome outgrowth of film use. Learner responses through class discussion, paper-and-pencil evaluations, and the formulation of essay-type or other written comments and questions definitely are valid and desirable. However, other forms of highly interesting learner responses can now be made possible, largely by diversifying the manner in which films are used, that is, by using them not only as information sources but also as the means

FIGURE 11.17

(a) A boy begins his individual study of 8mm film loops by selecting his materials. (b) A curious and interested classmate joins him. What does this indicate about the nature of their involvement and the values they find in such experiences? What are your reactions to this learning strategy? What primary learning tenets do you see in operation here?

for producing exciting, observable, and measurable learner responses. These are now discussed.

Individualized film learning and response

Film learning experiences are now available in so many forms that they are completely accessible. There are cartridges—super 8mm silent film loops of 3 to 4 minutes, mounted in plastic containers; projection cartridges—slightly longer super 8mm films that are easily placed into or removed from film projectors; movie paks —special reels that can easily be pressed or slid into extremely simplified 8mm sound projectors; and, of course, the more traditional forms of 16mm films. Regardless of the form, size, or "package," any may be used as individualized or small-group learning experiences.

An example of the effective use of 8mm silent film loops in individualized skill learning is now appropriate:

Children at work in the Hawaii public schools are successfully performing self-instruction in handwriting at ages 4 to 8. While in more traditional programs, children are still struggling with *manuscript* writing, most of the Hawaiian students teach themselves how to write the *cursive* alphabet.[60]

"When the children come in the fall," a teacher explained, "I show them the cartridges, how to insert one in a projector, and how to turn it on and focus it. For most children it is as simple as that—they take quickly to this self-tutorial, continuous progress activity. They begin the process by selecting a letter—"

"Selecting a letter?" a visitor asked.

"Yes, each cartridge contains a 3-minute visual and silent description in motion of how one letter of the alphabet is formed—how each stroke is done—how high or how low the strokes go—"

The teacher paused and indicated one child who was approaching a shelf on which several dozen super 8mm film cartridges were arranged in a row. The boy—6 years old—was picking out the "M" loop and selecting the companion "cue" card; then he sat down to begin his task. The teacher continued, "He shoves the film in place, turns on the projector, watches the moving hand on the screen as it forms the letter 'M,' and imitates it on his own cue card."

That is just what he did. Using a pen, he wrote on the surface of a transparent plastic-coated cue card. The teacher continued, "Those cards offer him cues which help him. But the cues diminish line by line (see Figure 11.13). Finally, he's on his

own. When he thinks he's 'got it,' he'll ask me to check him—No, I spoke too soon. He's asking a friend to come over and look at what he's done."

One of the young boy's age-mates seated herself next to him and started busily comparing his handwriting with the cues on the card. At one point, she switched on the projector so that both could see a rerun of the film to evaluate the boy's work better. Thus not only can most of these 4- to 8-year-olds teach themselves to write by responding individually to such self-instructional materials—super 8mm films and cue cards—but they help one another in the process.

"Does it always work out this way?" the visitor asked.

"No—but when it doesn't—well, that's why I'm here, to help them over the rough spots."

The boy cleaned away the ink marks by using a damp sponge on the plastic-coated card. This done, he removed the film cartridge and returned it to its place on the shelf. The teacher smiled. "They all help with the housekeeping. And they really do it very well."

"When they don't?" the visitor asked.

"Well, that's also why I'm here."

A moment later, the boy was headed for another self-instructional station—this time, to try out the electric typewriter. The girl was seating herself at the self-tutorial materials in reading—tape cassettes that played leisurely and interesting "talk-throughs" which exactly paralleled selected books of progressive difficulty.[61]

In general, continuous loop film learning experiences are most effective when the materials are organized to present one understandable concept at a time. If the learner is slow to understand, he merely has to pay attention a little longer while

[60] The materials in self-tutorial handwriting have been developed by the Hawaii English Project (discussed in detail in Chapter 15) as part of a larger statewide curriculum plan. These materials are now being used in at least one classroom in each of the state's elementary schools. (A reader who plans a trip to beautiful Hawaii now has a further inducement—to see for himself how this self-tutorial system actually works.)

[61] For a discussion of self-tutorial audio reading modules, see Chapter 9, pages 272–275.

the film automatically repeats its message so that he can study it again; if necessary, he can watch it over and over until either his interest is exhausted or he has learned.

It is not surprising to find, therefore, that research done on the use of 8mm film loops indicates that they are particularly effective in the acquisition of manipulative skill learning. For example, such loops used in teaching correct clarinet fingering and mouth and hand positioning not only encourage favorable responses from students, but also help them develop skills at a significantly improved rate.[62]

Applications in countless other areas are available. In learning basic woodworking skills, a series of film loops offers instruction in the use of hacksaws and coping saws, mitre joints, sharpening techniques, operating drills, braces, bits, routers, planes, and so forth.[63] A similar series of loops has been produced on track events. Thus a track coach can refer interested team members to exemplary demonstrations on how to run the 100-yard dash, perform high jumps, low and high hurdles, the pole vault, the shot put—all demonstrated by Olympic record holders.[64]

A social studies teacher whose pupils were interested in reconstructing the skills used in homemaking during pioneer days procured a series of film loops which demonstrated pioneer crafts.[65] By watching the individual loops, the students observed how flax was woven into thread, how wool

was spun into yarn, how weaving was done, how butter was churned, bread baked, candles made, and so forth. The utter simplicity with which each child could give himself such experiences allowed each one to proceed at his own pace in the investigation of his own interests to any length he wished. Similar materials are available in teaching arithmetic skills, learning various swimming strokes, understanding geometric theorems, performing simple experiments in science, and observing nature study phenomena. (The two directories mentioned earlier in this chapter—Technicolor's and NICEM's—list thousands of other skill-teaching loops.)

But there are many wider uses for 8mm film experiences than skill mastery. A student teacher being introduced to the inventory of 8mm film loops available in an instructional materials center selected one of the film loops that struck her fancy, put it into the projector, turned it on, and focused it.

"Why, I've never dreamed such things could exist. It's spellbinding," she exclaimed as she watched an octopus hatch out of its egg and make its first primitive movements along the ocean floor. She saw the octopus progress through its sequential stages of change and, as it approached adulthood, hunt, capture, and enfold for nutriment lesser creatures that lurked in hiding places on the ocean floor. As the loop ended, she remarked, "It's so clear—yet so simply done—I can see why learners would love it."

Success in using self-tutorial 8mm materials can be assured only when they are reasonably accessible. When the materials in the learning resource center of a school include a selection of appropriate 8mm films, silent loops, and longer 16mm sound versions and the equipment with which to use them, students usually become completely involved (see Figure 11.17). In such circumstances, film learning resources are rich, varied, and very understandable.

[62] Robert M. Diamond and Thomas C. Collins. *The Use of 8mm Loop Films To Teach the Identification of Clarinet Fingering, Embouchure and Hand Position Errors*, Report No. 28, Office for the Study of Instruction, University of Miami, May 1966.

[63] *Basic Woodworking*, super 8mm film loops, silent, color, 4 min. each, Walden Film Corporation, 1968.

[64] 8mm film loops, silent, color, 4 min. each, Track and Field News.

[65] *Pioneer Craft Series*, super 8mm film loops, silent, 4 min. each, Ealing Films.

Small-group film-learning experiences

School learning resource centers today include inventories of 16mm and 8mm motion pictures and projectors. When students are encouraged to study such resources, they and their teachers find themselves with an intellectual bonanza. Under such circumstances, the middle way between individualized and large-group instruction—small-group learning activity—is feasible. This is a type of learning experience that has its own special advantages.

We can go to England for a particularly good example. At the Oxhey School, near London, the principal explained to his visitors from the United States:

We believe here that if we surround our students with many, many learning opportunities, they will find within themselves the curiosity and interest which will lead them to explore and to inquire and to learn. Our students move freely from their classrooms to our learning resource center. They know they will find there all manner of films, filmstrips, books, pictures, and related learning materials. The teacher assumes the role of the one who encourages students to pose their own problems, to search for answers in any of the learning resources we have here. Then they invent ways of using their new information in developing projects of their own creation.

We saw all of this happen. Students and teachers began the day by planning what they wished to investigate. We watched one group of five develop the idea of finding out about the British colony of Hong Kong. Suggestions were made to them about locating information, and they carried out a search in the school's resource center. The group found several filmstrips and a film entitled *People of Hong Kong.* Next, two of the group rounded up the needed equipment. They met at a previously arranged spot in a hallway, set up the equipment, and studied! No sooner had they seen the film than friendly differences of view were expressed over what they had seen and what they had not seen—varied interpretations had been made. It was agreed that they had to see the film again.

Then the youngsters took their notebooks of information and sketches back to their classroom, assembled in the study corner, and planned how they would present their newly discovered information to their classmates. Things were discussed and discarded, and a few of the best ideas were finally selected—a mock news report, a search made through picture-story magazines for pictures to be displayed along with their own sketches and maps and diagrams. A dramatization of one of the historical events was planned. Finally, they asked the teacher to listen to their ideas. The teacher then joined them and, as various proposals were made, her responses became part of the final plans (see Figure 11.18).

Later, on returning to the office of the principal, we discussed what we had seen and asked questions. The principal responded:

Not all of our learning experiences are found right "in school." We take advantage of moving out into the community. Though many of the ideas spring from film experiencing, we go wherever necessary to continue the quest. People from the community are invited to come in and work with us, speak with us, and describe where they have been and what they have seen. Or the reverse may be true—we may spend weeks planning an extended field trip out into the community, even over to the Continent on occasion.

Usually, as large groups become involved in initial film viewing, the presence of adequate and easily available film resources encourages small-group activity. Here is an example: As part of the social studies course, the teacher had helped the class prepare for the orderly learning experiences presented in the film *Our Changing World*.[66] Before studying the film the class had engaged in vocabulary work and developed questions they wished to investigate as they observed this film about the geologic ages through which the earth has passed. After this preparation and the actual viewing of the film, the discussion centered on the advancing and retreating ice cap and how these changes were associated with various geologic ages. Finally, the children decided what additional areas they would like to investigate.

The next day, one pupil reported his excitement on having read an article entitled, "The Continents Are Adrift."[67] As discussion continued, four other students expressed similar interests. Those five students were encouraged to conduct their own research as a group to discover additional information that might support the hypothesis that the continents are actually moving, very slowly to be sure, but about 2 to 6 feet a year in a number of directions. Other groups were intrigued with climatic changes; pupils in groups of from four to six announced their interest in the climatology of the equatorial regions, the earth's highest mountain ridges, and the areas of the ice caps. The search was on as they scattered to set about their own questing and discovering activities, some in the classroom, where they investigated reading resources, others in the learning materials center, where they looked though the inventories of films and examined catalogs that might lead them to sources not immediately available.

Later, the various groups reported their findings. During their exchange of information, globes were referred to, wall maps put in place and examined, and displays of flat pictures presented and ex-

[66] 16mm film, color, 14 min., Film Associates of California.

[67] *Reader's Digest*, April 1971.

FIGURE 11.18

These Oxhey School students show what invariably happens when easily accessible film-learning resources are available to students and class organization is "open" or flexible. (a) A discussion on the best place to set up the screen is in progress. (b) Projection arrangements are do-it-yourself affairs. (c) The film is studied—then, because of "pointed" differences, the film is run again. (d) Now plans are being made to put new-found information into creative form. (e) The teacher enters the experience on invitation; her role is to guide, evaluate, encourage, and help. What are your reactions? Would you be willing to incorporate such learning arrangements into your teaching plans?

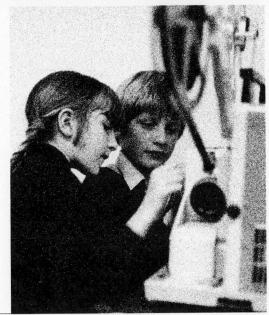

plained. One group, especially enthusiastic about their discoveries, included two projectors in their apparatus, using them alternately during their report to project scenes that could be compared. They thus introduced for comparison segments of films entitled *Adventure High Arctic* and *Visit to Antarctica*. All could witness visually and graphically these regions of desolation and cold at the "top" and "bottom" of the earth. Then, through the presentation of maps on overhead projectors, stage by stage other comparisons were made between the Arctic and Antarctica. When all of this was over, one student broke the silence by saying, "It just hit me—in the last few minutes I've been zigzagging back and forth, halfway round the world, and it's almost as good as if I'd really been there."

Regardless of the subject area being studied, when learners are given the opportunity to define their own interests and to conduct their own searches through learning resource inventories that are complete with film learning experiences and other related opportunities, the degree to which initiative is assumed and projects completed is beyond anything possible in the traditional large-group organization (see Figure 11.19).

Student-made motion picture films

By long tradition, the learner has been expected to express himself orally or in writing or in both ways when responding to instruction. There now is an exciting alternative—motion picture films produced by students. School administrators and teachers have evaluated and found promising the use by pupils of automatic motion picture cameras, along with simplified editors, viewers, splicers, and rewinds, to create films. They have observed how film-making actively stimulates and involves learners as they seek to plan and photograph their own ideas. This, of course, is an important element in *visual literacy*, discussed initially in Chapter 3.

One educator reports: "In a small number of schools, photography and film-making are encouraging an active, participatory type of education. There is evidence that film-making, linked in with film-watch-

FIGURE 11.19

This learning resource center provides space for film learning next to the materials. Note how films are intershelved with books. In this daylight environment, a special projection screen produces a clear, sharp image for small-group study. During further searches for information, related library materials are close at hand. What is your reaction to this kind of library-learning resource arrangement?

inventive, or creative projects, plans, or demonstrations.

It is only through an analysis of observable pupil responses to film utilization that a clear evaluation may be achieved. In the case of 8mm continuous loop skill instructional films, the obvious end result is mastery of the skill depicted. In the case of films dealing with more general areas of cognitive knowledge, many types of responses may be observed and evaluated: spontaneous quests for additional knowledge, the creation of stories and art work based on information gained from films, and so forth.

The manner in which films are used in the classroom no longer is limited to large-group learning experiences. Rather, the film often becomes a research tool to be used by the student as a member of a small group or as an individual.

If films are to be used as true learning source experiences, they should be easily available to students who wish to study them as discovery or questing activities. There is much evidence to support the idea that film learning resources are best used when they are most completely accessible to learners.

A dramatic innovation in film learning has come into use during the last decade—student-made motion picture films. Traditionally, learners relied on oral or written responses to give evidence of their behaviors resulting from instruction, but now the film offers a unique and exciting response opportunity. With the advent of virtually automatic cameras and projectors and simple film-editing tools, the teacher may proceed—while exercising adequate but restrained leadership—to encourage learners to use motion picture production as an individual and inventive medium through which each can communicate his ideas and observations. The steps involved in student-made motion pictures are simple and easily followed by pupils from primary grades up.

Most important is the realization that motion picture film experiences should be integrated with other media experiences to become a fundamental and important part of the multimedia learning environment.

Further learner response projects

1

Confer with the school district media specialist, audiovisual director, supervisor of the learning resource center, or school librarian for help in counseling catalogs and directors of 8mm and 16mm learning materials. Use as a guide the film catalogs listed in the References. As a result of your quest, draw up a list of titles and descriptions of potentially useful films. (Note source information: purchase or rental costs, local school ownership, or free materials.)

2

Through arrangements with the supervisor of the school learning resource center, school librarian, or local or regional director of the educational film library, secure and preview as many of the materials as possible on the list you drew up in Project 1. It is reasonable to undertake this as a group activity in which your pupils or fellow teachers participate. The long-range objective is to bring together a selection of the best possible learning resources. This can be a legitimate part of ongoing class activity or a project undertaken by your subject curriculum group. You may wish to exchange information with fellow students.

3

If you are currently teaching, invite your students to become members of such search or questing committees as these:

a   Locating and using motion picture projection equipment in our classroom.

b   Securing, evaluating, and using motion picture films in our classroom.

c   Examining, securing, and using super 8mm film production equipment in our classroom. Recommendations should be worked out jointly with your students and actually tried out. Do you have results to report?

4

Conduct a test in the area of film use procedures. If possible, secure the film entitled Fidelity of Report (see *Media References*). Without any preparation, ask fellow students to view the film. Immediately afterwards, give a written test of 18 or 20 items from the 100 questions that accompany the film. What is the average score of the students? What are your generalizations about the scores with respect to a teacher's responsibility when using a film?

5

With the cooperation of your class group, locate and use 16mm or 8mm films in a variety of ways—in a large-group situation, to start a project or a unit of work, in small groups of similar interests to search for information that answers their own questions. What results have you to report?

6

Help interested students to secure places and equipment in which to do individual study of 16mm or 8mm films. Report observable responses.

7

In terms of one particular subject-matter interest of your class (role-play this if you are not teaching now), select a film and plan for its use in a "study" situation. Incorporate into your plan:

a   An appropriate introduction to the film through pupil-teacher planning.

b   A diagram showing optimum projection conditions.

c   Evaluation of the film in terms of learner responses.

Report the kinds of creative follow-up activities that you feel are appropriate or that the students accomplished or should accomplish.

8

After you have studied the section on film technology in the accompanying Student Production Guide, arrange to visit your learning resource center or the offices of the school media specialist or audio-visual coordinator to examine various 16mm or 8mm projectors and motion picture production equipment. Visit a local dealer and compare what you feel you need (on the basis of your examination of the technology section) with what your school has available. The outcome may be a request to use certain equipment in your classroom or, if not available, a requisition addressed to your principal.

9

Put together a list of materials or things needed to make, with your students, an original super 8mm motion picture film. If necessary, borrow a camera from a parent or the athletic coach. (Or consult the audiovisual specialist or building coordinator). Put to the test this idea:

With proper leadership and reasonable encouragement and guidance from the teacher, students become excited about film-making and successfully communicate their ideas in this new and inspiring way which is all-absorbing and all-involving. Report your results.

10

Consider the possibilities of integrating film learning with other related media— tape recordings, for example—in adding sound tracks to silent films so as to create

a more complete environment for learning that is challenging to pupils of varied interests, levels of progress, and needs. Report your results.

References

Educator's Progress Service. *Educator's Guide to Free 16mm Films* (published annually).

HOUSER, ROLAND L., EILEEN J. HOUSER, and ADRIAN P. VAN MONDFRANDS. "Learning a Motion and Nonmotion Concept by Motion Picture versus Slide Presentations." *AV Communication Review*, Vol. 18, No. 4, Winter 1970, pp. 424–430.

LANDERS, BERTHA. *Film Reviews 1972 Source Directory*. Landers Associates.

MIERHENRY, WESLEY C. *Enriching the Curriculum Through Motion Pictures*. University of Nebraska Press, 1962.

National Audiovisual Center. *U.S. Government Films*. Washington, D.C., 1969.

National Information Center for Educational Media. *Index to 8mm Motion Cartridges*. University of Southern California, 1969.

SCHINDEL, MORTON. "The Picture Book Projected." *School Library Journal*, February 1968.

Service Press. *Guide to Government Loan Films*. Service Press, Alexandria, Va., 1971–1972.

Syracuse University Audio Visual Center. *Instructional Materials for Teaching Audio Visual Courses*. 3rd ed. In cooperation with the U.S. Department of Health, Education, and Welfare, Department of Education, 1971.

Technicolor Corporation. *Silent Film Loop Source Directory*. 6th ed. Technicolor Corporation, Commercial and Educational Division, 1970–1971.

WITTICH, W. A., and JOHN GUY FOWLKES. *Audiovisual Paths to Learning*. Harper & Row, 1946.

Media references

Children Make Movies, 16mm film, sound, b/w, 10 min. McGraw-Hill.

The 8mm Film: Its Emerging Role in Education, 16mm film, sound, color, 28 min. Du-Art Film Laboratories.

Facts About Film, 2d ed., 16mm film, color, 16½ min. International Film Bureau.

Facts About Projection, 2d ed., 16mm film, color, 16¼ min. International Film Bureau.

Fidelity of Report, 16mm film, b/w, 3 min. Pennsylvania State University.

Film Research and Learning, 16mm film, sound, b/w, 16 min. International Film Bureau.

Film Research and Learning, 16mm film, b/w,

15 min. Michigan State University.

How To Splice a Film, filmstrip, color, 38 frames. Bailey Film Associates.

How To Splice Film, 16mm film, b/w, 10 min. Encyclopaedia Britannica Films.

Making Films That Teach, 16mm film, b/w, 20 min. Encyclopaedia Britannica Films.

Sound Recording and Reproduction, 16mm film, b/w, 11 min. Encyclopaedia Britannica Films.

Super 8—A Unique Communication System, slides, tape, color, 30 min. Eastman Kodak Company.

Source references

See source lists in the Appendix; particularly relevant sections are: Film Indexes; Film Reviews; Film Sources, 8mm, 16mm; Projectors, 8mm, 16mm; Screens.

See *Student Production Guide,* Chapter 2, "Equipment Operation" (Motion Picture); Chapter 4, "Producing Photo and Sound Materials for Instruction" (Motion Picture Photography Concepts).

TWELVE
Instructional television

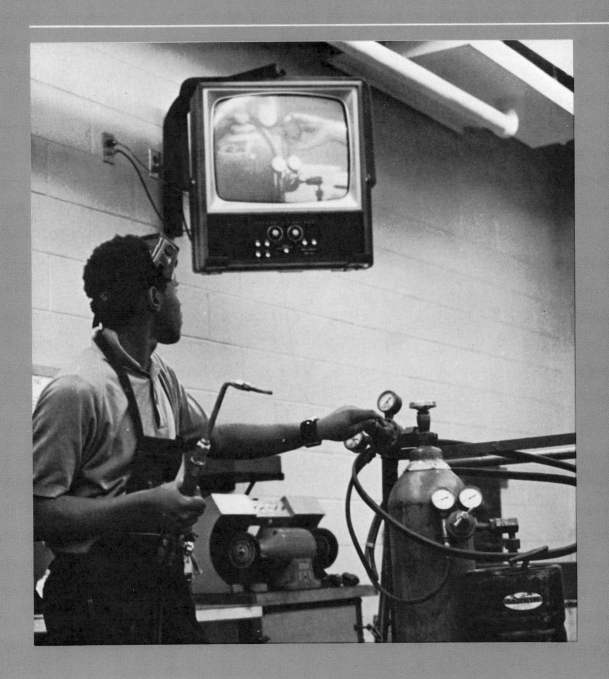

Objectives	Performance responses

1

To identify the characteristics and nature of ITV which enable this medium to bring to pupils, in a highly efficient manner, needed and desired learning experiences.

Identify persons or organizations in or near your school district which are sources of ITV lessons. Arrange to watch and evaluate several or a sequential series of such lessons and their accompanying study materials. See pages 526–537.

2

To identify the utilization responsibilities that pupils and teachers must recognize and assume if the greatest good is to be achieved from ITV use experiences.

Prepare an ITV lesson plan describing the televiewing objectives, pupil-teacher preplanning activities, viewing conditions, and follow-up learner response activities to be sought. Justify this plan by referring to at least three research studies, the finding of which support these procedures. See also pages 516 and 523–526.

3

To identify specifically an optimum classroom physical arrangement that would help to ensure effective ITV learning.

Draw a diagram of the seating, listening, and viewing arrangements needed to ensure, for learners, effective reception of ITV experiences.

4

To identify three kinds of innovative television learning experience arrangements in addition to broadcast ITV reception.

Prepare proposals for two kinds of classroom television activities in which pupils accomplish most of the planning, production, and informative presentations. State specific objectives and the communication activities. State how you will evaluate the results of such experiences. See pages 541–546.

5

To identify the role changes likely to occur as classroom teachers initiate television production activities in the classroom; that is, as they use videotape recording equipment as a pupil response device.

Actively participate in or observe others who use open-circuit, closed-circuit, and/or VTR retrieval ITV learning experiences. Report at least three observations about conditions that affect the teacher's role in initiating, guiding, and evaluating such instruction.

6

To identify specific role changes that reflect pupil involvement and response as they use television as the means through which skills, experiments, demonstrations, and information can be reported to age-mates.

Assist pupils with whom you work or can arrange to work actually to plan and use television as a personal communication experience.
Evaluate the results in terms of observable learner behavior changes. Describe objectives, process activities, and observed behavior, which you will evaluate against the learning tenets in Chapter 2, pages 46–74.

AS you consider the use of televised information in helping learners realize their goals, review your own experiences with this extraordinary medium.

The face and voice of the television newscaster are an experience that can be shared daily by at least 90 percent of those who live in North America and Europe and by smaller numbers elsewhere. At first, the telecaster appeared merely as a "talking face." Then he made his communication more precise by referring to and showing illustrative material—pictures, charts, maps, objects, and short sequences from motion picture films. Next, some telecasters became "anchormen," adding reports from fellow newscasters all over the country and film sequences from teams of photographers who roam the world to film persons, places, and things and events as they happen. In much the same way, instructional television has advanced from its small beginnings—pictures of "a good teacher at work"—to the production of teaching-learning experiences that represent the cooperative efforts of teachers, media specialists, and television personnel.

Only a generation ago, the viewing of a television image was something so novel that news magazines carried feature stories about such activities going on in the research and development laboratories of electronics industries. Contrast this with the worldwide television broadcasts which reported, instantaneously and both visually and audibly, what was happening and what was being said on July 20, 1969, during the first landing of man on the moon. It is estimated that 2 billion viewers saw those television reports as they watched alertly in the 62 countries of the world served by a combination of electronic facilities staffed by more than 40,000 technicians and programers. This staff worked "round the clock" in order to keep visual and sound reports flowing smoothly and observably through a system of satellites, earth stations, earth relays, and cable and microwave communications (see Figure 12.1). Today such communication sophistication can be, and often is, available to pupils and teachers in their classrooms.

As the teacher turns from the extra-school world of worldwide telecommunications to the classroom, a surprising variety of television developments and applications becomes apparent.

Often, television provides special-events broadcasts that schools can use as enrichment experiences to augment and personalize everyday teaching. Examples include the inauguration of the President, the opening of Congress, sessions at the United Nations, and speeches made by the President and other high officials. Some particularly useful television broadcasts are offered by the Public Broadcasting Service (PBS), a network of more than 200 television stations across the country, backed by the federally mandated Corporation for Public Broadcasting. For example, PBS has broadcast a series of public affairs programs, "The Advocates." It also has rebroadcast some of the British Broadcasting Corporation's series of "Masterpiece Theatre" multipart programs, including "The Forsythe Saga," "The First Churchills," "Civilisation," and "Jude the Obscure."

A very significant television program, "Sesame Street," created and produced

FIGURE 12.1

INTELSAT, the International Telecommunications Satellite Consortium, composed of 81 member nations, is gradually broadening the scope of worldwide telephone and television communications by means of an increasing number of orbiting satellites. NASA launches the satellites under contract to COMSAT, the American-owned Communications Satellite Corporation, which manages the technical aspects of INTELSAT, but the satellites are owned by INTELSAT. The satellites are all placed into orbit over the equator, 22,300 miles up. At that altitude they travel at the same speed as the earth's speed of rotation; thus each remains over the same place on earth. (a) Rockets—here an Atlas Centaur—boost the "fixed-position" satellites such as this (b) INTELSAT IV into orbit. (c) A drawing shows how three INTELSAT IVs will give global coverage. (d) INTELSAT has satellites in orbit that relay audio and video messages to more than 50 earth station terminals such as (e) this one in Hawaii.

by the Children's Television Workshop, has been broadcast by PBS since the fall of 1969. This outstanding effort to use television to teach the very young consists of 130 one-hour programs that use animation, film segments, and other arresting visual devices to attract and hold an audience estimated at more than 12 million preschool and primary-level children who learn the alphabet, words, numbers, and vocabulary concepts as they eagerly watch. The programs are constantly evaluated and revised. More recently, CTW has planned and produced another series, "The Elec-

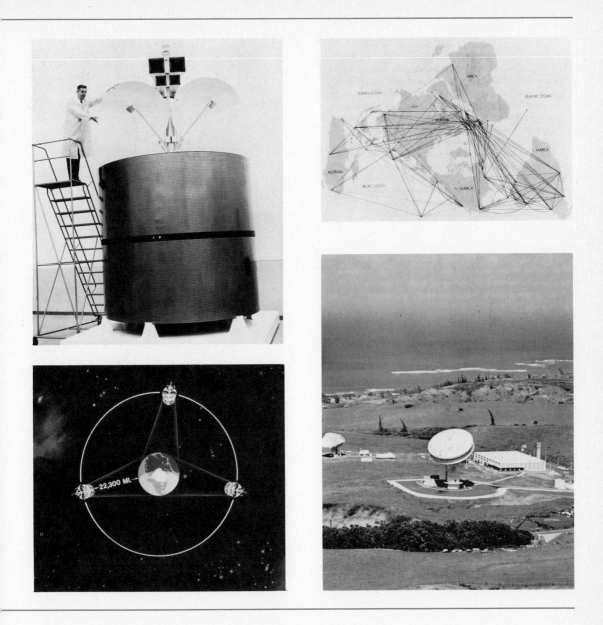

tric Company," which has been broadcast by PBS since the fall of 1971. This series of 130 half-hour programs is aimed at a higher level—children of ages 7 to 10; it emphasizes teaching basic reading skills to children who are beginning to have reading problems. In planning "The Elec-

tric Company," the producers made use of the intensive production experience "Sesame Street" had given them; they also drew on the evaluative judgments arrived at during research studies of the results of "Sesame Street" (see pages 523–526). Thus "The Electric Company," in at-

FIGURE 12.2

The television programs "Sesame Street" and "The Electric Company" are both designed for at-home as well as in-school viewing. The producers of both programs use all kinds of audiovisual media and communication devices to produce rapidly paced, changing, attention-sustaining experiences for children. The results in learning gains are uniquely positive. What is your response to this kind of instruction? (a) "Ernie" and "Cookie Monster," two of the many "Muppet" puppets that appear regularly on "Sesame Street," give a short lesson on the uses of the letter "D." (b) Word detective "Fargo North, Decoder" of "The Electric Company" attempts to unravel the meaning of a mysterious coded message that has been "processed" and flashed on the screen of the helpful "Opto-Spectometer." Taking clues from the context, Fargo and the girl decode the word, but since this takes them some time, their young viewers become involved in trying to beat them to it. (You undoubtedly have already guessed: "furpo" is "candy.")

tempting to combat some of the more elusive learning problems encountered by older children, incorporates all that is now known about making television communication reach children. In the format evolved to achieve this goal, the program makes heavy use of electronic computer-generated graphics and animation among its attention-sustaining techniques—hence its name. It also features vaudeville comedy routines, takeoffs on soap operas and game shows, and rock music (see Figure 12.2).

Supplementary television programs are originated in many school-financed and -staffed television studios in almost every large American and European city, bringing to classrooms in the area televised lessons given by outstanding teachers and teams of local resource persons who conduct demonstrations and explanations re-

lating closely to the basic curriculum plans being pursued by watching students and teachers.

In classrooms where television is used as related instruction, the circumstances for viewing and study vary from the most rudimentary provisions for seeing and responding to the most highly sophisticated provision for videotaping programs in advance and organizing them for easy access or retrieval for study purposes. They then can be arranged for student who view as members of groups or who choose to study independently (see Figure 12.3).

About her early impressions of instructional television (ITV), one teacher reports:

The day the door of my classroom opened and the technician rolled in our first television set, I was really shaken—I couldn't help but wonder if this was the way all instruction was going to be offered and if I, perhaps, would become dispensable. However, the more I used ITV lessons and observed how well planned they were—using appropriate demonstrations, visual explanations, motion picture film sequences, etc.—the more I realized that here was a dramatic new way of supplementing all the other learning experiences available to us in our classroom. And to get the most out of all this, I as a teacher was going to be more needed than ever before.

FIGURE 12.3

Televiewing is arranged to fit the needs of learners. (a) A small group studies away from others as they seek information of interest to them. (b) These pupils pursue independent study by dialing specific and available television programs (or films). What initiative and planning must be pursued in these cases by the administration, teachers, and pupils of these schools?

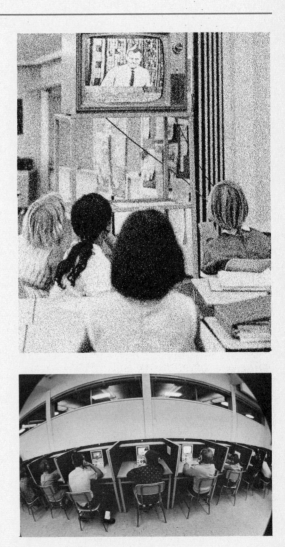

The *role* the teacher was referring to is one that is constantly described by researchers. Research studies indicate again and again that television learning opportunities become increasingly efficient for learners when the teacher and pupils become deeply involved, first in anticipating the nature of a forthcoming television learning experience, then in arranging the most effective kind of viewing conditions, and afterward in discussing the program in a true Socratic-style manner which fosters follow-up involvement and clarification.

A parent reports, "I'm glad television is finally being used in the classroom. Why, when I think of our living room just before dinner time—the youngsters sit 'glued' to the TV screen! That kind of interest should be incorporated into our classroom."

Why is television so fascinating? Why has it captured the attention and interest of children, teachers, and adults in general? How does it work? How are the best television programs produced? How may television become an effective part of day-to-day classroom instruction? Under what circumstances can teachers incorporate television into the broad spectrum of other media learning experiences? What new roles may be assumed whereby deep involvement may be achieved by both teacher and pupil?

This chapter answers some of these questions by describing the nature and use of instructional television, both closed and open circuit, as well as the very important new emerging area of pupil-teacher planned intraclassroom television communication— the use of simplified television recording and playback equipment whereby pupils and teachers may plan creative and inventive television communication experiences of their own.

Television—a multimedia learning experience

FOR years, teachers have known much more about what audiovisual tools they should have to provide needed classroom learning experiences than they have known about ways to *get* these new audiovisual tools for teaching. Films, models, slides, projectuals, charts, demonstration equipment—all these abound, yet, ironically, they are often very hard to acquire for classroom use. Educational television, at its best, has overcome much of this inaccessibility problem by serving as a tremendously effective carrier of needed learning experiences that have long been associated with the audiovisual field. During any one well-planned and well-presented series of school television programs, lessons may be communicated through the interrelated use of film clips—selected short but useful segments of 16mm films—chalkboard illustrations, slides, models, specimens, experiments or demonstrations, and short segments of tape recordings. Any or all of these may be referred to or explained by expert guests or by outstanding teachers who guide the course of television lessons. Thus educational television can make available many needed and heretofore inaccessible learning experiences—experience that most teachers quickly realize adds efficiency to classroom instruction.

Instructional television production creates many opportunities for cooperative planning by teachers, supervisors, learning materials experts, and skillful TV production teams. Instructional television at its best results from the combination of careful curriculum planning, subject content analysis, and the selection and interrelated use of the most appropriate instructional media.

The next step, evaluation, is invariably engaged in as teachers integrate the television programs into the stream of classroom instruction. As teachers and pupils discuss and use television, they quite naturally evaluate the quality of the content, its appropriateness to the age of the learners, and the clarity with which understandable and useful information and skill understandings are communicated. On the basis of such evaluations, teachers, subject experts, and ITV producers continue their recycling or revisions aimed at further improving television lessons, as well as plans for their use.

Throughout this cycle of production, classroom utilization, and evaluation, the weaker "links" in any television series are gradually replaced by more effective teaching demonstrations until finally the best instruction through television is realized.

One of the current remarkable demonstrations of multimedia educational television is "Sesame Street," the series of programs already mentioned. These programs, which are primarily intended to improve the range of concepts and vocabulary level of disadvantaged preschool children, take place amid the adults and children who live on "Sesame Street," who work and play there just like people everywhere. Although the programs are aimed at young children, adults "identify" with their realism and the "magic" of the content, which employs all kinds of fascinating visual and audio experiences: puppets; animated cartoons that show, for example, numbers grouping and regrouping themselves into many types of sets, each equal to 5 or 10 or another number; animated letters of the alphabet which move around and present themselves in a variety of forms; animated graphics and cartoons that explain vocabulary concepts by visualizing rather than verbalizing; and larger-than-life caricature birds and animals that move and "speak" for themselves. Little wonder that this program has attracted an audience of 12 million preschool and primary-grade children.

"Sesame Street" has emerged from several years of experience as one of the most intensively researched areas of television learning. The reason for this is that the producers first established educational goals for the program that involved specific readiness learnings, including these: knowledge of body parts, letters of the alphabet, and words; recognition and understanding of numbers; understanding of "relational" vocabulary, that is, amount relationships; understanding of size and "position" relationships, as in "through," "into," "over," "under," and so forth. Therefore these known ends could be observed and evaluated in the behaviors of children once television instruction was completed.

Present and future classroom teachers will be primarily interested in two broad areas of information resulting from research on the first two years of "Sesame Street." The first of these broad areas concerns the kinds of behavioral changes in performance that have been observed among children who have watched "Sesame Street" and who have, as a result, developed specific cognitive skills and awareness of cognitive information. The second broad area concerns the observed attitudes of these children once they have started their first formal school experience, usually in kindergarten.

Among the significant observable cognitive changes that have occurred, the following are the most important:

1. The "Sesame Street" programs did impart basic facts and skills to children aged 3 to 5, particularly to those who watched most frequently.

2. The programs were as effective for black disadvantaged children as for white disadvantaged children.

3. Disadvantaged children who were continuing viewers gained as much as advantaged children.

4. The 3-year-olds among the most frequent viewers gained more and ended with higher total scores than older children who viewed less frequently.

The second broad area of measurement, relating to attitudes, was undertaken particularly during the second year of the program. The measures of attitudes used showed definite gains in favorable attitudes toward school and toward people of other races among frequent viewers as compared with infrequent viewers.

Another significant result suggested by research on the second year of the program is this: although gains in vocabulary, mental age, and IQ have never been objectives of ''Sesame Street,'' as a side effect the program may be having a positive impact in those areas; at least, this is the conclusion that can be drawn from viewers' performance as measured by one of the standardized tests (Peabody Picture Vocabulary Test) used with preschool children.

The overall generalization made after the first year of ''Sesame Street'' and confirmed after its second year is that those children, regardless of age, who watched the most learned the most. The vitally important effects of this basic result on readiness for school are summarized in Figure 12.4.

Finally, one of the most important results of the second-year research is the finding that there is no basis for the fears expressed by some that ''Sesame Street'' viewers, accustomed to its fast-paced entertaining television format, would be ''turned off'' by conventional classroom instruction when they started school. Actually, quite the opposite is true: the degree of readiness provided by ''Sesame Street'' allows learners to slide smoothly and efficiently into the classroom interaction and other opportunities given them during formal instructional programs.[1]

[1] The discussion of research findings on ''Sesame Street'' is based on information in *A Summary of the Major Findings in ''The Second Year of Sesame Street: A Continuing Elevation''* (a report by Gerry Ann Bogatz and Samuel Ball), Educational Testing Service, Princeton, N.J., November 1971.

FIGURE 12.4

Teachers of children beginning school in the fall of 1970 who had "Sesame Street" "graduates" in their classes were asked to rank *all* children in their entering classes on the indicated seven different criteria relating to readiness for school. The teachers were not told which children were under study. Researchers summarized in this graph the teacher rankings of the children who had viewed "Sesame Street," dividing them into four degrees of frequency of viewing.

There is a still newer example of a television series that successfully involves children—in this case because children actually create the programs. The half-hour program, which is called ''Zoom,'' is produced by WGBH-TV in Boston and has been broadcast weekly over the Public Broadcasting Service network since the beginning of 1972. ''Zoom,'' aimed at children 7 to 12, is planned and created by a panel composed of seven representatives of the viewing audience (the panel is changed every 13 weeks). These seven children interact with adult adviser-editors, of course, but the children themselves make the final decisions about the content of each program. The result is a fast-moving series of programs that include animated and documentary films made by children and feature the panel members themselves in various ways—they all ''rap'' together on topics that interest children their age;

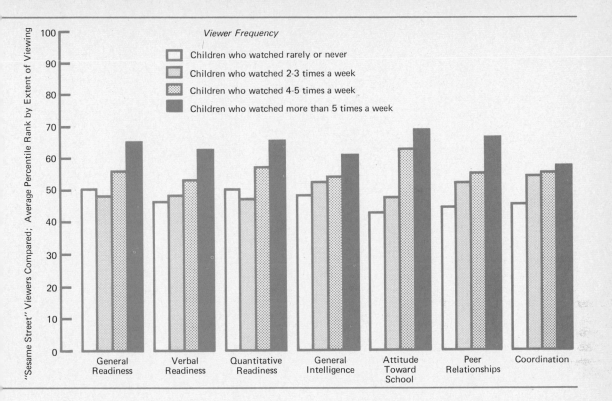

they put on dramatic skits; some or all of them do song-and-dance numbers. No adults appear on the programs. The panel members constantly invite their viewers to send in films, ideas for skits, and so on—and they do. Thus ''Zoom'' is apparently achieving its overall goals—to encourage creativity in children and to make television participatory. The program also is a striking example of successful interaction between children and adults as each group seeks to understand the other better.

Thus it has been proven that television is a powerful communication tool. Even so, it must be realized that pupils must be actively involved in it, as they must be in any type of learning. Rather than reducing viewers to a passive dreamlike state—which has happened—television, if it is to improve our entire learning environment, must continually devise ways to encourage the active response and involvement of the learner. How teachers may accomplish this will be discussed later in this chapter.

Nature and scope of instructional television

INSTRUCTIONAL television is a multimedia learning resource. Like films, filmstrips, models, community study, and related resources, it must be experienced to be understood and appreciated. The technical and scientific electronic processes by which televised images are actually captured, transmitted, and revisualized before the learner are significant and interesting (see the accompanying *Student Production Guide*). Nevertheless, it is the experience produced *in the mind of the learner* that is all-important. The validity and understandability of this experience are enhanced because it is essentially visual, employs motion, and, in most of the more recently established use situations, employs color in such a way as will enhance meaning and understandability.

The advantages to the learner of carefully produced and wisely used television thus include its high visual impact as it presents lifelike and realistic experiences. When television is available to teachers, it has the effect of enlarging instructional experiences, expanding curriculum learning opportunities, and stimulating both pupils and teachers. The obvious reason for this is that it is far beyond the energies or capacities of any one or a few teachers to match the literally hundreds of hours of planning and production and other professional work necessary for *good* television. All of these advantages must be evaluated realistically. This includes weighing them against several limitations, among which are the predetermined pacing of informational materials and experiences, the inability of studio teachers or producers to witness possible positive and negative reactions and responses from pupils, and the fact that class scheduling is upset by fixed broadcast schedules.

However, when teachers and administrators objectively evaluate both advantages and disadvantages of ITV, there are many ways, as will be described later, for capitalizing on its strengths and overcoming many of its weaknesses. Scheduling problems, for example, are overcome by prerecording and later playback on the latest easily operated electronic equipment. In any case, because the advantages so overwhelmingly outweigh any possible limitations, teachers in general and students welcome the television learning ex-

perience as a means of broadening their grasp of the bewildering environment of the world's people, places, and happenings.

International instructional television

A good communication idea is universal, and this is the case with instructional television. Instructional television development has taken place in many parts of the world.

In Sweden, as in Germany, Italy, England, Japan, France, and other countries, television production and broadcasting are the responsibility of the central government. Recently, in Sweden, 5,000 young people enrolled in a single electronics course in which television broadcast demonstrations were supplemented by small-group meetings to which students brought actual models assembled from packets of electronic parts distributed before the telecasts to all who were enrolled. The advantages of large-group communication were thus combined with a highly desirable degree of individual involvement and performance (see Figure 12.5).

The Inner London Educational Television Service currently broadcasts closed-circuit programs to more than 1,400 public and private schools in the London area. Unique in this operation is the number of school personnel who are involved not only in the decisions to broadcast certain information, but also, more important, in supervising and demonstrating good classroom utilization. Inner London television preceded its first broadcasts with two years of intensive study and media learning systems analysis. During this time, decisions were made concerning the subject areas to which televised information broadcasts could make the greatest instructional contribution, preliminary pupil performance behavioral goals were carefully outlined, and all kinds of interrelated media communication tools—films, models, charts, graphics, and so forth—were evaluated for

FIGURE 12.5

Teaching with instructional television is international. (a) Two professors examine one of eight packets of electronics parts to be assembled by each of 5,000 enrolled students to prove their new knowledge gained from participating in one Swedish national television course originating from (b) this studio in Stockholm. (c) These Japanese schoolchildren participate in the world's most comprehensive program of instructional television.

FIGURE 12.6

use. Only after these processes were completed did production go forward. Once broadcasting had begun, teams of intensively trained teacher-supervisors were deployed among the teachers in the schools using television to assist in effectively integrating television into ongoing classroom work, carry on evaluation of the efficiency of ITV, and assure that positive evaluation outcomes were recycled into improved ITV programing. Most of those involved in this process are classroom teachers who are given one- or two-year leaves to become involved in the planning, production, utilization, and evaluation of ITV for the Inner London schools. After such service most return to the classroom, and counterparts continue the cycles of work.

In Japan, where television is carried out under the direction of a national authority, instructional television occupies an important place in classroom instruction. Japanese national television has one great advantage: a monthly tax of about one dollar is collected on each of the approximately 24 million receivers. The proceeds are used to finance the network. The Japan Broadcasting Corporation (NHK) devotes most of its scheduling to educational programing—about 70 percent may be classified as formal or informal education. At present, about 100 relay stations interconnect with open broadcast circuits to provide the most complete educational television coverage in the world. More than 90 percent of all primary schools and more than 80 percent of all intermediate and high schools make use of the educational broadcasts, which continue during 10 hours of the day.

Instructional television in the United States

Instructional television which is directly identified with presenting information and experiences related to ongoing courses of study in curriculum plans pursued by local school districts is made available to most

ITV is a teaching device highly effective in explaining and demonstrating cognitive information. This Michigan State University professor uses TV and the telephone to communicate with his students who assemble in dormitory or campus TV study centers. At appropriate intervals he involves his students by answering or asking pertinent questions over the telephone. What effect does this kind of communication produce? What are your opinions?

of the nation's schools through 43 state networks. Because of television's efficiency, instruction is pursued through ITV means in 232 universities, 908 colleges, and more than 100 seminaries and institutes.

At Michigan State University, for example, more than 78,000 credit hours are offered each academic year through television. Closed-circuit television—signals sent through wires—is used at Michigan State instead of open-circuit television—signals sent through the air (see Figure 12.6). Cost studies have revealed that in addition to educational advantages there are economic advantages to this kind of instruction. Studies also show that the

achievement levels of students using ITV lessons are, in the majority of cases, similar to or higher than the accomplishment levels of students receiving traditional college instruction.

An overwhelming record of participation in television learning in the United States has been accumulated among the elementary, intermediate, and secondary schools of the nation. The 3,000 public school districts using ITV list nearly 16 million enrollments, the highest being in science, the social studies, language arts, and English. Smaller but still imposing enrollments of one million or more are recorded in music, art, and the modern languages. In all, nearly 7 million students are relying on television study for one or more of their classes.[2]

So successful has television been in capturing the imagination and active participation of Americans that public educational television broadcast facilities have been set up which are completely separate from the commercial television networks. The Public Broadcasting Service, as already mentioned, manages a network of 200 public television stations, making possible national programing of public tele-

[2] Lawrence McKuene, *National Compendium of Televised Education*, Vol. 15, Michigan State University Continuing Education Service, 1968.

TABLE 12.1

vision for adults and youth. National Educational Television, a national program production organization, provides a major portion of the adult evening programs seen on public television channels. Six regional television networks and 12 state networks link together geographically related stations and facilitate the exchange of programs for common broadcast.

The most recent development has been the establishment of the Corporation for Public Broadcasting (CPB), created by Congress in 1967 and operational since 1968. In effect, the act creating CPB states that the entire United States should have the benefits of strong public broadcasting —instructional as well as culturally educational. Under the auspices of CPB, the Public Broadcasting Service reaches nearly all the 50 states and territories of the United States. In furthering this program, CPB is the authorizing agency providing funds made available by Congress, but additional efforts are made through matching funds to incorporate financing from public foundations and trusts.

It is through such developments as these that high-quality, highly useful, and socially valuable television information is being made increasingly available to schoolchildren, youth, and adults.

Closed-circuit television

Television programs are distributed or "propagated" through two main avenues: open circuit (through the air) and closed circuit. Closed-circuit television uses a network of coaxial cables or wires through which the television signals are distributed from a source to the reception points, usually classrooms. An advantage of closed-circuit distribution systems is the high quality of reception that can be achieved. Open-circuit television, on the other hand, broadcasts its signals into the atmosphere to be retrieved by antennas at the reception points, from which signals are led into

Influence of classroom TV instruction on achievements in English and social studies by eighth-graders in Maryland

classrooms (see the technical explanation in the accompanying *Student Production Guide*).

One of the many well-established closed-circuit systems has continued in operation in Hagerstown, Maryland, since it first began in 1956. Thus one may see in Hagerstown high-quality educational television programs in widespread use. The success of educational television in Hagerstown has been verified by research studies carried on there; these studies represent one of the most comprehensive continuing investigations of television instructional work yet carried out (see Table 12.1).

One of the largest closed-circuit installations continuing in operation is in South Carolina. In 1960 the legislature of that state authorized $1 million for educational television installations. The educational television network of South Carolina ties together more than 100 schools in the Charleston and Columbia areas and 67 junior and senior high schools in most of the state's counties.

Other examples of closed-circuit tele-

	Hagerstown schools						Rural schools					
	Sept., 1957		May, 1958		May, 1961		Sept., 1957		May, 1958		May, 1961	
Grade 8	Grade equivalent	Percentile	Grade equivalent	Percentile	Grade equivalent	Percentile	Grade equivalent	Percentile	Grade equivalent	Percentile	Grade equivalent	Percentile
Vocabulary	7.59	(23)	8.13	(23)	8.44	(35)	7.06	(10)	7.30	(8)	7.89	(16)
Reading Comprehension	7.69	(19)	8.26	(18)	8.46	(24)	7.29	(10)	7.63	(8)	8.08	(14)
Spelling	7.56	(15)	8.18	(22)	8.61	(33)	7.17	(10)	8.05	(15)	8.14	(20)
Capitalization	8.10	(48)	8.65	(50)	9.18	(72)	7.37	(16)	7.94	(19)	8.38	(37)
Punctuation	7.44	(21)	7.98	(29)	8.60	(55)	6.93	(10)	7.63	(19)	7.82	(24)
Usage	7.37	(17)	7.89	(17)	8.27	(29)	6.67	(7)	7.47	(10)	7.65	(13)
Map Reading	7.95	(31)	8.52	(24)	8.86	(44)	7.65	(17)	7.99	(8)	8.49	(23)
Reading Graphs and Tables	7.79	(28)	8.52	(27)	8.76	(29)	7.51	(16)	7.93	(16)	8.20	(22)
Knowledge and Use of Reference Material	7.97	(39)	8.66	(43)	8.93	(57)	7.55	(18)	8.09	(16)	8.47	(31)

Source: *Washington County Closed Circuit Television Report,* Board of Education of Washington County, Maryland, 1964.

vision instruction may be found in hundreds of American and European schools. In the Horace Mann school in Munich, Germany, teams of teachers work together to prepare meaningfully arranged demonstrations which, once prepared, may be sent by closed circuit into three or four classrooms simultaneously for study; or they may be recorded on videotape for use repetitiously or later (see Figure 12.7).

In London, many schools are interconnected by closed-circuit television, as has been mentioned. ITV is used there to bring information that research has shown can be communicated effectively by television to thousands of widely scattered students. The television information is integrated by the classroom teachers in London into many kinds of interpretive, clarifying, learner-involvement follow-up activities. The nature of such activities varies as widely as do the interests and creative plans of teachers and pupils (see Figure 12.8).

In France, creative uses of closed-circuit television are being carried out in several designated research centers. In one of these, lessons taught by members of the teaching staff, assisted by technicians, originate in a production center located in the school. Classrooms are light-controlled so that they may be altered at a moment's notice to accommodate different types of media learning. Children at work in this school combine ITV learning experiences with other learning and response opportunities. They may refer to films, filmstrips, and so forth, which are available for their use in the school's learning resource center. They also may actively participate in the production of original ITV lessons (see Figure 12.9).

Closely akin to closed-circuit television is a limited broadcasting technique, the 2500-megahertz microwave system, more flexible than closed circuit but less universal than open circuit. It is necessary to apply to the Federal Communications Commission for permission to use this type of broadcasting, which reaches schools within 5 to 20 miles. At Bradley University, Peoria, Illinois, is one such installation, which has become a pattern for hundreds

FIGURE 12.7

This teacher in Munich is using a microscope and a television camera to enable groups at work in three remote classrooms to see in precise detail the cell section he is about to describe. What communication problems does this technique surmount?

FIGURE 12.8

These London schoolchildren and their teacher are pursuing their quest for further information by observing at firsthand to clarify ideas developed initially during a television series, *London Past and Present*. How may the teacher positively affect the usefulness of ITV?

of others. On the basis of such successful pioneering in the use of educational television, many state and regional networks have now been established which employ all three types of information distribution —open-circuit, closed-circuit, and 2500-megahertz microwave transmission. In addition, recorded television is extensively used to record and rebroadcast, to record on tape and then distribute programs by mail or other surface means, and to record in order to analyze and improve programs.

Recording and playing back instructional television

Videotape recording (VTR) permits the user to record for later playback the electronic counterparts of both images and sound on tape not unlike that used in a tape recorder. VTR recorders use wider tape, however, varying from ½ to 1 to 2 inches. (A detailed explanation of this process is included in the accompanying *Student Production Guide*.)

A very recent development that is a

FIGURE 12.9

ITV is one component in a system of interrelated learning experiences at Le Mar le Roi,
France. (a) The lessons usually originate in the
school's own production center. (b) Pupils may
continue their search by referring to other media
learning resources available to them in the
school's audiovisual center.

workable and efficient alternative to open-reel VTR recording-playback is the "video cassette" system. This vision and sound recording technique makes it possible to videotape anything and play it back immediately through any standard television set by simply inserting a cassette into a player. The cassettes, which run up to 60 minutes, may be in color or black and white. All that is necessary is a video camera and a special recorder-playback that immediately produces cassettes of ½-inch or ¾-inch videotape. The recorder-playback or a separate player unit is connected to the antenna input of the television set. Thus live audiovisual classroom learning experiences can be captured on videotape and immediately shown on the regular classroom TV set or stored for later reference. The simplicity of the cassette system enables students of any age to use the tapes for self-evaluation or for analysis of activities they have created. The cassettes may be quickly duplicated for simultaneous use in any classrooms equipped with players and TV sets. Also, films and videotapes in other forms and sizes may

FIGURE 12.10

Component parts of two current systems for recording and playing back televised information
are shown: (a) a video camera; (b) an open-reel
VTR recorder-playback and receiver; (c) part of
a VTR cassette system—cassettes and player
used with the standard TV set in the background.

be rapidly and inexpensively converted to cassettes that can be shown in this way. The opportunities for using this simple cassette system in innovative and creative ways in the classroom are limited only by the teacher's imagination (see Figure 12.10).

Another recent development in television recording is electronic video recording, or EVR. In this system, pictures and sound are stored for later playback on a thin film slightly less than ⅜ inch wide, packaged neatly in a small cassette. This film is usually divided into two parallel channels, each with its own magnetic sound track. In black-and-white EVR, each channel may be used for separate programs. In color EVR, however, one channel is used for image information and the other channel for color information. Unlike motion picture film,

EVR film has no sprocket holes. Synchronization is accomplished through tiny optical marks on the film itself.

A basic difference between VTR and EVR is at the stage of original recording. VTR permits a good deal of latitude, allowing recording and playback to go on within a classroom or television studio. The technique has been sufficiently simplified so that students and teachers can use it (as will be explained later). In the case of EVR, the original recording must be done under carefully controlled manufacturing and laboratory conditions. The playback phase of EVR, however, is extremely simple and versatile: completed cassettes of film are inserted easily into a playback mechanism for broadcast reproduction or use in a single classroom.

Instructional television: some research findings

INSTRUCTIONAL television has now played an increasingly important part in the American educational scene for two decades. Those who have been and are responsible for its development and use during this time must be credited for their integrity in refusing to become complacent about ITV. That is, these people have never stopped searching for ways and means to improve the quality and effectiveness of this form of communication. As part of their efforts, they have carried out or sponsored more than 1,900 research investigations aimed at finding out how television can improve learning opportunities by continually expanding the types of useful experiences it provides and making them available to increasing numbers of learners.

Three general cycles of television research and development may be identified:

First, the "master teacher" idea expressed the theme of many of the early television efforts. It was hypothesized that if one could locate an outstanding teacher,

he might use television as the means of making that individual's skill in teaching available to wide numbers of students. The early role of television was thus characterized as capturing the teacher at work and broadcasting him as he was—and even the best of teachers was likely to rely excessively on verbal communication. Research examination of such early efforts revealed that the learners who responded to such instruction did about as well as—no worse than and no better than—those who were taught in traditional ways. In other words, this first research inevitably reported: no significant difference. It should be added that the advantages inherent in broadcasting "master teachers" were often negated by the feeling on the part of the local classroom teacher that he was being set aside and placed in a position of secondary importance and thus had no real responsibility, since the television teacher was literally "taking over."

An important result of this early research was that it came to be recognized that there is no magic in lessons just because they are televised. That is, *instructional television, to be effective, must employ the particular and specific strengths of the medium*—its ability to visualize, to magnify demonstrations and illustrative materials, to give every learner a "front seat," to bring into the classroom learning experiences that the local teacher cannot arrange (costly experiments, complicated demonstrations, visual excursions to remote or inaccessible places), to bring current events experiences instantaneously into the classroom, and so on. When such characteristics were actively utilized, when recognized learner needs were anticipated, and when methods were suggested for encouraging learners to respond actively to the experiences (pre- and post-television activities pursued by both local classroom teacher and pupils), research began to reveal more significant gains.

This new cycle of ITV production and use was characterized by careful planning by teams of television producers, directors, and assistants to achieve the best possible use of all kinds of interrelated and needed learning experiences in terms of the goals to be achieved. Thus models, objects, specimens, film clips, flat pictures, graphics, demonstrations, charts, and so forth, were all brought into televised learning.

The research of this period has been summarized by Chu and Schramm, who report that pupils can learn with improved efficiency from carefully produced and wisely used instructional television. For example, one study investigated the responses to television of more than 200,000 students at work in 800 public schools. These pupils, evaluated on their work in English, mathematics, science, and social studies, used television effectively to gain known goals and objectives.[3]

[3] Godwin C. Chu and Wilbur Schramm, *Learning from Television: What the Research Says*, Stanford University: Institute for Communication Research, December 1967. (Also ERIC-ED 014900, *Research in Education*, Vol. 3, No. 5, May 1968.)

In general, research results show that television can be used efficiently to teach any subject where one-way communication contributes to learning. However, to achieve its full effectiveness it depends on the participation of classroom teachers who arrange to use readiness as well as postviewing opportunities to discuss, clarify, and respond. In other words, once effective television learning experiences have been designed and produced, great reliance must be placed on the classroom teacher, who invariably is the ultimate influence that determines when and how the student is affected.

Accordingly, a third cycle of research has considered various ways in which the classroom teacher can actively involve the learner in television instruction. For example, such research has been conducted in Santa Clara, California, by television personnel who studied the relative effectiveness of three methods of classroom television utilization. Eight hundred fifth-grade students divided into three groups were exposed to 12 television lessons in science. In one group, the teachers were asked to use the Socratic approach—ask questions and ask the children to give immediate knowledge of correct responses—after each telecast. In the second group, the teachers were asked merely to explain to the students that they would proceed directly into television experiences without any preliminary question-and-answer session. In the third group, the teachers were provided with a programed guide and left to their own devices in using it or ignoring it. It was found that the teachers who used the Socratic or discussion method of instruction achieved the highest results with their pupils. The generalization is that teachers who conscientiously attempt to involve their students in the lesson and attempt to encourage them to respond actively to questions about the content achieve good results. That is, if the teacher, through his actions and behaviors in the classroom, gives evidence that television is an important and useful learning tool, students invariably accept the cue.[4]

Another investigation concludes that enthusiastic and conscientious handling of foreign language ITV lessons by classroom teachers invariably results in higher achievement by participating students. Its author states:

Far from the concept of letting the machine do all of the work, it is evident how little foundation there is to the fear that television will replace the teacher. On the contrary—and here findings of research projects agree—evidence mounts up that it is only with the aid of the teacher that television can be an effective means of teaching foreign languages in the elementary school.[5]

A study conducted in the Denver public schools shows that learners' progress in televised foreign language instruction in the elementary schools indicates that the degree of learner involvement in activities growing out of the television viewing is directly related to performance. (This study is described in more detail on pages 533–535.)

To sum up, research evidence that has been accumulated over the last 20 years yields these significant generalizations:

1. The use of instructional television in the classroom can result in statistically significant advantages when television is planned and produced in terms of the known principles of media learning systems analysis and application. (An outstanding example is Inner London television, which was preceded by two years of preliminary planning and is carried on concurrently with intensive in-service training of teachers, as already described.)

2. Goals and objectives to be achieved by learners from ITV must be known. That is, learners and teachers must know why they are using television and what purposes it will serve.

3. ITV is most likely to communicate effectively when lessons are so planned as to use, in context, interrelated and appropriate other visual and audio experiences needed by and useful to learners. (These experiences are provided by using films, audiotapes, community study, classroom discussion, classroom demonstrations, flat pictures, maps, etc.)

4. To be effective, televised material must be easily seen and heard. The best possible seeing and listening conditions must be provided for all students.

5. Television is most effective when it is in color. Color is inherently interesting; more important, it often provides the final clues essential to unlocking meaning and understanding.

6. The classroom teacher who accepts and uses television as a useful and effective means of more successfully accomplishing curriculum and course-of-study goals achieves significant results.

7. The classroom teacher who encourages ITV preparatory and follow-up activities and learner involvement in putting to use new-found information in creative and inventive ways achieves significant results.

Thus ITV, to be effective, must be an integral part of the overall classroom learning environment. When it is, it produces great student response and involvement.

Early in 1972, there was an International Seminar on the Content of Instructional Television, led by Wilbur Schramm, Ray Carpenter, and Arthur Lumsdaine. At the end of the seminar, these three men, who have long been generally acknowledged as preeminent in the field of media and television research, evolved a brief description of good instructional television. It would be difficult to find a more appropri-

[4] *The Effect of Different Television Utilization Procedures on Student Learning,* Santa Clara Office of Education, San Jose, Calif., 1968.

[5] S. E. Randall, *Research Results in Three Large Televised Foreign Language Courses in the Elementary School Programs.* Paper read at the International Conference on Modern Foreign Language Teaching, West Berlin, Germany, 1964.

ate way to close a discussion of ITV research than by quoting this statement that synthesizes the views of a panel composed of Schramm, Carpenter, Lumsdaine, and 12 other media research experts:

Good ITV programs hold the child's attention while leaving room for thinking; make use of proper repetition, variation, and sequence; bring out the creative potentialities and fun involved in learning;

and lead the child toward some activity after the program. Good ITV programs look toward freeing the child to find his own problems and answers. Good ITV is much more than content; television is actually part of a learning-teaching system. Thus the greatest function of ITV is to push and stimulate this much larger context of learning, of which television is always only a part.[6]

Selecting and using instructional television programs

Like all new media learning materials, instructional television carries with it its own teaching-related responsibilities. However, unlike other media learning materials, instructional television seldom carries with it opportunities for the teacher to preview it in advance and make preuse judgments. In order to offset this drawback at least partially, those who produce instructional television learning experiences usually prepare accompanying lesson plans and descriptions that are given to individual classroom teachers early in the semester. These preliminary announcements and lesson plans in ITV manuals usually describe content and set forth learner objectives and goals. On the basis of these, the teacher may decide in advance whether or not specific ITV lessons will be useful in meeting the needs of the viewers—his own students. Then when the television lessons are received into the classroom, the teacher may review his preliminary judgments.

Some suggested prebroadcast activities

Television, when it is used wisely, is brought into the classroom as a learning experience that is closely related to the curriculum, useful, and interesting. Lessons should not be used casually. If the teacher arbitrarily stops an °ongoing activity just because a given television program has been announced for a specific time, disaster may follow. One teacher unwittingly described this type of mistake when he was discussing his use of ITV: "We've given it a try. I watch the time— at three minutes before the hour, we stop whatever we're doing, turn on the set, and get ready for anything that 'comes over.' "

In contrast, consider the following situation:

The principal and his visitors moved toward the classroom. On the door was a sign: "Televiewing—Quiet Please." As they entered unobtrusively, tney saw that pupils and teacher were busily engaged in discussing the forthcoming television lesson, "Understanding the Pacific World." On the desks before them, manuals were spread out. The manuals included questions that students were expected to discuss in advance. Beyond this, however, the teacher encouraged students to raise their own questions that reflected their own interest—and he added one of his own.

The effects of earlier study about the Pacific countries were obvious. Learning

[6] *Intrachange* (newsletter), East-West Center, Jefferson Hall, Honolulu, February 4, 1972, pp. 3–4.

displays on two of the walls included large, colorful commercial maps surrounded by smaller charts produced by pupils. References were often made to these as pupils sought to relate information already learned to what was being anticipated in the questions about the coming lesson. Objects, pictures, and specimens that pupils had collected as the result of their past television study were displayed on two tables. These displays illustrated the activities of people at work in Hong Kong, Macao, and the Philippines. As pupils and teacher continued their discussion, the visitors sensed that this had become a highly personalized experience for all as the students added their own insights. The visitors concluded that such preliminary involvement could produce only good identification with the purposes of the anticipated instructional television experience.

Related pretelevision activities often include the study of special vocabulary items included in the telecast. Also, many study guides explain briefly the key concepts introduced in a lesson so that readiness may be established for understanding the details described in the telecast itself. This kind of preliminary procedure, in fact, is typical of good utilization practices with *any* media materials. (See the film utilization suggestions on pages 481–486.) Ordinarily, however, the television lesson appears only once. Its pace is rather rapid, and it is usually organized so as to present a series of developmental concepts. Thus unless the student is prepared in advance, he may lose out along the way, and the entire thread of the experience may be lost. Therefore it is even more important in television use to spend reasonable time and effort in preliminary discussion and readiness activities, including vocabulary study, examination of maps where appropriate, reviewing material in past lessons, and, above all, helping each pupil determine his own central purpose with respect to what is about to happen.

Assuring effective viewing conditions

Well before the actual television viewing time, all should be placed in readiness. Sun curtains should be drawn. Pupils and teacher should check to be sure that glare does not impair the viewing conditions of the television lesson. Wherever possible, the set should be tuned in before the actual lesson begins, focused, and adjusted so that all may see and hear clearly. The teacher must know how to manipulate the controls of the particular classroom receiver properly. Adjusting for proper contrast, focus, and horizontal and vertical hold is essential (plus, of course, adjusting the additional controls on a color set). In the upper grades, students can help adjust the receivers before and during broadcasts. Listening and seeing efficiency must be checked. The teacher should move around the classroom to be sure that all pupils can hear and see well.

Because of engineering limitations, television screens are just not big enough to carry images visible to those seated far away at the back of a room. When contrasted with the 50- to 60-inch-wide screens normally used for classroom viewing of films, filmstrips, and slides, television screens do seem inadequate. The only practical way to overcome this difficulty for whole-class viewing is to use several television receivers, arranged to form two- or three-group viewing centers in the classroom, so that all sit within effective visual range of one receiver. The best viewing area for a 24-inch (diagonal measure) receiver is diagramed in Figure 12.11—no closer than 8 feet and no farther away than 22 feet from the receiver, with a horizontal viewing angle of no more than 30 degrees.[7]

Children should not be asked to "crane their necks" or bend back uncomfortably to view television receivers mounted too

[7] *Design for ETV: Planning for Schools with Television* (rev. ed.), Educational Facilities Laboratories, 1968, pp. 32–33.

FIGURE 12.11

Effective and ineffective zones for comfortable viewing of 24″ classroom television receivers. At what height should the receivers be placed? What can the teacher do to remove undesired glare and lower surrounding light levels?

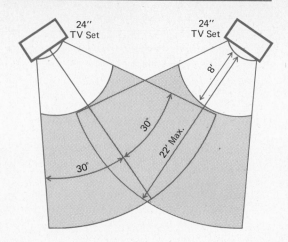

high above them. The receiver placed on a table may be viewed comfortably by small children who draw their chairs in a circle before it. Older students will learn through experimentation how best to group themselves around a receiver that is placed not more than 4 to 5 feet above floor level.

During televiewing, light levels should be kept high enough so that the teacher can be conscious of the facial expressions of the group. Facial or physical reactions often show that there are questions or that enthusiasm is high or low; other cues may signal opportunities for clarification after the broadcast is completed.

If the television-viewing conditions are not effective, the teacher should not hesitate to call on the administrator, the supervisor, or the audiovisual director.

Assuring learner involvement and response

In any teaching situation, it is the teacher's responsibility to arrange for all kinds of opportunities through which each learner becomes *involved* in what he is learning and *responds* by giving evidence that he can use his new-found information in constructive, creative, and exciting ways. This is particularly true of television.

Those who plan television learning guides are skilled in suggesting ways to involve learners, but it is the teacher who decides which of these ways to use. The following television lesson guide, which was prepared by and is used in the Milwaukee Public Schools, is quoted as an example of a well-planned TV lesson guide.

Unit X. Meteorology[8]

HOW IS THE ATMOSPHERE HEATED AND COOLED?

Preparatory Activities

Why is it colder in our latitude during the winter than during the summer?

In what geographic areas have the world's lowest and highest temperatures been recorded?

Why is it colder on top of a high mountain than at the base of the same mountain?

Vocabulary:

heat	*reflect*	*Fahrenheit*
temperature	*intensity*	*"greenhouse*
radiant	*centigrade*	*effect"*
energy		*thermometer*

[8] Quoted with permission of the Milwaukee Public Schools.

Content

The sun, either directly or indirectly, is the source of most of our heat.

The sun's energy is transferred from sun to the earth by radiant energy waves which will either be reflected from matter, transmitted through matter, or absorbed by matter and changed to heat energy.

The amount of heat energy absorbed by the earth and its atmosphere from the energy of the sun depends upon the following factors:

1   The intensity and duration of exposure to the sun's rays.

2   The angle of the sun's rays to the surface of the earth.

3   The distance from the sun to the earth.

4   The nature of the surface of the earth.

Heat can be transferred by a movement of air currents when cold air, being heavier than warm air, pushes down on the warm air, causing it to move upwards.

A thermometer measures the intensity of heat.

Classroom Activities

Construct an air thermometer. See A Sourcebook for the Physical Sciences, p. 393.

Calibrate a Fahrenheit thermometer with a centigrade scale. See A Sourcebook for the Physical Sciences, pp. 393–394.

Demonstrate convection of heat by warming a transparent vessel filled with water. Add a few drops of ink and observe the circulation of the currents. The continuous movement of the cold and warm portions of the liquid creates a convectional current similar to that taking place within the atmosphere when air is heated and cooled.

Demonstrate how heat is absorbed and reflected.

Secure several accurate thermometers and several different-colored pieces of cloth. Try to obtain a black cloth and also a white cloth among those to be tested. Place thermometers beneath each of the samples of cloth and place in direct sunlight for one hour. Compare the readings on the thermometers after the necessary time and determine which colored materials absorbed more heat and therefore record a higher temperature. Note also which colored cloth reflected most of the light and therefore recorded a lower temperature. Make comparisons at the conclusion of the experiment with the earth and how various materials reflect and absorb heat at different rates.

Suggested Reading

Exploring Earth Science, *Thurber & Kilburn, pp. 50–59.*

Science 1, *Davis, pp. 137–139.*

Science in Our World, *Carroll, pp. 92–94.*

Our Environment, How We Adapt Ourselves to It, *Carroll, pp. 21–45.*

Additional Suggestions to the Teacher

Activities:

A number of experiments and demonstrations related to heat may be found in UNESCO, 700 Science Experiments for Everyone, Garden City, N.Y., Doubleday & Co., Inc., 1956. See pp. 133–135.

Films:

4475   *Sun and How It Affects Us (11 min.)*

4469   *What Causes the Seasons? (12 min.)*

5694   *Why Seasons Change (11 min.)*

4140   *Inconstant Air (27 min.)*

Filmstrip:

V52139   *Weather*

FIGURE 12.12

As television producers work closely with seventh-grade science teachers in Atlanta, they seek to bring realistic firsthand experience opportunities to all classroom teachers and pupils so that instructional television can be used in a work-study manner. Before each science broadcast each classroom group is supplied with hundreds of fresh specimens. As pupils prepare to view the ITV lesson, they study the specimens; then they refer to them during the broadcast and use them for experimental and creative purposes of their own choosing after the broadcast. What ideas do these practices give you? (a) Plant propagation with bryophillium. (b) A study of carpellate and staminate cones in pinus taeda, Georgia's most prevalent pine. (c) Alternation of generations in mosses; upper right: male and female gametophytes and an asexual sporophyte.

Note that this guide includes many ideas for involving pupils. Activities are suggested which experience has shown are likely to encourage pupils to put their new-found information to the test. Thus they can construct something, calibrate scales, conduct demonstrations, choose and present for their classmates related demonstrations of their own, and search for more information by referring to suggested films, a filmstrip, additional readings, and so forth. In this way the television teaching lesson may become integrated into the mainstream of classroom instruction. How does the Milwaukee guide compare with guides that you may use? What is the implied relationship of this guide to the role of the classroom teacher? What is implied about instructional television and the use of related media learning materials?

Another illustration of the use of television learning experiences to challenge learners and inspire their involvement and response comes from the Atlanta public schools. Gil Tauffner, the television coordinator, describes their ITV series on plant reproduction as follows:

In addition to the usual lesson guides, we provide teachers and pupils with kits of science materials. These may include plant specimens, mushroom growth materials, packages of test tubes, agar-agar, pine cones, flowers, bulbs, seeds, and even sand. The Classroom teacher receives these well in advance of the actual broadcast date. As the television teacher conducts demonstrations, the students are encouraged to follow along by manipulating the equipment, specimens, or realia which they have before them on their desk tops.
When each telecast is over, students are then in a position to try out their new information by further manipulating these materials. Experiments are conducted, planting beds are prepared, and plantings
made of seeds or bulbs, etc. A sense of involvement is produced which "brings television instruction to life." Teachers and students report their enthusiasm. This kind of television activity has proved to be one of the most effective study devices associated with our instructional television programing in Atlanta.

Some of the projects undertaken by pupils are shown in Figure 12.12. Others experimented with planting seeds under various conditions and with the propagation of leafy plants. Still others carried on experiments in determining the growth patterns of rhizomes as these underground stems spread and develop new plants. Comparisons of asexual and heterosexual vegetative propagation forms were verified by other students.

As such follow-up involvement proceeds, pupils invariably discover that though basic information has been developed during the television lesson, they need much additional information. The search continues. In many cases, picture sets, filmstrips, and motion picture films are secured from school media centers or from the school district media offices. Thus the television broadcasts week after week inspire television teachers and planners, classroom teachers, and pupils to move ahead to expand the basic concepts initially presented in these same broadcasts.

In Los Angeles County, California, hundreds of young people become involved in inventive and creative projects that are "sparked" by core instructional broadcasts. For example, a television series evolved there, entitled "Living in the West," has been particularly successful in eliciting creative student responses (see Figure 12.13). The series is the result of long-range cooperative planning among television teachers, curriculum supervisors, classroom teachers, and curriculum committees. Such planning concerned not only the production of the instructional television programs for broadcast, but also the planning, writing, and distribution of the accompanying study guides; the guides stress learner involvement through follow-up projects, including field study and the use of community resource personnel, films, filmstrips, models, and specimens.[9]

During a survey of classroom teachers who had used "Living in the West," such representative evaluations as these were reported:

Our vocabulary study increased im-measurably. After each new lesson, one of our pupil activities was to discuss and record all of the new words we had learned.

. . .

Our question-and-answer periods were times of high interest. Students were eager to discuss their new-found information and to make their own statements about how their ideas had changed and grown.

. . .

Map study increased. We had a high purpose for turning to the maps to find the location of the harbors, freeways, and planned future airport and harbor developments.

. . .

We have gained greatly in our under-standing of the Los Angeles basin . . . how weather affects it, why transportation problems exist. . . . We now plan to take several field trips into outlying areas because we have great curiosity about things and want to find out for ourselves!

. . .

We have organized displays of models and specimens that we have gathered ourselves during our field excursions.

. . .

As the result of our television study, we have made maps, gathered specimens,

[9] *Guidepost to "Living in the West,"* Los Angeles County, Supt. of Schools, Los Angeles, Calif.

FIGURE 12.13

Those who planned and produced the instructional television social studies series "Living in the West" suggest that after each lesson the classroom teacher take the responsibility for helping the learners use their new-found information in creative ways. These pictures show how effective such plans can be in inspiring follow-up activities that go forward in the classroom. Then, as shown, some of the learner-created response projects come full circle when they themselves are integrated into a summary lesson that is being televised. What ideas do you have for integrating instructional television lesson experiences into your own teaching?

written "books," and collected pictures which relate to the television lessons.

. . .

A search for more pictures, slides, and models has been going on. We have ordered and used many related films and other learning resources that we can secure from our center.

. . .

We have arranged field trips and invited resource people into our classroom. We had not done this before. The television programs really provided the incentive. Before a guest arrived, we'd plan and even "rehearse" the questions we were going to ask and how we would behave.

. . .

We created audiotape reports—a wonderful language arts activity. It caused us to think and plan about what to record.

*The pupils decided that the best way
was to write their own ideas, then practice.
We had never taken such pains before.
The students were much more exacting
than I ever had been.*[10]

Effective television learning, then, does
does not end with turning the receiver off
and going back to "other work." Rather,
television can be, and should be, a stimulus. As learners gain additional understandings through instructional television
experiencing, they invariably gain incentives that are difficult to produce by traditional methods. In other words, the enriched learning environment provided by
instructional television and related experi-

[10] *Los Angeles Regional ETV Survey*, 1965, Educational Testing Service, Los Angeles office.

ences engenders the strong feeling among
normal learners of "wanting to know."

A final illustration, from the Denver
public schools, is a unique Spanish television lesson-demonstration series which
was used along with other learning experiences available in the classroom. A survey
of the need for Spanish instruction among
upper elementary students revealed that
most students wanted to study this subject.
Spanish instruction had traditionally employed electronic materials, including
transcriptions and prerecorded tapes,
work-study corners, called "Spanish corners," and the usual text materials. It was
decided that a series of 15-minute television programs would be produced and
used along with related classroom techniques. The instructional television lessons
employed active pupil-response forms dur-

ing studio production. That is, pupils in the studio worked with the studio teacher and also played parts in the instructional television programs. Pupils out in the classrooms could observe students like themselves at work studying.

The television lesson-demonstrations were videotaped so that they could be repeated. The decision to repeat the television lessons grew out of research findings of Charles F. Hoban and others.[11] Hoban concluded:

Repetition of whole films, repetition of scenes and sequences, repetition of illustrative examples, repetition of films and filmstrips, repetition of review and discussion of film content . . . all of these have been investigated and in general, all have resulted in increments in learning.[12]

In Denver, it was expected that repeating television lessons would help pupils learn more. This is what did happen.

The television programs were added to the classroom learning devices then in use—record players and earphones, tape recorders and prerecorded tapes; in addition, there was a specially produced programed instruction text in Spanish to which learners could refer. In assessing the value of repetition, the television programs were used throughout a semester in four different ways with four groups of fifth-graders. All four groups used the same additional learning devices and materials. The variations among the four groups were as follows:

[11] Charles F. Hoban, "The Usable Residue of Educational Film Research," *Teaching Aids for the American Classroom*, Stanford, Calif., Institute for Communication Research, 1960; Walter A. Wittich and John Guy Fowlkes, *Audiovisual Paths to Learning*, Harper & Row, 1946. Repeated broadcasts of given lessons are used elsewhere. In Hawaii, lessons over KHET are repeated twice a week; both teachers and pupils benefit from the increased learning efficiency.

[12] Hoban, op. cit., p. 105.

The first group viewed the television programs once.

The second group viewed the television programs and (because they had been videotaped) immediately repeated the viewings, thus devoting 30 minutes rather than 15 minutes a day to the experience.

The third group viewed the television programs and then repeated the viewings in the early evenings at home over open-circuit television. Parents were encouraged to join their children at the repeat viewings.

The fourth group viewed the television programs and then had 15 minutes of oral practice under the direction of the classroom teacher.

The accomplishment levels achieved by the four groups as shown in test scores are summarized in Figure 12.14. It is interesting to note that early research evidence on the repeated use of films, filmstrips, slides, and so forth, is now confirmed with instructional television. When ITV programs are repeated, learning efficiency is increased. When the repetition involved the participating parents, it was particularly effective in this case.

The greatest improvement in learning over those who merely viewed the programs once, however, was accomplished not by repetition of the ITV lessons but by oral practice after each lesson that was led by the classroom teacher. Thus again we see that the classroom teacher is all-important in learning.

One of the main conclusions drawn from overall assessments of the Denver experience is that the successful results could be attributed not so much to any one technique as to the great involvement of the learners that was achieved by means of all the techniques. That is, the *effective context* created for the television lessons resulted from a combination of repetition, parent participation at home, teacher participation and guidance, student participation in the programs themselves, and the use

FIGURE 12.14

The effects of four approaches to learner involvement in the television teaching of Spanish
among fifth-graders in a Denver school.

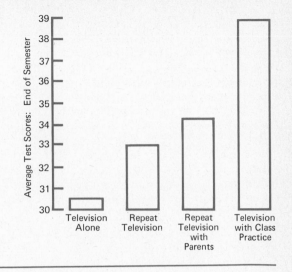

of many related learning materials. Thus the lessons were not something "done to" the students and teachers; rather, they became part of the learning resources of the schools, combined with the other techniques to form a new and more potent "package" that actively involved all concerned.

It should be emphasized, in conclusion, that the Denver experience shows yet again that the influence of the classroom teacher as arranger, counselor, and guide in supervising the work-study use of instructional television in the classroom is vital. In fact, the classroom teacher is the most significant single factor in achieving effective utilization of instructional television.[13]

Evaluating instructional television

The classroom management of instructional television must be subject to evaluation. The most effective means of accomplishing this is through the classroom teacher's observation of pupil reactions to instruc-

[13] Denver Public Schools, *The Context of Instructional Television—Summary Report of Research Findings, 1960–64,* Denver Public Schools, June 1964.

tional television as such. Pupil reactions and responses range all the way from clearly observable growth in discussion facility and vocabulary development to the desire to locate and study additional learning resources and plan and create classroom exhibits and displays.

Both those who *plan* and those who *use* instructional television must methodically pursue such evaluation. The producers and supervisors of instructional television are obligated to communicate constantly with classroom teachers to secure reactions to program content, quality of study guides, the manner of selecting and using educational media in television, and the nature of pupil behavioral changes resulting from instructional television utilization. The classroom teacher is obligated, in turn, to report his and the learners' evaluation to the proper television supervisory and program authorities. It does little good, on completing the viewing of a program, either to praise it or criticize it unless a specific affirmative or negative report is immediately and methodically sent to the local programing authorities. If such reports are not made, little constructive change can be expected. Thus the classroom teacher

ITV evaluation scale

1   Are instructional television program announcements, study guides, or annotated descriptions distributed to teachers well

ahead of the actual programs?
0% _____   50% _____   100% _____

2   Are the goals and objectives of the ITV programs made known to pupils and teachers in clearly stated form? (Usually included in

study guides or preliminary descriptive materials.)
0% _____   50% _____   100% _____

3   Do the published goals of the ITV programs relate directly and constructively to the subject, grade level, and interests of the

teachers and pupils who are expected to use the programs?
0% _____   50% _____   100% _____

4   Are study guide annotations or content descriptions of the ITV lessons adequate and clearly stated?

0% _____   50% _____   100% _____

5   Are cueing questions included in the study guide?

0% _____   50% _____   100% _____

6   Are there references in the study guide to related and useful supplementary media materials, including films, picture sets, film-

strips, models, etc.?
0% _____   50% _____   100% _____

7   Has the teacher conducted pupil-teacher discussion and planning to help pupils become aware of their reasons for viewing

the ITV lesson?
0% _____   50% _____   100% _____

Classroom Environment for ITV Utilization:

1   Has the teacher conducted beginning-of-the-year testing to ascertain the levels of visual and auditory acuity among pupils?

0% _____   50% _____   100% _____

should seek active participation not only in the planning of ITV but also in its continual evaluation and constructive recycling. Only through continual and objective evaluation can a higher quality of ITV and better multimedia ITV programing be achieved.

The ITV evaluation scale above is suggested as one that can be applied by the classroom teacher.

Instructional television: some innovative uses

As is often the case, what engineers and technicians invent for one purpose, creative teachers put to all kinds of unforeseen innovative uses. So it is with television cameras and new lightweight, easily operated videotape recording and playback equipment—equipment that records visual images as well as sound.

2 Is the visual environment of the classroom 　　　　　　　　etc.)
satisfactory? (Avoidance of glare, seating 　　　　　　0% _____　　50% _____　　100% _____
arrangements, viewing distance from screen,

3 Is the audio environment of the classroom 　　　　ments, distance from receiver, etc.)
satisfactory? (Avoidance of extraneous 　　　　　　0% _____　　50% _____　　100% _____
noises, room acoustics, seating arrange-

4 Can the television set be adjusted so as to 　　　　0% _____　　50% _____　　100% _____
attain completely clear and understandable
audio and visual signals or stimuli?

Post-Televiewing Evaluation Criteria:

1 Was the content of the television program 　　　　0% _____　　50% _____　　100% _____
suitable to the age level and subject interests
of the pupils?

2 Was the information presented in terms of 　　　clips, graphics, community resource
optimum communication techniques? 　　　　　personnel, etc.)
(Demonstrations, models, mock-ups, film 　　　　0% _____　　50% _____　　100% _____

3 Did the program organization and content 　　　experiences?
clearly refer to announced learning objectives 　0% _____　　50% _____　　100% _____
which related to needed classroom

4 Did the teacher encourage and stimulate 　　　found information?
follow-up activities which permitted the 　　　　0% _____　　50% _____　　100% _____
students to respond creatively to their new-

5 What evidences of desirable learner be- 　　　working with the ITV program?
havioral changes can be attributed to 　　　　　0% _____　　50% _____　　100% _____

Now that you have an evaluation instrument, you 　　**of putting it to use. Perhaps your local ITV or**
are encouraged to bring it to the attention of 　　　　**media specialist or principal may be helpful.**
local ITV authorities and seek ways and means

ITV for self-evaluation

In Chapter 8 we have discussed methods of using audio recording equipment to record and immediately play back, for purposes of self-analysis, one's own speaking or singing voice. Now we can record the voice or other sounds *and* visual images on tape and immediately play back the result. This kind of recording is often used by individuals or groups who wish to see and hear their own performances immediately. The response is dramatic as one is confronted by the living, speaking visual image of himself. Little wonder that departments of speech and dramatics often have students spend rehearsal time with a videotape recorder and playback so they can profit from the immediate self-analysis and resulting self-improvement (see Figure 12.15).

A special adaptation of this technique has proved useful in teaching language to hearing-impaired learners. Ralph S. White, director of the Speech Through Vision Project of the Clark School for the Deaf in Northampton, Massachusetts, reports using a videotape recording and playback arrangement with special pushbutton controls which made it possible for teachers

FIGURE 12.15

(a) These students at work in a performance analysis studio at a university can see themselves simultaneously on a TV monitor connected with the camera. At the same time, their performance is being videotaped so they can critique their own efforts later during repeated "run throughs." (b) These high school students are evaluating their own performance a few minutes earlier. Their teacher obviously enjoys watching their reactions. What possibilities does this technique hold for your teaching?

to start, record, play back, and repeat. Because deaf children have unique problems in attempting to understand and apply the instructions and suggestions given by their teachers, videotape playback has proved particularly useful (see Figure 12.16):

The child who bobs his head and weaves about on his feet while he talks really doesn't grasp the reason behind the teacher's corrections—until he sees himself on television. Videotape playback is unmercifully accurate. Suddenly, the student sees himself, and the teacher's corrections take on meaning.[14]

Videotape recording and immediate

playback are being used to enable teachers in training to see and hear themselves as they engage in practice teaching (see Figure 12.17). One professor of art education who uses the method comments:

VTR helps the student teacher gain insights into her personal teaching approach. By using VTR, the student teacher can come to see herself as the unique personality she is. Her strengths can be capitalized on and her weaknesses minimized. As we all know, the manner in which a teacher relates to her students is fundamental to the process of education. VTR, in this case, provides a valuable service by showing us the actual "face" of our behavior.[15]

[14] Ralph S. White, "Teaching Speech with Television," *Educational Television*, December 1970, p. 40.

[15] Don Cyr, "To See Ourselves," *Arts and Activities*, May 1970, Vol. 67, pp. 14–17.

FIGURE 12.16

A deaf pupil is about to observe her own efforts to speak correctly while videotaping proceedings. When desired, the teacher may stop the tape and repeat useful sections immediately, then resume recording. What applications are there for your own work?

This procedure is now used in most of the nation's teacher training institutions and agencies. Whatever the technique is called —"self-critique teaching," "microteaching," or "self-image teaching"—it integrates the basic opportunity to perform as a teacher at work in a live, realistic setting with, immediately afterwards, the opportunity to observe the "living" record of the practice teaching in a nearby conference or viewing room. Often the student teacher prefers to do this with other student teachers; because all are in the same situation, they encourage one another in their self-analysis, value judgments, and constant search for ways to improve. Another procedure often used is to view the playbacks with the critic teacher, who offers constructive suggestions.

VTR plays an important part in therapy at the Hawaii State Hospital, where creative sociodramas are videotaped for later playback. In this innovative situation, the participants are emotionally disturbed young people ages 14 to 19. Many are unable to respond normally to the realities of everyday social situations. Boys and girls working in small groups are encouraged to act out ways they would make a purchase in a store or restaurant, serve as a gas station attendant, ask for information, attend a party, make introductions, and so forth. As the confidence of the group grows, behaviors are videotaped and then played back. Animated evaluations and discussion follow as group judgments and self-judgments are made and rejected; in many cases, real insights into future behavior are the result.

Another use of VTR in helping emotionally disturbed teenagers is found at the Hawthorne Cedar Knolls School in Haw-

FIGURE 12.17

(a) This student teacher is being videotaped by the critic teacher as she works with children. (b) Immediately afterward, she watches the visual and audio record of her actions with the critic teacher and another student teacher. Co-operating teachers are just as surprised by the value of such experiences as the student teachers. How does this procedure impress you? Can you think of ways to use such techniques with the *pupils* with whom you work?

thorne, New York. The director of the educational communications center there describes some of the philosophy behind the VTR program and how it was begun and carried out as follows:

Emotionally disturbed youngsters will not function in an atmosphere that is not conducive to success. This success does not have to come easily, just as long as it is more readily apparent than in a normal situation. When our television studio was installed, the first students we had in class were mostly the old AV squad. I felt that the first few productions had to be simple, yet worthwhile enough so that the students would have a sense of achievement. We began with two programs in a "how to" series. These *were how to make a transparency and how to thread and operate a 16mm Graflex projector. Both pieces of equipment are simple, with straightforward steps that must be followed every time. The students wrote the scripts and handled all aspects of the production. They all knew how to operate these machines, and the transition to a full-scale television production was an easy one.*

Our next step was to move to a slightly more sophisticated format. Interview shows were something with which they were all very familiar. We took the obvious step from familiarity with content to familiarity with format. . . . The next stage in our attempt to raise the students' level of production sophistication was to direct them toward "personality" or "host"-type programs. . . .[16]

Inspired by the director, these students then branched out to creating personal types of television presentations that ignored standard procedures and formats. Some of the students, most of whom had met with failure within the traditional education system, found that this new medium enabled them to express themselves articulately and literally for the first time. Not many people have adequately explored the manipulative and production aspects of simple television programing to this extent. However, as this example shows, emotionally disturbed children (who are not necessarily, of course, dull or incompetent) may become sensitively and productively involved when they are exposed to exciting challenges that lead directly to tangible results.

There are many other examples of innovative VTR uses. The track coach uses video recording and playback to help the athlete see and instantly evaluate his performance of the Roll over the high-jump bar. This is done by setting up the equipment right on the track field and using its stop-motion (sometimes also slow-motion) capabilities. The swimming coach and the 100-meter sprinter record, watch, and correct the snap turn performed at the end of the first lap. Thus evaluation immediately follows the performance, and any errors may be seen and corrected.

If understanding does not occur immediately, the videotaped material may be played back as many times as needed. The shop instructor may record, at closeup distance, the delicate placement of wood blocks onto the lathe-chuck and then make this

[16] Peter M. Weiner, director, Educational Communications Center, Union Free School District No. 3, Hawthorne, N.Y., report presented at joint annual meeting, Connecticut and New York State Educational Communications Association, November 3, 1971.

experience available for immediate study and imitation by high school students. The use of video recording and playback during dramatics rehearsals, vocal music performances, band and instrumental performances—all these are highly refined but much more effective steps beyond the traditional uses of audio recording and playback during such situations which have long been familiar.

Individualized study of ITV recorded materials

Videotape recording and playback has been proved to be an effective means for visualizing, demonstrating, and explaining. Therefore, videotape recorded lessons can become valuable cognitive and skill learning experiences that can be used anytime and anywhere by groups or individuals.

One program of individualized instruction through television recording and playback is a continuing part of instruction in the Coatesville Area School District in Pennsylvania. Under this program, the student is offered much freedom in his own quest for information. He may find what he needs in the library by observing filmstrips, films, and so forth, or by reporting to a carrel where he is able to "retrieve" previously organized and planned videotaped lessons and demonstrations by dialing a selected code number. Not always does this experience go on in learning carrels, however. If it is more appropriate for the materials to be viewed in a laboratory or shop, this, too, is arranged. An industrial arts student may receive videotaped instructions as he stands before the welding equipment that he is learning to operate or the student learning how to operate a duplicating machine may retrieve needed videotaped instructions next to the machine (see Figure 12.18). For students studying English, special individualized videotaped lessons are available by dial access. Approximately 40 percent of these students seem to have made significant

FIGURE 12.18

This Coatesville student has "dialed" for a needed videotaped demonstration of the operation of a duplicating machine. This is video individualized instruction. How may this affect learner progress? How could you employ this technique?

gains beyond what would be expected in first-year programs. Further advantages reported include individual freedom to move about and progress at one's own pace. More than 75 percent of the students enrolled in journalism, English, the social studies, and mathematics reported that they learned more, progressed more rapidly, and at the same time developed stronger positive relationships with their teachers. Of this group, 80 percent reported that they would like to continue this kind of individualized instructional system.[17]

Videotaped information lends itself extremely well to demonstrations and instruction in skills or whenever the qualities of motion and vision are important to understanding and conceptualization. Because individual schools and school districts are constantly searching for highly individualized ways of making learning experiences meaningful and relevant, local resource experts, as well as teachers with special talents, are often invited to videotape explanations and demonstrations.

[17] H. Eugene Hollick, ''Dial Access Retrieval: The Future—Now!'' *Educational Television*, June 1970, p. 11.

Once this is done, the results may be subjected to tryout and, if the evaluation indicates it, revision. Through the process of recording, evaluation, and, where needed, improvement, a basic inventory of videotaped materials can grow into an inventory of tested and valuable instructional materials made available through dial access means (see Figure 12.19). Many schools now employ technicians and graphic art experts to work closely with instructors who wish to prepare learning materials of this nature.

Student-created ITV

Instructional television has too long been thought of as a medium for experts, something that could only be produced in an elaborately equipped television studio complete with technicians, soundproof glass booths, thousands of watts of light, and so forth. Fortunately, however, more and more teachers and students are realizing that television is an exciting new channel of communication that can be manipulated and used by *themselves*, even if at a rudimentary level. More and more teachers find that classroom ITV is a stimulating communication alternative and still another

FIGURE 12.19

(a) This student in a video carrel at a university is studying a lesson created by staff members who plan, record, evaluate, and recycle such individualized instructional experiences. The lessons dialed by the students are retrieved from (b) a central inventory of tapes which are activated electronically. (c) At a high school, students work individually in retrieval carrels. How does all this change the roles of learners? Of teachers? What are your feelings?

FIGURE 12.20

way to develop *visual literacy* skills. Classroom ITV offers an exciting change from the traditional dependence on writing and talking as the sole means of expressing ideas. Just as learners are thrilled with the opportunity to express themselves through overhead projectuals, 8mm motion picture films, and audiotape recorded reports—so instructional television has become useful as a creative tool of expression within the classroom environment. This is possible because easily operated, transistorized classroom versions of the more elaborate "studio" television equipment are now available.

An example of pupil-teacher-planned classroom television is drawn from the experience of one teacher in Hawaii who helped 44 elementary students to use classroom ITV to create original learning demonstrations in mathematics. This teacher undertook the classroom television project with no outside help whatsoever. She began by helping the children learn to operate the simple television cameras and videotape recorders as they discovered the capacity of the equipment for recording pictures and sound and then immediately played all of this back. The teacher found that the media specialist and the principal provided useful explanations as she and the pupils sought to gain confidence and precision in operating the equipment.

Of the group with whom the teacher worked, four boys and two girls turned out to be "naturals." They took to the machinery as ducks take to water and immediately began experimenting. Their enthusiasm spread to other members of the group, and before they knew it, an ITV lesson in mathematics was planned. It included visualized explanations and demonstrations by students. As a result of their own new insights, they planned and produced charts and diagrams with lines and print large enough to be seen on the receiver screen. They arranged demonstrations with objects that portrayed ideas in a

Given the opportunity, learners quickly master new ways to communicate. Using simple classroom television equipment, pupils created their own mathematics lessons. They planned and wrote and designed (a) visual explanations which were recorded by the television camera and evaluated on the receiver screen. (b and c) When their standards were satisfied, the entire lesson was videotaped, then (d) played back to be judged finally by classmates who approved it for use by other pupils "across the hall." What learning principles are at work here? Why is pupil involvement so high? What do you think?

very streamlined way, permitting them to condense formerly time-consuming verbal explanations (see Figure 12.20). Thus the students discovered an extremely relevant and very interesting new way to communicate their ideas. This kind of activity introduces learners to their contemporary world of technological communication.[18]

In another situation, the students at the Banks Model School in Alabama learned with enthusiasm how to operate classroom television cameras and videotape recorders. Some of these children came from homes where coal and wood fires provide the heating, but the latest color television set provides the entertainment.

[18] Antoinette Yamada, *Case Studies in Student Response Television*, a seminar report required for the master's degree in Educational Communications, University of Hawaii, August 1969.

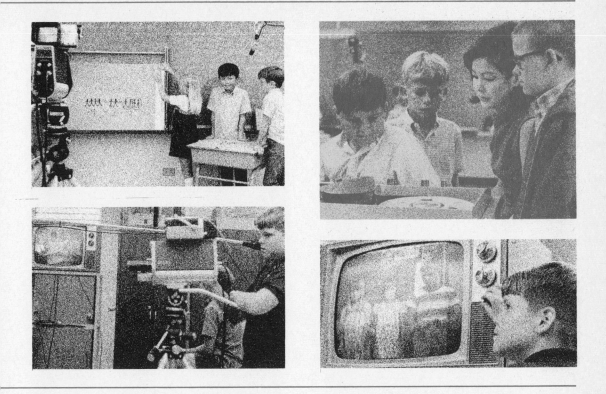

The introduction of VTR equipment into their classroom has brought a whole new creative world to them. These children control the entire sequence of instructional television, from planning to videotaping original lessons and ideas, and thus become involved in the kind of communication procedures found in the world around them (see Figure 12.21).

In many school districts around the nation, the production of actual ITV lessons is undertaken by teachers and learners who work together not only in manipulating television cameras and VTRs, but also in planning what then becomes an important activity in the life of the school.

As carried on in the Denison, Texas, public schools, pupil-teacher-planned ITV involves students and teachers in three ways. First, students help teachers develop and produce television lessons for the entire school district by setting up props,

working the cameras, and operating the console (see Figure 12.22). Second, selected pupils participate in actual television broadcasts arranged by teachers—by drawing, singing, doing demonstrations, or participating in vocabulary activities, and so forth. The third kind of student involvement in the Denison schools has been described as follows:

Teachers and principals arrange for children to describe, via ITV, their own accomplishments. Elementary students bring class projects they have made and describe these. Others exhibit pets, calves, chickens, lizards, and cats. Via ITV, high school students arrange and present newscasts and accounts of school life to their classmates and the community.[19]

19 Jerry Cunningham, "Denison Moves Ahead with ITV," in *Educational Resources and Techniques*, Fall/Winter 1970, pp. 7–9.

FIGURE 12.21

These students at the Banks Model School not only can use classroom TV cameras and VTRs; they can also stoke the potbellied stove! What observations can you make about the relevance of such television learning experiences?

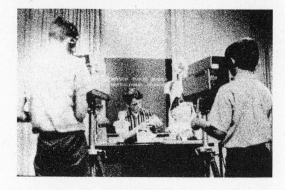

FIGURE 12.22

These Denison high school students are video-taping a pilot version of a television demonstration lesson on human anatomy to check distances and lighting and try out different ways to make the parts of the model clearly visible in an actual lesson. Students have become involved in every step of television learning—planning, arranging for the best communication devices to accomplish purposes, and operating the cameras and recording and broadcasting equipment, as well as participating as "talent." What advantages do you see in such uses of ITV?

Summary

Instructional television should be thought of as a multimedia learning experience that serves as a carrier vehicle for needed and useful subchannels: 16mm and 8mm motion picture films, filmstrips, models, live demonstrations, controlled experiments, graphics, charts, maps, diagrams, mockups, specimens, and so forth. When all of this is put together by a television media learning systems specialist, the highest kind of communication can result.

Current open-circuit public and commercial ITV ranges from the very successful "Sesame Street," which attracts audiences of millions of children, to quasi-instructional broadcasts of current news happenings—on-the-spot documentation of moon landings, presidential messages, and many kinds of social and cultural events and performances.

Instructional television is used internationally. Through centrally controlled broadcasting systems in Europe and Japan and through state, local, and independent school and university facilities in the United States, ITV is becoming responsible for larger and larger portions of "information-giving" in education.

Television is distributed largely by means of open-circuit broadcasting through the air, closed-circuit broadcasting through cable networks, and retrieval systems such as those in hundreds of school districts. Retrieval systems make it possible for students to engage in small-group and independent learning by dialing or in other ways retrieving ITV messages stored in central locations.

Instructional television uses have now been expanded through the rise of videotape recording and electronic video recording. VTR makes it possible to overcome the former scheduling difficulties and to develop great flexibility in terms of time and place usefulness.

During the last 20 years, research investigations concerned with instructional television have become increasingly refined. Early research findings often reported "no significant difference in the use of ITV versus traditional instruction in the communication of factual information." In recent years, more sophisticated television communication planning and production, along with highly refined definitions of responsibility assumed by people who guide and use television, have led to research outcomes that indicate superior results gained by those who pursue ITV learning opportunities. The most recent research evidence indicates that the classroom teacher who guides and interprets television learning resources is the single all-important factor in ITV use. When quality multimedia television learning materials are used by a teacher experienced in previewing and postviewing response activities, the highest gains in learning through instructional television are achieved.

Improvement in instructional television is virtually certain when classroom teachers participate both during the planning stages and in the final evaluation and reporting of learning outcomes. This procedure is used successfully by the producers of instructional television in London, Milwaukee, Honolulu, Hagerstown, and hundreds of other school districts of all types.

Student-created instructional television within the classroom is a promising new learning opportunity. In this activity, the new lightweight, easily operated TV cameras and VTR equipment are used by pupils and the classroom teacher in much the same way as 8mm motion picture cameras, overhead projectors, and slide projectors in creating original visual responses. More and more teachers now realize that videotape recording equipment can be used by pupils. Where once students relied on oral and written words to give accounts of demonstrations, processes, and skills, they can now use the exciting means of videotape recording. Thus demonstrations of skills and reporting of information gained through related simple research activities in the library and the community or through other courses can be created visually and audibly. Student groups may also plan and produce television lessons as such. The gains in learning are achieved because in order to produce a program, students must first have a clear grasp of the information they are attempting to interpret. As is the case with the production of 8mm silent or sound film, the production of classroom VTR reports depends largely for its efficiency on the pupils' abilities to visualize creatively.

In all of its many aspects, ITV has become a relevant, useful, and interesting means through which students learn and respond to learning.

Further learner response projects

1

Arrange to observe the classroom reception and use of an instructional television lesson or lessons, either open circuit or closed circuit. Evaluate what you see in terms of previewing activities, physical classroom arrangements for reception, and creative follow-up learner response activities. What were the roles of the pupils and teachers in carrying on all three of these areas of planning and involvement? Report your reactions.

2

Procure several instructional television study guides from an ITV program supervisor or learning resource center and examine them. As far as possible, secure those which have to do with your own grade level and subject interests. Read, study, and analyze the learning guides with respect to suggested previewing activities, arrangements for television reception, and suggested postviewing ways of employing newly learned information in creative and inventive pupil response activities.

3

Apply the evaluation criteria in this chapter, pages 526–537, to the classroom use of an ITV lesson you have used or observed being used. What are your overall reactions? What suggestions do you have for lesson content, improving the communication devices employed within the lesson itself, the use of verbal versus visual demonstrations, etc., and for improving the involvement of the learners and their interaction with the lesson?

4

Seek out your local ITV authority and report your findings in Project 3 to him. Report to your classmates and/or your instructor the results of your interview. What developments do you anticipate?

5

Explain to your pupils how television can be used in your own classroom and what it can become. Borrow the school's ½-inch videotape recorder. Demonstrate (or arrange with your audiovisual specialist to demonstrate) how the camera is operated, how videotape recording is done, how the receiver is adjusted, etc. Encourage the students to examine their own visual literacy experiences for ways and means of creating a small-group or class project in original television production and playback. Some suggestions: demonstrations of skills learned in science, home economics, industrial arts, etc. Use charts, models, mock-ups, etc. Use creative dramatic interpretations of literary episodes drawn from pupils' selected works, sociodramas about school affairs, musical performances. Encourage self-evaluation of these. What responses were gained?

6

Do the same, using as the core effort visual documentation of the students' school, neighborhood, and community. Encourage them to collect visual evidence: news pictures, magazine photographs, visual evidence secured from local businesses, advertisers, trade associations, or, best of all, photographed personally. These visual literacy experiences (see Chapter 4) can then become the core

information included in their television report. How did the pupils respond to this activity? What are your feelings about using television communication as the means through which learners expand their skills beyond using traditional spoken and written words to report their feelings, suggestions, and value judgments?

References

CHU, GODWIN C., and WILBUR SCHRAMM. *Learning from Television: What the Research Says.* Stanford University, Institute for Communication Research, December 1967. (Also ERIC-ED 014900, *Research in Education,* Vol. 3, No. 5, May 1968.)

CUNNINGHAM, JERRY. "Denison Moves Ahead with ITV." *Educational Resources and Techniques,* Fall/Winter 1970, pp. 7–9.

CYR, DON. "To See Ourselves." *Arts and Activities,* Vol. 67, May 1970.

Design for ETV Planning for Schools with Television. New York Educational Facilities Laboratory, 1960.

GORDON, GEORGE N. *Classroom Television: New Frontiers in TV.* Communication Arts Books. Hastings House, 1970.

HOBAN, CHARLES F. "The Usable Residue of Educational Film Research." In *Teaching Aids for the American Classroom.* Stanford University, Institute for Communication Research, 1960, p. 105.

HOLLICK, EUGENE. "Dial Access Retrieval: The Future—Now!" *Educational Television,* June 1970, p. 11.

McKUENE, LAWRENCE. *National Compendium of Televised Education,* Vol. 15. Michigan State University Continuing Education Service, 1968.

MURPHY, JUDITH, and RONALD GROSS. *Learning by Television.* Georgian Press, 1966.

SCHRAMM, WILBUR, JACK LYLE, and EDWIN B. PARKER. *Television in the Lives of Our Children.* Stanford University Press, 1961.

WHITE, RALPH S. "Teaching Speech with Television." *Educational Television,* December 1970.

WITTICH, WALTER A., and JOHN GUY FOWLKES. *Audiovisual Paths to Learning.* Harper & Row, 1946.

Media references

A Case Study in the Elementary School, 16mm film, b/w, 30 min. National Association of Educational Broadcasters.

Examples in the Secondary School, 16mm film, b/w, 30 min. National Association of Educational Broadcasters.

Preparing the Television Lesson, 16mm film, b/w, 30 min. National Association of Educational Broadcasters.

Promising Practices, 16mm film, b/w, 30 min. National Association of Educational Broadcasters.

The Role of the Classroom Teacher, 16mm film, b/w, 30 min. National Association of Educational Broadcasters.

Television, Line by Line, 16mm film, sound,

color, 11 min. International Film Bureau, 1969.

What Television Brings to the Classroom, 16mm

film, b/w, 30 min. National Association of Educational Broadcasters.

Source references

See source lists in the Appendix; particularly relevant sections are: Networks; Videotape Recorders.

See *Student Production Guide,* Chapter 4, "Producing Photo and Sound Materials for Instruction," Videotape Production.

THIRTEEN
Computers, simulation, and games

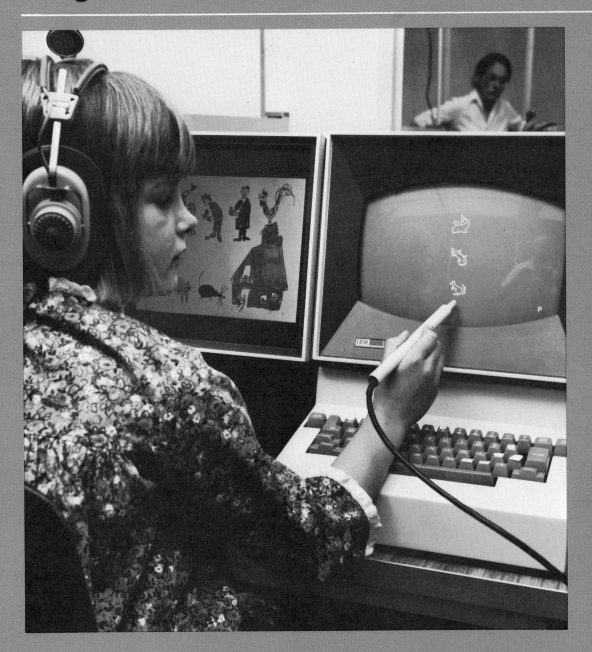

Objectives	Performance responses

1

To identify and discriminate among three or more distinctive types of computer use in instruction.

Given a set of six program printouts or descriptions, identify each according to the classification used in this chapter and write the reasons for your identification in each case. Divide your class into discussion groups of four to six students and exchange and critique the papers.

2

To assess the relative advantages and limitations of computerized instruction.

From a list of 15 statements supplied by the instructor, select 4 that correctly describe advantages, 4 that correctly describe disadvantages, and 4 that are inaccurate or inadequate statements of either strengths or limitations of computerized instruction.

3

To identify 10 administrative benefits of computer services in education.

Divide your class into six committees. Assign each committee the responsibility of investigating and reporting back to the class on one of the six pairs of administrative functions listed below in terms of (a) how the computer is applied to the indicated functions and (b) the benefits realized over former methods. The investigation should preferably include a visit to a computer installation and/or discussions with business officials of a school district or college using computer services. The functions are (1) payroll and personnel records, (2) purchasing and inventory, (3) budgeting and budget control, (4) student admissions and records, (5) class and classroom scheduling, (6) program planning and evaluation.

4

To assess the probable future role of the computer and of yourself in relation to it as a teacher in your school or college between 1975 and 1980, given a set of assumptions.

Using a planning team, plus the investigating teams set up in Response 3, have each of the latter prepare a one-page summary (based on a given set of assumptions) in the form of parallel items in two columns. The columns should be headed: "Probable future computer applications to instruction" and "Implications for changes in teachers' roles." The assumptions are: (1) Computer costs will come down to about the present per pupil costs of instruction. (2) Available dollars per pupil will increase slowly, if at all.

Objectives	Performance responses

(3) Emphasis on individualized instruction programs will increase. (4) Public pressure on the schools and colleges will continue undiminished. (5) Validated CAI programs will increase in number and quality. The planning team should arrange a critique session, a symposium, a debate, or other suitable activity to distill the essence of the findings for the class. Copies of the summary reports should be duplicated and given to each member of the class.

5

To identify learning activities particularly appropriate to computerized instruction, to simulation and gaming, and to neither, given a list of specified learning activities.

From a list of 10 or more learning activities supplied by the instructor, classify each according to appropriateness as specified in Objective 5 and supply justification for your selections. Use a format of three columns headed: "Activity," "Preferable medium," "Reason."

6

To describe and differentiate among the several types of stimulation and gaming.

Using the definitions and examples provided in the chapter, write descriptions of two or more different kinds of simulation and two or more different kinds of games. Then identify and list topics, in your own teaching area if possible, for which each type might be of significant value.

ALTHOUGH educators have long supported the principles of individualized instruction, they have, in general, done relatively little implementing of these principles. It is true that most teachers have tried to compensate for the lock-step classroom situation—every child doing the same thing at the same time—by giving special attention to certain children even at the expense of others. Nevertheless, such efforts have only limited success at best because it is impossible for one or two teachers to give the amount of attention to each student that individualized instruction implies or to keep track of the many details involved in relating each child's performance to a series of specific curriculum objectives. (Specific ways to individualize instruction within the context of our present technological capacities are discussed in detail in the next chapter.)

Computers

MOST individualized instruction efforts so far have concentrated on self-pacing alone; indeed, instituting even *that* change requires individualized scheduling and quite extensive records. Furthermore, when we go beyond self-pacing into providing different instructional objectives for different students, into program branching, and into letting some students select their own objectives and the learning resources needed to obtain them, the records and the scheduling problems become immensely complicated. For these reasons, educators are beginning to take a serious look at computers as the only practical and available long-term solution to such problems.

Looking toward future developments in education, Wayne Holtzman, psychologist and dean of the College of Education at the University of Texas, predicts the disappearance of the lock-step, self-contained classroom and the uniformly prescribed curriculum. Instead, he says, there will be learning resources centers with computerized libraries and individual study carrels hooked into remotely located computers (see Figure 13.1). Such centers will play a central role in educational programs extending from preschool through the continuing education of adults. He continues:

Computers will take over most of the drudgery of scheduling, allocating learning resources to individuals and groups, maintaining progress records while preserving their confidentiality where appropriate, compiling and scoring tests, providing easy access to files of information for reference or guidance by students and teachers, and a host of other management activities. For major segments of the curriculum, the computer will also provide direct interaction between the student and the subject matter to be learned, whether the instruction involves drill and practice in arithmetic or foreign language, tutorial interaction and dialogue, or problem solving and simulation of complex phenomena.[1]

[1] Wayne H. Holtzman, ed., *Computer-Assisted Instruction, Testing, and Guidance*, Harper & Row, 1970, p. 3.

FIGURE 13.1

Learner response centers can be used for a variety of teaching-learning experiences at all levels. (a and b) These pictures taken at the Responsive Environments Program Center in New York show computerized booth facilities and monitors. (c) This "talking typewriter" is a multisensory (sight, sound, tactile) computer-based synchronized learning system for teaching reading, typing, and other skills.

Many problems remain to be solved before such complete use of computers in education can become reality, including the primary ones of cost and the generation of vast amounts of validated self-instructional programs. But as educators in today's schools we must be aware of what is already going on and what is in prospect as we consider the potentials of computers in the improved educational programs that are so badly needed in our schools. One thing that is going on, as most of us know, is the extensive use of computers in business and industry and in military and space operations. Yet we may *not* be aware of the extent to which computers are already being used in education and the implications of these uses for future developments.

In this chapter, we deal with a number of computer applications in education. Most of them are still experimental, but some, such as those related to administration, are already in widespread use. As you read about the several kinds of computer applications, consider the implications that computers may have for your own school and for your own role as a teacher in the days that lie ahead.

What is a computer?

A *computer* is a power-driven machine equipped with keyboards, electronic circuits, storage compartments, and recording devices for the high-speed performance of mathematical operations.

As this definition implies, a computer is, in simple terms, a glorified calculator with the added capacity of storing or "memorizing" large amounts of information and producing, or retrieving, any of it when called for. The typical calculator, of course, does not have this "memory." A tape recorder does, however; the way information is stored on audiotape for later retrieval is similar in principle to the way the computer stores its information. Essen-

tially, then, what we have in a computer is a machine that stores and processes information and performs desired calculations electronically and at a very high rate of speed.

SOME GENERAL TERMINOLOGY Our discussion of computerized instruction avoids technical terms. This is intentional, since our basic purposes are to introduce the subject of computers in education and to develop certain concepts with respect to their current and future potentials. For these purposes, technical terms are unnecessary; indeed, they might even be distracting, particularly since a number of computer terms do not have standard meanings.

The most commonly used label for computer uses in instruction at the present time is *CAI* or *computer-assisted instruction*. Others include CBI (computer-based instruction), CMI (computer-managed instruction), and CAL (computer-assisted learning). Such names may derive from particular uses of computers or certain university projects or specific computer manufacturers. As a result, any single term can mean different things to different readers. Karl Zinn, one of the leading authorities and author of a comprehensive survey of the field, points out that most uses of the label CAI represent a fairly narrow definition of computer use, namely, drill and practice and tutorial modes[2] (see Figure 13.2). Others, however, use the term to represent the whole field of computer use in instruction. It is important, therefore, to ascertain the intended meaning

[2] Karl L. Zinn, *An Evaluative Review of Uses of Computers in Instruction*, Project CLUE (Computer Learning Under Evaluation), Final Report, USOE Contract No. OEC–5–9–32–509–0032, University of Michigan Press, Ann Arbor, December 1970, p. 3. (Copy available from ERIC Clearing House on Educational Media and Technology, Institute for Communication Research, Stanford University, Stanford, California 94305.)

FIGURE 13.2

The drill-and-practice use of computers illustrated here is one of their simplest instructional
applications. If this were the only kind of application of computers in a school, what questions
might logically be raised?

or scope in interpreting such general terms.
For those who wish to become familiar with
some of the more technical terms, glossaries
are available.[3]

HOW COMPUTERS FUNCTION   One of
the most obvious and generally understood
advantages of computers is their speed

[3] A particularly useful glossary in which terms are
defined from an educational orientation has been
prepared by Zinn, op. cit., Appendix E. Two longer
glossaries with complete technical definitions are:
Vocabulary for Information Processing, American
National Standards Institute, 1430 Broadway,
New York, N.Y. 10018, 1970; *Automatic Data
Processing Glossary*, Bureau of the Budget, Washington, D.C., Government Printing Office, 1964.
Shorter and less technical glossaries are available
from most computer manufacturers and some
professional associations.

and accuracy in solving mathematical
problems of all levels of complexity. Let
us digress for a moment and explore this
mathematical capacity a bit further, using
as an example a very practical problem—
assigning classes to teachers.

A typical problem that computers are
especially helpful in solving involves getting the most out of limited resources. For
example, consider a science department
chairman who is faced with the problem
of assigning five teachers in five subjects
—general science, biology, chemistry,
physics, earth sciences—so that the best
possible job will be done. All five teachers
can teach all five subjects, but each one is
much better in some subjects than others,
as indicated in Table 13.1, which shows
their relative ratings in teaching abilities.

TABLE 13.1

The chairman's problem is to assign one teacher to each subject so as to make the best overall use of all five. Obviously, he cannot assign each one to his best subject because teachers A and C are both best (6) in earth sciences. There is little choice with teacher D, who is "good" (4) in one subject only, but quite a lot of choice with teacher C, who is "good" or better all around. Thus there must be some sort of compromise to get optimum use of all five teachers. By using some fairly elementary arithmetic and what mathematicians call a *5 × 5 matrix*, it is possible in 5 or 10 minutes with a paper and pencil to come up with the solution indicated by parentheses in Table 13.2. Note that three teachers are assigned to their second-best courses and two to their best courses. In the assignment pattern as a whole, however, every class has a teacher whose rank is at least "good" (4) on the scale.

The problem just described is a relatively simple one. With more complex problems, a computer is indispensable. For example, the five-teacher problem involves only 120 possible combinations, but if there were 10 teachers involved and the task was to assign these 10 persons optimally to 10 positions, there would be 3,628,000 possible patterns from which to select the best one. It could still be done manually, but it would take many hours at best, whereas the computer could do it in minutes or less.[4] In any case, much larger than 10 × 10 matrices are commonly run on computers —matrices that would take months or years to solve with a desk-type calculator.

The computer's power to process huge masses of information and to solve complex problems is difficult to comprehend. Commenting on this point, John Pfeiffer draws the following helpful analogy:

[4] John Pfeiffer, *New Look at Educational-Systems Analysis in Our Schools and Colleges*, Western Publishing Co., 1968, pp. 34–36.

TABLE 13.2

Perhaps the critical fact is that today's fastest models are some one to two million times faster than a man at a desk-type adding machine, which is about the difference between a day and a millennium and means that studies are being undertaken routinely that were unthinkable less than a decade or so ago.[5]

Assuming that the reader is properly impressed but still somewhat skeptical, his next thought probably is, "Fine, but as a classroom teacher I have very little need to solve complex mathematical problems of any kind, so what does all of this have to do with me and my teaching" The answer is that most of what the computer *does* is done in mathematical terms. Even the scanning of literature or the retrieval of textual information by computer requires a translation into mathematical terms first. In other words, information and

[5] Ibid., p. 37.

	General science	Biology	Chemistry	Physics	Earth sciences
Teacher A	1	3	2	3	6
Teacher B	2	4	3	1	5
Teacher C	5	6	3	4	6
Teacher D	3	1	4	2	2
Teacher E	1	5	6	5	4

Source: John Pfeiffer, *New Look at Education-Systems Analysis in our Schools and Colleges,* Western Publishing Co., 1968, p. 35.

Note: Rating scale: from 6 = Excellent to 1 = Poor.

	General science	Biology	Chemistry	Physics	Earth sciences
Teacher A	1	3	2	3	(6)
Teacher B	2	(4)	3	1	5
Teacher C	(5)	6	3	4	6
Teacher D	3	1	(4)	2	2
Teacher E	1	5	6	(5)	4

Source: Pfeiffer, op. cit., p. 35.

problems of whatever type are translated via computer languages into numerical terms, along with the procedures and formulas necessary to process the information when the computer is called upon to do so. At that point, and with the additional input supplied by the student at the console, the computer performs the necessary calculations, translates the answer back into ordinary English, and types it out on the student's teletypewriter for him to read. And normally this all takes place in far less time than it has taken you to read the last two sentences!

Whether we shall one day seriously put this power to work in instructional programs remains to be seen. But computers certainly are here and here to stay. Though relatively few school systems now own their own computers, many are hooked up by telephone lines or other means with commercial computer services on which they buy time for administrative functions.

These uses and a few more general uses are briefly described next.

COMPUTER USES IN ADMINISTRATION
An important factor to keep in mind as we consider possible computer uses in instruction is the fact that large numbers of educational systems already use computers for a variety of administrative purposes. Holtzman cites several applications adapted from business and industry:

The most immediate applications in public school systems and higher education involve the simple transfer and adaptation of techniques developed successfully in business and industry. Such daily transactional activities as purchasing, payroll, inventory, personnel records, and auditing are being rapidly computerized. In the larger, more sophisticated systems, operations research and improved methods of forecasting are being developed. Pro-

gram planning, budgeting, and control, as well as improved estimation of cost effectiveness, require greatly improved processing of information.[6]

In addition to typical business management applications, computers are also widely used to serve a variety of administrative needs which are unique to education. These include such operations as the processing of information for student admissions, continuous updating of student records, scheduling of classes, registration of students, maintaining certain personnel and guidance records, and the storage and retrieval of much information traditionally found in libraries.

Computers are costly machines; thus their purchase or lease can be justified only in terms of values received which are clearly above and beyond those that could reasonably be achieved without them. Such justification has been well established for administrative purposes. Many computerized information-processing operations actually cost less than formerly and yet are accomplished with infinitely greater speed and convenience. More important, however, are the many new operations the computer has made possible which could not be achieved without it at any price. The instantaneous processing of election returns is a familiar example. Man's flights to the moon and other space explorations are more dramatic examples. There are hundreds, perhaps thousands, of routine, unspectacular examples of information processing performed by computers without which administrators in government, industry, and some sectors of education could not function at comparable levels of effectiveness.

Thus availability per se is not the central question as we think about computer uses in instruction. The computers are already there and widely used for administrative purposes, though there are

additional costs for whatever additional time is used on them for instruction. Under these circumstances, therefore, the central question becomes one of the legitimacy and feasibility of the educational uses to which computers can be applied. Let us take a look at some examples.

Instructional uses of computers

There are a variety of legitimate instructional uses for computers. These can be conveniently classified in four groups: drill and practice; tutorial and dialogue; simulation and gaming; and aids for information handling. We shall examine each of these types briefly, plus a fifth and different kind of use, that is, the use of the computer as a subject of instruction in itself.

Typically, the student sits at a specially designed electric typewriter which is connected to a computer by telephone lines. He identifies himself by a code number and his name, the machine types out the first question, he types the answer—and the lesson is under way.

DRILL AND PRACTICE   The following example of a computerized drill comes from an elementary mathematics drill-and-practice program developed by Patrick Suppes at the Institute for Mathematical Studies in the Social Sciences at Stanford University during the mid-1960s. Along with a language skills curriculum by Suppes and Richard Atkinson, the mathematics curriculum was tested initially in the schools of Palo Alto, California; McComb, Mississippi; Waterford, Michigan; and New York City. In the following drill, the computer, after printing out each problem, positions the typewriter to accept the response in a blank. The fact that the computer goes on to a new problem tells the student he has answered correctly. In this drill the student's responses are underlined.

[6] Holtzman, op. cit., pp. 5–6.

Sample Printout of a Lesson Taken by a Fifth-Grade Student

Please Type Your Name
Mike O'Dell
    Drill Number 509013
$(42 + 63)/7 = (42/7 + (63/7)$
$48 - 38 = 38 - 48$
    Wrong
$48 - 38 = 38 - 4$
    Wrong, Answer is 28
$43 - 38 = 38 - 28$
$76 - (26 - 10) = (76 - 26) + 10$
$4 \times (7 + 13) = (4 \times 7) + (4 \times 13)$
$(53 - 20) - 11 = 53 - (20 + 11)$
$32 + (74 + 18) = (32 + 74) + 18$
$51 \times (36 \times 12) = (51 \times 36) \times 12$
$17 \times (14 + 34) = (17 \times 14) + (17 \times 34)$
$362 + 943 = 943 + 362$
$(5 + 8) \times 7 = 5 \times 7) + (8 \times 7)$
$(90/10)/3 = 90/(10 \times 3)$
$(72/9)/4 = 72/(9 \times 4)$
$(54 + 18)/6 = (54/6) + (18/\underline{\quad})$
    Time Is Up
$(54 + 18)/6 = (54/6) + (18/6)$
$60 - (19 - 12) = (60 - 19) + 12$
$72 \times (43 \times 11) = (72 \times 43) \times 11$
$(63/7) + (56/7) = (63 + 7)/7$
    Wrong
$(63/7) + (56/7) = (63 + 56)/7$
    End of Drill Number 509013
13 May 1966
16 Problems

	Number	Percent
Correct	13	81
Wrong	2	12
Time Outs	1	6
Wrong		
2		
16		
Time Outs		
13		

222.7 Seconds This Drill
Correct This Concept—81 Percent, Correct to Date—59 Percent
4 Hours, 46 Minutes, 59 Seconds Overall

Goodbye Mike[7]

7 Patrick Suppes, Max Jerman, and Dow Brian, *Computer-Assisted Instruction: Stanford's 1965–66 Arithmetic Program*, Academic Press, 1968, p. 29.

This lesson is an example of one of the simpler forms of computer uses in instruction, but, as you can readily see, the availability of such drill-and-practice exercises on a computer terminal could materially relieve the teacher of having to administer such work himself. More important, it would make unnecessary much routine paper marking and record keeping, since the computer keeps track of each student's performance and can "read back" to the teacher a summation of each student's work whenever he wants it.

As you also noted, whenever the student makes an error, the computer immediately calls it to his attention; the student then knows that he should try again. Depending on the program in the computer, after a predetermined number of "wrongs" the student might be referred or "branched" to a remedial exercise if necessary. In the quoted drill, however, the computer has been programed merely to give the correct answer after two wrong answers. In any case, the successful student can move ahead to new material as rapidly as his performance warrants. Just as in programed instruction, the student moves at his own pace, gets immediate feedback on his efforts, and receives individual tutoring if needed (see Figure 13.3).

The Stanford programs are still in development stages as this is written, but there is clear evidence that they have resulted in effective learning. Interestingly enough, students with lower-level intellectual skills and poor motivation have shown greater gains under the Stanford programs than in standard classrooms.[8]

TUTORIAL AND DIALOGUE Tutorial programs differ from drill-and-practice programs in that the subject content is literally "taught" by the computer program. Information may be presented much

8 Zinn in Holtzman, op. cit., p. 278.

FIGURE 13.3

In well-designed computer lessons a kind of interaction takes place between the lesson and the student which is not unlike that between teacher and student.

as it would be in a programed instruction text. In fact, in designing computer programs of this nature, the same precise analysis of the learning task and specification of objectives must be used as is used in designing programed instruction lessons.

The computer, however, may provide various options not usually present in programed texts. For example, explanations may be given orally via audiotape and needed visuals presented on a cathode ray tube (CRT) very much like the tube in a television set. The student may respond to questions on a typewriter keyboard or by pointing or drawing with a light pen on an electronic screen or CRT in his study carrel (see Figure 13.4). The computer, in turn, reacts to the student's response by indicating that it is correct or by "talking" to him in some manner if it is not

(immediate feedback). The student then makes a further response. Thus a kind of dialogue takes place between the student and the machine.

The Brentwood Tutorial Mathematics Program is one of the better known examples of computerized tutorial programs. This program also was developed by Patrick Suppes at the Institute for Mathematical Studies in the Social Sciences at Stanford University, during the middle and later 1960s. Under this system, which is used to teach mathematics to first-graders, some 400 lessons were developed covering the topics of counting, numerals, addition, subtraction, linear measure, set notation, and geometry. Each student responds to questions and practice problems either on his typewriter or by using a light pen to touch one of the answer choices presented on the CRT. He receives audiotaped instructions and directions through a headset. Also, if he responds incorrectly or fails to respond within a reasonable time, he receives special additional audio instructions. An example from one of the lessons illustrates how the program unfolds:

For one problem, a drawing of a car and a drawing of a truck surrounded by set braces and followed by an equal sign were presented on the CRT; this problem was accompanied by the audio message, "There are two members in this set." After this message, two more sets, one empty and one

FIGURE 13.4

Student responses to computer-presented questions or directions can be drawn or written with a light pen in some cases, in addition to the usual use of an electronic typewriter keyboard.

containing a train and a steam shovel, each preceded by a box, were displayed below the initial set; the choices were accompanied by the audio instructions, "Find another set with two members." At this point a small "p" (for pen) was displayed in the corner of the CRT as a signal to the student to respond. If the student touched his light pen to the box in front of the correct choice, a smiling face was displayed and he heard, "Yes, the sets have the same number of members," and proceeded to the next problem.

If the student did not respond within 20 seconds, he heard, "Which set below has two members?" If the student responded incorrectly, he heard the audio message, "Point to the box next to the set with two members," and saw a sad face. For most problems in the curriculum, students were allowed three chances to produce the correct answer.[9]

In most of the lessons, the number of initially correct responses is accumulated

[9] Patrick Suppes and Mona Morningstar, "Four Programs in Computer-Assisted Instruction" in Holtzman, op. cit., p. 243.

FIGURE 13.5

When remedial assistance is needed in a computerized learning situation, the computer calls the teacher.

on the computer, and as soon as the student reaches a specified number of correct responses, he is permitted to skip the rest of the problems and go on to the next lesson.

As mentioned, both explanations and practice problems contain special audio messages heard only by students not performing up to predetermined standards. Furthermore, if the student makes a certain number of errors during a lesson, he is branched to a remedial lesson containing the same kinds of problems but with a slower development of ideas and simpler vocabulary. If a student fails to meet the remedial criterion, the computer automatically calls the proctor or teacher to come and assist (see Figure 13.5).

Computerized tutorial and dialogue programs have been developed in many subject areas. The following example is one of a series used in English grammar for intermediate-grade pupils as part of a computer-based individualized instruction program called INDICOM used in the Waterford Township Schools near Pontiac, Michigan (see Figure 13.6). The computer's parts of the dialogue with the student are in capital letters.

SIMULATION AND GAMING   Computers also are useful in simulation and gaming exercises. Simulation and games constitute a broad area of instructional method which is discussed in more detail later in this chapter. Simulations are representations of real-life situations with some of the real elements removed for such reasons as safety (driver or pilot training), unavailability of equipment because of expense or complexity (the cyclotron) or length of time involved (genetic or population studies). Games are employed in many simulated exercises in order to introduce an element of competition for teams or individuals.

For example, experts at the Huntington Computer Project in New York have been working with a number of high schools for several years on explorations of various

OBJECTIVE: YOU WILL BE ABLE TO SELECT THE SUBJECT FROM A GIVEN SENTENCE.
THE SUBJECT OF A SENTENCE DOES SOMETHING. EXAMPLE: THE GIRLS PLAYED CARDS. GIRLS IS THE SUBJECT BECAUSE THEY ARE DOING SOMETHING. TYPE THE SUBJECTS IN THESE SENTENCES. JANE MADE A PIE.

Jane

JANE IS THE SUBJECT BECAUSE SHE IS DOING SOMETHING.
TOMMY SAT ON A TACK.

Tommy

THE SUBJECT OF A SENTENCE NAMES A PERSON, PLACE, OR THING. IN THE EXAMPLES ABOVE WHAT DID THE SUBJECTS NAME: PERSONS, PLACES, OR THINGS?

persons

WHAT IS THE SUBJECT IN THE NEXT SENTENCE? HIS RED WAGON IS BROKEN.

wagon

WAGON IS A THING. IS THE SUBJECT IN THE NEXT SENTENCE A THING?
COLUMBUS IS THE CAPITAL OF OHIO.

no

WHAT IS IT?

place

A WAY OF FINDING THE SUBJECT IS TO SAY WHO DOES SOMETHING. WHAT WORD ANSWERS THAT QUESTION IN THE NEXT SENTENCE?
SALLY SAW HER DOG.

Sally

LOOK AT THE NEXT SENTENCE: THE CLOCK STRUCK THREE. SINCE CLOCK CANNOT ANSWER THE QUESTION WHO DOES SOMETHING, SHOULD YOU ASK INSTEAD WHAT DOES SOMETHING?

yes

TO FIND THE SUBJECT YOU MIGHT ASK WHO OR WHAT IS DOING SOMETHING.

008 PROBLEMS 008 CORRECT 100 PERCENT 02 MIN. 54 SEC.

THAT IS ALL FOR TODAY. 14:44:48
& C M S P L A PROGRAM
WATERFORD SCHOOLS—ESEA TITLE III
TEAR OFF ON DOTTED LINE[10]

[10] Communications Math Skill Program—Language Arts. Produced by INDICOM Project, Title III, ESEA, Waterford School District, Pontiac, Mich.

FIGURE 13.6

The degree of concentration and involvement of students in the Waterford, Michigan, INDICOM project is readily apparent in these pictures.

simulation uses of the computer in the classroom. They have experimented with computer simulations in biology, chemistry, earth science, physics, and social studies. Some simulations are used to enrich existing experiments and other classroom activities; others, however, are used to provide experiences which would otherwise be impossible to achieve within the high school classroom.

Examples of the latter include a program in evolution, called STERL, which permits the student to experiment with control of pests through a combination of pesticides and the injection of sterilized males into the community. Another program, called EDER1, permits the student to explore the concepts of scarcity, opportunity, and allocation of available resources. The EDER1 program is designed as a game against nature in a Robinson Crusoe environment—the student is placed on an uninhabited island 48 hours before a severe hurricane is due and must use the natural resources of the island to secure adequate food, water, and shelter before the hurricane hits.[11]

In addition to providing cognitive learning, simulation and games can provide practice in decision-making skills as well as theoretical tests of hypotheses in quite abstract situations. One familiar example is the predicting of future economic developments. Because a number of variables can readily be manipulated on the computer, it is possible for the student to test out various hypotheses.

In one such simulation problem, the student must decide on the best course of action to follow in planning for future sales of projection equipment. To begin with, he has access to several types of information, such as past sales of this equip-

[11] L. Braun, *The Digital Computer as a General-Purpose Simulator*, Huntington Computer Project, Polytechnic Institute of Brooklyn, Brooklyn, N.Y., 1970.

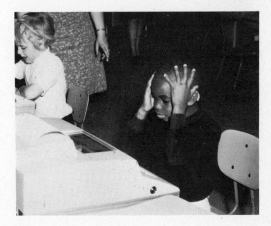

ment, market trends, enrollment growth in the schools, costs of manufacturing the equipment, and costs of sales to this point. With the computer, he can rather quickly test out a series of assumptions or "ifs" to help him make the best decisions. If, for instance, school income stays about the same, but school costs increase by 5 percent during the next 12 months, what is the likely effect on sales of this equipment? If, on the other hand, school income increases by 5 percent and costs go up 6 percent, what is likely to be the net effect on such sales? Clearly, there are other factors to consider than just these two variables, and a good simulation program would have them built in. But the point is that such variables and various combinations of them can rather readily be tested out with a computer, whereas such testing would be far more difficult without it.

Simulation on economic principles has even been tested with sixth-graders by the Board of Cooperative Educational Services in northern Westchester County, New York. Two simulation games were developed, each involving one person playing against a computer.[12] In the Sumerian game the student plays the role of the priest-ruler of a city-state in ancient Mesopotamia. He must make decisions on how to allocate resources, apply surplus grain to the development of crafts, and promote trade. The Sierra Leone Development Project transforms the student into a member of the Agency for International Development making decisions on how best to allocate funds to help solve the economic problems of a newly emerging nation.[13] Both slides and audiotape were used in these simu-

[12] R. L. Wing, "Two Computer-Based Economic Games for Sixth-Graders" in *Simulation, Games and Learning*, Sarane S. Boocock and E. O. Schild, eds., Sage Publications, Beverly Hills, Calif., 1968.

[13] Both games are available by special arrangement with the Board of Cooperative Educational Services, 845 Fox Meadow Road, Yorktown Heights, N.Y. 10598.

lations, along with the computer program. Three computer consoles were available so that three students (or three small groups) could play the game at a time. The games were designed for individualized instruction and thus provide a considerable variety of options, not only in terms of self-pacing, but also by means of variations in content, difficulty of problems, style, and modes of presentation. A research study on the programs showed that in comparison with conventional classroom teaching on the same topics, the students working on computers achieved about the same amount of learning in considerably less time.

An example of simulation applications of the computer at a higher level involves a student exploring a simple concept in wildlife management. The setting is a salmon-fishing operation. Zinn thus explains the game:

The object of the game is to build up and maintain a population which will maximize the catch taken by the fishery. The size of the run for the coming year is determined by the computer in some way not known to the student, although he does know it depends on the previous year's escapement.

To the following printout of a "conversation" between computer (in capital letters) and student are added Zinn's comments in the right-hand column.

INFORMATION HANDLING A fourth general type of computer use in instruction is the handling and processing of information so that it can be called upon by the learner, teacher, counselor, or researcher as needed. Although computers have the capacity of storing and retrieving large masses of information on any subject desired, we are still some years away from totally computerized libraries in which information on almost any subject can be retrieved at will (some efforts to move toward this goal are described in Chapter 10).

Conversation

WHICH MANAGEMENT STRATEGY DO YOU WANT
TO ADOPT?

    catch

CATCH FOR 1969
    16,000

ESCAPEMENT = 2,000

CATCH FOR 1970
    10,000

ESCAPEMENT = 1,000

CATCH FOR 1971
    5,000

ESCAPEMENT = 1,000
THE MEN AT THE FISHERY ARE DISTURBED
ABOUT THE LOW CATCH

CATCH FOR 1972
    10,000

NO FISH ESCAPED. LET'S START OVER AGAIN

WHICH MANAGEMENT STRATEGY DO YOU WANT
TO ADOPT?

    escapement

ESCAPEMENT FOR 1969?
    15,000

CATCH = 3,000
THE MEN AT THE FISHERY ARE FURIOUS ABOUT
THE LOW CATCH

ESCAPEMENT FOR 1970?
    15,000

CATCH = 11,000

ESCAPEMENT FOR 1971?
    10,000

CATCH = 15,000

ESCAPEMENT FOR 1972?
    9,000

CATCH = 21,000

ESCAPEMENT FOR 1973?
    9,000

CATCH = 19,000

YOUR TOTAL CATCH FOR THE LAST FIVE YEARS
HAS BEEN 68,000 SALMON—13,600 PER YEAR.
DO YOU WISH TO DISCUSS THE OPTIMUM
STRATEGY NOW?

Commentary

The player has the choice of setting either
escapement or catch.

The player sets the catch at 16,000 fish.

The computer supplies the size of the escapement and asks about the next year.

The student notes that when 2,000 escape
(1969, above) the next year's run is 11,000
(catch of 10,000 plus 1,000 escaping).

The student should have kept the catch down
until the population had recovered.

This time he will try the safer strategy of setting
the number of fish which must be permitted to
escape to spawn before the fishery can begin to
catch.

The student holds firm because he expects a
much bigger run the next year.

The student graphs the data so far, infers a
relationship between escapement and the run the
following year, and is ready to switch to a sub-
program which will "discuss" with him the
optimum strategy.[14]

---

[14] Zinn, Project CLUE Report, op. cit., pp. 18–19.

Nonetheless, as already indicated, information and programs on a great many selected topics or units can readily be stored in a computer, and use of this "filing" capacity, though expensive, may be warranted for specialized information which might otherwise be difficult to obtain, such as statistical tables on employment, production, and population and other types of data which are continually updated. Computerized management of documents in libraries is already in process, and computer programs that manage all of the major activities of a library, from ordering to file search and revision, are only a matter of time. When such systems have been inaugurated by properly computerized major libraries, such as the Library of Congress, the establishment of data banks for smaller libraries will be a relatively simple matter that can be expected to proceed fairly rapidly.[15]

One of the areas in which the information-handling capacity of computers is being used to advantage is counseling and guidance. Whether a machine can in fact be programed to "counsel" is still an unanswered question, but there is no question that the data storage and processing capacity of computers can be a tremendous aid to both students and counselors:

The counselor of today is often caught in a paradoxical situation. He spends ever more time collecting, recording and evaluating data about his students, and ever less time relating to those students as human beings. Yet, today's advanced information processing technology should enable him to shift to the computer the burden of data handling, freeing him to fulfill his unique function as a counselor.[16]

The essence of the guidance systems now in use or under development is that the computer can store complete cumulative records (IQs, grades, test scores, extracurricular activities, interest inventories, etc.) and match them with a wide range of occupational or educational choice requirements so as to indicate probabilities of success. For example, the School District of Philadelphia and the Willowbrook High School, a large comprehensive high school outside Chicago, use computer technology to give students and counselors information about occupational opportunities in the area, educational and training programs necessary, and other facts helpful in making curriculum choices.

The Palo Alto Unified School District provides computer-based course selection assistance by means of a dialogue between the student and the computer; the computer is programed to include information about the success of former students on college entrance examinations, various kinds of jobs, and pertinent course information in later high school grades. The City School District of Rochester, New York, uses a multimedia package, including occupational materials on microfilm and related information and training units, to help students in making occupational or educational decisions. Still more sophisticated automated guidance systems are under development at Harvard University[17] and at the Systems Development Corporation in Santa Monica.[18]

The above examples of how the information-handling capacity of the computer can be effectively applied are but initial in-

[15] Holtzman, op. cit., p. 8.

[16] *Layman's Guide to the Use of Computers*, Association for Educational Data Systems, 1201 16th St., N.W., Washington, D.C. 20036, 1971, pp. 5.21–5.25.

[17] Allan B. Ellis and David V. Tiedeman, "Can a Machine Counsel?" in Holtzman, op. cit., pp. 345–373.

[18] *Layman's Guide to the Use of Computers*, op. cit., pp. 5.22–5.23; John C. Flanagan, "Program for Learning in Accordance with Needs," *Psychology in the Schools*, Vol. 6, No. 2, April 1969, pp. 133–136.

dicators of some of the changes that computers can bring about in education during the next decade. Furthermore, a number of experimental systems are already being tried (though they are still quite expensive) which will enable students to organize and use large blocks of information by means suited to their own interests.[19] The importance of this development to individualized instruction is obvious. It also suggests that it is increasingly important for today's students to become familiar with the use of computers as a fundamental tool of learning. When we consider also the administrative and instructional uses described earlier and the vastly more numerous and extensive applications of computers in industry and government, it is easy to see why computers themselves have become important as a subject of study.

COMPUTERS AS A SUBJECT OF INSTRUCTION The growth of the computer in American society has been phenomenal. There were 30,000 computers in operation in the United States in 1965, 50,000 by early 1968, and 60,000 by mid-1970, a rate of increase almost twice that predicted by 1965 by the American Federation of Information Processing Societies. This expansion of the computer into an influence on virtually all walks of life clearly will increase as time goes on.

Therefore, it is not surprising that computers have become an important part of the curriculum, not only in higher education but also in secondary and technical schools. Departments of computer or information sciences have developed rapidly in our universities during the past decade. Students can major in the field and many do, but large numbers from other departments study computer languages and applications so that they can make use of them in their own fields of work. Holtzman reports that in junior colleges, technical

[19] Zinn, Project CLUE Report, op. cit., pp. 10–20.

schools, vocational institutes, and many high schools, the field of data processing by computers is proving an attractive occupational opportunity for students.[20] This is borne out by the following summary of estimates made in the summer of 1970 at the first World Conference on Computer Education, held in Amsterdam, of the numbers of well-trained people who will be needed by 1975 to fill jobs at several levels in information processing:

The presentations and discussions on the problems of professional training included some striking points on need:
—a realistic estimate of the need for well-trained personnel in the field of automation indicates that by 1975 the USA will need 450,000 operators and 1,500,000 programmers; the estimates for the UK are for 65,000 programmers by 1975.

These figures made it clear that efforts in training people in these areas should be raised by establishing informatic schools at the non-university level.[21]

Availability of a computer for the training purposes implied by these trends

[20] Holtzman, op. cit., p. 8.

[21] Bob Scheepmaker and Karl L. Zinn, eds., *General Report of the First International Federation for Information Processing* (IFIP), World Conference on Computer Education, 1970, copyright IFIP, Amsterdam, 1970; distributors: Science Associates/International, New York, p. 1/125. *Note:* The term "informatics" may be coming into use as a more comprehensive term than "computer science" in that it encompasses the software and application elements as well as the technological aspects of computers. *Informatics* is defined thus: "The science of the systematic and effective treatment, especially by automatic machines, of information seen as the medium for human knowledge and for communication in the technical, economic and social contexts" (World Conference *Report*, p. 1/121). The Conference recommended to education authorities that they provide an early introduction to informatics as an integral part of general education in the secondary and primary schools (World Conference *Report*, p. 1/127).

and needs is, of course, essential. In fact, it seems inevitable that computer systems will come to be viewed as vital to the functions of any major educational institution. Because of the costs involved, it appears that multipurpose computer systems will develop, along with regional networks to make it possible for smaller institutions to benefit from large, remotely located central computers which will serve at once to extend capacity and reduce costs. This leads us to the question of computer costs and how these costs are likely to affect their introduction and use in our schools.

Costs of computer use in instruction

Computers are expensive. Many people feel that they are far too expensive to be seriously considered for regular use in our schools. But education itself is expensive, costing in the United States something over 80 billion dollars a year in all its forms. Most of this expenditure goes to public education, and costs are rising every year. At the same time, education is being subjected to its severest criticism in history. In the minds of many, education's future, at least in its present form, is very much in doubt. Under these circumstances, the question of computers becomes less one of costs than of cost-effectiveness—the relative results achieved per dollar invested in comparison with other uses to which these dollars might be put.

In discussing the future of learning and teaching, John Goodlad points to a fundamental need to change the human-to-human instruction pattern which dominates current educational practice in our schools:

The era of instruction that will supersede the era of human-based instruction is to be one of man-machine interaction. And the machine is the computer. We have lived in the shadow of the computer long enough now but used it so little in

instructional affairs that we may be inclined to believe its future and our own to be things apart. Nothing could be further from the truth. . . .

The era of human and machine-based instruction is soon to be upon us. If we turn our backs on the computer, we may delay computerized instruction a little. But we may destroy the school and the influence of the education profession in the process. It is imperative that we explore the most appropriate roles of man and machine and that we legitimize them.[22]

Nonetheless, there *are* costs involved, and we need to have some grasp of their size and significance in order to think intelligently about computerized instruction.

In a careful study of costs of traditionally administered instruction (TAI) in the public schools versus computerized instruction (CAI), the cost of CAI was estimated in 1968 as $3.73 per student hour as compared with approximately 36 cents per student hour for TAI for a class of average size.[23] This wide difference was caused in part by the limited amount of computer use possible in a typical six-hour school day and with traditional school organization, but it did mean that unless CAI could be shown to be at least 10 times more effective or efficient than TAI, the change to CAI did not seem to be warranted at that time in the public schools. In higher education, on the other hand, because of the much higher costs of instruction and the far greater flexibility of operation and hours of possible use,

[22] John I. Goodlad, ''The Future of Learning and Teaching,'' *AV Communication Review*, Vol. 16, No. 1, Spring 1968, pp. 7, 10–11.

[23] Felix F. Kopstein and Robert J. Seidel, ''Computer-Administered Instruction Versus Traditionally Administered Instruction: Economics,'' *AV Communication Review*, Vol. 16, No. 2, Summer 1968, p. 163.

FIGURE 13.7

This is a schematic diagram of the plasma panel being developed for use in the Plato IV system at the University of Illinois. The device combines the properties of image retention, versatile display, and high brightness at low cost. In contrast with the cathode ray tube, on which images must constantly be regenerated, the plasma panel holds its own images and responds directly to computer signals; thus it makes separate communication lines for visual displays unnecessary.

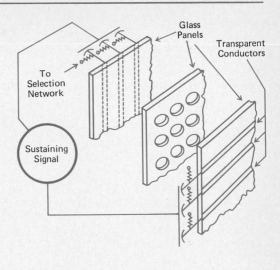

CAI was judged to have a competitive advantage over TAI in larger institutions. This was particularly true in the professional schools.

At the University of Illinois, a computer-based educational system called Plato has been in use since 1960. The present third version, Plato III, uses 20 learning stations in a computer classroom giving instruction in a number of subjects. They have logged more than 70,000 student contact hours of credit teaching with a variety of teaching strategies ranging from drill and practice to student-directed inquiry. Although most of the use has been with college students, a 20-terminal system has also been placed in a community college and a high school near Urbana, Illinois, and adult education as well as preschool groups have cooperated in trial use of the system.

That experience, along with some new engineering developments, led to the design of a new system, Plato IV, which it is believed will reduce direct operating costs of instruction to about 25 cents per student hour. Notable among the new engineering developments is a plasma display panel (see Figure 13.7) that would greatly reduce the cost of visualizing as compared with the cost of the cathode ray tube. The panel contains a rectangular array of small gas cells that can be selectively ignited by impulses from the computer so as to form displays. The system involves a very large computer with 4,000 student terminals which could be located at any distance from the central computer. The student terminals would each consist of the plasma display device, a special microfiche slide card image selector combined with a projector, and a typewriter keyboard (see Figure 13.8). The system also provides for random-access audio devices, films, lights, and random-access slides.

Assuming 300 days of use per year at eight hours per day, it has been calculated that Plato IV could be put into use at a cost per student contact hour that would be comparable to the cost in conventional elementary school classrooms, which is about 27 cents per student contact hour. This figure does not include the potential income from the computer during the other 16 hours each day and during idle time between student requests. The system is

TABLE 13.3

planned for activation in the early 1970s.[24]

Experts in the computer sciences have raised many questions about the adequacy of the Plato IV cost estimates in such terms as contemplated modes of use, the realism of assuming eight hours of use per day of each student station, and the use of one central computer system rather than a combination involving satellite systems. Nevertheless, the fact remains that even if the cost estimates are off by as much as a factor of two or three (which remains to be demonstrated), they still represent a substantial reduction over the results of earlier cost studies and may portend the kind of breakthrough necessary to make computer use feasible on a large scale in the public schools. The estimated Plato IV specific cost breakdown in Table 13.3 also provides some useful general information

on the initial costs of computers and the continuing costs of preparing programs (software) to use on them.

Another experimental project is also aimed at achieving low-cost effective operation, though by a means different from the Plato project. The MITRE Corporation has combined television with computer tech-

[24] Donald Bitzer and D. Skaperdas, ''The Economics of a Large-Scale Computer-Based Education System: Plato IV'' in Holtzman, op. cit., pp. 17–29.

FIGURE 13.8

This is a schematic drawing of the student terminal in the Plato IV system. Computer-generated information can be shown on the plasma display panel; also, information pre-stored on a microfiche slide card can be super-imposed on the transparent panel at the same time by means of a random-access slide selector and an optical projector, as shown.

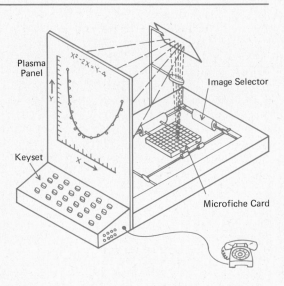

Item	Total costs, millions of dollars	Cost per year, millions of dollars (5-year amortization)	Cost per student contact hour, cents
Computer and extended memory	4.5	0.9	8
Software	1.5	0.3	4
4,000 student terminals	7.5	1.5	15
Subtotal	13.5	2.7	27
Lesson material	—	—	3
Data distribution lines	—	—	4
Total			34

Source: Donald Bitzer and D. Skaperdas, "The Economics of a Large-Scale Computer-Based Education System: Plato IV" in Holtzman, op. cit., p. 28.

nology to provide a computer-based instruction system which is small in comparison with Plato IV, having perhaps 200 terminals instead of 4,000. At this writing, the development plan is not entirely fixed, but the system may be in use on a trial basis in two community colleges by the time this book is published. This system, which is called TICCIT (Time-Shared Interactive Computer-Controlled Information Television), uses relatively low-cost minicomputers, ordinary television receivers to provide computer-generated sound, pictures, and text to the student, and newly developed data-transfer hardware and software structures which have promise of very fast response times and a high level of flexibility (see Figure 13.9). Based on a school population of 1,200 students, 120 terminals, and a 10-hour day, the TICCIT system would provide one hour of terminal service per day per student at a cost of about $40 per student per year or 20 cents per terminal hour.[25]

[25] Kenneth J. Stetten, "The Technology of Small, Local Facilities for Instructional Use" in R. E. Levien, ed., *Computers in Instruction: Their Future for Higher Education*, Proceedings of a conference sponsored by the National Science

Advantages and limitations of computerized instruction

As you read our rather brief discussion of instructional uses of computers, you probably became aware of some of the unique benefits to be derived from their use. You probably also found that you had some questions. In summing up our consideration of computers, therefore, it might be helpful to take a look at the pros and cons through the eyes of some representative learning psychologists, educators, educational researchers, and computer specialists.

UNIQUE CONTRIBUTIONS OF COMPUTERS   Speaking of the solution of learning problems by using computers, John Feldhusen, an educational psychologist, is clearly an enthusiast, affirming:

The evidence clearly indicates that CAI teaches at least as well as live teachers or other media, that there is a saving in time to learn, that students respond favorably to CAI, that the computer can

Foundation, the Carnegie Commission on Higher Education, and the Rand Corporation, Report #R–718–NSF/CCOM/RC, the Rand Corporation, Santa Monica, Calif., July 1971, pp. 35–41.

FIGURE 13.9

The TICCIT system employs another approach to providing low-cost computer instruction. As shown here, the display device is an ordinary portable television set. The use of standard TV receivers and other special engineering developments opens additional potentials for practicable CAI use in schools.

be used to accomplish heretofore impossible versatility in branching and individualizing instruction, that true, natural instructional dialogue is possible, and that the computer will virtually perform miracles in processing performance data.[26]

In a report on CAI research and development, Feldhusen discusses the capabilities of CAI in comparison with other media:

There are some things which CAI is able to do better than other media: (1) Secure, store and process information about the student's performance prior to and/or during instruction to determine subsequent activities in the learning situation. (2) Store large amounts of information and make them available to the learner more rapidly than any other medium. (3) Provide programmed control of several media such as films, slides, TV, and demonstration equipment. (4) Give the author or teacher an extremely convenient technique for designing and developing a course of instruction. (5) Provide a dynamic interaction between student and

instructional program not possible with most other media.[27]

Lawrence Stolurow stresses the individualized instruction potentials of CAI in contrast with other media:

Computer-assisted instruction is distinct from media in that it is a potential means of making instruction a truly individualized process through the use of a variety of media to support a system of instruction. While programed instruction and language laboratories appear to individualize instruction, they actually only take the first baby step in that direction by allowing the student to proceed at his own rate. Mass media approaches have provided an illusion of economy; hidden are costs of revision required to reach different students of the total audience; with CAI we could individualize materials electronically rather than by hand.[28]

[26] John Feldhusen and Michael Szabo, ''The Advent of the Educational Heart Transplant, Computer-Assisted Instruction: A Brief Interpretative Review,'' *Contemporary Education*, Vol. 50, No. 5, April 1969, Indiana State University.

[27] John Feldhusen, ''A Position Paper on CAI Research and Development,'' OE-ERIC Clearing House on Educational Media and Technology, Stanford University, 1969.

[28] Lawrence Stolurow, ''Computer Assisted Instruction,'' in *The Schools and the Challenge of Innovation*, Committee for Economic Development, Supplementary Paper No. 28, McGraw-Hill, 1969, pp. 270–319.

In his book on applications of the systems approach to the solution of many of today's educational problems and the role of the computer in that effort, John Pfeiffer points to a generally accepted and important fringe benefit of computer use. This benefit arises from the fact that before computers can be of any use at all, they must be carefully programed to perform desired functions. This act of programing requires a prior thinking through of problems and needs with a degree of thoroughness and specificity not commonly associated with educational planning. Pfeiffer aptly describes the result thus:

Incidentally, there may be an interesting relationship between our increasing emphasis on the need to define objectives and our increasing experience with computers. Computers are notorious for their simple-mindedness among other things. They demand instructions spelled out in excruciating detail, and dealing with them has probably forced us to become more explicit and exact in dealing with one another. We can be brilliant but rather sloppy thinkers; computers are stupid but accurate. It seems that during the course of time, in the evolving symbiosis between man and machine, we are destined for better or for worse to become somewhat more precise (and, of course, the computer · will inevitably become somewhat more intelligent).[29]

LIMITATIONS OF COMPUTERS The cost of the computer is the drawback most often cited as a serious one. Nevertheless, many authorities such as Karl Zinn consider misuse or inappropriate use of the computer as far more fundamental in significance. For instance, the National Council for Educational Technology in England comments:

It is important not to consider CAI as a learning process which involves the computer solely: the "system" could include, for example, teachers, printed material, and linear programed texts. Many experimental developments of CAI have been ineffective because they have attempted to put the whole process on the computer rather than selecting those parts for which it is most applicable.[30]

There is also concern that computers may inject an inhuman quality into educational programs (see Figure 13.10). In an article advocating the development of a realistic perspective against which technological innovations in education can be viewed objectively, Anthony Oettinger and Sema Marks comment pointedly on a possible underlying danger that such innovations could bring with them—particularly those that prove highly efficient and effective:

If, as is true of all computerized systems of "individualized" instruction now visible as prototypes as well as of many others based on explicit definitions of "behavioral objectives" (BO's), the intent is to instruct students in such a manner that all will achieve a final level of competency which meets (or surpasses) the same set of minimally acceptable performance criteria, with variation only in style, speed, or level of achievement, the objective cannot be the cultivation of idiosyncrasy. It is, rather, what an industrial engineer might call mass production to narrow specifications with rigid quality control. Each pupil is free to go more or less rapidly exactly where he is told to go.[31]

[29] Pfeiffer, op. cit., p. 14.

[30] National Council for Educational Technology (NCET), *Computer-Based Learning Systems: A Programme for Research and Development*, 160 Great Portland Street, London W.1, England, 1969.

[31] Anthony G. Oettinger and Sema Marks, "Educational Technology—New Myths and Old Realities," *Harvard Educational Review*, Vol. 38, No. 4, Fall 1968, p. 701.

FIGURE 13.10

This is one view of possible future problems with computers. Some scientists believe that computers may one day reach the point where they can think for themselves. Others scoff at this view, saying, "We can always pull out the plug!"

There are others, however, who disagree, including Wayne Holtzman, who says:

Contrary to the skeptical criticism of some alarmists, there is no reason to believe that this new technology will necessarily dehumanize man. There are many things in this world that can be done better by machines than by human beings. The advent of the computer, and the educational technology related to it, clearly points the way to major changes in education that will free the individual, both teacher and student, to interact in more human ways than ever before.[32]

Sources of computer information

It is obvious that computer technology and applications in education are undergoing extensive development and rapid change. These changes can be expected to continue

[32] Holtzman, op. cit., p. 13.

for the next decade or more. Thus students in educational technology who are interested should certainly keep up to date on major developments, experimental programs, and new educational applications of computers. One continuing source, of course, is the publication output of professional associations such as the Association for Educational Communications and Technology (AECT), the Association for Educational Data Systems (AEDS), the American Educational Research Association (AERA), and the International Federation for Information Processing (IFIP).[33] The best single source, however, is Karl Zinn's *Guide to the Literature on Interactive Use of Computers for Instruc-*

tion.[34] This guide is really a continuing source of sources which Zinn and his associates revise from time to time; it includes, in convenient form, a wide variety of annotated listings of significant reports of projects and conferences, publications, and program sources, as well as helpful analyses of current developments in the educational uses of computers.

Also see the sources listed in the Further Learner Response Projects at the end of this chapter.

[33] AECT, AEDS, and AERA are all at 1201 16th St., N.W., Washington, D.C. 20036; IFIP, Congress Office, 23 Dorset Square, London N.W. 1, England.

[34] Karl L. Zinn and Susan McClintock, *A Guide to the Literature on Interactive Use of Computers for Instruction*, 2nd ed., 1970, Center for Research on Learning and Teaching, University of Michigan. Distributed by ERIC Clearing House on Educational Media and Technology, Institute for Communication Research, Stanford University, Stanford, Calif. 94305.

Simulation and games

As indicated earlier in this chapter, one valuable application of computers in instruction is in simulation and games. We should emphasize, however, that in connection with simulation and games, as in all its other uses, the computer is primarily a means of storing information which has been given to it and processing this information. The computer does not "play" games, in other words; it merely enables people to simulate situations or play games. Thus in simulating a management situation, a computer which has been programed properly can quickly show, for example, the results of management decisions to hire 10 new salesmen, buy out a competing company, or introduce a new product. In other words, because of its capacity, speed, and accuracy, the computer *facilitates* certain simulation and game exercises that might otherwise not be practical. On the other hand, in the great majority of educational simulations computers are unnecessary.

Nature of simulation and games
Simulations are concentrated learning exercises specifically designed to *represent* important real-life activities by providing the learner(s) with the *essence* or essential elements of the real situation without its hazards, costs, or time constraints. Simulations are frequently cast in the form of competitive games to add motivation and interest.

Games are contests based on skill and/or chance that are played according to rules.

Thus a simulation, by capturing the essence or essential elements of a real-life situation, provides the learner with experience which will help him to understand and to function better in that situation or in comparable situations later on.

Simulation and games are actually a method of learning which has been around a long time. The make-believe store run by kindergartners, little girls dressing up in mother's clothes and playing with dolls—these are examples of a kind of simulation. This make-believe is a normal and natural characteristic of young children which has marked learning potentials.

It is only in the last decade or so, however, that the possibilities of simulation and games for older students and adults have been seriously investigated, though there is one marked exception in the area of skills and tactical training. During and since World War II, extensive use has been made of psychomotor skills training with simulators in such areas as aircraft training, driver education, and weapons systems operation; at the command level, intensive use has been made of war games for tactical training. On the other hand, simulations in such areas as the social studies, teacher education, and management decision-making are largely a product of the 1960s and early 1970s.

Commercial television has done much to familiarize the public with the values of simulation, particularly in its coverage of the NASA space projects. Extensive "live" color coverage of lunar explorations was first provided during the Apollo 15 moon flight, but even then considerable use was made of simulated demonstrations of various phases of the astronauts' journey so that home viewers could better understand what was going on.

Some simulators such as those used in pilot training appear exactly like the pilot's cockpit in a real plane, including all controls and instruments (see Figure 13.11). Furthermore, the controls and instru-

FIGURE 13.11

The value to potential pilots of a full-scale model of a real airplane like this Link trainer is obvious. Trainers of this type are often programed to simulate takeoffs and landings and flight problems. The "plane" responds to the student pilot's handling of the controls so that he gets the feel and experience of actual flight conditions without the hazards.

PLATE 11.2

Research studies on the selections pupils make
from alternative learning materials presented in
black and white and color indicate preponderant
selections of color. Color is inherently attractive.
However, what additional values of color do you
see in these stills from representative color
sound motion picture films?

PLATE 11.3

Many color motion picture films are available (though at somewhat higher cost than black and white). Examine each of these stills carefully, first in its black-and-white form, then in its original color. What information is transmitted by each color version that is not transmitted by the black-and-white version? Which stills contain relationships that depend solely on color for meaning? Are there other values to the color versions of these films? How, in your observation, do students ordinarily respond to color versus black-and-white films? Is this important?

PLATE 15.1

This is the beginning of the Battle of the Little Big Horn on June 25, 1876, as reenacted in the feature film *Little Big Man*. George Armstrong Custer (in light coat and hat) leads his men of the Seventh U. S. Cavalry against the Sioux and Cheyennes, led by Sitting Bull and Crazy Horse. Custer and all the men of his battalion were killed in the battle.

PLATE 15.2

We see, on the one hand, what man has done as he has sought the benefits of technology without considering the effects of this technology on the environment. We see, on the other hand, what man used to have around him and what he wishes to have again. What can the individual student, working with his teacher, hope to achieve in correcting this present imbalance?

PLATE 15.3

One of the many films that are valuable as source
material during a unit on Africa is *Continent of
Africa.* This frame is from a sequence showing
native women picking plantains.

ments respond to the trainee's actions in the same way as they do in a real airplane. All this is necessary so that the trainee's physical response to possible actual problem situations later on will be precise and accurate. In this situation, the appearance of the real thing is important. In other kinds of simulations, however, the appearance may be relatively unimportant. Children playing store in kindergarten play the game wholeheartedly in a "store" made of a few boards and boxes. The classroom does not have to look like a legislative chamber for students to play the roles of representatives, giving speeches and bargaining with other players. The essential elements, in other words, are something other than appearance in the latter two examples.

Emphasis on the "essence" or essential elements of learning situations accordingly suggests that simulations should omit some elements of the real-life situation. The elements omitted, of course, are unimportant to the specific purpose of the simulation or game; leaving them out, in fact, simply avoids unnecessary complexities or confusion which might otherwise occur. Thus in the Democracy (Legislature) game,[35] not only is the appearance of a legislative chamber unnecessary; also unnecessary are such extraneous details as the pages, the hearings reporter, and the more intricate elements of Robert's Rules of Order which sometimes come into play in real-life legislatures. In other words, irrelevant or unimportant elements are omitted so that the learner can more easily acquire the *specific* learning for which the simulation is intended.

Types of simulation and games
Simulation and gaming have at least three ancestors: simulator trainers, games, and

role-playing.[36] *Simulator trainers*, sometimes called mock-ups, were first discussed in Chapter 4, "Three-Dimensional Teaching Materials." In this context we have already mentioned pilot training simulators and illustrated a light-plane trainer. Commercial pilots, as one might expect, are trained and retrained at frequent intervals. Pilots learning to fly the huge 747 jet or the DC-10, for instance, "fly" in a simulator trainer that looks, acts, and feels exactly like the real thing—though it never gets off the ground (see Figure 13.12). These trainers simulate the actual flying of a 747 or a DC-10 in every particular without risking any of the hazards or costs that would be involved if an actual airplane were used. The driver education trainer is a familiar example in high schools where some of the same problems of hazards and costs apply as in pilot training (see Figure 13.13).

Games of one sort or another are probably as old as man himself. All cultures tend to play games that are competitive in nature—they have winners and losers and depend on some degree of skill or chance or both. Many simulations use a game format for purposes of motivation and interest stimulation; thus the term *simulation and gaming* is frequently used in combination to describe systematically designed simulations involving competition among teams or individuals.

There is also a category of educational games which are competitive but which do not involve simulation and thus are called "nonsimulation games." Examples are Wff 'n Proof, a game designed to teach mathematical logic to children 6 years old and older; Equations, a series of five games designed to teach basic computational skills

[35] Developed at Johns Hopkins University by James S. Coleman. Available from Western Publishing Company, Inc., School Library Department, 850 Third Avenue, New York, N.Y. 10022.

[36] Paul A. Twelker, "A Basic Reference Shelf on Simulation and Gaming" in David W. Zukerman and Robert E. Horn, *The Guide to Simulation Games for Education and Training*, Information Resources, Inc., Cambridge, Mass., 1970, pp. 313 ff.

FIGURE 13.12

Commercial pilots undergo continuous training and retraining throughout their careers. (a) This 747 Flight Simulator is hooked up to a computer programed to simulate every conceivable flight situation or problem which might be experienced; it also precisely records the pilot's reactions for assessment. The motion picture projector projects a 70mm film in front of the cockpit that provides low-altitude visual cues for pilots in training. (b) This DC–10 Flight Simulator uses a color TV projection system to provide visual cues for training. Two control panels, linked with computers, establish aircraft system and flight variables for specific training problems. The panel on the left controls the visual system, a record and playback feature, and performance measurement. The panel on the right controls mechanical malfunctions. Thus any possible flight situation can be simulated and played back for critique or demonstration purposes, and all crew reactions are automatically evaluated.

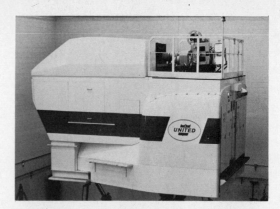

FIGURE 13.13

This photograph of a driver-trainer installation shows the essential elements of this simulator trainer. Students respond to filmed driving situations and their reactions are timed and recorded as they do so for immediate or follow-up evaluation of their progress.

from the primary grades on up; and The Propaganda Game, in which junior and senior high school students learn the techniques used by professionals to mold public opinion.[37]

Role-playing has many definitions, ranging from simple make-believe and play-acting to sociodrama. As used in simulation and gaming, however, role-playing is closely associated with interpreting the feelings and actions of others, as in the Democracy (Legislature) game for high school and older students. Students who get into the spirit of the game literally try to "become" senators or representatives and to act and react as they conceive that such persons would.

The simulator for training, the game for motivation and interest, and role-playing for better understanding of one's self and others are, individually, valuable kinds of learning experiences. When these are appropriately combined in simulation activities, there is clearly an opportunity for unique and even more significant learning to take place.

Design and evaluation of educational simulation

Educational simulations and games, like other well-organized learning experiences, must be carefully designed around clearly specified objectives. The objectives must have been derived from a careful analysis of what is to be learned and a determination that a simulation exercise is particularly appropriate as a method of providing the needed learning experience.

The design consists, in brief, of the following steps: (1) a systematic analysis of the problem, process, or situation to be taught; (2) the selection of a suitable model (format) for the game; (3) setting up the "parts" or roles to be played in

simulating the model; (4) establishing necessary rules for operating the game so it will function effectively toward the specified objectives; (5) determination (and, if necessary, preparation) of the materials and information needed by the players; (6) a tryout period of testing with representative groups of students and reworking as necessary until everything about the game functions as intended.

In other words, an Instructional Development approach is needed to design and construct good educational simulations —a task which requires some expertise and a considerable amount of time and patience. (Instructional Development was discussed briefly in Chapter 3 and is described at some length in Chapter 15.) In consequence, most such games are developed by simulation and content specialists working together; many companies, including textbook publishing houses, have therefore moved into the field of simulation development and distribution.

Two points should be made now. First, though we stated that an Instructional Development approach is needed in developing educational simulations and games, this statement should not be construed to mean that simulation experts in fact do use an I.D. approach. In many cases and for a variety of reasons—such as the lack of access to data to establish what materials are really needed and the practical necessity of getting materials on the market that will sell—they have not. Instead, as is still true with most instructional materials, they have proceeded, on the basis of their own experience and the best advice they could get from educators, to identify topics and problems in which simulation and games are potentially valuable and then they have gone ahead and produced the material.

Second, as noted by one expert, students can, should, and occasionally do design games, and it can be a stimulating and valuable learning experience for

[37] All three games are produced by Wff 'n Proof, 1111 Maple Ave., Turtle Creek, Pa. 15145.

FIGURE 13.14

them.[38] Clearly, students are rarely in a position to use an I.D. approach. Their teacher, however, might be involved with an I.D. team and, if so, could better guide students toward topics in which games had been systematically identified as desirable learning strategies. In such a situation, the values that result in any case from active student participation would be significantly enhanced. Accordingly, teachers who become interested in games and, on occasion, in having students design them should become sufficiently familiar with the game medium to be able to decide whether or not certain topics under consideration in their courses are both appropriate for game treatment and important enough to warrant the necessary expenditures of time and energy.

As we shall see shortly, many simulations and games are now available for schools and colleges in a wide range of subjects and grade levels. One caution should be noted here. Because it is quite possible for a game to be interesting but nevertheless involve little tangible learning, it is important in considering such simulation materials to ascertain the extent to which they have been tested, refined, and validated. Companies that sell educational games should be able to provide the data necessary to make a judgment on their values for cognitive learning.

It should also be noted, on the other hand, that learning from educational games can take a number of forms, of which cognitive learning is only one. The learning of processes and experience with the relative risks and potential rewards of alternative strategies and decisions are also important, and these values are more difficult to measure. The learning of processes and experience in decision-making both contain affective elements of considerable value. Games involving social interactions

Games, which have an appeal for all ages and achievement levels, may contribute much to social as well as cognitive learning.

inherently require forms of cooperative activity among participants which in themselves are important educational goals (see Figure 13.14). On elements such as these, a teacher may have to make intuitive judgments or base his selections on the experience and testimony of other teachers until he can try out the simulations for himself.

Advantages and limitations of simulation gaming

As is the case with any other teaching material or technique, simulation exercises should be chosen and used so as to maximize their advantages and minimize their limitations. Simulation gaming has four primary advantages and two primary limitations that must be balanced against each other in any specific situation.

[38] John Raser, *Simulation and Society,* Allyn and Bacon, 1969, p. 131.

ADVANTAGES OF SIMULATION GAMING

One of the marked advantages of effective simulation is *increased motivation and participation*. Social studies teachers have reported that games such as Democracy, which has been mentioned, and Empire, which is described below, produce general enthusiasm and involvement of practically all students in a class. As any experienced teacher knows, this extent of student interest and involvement is a rarity in normal classroom procedures. The high interest level is definitely connected with the relevance and real-life characteristics of such games, the social interaction and co-operative endeavor necessary to play them, and the learning of processes or "how things get done" in the real world. In this last context, it is notable that culturally impoverished students tend to come off very well in these games. One thing students from ghetto areas have learned is the importance of discovering how to survive in their own environment. Thus they tend to take quickly to "operating" in the game environment and to do well at it. Though this tendency is certainly not limited to disadvantaged students, it is more noticeable in their case, since they do not normally respond as well to traditional classroom practices as their more fortunate classmates.

Another benefit attributed to good simulations is the *social interaction* they generate. In educational simulation a player must not only think out his own best moves on the basis of the information he has, but he must also persuade his teammates of the probable effectiveness of those moves. Thus players tend to learn how to operate more effectively within the group. Those individuals who get too far out of line either through overaggressiveness or apathy tend to be "straightened out" by their peers.

Still another advantage of simulation games is that individual games can *accommodate a broad range of student ages and achievement levels*. As one writer points out, the slower students tend to learn from faster ones, sometimes better than they do from teachers, and both share social interaction benefits from such games while sometimes learning from them at quite different cognitive levels. This writer also mentions the specific advantages for culturally deprived students, saying that they "respond relatively better to game teaching than to less dynamic, more expository methods." He adds: "For this and other reasons, games may be able to test the comprehension and solution of complex problems better than purely verbal tests, as well as offering highly motivated, self-directed learning."[39]

We have mentioned another reason for the appeal of games to students of a wide range of abilities: well-designed games *approximate reality* far more closely than conventional classroom procedures. This realism extends both to the substantive and the process aspects of simulations. For example, the following description of the Empire game makes clear how information about the nature and importance of trade in the British Empire might be vitalized and sharpened for junior high school social studies students playing the game. Teams of students play the roles of London merchants, New England merchants, European merchants, Colonial farmers, Southern planters, and British West In-

dian planters in the mid-1700s. The entire class engages in trading, using goods, prices, tariffs, and the transportation of that time. They experience competition, political influence, negotiation, smuggling, piracy, and law enforcement. The general purposes of the game are to show how the trading system of the eighteenth-century British Empire operated and the decision-making roles of interest groups within it. The specific objective of the game is to trade your own products advantageously for necessary products not grown or manufactured where you live. Decisions must be made and consequences experienced in terms of with whom to trade and how much to charge or pay.[40]

LIMITATIONS OF SIMULATION GAMING
As with all teaching-learning techniques and materials, there are also limitations and disadvantages to simulation and gaming. One is the fact that *some games take considerable time* to play. A review of 29 historical games for junior and senior high school, for example, shows a range of from 1 to 30 hours required, with an average of approximately 4 to 5 hours for each game. Many primary and middle-grade games in reading, phonics, and mathematical skills topics, on the other hand, call for only 15 to 20 minutes per exercise. The time required must naturally be equated with the learning values that can be realized.

A possible limiting characteristic of simulation for some teachers is the fact that games are *occasionally somewhat complex and demanding of the teacher* in terms of the planning and monitoring necessary to make a game function successfully. This is simply to say that setting up and conducting effective simulations and games requires the added "know-how" that can be acquired from study of the directions which normally accompany these materials

---

[39] Clark Abt, "Games for Learning," Occasional Paper No. 7, The Social Studies Curriculum Program, Educational Services, Inc., 1965, p. 19.

[40] Available from Educational Development Center, 15 Mifflin Place, Cambridge, Mass. 02138.

and care in applying them. Again, it is a question primarily of the values to be derived—and you won't know until you try.

. . .

Research on the effectiveness of simulation and games in most school subjects is still spotty and inconclusive.[41] It is difficult to prove statistically that simulation and games are inherently valuable classroom activities. Nevertheless, experience seems to demonstrate that worthwhile learning does take place and that there are sufficient beneficial effects in increased motivation and involvement to warrant using simulation and games from time to time in our classes (see Figure 13.15). Teachers experienced in using games report their best results when such materials are carefully incorporated in an overall plan involving coordination of a variety of study techniques and media. Such coordination, of course, should be standard practice with

any materials or techniques of teaching and learning; furthermore, it is a natural outcome of Instructional Development analysis and planning as it is referred to throughout this book.

Sources of simulation games

If you want to try out a simulation game, where can you get one? In what subjects and grade levels are games available? Where can you find out about them? What do they cost?

As is the case with most media and materials, there are many sources, types, and grade levels of educational games. Your school supply company is a good place to start, along with professional magazines, in which game publishers' advertisements appear regularly. The school's resource center or library may have some games on hand. There is also a good and quite comprehensive guide which contains descriptions and much additional information on some 400 educational games classified in numerous subject areas.[42] The au-

[41] Robert H. Davis, review of *Simulation and Gaming in Education* by P. J. Tansey and D. Unwin, Methuen, London, and Barnes and Noble, New York, 1969, in *Simulation and Games*, Vol. 1, No. 4, December 1970, p. 43; Paul A. Twelker, "Simulation and Media," unpublished manuscript, Teaching Research Division, Oregon State System of Higher Education, 1971, p. 39.

[42] David W. Zuckerman and Robert E. Horn, *The Guide to Simulation Games for Education and Training*, Information Resources, Inc., 1675 Massachusetts Ave., Cambridge, Mass. 02138, 1970, 336 pp., $17.00.

FIGURE 13.15

One way to increase motivation and participation in games is to extend the range of the competition. There now are national tournaments for teams from junior and senior high schools. Here, for example, students from three high schools playing the Equations game are engrossed in "brain-to-brain" combat during the Fifth National Academic Games Olympics in New Orleans in 1970.

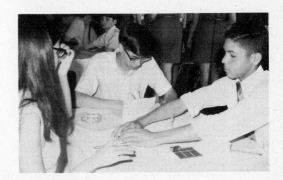

thors plan to publish supplements or a new edition annually (they expect to add 200 or more games in the second edition). The following entry is representative:

The Community
Erwin Rausch

PLAYING DATA

Age Level	High School College Management/ Administrative
Number of Players	Minimum 3, no maximum
Playing Time	2 to 5 hours in 30-minute periods
Preparation Time	1 hour at first only

MATERIALS

Components	Players' manuals Administrator's manual Worksheets

Supplementary Material "A Guide to Teaching"

COMMENT

THE COMMUNITY is the only game we've encountered which gives students a chance to experience the problems of the local, tax-supported economic systems in which they live. The problems of limited funds and competing priorities with which it deals lie close to the root of our national turmoil; I'd like to see every student playing the game from time to time. THE COMMUNITY is an interactive game, and calls for cooperation as well as competition and conflict; too many economics games—and business games as well—ignore the cooperative aspects of man's admittedly self-

oriented interactions. Further, I think that of all economics games THE COMMUNITY makes the most significant use of role-playing to increase learning. Game events are deterministic, with quantitative (zero sum) outcomes. Play is by teams, and calls for rapid thinking, coalition formation, bargaining and decision making. Results of outside evaluation are available from Didactic Systems, but not from SRA. (D.Z.)

SUMMARY DESCRIPTION

Roles	The players represent in turn the taxpayers of the community, the employers and employees, the elected officials
Objectives	To earn point credits for achievements and avoid demerits and losses: to build the "best" community
Decisions	Determining wage rates Determining tax rates and allocation of public revenues to public needs Deciding which improvements to approve
Purposes	The game is intended to acquaint students with the public sector of the economy It illustrates the basic problems of selecting and financing public services

Cost	1	$1.25, $1.50 for teacher's guide
	2	$1.87 for six players, minimum order $10.00 must include teacher's guide
Producer	1	Science Research Associates, Inc. 259 East Erie Street Chicago, Illinois 60611

2 Didactic Systems, Inc.
Box 500, Westbury,
New York 11590

Twelker has published an annotated bibliography on Instructional Simulation Systems including about 1,500 references and descriptions of simulation exercises and games with information on subject, learner population, price, materials furnished, and other relevant facts of interest to the teacher or resources librarian.[43]

Finally, the professional and other journals listed in the References at the end of this chapter provide reviews and listings of recently produced simulation exercises.

Summary

Already in use for administrative purposes in many colleges and school systems, computers have promise as well for future instructional programs in the schools. Instructional uses to this point have been largely experimental, but they have demonstrated that (1) effective learning takes place, frequently with considerable savings in time; (2) individualized instruction can be greatly facilitated. Computerized instructional programs are principally of four types: drill and practice; tutorial and dialogue; simulation and gaming; information handling.

The primary attributes of computers are their capacity to record and process huge amounts of information and to perform complex mathematical computations with great speed and accuracy. These capacities make individualized instruction feasible in a variety of forms and free the teacher from substantial amounts of record keeping and processing. *Any* use of the computer requires careful programing, in itself probably an educational dividend.

Heavy costs of computer use are most often cited as barriers to its application for instructional purposes, but there are signs that substantial reductions in costs are not far distant. Misuse or inappropriate applications, in Instructional Development terms, may be a more fundamental hazard; some educators also point to the danger that computers may inject mechanical and inhuman qualities into education.

Simulation and games have come into prominence in education since the early 1960s. They incorporate elements from simulator trainers developed during and since World War II, from games of various kinds, and from role-playing in a variety of contexts. Although research evidence is sparse, significant benefits of simulation gaming appear to include increased motivation and participation, social interaction and cooperation among students, the accommodation of a wide range of student age and achievment levels, and the addition of realism and relevance to learning experiences. Like the computer, gaming can be overused or misused; it requires careful planning and application to be effective; some games also take considerable time and are complex in their administration. The potential benefits of simulation and gaming, however, are sufficient to warrant their careful consideration and use by teachers interested in improving the quality and relevance of instruction in today's schools.

43 Paul A. Twelker, *Instructional Simulation Systems: An Annotated Bibliography*, Continuing Education Publications, Waldo Hall 100, Corvallis, Ore. 97330, 1969, 268 pp., $6.75.

Further learner response projects

1

The field of computer applications in education is changing rapidly and will probably continue to do so. To keep abreast of current developments, secure sample copies from one or more of the newsletter sources listed below and make them available for examination by interested class members.

CAI Reporter, Computer Publications Division
Capitol Publications, Inc., Suite G-12
2430 Pennsylvania Avenue, N.W.,
Washington, D.C. 20037
(biweekly, $45 per year)

Automated Education Letter
Box 2658
Detroit, Michigan 48231
($18 per year)

ENTERLEK News About Computer-Assisted Instruction
42 Pleasant Street
Newburyport, Massachusetts 01950
(free)

EDUCOM Bulletin
Box 364, Rosedale Road
Princeton, New Jersey 08540
(free to members, $5 per year to educators, $10 per year to others; relates to higher education only)

2

Information about available computer programs can be secured from several sources. Aside from sources mentioned in the chapter, the computer manufacturers provide lists of programs available for their own computers. Interested students in the instructional technology class should write for lists from the sources listed below and share them with others in the class.

National Cash Register Company
Main and K Streets
Dayton, Ohio 45409

Univac Division, Sperry Rand Corporation
Peripheral Sub-Systems
Jolly Road
Whitpain, Pennsylvania 19422

Burroughs Corporation
Industrial Marketing Division
Second Avenue & Burroughs Road
Detroit, Michigan 48232

Honeywell Information Systems, Inc.
60 Walnut Street
Wellesley Hills, Massachusetts 02181

International Business Machines Corporation
Highway 52 & Northwest 37th Street
Rochester, Minnesota 55901

Xerox Data Systems
701 South Aviation Boulevard
El Segundo, California 90245

Hewlett Packard
Palo Alto, California 94304

3

Invite a representative of the computer science department on your campus or another person familiar with CAI to come in and discuss recent developments in computer applications to instruction.

4

Write to the Northwest Regional Educational Laboratory, Division of Dissemination and Installation, 710 S.W. Second Avenue, Portland, Oregon 97204, or to Tecnica Education Corporation, 655 Sky Way, San Carlos, California 94070, *for information on three packaged "hands-on" concentrated courses on uses of the computer in teaching and administration. Be on the lookout for similar training opportunities available to interested individuals or school systems.*

5

Secure a simulation game exercise that is suitable for your teaching area, try it out *with your students, and report the results to your instructional technology class.*

6

Invite a faculty member (probably from the department of psychology or the College of Education) who has done special work with simulation and gaming *to come in and discuss his experience with the class and perhaps illustrate the techniques involved with a sample simulation game exercise.*

References

ABT, CLARK C. *Games for Learning.* Educational Services, Inc., 1966.

AHL, DAVID, and JAMES BAILEY. "Computers Are for Kids—Not for Geniuses." *School Management,* April 1971, p. 26.

ALLEN, LAYMAN E., ROBERT W. ALLEN, and JAMES C. MILLER. "Programmed Games and the Learning of Problem-Solving Skills: The WFF'N PROOF Example." *Journal of Educational Research,* September 1966.

ATKINSON, R. C., and H. A. WILSON. *Computer-Assisted Instruction: A Book of Readings.* Academic Press, 1970.

BOOCOCK, SARANE S., E. O. SCHILD, and C. STOLL. *Simulation Games and Control Beliefs.* Johns Hopkins University, 1967.

BOOCOCK, SARANE S., and E. O. SCHILD, eds. *Simulation Games in Learning,* Sage Publications, Inc., 1968.

CHERRYHOLMES, CLEO. "Developments in Simulation of International Relations in High School Teaching." *Phi Delta Kappan,* January 1965, pp. 227–231.

Commission on Instructional Technology. *To Improve Learning: A Report to the President and the Congress of the United States.* U.S. Government Printing Office, 1970.

CRAWFORD, JACK, and PAUL A. TWELKER. "Affect Through Simulation: The Tamesman Technologist." *Contributions of Behavioral Science to Instructional Technology, 1, The Affective Domain.* Communication Service Corporation, 1970.

CRAWFORD, JACK, and PAUL A. TWELKER. *Instructional Simulation: A Research Development and Dissemination Activity.* Teaching Research, Monmouth, Ore., 1969.

CRUICKSHANK DONALD E. *Inner City Simulation Laboratory.* Science Research Associates, 1969.

CRUICKSHANK, DONALD E. "Simulation: New Direction in Teacher Preparation." *Phi Delta Kappan,* September 1966, pp. 23–24.

DUKE, RICHARD. *Gaming—Simulation in Urban Research.* Michigan State University Press, 1964.

FELDHUSEN, JOHN, and MICHAEL SZABO. "A Review of Development in Computer-Assisted Instruction." *Educational Technology,* April 1969, pp. 32–39.

GAGNE, ROBERT M. *The Conditions of Learning.* Holt, Rinehart and Winston, 1965.

GAGNE, ROBERT M. "Simulators." *Training Re-*

search and Education. Wiley, 1965, pp. 223–246.

GUSTAFSON, KENT L. "Simulation of Interpersonal Relations." *Audiovisual Instruction,* January 1971, pp. 35–37.

KAGAN, NORMAN, et al. *Studies in Human Interaction.* Michigan State University, 1967.

KERSH, BERT Y. *Classroom Simulation: A New Dimension in Teacher Education.* Teaching Research, Oregon State System of Higher Education, 1963.

KERSH, BERT Y. "Simulation in Teacher Education." *Programed Instruction,* Vol. 2, 1963.

Layman's Guide to the Use of Computers. Association for Educational Data Systems, N.E.A., 1971.

LEKAN, HELEN M. *Index to Computer-Assisted Instruction,* 3rd ed. Harcourt Brace Jovanovich, Division of Instructional Systems, 1972 (information on programs in 70 subject areas, cross-referenced by subject matter, central processor, computer language, instructional logic, and source).

MARGOLIN, JOSEPH B., and MARION R. MISCH, eds. *Computers in the Classroom: An Interdisciplinary View of Trends and Alternatives.* Spartan Books, 1970.

RASER, JOHN R. *Simulation and Society: An Exploration of Scientific Gaming.* Allyn and Bacon, 1969.

SILBERMAN, HENRY F., and ROBERT T. FILEP. "Information Systems Applications in Education." *Annual Review of Information Science and Technology.* Vol. III. Eycyclopaedia Britannica, Inc., 1968, pp. 357–395.

SILVERN, LEONARD C. *Systems Engineering of Education VI: Principles of Computer-Assisted Instruction Systems.* Education and Training Consultants Company, 1970.

Simulation and Games (quarterly journal). Sage Publications, 275 South Beverly Drive, Beverly Hills, Calif. 90212.

Simulation/Gaming News (five issues during school year; $4.00 per year), Box 8899, Stanford University, Stanford, Calif. 94305.

STEWART, E. C. "The Simulation of Cultural Differences." *The Journal of Communications,* December 1966, pp. 291–304.

STOLUROW, LAWRENCE M. "Computer-Assisted Instruction." *The Schools and the Challenge of Innovation.* McGraw-Hill, 1969, pp. 270–319.

Strategy and Tactics (bimonthly magazine). Simulations Publications, Inc., 44 East 23rd Street, New York, N.Y. 10010.

TANSEY, P. J., and DERICK UNWIN. *Simulation and Gaming in Education.* Methuen Educational, Ltd., 1969, and Barnes and Noble, New York, 1969.

TICKTON, SIDNEY G., ed. *To Improve Learning, An Evaluation of Instructional Technology.* Volume I. Bowker, 1970.

TICKTON, SIDNEY G., ed. *To Improve Learning, An Evaluation of Instructional Technology.* Volume II. Bowker, 1971.

TWELKER, PAUL A. "Classroom Simulation and Teacher Preparation." *The School Review,* September 1967, pp. 197–204.

TWELKER, PAUL A. "Simulation: An Overview." *Instructional Simulation: A Research Development and Dissemination Activity.* Teaching Research, Oregon State System of Higher Education, 1969.

TWELKER, PAUL A., and KENT LAYDEN. *Instructional Simulation/Gaming.* ERIC at Stanford. Palo Alto, Calif., 1972.

WFF'N PROOF Newsletter (quarterly on games, $1.00 per year), 1111 Maple Avenue, Turtle Creek, Pa. 15145.

WING, R. L. "Two Computer-Based Economic Games for Sixth Graders." *Simulation Games in Learning.* Sage Publications, 1968.

ZINN, KARL L. *An Evaluative Review of Uses of Computers in Instruction.* Project CLUE, Final Report, USOE Contract No. OEC–5–9–32–509–0032. University of Michigan Press, Ann Arbor, December 1970.

Media references

Apollo Reentry Simulation, 16mm film, color, 11 min. NASA.

CAI, 16mm film, color, 17 min. RCA.

Class of '01: The College of Tomorrow, 16mm film, color, 25 min. McGraw-Hill.

Computer in the Classroom, 16mm film, b/w, 13 min. Rand Corporation.

Computers and the Mind of Men: Managers and Models, 16mm film, b/w, 30 min. NET.

Flight Simulation, 16mm film, color, 20 min. IBM.

Gemini Mission Simulator, 16mm film, color, 9 min. NASA.

Kagan Stimulus Film, I & II, 16mm film, b/w, 56 min. Michigan State University.

Living Machine, 16mm film, b/w, 57 min. NFBC.

The Process of Communication, 16mm film, b/w, 45 min. Ohio State University.

Sign On/Sign Off, 16mm film, color, 24 min. Pennsylvania State University.

Source references

See source lists in the Appendix; particularly relevant sections are: Computers and Programs; Simulation and Games.

FOURTEEN
Individualized instruction and technology

Objectives	Performance responses

1

To identify and describe four types of individual differences which should be considered in designing programs for Individualized Instruction (I.I.).

Review the four principal types of individual variables. (a) Write a brief description of each type. (b) List examples of each type in relation to learning (c) Check your work against that of two or more of your fellow students and reconcile your interpretations if necessary.

2

To define Individualized Instruction and identify at least three basic distinctions between I.I. and group- or class-oriented instruction.

Write a definition of I.I. in your own words and list three or more differences between an I.I. program and a typical class program in a school.

3

To identify major types of existing I.I. programs in terms of who determines the objectives and the methods of achieving them.

List four major types of I.I. in terms of the criteria in Objective 3 and describe at least one way in which each differs from the other three. Check as in Response 1.

4

To identify three major differences in philosophy between I.I. and traditional instruction and trace the effects of these differences on the objectives defined for I.I. programs.

Review the section on "Differences from Traditional Instruction" (pages 610–612). (a) In one column labeled "Philosophies" list the three major points of view—or philosophies reflected —with a brief note of explanation of each. (b) In a second column labeled "Objectives" write a brief explanation of how the corresponding objectives differ under these three philosophies. (c) Compare notes with two fellow students. Question one another (and the instructor, if necessary) until substantial agreement is reached.

5

To identify and explain four key problems that must be considered in establishing an I.I. program in a school and to find a viable solution for each.

Select a committee to explore administrative problems involved in establishing I.I. programs. Have the committee conduct a panel discussion during which (a) key problems are listed on the chalkboard (and by each student in his notebook during the course of the discussion) and (b) one or more practical solutions for resolving each of the problems are presented and listed.

6

To specify and illustrate at least three ways in which educational technology can make *unique* contributions to the success of I.I. programs.

Appoint several committees to examine case studies of I.I. programs taken from the Edling survey or other sources. (a) Find three or more illustrations of educational technology applications without which the I.I. program either could not function at all or would function with significantly less efficiency and/or effectiveness. Write a one-page description of each example selected. (These illustrations should show media contributions above and beyond the usual benefits of audiovisual materials to learning which would apply in *either* I.I. or traditional classroom instruction.) (b) Each committee should then present and defend its reports before another committee (or a small group from the class). (c) During or after these discussions, the reports should be revised as necessary for clarity and adequacy. Copies of the revised reports should be distributed to all members of the class.

AS we pointed out at the beginning of the last chapter, Individualized Instruction is one of those elusive goals that educators have *talked* about for years, but, with a few notable exceptions and until recently, one that they have *done* relatively little about. Actually, concern for the individual in learning is almost as old as education itself. Aristotle, Plato, and other early Greek scholars typically conducted their discourses with a select few. During the periods of the Roman Empire and the Middle Ages, instruction was carried on by tutors for sons of the well-to-do, individually or in small groups. It was not until after the development of universities in the Middle Ages and the advent of printing in the Western World in the mid-fifteenth century that lecturing to large groups came into prominence.

As efforts increased during and after the Colonial period in this country to make education available to more and more young people, it was inevitable that group or class techniques would predominate and that therefore the teacher would control the learning experience. In essence, that is the system that has remained as an almost universal pattern for education across the world today.

Much of the present widespread criticism of education appears to be based on a combination of factors—rapidly increasing costs, on the one hand, and inadequate or questionable results of the whole education enterprise, on the other. We hear much of "accountability" as a requirement for continued public support of our school and college programs. For the good

of education this pressure is probably long overdue, for it is forcing us all to look with new intensity at all that we are doing in education, including how we conduct our instructional programs. Though the problem may be broader than instruction alone, there is no question that much of it is centered there.

Reliance on instruction in class-size groups as the primary model for education has long been a target of criticism both within and outside the educational profession. A leading clinical psychologist, for example, decries the manner in which youthful enthusiasm and curiosity tend to become lost in our schools:

The young human being is intrinsically motivated to a high degree. He is curious, eager to discover, eager to know, eager to solve problems. A sad part of most education is that by the time the child has spent a number of years in school the intrinsic motivation is pretty well dampened. Yet it is there and it is our task as facilitators of learning to tap that motivation, to discover what challenges are real for the young person, and to provide the opportunity for him to meet those challenges.[1]

Numerous efforts are being made, as we shall see, to correct some of the deficiencies present in our schools and colleges by individualizing instruction in various ways. These efforts are characterized by rather complete changes in perspective among curriculum planners, teachers, and

[1] C. R. Rogers, *Freedom To Learn*, Merrill, 1969, p. 131.

administrators in relation to both what is important for students to learn and how it can be organized and taught (see Figure 14.1). Most such efforts are heavily dependent also on instructional technology in a variety of forms, including instructional development procedures that involve careful diagnosis of the problems and needs of individuals and groups as a basis for designing viable solutions.

Basically, Individualized Instruction (I.I.) means adapting instructional materials and techniques to the individual differences found among learners. In order to develop effective programs of individualized instruction, therefore, we must first be aware of the various kinds of individual differences that exist, so that we may then deal with them in some kind of orderly fashion. Ideally, perhaps we should be able to design a different set of learning materials and experiences for each and every student. The impracticality of such a solution is fairly obvious. In any case, students clearly have many common characteristics and needs, as well as individual differences, that must be accommodated. The task is therefore one of accommodating both the common *and* the

individual needs—and achieving the proper balance between these is both a more viable and a more manageable possibility. As we shall see, even in the face of a long tradition of group instruction, noteworthy and successful efforts are being made to introduce Individualized Instruction programs into our schools—and to move toward a better balance between group and individual needs. Actually, group work is a normal, in fact, essential, part of many Individualized Instruction programs. Some programs start a unit with a general presentation, and students then select individual topics or contracts to pursue. In other cases (typing, for example), students are entirely on individual tracks but meet together to use the equipment.

One important thrust toward providing for individual differences is programed instruction. As shown by his pioneering and extensive work in programed instruction, the noted psychologist B. F. Skinner places considerable importance on individual differences in education; in fact, he regards accommodating them as critical to increasing the effectiveness of current educational programs: "Failure to provide for individual differences among students

FIGURE 14.1

Many schools that have Individualized Instruction programs use contracts, as in the Cashton, Wisconsin, Elementary School. When a contract suggests that a pupil might listen to a record to learn a concept, there is no reason why he must listen alone. Other students working on the same contract may choose to listen at that time merely because it is convenient.

is perhaps the greatest single source of inefficiency in education.''[2] Even so, there is much evidence that Skinnerian self-teaching programs actually leave the teacher in complete control—that the only variable in such programed instruction that truly individualizes it is self-pacing. In point of fact, programed instruction as such has shown little improvement over other methods in adapting learning ex-periences to the aptitudes, interests, learning styles, or other intrinsic characteristics of individual learners. Nonetheless, potentially, through technology and different means of organizing learning experiences, it is possible to provide for many more of the individual differences among learners than the pace at which they can learn. What are some of these other differences?

Types of individual differences

THE magnitude and complexity of the task of adapting instructional programs to individual differences become evident when we look at the various types of differences which have been and are being studied by psychologists in relation to learning. For example, one researcher has listed more than 50 studies dealing with one or more of four basic and distinct types of individual differences—personality, cognitive, inquiry, and sequencing variables.[3] These four variables and a few of the findings relating to planning instruction to accommodate individual differences merit further discussion.

1. Personality variables

Common sense tells us that personality traits have a marked influence on how students react to various kinds of instruction, but many research studies also support this conclusion. For example, students who are flexible in their thinking and who are able to cope with ambiguity and inconsistency seem best able to profit from the give-and-take of class discussion and/or prob-lem-solving situations. On the other hand, students who seek definite, concrete, ordered, and consistent patterns of thinking and who see themselves in more or less stereotyped ways tend to be more comfortable and content in more highly teacher-centered and specifically directed kinds of activities.

Numerous studies bear out the fact that there are distinctive learning styles which seem to correlate rather closely with personality characteristics. For example, students having a strong interest in social acceptance and a corresponding need for it have been found to perform poorly with programed instruction, while learners who appear to be more withdrawn, less self-reliant, and more test-anxious perform successfully with it.[4]

Another study shows that students tend to react quite differently to, on the one hand, content that is governed by logical and inherently ''meaningful'' rules and, on the other, content that is governed by ''arbitrary'' rules. The difference in reactions correlates highly with whether

[2] B. F. Skinner, *The Technology of Teaching*, Appleton-Century-Crofts, 1968, p. 242.

[3] John P. Fry, *The Effect of Student-Controlled Instruction on Learning*, unpublished dissertation, Michigan State University, 1970, pp. 34–44.

[4] B. A. Doty and L. A. Doty, ''Programmed Instruction Effectiveness in Relation to Certain Student Characteristics,'' *Journal of Educational Psychology*, Vol. 55, 1964, pp. 334–338; M. W. Traweek, ''The Relationship Between Certain Personality Variables and Achievement Through Programmed Instruction,'' *California Journal of Educational Research*, Vol. 15, 1964, pp. 215–220.

the students are extrovert or introvert types, high or low on test anxiety, and high or low on technological and social-esthetic interests.[5] A study of a group of 16-year-olds confirms the fact that extroverts seem to learn best with unstructured material and situations such as the "discovery method," whereas introvert-type students seem to learn best with structured and prompted learning situations.[6]

2. Cognitive variables

Individual differences dealing with knowledge, perception, and understanding of material at various levels of sophistication have probably been studied more extensively than any other, since they relate most directly to the traditional objectives of education. These studies have typically shown contradictory results. For example, the correlation between the results of general ability tests such as the IQ test and individual learning performance has generally been negligible.[7] On the other hand, when specific relevant abilities such as adding, subtracting, or following directions are studied, the correlation between these abilities and performance is clearly positive.[8]

These findings strongly suggest the importance of careful and relevant diagnostic procedures as a preliminary to designing Individualized Instruction. For example, when three researchers recently investigated the interaction between individual differences and several methods of presenting programed instruction, they made a significant discovery. This was that of two specific sources of individual differences, prior learning and general abilities, the former appears far more useful in determining the best instructional method to employ with a given student.[9] These researchers join the psychologist Robert Gagné in viewing prior conditioning, transfer, and "learning sets" as accounting for most individual differences in cognitive learning.[10]

3. Inquiry variables

Differences among individuals in curiosity traits have received increasing attention in recent years as educators have undertaken to open up the lock-step, teacher-dominated patterns of classroom instruction by means of flexible scheduling, team teaching, the "discovery" method, and differentiated staffing.

For example, Lee Shulman and his associates studied the inquiry process among teachers in training in a situation which, though simulated, was sufficiently realistic to achieve a fairly high degree of emotional involvement. They discovered significant and important differences between effective and ineffective "inquirers."[11] The

[5] G. K. Tallmadge and J. W. Shearer, "Relationships Among Learning Styles, Instructional Methods, and the Nature of Learning Experiences" *Journal of Educational Psychology*, Vol. 60, 1969, pp. 222–230.

[6] G. O. M. Leith, "The Acquisition of Knowledge and Mental Development of Students," *British Journal of Educational Technology*, Vol. 1, No. 2, May 1970, pp. 116–128.

[7] R. P. Carver and P. H. DuBois, "The Relationship Between Learning and Intelligence," *Journal of Educational Measurement*, Vol. 4, No. 3, 1967, pp. 133–136.

[8] R. M. Gagné and N. E. Paradise, "Abilities and Learning Sets in Knowledge Acquisition," *Psychology Monographs*, Vol. 75, Monograph 218, 1961.

[9] R. H. Davis, F. N. Marzocco, and M. R. Denny, "Interactions of Individual Differences with Modes of Presenting Programmed Instruction," *Journal of Educational Psychology*, Vol. 61, 1970, pp. 198–204.

[10] R. M. Gagné, "The Acquisition of Kowledge," *Psychology Review*, Vol. 69, 1962, pp. 355–365.

[11] L. S. Shulman, M. J. Loupe, and R. M. Piper, *Studies of the Inquiry Process: Inquiry Patterns of Students in Teacher Training Programs*, USOE Cooperative Research Project No. 5–0597, Michigan State University, 1968.

pattern of study employed in this experiment reflected some of Shulman's convictions on how to stimulate curiosity and on the nature of the ability to inquire effectively, as he had expressed them earlier:

The "real world" does not consist of carefully constructed situations that are presented to individuals as problems for solution. Instead, individuals move through an array of stimulus situations, which are potentially problematic in varying degrees, selectively reacting to some and not to others. Those situations which are problematic do not present themselves one at a time in a predetermined numerical order but derive both their definition and the order in which they are handled from cognitive activity of the inquirer.[12]

In pursing the study, Shulman and his associates developed a battery of some 17 tests; they found that five of these proved to be good predictors of inquiry performance. Their findings characterized the effective inquirer as: "high in associational fluency; . . . high in cognitive complexity, preferring the ambiguous, the asymmetrical, and the unexpected to the regular, articulated, and predictable; liberal in political values, willing to risk on a test of logical thinking; high in verbal problem-solving; and low in expressed test anxiety.[13]

The parallels between the inquiry variables suggested by what has just been said and the personality variables discussed earlier are clearly evident.

4. Sequencing variables

A considerable number of studies have been done on programed instruction materials to assess the relative effect on achievement of random versus logical se- quences. Though it might seem obvious that logical steps or sequences would be essential to effective learning with programed instruction, actually this appears not to be the case with most of these materials that have been employed.[14] On the other hand, a more recent study showed no differences between random and logical sequences and between high- and low-ability students on low-order tasks but did find that logical-sequence students did better than random-sequence students on high-order, complex, problem-solving programed instruction sequences.[15] In consequence, at least one researcher has suggested that randomly arranged learning experiences of other types may also be more beneficial than systematically arranged instruction.[16]

From a frame of reference similar to Shulman's, John Fry undertook to test the hypothesis that inquisitive individuals can control their own learning or instructional strategies and thereby learn more and be more satisfied than by conventional means. He ascertained that individual differences do appear to exist among students within this specific dimension of student control of instructional functions. He found further that highly inquisitive students who are also high in aptitudes can function to advantage in controlling their own learning. However, students with less aptitude, even though highly inquisitive, appear to do better when the sequencing and control of the learning experience are performed by the instructor.[17] Fry also found that the random-sequence treatment was highly effective with his high-aptitude, high-in-

[12] L. S. Shulman, "Seeking Styles and Individual Differences in Patterns of Inquiry," *School Review*, Vol. 73, 1965, p. 258.

[13] Schulman, Loupe, and Piper, op. cit., p. 94.

[14] F. C. Niedermeyer, "The Relevance of Frame Sequence in Programed Instruction: An Addition to the Dialogue," *AV Communication Review*, Vol. 16, 1968, pp. 301–317.

[15] J. L. Brown, "Effects of Logical and Scrambled Sequences in Mathematical Materials on Learning with Programmed Instruction Materials," *Journal of Educational Psychology*, Vol. 61, 1970, pp. 41–45.

[16] Leith, op. cit.

[17] Fry, op. cit., pp. 151–161.

quiry students. Finally, his results indicate clearly that in addition to prior learning experiences and basic abilities, the predominant sources of individual differences, there are distinct differences in learning styles which must be taken into account in designing instructional strategies.

To sum up briefly, we have noted that there are several important types of individual differences that affect learning. The first and most obvious of these is the different paces or speeds at which different individuals learn. However, there are at least four other types of important variables among individuals that influence learning: personality variables, cognitive variables, inquiry or curiosity variables, and variables in how individuals respond to logical as opposed to randomly sequenced learning experiences. The fact that any two individual students are likely to differ significantly from one another in several or more of these variables suggests how *very* complex the task of truly individualizing instruction can be. It also explains why most I.I. programs developed to date have been able to deal most effectively with only the first kind of differences—the different speeds or paces of learning among individuals. Nonetheless, many school systems are making determined efforts in their I.I. programs to accommodate some of the other types of variables as well, and we shall describe a number of these efforts later in this chapter—noting as we do so how educational technology contributes to these I.I. programs.

Nature and characteristics of Individualized Instruction

IT is clear that our educational system has been dominated for several generations by group or class techniques and that it has been assumed that the individual student will somehow learn from these techniques. And somehow most do, but too many—and particularly those with learning deficiencies—do *not* learn or learn less than they must to survive in the system and in our society. At best, group instruction is less effective than it needs to be to provide optimum development for individual learners, whether they are good, average, or poor learners.

Much of the argument for improvement of our schools falls back on the traditional belief that lower pupil-teacher ratios would somehow solve the problem. This position is based on the theoretical assumption that with fewer pupils the teacher could somehow give sufficient individual attention to each of his pupils to correct whatever deficiencies may exist by reason of inadequate prior learning, inadequate economic and cultural background, or curriculums inadequate to the needs of today's students. The assumption is naive on two counts. First, the problem is not all that simple; second, no teacher can deal adequately with the myriad individual, personal, social, and academic needs of even 20 or 25 pupils!

Furthermore, and unfortunately for the small-class proponents, there is little evidence that the pupils of 20 or 25 years ago (when classes typically were limited to 25 or 30 pupils) learned more or learned it better than pupils today in crowded classrooms of 35 to 45 pupils. As a matter of fact, with the sole exception of spelling, the students of today, with all their problems, appear to be averaging more than a grade level ahead of where their parents were at the same age, according to comparable achievement test records. The problem, in short, lies elsewhere than in pupil-teacher ratios.

One source of the problem, actually, is that the need to know has advanced considerably more than one grade level in the past generation, as attested by the complexities and demands of our rapidly changing society—and troubled educators are concluding that the educational system as it has been is inadequate to meet this challenge. More and more school systems therefore are turning to Individualized Instruction programs as one part of the solution. But in the "real world" of tight dollars and demands for increasing accountability, there is *no way* for I.I. programs to be adequately financed without counterbalancing applications of large-group and small-group instruction, self-instruction, and other cost-effective techniques (including the use of mass media), where these are adequate for other parts of the solution.

Thus the educational system itself must change. We will hear more and more of accompanying organization, curriculum, and staffing changes during the years ahead. Teacher aides, differentiated staffing, flexible scheduling, community schools that *really* involve the community, and competency-based certification are representative of other changes yet to come. In curriculum and instruction we may expect Instructional Development procedures (discussed in the next chapter) to come into wide use as a more systematic means of identifying and solving complex educational problems in the most cost-effective manner. And we may also expect educational technology to become an essential component in the educational systems of the future, with machines taking over those parts of the instructional and management processes which they can handle effectively, thus freeing the talents and energies of teachers for the more creative and vital aspects of teaching—student development and the design and preparation of the all-important software to be used in the machines.

Within this context, Individualized Instruction can perhaps be viewed in a new light as part of a new educational system which is already in the making. We now proceed to pin down more precisely what we mean by Individualized Instruction and to identify some common characteristics as well as distinctive differences found among current I.I. programs—as a basis for looking more meaningfully at what is happening in many school systems across the nation.

Definition of Individualized Instruction

Individualized Instruction consists of learning experiences specifically designed for individual students on the basis of diagnostic procedures employed to determine individual interests and needs; once established,

FIGURE 14.2

During 1968–1969, some 600 school districts across the United States reported having Individualized Instruction programs. This map shows the locations of the 46 programs visited and reported on by Jack Edling.

these learning experiences are largely self-directed, self-administered, and, within broad limits, self-scheduled according to the interests and convenience of the learner.

Clearly, such a program as just defined is a far cry from the kind of schooling most of us have ourselves experienced. Further, it raises immediate questions both as to how such a system can be made to work in today's schools and whether the results are, in fact, all that much better than group- or class-oriented instruction.

Perhaps one of the best answers comes from Jack Edling. After a preliminary survey of some 600 school systems with identified Individualized Instruction programs, Dr. Edling, who was then director

of the Teaching Research Division of the Oregon State System of Higher Education, made personal visits to observe and report on 46 of these programs in 24 states in all sections of the United States (see Figure 14.2). He interviewed key teachers and administrators in those systems, observed and photographed programs in action, and collected and analyzed vast numbers of reports, achievement records, and other data. His general conclusion was that reactions to these Individualized Instruction programs have been highly favorable for the following reasons:

The favorable reactions of schools which have made even a partial transition to an

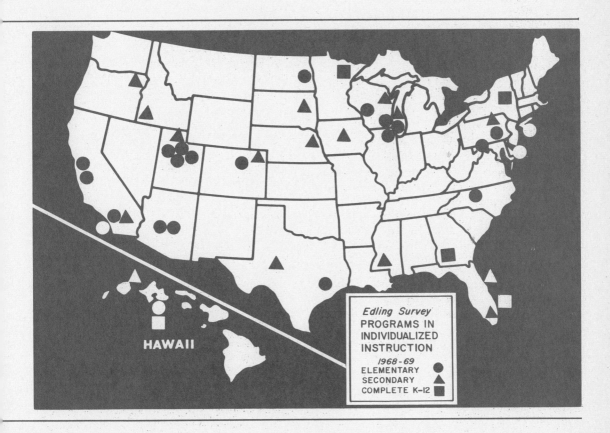

individualized instructional program may be attributed to a number of factors. First, student response has been positive. Some students have difficulty in making the transition, and others try to discover ways to take advantage of it, but most act as if it were too good to be true. Second, teachers report that while they are working harder than before they are more satisfied. Traditional disciplinary problems virtually disappear and attendance is improved. The teachers also appreciate their students' renewed interest in academic activities and in school in general. Third, the enthusiasm of students is being passed along to parents, and the favorable experience of teachers and administrators is being acknowledged by school boards. Thus, schools are receiving renewed attention, encouragement, and approval from their communities when previously they had been more or less accepted as a necessary community responsibility.[18]

Types of Individualized Instruction

By definition, Individualized Instruction programs are oriented toward individual rather than toward groups or class techniques. Theoretically, all kinds of individual differences are taken into account in designing I.I. programs, but in actual practice the one common characteristic found in Edling's survey was self-pacing. In other words, the student can take as much time as he needs to complete an assignment or a unit of work. Depending on how a specific program is designed and administered, however, variables other than speed of learning alone may in some cases also be accommodated. Under many of the programs, it would appear possible to ac-

commodate, in addition to pacing, individual differences in personality, learning styles, curiosity or inquiry levels, and perhaps in the ordering and sequencing of learning experiences. Accordingly, let us keep these additional factors in mind as we examine the several types of existing I.I. programs.

Edling identifies four major types of Individualized Instruction, based primarily on who determines what the objectives should be and who determines the methods, materials, and media to be used in achieving them.[19]

1. INDIVIDUALLY PRESCRIBED I.I. Many school systems which have I.I. programs establish common learning objectives. In such schools all children may be required to achieve a certain proficiency in reading, spelling, mathematics, and so forth, and to go through a specified series of materials and exercises to attain the desired levels of performance. The principal individualization in this instance is that the student does the work at his own pace (see Figure 14.3). In these schools, behavioral objectives are clearly specified, and well-defined systems of materials and methods of instruction have been developed based on careful diagnosis of individual pupils and their learning needs. This is known as Individually Prescribed Instruction (IPI). In placing students at the proper level in each subject area and in prescribing an individual learning sequence for each child, the West Dover, Delaware, Elementary School, for example, uses placement tests, pretests, skill booklets, and curriculum-embedded tests.

In addition to the West Dover Ele-

---

[18] Jack V. Edling, *Individualized Instruction: A Manual for Administrators*, Continuing Education Publications, Oregon State University, Corvallis, 1970, p. 1.

[19] Much of the information in the rest of this chapter is drawn from Edling's recent survey of I.I. programs in U.S. school systems, which has been described. Aside from direct quotations, therefore, further footnotes to his report, cited in footnote 18, will be omitted in order to avoid redundancy.

FIGURE 14.3

One of the great advantages of Individually
Prescribed Instruction is aptly expressed by this
bulletin board.

mentary School, the Downey Elementary
School, Harrisburg, Pennsylvania, uses
this plan, as do the Hillsdale High School,
San Mateo, California, in its reading pro-
gram and the Harry A. Burke High School,
Omaha, in its physics program.

2. SELF-DIRECTED I.I. In self-directed
programs, the school still sets the objectives
but gives the learner degrees of latitude
in determining how he will achieve them.
Typically, such schools have learning laboratories or resource centers with wide
varieties of pertinent learning materials
available. These schools provide varying
degrees of guidance, but the individual student is left largely to his own resources in
selecting the materials he will use and in
seeking assistance when he desires it. The
faculty members in these schools place
high value on individual learning styles
and on individual differences in approaching solutions to learning problems. They
feel that prescribed sequences or systems
preclude the individual's development of
his own unique interests and talents and
deny him the freedom to find his own
best methods of learning. Such Individualized Instruction programs are characterized
by well-developed testing programs, clearly
stated objectives, and well-equipped and
well-developed learning resource centers
(see Figure 14.4).

Examples are found in the Mary
Louise Aiken Elementary School, West
Hartford, and the Granada Community
School, Corte Madera, California.

3. PERSONALIZED I.I. The prescribed
and self-directed types of Individualized
Instruction discussed were typically found
in required subject areas such as language
arts and mathematics. A third type called
"personalized" is most often found in
some of the sciences, the social studies,
and in elective courses. Here the student
chooses his own objectives from a sizable
list of possible objectives—in other words,
he selects the objectives that appeal to his
interests. Once these are selected, however, he follows a prescribed program with
specified materials.

Edling found this selective type of individualization in a number of secondary
schools including the Roy, Utah, High
School and the Miami Springs, Florida,
High School. Instead of the usual world
and American history and American problems courses, the Roy High School offers
a choice of more than 40 options in the
social studies. In Miami Springs, students
essentially select their own programs except for requirements in English and math,
and even in those subjects, they select the
level of difficulty desired. The L. E. Ber-
ger Middle School, West Fargo, North Da-

FIGURE 14.4

The focus in self-directed I.I. is on independent learning. Objectives are specified, as in IPI programs, but students may choose how to go about achieving them. Clearly this requires enough alternatives to be meaningful; such schools typically have well-stocked learning resource centers.

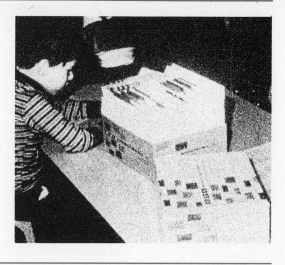

kota, likewise provides options so as to give the pupil opportunities to practice his own decision-making. Once a decision is made, he enters into a contract incorporating (1) specific objectives, (2) resources, and (3) instructional procedures; he fulfills the contract by completing a prescribed test or other evaluation procedure.

We should note here that "contract" in this sense has a special meaning; it is an agreement that a student enters into with his teacher specifying what he will undertake and what he will achieve in furthering some specific aspect of his own learning at his own pace. The term was widely used a generation or more ago in a related context—contracts for different levels of work for specified marks or grades. Because this early contract plan was used primarily in a traditional class situation, with the necessity of keeping the class together on the same topics, however (as well as for other reasons), it proved unsuccessful. Within the context of Individualized Instruction, on the other hand—without the same time constraints and with quite different motivations—the

present contract idea appears to work very well.[20]

4. INDEPENDENT STUDY This type of Individualized Instruction provides the most complete degree of freedom in that students pick both their objectives and their methods of study. It is not surprising that this type of program is typically reserved for the above-average student. For example, in the Urbandale, Iowa, High School, only 33 students out of an enrollment of 560 independently designed their own programs of study. In

[20] This type of contract should not be confused with "performance contract," a very different kind of agreement between a public school and a private concern; under such an arrangement the private concern undertakes certain types of teaching (sometimes remedial teaching of disadvantaged children) at the school, promising to produce certain results in terms of grade-level gains and contracting to accept payment geared to student achievement. Incidentally, after fairly extensive trials in a number of states, performance contracting has proved to be of dubious value (see, for example, "Learning Plan Test Is Called a Failure," *New York Times*, February 1, 1972, pp. 1 ff.).

the Melbourne, Florida, High School, exceptional students are released either part- or full-time to study anything they wish that is not offered in the curiculum (see Figure 14.5). Interestingly enough, this freedom is also extended to some students with creative imaginations who may not have a particularly strong academic background. Among elementary schools, the Lakeside School, Merrick, New York, and the Kahala School, Honolulu, provide comparable freedom to pupils both in objective selection and in the choice of materials and methods with which to pursue their interests.

It should be noted that use of any one of these four types of Individualized Instruction does not exclude the use of another type in the same school; in fact, most school systems that use any I.I. use more than one type. The philosophies of a par-

ticular school, of course, influence the degree of freedom permitted. Typically, a school may begin an individualized instruction program with a carefully developed diagnostic program and specified goals and move, as did the Roy High School, to increasing the options in certain areas of study. In either case, however, in that school the means and materials of learning are prescribed once the options have been chosen.

School systems placing high values on self-direction and individual learning styles range from those that require students to select from a predetermined set of behavioral objectives and curriculum goals but then permit the student to select his own means of attaining them to those in which some students are left quite free to establish both their goals and the means of achieving them.

FIGURE 14.5

Self-directed independent study opportunities are provided for exceptionally capable students in some schools, along with other types and levels of I.I. programs for others. Where such programs exist for gifted students, they fill a need that usually is ignored in traditional schools.

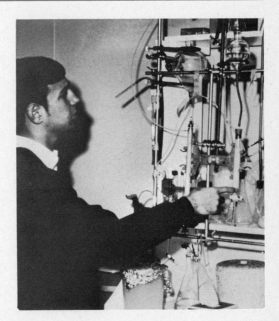

Differences from traditional instruction

WHATEVER pattern or patterns of Individualized Instruction school systems may pursue, there are three clear distinctions between this plan of instruction and traditional group or class patterns.

1. Differences in specification of objectives

In objectives, there is a strong tendency for schools having Individualized Instruction programs to extend and specify their objectives in behavioral terms even when the school's objectives are traditional in terms of content and skills to be attained. In some schools, the objectives have been systematically developed under an Instructional Development type of approach (see Chapters 3 and 15), with phases or levels of difficulty. For example, at the Melbourne, Florida, High School, very detailed statements of objectives have been formulated in mathematics, English, science, and the social studies. In each of these, several levels or phases of difficulty have been designated, with objectives specified for each phase:

Phase 1. *Designed to provide the student with remedial work in basic skills; organizational emphasis is on a ratio of no more than 12 to 15 students to a teacher.*

Phase 2. *Designed to develop existing but limited skills; the curriculum focuses on small-group work and directed readings.*

Phase 3. *Classes are designed for students of moderate ability; attention is paid to depth study and self-directed learning.*

Phase 4. *Involves in-depth study and emphasis on small-group and independent work at an advanced level.*

Phase 5. *Involves advanced placement courses at a highly intense depth level.*

Phase Q. *Provides for students interested in independent study.*

Phase X. *This is the designation given to courses outside the major disciplines for which there are no standardized criteria (such as typing and physical education); these courses are nongraded and unphased.*

2. Emphasis on individual development

Optimum individual development is emphasized in approximately one quarter of the schools in the Edling survey. In these schools, perhaps best exemplified by the John Murray Junior High School, Pendleton, Oregon, the emphasis is on developing self-confidence and a positive self-image that leads to more effective learning:

The goal is to try to change the self-image of learners who are average or above average in ability, but who are under-achieving. For those children, for whom the present curriculum has failed, we have de-emphasized subject matter as it is commonly understood and have said to ourselves "let's make our objective the development of this person as a person!"[21]

In the course of this deliberate effort to improve the self-image of underachievers, various unconventional activities, including Monopoly and other games, are used at the Murray School. As better images of school and self are developed, the curriculum is broadened to include basic skills and additional concepts that the student is now ready to learn. The system is based on Abraham Maslow's theory that a child has certain physical, emotional, and psychological needs which must be satisfied before he can do full justice to learning.

[21] Edling, op. cit., p. 13.

Thus, to the extent feasible, emphasis is placed on diagnosis and treatment of these needs rather than upon academic achievement.

The UCLA University Elementary School likewise emphasizes personal and social development factors in an ungraded curriculum which undertakes to strike a balance between personal and social growth of the individual child and achievement of the academic tools which he will need in all future learning. The program is organized into four phases: early childhood, lower elementary, middle elementary, and upper elementary, and pupils are placed in the phases which best accommodate their needs in both the personal and academic sense.

3. Emphasis on learning how to learn

Lifelong learning objectives receive primary emphasis in another group of schools constituting about 20 percent of the schools visited. The point here is one of positive attitude formation. These schools may use fairly traditional content but, as Edling points out, there is a subtle but highly important difference between them and the schools whose I.I. programs focus primarily on content learning:

The underlying philosophy has little to do with traditional concepts of achievement testing, acquiring an organized body of knowledge in the sense of the present academic disciplines, or of any structured curriculum which defines objectives in terms of content to be learned. The emphasis is on learning processes, and learning to enjoy the behavior of learning. The objective is to build an atmosphere, an attitude, an approach to learning, not a sequenced, structured, predetermined series of learning experiences. While many of these schools do employ contracts and other structured aids in learning, the attitude

toward their use is different from schools which are oriented toward student academic achievement.[22]

Among the best examples of this philosophy carried into practice is the Duluth, Minnesota, school system, whose superintendent states:

We have an end goal that says we want life-long learners, and this implies that if one is going to be a life-long learner, one has to have a very active role in his own learning processes. It also implies that learning is not drudgery; rather, it should be exciting. So this is the end product we're looking for: an attitude toward learning. This is the major goal of our instruction.[23]

The Kahala School, Honolulu, has a highly developed independent study program, the underlying objective of which is to have "children learn to learn, and to enjoy learning."[24] The Miami Springs, Florida, Senior High School has an ungraded I.I. program that emphasizes creating positive attitudes toward learning. At Miami Springs, freedom of choice in selecting courses and levels is stressed in the independent study program. Along with this freedom, however, goes a reassuring emphasis on the responsibilities that must accompany individual freedom. It is the school's philosophy that "one learns to handle responsibility by handling responsibility." As the principal puts it:

We need to develop some degree of social emphasis on individualization because there are idiosyncrases within each of us, and that's fine; but I also think there are commonalities among us and these also must be emphasized. If we are graduating students with the idea that life is one

22 Edling, op. cit., p. 17.

23 Edling, op cit., p. 17.

24 Edling, op. cit., p. 18.

person doing his own thing, and each one doesn't feel any sense of responsibility for those who have difficulties and are in trouble, then I think we are educating half a person. We think an equally important objective is to develop experiences in school to help students learn that they have responsibilities beyond themselves.[25]

As we have seen, there are significant differences in the philosophies and in the objectives arising from them in various Individualized Instruction programs. A majority of schools with I.I. programs are concentrating on doing a better job of specifying and dealing with traditional content objectives. Other schools, however, are placing their priorities on attitudinal objectives such as improving the individual's self-image, on stimulating and nurturing each student's natural curiosity, on making learning an enjoyable and continuing experience—in short, on optimal development of the individual's personal, social, and intellectual characteristics. Within that rather wide range, there are numerous schools with elements of both types of objectives. Furthermore, many schools with purely content-oriented programs have tended to move toward attitudinal objectives as they become more successful with and confident of the programs already under way.

One positive effect of the I.I. movement has clearly been a great improvement in the precision with which objectives of all types are defined. As we noted earlier in our discussion of Instructional Development (Chapter 3), such exact specification of objectives is an essential element in any soundly based instructional improvement.

Procedures and facilities for Individualized Instruction

As noted, the objectives found in various Individualized Instruction programs vary considerably. The instructional procedures and facilities used to put these into practice vary even more—from highly prescribed activities in regular classroom settings on a fixed class-period schedule to situations in which some students have complete freedom of choice as to the topics they will study, the materials and methods they will use to study them, and when, where, and how long they will study them. In between are all possible combinations of the elements of how the work is laid out, the settings in which the student does his work, and the kind of time blocks and time allowances made. A considerable variety of configurations could obviously be expected; such variety does, in fact, exist in schools around the country that have I.I. programs. For example, the East Elementary School, Tooele, Utah, uses the Continuous Progress Plan and an ungraded system in which emphasis is placed on providing *appropriate* learning experiences for each individual child; these experiences are designed by the teacher, who encourages the child to participate and then works with him, guiding him to achieve maximum growth through the experiences.

Some inherent constraints on I.I.

It is important to note that in any given school, Individualized Instruction is seldom provided for all students, nor are I.I. programs set up in all subjects. This situation is a natural product of three primary constraints.

1. SIZE OF THE TASK The first constraint on I.I. arises from the obvious fact

[25] Edling, op. cit., p. 19.

that starting an Individualized Instruction program in a traditional school is a sizable task. Though some materials for Individualized Instruction are available commercially in a few subjects, most materials must be generated "from scratch" within the school system. As might be expected, therefore, a school starting an I.I. program usually begins with an area of critical need, such as reading or mathematics, and expands gradually from there. For example, at the Cashton, Wisconsin, Elementary School, contracts are used in mathematics, social science, and English. Each of the three teachers developed contracts, spanning several grades, for her subject-matter area. The teacher remains in a self-contained classroom while the children rotate classes. However, within any class children are working together on various levels or "grades" of contracts.

2. ADAPTABILITY OF TEACHERS The second constraint on I.I. arises from the fact that some teachers are better suited to working in I.I. programs than others; in consequence, some school systems have I.I. sections along with traditional sections in the same subject. If the system is to function effectively, teachers frequently need to coordinate their efforts as members of a team and to change their familiar role—controlling instruction—to an unfamiliar role—facilitating individual learning. Some teachers (as well as some learners) may find these transitions uncomfortable and difficult. Recognizing such difficulties, many administrators deliberately avoid forcing the issue, knowing that teacher cooperation is essential to successful innovation. On the other hand, there doubtless are many administrators who, for one reason or another, fail to take the initiative in moving toward I.I., though many of their teachers would welcome it.

3. SUITABILITY OF SUBJECT CONTENT The third constraint on I.I. arises from the fact that there are subjects which by nature require group activities, as in some aspects of physical education and dramatics and in group singing, band, and orchestra. Also, to a substantial degree, small- or large-group activities are important in many subjects where the give and take of discussion, the socializing influence of cooperative projects, and the consensus of group decisions provide important lessons to be learned. In consequence, many school systems with I.I. programs arrange for some group activities along with individualized learning. This pattern normally requires flexible time scheduling plus individual contracts involving several or more levels of difficulty, so that most students can profit from both individualized and group work on the same topic (see Figure 14.6).

Elements to be accommodated in I.I.

Before looking at a few representative examples of I.I. programs, it will be helpful to consider briefly three basic elements which must be accommodated in any I.I. program.

1. HOW LEARNING ACTIVITIES ARE DIRECTED OR PRESCRIBED Learning activities may be prescribed in considerable detail by the teacher or by the materials themselves. Or, as we have seen, the learner may have considerable latitude in selecting his objectives as well as the methods and materials he will use to attain them.

2. INSTRUCTIONAL SETTING The instructional setting may range from an individual classroom containing materials for a single discipline, staffed by a single teacher, to multiple learning areas with wide ranges of equipment and materials, staffed by teams of teachers occasionally supplemented by teacher-aides and other assistants (see Figure 14.7). Of the 46 school districts in Edling's personal survey,

FIGURE 14.6

Individualized Instruction with large enrollments becomes feasible only when appropriate combinations of large- and small-group activities are coupled with self-instruction and individual guidance as needed. Further, some subjects require group interaction, as in this social studies class in the Huron, South Dakota, Senior High School.

FIGURE 14.7

(a) Learning resource centers such as this one in the East Elementary School, Tooele, Utah, facilitate I.I. programs by enabling the materials to be distributed from a central location. Some schools have several centers, each of which contains materials for different clusters of subjects. Still others manage with materials collections in a part of the classroom. (b) In the Matzke Elementary School, Cypress, Texas, students have individual trays in which they collect materials from a number of areas; they then proceed on their own to work with the materials.

24 used single learning areas, while 22 had large multidiscipline learning areas, the latter being the pattern found in most of the elementary schools, along with team-teaching.

3. TIME SCHEDULING A time schedule may be set up for an individual student or for the subject he is studying; or he may have a large block of time, schedule several activities within this time block, and use it without reference to a detailed schedule to study or work on whatever he wishes. Flexible scheduling and/or continuous progress plans are characteristic of most I.I. programs.

Some representative examples of I.I.

The Meadow Moor Elementary School, Salt Lake City, has a continuous progress plan for skill subjects and prescribed learning activities which are sequenced. Though each student's time is scheduled, the procedure is not lock-step, and children are free to alter the sequence, particularly in science and the social studies. Their interests are a dominant factor in choosing activities. Teachers and support staff pre-pare a folder of materials for each child for each day's work, based on a diagnosis of his previous work and needs. Multiple-learning areas are used, and teams of teachers are assigned to work with individual students as needed. Group activities also are employed from time to time, though on a very flexible basis. This plan leads to a highly effective use of staff and also of student time.

In the Niskayuna School District, Schenectady, New York, which uses I.I. in selected areas from kindergarten through grade 12, there are centralized learning areas that employ considerable amounts of media materials (see Figure 14.8). Teams of two teachers and three aides are each assigned to a group of about 85 learners. In the elementary grades, the learning is directed by an instructional team, while in the high school the students direct their own instruction—that is, they have more freedom to select the units on which they will work, although all objectives are prescribed and the activity guides spell out procedures and materials to be used. At both elementary and secondary levels, students schedule their own time and assume increasing responsibility for

FIGURE 14.8

In the Niskayuna School District, the I.I. system is planned so that the elementary grades use directed self-instruction while the high school stresses self-directed instruction. At both levels students schedule their own time and use a considerable amount of technology.

achieving prescribed objectives (see Figure 14.9).

In general, elementary schools tend to use learning resource centers as the core or hub of I.I. programs. In the newer elementary schools, in fact, such resource centers are located centrally, with classrooms and other activity spaces extending outward around them.

On the other hand, junior and senior high schools tend to continue to use traditional classrooms as learning areas for individual subjects. In the Milton, Pennsylvania, Junior High School, for example, rooms are assigned for each subject and students are scheduled there for specific class periods in the usual manner. Each child in the room, however, works on an individual activity and at his own pace. He uses materials for the most part designed and prepared by the teachers. Behavioral objectives have been carefully spelled out and special materials prepared at various levels in mathematics, social science, science, and language arts. The student is placed at the level deemed best by the teacher in charge but may transfer to

any other level at any time, depending on his performance. He must complete a unit satisfactorily, however, before moving to a more advanced objective or unit.

When students are allowed to select their own activities—as in schools which stress that students learn how to learn and plan their own learning—instructional procedures, of course, are modified from the prescribed situations described. Yet there are some schools, such as the Duluth Public Schools, which operate independent learning plans on a time-scheduled basis. There each child at the beginning of each day maps out how he plans to spend his day, and his plan is checked and his progress monitored by a teacher. Though the student thus decides what contract he will work on, if desired materials happen to be unavailable, an alternative is worked out with him by the teacher. The student is required to stay with the time schedule worked out at the beginning of the day. This arrangement has the advantage of optimum use of resources, which are extensive—many different learning materials are available in the large learning areas.

FIGURE 14.9

Students adapt readily to the new procedures and responsibilities inherent in I.I. Where lessons are individually prescribed, students often go, as shown here, to a designated file, pull out the material they are to work on, check it later with an answer sheet, seek help if needed, return the material to the file when completed, and go on to the next assignment. No problem!

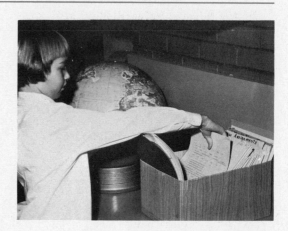

The Martin Luther King Jr. Elementary School, Evanston, Illinois, starts out the day with group activities, but as soon as the initial objectives for the day have been attained, students move into small-group "mini-labs" where they work on projects or topics of their own choice, in the process selecting their own media and other learning materials. Each of these mini-labs is organized by a teacher who is a member of a team and a specialist in one of four subjects—social studies, science, mathematics, or language arts. Learning centers contain mini-labs in all basic subjects, and within each mini-lab, students have almost complete freedom of choice in selecting their own learning activities. There is also a team of teacher specialists in music, dramatics, and physical education who organize group work.

Thus various patterns and plans are found in schools that have moved into Individualized Instruction programs. The nature of the approach used in each case is influenced primarily by the philosophy of the school. So far, most programs have continued to emphasize content objectives; nevertheless, instead of simply giving lip service to them, they specify their objectives and carefully try to design programs which provide assurance that these objectives will be met by each individual student. In the process and to the extent that they are successful, such content-focused programs doubtless contribute also to more positive attitudes of students toward learning and toward school and toward their individual self-images. Other schools, however, make the latter type of more intangible but vitally important objectives a primary focus of their programs and design learning activities to contribute directly to their attainment. For example, at the Meadow Moor Elementary School, Salt Lake City, the children operate a unique bank. Tokens are awarded for academic achievement and in turn are used to pay fines or purchase special privileges. Also, citizenship is involved, for students are paid in tokens for special work such as library work, cleaning, or being bank tellers, and each class pays regular taxes in tokens to support these school workers. There is much enthusiasm for the system and for maintaining all accounts accurately.

Time, money, and resource restraints are very real, but it is important to note that many school systems have managed in spite of such limitations to develop effective I.I. programs which, though less perfect than they might like, are nonetheless a decided step forward from their former traditional, group-oriented programs.

Role of media and technology in Individualized Instruction

THUS far, as you undoubtedly have noted, we have said relatively little about media and educational technology in I.I. programs. This is intentional—until one has carefully diagnosed the individual needs of his students and has clearly specified his objectives, he is in no position to select the alternative materials and methods which are most likely to help students to achieve the objectives successfully.

Need for systematic development procedures

The perceptive reader will have sensed already that in our discussion of Individualized Instruction, with our emphasis on diagnosis of individual needs and specification of objectives, we have been saying many of the same things said earlier in the discussion of Instructional Development. In fact, I.I. programs can be excellent examples of Instructional Development when they are planned, designed, developed, and validated with sufficient care.

So far, it has been first things first, for the most part, in introducing I.I. programs. That is, the need to overcome the problems involved in simply developing or acquiring the large amounts of materials necessary for I.I. programs and planning their uses has tended to overshadow the need to test and validate these materials and methods for specific types and levels of learners. That the materials now in use usually *work* we do know; and that I.I. programs in general are an improvement over previous traditional group instruction practices we also know. But how *much* better these programs are and whether there are not still better I.I. options available remains to be determined.

These comments refer to both materials prepared locally by teachers and materials commercially produced which teachers select and adapt for I.I. purposes. Materials specially developed as a part of funded or cooperative I.I. projects are more likely to have been tested and revised, but such testing is likely to be limited to content achievement objectives alone and to student populations in a single area. Because of those factors and because of objectives which may be unique to individual schools, there is no real substitute for teaching staffs that first identify and specify their own objectives and then identify and test the materials and procedures to be used in attaining those objectives. Such efforts are time consuming and demanding, but they are essential to effective Individualized Instruction programs.

Nature and amounts of materials required

Questions of materials and methods are complex enough with well-designed group-oriented instruction; with I.I. programs, the complexity is multiplied. Since I.I. programs require, if nothing else, that the student work at his own pace, each student must have his own set of materials to work with. When I.I. programs encompass differences in addition to pacing alone, still greater amounts and varieties of materials are likely to be required. For example, if students are to be encouraged to explore and develop their varied interests independently, access to a wide range of relevant learning materials is clearly necessary.

It is not to be expected, of course, that all possible avenues of independent inquiry can be anticipated and accommodated within a school. Fortunately, the bright, inquisitive youngster, if given the opportunity and variety of materials such as are available in well-stocked learning resource centers, can usually proceed very well on his own and move on to outside sources if necessary. The needs of most pupils, on the other hand, are more likely to be met by carefully designed, sequenced materials—particularly in programs where a substantial portion of the activities is prescribed.

As indicated earlier, there are some good I.I. materials in a number of subject areas available from commercial sources (see the source lists in the Appendix). For the most part, however, individual teachers or groups of teachers must generate the bulk of the materials to be used through creating new materials or through selecting and adapting existing materials. In such circumstances, teachers tend normally to employ the medium they know best, that is, the written and spoken word. Thus many programs initially consist largely of printed excerpts from texts and workbooks, teacher-prepared mimeographed materials, and audiotapes (see Figure 14.10).

Once a program is moving along, however, its designers begin to see how improvements and shortcuts can be made and they begin to become more sophisticated in presenting ideas in graphic, pictorial, film,

FIGURE 14.10

The name of the game and the biggest single problem in I.I. is *materials,* large quantities of which are needed. Initially, most verbal materials are teacher-made or adapted from commercial materials. Both are coordinated to develop specific skills and concepts at various levels.

or recorded form. Consequently, many learning centers now have packets of self-instructional materials containing locally produced audiotapes which provide directions to the student, along with workbooks, sequences of programed instruction, and such illustrative materials as slides, filmstrips, and 8mm cassette motion picture film loops (see Chapters 9, 10, and 11 for detailed descriptions of these types of learning materials).

It is important also to keep in mind that I.I. programs seldom are completely individualized. There are some small-group and occasionally some large-group activities for which more traditional uses of films and other media are appropriate. But most I.I. activities *are* individual, and it is here that media, used creatively and carefully combined with reading materials and programed materials, can make their major contributions.

Programs emphasizing technology

Although most schools, when starting an I.I. program, tend to interpret their materials needs largely in verbal terms, the Niskayuna School District, Schenectady (with the help of an ESEA Title III grant), began early to place an emphasis on resource materials other than printed ones. Students in the Niskayuna schools have ready access to media centers where they consult filmstrips, slides, films, and tapes (see Figure 14.8). This emphasis on using technological sources of information such as information processing systems is expected to result in the replacement of a substantial portion of current book materials as time goes on.

Niskayuna is also an example of a system employing both prescribed and self-directed activities. As has been noted, in the early grades, the program is of a prescribed nature, but as the student progresses in his ability to handle resource materials, the program becomes more nearly a self-directed type in which the student follows major guideposts in the curriculum but directs his own learning activities. By the time a student reaches high school, if the system works as planned, it should be possible for a teacher to indicate an objective and for the student then to pursue independently his own means of meeting that objective. In the process, Niskayuna High School students are making considerable use of cameras and media in generating their own report, study, and developmental materials (see Figure 14.11).

To give another example, the Punahou School, Honolulu, one of the largest and most distinguished college preparatory schools in the United States, has moved into the use of videotape recorders and other audiovisual materials in its I.I. programs in physics, economics, art, music, and languages. They use this equipment for a variety of student purposes, as well as for teacher self-evaluation.

The Waterford Township Schools near Pontiac, Michigan, noted over a period of years for their innovative programs, undertook a substantial Individualized Instruction program in the late 1960s based on computer-assisted instruction (CAI). Aided by an ESEA Title III grant, the schools have undertaken a series of programs in mathematics, science, business, humanities, industrial arts, language arts, reading, the social studies, guidance, and classroom management (a computer printout from an English grammar series used in the Waterford schools is quoted in Chapter 13). This project, called INDICOM—an acronoym for "individualized communication"—has been able to extend student achievement in mathematics and language arts significantly at both the elementary and high school levels (see Figure 14.12). The CAI system, which includes both visual and audio components, is located in the Instructional Media Center, where access is provided to films, filmstrips, tapes, and other media materials, as well as books and reference materials.

Types of materials used

COMMERCIALLY PRODUCED MATERIALS As we have noted, in schools developing new I.I. programs, most of the instructional materials employed, especially in the beginning, are those with which teachers are already familiar—*commercially produced* printed and audiovisual materials of various types. Because many of these materials are designed for traditional class or group use with a teacher present most of the time, rather than for individual self-instruction on a more independent basis, much of the material has to

FIGURE 14.11

Technology in the Niskayuna Schools is used not only for instruction of students; it is also used for reports and for instruction *by* students.

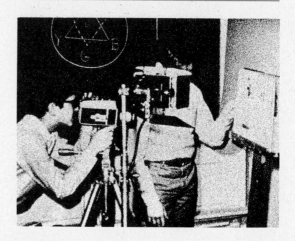

FIGURE 14.12

The Waterford Township INDICOM project uses CAI effectively in a variety of subject areas and grade levels. One general advantage is ready access to individual attention when needed, as shown here.

be adapted to the new instructional format. This adaptation typically takes two forms: (1) modifying the physical form and organization of the material itself, particularly in the case of printed materials; (2) supplementing the material with written or taped directions, and so forth, to make it more suitable for independent use by the student. The examples that follow illustrate both kinds of adaptation.

As noted earlier, printed and mimeographed materials are the most commonly used types in I.I. programs. Teachers have found ingenious ways to adapt familiar printed materials for Individualized Instruction when they cannot get copies for all students. In some schools, for example, teachers take two copies of a workbook or text, mount the pages on cardboard, and place the mounted pages in a file readily accessible to students. In this way, they are able to make one workbook do for some 20 students (see Figure 14.13). This practice, of course, is not ideal, but it does

meet an immediate need for materials in an inexpensive manner—frequently an essential requirement in initiating new programs. Under this system, students write their responses on their own paper and then compare them with the answers in the teacher's manual, which is mounted in a similar manner.

Among traditional audiovisual materials, audiotapes are probably used more than any other type, according to Edling's survey (see Figure 14.14). Some of these tapes come in convenient, foolproof cassette form, used with small recorder-playbacks. Various commercial tapes such as poetry recordings and language materials are widely used, often as part of learning contracts. These tapes may either be checked out to the student to be used in his study carrel or, in some schools, provided through a dial-access system. The Burke High School, Omaha, for example, uses a dial-access system in its I.I. program. Students go to the library, choose what they

FIGURE 14.13

When workbook pages and answer sheets are
mounted on cardboard, costs are held down and
students can check their own work.

FIGURE 14.14

The individualized program at the Urbandale,
Iowa, Senior High School does not preclude
small-group activities. Many audiovisual devices
and materials are used in instruction while the
teacher may be working individually with another
student.

want to hear from a catalog of recorded
materials, and listen immediately in individual carrels by dialing the indicated
number. Selections of phonograph records
are used extensively in many schools, particularly at the junior and senior high
school levels.

Filmstrips are the next most frequently used audiovisual item found in
Edling's survey. These are easily handled
and used with small rear-view projectors
or desk-top viewers; they are available in
great numbers on many individual topics.
In addition, slide sets, maps of various

kinds, selected study prints, and other flat
pictures are commonly used in I.I. units
(see Figure 14.15).

Thus, in printed, tape, and filmstrip
form, large amounts of commercial instructional materials are used in I.I. programs.
It should be emphasized, however, that the
commercial materials typically are used
in new ways and for somewhat different
purposes than those for which they were
originally designed. In brief, they are
adapted from their original formats and
used more or less independently by individual students in new patterns designed

622

for highly specific objectives. Frequently, a single sequence from a filmstrip or recording is used, rather than the complete form, and individual slides or pictures are selected from sets to illustrate highly specific points. Although such adaptation is also made in traditional class instruction on occasion, it is more characteristic of well-designed I.I. units. In adapting commercial materials, teachers also often supplement them with teacher-prepared materials such as those discussed next.

TEACHER-PREPARED MATERIALS The next most frequently used mateials in I.I. programs are *teacher-prepared,* rather than commercially produced. The range of materials in this category is almost unlimited. In reading, for example, primary students frequently tell stories to the teacher, who types them "from dictation" on a primary typewriter and binds them in a folder which is put in the students' library. Since each student is familiar with his own story, this procedure makes for a ready association of oral words with written symbols. As they read each other's stories in fact, young students often develop rather large sight-reading vocabularies.

Teachers use audiotapes in many ways in preparing materials tailored to their own students. They record directions, explanations of problems, oral tests, practice exercises, and various other things that teachers usually talk about. Many use students or aides or both to record such materials. Actually, directions and explanations are often more quickly and effectively conveyed on tape than in printed or mimeographed form, and the familiarity of the teacher's voice may often be an added advantage. Experience at the Nova School, Fort Lauderdale, Florida, for example, suggests that students feel more security because they are listening to their teacher's voice and thus sense that they can readily get additional information or help whenever they need it.

Teachers and librarians normally collect magazine and newspaper articles and illustrations on numerous aspects of science, the social studies, and other areas. These single-topic materials are teacher-prepared materials which become valuable reference sources. Teachers also find or

FIGURE 14.15

In the Duluth I.I. program students are taught to operate audiovisual equipment so they can use it actively in their individual learning activities. This boy has selected his own instructional materials and is using them as easily as if he were using books.

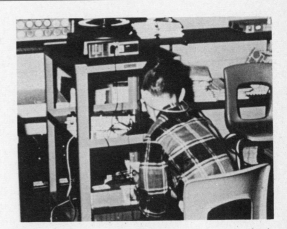

generate games and other devices to give students practice in basic skills. Students are then often inspired to bring their own games from home to share with their classmates.

PROJECT-DEVELOPED MATERIALS   A third and highly important source of I.I. materials is *special projects* undertaken to develop materials and techniques specifically for I.I. programs. Most of these projects involve carefully coordinated developmental programs in which a number of school systems are involved. For example, the Kettering Foundation has established a bank of teacher-prepared instructional contracts. These are available to member-schools which contribute to the collection; thus each contract gets a variety of users, and the whole program is a helpful beginning on solving the problem of duplication of effort. Although such contracts may well have to be modified and adapted to accommodate local needs, it makes little sense for everyone wishing to establish an I.I. program to have to start from scratch and "reinvent the wheel" all over again.

Project PLAN (Program for Learning in Accordance with Needs) is being widely used as a comprehensive system that makes extensive use of existing instructional materials and resources in individualizing education. The Brittain Acres Elementary School, San Carlos, California, began development of the plan in 1967 with the assistance of 14 cooperating school districts. By 1970 alternative sets of materials appropriate to different levels of achievement within each grade level had been completed for many units of instruction for grades 1 through 12. At the Brittain Acres School, Project PLAN materials are used as a guide to conventional materials. They clarify instructional objectives, offer a choice of learning modes and materials, and provide evaluative procedures (see Figure 14.16).

An example of a thoroughly developed instructional system in reading, mathematics, and science is the Individually Prescribed Instruction (IPI) program being developed by the Learning Research and Development Center at the University of Pittsburgh and the Regional Education Laboratory in Philadelphia. The IPI materials, which are tested in a substantial number of schools, include pretests, posttests, instructional units, and diagnostic materials.

Validated I.I. materials are also be-

FIGURE 14.16

At the Brittain Acres Elementary School, a computer system is used to keep track of pupil progress and to prescribe learning activities in terms of diagnostic data on interests and past achievements.

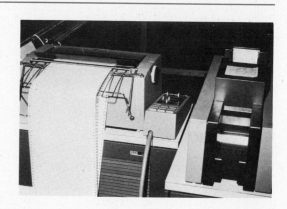

ing developed at various other locations. Examples are found in the teaching of spelling in Utah's Continuous Progress Plan; in the Nova Schools, Fort Lauderdale, where games and simulations are being used; and in the Wisconsin State Department of Education, where an elementary language arts program has been developed. An extensive program in English for kindergarten through grade 12 has been under way in Hawaii since 1966 that involves language skills, language systems, and literature (see Chapter 15). Although the program is not solely designed for Individualized Instruction purposes, during its evolution and use many materials that can be used effectively in I.I. programs have been developed and validated. As this is being written, Hawaii English materials are in use in the Berryessa Unified School District, San Jose, California, as well as in Guam, the Trust Territories, and American Samoa. Thus more and better materials are constantly becoming available as innovative projects multiply, and the pace of new development can be expected to increase.

It should not be expected, however, that "imported" systems of materials can achieve adequate individualization of instruction in any specific school. By definition, I.I. requires diagnosis of *individual* learner needs. In these terms, therefore, teaching staffs must identify their own objectives and then identify the materials that they are sure are adequate for attainment of those objectives. Many of the project materials mentioned were, of course, prepared for special areas and conditions. Nevertheless, many have wide applicability. In other words, it is probable that some combination of commercially produced, teacher-prepared, and project-developed materials will continue to be necessary for implementing effective I.I. programs.

Summary

The individualization of instruction has long been a goal of professional educators. Only in recent years, however, has a combination of external and internal pressures on the schools led to serious efforts to develop Individualized Instruction programs. Most of these programs currently concentrate primarily on accommodating individual differences in the speed of learning. There are other important individual differences, however, including personality variables, cognitive variables, inquiry variables, and sequencing variables; various I.I. programs in schools are attempting to accommodate such differences, also.

Individualized Instruction requires much more than personal attention of teachers or a small pupil-teacher ratio. It consists of learning experiences specifically designed for individual students on the basis of diagnostic procedures employed to determine individual interests and needs. Hundreds of school systems have embarked on one degree or another of I.I. program development. Most of these programs are prescribed and content-oriented. Many, however, have moved into self-directed, personalized, and independent study programs which emphasize variables other than the pace of learning alone. Although the impact of introducing an I.I. program on school organization, schedules, and facilities is considerable, it should be noted that I.I. typically is not provided in all subjects nor for all pupils in a school.

The more advanced I.I. programs make extensive use of media and technology, and marked increases in the use of educational technology are likely as the I.I. movement progresses. As programs improve, systematic planning and Instructional Development procedures will increasingly characterize the efforts applied to these programs. At the present time, a primary problem lies in the availability of suitable materials in sufficient variety to make truly individualized programs possible. Cooperative project-developed and -validated materials are beginning to emerge, however, as are new commercially produced I.I. materials. These, combined with teacher-prepared and teacher-adapted materials, plus more sophisticated use of educational technology, seem most likely to hold the key to solution of the materials problem.

Further learner response projects

1

A group or committee with particular interests or experience in diagnosis and testing for individual differences should secure examples of representative tests or other instruments for measuring personality variables, cognitive variables, and inquiry variables. Prepare a suitable display of the materials and arrange for a discussion in class if time permits. Also, prepare a representative list of sources of the three types of instruments and give a copy to each class member.

2

Arrange to have a resource person from the department of psychology or the tests and measurements bureau come into the class and discuss the topic of testing for individual differences of several kinds.

3

A low pupil-teacher ratio (25:1 or lower) has long been advocated as a fundamental requirement for effective individualized instruction in public schools. A group of three or four students should examine this thesis and prepare arguments for or against it. Present the arguments in a panel discussion for the instructional technology class.

4

Select from among Edling's case studies on Individualized Instruction programs described in this chapter (and/or from other sources) two or three that are of particular interest. Write, call, or visit the schools involved to secure information from each on the following: (a) the current status of the I.I. program; (b) the successes or failures of the programs to this point and the reasons for them; (c) what advice the administrators or other key figures in the program would give to others wishing to start an I.I. program in their own schools today.

5

Most I.I. programs to date have provided primarily for differences in the speed at which different individuals learn. Identify two or more additional variables that a good I.I. program should also accommodate and prepare a list of practical suggestions on how each of the additional variables might be dealt with in such a program.

6

Accountability and cost effectiveness (see Chapter 10, page 393) are important considerations for educators at all levels and will probably continue to be so for the foreseeable future. Prepare an

outline of the principal points you would make—in terms of (a) accountability and (b) cost effectiveness—in urging the P.T.A. to support establishing an I.I. program in your school or school district.

7

Some schools use substantial amounts of technology in their I.I. programs; others do not. In terms of what you know about learning and about the contributions

media can make to it, what position would you take on involving media in an I.I. program in your school and for what reasons?

References

ABBOTT, JANE. "Auto-Tutorial Systems—Students Prepare Some Dandies." *The Science Teacher,* Vol. 37, December 1970, pp. 19–22.

BURKMAN, ERNEST. "ISCS: An Individualized Approach to Science Instruction." *The Science Teacher,* Vol. 37, December 1970, pp. 27–30.

DeCECCO, J. P., ed. *Educational Technology.* Holt, Rinehart and Winston, 1965.

DENLON, FLOYD G. "A Field Test of Computer-Assisted Instruction in First Grade Mathematics." *Educational Leadership,* Vol. 28, No. 2, November 1970, pp. 170–180.

FAGAN, EDWARD R., and JEAN VANDELL, eds. *Humanizing English: Do Not Fold, Spindle or Mutilate. Classroom Practices in Teaching English, 1970–71.* National Council of Teachers of English, Champaign, Ill., 1970, 103 pp.

FRENCH, RUSSELL L. "Individualizing Classroom Communication." *Educational Leadership,* Vol. 28, No. 2, November 1970, pp. 193–196.

GAGNE, R. M. *The Conditions of Learning.* Holt, Rinehart and Winston, 1965.

GROPPER, G. L., and G. C. KRESS. "Individualizing Instruction Through Pacing Procedures." *AV Communications Review,* Vol. 13, No. 2, 1965, pp. 165–182.

HENRY, NELSON B., ed. *Individualizing Instruction.* National Society for the Study of Education, 61st Yearbook. University of Chicago Press, 1967.

LANGE, PHILLIP C., ed. *Programed Instruction.* National Society for the Study of Education, 66th Yearbook, Part II. University of Chicago Press, 1967.

LEVIN, G. R., and B. L. BAKER "Item Scrambling in a Self-Instructional Program," *Journal of Educational Psychology,* Vol. 54, 1963, pp. 138–143.

MAGER, R. F., and C. CLARK. "Explorations in Student-Controlled Instruction." *Psychology Reports,* Vol. 13, 1963, pp. 71–76.

MINADEO, LOUIS. "Self-Paced Training Program," *A-V Communications,* December 1969, pp. 16 ff.

MITZEL, H. E. "The IMPENDING Instruction Revolution." *Phi Delta Kappan,* April 1970, pp. 434–439.

PACE, ARTHUR L. *Coordination of Organic Curriculum Development in the Public Schools of Houston, Texas.* ERIC, Ed. 044 806, Bureau No.—BR–8–0162, September 1970.

PATTERSON, MARVIN D. "Individualizing Science Instruction Within Project PLAN." *The Science Teacher,* Vol. 37, December 1970, pp. 33 ff.

READ, EDWIN A., ALLRED A. RUEL, and LOUISE O. BAIRD. *Continuous Progress in Spelling—An Individualized Spelling Program.* Brigham Young University, Provo, Utah, 1968.

ROE, K. V., H. W. CASE, and A. ROE. "A Scrambled Versus Ordered Sequence in Auto-Instructional Programs," *Journal of Educational Psychology,* Vol. 53, 1962, pp. 101–104.

SHULMAN, L. S. "Seeking Styles and Individual Differences in Patterns of Inquiry." *School Review,* Vol. 73, 1965, pp. 258–266.

SKINNER, B. F. *The Technology of Teaching.* Appleton-Century-Crofts, 1968.

SMITH, K. V., and M. F. SMITH. *Cybernetic Principles of Learning and Educational Design.* Holt, Rinehart and Winston, 1966.

SUPPES, PATRICK. "On Using Computers To Individualize Instruction." In Don D. Bushnell and Dwight W. Allen, eds., *The Computer in American Education.* Wiley, 1967, pp. 11–24.

SUTTER, E. G., and J. B. REID. "Learner Variables and Interpersonal Conditions in Computer-Assisted Instruction." *Journal of Educational Psychology,* Vol. 60, 1969, pp. 153–157.

WASHBURNE, CARLETON W., and SIDNEY P. MARLAND, JR. *Winnetka.* Prentice-Hall, 1963.

Sources of specially developed materials for Individualized Instruction

Continuous Progress Plan Materials, Utah State Department of Public Instruction, Division of Research and Innovation, Salt Lake City, Utah 84101.

Hawaii English Project Materials, Office of Curriculum Development and Technology, 1750 Wist Place, Honolulu, Hawaii 96814.

An Individualized Spelling and Language Arts Program, Wilson School, Janesville, Wis. 53545, and Wisconsin Research and Development Center for Cognitive Learning, University of Wisconsin, Madison, Wis. 53706.

Individually Prescribed Instruction Materials, Learning Research and Development Center, University of Pittsburgh, Pittsburgh, Pa. 15222, and Research for Better Schools, Inc., 1700 Market St., Philadelphia, Pa. 19104.

Lessons for Self-Instruction in Basic Skills, California Test Bureau, Del Monte Research Park, Monterey, Calif. 93940.

Project PLAN Materials, Westinghouse Learning Corporation, 100 Park Avenue, New York, N.Y. 10017.

A Statement of Skills and Objectives for the Wisconsin Prototypic System of Reading Skill Development, Wisconsin Research and Development Center for Cognitive Learning, University of Wisconsin, Madison, Wis. 53706.

The Wilson Manual for Individually Guided Reading, Wilson School, Janesville, Wis. 53545, and Wisconsin Research and Development Center for Cognitive Learning, University of Wisconsin, Madison, Wis. 53706.

Winnetka Curriculum Materials List, Winnetka Public Schools, Winnetka, Ill. 60093.

Media references

Charlie and the Golden Hampster, 16mm film, color, sound, 13 min. IDEA, 1968.

Continuous Progress Learning, 16mm film, color, sound, 22 min. IDEA, 1968.

Individually Guided Education for all Children, 16mm film, color, sound, 22 min. Research and Development Center for Cognitive Learning, University of Wisconsin, 1969.

Rx for Learning, 16mm film, color, sound, 29 min. Learning Research and Development Center, University of Pittsburgh, 1968.

The Oakleaf Project, 16mm film, b/w, sound, 30 min. Learning Research and Development Center, University of Pittsburgh, 1968.

The Poor Scholar's Soliloquy, 16mm film, color, sound, 6 min. Michigan State University, 1971.

Source references

See source lists in the Appendix; a particularly relevant section is Individualized Instruction.

See *Student Production Guide,* any pertinent production references for self-instruction materials.

FIFTEEN
Multimedia instructional development

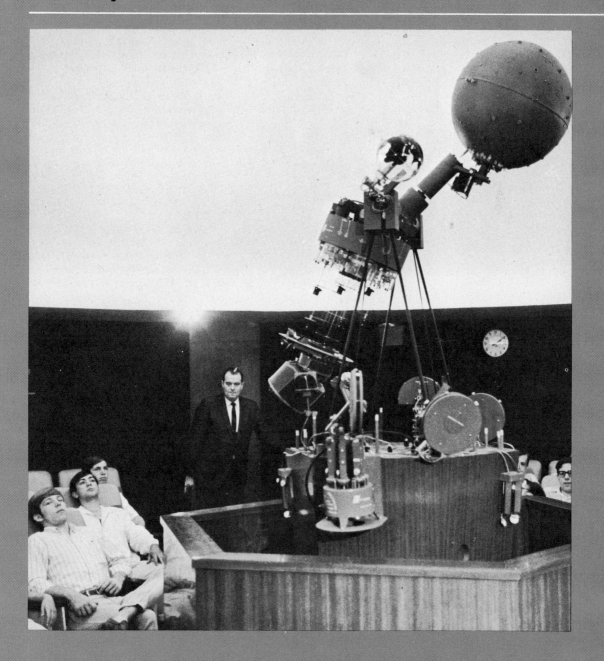

Objectives	Performance responses

1

Given six examples of effective multimedia use, identify specific procedures which together produce desired changes, as shown by learner response.

Prepare in diagrammatic form (preferably on a projectual) a graphic portrayal of the inter-related and sequential steps which together constitute an Instructional Development learning organization. Prepare such diagrams for at least two of the examples of multimedia use described in this chapter.

2

Given specific examples of the steps through which an individual teacher and learners must pass while accomplishing a mediated Instructional Development strategy, demonstrate your ability to apply these steps to an I.D. plan of your choice.

Develop for use in a hypothetical or real situation a feasible Instructional Development plan that is closely related to your subject field of interest and grade level of present or future teaching responsibility. Activate this prototype and evaluate its worth in terms of pupil-response changes which you believe may be accomplished or actually observe being accomplished. (If it is not feasible to activate the prototype with actual pupils, explain your plan to your fellow-students, note their constructive suggestions, and respond in terms of changes you feel are possible and desirable.)

IN this book we have been dealing with a wide range of individual media, their characteristics, and ways in which they can be used effectively in teaching and learning. The point has been made frequently that media are best used when they are used in combination with a variety of other instructional materials and techniques, each of which is chosen because of the particular contribution it can make to the total learning experience. Now it is time to pull together some of the key ideas discussed in the preceding chapters. We do this in this chapter by examining six actual teaching-learning situations in which media have been incorporated as *inherent* elements in the total learning experience.

In considering these six examples of effective multimedia use, it will be helpful to keep two important points in mind. First, media and technology are no longer the prerogative of the teacher alone. Students can, should, and *do* use media for a variety of purposes. Both teachers and stu-

dents have become increasingly innovative and sophisticated in the ways in which they put a variety of media together with other materials and techniques; the resulting experiences range from basic visual literacy activities to fairly complex Individualized Instruction sequences to two- and three-screen large-group presentations which may have emotional impact or present information in a new context, or both.

A second point to keep in mind as we consider the more complex matters involved in actually combining media and materials of many kinds to achieve improved learning results is this: There is an explicit need for a new kind and level of planning to help assure that our efforts will be successful and effective. We have referred to this kind of planning a number of times earlier in this book as Instructional Development. Accordingly, it will be worth our while to consider the several steps in the I.D. process in some detail before we go on to our examples of effective multimedia use.

The Instructional Development system

BY definition, Instructional Development means *the application of an instructional systems approach to the analysis of and development of practical solutions to teaching and learning problems.* Each of the steps suggested in Chapter 3 for the seventh-grade science teacher undertaking to improve the performance of his students has rather precise requirements; also, there are substeps and additional steps that need to be followed if the true benefits of the

Instructional Development process are to be achieved.

For example, in defining the problem we suggested that the science teacher must use considerable care in his analysis of *what the problem really is,* particularly when working on his own. There is always the temptation to skip this step, under the assumption that we already know what the problem is, and to proceed rather directly to the business of finding practical answers.

Though such a procedure is undoubtedly necessary at times to meet immediate operational needs, it is quite inadequate for dealing with the fundamental underlying problems of curriculum and instruction.[1] This is so because a brief or cursory analysis of the problem risks committing large amounts of time, energy, and resources to treating symptoms, rather than causes, or, to put it another way, to find answers to the wrong questions. In other words, the problem definition or identification step is particularly critical, since everything that follows is based on decisions made then, and this is therefore the point at which most problem-solution attempts in education have gone awry. Experience with successive steps in the Instructional Development process has likewise shown that rather rigorous ground rules need to be followed if adequate solutions are to be found. Yet without specialized training, experience, and expert assistance in the Instructional Development approach—which relatively few educators have had an opportunity to acquire—a breakdown in one or more steps of the process is almost inevitable.

In an attempt to remedy this situation, with the support of the U.S. Office of Education, a Consortium of four universities with strong programs in Instructional Development and Technology has concentrated for several years on the development of a tested training program for teachers, administrators, policy makers, and specialists in curriculum, content, and media areas that enables teams of educators within schools or school systems to acquire initial competencies in Instructional Development principles and methods. This training program is carried on in the form of Instructional Development Institutes (IDIs) which are particularly designed for school systems having large numbers of economically and academically deprived students, limited resources, and a real desire to find solutions to serious educational problems (see Figure 15.1).

The Consortium, known as the Na-

FIGURE 15.1

This nine-step Instructional Development model is in use in Instructional Development Institutes being offered by NSMI and the USOE for school systems in all parts of the United States (see also the popularized version of this model shown in Figure 3.32).

---

[1] Instructional Development is properly a *team* effort involving teachers, administrators, and specialists in subject, curriculum, technology, and other areas—and in some cases members of the Board of Education. Yet an individual teacher *can* apply I.D. principles in his daily work and in some instances carry them out on limited topics. In the process, he can gain valuable experience as well as improved learning results.

tional Special Media Institutes (NSMI),[2] used the instructional systems approach in designing and developing materials and

techniques to be used in IDIs in school systems across the nation. During the initial development period, the IDI program was tested in prototype institutes in three major school systems—Detroit, Phoenix, and Atlanta. During these prototype institutes, representatives of 11 teacher education agencies other than the NSMI institutions participated and received additional specialized training so that they could repli-

[2] The NSMI Consortium now consists of Michigan State University, where the national office is located, Syracuse University, the U. S. International University, Corvallis, Oregon, and the University of Southern California. As of 1973–74, NSMI changed its name to the University Consortium for Instructional Development and Technology and the University of Indiana became a member.

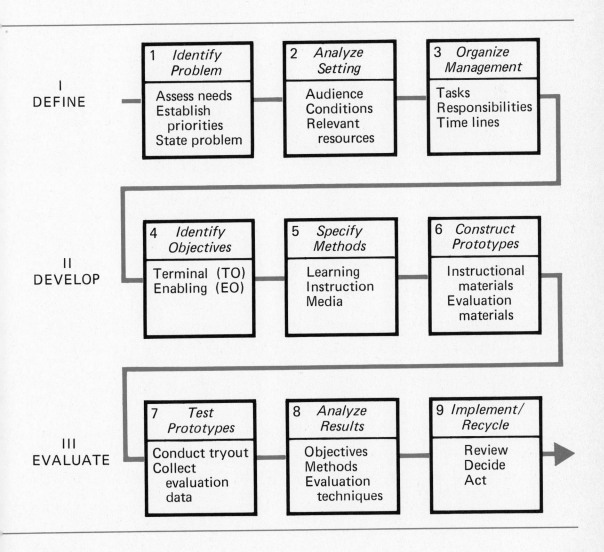

FIGURE 15.2

The process of Instructional Development outlined in the nine-step model has numerous substeps and decision points, as suggested here. Each of these, in turn, has rather precise requirements which must be observed if the system is to function effectively.

cate the IDIs in school systems in their respective regions of the country, using the materials and procedures which had been validated and provided to them by NSMI.[3] Ten of the 11 agencies were further designated and prepared to train additional trainers of school systems in Instructional Development.

More recently, the Office of Education has selected a number of additional multiplier agencies (IDAs), the aim being to have available eventually enough qualified agencies to conduct IDIs throughout the 50 states and the Trust Territories—a multiplier effort which may be expected to continue to expand. The NSMI group is providing training for the IDAs and other multipliers, plus continuing evaluation and revision of the materials and other follow-up assistance as needed. Various other teacher education agencies are indicating active interest in the IDI program, a development which suggests that Instructional Development may become an integral part of future teacher education programs. In short, the use of Instructional Development in some form appears likely to become common practice in many school systems across the nation during the 1970s.

A detailed discussion of the IDI program is unnecessary for our purpose here, which is simply to provide an introduction to the I.D. concept and some idea of its potential significance in the improvement of teaching and learning. In that context, however, it is worthwhile to note the principal steps in the Instructional Development process which an individual or an I.D. team

[3] These initial Instructional Development Multiplier (IDM) agencies were the U. S. Bureau of Indian Affairs, the California Teachers Association, Clarion State College, Florida State University, Georgia State University, the Minnesota State Department of Public Instruction, the New York State Teachers Association, Southern University, the University of Toledo, Virginia State College, and the Washington State Department of Public Instruction.

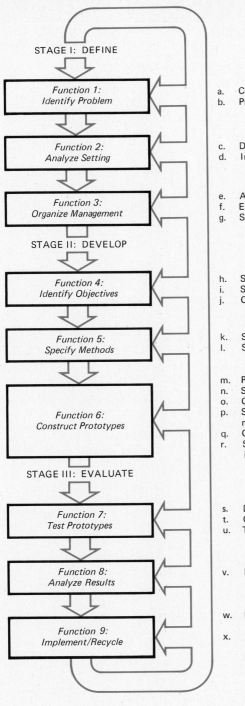

STAGE I: DEFINE

Function 1:
Identify Problem

a. Compare status quo to ideal
b. Propose tentative solution

Function 2:
Analyze Setting

c. Determine learner characteristics
d. Inventory school/community resources

Function 3:
Organize Management

e. Assign TAPS team responsibilities
f. Establish lines of communication
g. Specify project planning and control procedures

STAGE II: DEVELOP

Function 4:
Identify Objectives

h. State terminal performance objectives
i. State enabling objectives and determine relationships between objectives
j. Construct performance measures

Function 5:
Specify Methods

k. Specify instructional strategies and media forms
l. Specify alternative methods

Function 6:
Construct Prototypes

m. Prepare comprehensive description of instructional design specifications
n. Specify design for evaluation of instructional and evaluation designs
o. Conduct technical review of instructional and evaluation designs
p. Specify procedures for collection and development of instructional materials
q. Construct and assemble instructional materials
r. Specify procedures to be used by personnel during tryout of instructional prototype

STAGE III: EVALUATE

Function 7:
Test Prototypes

s. Determine the type of tryout (i.e., developmental, validation, field trial)
t. Carry out evaluation as planned
u. Tabulate and process evaluation data

Function 8:
Analyze Results

v. Determine relationships among results, methods, objectives, and goals

Function 9:
Implement/Recycle

w. Indicate what kinds of revisions (if any) are suggested by the interpretation of results, methods, objectives, and goals
x. Determine if suggested revisions indicate that the prototype is to be recycled or if the design can be implemented without major revisions

needs to go through, as diagramed in Figure 15.1, and the summary of decision points in Instructional Development shown in Figure 15.2. The following discussion amplifies and clarifies these two figures.

(For those wishing to pursue the subject further, several helpful sources are included in the References at the end of this chapter.)

The Instructional Development process

Stage I: Define

1. IDENTIFY PROBLEM   This beginning definition step, as suggested earlier, is of critical importance. It involves the following: assessment of needs not only in terms of what is perceived to be the status quo and what the ideal situation might be, but also in terms of underlying causes of the problem situation; identification of causes of the problem that can be rectified and determination of their relative importance or priority; then, in those terms, if the decision is affirmative, a commitment to apply the necessary time, energy, and resources to carry through to an adequate solution. The definition step may require considerable time and study since it almost invariably necessitates the gathering of substantial amounts of relevant information beyond that currently at hand before a valid decision can be reached. It should be noted that in the course of defining the problem, information and factors relating to other phases of the I.D. process are also under consideration by the I.D. team. Thus the I.D. process is not strictly a linear or 1–2–3, etc., process; that is, the several stages must be dealt with not only consecutively but also simultaneously during the process.

2. ANALYZE SETTING   Analysis of the setting deals primarily with the human and functional factors involved in any significant change in the existing system. If a change is to be brought about successfully, we need to be able to recognize and identify the people in the school or school system

who serve as "gatekeepers," decision makers, opinion leaders, and change agents. Further, how they carry out these functions is greatly influenced by such human factors as whether they are inclined to be

FIGURE 15.3

This is a sample of a PERT (Program Evaluation Review Technique) chart. Though it looks somewhat like any other time line, the difference lies in the precision with which the planning is done. This is accomplished by beginning with the final completion date and working backward to establish when each component and subcomponent must be completed to achieve the final goal on time. Furthermore, the system provides in its planning for possible problems, unexpected delays, and any necessary adjustments. (This chart is adapted from a formal PERT format so as to show time relationships more clearly and be more intelligible to the average reader. A true PERT chart utilizes a formal symbol structure and is both more comprehensive and more detailed than the chart shown here.)

early, middle, or late adopters of new ideas and whether they go about dealing with problems in a creative, a defensive, or an emotional manner—and to what degree. Such analysis is, of course, essential to planning the approaches or strategies needed to gain support for the changes which may be proposed. We make such analyses in a rather casual way all the time in our normal relationships with people— and particularly in our relationship with the people with whom we work—but we must do so with much more care and thoroughness when an important new program is at stake.

3. ORGANIZE MANAGEMENT   As a systematic process, Instructional Development requires well-defined organization, management, and scheduling. This is particularly true when a group of people are working together on a significant problem or new program,[4] but the same principles apply if a teacher is working on solving a problem by himself. Controls must be established to

[4] In order to facilitate constructive change, a cross section of educational personnel must be trained. Thus one of the requirements of an IDI is that TABS teams—teachers, administrators, board members, and specialists—be trained together in I.D. principles and practices.

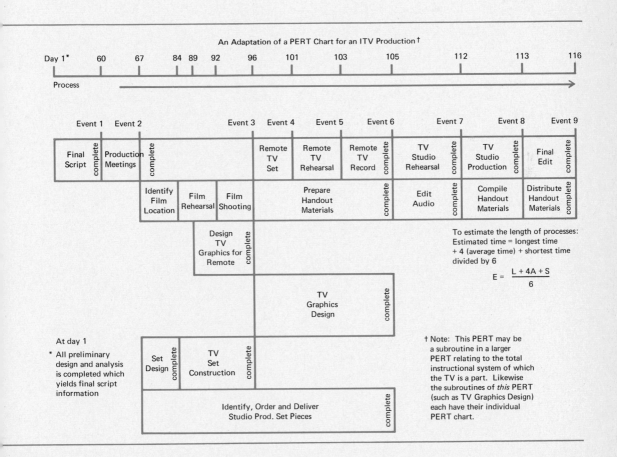

An Adaptation of a PERT Chart for an ITV Production †

Day 1*   60   67   84 89   92   96   101   103   105   112   113   116

Process

Event 1   Event 2   Event 3   Event 4   Event 5   Event 6   Event 7   Event 8   Event 9

| Final Script | complete | Production Meetings | complete | | Remote TV Set | Remote TV Rehearsal | Remote TV Record | complete | TV Studio Rehearsal | complete | TV Studio Production | complete | Final Edit | complete |

| | | Identify Film Location | Film Rehearsal | Film Shooting | Prepare Handout Materials | | | complete | Edit Audio | complete | Compile Handout Materials | complete | Distribute Handout Materials | complete |

Design TV Graphics for Remote | complete

TV Graphics Design | complete

To estimate the length of processes: Estimated time = longest time + 4 (average time) + shortest time divided by 6

$$E = \frac{L + 4A + S}{6}$$

At day 1
* All preliminary design and analysis is completed which yields final script information

Set Design | complete | TV Set Construction | complete

Identify, Order and Deliver Studio Prod. Set Pieces | complete

† Note: This PERT may be a subroutine in a larger PERT relating to the total instructional system of which the TV is a part. Likewise the subroutines of *this* PERT (such as TV Graphics Design) each have their individual PERT chart.

assure that task assignments are carried out, that expert assistance is identified and arranged for when needed, and that appropriate communications take place with others on ideas, problems, and other developments as they occur. In order to assure task completion by an agreed time, time lines must be set up to indicate target dates for finishing each of the elements involved in the process. Typically, such target dates are established by using the PERT (Program Evaluation Review Technique) method, which starts with the ultimate completion date and works backward to establish the dates when other elements must be ready if the final date is to be met. An example is shown in Figure 15.3.

In short, when a group or team is working on an Instructional Development problem, the following management factors are of major importance:

a   Who *is given responsibility* and the necessary authority *to accomplish each specified task?*
b   What *instructional alternatives are to be considered and what personnel and material resources can be brought to bear?*
c   When *in sequence are they to be brought to bear in order to meet the proposed objectives and in order to meet indicated deadlines?*
d   How *are personnel and material re-resources to be organized and how is the total system to be organized to function in an effective manner as measured by predetermined specified criteria?*

Stage II: Develop
4. IDENTIFY OBJECTIVES   As indicated earlier, if objectives are to be useful, they must be spelled out in terms which will permit determination of whether or not they have been met. There are several kinds of objectives, but there are two, in particular, which are important in the I.D.

process. These are *terminal* performance objectives (TOs) and *enabling* objectives (EOs), the latter being necessary intermediate steps to attainment of the terminal or ultimate objectives. The terminal performance objectives must be spelled out first and then the enabling objectives; finally, performance measures must be constructed for each objective of each type so that we can know definitely whether or not it has been achieved.

5. SPECIFY METHODS   Once objectives have been established, we reach the point of decision—the point when we determine what are likely to be the best methods and materials to employ under the circumstances in order to attain those objectives with our pupils. The range of possible methods and materials is extensive, but not unlimited; in other words, this is when we have to face up to what is practicable in terms of available resources, personnel, equipment, and facilities. Frequently, "trade-offs" must be made to reach a workable decision—for example, it might be desirable to introduce computers for individualized instruction at this stage, but if a computer system is not available or is out of reach financially, we have to find the best practical alternative. This is the stage at which we first become concerned with media, along with other materials, and decisions are made in terms of both the specific needs of the learning situation and the particular advantages of the various media in satisfying those needs (see Figure 15.4).

6. CONSTRUCT PROTOTYPES   This is the design, procurement, and production phase. Having decided on the kinds of learning experiences and materials most likely to be effective for our purposes, we proceed to spell them out in detail, specifying the readings, tapes, films, exercises, and other activities to be tried. This may involve considerable review and examination of avail-

FIGURE 15.4

In Instructional Development the aim is to arrange that the learner may "quest" his way through any number of needed learning experiences—to conceptualize, to understand, to become involved, to respond with performances which show how and when he has achieved his objectives. When we specify methods we begin to consider media and other materials: (a) In cooperative staff and teacher planning sessions, specific media and equipment are evaluated for specific purposes and (b) prototype materials also are assessed.

able materials as well as consideration of a variety of instructional approaches. In some cases, where no suitable materials exist, it may be necessary to produce them. While this process is going on, a part of the I.D. team should be designing the evaluation to be applied.

Stage III: Evaluate

7. TEST PROTOTYPES   Assuming that the preceding steps are reasonably complete, we are now ready to try out the "package" we have created. This may be done with a representative group of our own students or with a comparable group from another school. In either case, it is important that we collect evaluation data on what works, what doesn't, and why. It is probable that certain revisions will be needed before we try the new system in a regular class—the next step in the process.

8. ANALYZE RESULTS   Once a full-scale tryout is under way, we need to observe all aspects closely and note further adjustments that may be needed either in the instructional design or in the materials used. It is important to test along the way to ascertain how well our enabling objectives are being met and, at the conclusion of the unit, how adequately the terminal objectives have been achieved. Taken together, these several kinds of data provide the in-

formation for an overall assessment and evaluation by the I.D. team.

9. IMPLEMENT/RECYCLE On the basis of the results of the full-scale tryout we are in a position to decide whether the new system is ready to be put into regular use in our schools. It may be ready; more than likely, however, it will require certain revisions and retesting before our I.D. team is satisfied. In any case, provisions should be made for continued evaluation and modification even after it does go into regular use.

. . .

Now consider the following six examples. These provide many techniques teachers have actually used in carrying out the interrelated use of media, materials, and various teaching and learning strategies to create effective learning experiences for their students. The examples consist of a primary-level English program; a sixth-grade social studies unit on Custer; a junior high school unit on ecology and pollution;

a high school unit on Africa; science and business education applications in two community colleges; and uses of planetariums and multi-image learning experiences in secondary schools and colleges. Although several of the examples are from Hawaii and Michigan, where the authors have observed them personally, all the examples are representative of good teaching that can be found in all parts of the country.

In some of these cases, Instructional Development principles and procedures were used in the design of the programs; in other cases, they were not used. As you read the cases, note (1) where I.D. principles *were* applied to advantage; (2) where and how I.D. principles *could have been* applied in cases where they were not and thus where they could be applied in developing a similar unit or program; (3) the many creative uses of media in effective and natural combination with other learning materials and methods.

Example 1: Learning English skills

T HOUGH many innovations in Instructional Development occur under the impetus of the individual teacher and are therefore rather modest in nature, there are illustrations of much more comprehensive developments. One of these is the Hawaii English Program.[5] The development and use of this program have involved the long-range participation of hundreds of the state's educational administrators, teacher trainers, curriculum supervisors, teachers, and parents, and, as this is written, 49,000 elementary-grade students. As the program progresses into the high schools, the target

is the participation of "all learners." The program itself is administered under the direction of the Curriculum Development and Technological Branch of the Hawaii Department of Education.

The task was to design an entire program of English instruction. The design began with defining goals; as the work proceeded, many teaching materials were created and put to use in the hands of real teachers and real children at work in real classrooms. The program is a continuum of creative media learning experiences from kindergarten through the twelfth grade. The instructional materials as a whole provide learners with highly individualized experiences with the English language—its skills, systems, and literature. However, because the entire language skills program is

[5] *The Hawaii English Program: Its Design and Evaluation,* Curriculum Development and Technological Branch of the Hawaii Department of Education, Manoa Campus, University of Hawaii, Honolulu, 1971.

so comprehensive, the description here is limited to the language skills program for the primary grades—a program now installed in at least one classroom in every elementary school in the state of Hawaii.

The English program was undertaken by teams representative of school personnel, teacher trainers, and lay people. The initial task these committees undertook was to meet together to agree on a working definition of English as a subject and the nature of language skills specifically: reading, speaking, writing, listening, and creative speaking and writing through literature. The committees worked jointly under the aegis of the Hawaii Department of Education and the College of Education of the University of Hawaii. Committee actions included meticulous consideration of the basic stages of learning systems development: statements of goals; creating, sequencing, and assembling learning materials; actual trial use of the materials under a variety of teaching strategies within the classroom; evaluation and recycling. In addition, detailed plans were made for the training of the teachers who were to be responsible for actually installing and evaluating materials and equipment in connection with the use of the newly developed teaching strategies during on-going classroom programs.

During the last four years the program has been subjected to a variety of field tests and to evaluation and constant recycling. The description that follows thus represents a current plan which has been brought to a remarkable stage of sophistication as shown in innovative teaching and pupil response.

The overall goal of the language skills program is to help students toward progressively greater control over the nature of their language performance, including reading, speaking, writing, and listening.

Enabling objectives describe how each child may progress from his entry level toward attainment of his terminal objectives by means of responding to sequences of independent learning experiences in the language arts. The program assumes that the child is the decision-maker and that once he has decided on his course, someone or something in his immediate environment (either the teacher or appropriate media learning experiences) will be available to respond to his decisions. The program assumes that children differ in interests, styles of learning, pace of learning, aptitude, thresholds of boredom, educational needs, and, above all, that they differ in need for success through mastery of tasks.

Specific objectives have been clearly worked out which include such as the following: (1) to learn to distinguish between the basic sounds of the English language and to apply these to reading and speaking tasks; (2) to learn to write cursive letters clearly and legibly; (3) to develop interest in learning to read; (4) to learn to read; (5) to develop interest in reading widely and comprehensively; (6) to listen attentively to sounds and words and to respond correctly to these. Many other subskills are also defined as objectives.

In general, all of the specific objectives for the language skills program are organized in two basic areas: listening and reading skills and oral and writing skills. The actual learning materials used by students who seek to attain these overall objectives have been organized to reflect the nature of the various specific objectives included within them. However, as these are used in the classroom, they are closely interrelated and thus become part of a *total* experience which carries each child toward accomplishing desired behaviors.

Materials and strategies
MATERIALS OF THE CURRICULUM A unique characteristic of the program is the variety of communication means used to convey information about language skills to each learner. These materials are classified according to the nature of the material and the sense primarily employed by the

FIGURE 15.5

As you examine these "modes," can you identify the task for which each was selected? While such learning goes on, the teacher assumes the role of humanitarian. Do you agree? What are the roles of pupil and teacher in relation to each of the situations shown? (a) Teacher and pupil work with a picture word stack. (b and c) The audio card reader is used to identify sounds of letters. (d) With this equipment a pupil will learn by observing visual cues produced by a continuous-loop 8mm film. (e and f) Tape-recorded books become a listening, looking, and learning experience. (g) By following the cues on the diagrams, the child learns typing skills. (h) The alphabet is learned by feeling and visualizing the flocked surfaces of letters. (i) Records of songs "speak" and "demonstrate" to children, then "ask" for their participation. It is not unusual to walk into a classroom in mid-morning and see two or three children singing away by themselves. (j) Many game situations help in developing manipulative and visual identification skills. Could any one teacher even hope to arrange such varied and essential self-tutorial or peer-relationship learning experiences working by himself within the limited resources of the traditional classroom?

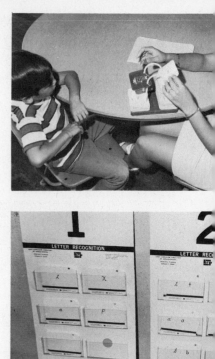

learner in responding to it (audio, visual, tactile). The materials are called "modes." The chief modes are (see Figure 15.5):

Stock mode A series of punched cards stacked on rods attached to a base. The learning materials are programed into the stack in such a way as to permit two or more children or a teacher and child to work together; primarily visual.

Audio card-reader mode An audio card-reading device which records and/or plays back sound; primarily audio, but also visual.

Film mode A continuous-loop 8mm motion picture film in a cartridge, in most cases without sound; visual if no sound.

Book mode Visual or, when accompanied by an exact parallel audiotape, visual-audio.

Typewriter mode Primarily visual, but also tactile.

Paper and/or pencil mode Primarily visual.

Flocked-card mode Cards with letters or numerals in textured or raised material; tactile-visual.

Tape-recorder mode A tape recorder that uses cassettes; audio. See book mode, also used in creative audio response.

Phonograph and disc mode Audio.

Game mode Varied devices, such as lotto or playing cards, to carry out task-oriented, competitive or self-evaluative activities.

Most of the materials of the curriculum are conveniently packaged in individual containers that can be easily handled and stored. There are a great many items in the total skills package, but the problem of management is reduced considerably by students who assume responsibility for proper storage after use. This they do very expertly because housekeeping skills are specifically taught.

A detailed instructional manual for the teacher accompanies the program. This manual includes discussions of (1) conceptual framework, (2) the learning environment, (3) the various subprograms, (4) learner goals for each element, (5) entry and exit behaviors, (6) the learning procedure, (7) next steps, (8) record keeping.

All of these materials have been subjected to intensive classroom tryout. As might be expected, weaknesses have often been discovered; these weaknesses, however, have then become the subject of intensive study resulting in appropriate reorganization for subsequent tryouts.

TEACHING STRATEGIES: METHODS As we have said, the Hawaii language skills program is distinctive because it provides *differentiated* learning opportunities and because it frees and encourages each child to assume greater responsibility for his own learning. Nevertheless, not surprisingly, these distinctive aspects of the program produce problems during transition periods. When teachers who are accustomed primarily to large-group teaching first face the responsibility of providing differentiated learning to children who also are accustomed primarily to large-group teaching, many dilemmas and uncertainties are likely to come up in the course of bringing about the many necessary changes. These transitional problems are frankly recognized in Hawaii and dealt with by means of learning demonstration centers which are set up during both the school year and summer sessions. These classroom "installation training" centers become, in effect, laboratories where teachers observe, participate, and themselves learn. As a result, teachers follow the program with confidence and enthusiasm. When they do, the children do, too.

We have discussed the differentiated learning materials and opportunities that are part of the program in Hawaii. In implementing the other primary attribute of the program—encouraging each child to assume responsibility for his own learning—provisions are made for a surprising amount of peer teaching. Children, once they have mastered a skill or technique, are encouraged to teach others. The feelings of responsibility, purpose, and self-fulfillment which result from teaching others are highly important and gratifying to the young tutor. In other words, gains are achieved not only by the child who is taught by his peer, but, even more important, also by the child who teaches. Helping another to learn is a chance to review—to review in a gamelike situation and yet with an adult-type purpose to enhance the activity. Such activity also becomes an additional review test of the tutor's own learning.

Peer instruction is welcomed by children also as a contrast to carrel-based instruction. The use of carrels must not be overdone, for too much carrel-based teaching often results in a dampening effect. Some children become bored when they must spend unduly long periods of time by themselves. They are apt to miss human interaction—and this is remarkably well provided by pupil-identified peer-teaching. In sum, the teaching-learning peer groups of two and three that are used in the skills program provide great benefit for each child, whether learner or tutor.

Classroom organization for the language-skills activities moves usually from whole class to small group or individual and back again to whole group. The activities that initiate each of the three-week units usually begin with a large-group discussion, with the teacher introducing the key questions that bring out what is to be learned. How things are to be learned is then made

the subject of individual response and selection. During these planning periods, students listen, ask questions, and then select the individualized learning materials and activities they would like to pursue.

As the actual learning proceeds, the teacher becomes counselor, helper, problem-solver, encourager, and *evaluator*. During individualized activity, additional time obviously is available to the teacher. Thus he can constantly observe and evaluate and give individual attention to those who want or need it, or both. Through this close interrelationship with each individual learner, evaluation is constantly being pursued. *Performance* becomes the key criterion in an environment which rewards productive and desirable behavior.

Usually, groups are re-formed when questions arise which the teacher feels are of interest to many. Also, this calling together may occur when individuals have developed performance skills that are worthy of being shared with the group. Thus large groups observe as small-groups and individuals exhibit their accomplishments in reading, singing, typing and handwriting, telling original stories, or performing creative dramatic versions of things learned as a result of reading with tape-assisted books (see Figure 15.5).

Tryout and evaluation

An evaluation of the program during the 1970–71 phase of classroom tryout was based on the performance of students randomly selected to represent various grade levels and groupings, classroom organizations, and school and class sizes from all districts of the state.[6] Tests were selected on the basis of objectivity, reliability, and suitability, as well as cost in terms of time elements. Variables such as attitudes

[6] *Evaluation Report of the English Skills and Literature Program*, Hawaii Curriculum Center, Honolulu, November 1971.

toward the program were also considered and reported.

The overall report is that the program works phenomenally well. Of the students polled, 86 percent reported that they liked their lessons, including 36 percent who liked them *very much*. The remainder were neutral or negative. Varieties of interest were reported. For example, 34 percent of the children reported that they liked reading best, 12 percent liked writing, 6 percent liked listening. Typing was the most popular skill, having been selected by 45 percent of the children. The evaluation of the success of self-directed instruction indicated that 55 percent of the students reported that they chose their classroom activities independently, 82 percent of the students reported that they liked to tutor, and 79 percent liked to be tutored. In actuality, 70 percent participated frequently as tutors and 79 percent frequently received tutoring.

The nature of the children's work habits as shown in these reports indicates the great departure from traditional classroom practices. We might well ask ourselves this question: How can we be satisfied any longer with the traditional unilateral communication that is characteristic when one teacher leads the discussion of 30 or 35 students?

The numbers of books read by Hawaii English Program students and non-HEP students were assessed to determine the amount of reading activity. Over a three-month period, among 128 HEP students, the third-graders read an average of 51 books each, second-graders 10 books each, and kindergartners and first-graders 1 book each. The overall average was 10 books read per pupil, with a range from 0 to 114. When this same information was secured from 188 non-HEP students, the following results were reported: averages by grade were: third grade, 8 books each, second grade, 2 books each, first grade, 1 book

each, kindergarten, less than one. The overall average was 2 books read per pupil, with a range from 0 to 30. The books read by both groups were considered generally comparable (most of them contained 30–100 pages).

There is a point that should be emphasized here. Traditionalists often ask: "Will reading suffer when large amounts of time are spent on new media instructional experiences?" This question obviously has been answered. There is ample evidence that significant gains are accomplished in reading comprehension and interest in reading and that they are accomplished because, through the use of interrelated media-oriented learning materials, greater backgrounds of information and concepts are available to be applied to the *interpretation* of the printed page. Thus an interrelated program of media learning experiences has beneficial effects on reading comprehension and, as a result, on attitudes toward reading and reading interests.

Evaluation and recycling are standard procedures as the Hawaii English skill project continues (the 1971–1972 year was its sixth year of operation). Nothing is accepted as completely satisfactory. Rather, the goal of the project is constantly in the direction of recycling out the least effective materials and incorporating better materials.

To sum up, we quote an evaluative judgment of the skills program made by the director of the Hawaii Curriculum Center:

Many people are not aware of the size of this program. Actually, the Hawaii Department of Education has never performed such a big task before. It involves fully 40 percent of the elementary curriculum. Yet in relation to the size, the problems have been small. So while people elsewhere are still talking about systems learning development, instructional development, and all the rest, we here in Hawaii have put these ideas to the practical test of use *in our English skills program. It is highly successful.*[7]

One extremely fascinating outcome is the use of this skills program by the schools of American Samoa. During the summer of 1972, teams of Samoan teachers met to work in the training centers with Hawaii's teachers. Their goal is now being accomplished—to assimilate into the large-group Samoan television teaching program for use by elementary school teachers the important next stage, that is, classroom learning experiences which complete the two-pronged teaching approach. Thus by combining the advantages to learners of the island-wide television lessons broadcast six times a week with the advantages of the materials of the Hawaii English skills program, the best of two innovational learning experience systems is provided to learners. Also now made available are the benefits to learners of small-group and individualized continuous learning opportunities conducted most effectively under the direction of a classroom teacher and in a climate of self-tutorial and peer-teaching opportunity. Similar in-service training plans are being set up for teachers who will use this skills program in Guam, the Trust Territories, and San Jose, California.

At this point, we might mention Horace Greeley's axiom, "Go West, young man." If you would like to observe first-hand some of the most exciting applications of Instructional Development which employ all kinds of modern conceptualizations relating to learning strategies and inter-related media learning strategies—go West.

Example 2: A unit on Custer

AN exciting educational experience involving a variety of media began one winter day in Roy Shehab's sixth-grade social studies class in the Crescentwood Elementary School in East Detroit. It was a unit on George Armstrong Custer—a new topic, never before studied in that school. Before it was over, a city council, a police department, a parks commission, two newspapers, a television station, a radio station, a historical museum, a public library, and the people of two communities were to become much involved in the work of this group of sixth-graders.

Normally, world history and ancient history are taught in the sixth grade in that school system, and the students *had*, in fact, been studying about key historical events and people—from the Roman Empire and Julius Caesar to Churchill, Franklin Roosevelt, Stalin, and many others in between. As they studied these prominent figures and their times, the students began to realize, under the skillful guidance of their teacher, that very often there are strongly divergent points of view about important people and events. While seeking a way to carry this idea forward with his students, Shehab noticed an article in a Detroit newspaper based on the facts that General George Armstrong Custer had lived for some 11 years in Monroe, Michigan, not far from Detroit, that the public library and the county historical museum in Monroe possessed unique collections on Custer's life and times, and that a new feature film

[7] Shinkichi Shimabukuro, memorandum. Requests for further information about this extremely comprehensive program should be directed to Dr. Shimabukuro, Hawaii State Department of Education, Honolulu. It has been the purpose here to outline in general the nature and scope of the program. Volumes of additional explanatory information are available to those who seek it.

entitled *Little Big Man,* in which Custer is a major character, was soon to be released.

Materials and strategies

After discussing the article with his students and finding them much interested in discovering more about the famous Indian fighter, Shehab secured permission from his principal to develop a new unit with his class on the colorful and controversial general. He then asked Lewis Saks, the system's director of learning resources, to help him and his students in finding suitable study materials (see Figure 15.6). The school libraries had little, so the search was widened to public libraries, university libraries in the area, homes in the community, and the library and historical museum in Monroe. A few instructional films and many pictures of the Battle of the Little Big Horn were available, and, of course, there was the feature film to be shown in a few weeks.

Since a primary purpose of the unit was to highlight the fact that there are conflicting opinions on controversial figures, the teacher divided the class in half—one group to search for information and views favoring Custer and the other group to seek evidence which presented Custer in a less favorable light (see Figure 15.7). Every student became involved, and many undertook special projects such as building a scale model of the battlefield where Custer made his last stand and studies of his careers at West Point and in the Civil War, his reputation as an Indian fighter, and his personal characteristics.

As they moved more deeply into the unit with such activities, the students became more and more absorbed in what they were doing. Many sought additional information on their own, and all looked forward to seeing *Little Big Man.* Here the parents, the school administration, and the theater management became involved, since permissions to see the film obviously were necessary, particularly in this case, because the film was rated unsuitable for children. Nonetheless, the necessary permissions were secured and the class went as a group to

FIGURE 15.6

Lewis Saks, the learning resources director, took an active interest in the Custer unit and provided considerable assistance to both teacher and students.

FIGURE 15.7

Any child is blessed with an imagination which can flourish or be turned off, depending on how we nurture it. Who knows what thoughts of the Battle of the Little Big Horn this boy may be having or where they may lead?

see it (see Plate 15.1, following page 580).

By that time the pupils had already learned a good deal about Custer, a fact reflected in their discussions following the film (which is strongly anti-Custer). Many were able to point out inaccuracies in the film's story line. Many others, particularly those who were seeking evidence on the positive side, pointed out that the general as portrayed in the film was quite a different character than their information had led them to believe. These discussions led to further activities in which the pros and cons on a number of controversial points were debated. They also led to questions on why the film took such liberties not only with the characterization of Custer but with numerous points of historical fact. Quite on their own, the sixth-graders came to the conclusion that the purpose of the film was to entertain and make money rather than to present accurate information.

At this point the members of the class decided they needed more information. Two knowledgeable people from Monroe—the director of the Monroe County Library and the county director of learning re-sources—were invited to come to East Detroit to discuss Custer with the class. Their presentations were greeted with such a variety and level of questions as to impress the visitors and to cause them to invite the class, in turn, to come and visit the library and the Monroe County Historical Museum, where much more information on Custer could be found. The class responded enthusiastically and, with their teacher, began at once to make plans for the visit.

The trip proved to be an exciting and valuable learning experience for the students. Also, because of the imagination and initiative of Lewis Saks, who made the arrangements, the trip generated considerable general interest in both communities. The school bus bringing the students from East Detroit was met at the Monroe city limits by a police escort. The City Council gave permission for pictures to be taken from the top of the statue of General Custer in the public square (see Figure 15.8). The local newspapers ran stories on the visiting students, and the local radio and television stations conducted interviews with them and used excerpts in their evening newscasts. A motion picture photog-

649

FIGURE 15.8

Such statues of heroes appear in public squares the world over. How they came to be there and what they represent can be important clues to understanding a culture.

FIGURE 15.9

Research can be a "drag" or a stimulating and absorbing activity. (a) Here in the Monroe County Public Library students learn some of the lore behind the facts about a famous man. (b) What one brings *to* a museum display can make all the difference. These Custer realia would be just dead relics to many children, but to these young investigators with a background and a purpose, they are fascinating and "alive."

rapher came in to document the proceedings, and the children themselves also took many pictures. Monroe High School history classes had representatives observe the proceedings and report back to their classes. In short, interest and involvement in this project of the schools ran high in both communities.

The reaction of the students to the experience was highly positive—in part because of the care with which the plans for the trip had been made, but also because they had by this time learned enough about Custer and the whole problem of differing points of view to be genuinely and deeply interested in the subject. They were able to find many new source materials at the public library, including letters, documents and official reports. At the museum, they were able to sit at Custer's desk, in his chair, and even in the saddle he used; they also inspected a life insurance policy of Custer's. The children surprised some of the local experts with their questions and with the extent of their knowledge. Some examined official documents—reports of campaigns, including the Battle of the Little Big Horn, records of court martial cases in which Custer was involved, and records of his time at West Point (see Figure 15.9).

A notable learning development which had begun earlier but which was enhanced by the trip was this: The more the students learned and heard and saw, the more difficult they found it to decide what to *believe* about the nature, the character, and the acts of the legendary general. They learned that he was indeed an avid Indian fighter, but they also learned that he had a reason. They learned that he had indeed gone AWOL during his military career, but that here, too, perhaps he had a justifiable reason. On their own they began to draw comparisons with the tangled trials of Lieutenant Calley and others resulting from My Lai. They were beginning to learn, in short, the valuable lesson that seldom are there simple or final answers to such questions. As one young girl put it, "How am I ever going to get at the truth?" (See Figure 15.10.)

Evaluation

At the end of the unit, Lewis Saks asked the students to write him letters telling what they had learned from their study of General Custer. Two representative letters follow:

Dear Mr. Saks,

I think our class had a real opportunity to do the Custer project and to get our pictures in the paper.

When we started the Custer project, I was disappointed because I was for him and they put me on the against side. After I found out the bad points about him I was really glad that I was against him.

When we finished our reports we saw the movie Little Big Man. *I think I speak for most of the class that Custer did not do all the things they say he did. I think half the class is still confused.*

I would like to thank you, Mrs. Daume, Mr. Cookingham, and the rest of the staff that made us famous.

> *Thank you again,*
> *Theressa Frasard*
> *6th Grade*
> *Crescentwood School*

P.S. Most of the credit should go to Mr. Shehab for letting us do the project and the rest of the staff.

• • •

Dear Mr. Saks,

I learned very much by working on a report and by helping make a map. I learned to work with others, to look up information quicker, and how to work in a debate. I learned that in everything there's a good and a bad, and that people are almost always for something or against something.

> *Sincerely yours,*
> *Joseph Evangelish*

From the standpoint of the teacher and the school it is clear that there were valuable outcomes:

1   *The students learned much about methods of inquiry and about formulating their own judgments.*
2   *They learned about differing points of view on practically everything that is important.*
3   *Every child was involved and, for the most part, interest deepened throughout the unit.*
4   *The use of media throughout the unit was natural, meaningful, and highly effective.*
5   *The parents, other schools and teachers, and two communities were much involved. The newspaper, television, and radio publicity was healthy in two respects:*
    a   *The general benefits deriving from favorable publicity for the schools;*
    b   *The particular benefits deriving from publicizing the teaching-learning process.*

This unit on Custer in the Crescentwood School was not planned in Instructional Development terms. Rather, it evolved from the combination of an excellent teacher, a learning resources director with creative imagination and extraordinary resourcefulness, and a series of favorable circumstances, such as the timing of release of the feature film. As the teacher put it, "One thing led to another!" Perhaps the most important point is that these things *did* lead to something—that this was not left to chance. Something good was *made* to happen, and in the end it benefited not only the students, but also the schools and communities involved.

Another time, Instructional Development principles are more likely to be used. In retrospect, the teacher and other educators involved feel that future units of this kind can be made even *more* effective by greater specification of objectives and methods and by building in an evaluation system from the start to make possible a better judgment on the values of the time spent (an hour and a half per day on the average for about six weeks) and a better assessment of the learning results achieved. And they feel that this can be done without sacrificing the spontaneity, interest, and degrees of freedom and involvement achieved in the Custer unit. In short, a good instructional system need not be sterile simply because it is carefully and precisely planned; actually, a *good* instructional system cannot be sterile, because if it is to achieve the superior effectiveness of which it is capable, flexibility and human factors must be built into it.

FIGURE 15.10

Where lies the "truth"? The students who summarized these points about Custer are less than sure—and by that very fact they have learned an important lesson.

Example 3: Ecology and man's deteriorating environment

I N today's society, the problem of the deterioration of our environment has at long last been recognized as the price of man's efforts to win for himself the benefits of an increasingly complicated technology. How to utilize the advantages of technology without sacrificing the balances of natural ecologies has finally become a primary social concern among people around the globe.

As a result, teachers are being called on to help learners understand the complexity of the dilemma. Up to the present time, some beginning, fragmented attempts have been made to restore our deteriorating environment by halting the ravages of our technology. To bring about further change, school people, students, and lay people will need to work hard. They must first become aware of pollution and ecological destruction. They must then *decide* on actions that will demand the expenditure of great amounts of energy and dollars, actions that will nevertheless be necessary if solutions are to be found which will stop the onward sweep of land, air, and water deterioration (see Plate 15.2, following page 580).

As they began to consider these problems, a teacher in a midwestern community school and the members of the junior high social studies class were searching for the meaning of Ralph Waldo Emerson's prophecy, "The end of civilization will be that it will eventually die of civilization." A listing of all of the sociological and scientific benefits of civilization was in progress. The list included many elements of our "advanced" society—communication, transportation, creature comforts, and so forth. One student referred to Henry David Thoreau's belief that in order to enjoy life, one must attempt to keep it as simple as possible.

"But that would get boring," the student continued "Who wants things simple? I like it the way it is—television, jet planes, hard rock on radio, my car, drag races—Why, my mother would never give up her washer, dryer, refrigerator, air conditioning—and Dad has to get a new car every third year, and we all drive out to the national parks every summer—"

The teacher had been searching for ways to introduce the idea that all this high-pressure "consuming" could soon lead us to destroying our environment and therefore ourselves as we relentlessly satisfy our desires. He had previewed many films on the subject, and just to get things started in that direction, he screened selected excerpts from two films which illustrated what happens when man upsets, through his great appetite, any of the three great ecological balances. The first excerpt was from *What Is Ecology?* and the second was from *Ecology of Man.*[8]

The first excerpt explained the natural balances that exist where forest and water plants and animals survive together in their natural environment and how, when these balances are upset, chaotic destruction takes place. The other excerpt had to do with defining and demonstrating the interrelationships of the elements of ecology—temperature, water, minerals, land, food supply, and so forth. Both excerpts showed dramatic examples of what happens when

[8] See the list on page 656 for details on these films.

man's activity interferes with and upsets or destroys the ecological balances.

The teacher continued, "All of us live in community or neighborhood environments that are characterized by balances and encroaching imbalances. Unfortunately, however, most of us accept things as they are, not realizing that we live in the midst of changes which developed slowly and were very often unnoticed. The beaches close early because the water is polluted, and all we say is, 'Oh well, it just happened this summer.' For days we notice that the air is heavy and the sun not bright, but we say, 'The sun's been a little hazy recently, but the air will clear.' "

Like many, the school in question was in a very typical mid-American district where a relatively high standard of living was available to most of the students. The teacher "taught" a social studies curriculum in which 75 percent of the time was to be spent on required units of work. Beyond that, the teacher was encouraged to investigate related areas of social significance and importance which his discretion and interest prompted him to develop out of the observations he made about the nature and needs of his students. Thus the teacher had decided to pursue with the group the local area problems relating to ecological balances and imbalances and what might be done about the latter.

As he had hoped, the showing of the excerpts and his comments opened up a lively discussion and led to the formation of a "steering committee" of interested students who would, with the teacher, recommend to the whole group what might be pursued, investigated, and accomplished. Later, an objectives committee was assigned the responsibility of acting for the class in developing feasible plans.

One of the members of the steering committee reported during a later meeting, "First of all, we have to know something—the entire world of land, water, and air must be in balance."

A second student picked up the idea: "But there are many sub-balances, small ecologies, that occur."

A third student added, "The greatest balance is the earth's weather system. It is in balance even though there may be violent storms raging over one area and calms in other places." He pointed to the aquarium and continued, "And, of course, that's a little 'ecology'—snails, plants, fish, and things."

The teacher had been noting the flow of discussion and occasionally contributed an idea or a modification. He summarized at one point by writing on the chalkboard: "Given information about the nature of ecological balances in the world's environments, locate and understand some of the balances that exist within landforms (deserts, forests, prairies) and in microcommunities in water (oceans, ponds, rivers, lakes, streams). Be able to relate all of this to how these balances affect our lives in the villages or cities."

He addressed the class, "Is this too big a job or is this really what it is all about?"

"No, and yes," came back the responses.

But how would students in groups demonstrate that they knew what ecological balances were all about? Suggestions for terminal projects were volunteered.

"If we really understand these balances, we ought to be able to at least diagram them," a student began.

Another added, "One good way to do this is to diagram them on projectuals. Then we could show them to all of us at once and describe, question, and discuss, or whatever—"

"Why not ask some of our community experts—the forest rangers, the agricultural agents, the weatherman, the conservationists—to be here when we make our reports and add their own ideas?"

Later, after class, the teacher assembled from his notes the substance of the goals and desired terminal behaviors:

1. Has man behaved intelligently in developing the present urban technological society? Given information about natural ecologies—lakes, streams, prairies, forests—choose one and describe at least five ways in which man has changed, supported, or threatened to destroy its balance through his actions.

2. What can one person, a member of our class, do to understand and, on this basis, help restore desired ecological balances to some aspect of his immediate environment—streams, forest areas, business neighborhoods, the school community, the air which surrounds the school or community, etc.?

Next, such broad objectives needed to be broken down into much smaller areas. For example, given the information that our air environment (the lower troposphere) is composed of a blanket of nitrogen, oxygen, neon, and carbon dioxide varying up to 3 miles thick around the earth's surface, what natural forces are at work which maintain pure air? What technological developments has man engaged in that threaten the natural balances that ensure pure air? What steps can the individual or members of the community take to correct practices that threaten pure air? Similar objectives were then worked out for water and land balances—man's responsibilities for understanding threats to natural balances and carrying out corrective actions where necessary.

The teacher considered the kinds of learning experiences needed if the members of his class were to conceptualize all the attendant understandings. The school had an Instructional Resources Center which included selected filmstrips, prerecorded tapes, graphics, diagrams, specimens, wall charts, flat picture collections, and, most important, comprehensive directories of local sources of 16mm films, 8mm film loops, videotaped television materials, and so forth.

Not all of this, but a surprising amount

of it could become available to the students. In addition, there were the resources of the community and here, the teacher decided, would be the place to start. Naturally, if one is to come to grips with one's environment, the first steps are to investigate it, to respond to it, to understand it, and to plan for its possible improvement.

Materials and strategies

MATERIALS FOR INSTRUCTION   The teacher identified two kinds of learning resources to be drawn on: those that could be located and responded to by the class members themselves and those he and the school's media specialist would arrange to secure. These last, the teacher announced, would be collected as the "Ecology Box."

Anything in the "Ecology Box" could be investigated by any class member as he carried on his quest for information, either as one of a group or individually.[9] The "Ecology Box" was placed in the school's social studies learning resource center, where the media librarian supervised its day-to-day use. The "box" included such questing materials as follows:

16mm sound motion picture films

Audubon Wildlife Series: Living Wilderness, color, 26 min. AV Explorations.
Audubon Wildlife Series: These Things Are Ours, color, 26 min. AV Explorations.
Ecology of Man, color, 18 min., DuArt.
Element 3, Parts 1 and 2, color, 48 min. 1966, International Film Bureau.
The Garbage Explosion, color and b/w, 16 min. Encyclopaedia Britannica Educational Corporation (EBEC).
The House of Man: Our Crowded Environ-

ment, color and b/w, 11 min. EBEC.
Man Makes A Desert, color, 10 min. Film Association.
Nature's Last Stand: The Desert, color, 28 min. Films, Inc.
Nature's Last Stand: The Everglades, color, 28 min. Films, Inc.
Nature's Last Stand: Point Pelee, color, 28 min. Films, Inc.
Nature's Last Stand: The Rocky Mountains, color, 28 min. Films, Inc.
Our Endangered Environment, color, 17 min. Environmental Films.
Our Land Needs Your Help, color, 13 min. Arthur Barr Productions.
Problems of Conservation: Our Natural Resources, color and b/w, 11 min. EBEC.
Problems of Conservation: Water, color and b/w, 16 min. EBEC.
Population Ecology, color and b/w, 19 min. EBEC.
The River, b/w, 38 min. U.S. Department of Agriculture (USDA).
Say Goodbye, color, 52 min. Films, Inc.
The Third Pollution, color, 22 min. Stewart Finlay.
What Is Ecology? color and b/w, 11 min. EBEC.
Your Environment Is the Earth, color, 12 min. Journal Films.

Filmstrip

Introduction to Ecology, color, McGraw-Hill.

Filmstrips with accompanying record or prerecorded tape

Environment: Changing Man's Values, 2 filmstrips, 2 tape cassettes, discussion guide, Guidance Associates.
Our Environment 1: Fresh Water Communities—Streams, Rivers, Ponds, Lakes, 4 filmstrips, 4 records, teacher's guide, and transparencies, 2 diagrams, EMC Corporation.

[9] Adapted from "The Thirties Box" (information sources on the 1930–1940 decade), Ontario Institute for Studies in Education, 252 Bloom Street W., Toronto, Ontario, Canada.

Our Environment 2: Sound and Noise, 2 filmstrips, 1 cassette, 1 diagram, teacher's guide, EMC Corporation.

Our Environment 3: Aesthetics, 2 filmstrips, 1 cassette, teacher's guide, 2 diagrams, EMC Corporation.

Our Environment 4: Atmosphere, 4 filmstrips, 2 cassettes, teacher's guide, student workbook, student activity sheets, 4 diagrams, transparencies, EMC Corporation.

Transient materials A sampling of materials gathered by the social studies learning resource center supervisor is as follows: "Noise: The Third Pollution," "Clean Water, It's Up to You," "Needed: Clean Air," "Community Action for the Environment," "Youth Takes A Lead in Ecology," "It's Up to You to Save Your Environment," etc.

Community resources Local committees: Life of the Land, Citizens Against Noise, the Sierra Club. Local offices of government and civic agencies: the Bureaus of Fisheries and Wildlife, Forestry, and Reforestation; Wildlife and Game Control; Water Control and Reclamation; Sanitation and Refuse Collection; Clean Air Control; etc.[10]

TEACHING STRATEGIES: METHODS Even when, as in this situation, one teacher works with a group of 35 students, unique opportunities are available. Recall how, at the beginning of the unit, two film excerpts were used to trigger interest in and discussion about further investigation of ecological balances, imbalances, and current

[10] Titles indicate areas of local community concern and official action. In most communities, these areas are represented through legally authorized or publicly organized offices, committees, or personnel. Because the names or specific designations are regional, teachers and students should refer to local city directories or telephone directories for specifics.

conditions of our environment. Now the teacher made another suggestion:

"Here are three battery-operated tape recorders—field recorders, we'll call them—4½ pounds, complete with cassette. Is that going to stop any of you from taking them outside and putting them to use? Any ideas, anyone?"

A pause followed and then, "Sure, we'll go record sounds—"

Another pause, then another voice: "What sounds"

A third voice chimed in: "The sounds we live with in the morning, during the day, and at night."

Still another student suggested: "How about good sounds and, well, sounds we can do without."

A lively discussion followed as the invitation to explore our environment of sounds was picked up. The idea was accepted with enthusiasm and was put into effect as the students appointed three two-man committees to go to work.

The next day, the teacher spread out an array of inexpensive black-and-white cameras gathered together from all over the school—from the art, science, and physical education departments, and others.

"Let's call this 'Operation Power Picture,'"[11] he began. "Rather than go into a long discussion, I'll just say this: Get out into our neighborhood—yes, into the city and countryside—take pictures of things as they are, things you like, things you don't like, things you would change if you could."

Again a jumble of voices poured forth ideas:

"Those power lines and poles that cut across the corner of the school grounds!"

"That real nice spot down by the pond where we often eat lunch."

[11] Adapted from "Environmental Studies," the American Geological Institute, Boulder, Colorado, 1971.

"How about those traffic jams we fight on the way to school?"

"I should have had one of those cameras with me this morning! You should see the Monday morning trash in Clements Park."

Cameras and film were issued to small groups. However, over in one corner another small group remained apart. It turned out that they were examining the possibility that they would want to quest their way first through the exciting "promises" within the "Ecology Box." We have already discussed the types of classroom organization that provide freedom for small groups to do different things while individual questing goes on, also. This is a good example.

The group periodically returned to more formal sessions. During such meetings of the whole class, they examined again their objectives and the appropriateness of the terminal reports and projects being planned. The questions about who wished to do what led directly into a projected classroom organization for the next three weeks. Two groups volunteered to go through the materials, carry on their own previewing, and come up with things they would like the entire group to see. They also would assume responsibility for including background information, study questions, and statements of purpose to be kept in mind while the actual materials were being presented to the large group.

In addition, opportunities to participate individually were given to those who had not yet found their way naturally into one of the several small groups that had been organized to pay particular attention to such matters as the county's water supply, recreation facilities, forests and fields, streams and lakes, population trends, traffic problems, refuse disposal, status and care of parks, wildlife preserves, fish and game resources, and so forth.

The initial weeks were spent largely in questing for cognitive information by means of the audiotapes, the photographs showing evidence of both ecological balances and deterioration in the community, first-hand visits with concerned community lay persons and officials, and by gathering statistics. Then the time soon came to present their new-found information through terminal reports, demonstrations, or exhibits of evidence—charts, pictures, tapes, selected film clips, and so forth. Thus the culminating stage of the activity was attained as such creative and purposeful pupil responses as the following were presented to the class group by various members.

Evaluation and recycling

The pupil committees on sound recording and visual documentation opened the reporting by presenting the evidence they had collected and carefully edited to include only what they thought was most effective. First the "sounds" committee asked their classmates to listen to the sounds of confusion and annoyance which had been recorded near the school grounds before, during, and after school. Their question then was, "Is this the way we want things to be, or can something be done about controlling all this?"

A member of the Student Council responded, "*We* make a lot of the noise on the school grounds and in the corridors! I'll take the responsibility to report this at the next meeting of the Student Council. Will you help by bringing in the 'sounds'?" The answer was, of course, an enthusiastic affirmative.

Two students volunteered to contact the Department of Traffic Control to present their recorded evidence and ask that some rerouting of the heavy traffic be done during the school days. The reports continued.

"These pictures we took speak for themselves," began the next student, indicating an attractively mounted display of

5 × 7 black-and-white enlargements. Litter scarred the school grounds, the park area across the street, downtown street intersections, and nearby identifiable lake and stream shores; all this was pointed out and became the subject of animated discussion.

"It's not exactly the way the Indians left it," a student admonished and suggestions flowed about what individuals could do to stimulate interest in cleaning up the environment and, even more important, how they could ask for help from the community to correct the situations.

The report on sanitation and refuse disposal included an account of visits to the Department of Sanitation and the trash disposal area and interviews with the department's personnel. A 3-minute film clip was presented which portrayed dramatically the dilemma posed by too much "consuming" and too little collecting and disposing of mountains of trash.[12] The discussion that followed centered on the alternatives of recycling or reclamation of trash or waste material, what could be done about the condition of the school grounds, and to whom in the community members of the group could report and seek solutions from.

As other reports were given, students presented exhibits of information, statistics, their own photographs, and panels of pictures they had secured either from the learning resources center or from maga-

zines. Statistics on population growth, information on trends in consumption of goods, data on the wasting nature of our mineral and forestry resources, evidence of extermination of whole species of birds and game animals—all of this was in graphic forms, often through the use of carefully drawn charts shown as projectuals.

More and more, the true meaning of Emerson's dictum about the dilemma of civilization versus technology became meaningful to students and teachers. The students understood that individual action must be the begining. Also, they planned how to bring their information to the attention of appropriate community agencies.

The teacher and those of the staff who had cooperated with him began an evaluation by reviewing the apparent usefulness to pupils of the questing materials. They decided what would be discarded as being irrelevant and what needed to be added so as to give more and more opportunities to each learner to continue his broadening search to discover his own role in a technology threatening to destroy itself. An overall problem that did not relate to the materials was identified: information about pollution and the deterioration of the environment is easier to assemble than to act on. The continuing challenge is to present this information to appropriate community agencies, to discover their plans for action, and to become constructively involved.

Example 4: African struggles for independence

CONTINUING pupil-teacher planning is the method used to implement the principles of Instructional Development in this example. In evolving new courses and units at the high school level, the ongoing responsibility for instructional organiza-

tion and the use of interrelated media rests with a committee composed of three to five social studies teachers, representatives selected from various participating groups of students, and parent representatives (when the latter are available). This committee work, which continues year after year, has resulted in the formulation of many exciting new courses and units, in-

12 "The Garbage Explosion"; see the list on page 656.

cluding a unit called "Africa Today."[13]

Many of the innovative units and courses have grown out of comparisons drawn between episodes in American history and their counterparts elsewhere in the evolving and developing nations of the world. One of the most rewarding of these comparisons was "discovered" by a junior student, who reported: "The more I've investigated, the more I believe that the people of the emerging African nations have faced many of the same kinds of problems and opportunities as the colonists at the time of the American Revolution around 1776." This central theme was accepted by the committee as the starting point for a new unit, "Africa Today," that would be part of the "America and the World" course that already existed.

Later, 28 broad objectives for the unit were formulated by the committee. Following are five of them:

1. Given the knowledge that, beginning with Ghana in 1957, 34 new African countries took their places among the family of nations between then and 1968, draw parallels between three events which led to the struggle for independence by the American colonists and three key events in the recent history of one of the following countries: Nigeria, Uganda, Ghana, Tanzania. Report your conclusions in a manner similar to that of current mass media—use the methods of television, newspapers, magazines, advertising, and so forth. For example, you might play the role of a television news commentator and discuss the three pairs of points, bringing out both similarities and differences.

2. Given information about similarities and differences in area, climate, and landforms of the United States and the continent of Africa, report your new-found information to classmates by using contemporary communications techniques; that is, construct, with the help of some of your classmates, a sand table, a papier-mâché map, or a two-dimensional map of the two areas or prepare your information entirely in projectual form. As you report your ideas about differences and similarities, refer to your exhibit or project the transparencies on an overhead projector.

3. Having achieved understandings about the nature, use, and development of means of transportation and communication in both the United States and the emerging areas of Africa from 1776 to the present, report your conclusions by assembling a pictorial comparative display in which you incorporate your own original drawings or pictures secured from library or magazine sources. As an alternative, create projectuals to visualize your descriptions and explanations.

4. During your study of American history you have acquired understandings of music, dance, art, and craft forms developed and practiced by the American Indians. Acquire the same type of information about similar cultural forms as developed and practiced by such African tribes as the Swahili, Digo, Shirazi, or Masai. Obtain from the school, a local museum, or other community sources drums, xylophones, and rattles and present a demonstration and explanation of one basic African music form, comparing and contrasting it with one basic American Indian music form.

5. Again using your knowledge of American Indian culture, present similar demonstrations and comparisons of African dance art, or craft forms. You may find it advisable to seek help and advice from teachers in the music and physical educa-

[13] This example describes a composite instructional plan worked out by three members of the 1971 Hawaii Media Leadership Training group. The plan is an "optimal unit" using interrelated media which is, in a sense, a recycled and expanded plan of instruction adapted from instructional work then going on at the Kailua High School in Honolulu. Thus when events at a specific high school are referred to in this account, the school is the Kailua High School.

tion departments and perhaps also from an expert in the community.

Additional objectives originated by the committee concern understandings about the following: African trade, religion, and education; the political problems caused by the fact that arbitrary geographical boundaries violate old tribal boundaries; the plight of some 10 remaining dependencies caused by unresolved problems with, particularly, Portugal and Spain.

Materials and strategies

SELECTION OF LEARNING MATERIALS Now the members of the committee set about methodically choosing and examining some of the materials listed in James E. Parker's remarkable bibliography of media learning materials relating to the black man.[14] Using this source, together with catalogs of films, filmstrips, maps, and prerecorded tapes produced by commercial publishers of learning materials, the committee obtained, previewed, and evaluated needed resource materials. (See the selection criteria, pages 382–385, 422–423, 536–537.) Such materials as the following were found valuable:

16mm sound motion picture films

The Old Africa and the New: Ethiopia and Botswana (Africa Series), b/w or color, 17 min. McGraw-Hill Text-Films.

Continent of Africa (The Four Regions), color, 15 min. McGraw-Hill Text-Films, 1963.

The Economy of Africa (Africa Series), b/w or color, 13 min. McGraw-Hill Text-Films.

East Africa: Tropical Highlands (Africa Series), b/w or color, 15 min. McGraw-Hill Text-Films.

Discovering the Music of Africa, color, 20 min. Film Association, 1967.

Republic of the Ivory Coast (Africa Series), b/w or color, 20 min. Universal Education and Visual Arts, 1962.

Republic of Niger (Africa Series), b/w or color, 20 min. Universal Education and Visual Arts.

Republic of Chad (The Peoples of Africa Series), b/w or color, 20 min. Universal Education and Visual Arts.

African Continent: An Introducton, color, 14 min. Coronet Films, 1962.

Africa: Living in Two Worlds, color, 14 min. Encyclopaedia Britannica Educational Corporation (EBEC).

The African Scene: Two Boys of Ethiopia, color, 20 min. EBEC.

The African Scene: Boy of Botswana, color, 17 min. EBEC.

The African Scene: Youth Builds a Nation in Tanzania, color, 18 min. EBEC.

The African Scene: A Family of Liberia, color, 17 min. EBEC.

Building a House (Julien Bryan). International Film Foundation.

Hunting Wild Doves (Julien Bryan). International Film Foundation.

Filmstrips on Africa were selected from catalogs issued by McGraw-Hill, Encyclopaedia Britannica, and Walt Disney Enterprises. An outstanding multimedia kit was selected which includes filmstrips, prerecorded tapes, and 33 rpm records.[15]

All the materials were assembled and made ready for use in the school's social studies learning resources center (see Plate 15.3, following page 580). The key to the success of such an arrangement lies in easy and dependable access by students and teachers to the materials. Comparable arrangements, which are to be found in many school districts, are fundamental to the success of new, flexible scheduling plans. The student, in such a situation,

[14] James E. Parker, *Media Relating to the Black Man,* North Carolina College, Durham, N.C., May 1969.

[15] *Zanjafrica: An Ecological View of Coastal Africa,* EMC Corporation, St. Paul, Minn.

markedly increases his use of "software" as he pursues his questing, individually or as a member of a group. (When such a program does fail, in fact, the failure usually is attributable to lack of accessible learning resources.)

TEACHING STRATEGIES: METHODS Which of the many available media learning materials should be used? In what order should those selected for use be presented? That is, which materials lend themselves to beginning or introductory aspects of the learning sequence and which materials are detailed in nature and lend themselves to individualized quests for information? These are questions that always underlie decisions about arranging materials for instruction. And, after all has been said and done, it is the teacher who must make these decisions final and then initiate their implementation.

The strategies employed in presenting "Africa Today" are feasible whenever modular scheduling is used.[16] During an

initial large-group meeting, the planning committee presented a report on its work. The statements of objectives were passed out and explained, and student members of the committee described briefly how the objectives were determined and how materials were selected. The second part of the meeting was used to introduce and alert the assembled students to the nature of the people, landforms, and climate of Africa.

FIGURE 15.11

Those who studied the multimedia learning resources as they tried to understand Africa today encountered a kaleidoscope of new information and ideas. (a) Africa is no longer the "dark continent" abounding in exotic beasts. (b) Rather, more and more people are crowding into the cities, seeking opportunities to improve themselves but also experiencing frustrations as they lose the freedom they had living in small tribes spread over the vast areas of the hinterland. (c) Yet, basically, people are the same everywhere, whether in tribes or in the old sections of the cities, as here. In the cities, increasing numbers find their way into newly organized schools, while (d) their parents are at work bringing twentieth-century communication, transportation, and industry to the immense open areas of the continent. In sum, the students learned that Africa is after all a reality, a living, moving part of the world—a part of us all.

---

[16] The term "modular scheduling" here refers to the following system of programing: The school day is divided into 20-minute time modules (or "mods"), 20 per day. Each student is scheduled for participation as a member of a large group, medium-size group, or small group for 50 percent of his day; he devotes the other 50 percent to planning his own work at an instructional materials center, where he does independent or small-group questing through materials (sound motion picture films, 8mm film loops, filmstrips, prerecorded tapes, maps, charts, books, transient sources, etc.), at the same time arranging for participation in other school activities as well as seek-free time to devote to individual conferences and assistance. The teachers also plan their time according to modules; this planning varies with subject area, but each group of teachers decides how their school day will be divided between actual instruction of large groups, medium-size groups, or small groups; individual counseling and evaluation; and also participation in school activity leadership. Some time modules are as long as five 20-minute periods; thus, when necessary, a large group can meet for more than an hour and a half.

The films *African Continent: An Introduction* and *Africa: Living in Two Worlds*[17] were presented. Each film was introduced by a student panel and followed by discussion by another group acting as a response panel—a group selected from the whole group. This kind of extended large-group activity is typical of the flexible

scheduling strategies used at this high school.

Finally, there was a summary statement by a local parent who frequently made lengthy business trips to Africa and who thus was able to present several eyewitness reports and respond to questions from the group. The closing moments of the session were devoted to permitting students to choose membership in small

[17] See list on page 661.

groups in order to become identified with a variety of questing projects, including: "The Landforms of Africa," "The People of Africa," "African Languages," "African Culture," "African Religion," African Business," "African Agriculture," "African Mining," "African Animal Husbandry," "African Education," "African Arts and Music," "The New Nations of Africa," and "Sports and Recreation in Africa."

The selected films, filmstrips, filmstrip sets, maps, and charts, along with government brochures published by the Department of State and by the emerging African nations themselves, were arranged in the social studies learning resources center on open-access shelves. Within the large comfortably furnished room, which contains carrels and viewing corners, prerecorded tapes, records, and transcriptions also were made available. The films included special ones providing in-depth treatments of music, the dance, art forms, religious and political problems of the emerging nations, and so on. All of these materials could be studied by individuals or members of small groups (see Figure 15.11).

During the following month, weekly large-group meetings were scheduled (within the school's flexible modular system) to encourage progress reports and the exchange of information resulting from the interaction among the members of each of the small groups at work. For example, at the third large-group meeting a series of reports on the complex problems of the emerging African cultures was presented. Members of several groups had discovered a multitude of intricate, interacting influences, among them these: a land area that is one-fifth of the world's surface and nearly four times that of the United States; a climate that encompasses the extremes —temperature and rainfall conditions that vary from scorching heat to subzero and deluge to desert; language problems cre-

ated by 1,000 dialects, of which only 10 are spoken by more than one million people of the nearly 300,000,000; religious problems enmeshed in the interplay between Christianity, Islam, and distinctive local tribal religious beliefs and mystical observations; and, finally, the conflicts created when large numbers of untrained, uneducated, though intelligent, people are given their independence and cast on their own after years of domination by Europeans, Arabs, and Hindus. The reports were multimedia in nature, and many of them were reinforced with descriptions and explanations worked out specially by the students. Such explanations were used to introduce and/or to summarize information presented in film and audiotape segments and to explain projectuals and slides.

Once the process was under way, the three teachers spent most of their available time "listening in" on the small groups and helping them, when necessary, to reformulate their directions and their methods of searching for additional information. As the research continued, letters were written to government agencies and personal calls were made on qualified members of the community who had special knowledge of African art, music, political affairs, and cultural backgrounds.

The fourth large-group meeting was a culmination meeting that consisted of presentations of the discoveries made by representatives of the groups—and by three individual students who had become especially "turned on" and had pursued "extra" investigations on their own. Enthusiasm mounted during demonstrations of the true nature and complexities of African music. A local black musician, well versed in African music, had been prevailed on to help several students prepare demonstrations and explanations of the nature and meaning of the rhythms of tribal dance forms, using drums, rattles, bells (both single and double), and the African xylophone. The students introduced their demonstration by showing excerpts from the film *Discovering the Music of Africa*.[18]

Other culminating projects, highly creative in nature, were presented at another large-group meeting. These included a spirited debate between two teams on the question, *"Resolved:* The emerging nations of Africa are incapable of governing themselves," and a lively demonstration of African dance influences on American culture performed by two teams of pupils who simulated the original African forms and then demonstrated the contemporary variations well known to youthful Americans—with uproarious results. Several students used projected charts and graphics to visualize their own oral interpretations of land utilization in Africa, reasons for the locations of centers of population density, climatic variations, changes in literacy rates since independence.

Evaluation

During the student and teacher evaluation that followed, the key question was: To what extent did the 150 members of the combined classes become profitably involved in conducting their own questing and reporting their findings? The consensus was that the combination of multimedia learning resources, teaching strategies, dramatic learning experiences, and modular scheduling had produced more involvement than was usual. On the negative side, some 18 to 20 students had been very casual about the whole thing, doing little more than "put in time." All concerned realized that not everyone can become profitably involved in all activities—that some, for various personal reasons, remain aloof or indicate their lack of interest in other ways. Nevertheless, since noninvolvement should, of course, be prevented as far as

possible, the committee then turned its attention to ways and means of cutting down on the number of uninvolved students during the next trial of the unit.

During one of the recycling conferences attended by teachers and some interested students, one probable factor leading to some of the noninvolvement came out. A student began the discussion: "When we do our own searching, previewing, and—" "Questing?" a teacher prompted. "Yes," the student replied, continuing, "Well, when we're trying to get facts, the social studies resource center just runs out of good things—there aren't enough things for us to use." The discussion that followed resulted in a consensus that good materials and useful materials of all kinds, including media resources, must be in greater supply than ever before when open or flexible scheduling is used.

Open scheduling of course permits a variety of student activities—as members of large groups, working together in small groups, and using large blocks of time for independent study and questing. Thus by its very nature open scheduling allows individual students to race ahead, free to indulge their inherent and voracious appetite for information—information they can only get from *materials*. In other words, any realistic and comprehensive application of Instructional Development principles that capitalizes on flexible or open scheduling depends for its success on the availability of many learning resource materials, all made readily accessible to students who wish to take advantage of small-group or independent questing opportunities. As a result, every year, during innovative teaching programs such as those we have described, teachers, supervisors, media personnel, and librarians constantly search for additional learning resource materials relating to subjects planned for continuing study.

• • •

We have now described four specific

---

[18] See list on page 661.

examples of effective multimedia use in teaching. These examples make it obvious that the application of Instructional Development strategies varies greatly in individual situations. Nevertheless, it should also be obvious that Instructional Development is, in a broad sense, a way of thinking logically about alternative ways of analyzing problems and alternative ways of using interrelated media to provide learners with alternative experiences that help them conceptualize and understand. Providing these alternative experiences by means of a variety of sources is one of the most inspiring of the challenges presented to teachers.

Example 5: Instructional Development in two community colleges

DURING the past decade, the number of junior colleges and community colleges has rapidly increased. Since these colleges are for the most part new, they have designed new kinds of curricula and learning experiences in response to new kinds of needs. With no tradition of conventional teaching methods to impede them, community colleges have frequently come up with unique and innovative instructional programs. We shall describe two of these which have quite different but highly successful programs.

Lansing Community College AVT Program

The Lansing Community College in Michigan has chosen a highly individualized form of instruction called the AVT program which dispenses with regular classes in numerous subject areas (see Figure 15.12). AVT, which stands for Audio-Visual-Tutorial, indicates a program that is an outgrowth of the Audio-Tutorial plan developed at Purdue University during the 1960s by Dr. S. N. Postlethwait, a noted biologist (see Chapter 9). Variations of this and other self-instruction plans, such as the SLATE (Structured Learning and Teaching Environments) plan developed by Dr. Robert Davis at Michigan State University and the Mastery Model developed by Dr. Fred Keller, initially at Columbia University, have been adopted by higher institutions across the country and particularly by the junior and community colleges.

The AVT plan at LCC began in the natural sciences in 1966. Dr. David Shull and his staff spent months intensively developing and testing the original units before the new college opened its doors. Instructional Development principles and procedures were used from the outset, with precise statements of objectives, careful development and testing of materials, and validation of results. There was considerable revision of the materials over the first several years. Meanwhile, with the help of a strong audiovisual support program, other departments, including business, social science, English, mathematics, and technology, moved into use of the AVT program in their basic courses (see Table 15.1).

An illustration from the business department suggests the extent to which the AVT technique serves individual needs. Recently a woman came to the department with a special request for instruction on a particular business machine with which she had had no experience but which she would have to operate in a position she was seeking. Although the term was already three weeks old, she was allowed to register at once for the one part of the office machines course she needed. She set up her own schedule of training at dif-

FIGURE 15.12

Highly efficient Individualized Instruction is used in a variety of courses at Lansing Community College. (a) A student studies a natural science course by means of a sequence using slides, a sound tape, and a lesson guide. (b) A student works to improve her reading speed.

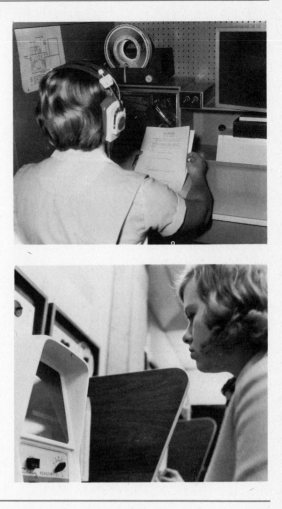

ferent times between 8:00 A.M. and 10:00 P.M. and received her instruction in a special carrel with 8mm sound films in continuous-loop cartridges. In less than two weeks she had finished her course, passed the final test, and accepted her new job—all without further teacher contact.

How is such individualization possible in a department with a heavy enrollment? It is possible because hundreds of teaching units in typing, business machines, secretarial machines, and accounting have been developed expressly for courses of instruction which are completely individualized. No two students are required to follow the same path or to progress at the same speed; yet all are able to seek the same goals and to reach them with better skills, more competencies, and fewer "gaps" in their knowledge than a traditional curriculum and materials approach could produce. Each subject is divided into large numbers of programed tutorial units lasting from 5 to 7 minutes each, rather than a relatively few blocks of related information units lasting 30 to 40 hours.

TABLE 15.1

Individualized instruction courses taught by audiovisual tutorial methods, Lansing Community College, 1972

Discipline	Course
Science	Natural Science 101—Botany/Zoology
	Natural Science 102—Chemistry/Physics
	Natural Science 103—Astronomy/Geology
Social science	Introduction to Psychology
English and languages	Writing
	Reading
	Spanish
	French
Mathematics	Basic Arithmetic
	Beginning Algebra
	Plane Geometry
	Intermediate Algebra
Business	Data Processing: Fortran
	Data Processing: Basic Cobol
	Law Enforcement
	Typing I, II, III
	Business Machines I, II
	Accounting I, II, III
	Secretarial Machines
Technology	Drafting
	Automotive
	Nursing
	Dental

Note 1: All courses listed are taken entirely in AVT lab format except the technology courses, which are supplemented with AVT lab material.

Note 2: Programs are under development in economics, art, and library technology, as well as additional programs in technology.

When a student comes in, an educational specialist in the secretarial sciences interviews him and helps determine the learning experiences needed. The student is then given one or more placement tests to determine how much of each sequence is actually needed for desired performance —as was the case with the woman needing instruction on a particular business machine. The student is then given a prescription sheet indicating all the units of instruction he is to take. This sheet is presented to the AVT laboratory attendant, who provides the necessary package of materials for one phase of a unit—usually either a sound film or a set of slides with an accompanying tape—and assigns the student to a carrel containing the necessary equipment for his instruction on each sequential concept (see Figure 15.13). When that phase of the unit is absorbed, the student returns the material to the attendant and goes to another area in the lab where related practice or application work is carried on. If the student encounters difficulties, he has two alternatives:

review the short instructional unit in the carrel or get assistance from one of the instructors in the laboratory. The instructors are available at all times for individual help and also to go over finished work with students immediately on completion.

Progress-check tests are included at intervals throughout a course. Each one is a self-administered test accompanied by an answer sheet, so the student can check his own paper. A record is kept of his progress and, if necessary, he is invited to make an appointment for a counseling session. On completion of all segments of a particular course, the student takes a test that covers the complete course. This test is administered by department personnel, but checked by the student's adviser.

In summary, programed instructional units are put on automated audiovisual media for individual use, with qualified tutorial assistance whenever necessary. The units and carrels are available 14 hours a day, five days a week, and also on Saturday mornings. Each course begins when the student is ready, is taught when the student requests, and ends when the student has achieved the degree of competence set for the course.

LEARNING AND COST EFFECTIVENESS
The mediated tutorial system in use at Lansing Community College has demonstrated its effectiveness in two significant ways. The first relates to learning results; the second relates to costs. In a study done by Ronald Edwards, chairman of the accounting and office programs department, before the complete changeover to AVT methods, students in both the beginning typing and business machines AVT lab sections did significantly better on final performance tests than did students in the traditional classroom instruction sec-

FIGURE 15.13

A student learns to operate a calculator in a carrel, using an 8mm cassette film, a sound tape, and a lesson guide. The same types of materials are used in typing instruction.

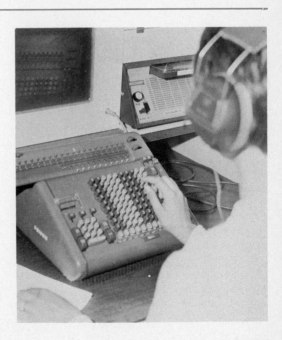

TABLE 15.2

Comparison of final performance test scores between AVT and conventionally taught sections in Business Machines I at Lansing Community College, 1968

	Number	Mean score
Control Group	26	76.3076
Experimental (AVT) Group	26	79.3846
t-ratio	*df* = 50	1.8040[a]

Source: Ronald K. Edwards, *An Experimental Pilot Study To Explore the Use of an Audio-Visual-Tutorial Laboratory in the Secretarial Skills Area,* Lansing Community College, Lansing, Mich., 1968, p. 9.

[a] A *t*-ratio over 1.677 is significant at the .05 level.

Authors' Note: A reader unfamiliar with the statistical terms "*t*-ratio," "*df*," and "significant at the .05 level" can find explanations in various sources, including textbooks in psychological testing and statistics. In any case, the meaning of these tables is apparent without an exact knowledge of the meaning of the technical terms.

---

tions (see Tables 15.2 and 15.3). In addition, there was a clear preference among the students, as measured on an attitude scale, for the individualized AVT system —a preference apparently attributable mostly to the freedom of scheduling and easier availability of machines and instructors under the AVT plan.[19]

As to costs of the AVT system, there is, of course, a substantial investment of time, energy, and money in the original development, testing, and recycling of units to be sure they work. This cost varies according to both the complexity of the learning problem to be solved and the experience and expertise of the designers; actually, materials costs may or may not be higher than they would be for good traditional class programs in the sciences or, as we shall see, in some business courses. In any case, such design and production costs as there are can be amortized over at least several years. Furthermore, once

they are designed and tested, such units can produce considerable savings in teacher and learner time; in efficient use of classroom or laboratory space and equipment; and, possibly, in the need for less equipment that would be used for a comparable number of students under a traditional system.

Edwards made an analysis of the actual costs of the AVT system used in the typing and business machines courses compared with the costs that would have been

TABLE 15.3

Comparison of final performance test scores between AVT and conventionally taught sections in Typing I at Lansing Community College, 1968

---

[19] Ronald K. Edwards, *An Experimental Pilot Study To Explore the Use of an Audio-Visual-Tutorial Laboratory in the Secretarial Skills Area,* Lansing Community College, Lansing, Mich., 1968, pp. 8–18.

incurred under the traditional system for the same number of students. He concluded that there were substantial savings in the use of the AVT system. Using the winter term, 1969, as a basis, the enrollment of 292 students in Typing I, II, and III and Business Machines I and II, would have required, under the traditional system, 13 sections, at least three classrooms, and three faculty members, for a total of 45 contact hours. By comparison, under the AVT arrangement, no sections as such are required, since students can come to the lab any time between 8 A.M. and 10 P.M. for totally Individualized Instruction. Once the AVT system was fully developed, one faculty member rather than three would be required (though he would need several assistants), and he could perform his necessary functions in about five hours a week instead of 45 under the traditional system. Faculty and staff costs under the traditional system were calculated at $11,000 per term; those under the AVT system, including all assistants needed, at $5,350. Equipment costs under the traditional system would have totaled $44,000 for typewriters and business machines. Under the AVT system employing nine carrels, several sets of Individualized Instruction materials and all machines necessary for both the carrels and the practice areas would total $14,800. If the costs of the additional rooms required under the traditional system are also figured in at $35,000 each, the cost differences become almost astronomical.

Although there are more elements involved in a careful cost accounting analysis than these alone, there appears little question that the AVT system in use at the Lansing Community College is indeed highly cost effective in the department of business.

Oakland Community College PEP Plan

In Chapter 14 on Individualized Instruction we pointed out that there are many individual differences other than speed or pace of learning. At the Oakland Community College near Pontiac, Michigan, some of these other differences are grouped as the ''cognitive style''—an overall factor relating to learning. An experimental program, the Personalized Education Program (PEP) is being conducted at Oakland in which the cognitive style of the student is matched with the methods and media by which he receives instruction.[20] His cog-

20 Joseph E. Hill and Betty D. Setz, *Educational Sciences at Oakland Community College*, Oakland Community College, Pontiac, Mich., October 1970.

	Number	Final exam (cognitive)	3-minute speed test	Writing errors
Control Group	20	76.850	41.700	5.850
Experimental (AVT) Group	23	82.638	40.957	2.780
t-ratio	*df* = 41	1.604[a]	.278[a]	3.042

Source: Edwards, op. cit., p. 12.

[a] A t-ratio of 1.683 is necessary in this situation to indicate significance at the .05 level; thus only in writing errors was the difference statistically significant. However, these groups included students both with and without previous typing exposure. When only those 21 students without previous typing exposure were compared, the AVT group proved significantly superior on all three tests.

FIGURE 15.14

nitive style is determined on the basis of a battery of diagnostic tests which measure (1) his ability to derive meaning from symbols, (2) cultural influences (family, associates, and individuals) on his perceptions (3) his reasoning patterns. (Another battery of tests concerning certain chemical and physiological aspects of memory is under development.) The results of these tests are fed into a computer which is programed to provide a printout based on some 2,300 items derived from the tests. The printout is summarized in a chart which indicates to the student, his counselor, and his instructors the instructional strategies that will work best in his particular case. In turn, instructors, counselors, and administrators are diagnosed in the same manner as the students, and students are assigned to instructors with comparable or complementary cognitive styles. The potentials of such matching are clear, but individualization does not stop there.

Following an introductory lecture-discussion on the opening day of a new unit, students are assigned for the next three days, according to needs and cognitive styles, to one or more of seven parallel tracks called Prescription Centers. In each of these tracks the same concepts are presented in different form—programed instruction, discussions, seminars, and so on (see Figure 15.14). Each student must then pass a test on the 5–10 concepts involved at a 90 percent level of achievement; he may repeat parallel forms of the test several times and secure additional help in between, if necessary, but must master the unit before going on.

CAMPI (Computer-Assisted Management of Personalized Instruction) is used to (1) design the modes of presentation associated with the Prescription Centers, (2) match the cognitive style of the student with the mode of presentation best suited to him, (3) administer an entry-level test and the final test, score both, and report the results to the student, the instructor,

Under the PEP program, students at Oakland Community College are channeled in various tracks and with particular instructors according to carefully analyzed needs and cognitive styles. (IPLL: Individual Programed Learning Lab; CA: Carrel Arcade; YTY: Youth Tutor Youth; LRC: Learning Resources Center.)

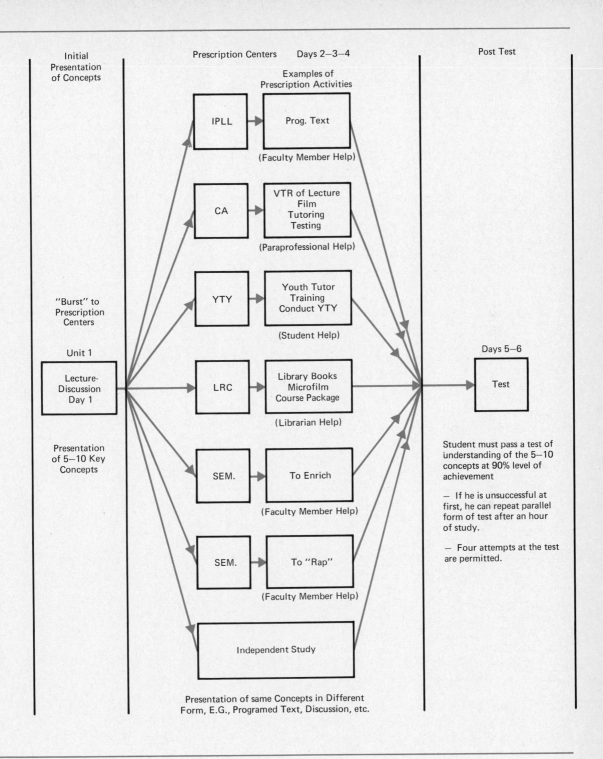

Initial
Presentation
of Concepts

Prescription Centers   Days 2–3–4

Examples of
Prescription Activities

Post Test

IPLL

Prog. Text

(Faculty Member Help)

CA

VTR of Lecture
Film
Tutoring
Testing

(Paraprofessional Help)

"Burst" to
Prescription
Centers

YTY

Youth Tutor
Training
Conduct YTY

(Student Help)

Unit 1

Lecture-
Discussion
Day 1

LRC

Library Books
Microfilm
Course Package

(Librarian Help)

Days 5–6

Test

Presentation
of 5–10 Key
Concepts

SEM.

To Enrich

(Faculty Member Help)

Student must pass a test of
understanding of the 5–10
concepts at 90% level of
achievement

— If he is unsuccessful at
first, he can repeat parallel
form of test after an hour
of study.

— Four attempts at the test
are permitted.

SEM.

To "Rap"

(Faculty Member Help)

Independent Study

Presentation of same Concepts in Different
Form, E.G., Programed Text, Discussion, etc.

673

and the Prescription Center, (4) diagnose test results to the point of predicting probable points of subsequent success and difficulty.

The Foundational Studies course in the Natural and Life Sciences, for example, is an introductory science course for students without a high school science background. The students attend a weekly lecture on one day and a lab session on another. During the other three days, each student is assigned to individually prescribed learning activities. Some are assigned to the Individual Programed Learning Lab to work on programed instruction packages. They are tested on the material at the beginning and end of each session in the learning lab, and the results are sent to the instructor. Other students attend small-group seminars led by students or by the instructor. Still others go to the Carrel Arcade to work on instructional packages developed by the instructors to fit particular cognitive styles. The packages may emphasize visual or aural elements or a combination of these, depending on how the student's learning style is oriented. Students can work either as individuals or in small groups (see Figure 15.15), and instructors are available for individual assistance as needed. The students work at their own pace for as long or as short a period as desired and, as in the learning lab, they are tested at the beginning and end of each session.

Adaptation of materials and methods to carefully determined individual learning styles—the crux of the PEP program—appears to be achieving marked success. Some 98 percent of the students in this program attain the objectives for the foundational science course, as compared with about 70 percent of the students in the comparable courses in the college taught by traditional means; also, students coming from the experimental program do at least as well in advanced science courses as students coming from a strong high school science background. When the cognitive ''mapping'' technique is applied to individualizing such vocational-technical courses as electronics, automotive engineer-

FIGURE 15.15

Oakland students learn science terminology, using an audio card-reader, cards with the words both printed and spoken on the audio strip, and workbooks.

FIGURE 15.16

Oakland students have available to them a variety of specialized training facilities and equipment in such vocational-technical programs as (a) electronics and (b) automotive engineering.

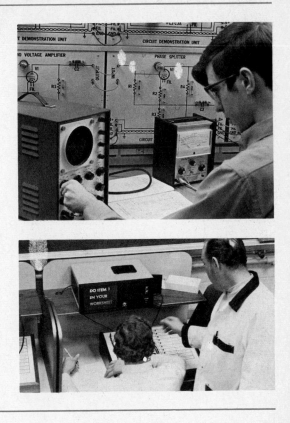

ing (see Figure 15.16), and climate control, comparable success is achieved.

Although many schools use a variety of media and methods in designing learning experiences, the Oakland program is unique in its extensive and thorough diagnosis of learning styles as determinants of the media and methods employed to meet individual student learning needs. As in the Lansing Community College AVT program, all learning units have been carefully developed and tested according to Instructional Development procedures.

Example 6: Planetariums and multi-image presentations— a preview of the future

UNTIL recent years, planetariums have been located mostly in large cities and on a few university campuses. With the advent of the space age, however, and the need for a whole new set of perspectives and concepts, there has been a surge of interest in making planetarium experience available to students in schools. High schools, particularly, are installing planetariums in both new and old buildings in

FIGURE 15.17

Even a small planetarium installation like this one is capable of opening new worlds to students. This simplified Apollo Planetarium is relatively inexpensive and can be installed in a fairly small area. It consists of the projector and control panel and a 10-foot hemispherical screen under which about 15 people can be seated. The planetarium may be operated manually or automatically or both during any presentation. Curriculum-related program packages for automatic presentations are available in earth-space science, the social studies, humanities, biography, and mathematics.

steadily increasing numbers (see Figure 15.17). It was estimated in 1967 that about 1,000 small planetariums were in use in school systems across the United States.[21] Although these planetariums for school use are very small and simple compared to the great planetariums, such as the Hayden Planetarium in New York and the Adler Planetarium in Chicago, they are quite adequate for developing understandings of basic space concepts.

A planetarium consists essentially of a dome, usually mounted on the ceiling, which represents the sky overhead and a special projector that displays images of the celestial bodies on the dome, under which the viewers are seated (see Figure 15.18). The projector itself consists of various individual units for projecting representations of the sun, moon, planets, and stars; these are moved by motors and precision gear systems to reproduce accurately the motions of the heavenly bodies.[22] When the lighting has been dimmed, night and day effects can be produced, and the moon, sun, stars, and planets can be shown on the dome as they appear at any point in time, from the present back to the distant past and forward to the distant future, and from any location on the earth or in space. Furthermore, the motions of the heavenly bodies can be dramatically speeded up or slowed down when desired. When appropriate narration and sound effects, including music, are added to such a presentation, the impact on viewers can be great. Even more important, a planetarium can teach concepts that are particularly significant in today's space age—and it can teach them to learners of any age.

A variety of teaching materials are available for teaching space science concepts at both elementary and advanced grade levels. These range from minimodels

[21] Maurice Gene Moore, ''The Planetarium—An Instructional Medium,'' *The Journal of Geography*, Vol. 66, October 1967, pp. 378–379.

[22] The term ''planetarium'' is often used in a restricted sense to mean only the projector or, in some cases, an operating model of the solar system.

FIGURE 15.18

(a) At the Coldwater, Michigan, Junior High School, the planetarium, consisting of a Spitz projector and large dome, is used in a science program in which students from various grade levels are very much involved. An active planetarium program can be much more than interesting observational experiences. (b) Celestial charts such as this one displayed near the dome are all prepared by Coldwater students. (c) Students are motivated to study the real night sky for themselves. This boy is examining one of the Coldwater school's telescopes in preparation for some night observing.

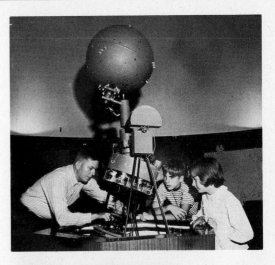

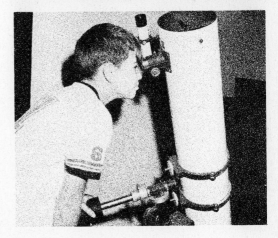

of the solar system which can be held on the palm of the hand through portable and inflatable planetariums which can be transported from school to school in a district to large observatory-type planetariums with sophisticated computerized projection units, complete with all necessary audio systems and packaged programs.[23]

Although it might seem that planetariums are suited primarily to the study of astronomy and space sciences, they are also being used effectively in a variety of other subjects at various grade levels. In the Tamaqua, Pennsylvania, High School, for example, ninth-grade classes use the planetarium daily for instruction in astronomy and space science, but the planetarium is also used in the following ways: Students from 10 elementary schools are brought to the planetarium regularly for carefully designed lessons in science, language arts, and the social studies; classes in physics, English, mathematics, and geometry often use the planetarium; during evenings and Sunday afternoons, adult groups and the general public use the facility.

Students are also involved in developing programs for the Tamaqua planetarium. The director of the planetarium has students construct scale drawings of scenes needed, photograph and enlarge or reduce those scenes, research and authenticate factual information used in special programs, and select the music and sound effects needed to correlate the scripts. Industrial arts students help construct motor supports and auxiliary projector mounts and bore holes necessary for the correct angle projection.[24]

In the Plymouth Meeting, Pennsyl-

vania, school district, the planetarium has been found to be of benefit to slow learners, perhaps because of its real-life quality and the vividness with which it can illustrate difficult concepts:

The planetarum acts as a sky laboratory for the student. Time can be adjusted to the need of the teacher; an entire day can be seen to go by in three minutes while the students note what happens during that day. The motion of the moon can be seen in a few minutes. . . .

One interesting point for the slow learner is that he will go see for himself in his own sky at home. The slow learner has

FIGURE 15.19

This unique Special Experiences Room at the McDonald Elementary School combines the usual planetarium offerings with a wide range of visual, audio, and other sensory experiences. The floor is carpeted so that viewers may comfortably sit or lie on it as they are enveloped in 360-degree panoramas of light, sound, and color.

[23] Philip Lewis, ''School Planetariums Propel Pupils into Space Science,'' *Nation's Schools,* Vol. 84, No. 3, September 1969, pp. 64–68.

[24] H. B. Geiger, ''How To Integrate Planetarium Usage into the Educational Program,'' *Nation's Schools,* Vol. 85, May 1970, pp. 112–113.

never been a big advocate of homework; it is just one more frustration for him. But he will try to estimate the altitude of Mars in his sky after he has learned to estimate angles in the sky. . . . Regardless of how educationally or culturally disadvantaged, everyone has a sky.[25]

The Special Experiences Room at the Everett A. McDonald Comprehensive Elementary School in Warminster, Pennsylvania, combines space science courses with

[25] Robert N. Kratz ''Everyone Has a Sky—A Planetarium Helps the Slow Learner,'' *The Clearing House*, Vol. 43, No. 6, January 1969, p. 349.

a whole range of additional and quite different types of experiences. Since the planetarium projector can be lowered into the floor when not needed, other types of projection can also be used, including a 360-degree projection pattern, if desired, on the entire dome (see Figure 15.19).

Several slide or film projectors are required to form the 360-degree cyclorama, but when the images from them are coordinated, there are unparalleled panoramas of landscapes, animal life, or other natural phenomena. The cyclorama projection system also makes possible ''ballets of light'' with a variety of fascinating light and color experiences; shadow silhouettes of various

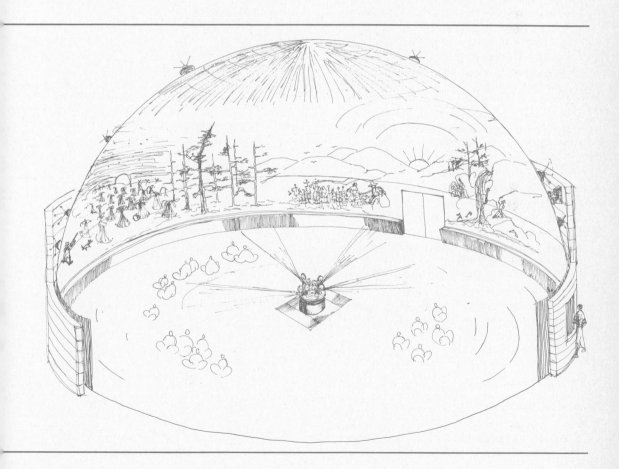

types and objects, including live swimming fish projected on the walls; the use of polarization techniques and time-exposure photography, plus music and other appropriate sound effects, to bring light and color, art and science together. Combinations of media permit a variety of other unique projection techniques. A bird or airplane, for example, "flies" around the room as an image projected from a rotating stand. Looking up at the top of a cathedral or tree can be experienced, since the image can be projected 30 feet upward onto the dome—or projection can sweep from eye level to the top of the dome to create the sensation of watching a crane hoist building materials high into the sky during construction of a skyscraper office building.

Curriculum Development Program The director of teaching and learning resources for the Warminster school district reports that an extensive curriculum development program has been under way for the past several years to add to the potential uses in innovative teaching and learning of the Special Experiences Room. Objectives include the following:

1 *Exploring contemporary theories, such as those advanced by Marshall Mc-Luhan, relating to the social and instructional impact of media;*
2 *Acquiring a feeling for simulation techniques;*
3 *Becoming acquainted with some of the relationships between science and esthetics;*
4 *Becoming involved with selected aspects of advances in educational technology;*
5 *Orienting teachers to the rich area of industrial arts and its curricular implications.*[26]

[26] Henry W. Ray, "Designing Tomorrow's Schools Today: The Multi-Sensory Experience Center," *Child Education*, February 1971, pp. 255–258.

At this writing, it appears doubtful that Instructional Development techniques have been employed in designing the planetarium programs described so far. Clearly, there is no reason why they could not be used in such programs, but at this stage it appears that the primary emphasis is on exploring the many unique applications of which planetarium-type spaces themselves may be capable—obviously a necessity before it can be established which learning activities can best be designed for and presented in these facilities.

As we have said, many school systems throughout the United States now have planetariums in which a variety of useful programs are carried on. Many of these programs, of course, are in the space sciences, designed to help explain the nature of the universe as it was in the past, as we know it today, and as it is likely to be in the future, and also to develop a reasonably clear picture of the earth's place within the universe. In addition, however, many schools and colleges are finding interdisciplinary and extracurricular applications for the planetarium.

For example, at the Lansing Community College, the 100-seat planetarium auditorium is used for dramatic presentations, fashion shows, and musical events. The science department uses the planetarium for parts of the 5-hour sequence in astronomy-geology that is required for freshman science. The art department uses it for art, color, and sound displays. The sociology department uses it to present a "sensitivity experience" showing what the world will become unless pollution is controlled. There, in the planetarium, in a program presented by a musical group, the "Hallelujah Chorus" dominates the sound, but pop music is woven into a second stereo channel, and flashed images of the Crucifix are interspersed with dynamic colored lights playing on the dome. It is a room in which the English department dramatically re-creates the courtroom scene of Weiss'

The Investigation—with flashes of back-room scenes projected simultaneously throughout the hemispheric area (see Figure 15.20).

In short, the planetarium is being explored in many places for a variety of learning experiences that go well beyond its original conception as a facility to study the universe. The latter purpose is, of course, highly significant and will doubtless increase in importance as the space age develops. But it may well be that the additional possibilities inherent in this truly multisensory instructional space will likewise prove highly important. It is a place where a projected slide that would cover an area only 3½ by 5 feet on a normal classroom screen can be blown up to 10 or more times that size; it is also a place where several such slides shown side by side on the walls and ceiling as a cyclorama can literally surround the viewer; it is also a place where films, multistereo sound, and even smells can envelop the viewer to create effects heretofore found only in expositions or rare experimental theaters.

One senses that we are on the brink of—if we have not already entered—an era in which experiences in schools can begin to transcend what even most adults have ever experienced. This may, indeed, be a reflection of a trend that McLuhan has aptly characterized:

The mark of our time is in its revolution against imposed patterns. We are suddenly eager to have things and people declare their beings totally. There's a deep faith to be found in this new attitude—a faith that concerns the ultimate harmony of all being.[27]

As the "revolution against imposed patterns" begins to take effect in the schools, one evidence of which is more sophisticated and more extensive applications of educational technology, we can expect problems of a different order and type to arise. One of these is brought out in questions raised by Robert Travers, a leading psychologist, on the learning effectiveness of simultaneous multisensory stimuli such as those

[27] Marshall McLuhan, *Understanding Media: The Extension of Man*, McGraw-Hill, 1965, p. 21.

FIGURE 15.20

A room—even a planetarium—can be just a room. Or it can be the setting for dynamic, dramatic, and moving experiences of many kinds. The difference lies in the creative imagination of those who use the room.

found in slide-tape presentations, sound motion pictures, and, most prominently, of course, in multiple-screen, multi-image presentations. Travers suggests that the mind tends to attend to one stimulus to the exclusion of others—that simultaneous audiovisual stimuli tend to have a cancellation effect on one another.[28] On the other hand, when Donald Perrin, a leading scholar in the area of multi-image displays, commented on Travers' findings, he pointed to the basic differences between the nature and function of multi-image presentations and the nature and function of the kind of material used in Travers' research. The Travers studies were done under laboratory conditions, using materials that were inherently uninteresting and purposely devoid of motivational character or similar variables. Perrin goes on to comment specifically on the need for evaluation criteria for "commercial" materials that are different from the criteria that can be applied to materials used in a rigorous research setting.

The confusion between research and commercial productions can be easily explained. The purpose is different, the approach is different, and the communication symbols themselves are different. The commercial productions of Eames and Fleischer are designed to achieve high visual impact, interest, involvement, motivation, and concentration—in modern terminology, to "turn on" the audience. Research works at low levels of motivation comparable to vigilance tasks; the learning of cognitive associations of nonsense words and symbols is certainly not too stimulating by comparison. Thus, producers and researchers are working at opposite ends of the motivation scale, and at opposite ends of the real/

abstract continuum. And while research is studying just a single variable, the commercial producer involves the whole visual sensorium.[29]

In other words, we are likely to find ourselves in a new "ball game" as we investigate the learning potentials of multimedia, multisensory imagery which are just beginning to unfold. The impact of this kind of imagery, in fact, may well be largely in the affective domain of the emotions and attitudes and its vehicle a product of artistry as much as reason. In any case, we can be sure it will have an impact.

As we think about multisensory imagery—indeed, as we think about the whole vital, stimulating, and burgeoning field of instructional technology that has been described in this book—we can be sure of one thing: The imaginative, creative teacher who refuses to be hemmed in by today's constraints, the teacher who looks on instructional technology as the essential tool he can use to help him free himself of these constraints—such a teacher and his pupils have a most exciting future ahead of them.

[28] Robert M. W. Travers et al., *Research and Theory Related to Audiovisual Information Transmission,* USOE Contract # 3–20–003, July 1, 1964. Available from Western Michigan University Bookstore, Kalamazoo, Mich. 49001 (ERIC–ED–003–625).

[29] Donald G. Perrin, "A Theory of Multiple-Image Communication," *AV Communication Review,* Vol. 17, No. 4, Winter 1969, pp. 379–380. Charles Eames, a noted designer, is the gifted and imaginative producer of such multi-image productions as the seven-screen U.S. Information Service show at the 1959 Moscow Fair, the six-screen U.S. Science Exhibit at the 1962 Century 21 Exposition in Seattle, and the 16-screen IBM Exhibit at the 1964–1965 New York World's Fair; in the IBM Exhibit, both still and motion pictures were projected. Richard Fleischer is a well-known cinematographer who produced *The Boston Strangler* in 1968 as one of the first multi-image feature theatrical films. Fleischer was among those inspired by the use of multi-image presentations at Expo '67, the international exhibition in Montreal; the 14 major multi-image, wide-screen or multiscreen, and multisound-channel productions exhibited there had a striking impact on the entire film industry. In *The Boston Strangler,* multiple images were used during about 35 percent of the entire film as an integral means of presenting the story.

Summary

Most educators today are far more willing than they were even a few years ago to accept media and technology as something more than peripheral aspects of their educational programs. One reason for this is their increased experience with more sophisticated applications of technology that demonstrate actual and potential gains in learning effectiveness. Particularly is this true in Individualized Instruction and other self-instruction programs which literally could not function without tape recorders and projection systems which are operated by the students themselves. Technology has also proved itself in those innovative school systems in which large-group and small-group instruction are employed as components of an overall system of instruction in which various forms of media have a natural and effective role to play.

Most of all, however, educational technology has proved itself in the instructional systems approach to solving teaching and learning problems. The meticulous kind of planning inherent in Instructional Development is in itself fundamentally sound and appealing to educational decision-makers in that it provides a degree of confidence beyond that normally found in educational planning. This confidence is derived throughout the process, from the careful definition of the problem that is required, through making selections from viable, practical alternative solutions, to the testing and recycling necessary to assure effective results. In the process, the alternative solutions invariably call for a variety of methods and materials, including pertinent applications of media. The various forms of media and mediated materials, along with other materials and methods, play a coordinated role in which effectiveness is a built-in performance criterion.

The specific examples in this chapter show patterns of use incorporating a variety of media and methods from primary to community college levels and a variety of degrees of application of Instructional Development principles. The principles demonstrated apply with equal validity at university and adult education levels since they are essentially based on the principles of how people learn and on how conditions for such learning can be optimized.

Example 1. An entire school district was mobilized to carry on a very comprehensive instructional program. The result was the reorganization of curriculum content and, more important, the development of continuing self-tutorial instructional materials and techniques that allow children to show continuing initiative and progress in terms of their own interest and enthusiasm.

Example 2. An individual teacher capitalized on some area history and fortuitous events to organize an exciting unit around a specific topic, relying heavily on area resources, pupil-teacher planning, and extensive community involvement and assistance.

Example 3. Again an individual teacher organized a program around a specific, though broader, topic. All the activities were evolved during pupil-teacher planning. The quest for alternative interrelated media opportunities was pursued with particular effectiveness. Again the reliance on community involvement was great.

Example 4. A group of teachers working independently within their own social studies department applied Instructional Development techniques during the formation and use of an instructional unit. In this case, pupil-teacher planning was an enlarged activity that involved teachers, students, and community representatives. The basic factor in the success of this unit was modular scheduling of appropriate learning strategies built around four types of instructional organization (large groups, medium-size groups, small groups, Individualized Instruction). This example underscores the fact that many and varied learning resource materials are vital to the success of Individualized Instruction. This application of Instructional Development principles is an example of the cooperative and continuing involvement of the members of one department in upgrading their own instructional plans, teaching strategies, and learning resources.

Example 5. Some unique, innovative, and specific applications of Instructional Development techniques in business education and the natural sciences are described

as developed and applied in two dynamic community college programs. These examples show how instructional programs can be adapted to a wide range of individual differences and needs and how media in a variety of forms can be used as integral rather than supplementary elements in the instructional process. Cost and evaluation data are included for one subject area.

Example 6. Planetarium and multi-image presentation programs in a number of school systems are described and discussed, with emphasis on their creative potentialities for a variety of new and significant kinds of learning experiences, in addition to the natural applications of planetariums for study of the universe.

Further learner response projects

1

Set up a committee of three or more with particular interest in the potentials of planetariums in teaching. Visit a nearby planetarium, if there is one, or write or phone for information and examples of

unique learning experiences made available through planetariums in various subjects and grade levels. Follow up with a presentation or report to your media class. (See the source lists in the Appendix.)

2

Analyze one of the teaching examples in the chapter (or another of your choice) according to the steps in the Instructional Development model. So far as the informa-

tion given indicates, which I.D. requirements appear to have been adequately met, which appear to have been ignored, and which fall somewhere in between?

3

Choose a typical teaching-learning example about which there is no evidence that I.D. principles have been applied in its planning and development and apply the same analysis as in Project 2. Make a list of the

similarities between the two situations and another list of the differences between the two. What conclusions can you draw from the comparison?

4

Can you tell by observing a teaching unit in use whether or not I.D. principles have been employed in its planning and development? If not, how can you tell—that is, what evidence is necessary? Finally, what

difference does it make whether I.D. is used or not? What real advantages does I.D. have over other less precise types of educational planning?

References

BRIGGS, L. J., et al. "Methods—Media Selection in Education." American Institutes for Research, Pittsburgh, Pa., 1967.

DAVIS, ROBERT H., LAWRENCE T. ALEXANDER, and STEPHEN L. YELON. *Learning System Design*. McGraw-Hill, 1973.

GEIGER, H. B. "How To Integrate Planetarium Usage into the Educational Program." *Nation's Schools,* Vol. 85, May 1970, pp. 112–113.

KAUFMAN, R. A., "Accountability, A Systems Approach and the Quantitative Improvement of Education—An Attempted Integration." *Educational Technology,* January 1971, Vol. 11, No. 1, pp. 21–25.

KAUFMAN, R. A. "A System Approach to Education: Derivation and Definition." *AV Communication Review,* Winter 1968.

KELLER, FRED S. *Learning: Reinforcement Theory*. Random House, 1954.

KRATZ, ROBERT N. "Everyone Has a Sky—A Planetarium Helps the Slow Learner." *The Clearing House,* Vol. 43, No. 6, February 1969, pp. 349–350.

LEWIS, P. "School Planetariums Propel Pupils into Space Science." *Nation's Schools,* Vol. 84, No. 3, September 1969, pp. 64, 66, 68.

MIALARET, G. *Psychology of the Use of Audio Visual Aids in Primary Education.* UNESCO, 1965.

MOORE, M. G. "Planetariums: An Instructional Medium." *Journal of Geography,* Vol. 66, October 1967, pp. 378–379.

ROBERTS, J. M. "Planetariums as an Interdisciplinary Teaching Aid." *Science Teacher,* Vol. 37, October 1970, pp. 57–58.

SILVERN, L. "Cybernetics and Education K–12." *Audiovisual Instruction,* March 1968.

SYMONDS, P. M. *What Education Has To Learn from Psychology*. 3rd ed. Teachers College, Columbia University, 1968.

TEUSCHER, H. "Put Stars in Your Curriculum." *Educational Screen and AV Guide,* Vol. 48, No. 1, January 1969, pp. 20–21 ff.

WARNEKING, G. E. "Planetarium Education in the 70's: Time for an Assessment." *Science Teacher,* Vol. 37, October 1970, pp. 14–15.

WATSON, G. B. *What Psychology Can We Trust*. Teachers College, Columbia University, 1961.

Media references

AV Forum, tape cassette, monthly report on current topics in instructional technology. AV Forum, 23434 Industrial Park Court, Farmington, Mich. 48024.

Child of the Future, 16mm film, b/w, 58 min. NFBC, 1963.

Designing Effective Instruction, color slides or tapes. General Programmed Teaching, 424 University Avenue, Palo Alto, Calif. 94301 (1968). Unit titles follow:
—Introduction to Basic Principles
—General Goals, Affective Objectives, Cognitive Objectives
—Main Components of an Objective
—Classification of Objectives
—Criterion Tests
—Determining Entry Level
—Entry Level Tests
—Stimulus and Response
—One-Way and Two-Way Stimulus—Response Pairs, Single and Multiple Discriminations
—Content Analysis
—Stimulus-Response Pairs in Chain Activities
—Influence of Objectives on Content
—Developing Objectives and Deriving Content
—Programmed Lesson Plans and Instructional Media
—Validation

Galaxy of Motion Picture Documents on Communication Theory and the New Educational Media, 16mm films, color. Ohio State University, 1966 (35 titles).

Individualized Instruction, color slides with tapes. AECT, 1970 (24 titles).

Instructional Development, 16mm film, b/w, 17 min. Indiana University, 1971.

Instructional Development: The People, 16mm

film, color, 19 min. Michigan State University, 1971.

Instructional Development: The Process, 16mm film, color, 26 min. Michigan State University, 1972.

Instructional Development: The Results, 16mm film, color, 10 min. Michigan State University, 1971.

Introduction to Feedback, 16mm film, color, 12 min. IBM, 1963.

Make a Mighty Reach, 16mm film, color, 56 min. IDEA, 1967.

Planning and Organizing for Teaching, 35mm filmstrip, sound, b/w, 110 frames. NEA, 1965.

Programming Is a Process, 16mm film, color, 32 min. University of Illinois, 1967.

Systems Engineering of Learning, 35mm filmstrip, sound, color, 114 frames. Educational and Training Consultants Company, 979 Teakwood Road, Los Angeles, Calif. 90049, 1964.

Using Motion Film in the Classroom, 16mm film, color, 11 min. Educational Media Labs, 4101 South Congress Avenue, Austin, Tex. 78745, 1968.

VIMCET Series, 35mm filmstrips, sound, color.

VIMCET, P.O. Box 24714, Los Angeles, Calif. 90024 (1969). Unit titles follow:
—Systematic Instructional Decision Making
—Educational Objectives
—Selecting Appropriate Educational Objectives
—Establishing Performance Standards
—Appropriate Practice
—Perceived Purpose
—Evaluation
—Curriculum Rationale
—Defining Content for Objectives
—Identifying Affective Objectives
—Analyzing Learning Outcomes
—Knowledge of Results
—Teaching Units and Lesson Plans
—Teaching of Reading
—Discipline in the Classroom
—Modern Measurement Methods
—Instructional Supervision
—Experimental Designs for School Research
—Behavioral Objectives Debate
—Criterion-Referenced Instruction

What Is an IDI? 16mm film, color, 18 min. National Special Media Institutes, Syracuse University, 1971.

Source references

See source lists in the Appendix; particularly relevant sections are: Furniture and Facilities; Learning Resources Facilities; Listening Laboratories; Individualized Instruction; Multimedia Equipment and Materials; Planetariums; Programed Instruction.

See *Student Production Guide,* Chapter 4, "Producing Photo and Sound Materials for Instruction," particularly the multi-image sections of Photo and Sound Materials: Design and Use, Photographic Slide Production, and Filmstrip Production.

APPENDIX
Source lists

ONE testimony to the rapidly growing use of media and technology in various forms is the expanding number of sources from which materials can be obtained. This rapid increase produces both benefits and problems for the teacher or resources librarian. The benefits, of course, lie in the opportunity today to find not only many more mediated learning materials than ever before but also better ones; the chances of locating just the *right* film, filmstrip, transparency, or other material for a specific purpose (or of finding several suitable alternatives) are vastly improved over what they were even a few years ago. The problems, however, arise from the same source as the benefits. The amounts of useful materials now available are so great that it is increasingly difficult to find out what materials even exist on any given topic, and then we must face the almost equally complex problem of finding where they may be conveniently obtained. There are more than 4,000 producers and distributors of instructional films, for example, and relatively few of these provide a rental service for their films. Thus the user must go to the catalogs of university, school system, or regional center film libraries to find a convenient source.

One day, perhaps in the not too distant future, there will be computerized catalogs on a vast number of topics in practically all subjects and grade levels. These catalogs, including rental source information where appropriate, may be located in local or regional Education Centers now being planned by the U. S. Office of Education to be established through State Departments of Education, along with a system of Educational Extension Agents whose duties will include making such information readily available to individual schools or school systems.

Even now, comprehensive source guides for

35mm filmstrips and 8mm and 16mm motion pictures are being compiled by such agencies as the National Information Center for Educational Media at the University of Southern California and published by the R. R. Bowker Company, 1180 Avenue of the Americas, New York, N.Y. 10036. These and similar comprehensive listings, such as the monthly Schwann LP record catalog, available in all record shops, and the National Audiotape Catalog, available from the Association for Educational Communications and Technology, 1201 16th Street, N.W., Washington, D.C. 20036, are important steps forward.

For the vast majority of teachers, however, who often do not have such comprehensive catalogs readily available to them, there is still value and convenience in a listing of major sources for various types of media equipment and materials such as this one which we have compiled. For the reader's convenience, these source lists are organized like the "Yellow Pages" in the telephone directory—with major headings, subheadings, and cross references throughout. Thus under the heading Display Surfaces and Supplies are listed major sources of Bulletin Boards, Chalkboards and Magnetic Boards, and Easels, Flannel Boards, Feltboards, and Hook-and-Loop Boards. Major headings identical to those in these lists are included in the References at the end of each chapter, references to specific lists in this Appendix.

Even though they are extensive, these source lists are not intended to be exhaustive. In an effort to keep the lists to manageable and useful proportions, only major sources have been included. Inevitably, other valuable and useful sources, particularly regional and local sources, have been omitted.

Acoustical materials
See **Furniture and facilities**

Adhesive mounting materials
See **Graphic materials**

Adhesives
See **Graphic materials**

Animals, 3-D
See **Three-dimensional materials**

Aquariums, 3-D
See **Three-dimensional materials**

Art, clip
See **Graphic materials**

Art supplies—general
CCM Arts and Crafts, Inc., 9520 Baltimore Avenue, College Park, Md. 20740.
Dick Blick, P.O. Box 1267, Galesburg, Ill. 61401.
Milton Bradley Company, 74 Park St., Springfield, Mass. 01105.
Arthur Brown and Bros., Inc., 2 W. 46th St., New York, N.Y. 10036.
Creative Playthings, Inc., Princeton, N.J., 08540.
Easter Handicraft Supply Company, Inc., 151 Spring St., New York, N.Y. 10012.
M. Grumbacher, Inc., 460 W. 34th St., New York, N.Y. 10001.

Audio equipment and materials

RADIO NETWORKS
American Broadcasting Company, 1330 Avenue of the Americas, New York, N.Y. 10019.
Columbia Broadcasting System, 51 W. 52nd St., New York, N.Y. 10019.
Mutual Broadcasting System, 135 W. 50th St., New York, N.Y. 10020.
National Broadcasting Company, 30 Rockefeller Plaza, New York, N.Y. 10020.

RECORD PLAYERS, TRANSCRIBERS,
RADIO RECEIVERS
Allied Radio Corporation, 100 N. Western Ave., Chicago, Ill., 60612.
Audio-Master Corporation, 121 W. 45th St., New York, N.Y., 10036.
Audiotronics Corp., 7428 Bellaire Ave., N. Hollywood, Calif. 91603.
Bogen Company, Division of Lear-Siegler, Inc., P.O. Box 500, Paramus, N.J. 07652.
DuKane Corp., 103 N. 11th St., St. Charles, Ill. 60174.

Newcomb-Audio Products Co., 12881 Bradley Ave., Sylman, Calif. 91342.

Radio-Matic of America, Inc., 760 Ramsey Ave., Hillside, N.J. 07205.

Rheem-Califone Division, 5922 Bowcroft St., Los Angeles, Calif. 90016.

U.S. Recording Co., 1347 S. Capitol St., Washington, D.C. 20003.

V-M Corp., P.O. Box 1247, Benton Harbor, Mich. 94022.

Webcor Sales Co., 5610 W. Bloomingdale Ave., Chicago, Ill. 60639.

Zenith Sales Corp., 1900 N. Austin, Chicago, Ill. 60639.

RECORDINGS AND TRANSCRIPTIONS

American Library Association, 50 E. Huron St., Chicago, Ill., 60611.

Audio Cardalog, Box 989, Larchmont, N.Y. 10538; $30.00 annual subscription.

Caedmon Records, 461 Eighth Ave., New York, N.Y. 10001.

Capitol Records Distributing Corp., 1750 N. Vine St., Hollywood, Calif. 90028.

Jack C. Coffey Co., Inc., P.O. Box 131, Waukegan, Ill. 60085.

Columbia Records, Educational Division, 51 W. 52nd St., New York, N.Y., 10019.

Decca Records, Inc., 50 W. 57th St., New York, N.Y., 10019.

Walt Disney Educational Materials Co., 800 Sonora Ave., Glendale, Calif. 91201.

EMC Corporation, Educational Materials Division, 180 E. 6th St., St. Paul, Minn. 55101.

Enrichment Materials, Inc., A Division of Scholastic, 50 W. 44th St., New York, N.Y. 10036.

Enrichment Teaching Materials, Inc., 71 E. 23rd St., New York, N.Y. 10010.

Epic Records, 51 W. 52nd St., New York, N.Y. 10019.

Folkways Records and Service Corporation, 50 W. 44th St., New York, N.Y. 10036.

Ginn and Co., 125 Second Ave., Waltham, Mass. 02154.

Harcourt Brace Jovanovich, 757 Third Ave., New York, N.Y. 10017.

Linguaphone Institute, 437 Madison Ave., New York, N.Y. 10022.

London Records, 539 W. 25th St., New York, N.Y. 10001.

National Council of Teachers of English, 704 S. Sixth St., Champaign, Ill., 61820.

RCA Victor Division, Radio Corporation of America, Audio Visual Marketing Division, Front and Cooper Sts., Camden, N.J. 08102.

Scholastic Magazines, Inc., 50 W. 44th St., New York, N.Y. 10036.

Schwann LP Record Catalog, 137 Newbury St., Boston, Mass. 02116.

Spoken Arts, Inc., 310 North Ave., New Rochelle, N.Y. 10801.

H. Wilson Corporation, 555 W. Taft Dr., South Holland, Ill. 60473.

Young Peoples Records, Children's Record Guild, 225 Park Ave. S., New York, N.Y. 10003.

TAPE MANUFACTURERS

Ampex Corp., 2201 Lundmeier Rd., Elk Grove Village, Ill. 60007.

E. I. DuPont de Nemours & Company, Wilmington, Del., 19898.

Memorex Corp., San Towas at Central Expressway, Santa Clara, Calif. 95052.

Radio Corporation of America, Audio Visual Marketing Division, Front and Cooper Sts., Camden, N.J. 08102.

Reeves Soundcraft Corporation, 15 Great Pastures Rd., Danbury, Conn. 06810.

Sony Superscope, Inc., 8150 Vineland Ave., Sun Valley, Calif. 91352.

3M Company, 3M Center, St. Paul, Minn. 55119.

TAPE RECORDERS

Ampex Corp., 2201 Landmeier Rd., Elk Grove Village, Ill. 60007.

Audiotronics Corporation, 7428 Bellaire Ave., North Hollywood, Calif. 91603.

Bell and Howell Company, 7100 McCormick Rd., Chicago, Ill. 60645.

Newcomb Audio Products Co., 12881 Bradley Ave., Sylmar, Calif. 91342.

RCA Victor Division, Radio Corporation of America, Audio Visual Marketing Division, Front and Cooper Sts., Camden, N.J., 08102.

Rheem-Califone Division, 5922 Bowcroft St., Los Angeles, Calif. 90016.

Sony Superscope, Inc., 8150 Vineland Ave., Sun Valley, Calif. 91352.

Tandberg of America, Inc., 8 Third Ave., Pelham, N.Y. 10803.

Telex-Communication Div., 9600 Aldrich Ave. S., Minneapolis, Minn. 55420.

3M Company, 3M Center, St. Paul, Minn. 55119.

V-M Corporation, P.O. Box 1247, Benton Harbor, Mich. 49022.

Webcor Sales Co., 5610 W. Bloomingdale Ave., Chicago, Ill. 60639.

TAPE SOURCES

In every community there are individuals who have audiotape or record collections and who are willing to work with interested students. College or university film libraries frequently also have audiotape libraries and an inexpensive duplicating service for schools. Possible sources of both types should be checked locally.

Academic Recording Institute, P.O. Box 22961, Houston, Tex. 77027.

Allied-Radio Shack, 1515 So. University Dr., Ft. Worth, Tex. 76107.

Ampex Corp., 2201 Landmeier Rd., Elk Grove Village, Ill. 60007.

Associated Educational Materials Co., Inc., 14 Glenwood Ave., Raleigh, N.C. 27602.

Capitol Records Distributing Corp., 1750 N. Vine St., Hollywood, Calif. 90028.

Educational Activities, Inc., P.O. Box 392, Freeport, N.Y. 11520.

Educational Development Laboratories, Inc., Huntington, N.Y. 11743.

EMC Corporation, Educational Materials Division, 180 E. 6th St., St. Paul, Minn. 55101.

Imperial International Learning Corp., P.O. Box 548, Kankakee, Ill. 60901.

International Film Bureau, Inc., 332 S. Michigan Ave., Chicago, Ill. 60604.

National Association of Educational Broadcasters, 1346 Connecticut Ave., N.W., Washington, D.C. 20036.

National Tape Repository, Bureau of Audiovisual Instruction, Stadium Bldg., 348, University of Colorado, Boulder, Colo. 80907.

Spoken Arts, Inc., 319 North Ave., New Rochelle, N.Y. 10801.

Tapes Unlimited, 13001 Puritan Ave., Michigan 48227.

World Tapes for Education, Box 9211, Dallas, Tex. 75215 (Recordings from students, teachers, and others from various parts of the world.).

Audiotape libraries
See **Audio equipment and materials: tape sources**

Audiotape manufacturers
See **Audio equipment and materials**

Automatic filmstrip projectors
See **Projectors: filmstrip projectors**

Building equipment
See **Furniture and facilities**

Bulletin board materials.
See Display surfaces and supplies

Cameras, motion picture
See Photographic equipment

Cameras, still
See Photographic equipment

Chalkboard supplies
See Display surfaces and supplies

Chalkboards
See Display surfaces and supplies

Charts and graphs
See Graphic materials

Coloring and shading materials
See Graphic materials

Comics
Children's Television Workshop, 1 Lincoln Plaza, New York, N.Y. 10023.

General Electric Co., Educational Relations, 570 Lexington Ave., New York, N.Y. 10022.

Commerical transparencies
See **Transparencies**

Computers and programs
Control Data Corp., 8100 34th Ave. South, Minneapolis, Minn. 55440.

Digital Equipment Corp., 146 Main St., Maynard, Mass. 01754.

Entelek, Incorporated, 42 Pleasant Street, Newburyport, Mass. 01950.

Honeywell, Inc., Wellesley Hills, Mass. 02181.

IBM, Thomas J. Watson Research Center, P.O. Box 218, Yorktown Heights, N.Y. 10598.

Information Systems—Education, General Electric Company, 13430 North Black Canyon Highway, Phoenix, Ariz. 85023.

Information Transfer Corporation, 214 Worcester Rd., Wellesley, Mass. 02181.

Philco-Ford, C and Tioga Streets, Philadelphia, Pa. 19134.

RCA, Instructional Systems Division, 530 University Ave., Palo Alto, Calif. 94301.

Remington Rand, 1290 Avenue of the Americas, New York, N.Y. 10019.

Copiers, slide
See **Photographic equipment: slide copiers**

Copying equipment
See **Reproduction equipment**

Demonstration science equipment
See **Three-dimensional materials**

Display surfaces and supplies

BULLETIN BOARDS AND SUPPLIES
Acme Bulletin Board and Directory Company, 37 E. 12th St., New York, N.Y. 10003.

Advance Products Co., 2300 E. Douglas Ave., Wichita, Kansas 67214 (easels).

Bangor Cork Company, Williams and D Sts., Pen Argyl, Pa. 18072.

Beckley-Cardy Company, 1900 N. Narragansett St., Chicago, Ill. 60639.

Brooks Manufacturing Company, 11333 Williamson Road., P.O. Box 41195, Cincinnati, Ohio 45241 (plastic reusable adhesive).

Brunswick Corporation, 2605 E. Kilgore Rd., Kalamazoo, Mich. 49003.

Bulletin Board Styx, Lea Audio-Visual Service, 184 Audly Dr., Sun Prairie, Wis. 53590.

Bulletin Boards and Directory Products, Inc., 724 Broadway, New York, N.Y. 10003.

Eberhard Faber, Inc., Wilkes-Barre, Pa. 18701.

Leah Audio-Visual Service, 184 Audly Dr., Sun Prairie, Wis. 53590.

Magnetic Aids, Inc.., 11 W. 42nd St., New York, N.Y. 10036.

Magnet Sales Co., 3935 S. Vermont, Los Angeles, Calif. 90037.

Masonite Corporation, 29 No. Wacker Dr., Chicago, Ill. 60606.

Silver Burdett Company, 460 S. Northwest Highway, Park Ridge, Ill. 60068.

Visual Crafts Supply Co., 640 N. Willow St., Kent, Ohio 44240.

Visual Specialties Co., 127 S. Saginaw St., Byron, Mich. 48418.

CHALKBOARDS, MAGNETIC BOARDS, AND SUPPLIES
A-1 School Equipment Co., 2511 East Imperial Highway, Los Angeles, Calif., 90059.

Beckley-Cardy Co., 1900 N. Narragansett St., Chicago, Ill. 60639 (Slato Steel chalkboard: porcelain or vitreous surface, steel, magnetic).

Brunswick-Corp., 69 W. Washington, Chicago, Ill. 60602.

Brunswick Corporation, 2605 East Kilgore Road, Kalamazoo, Mich. 49003 (chalkboard school equipment).

Com-Pak Chemical Corporation, 223 South Holmes St., Shakopee, Minn. 55379.

Corbett Blackboard Stencils, 548 Third Avenue, North Pelham, N.Y. 10803 (chalkboard stencils: ready-made, perforated patterns of maps, graph outlines, etc.).

Educational Aids, Inc., Union Hill Bldg., West Conshohocken, Pa. 19428.

Ronald Eyrich Co., 560 N.E. 42nd St., Ft. Lauderdale, Fla. 33308.

Ideal School Supply Co., 11000 So. Ravergne Ave., Oak Lawn, Ill. 60453.

Madison A-V Co., 62 Grand St., New York, N.Y. 10013.

Maggie Magnet Visual Aids Corp., 11 W. 42nd St., New York, N.Y. 10036.

Magna Visual, Inc., 1200 N. Rock Hill Road, St. Louis, Mo. 63124.

Johns-Manville, Greenwood Plaza, Denver, Colo. 80217.

Charles Mayer Studios, Inc., 776 Commins St., Akron, Ohio 44307.

Miami Magnet Company, 7846 West 2nd Court, Hialeah, Fla. 33014.

Oravisual Company, Inc., P.O. Box 11150, St. Petersburg, Fla. 33733.

United States Plywood Corp., 55 W. 44th St., New York, N.Y. 10036.

Weber-Costello Company, 1900 N. Narragansett Ave., Chicago Heights, Ill. 60639.

EASELS, FLANNEL BOARDS, FELT-
BOARDS, HOOK-AND-LOOP BOARDS

Arlington Aluminum Co., 19303 W. Davison Ave., Detroit, Mich. 48223.

Chartpak, One River Road, Leeds, Mass. 01053.

Educational Supply and Specialty Co., 2833 Gage Ave., Huntington Park, Calif. 90255.

Follett Educational Corp., 1010 W. Washington Blvd., Chicago, Ill. 60607.

GAF Corporation, Industrial Products Division, 140 W. 51st St., New York, N.Y. 10020.

Holt, Rinehart and Winston, Inc., 383 Madison Ave., New York, N.Y. 10017.

Judy Company. *See* Silver Burdett Company.

Maharam Fabric Corp., 130 W. 46th St., New York, N.Y. 10036.

Charles Mayer Studios, Inc., 776 Commins St., Akron, Ohio 44307.

Ohio Flock-Cote Co., 13229 Shaw Ave., East Cleveland, Ohio 44112.

Oravisual Company, Inc., P.O. Box 11150, St. Petersburg, Fla. 33733.

Program Aids Co., Inc., 550 Garden Ave., Mt. Vernon, N.Y. 10553.

Reynolds Metals Co., 2000 S. Ninth St., Louis-ville, Ky. 40208.

Silver Burdett Company, 460 So. Northwest Highway, Park Ridge, Ill. 60068.

Dry mounting materials
See **Graphic materials: mounting materials**

Duplicating equipment
See **Reproduction equipment**

Easels
See **Display surfaces and supplies**

8mm film sources
See **Films**

8mm projectors
See **Projectors: motion picture projectors, 8mm**

Facilities, furniture, etc.
See **Furniture and facilities**

Feltboards
See **Display surfaces and supplies**

Film indexes
See **Films**

Films

GENERAL SOURCES

Academy Films, 800 N. Seward St., Hollywood, Calif. 90038.

Association-Sterling Films, Inc., 866 Third Ave., New York, N.Y. 10022.

The Athletic Institute, 805 Merchandise Mart, Chicago, Ill. 60654 (physical education films).

AV Explorations, 505 Delaware Ave., Buffalo, N.Y. 14202.

Avis Films, Inc., 2408 W. Olive Ave., Burbank, Calif. 91506.

Bailey-Film Associates, 11559 Santa Monica Blvd., Los Angeles, Calif. 90025.

Arthur Barr Productions, 1029 N. Allen Ave., Pasadena, Calif., 91104.

Campus Film Distributors Corp., 20 E. 46th St., New York, N.Y. 10017.

Carousel Films, Inc., 1501 Broadway, New York, N.Y. 10036.

Chandler Publishing Co., 124 Spear St., San Francisco, Calif. 94105.

Churchill Films, 662 N. Robertson Blvd., Los Angeles, Calif. 90069.

John Colburn, Associates, Inc., P.O. Box 187, Lake Bluff, Ill. 60044.

Columbia University Press, Center for Mass Communication, 1125 Amsterdam Ave., New York, N.Y. 10025.

Contemporary Films/McGraw-Hill, Leo R. Dratfield, President, 330 W. 42nd St., New York, N.Y. 10036.

Coronet Films, 65 East South Water St., Chicago, Ill. 60611.

Walt Disney Films, 800 Sonora, Glendale, Calif. 91201.

DuArt Laboratories, Inc., 245 W. 55th St., New York, N.Y. 10019.

Ealing Corp., 2225 Massachusetts Ave., Cambridge, Mass. 02140.

Encyclopaedia Britannica Educational Corp., 425 N. Michigan Ave., Chicago, Ill. 60611.

Environmental Films, Inc., 8228 Sulphur Mt. Rd., Ojai, Calif. 93203.

Films, Inc., 1144 Wilmette Ave., Wilmette, Ill. 60091.

Films of the Nations, Inc., 305 E. 86th St., New York, N.Y. 10028.

Frith Films, 1816 N. Highland Ave., Hollywood, Calif. 90028.

Harper & Row, Media Dept., 10 East 53rd St., New York, N.Y. 10022.

Heidenkamp Nature Pictures, 538 Glen Arden Dr., Pittsburgh, Pa. 15208.

Paul Hoefler Productions, P.O. Box 1313, La Jolla, Calif. 92037.

Ideal Pictures, Inc., 15924 Grand River Ave., Detroit, Mich. 48227.

Indiana University, Audio-Visual Center, Bloomington, Ind. 47401.

International Film Bureau, 322 S. Michigan Ave., Chicago, Ill. 60604.

International Film Foundation, 475 Fifth Ave., New York, N.Y. 10017.

Johnson Hunt Productions, La Canada, Calif., 91011.

Journal Films, Inc., 909 W. Diversey Parkway, Chicago, Ill. 60614

Carl F. Mahnke, Productions, 215 East 3rd St., Des Moines, Iowa 50309.

McGraw-Hill Book Company, Text-Film Division, 330 West 42nd St., New York, N.Y. 10036.

Michigan State University, Instructional Media Center, East Lansing, Mich. 48823.

Modern Learning Aids, 1212 Avenue of the Americas, New York, N.Y. 10036.

Moody Institute of Science, Educational Film Division, 12000 E. Washington, Whittier, Calif. 90606.

National Film Board of Canada, P.O. Box 6100, Montreal 3, Canada; Suite 819, 680 Fifth Ave., New York, N.Y. 10019; or Suite 2320, 230 N. Michigan Ave., Chicago, Ill. 60601.

New York University Film Library, Distribution Department, 26 Washington Pl., New York, N.Y. 10003.

Pennsylvania State University, Audio-Visual Services, Pattee Library, University Park, Pa. 16802 (also Psychological Cinema Register).

Purdue University, Audio-Visual Center, Lafayette, Ind. 47907.

Society for Visual Education, Inc., 1345 Diversey Parkway, Chicago, Ill. 60614.

State University of Iowa, Bureau of Audio-Visual Instruction, Extension Division, Iowa City, Iowa 52240.

Sterling Educational Films, Inc., 241 E. 34th St., New York, N.Y. 10016.

Sutherland Educational Films, 201 N. Occidental Blvd., Los Angeles, Calif. 90026 (elementary and secondary science).

Syracuse University, Center for Instructional Communications Bldg. D–7, Colvin Lane, Syracuse, N.Y. 13210.

Teaching Film Custodians, Inc., 25 W. 43rd St., New York, N.Y. 10036.

Technicolor, Inc., 1300 Frawley Dr., Costa Mesa, Calif. 92627.

Thorne Films, Inc., 1229 University Ave., Boulder, Colo. 80302.

U.S. Department of Agriculture, Motion Picture Service, Office of Information, Washington, D.C. 20250.

U.S. Department of Interior, Bureau of Commercial Fisheries, Washington, D.C. 20242.

U.S. Department of Justice, Federal Bureau of Investigation, Washington, D.C. 20535.

U.S. Forest Service, A-V Branch, 12 Independence Ave., Washington, D.C. 20003.

Universal Education and Visual Arts, 221 Park Ave. S., New York, N.Y. 10003.

University of California, Extension Media Center, Film Distribution, 2223 Fulton St., Berkeley, Calif. 94720.

University of Michigan, Audio-Visual Education Center, Frieze Bldg., Ann Arbor, Mich. 48104.

University of Minnesota, Audio-Visual Education Service, Wesbrook Hall, Minneapolis, Minn. 55455.

University of Nebraska, Bureau of Audio-Visual Instruction, University Extension Division, Lincoln, Nebr. 68508.

University of Oklahoma, Audio-Visual Education, Norman, Okla. 73069.

University of Southern California, Department of Cinema, Filmstrip Distribution Unit, University Park, Los Angeles, Calif. 90007.

University of Wisconsin, Bureau of Audio-Visual Instruction, University Extension, 1312 W. Johnson St., Madison, Wis. 53701.

Wayne University, Audio-Visual Materials Bureau, Detroit, Mich. 48201.

Wexler Film Productions, 801 N. Seward St., Los Angeles, Calif. 90038.

See also Free and Inexpensive Materials.

INDEXES

Educational Television Motion Pictures, NET Film Service, Audio-Visual Center, Indiana University, Bloomington, Ind., 47401 (catalog of programs available in 16mm film and on videotape).

8mm Film Directory, published by Comprehensive Service Corp., 250 West 64th St., New York, N.Y. 10023, in 1969, $10.50.

Index of 8mm Educational Motion Cartridges, published by R. R. Bowker Co., 1180 Avenue of the Americas, New York, N.Y. 10036, in 1969, $16.00 (lists more than 9,000 items).

Index to 16mm Educational Films, prepared by the National Information Center for Educational Media, is available from R. R. Bowker Co., 1180 Avenue of the Americas, New York, N.Y. 10036, for $39.50.

Library of Congress Catalog: Motion Pictures and Filmstrips began in 1953 and has been cumulative since that date. It includes listing by title and subject of all educational motion pictures and filmstrips released in the United States and Canada and cataloged on the Library of Congress printed cards.

REVIEWS

EFLA Evaluations, Educational Film Library Association, 17 West 60th St., New York, N.Y. 10023. 1948–1964—$30.00 ; 1964–1967 —$12.00 ; Membership $50.00/Year.

Landers Film Reviews, P.O. Box 69760, Los Angeles, Calif. 60069. Subscription rate $33.50/Year, except July and August, Vol. 6–11—$37.00, Vol. 12 & up—$33.50.

Filmstrip projectors
See **Projectors**

Filmstrips

The major source guide for 35mm filmstrips is the Index to 35mm Educational Flmstrips published by R. R. Bowker Co., 1180 Avenue of the Americas, New York, N.Y. 10036. It sells for $34.00 and is scheduled to be updated by means of regular supplements. It has been compiled by the National Information Center for Education Media at the University of Southern California.

BFA—Educational Media, 2211 Michigan Ave., Santa Monica, Calif. 90404.

Coronet Films, 65 E. South Water St., Chicago, Ill. 60601.

DuKane Corp., 103 N. 11th Ave., St. Charles, Ill. 60174.

Educators Guide to Free Filmstrips, Educators Progress Service, Randolph, Wis. 53956. $7.00 (issued annually).

EMC Corporation, Educational Materials Division, 180 E. 6th St., St. Paul, Minn. 55101.

Encyclopaedia Britannica Educational Corp., 425 N. Michigan Ave., Chicago, Ill. 60611.

Enrichment Materials Inc., A Division of Scholastic, 50 W. 44th St., New York, N.Y. 10036.

Eye Gate House, Inc., 14601 Archer Ave., Jamaica, N.Y. 11435.

Filmstrip House, Inc., 432 Park Ave. S., New York, N.Y. 10016.

Guidance Associates, 23 Washington Ave., Pleasantville, N.Y. 10570.

Imperial Film Company, 4404 South Florida Ave., Lakewood, Fla. 33803.

Informative Classroom Pictures, 31 Ottawa Ave., N.W., Grand Rapids, Mich. 49501.

Jam Handy Organization, 2843 E. Grand Blvd., Detroit, Mich. 48211.

Time/Life Education, Time/Life Building, Rockefeller Center, New York, N.Y. 10020.

McGraw-Hill Book Company, Text-Film Division, 330 West 42nd St., New York, N.Y. 10036.

Moody Institute of Science, Educational Film Division, 12000 E. Washington Blvd., Whittier, Calif. 90606.

National Film Board of Canada, 680 Fifth Ave., Suite 819, New York, N.Y. 10019.

New York Times, Library Services Division, 229 W. 43rd St., New York, N.Y. 10036.

Popular Science Publishing Co., Audio-Visual Division, 355 Lexington Ave., New York, N.Y. 10017.

Sandak, Inc., 4 E. 48th St., New York, N.Y. 10017.

Society for Visual Education, Inc., 1345 W. Diversey Parkway, Chicago, Ill. 60614.

Stanley Bowmar Co., 4 Broadway, Valhalla, N.Y. 10595.

Technicolor, Inc., 299 Kalmus Drive, Costa Mesa, Calif. 92627.

Universal Education and Visual Arts, 221 Park Ave. S., New York, N.Y. 10003.

Weston Woods Studio, Inc., Weston, Conn. 06880.

Flannelboards
See **Display surfaces and supplies**

Flat pictures

Local resource people often are excellent sources of flat pictures. For example, fellow teachers and/or parents who have taken vacation trips may have good pictures available. Business and industries in the community are also immediate possibilities. Other useful sources include national magazines, service organization publications, libraries, historical societies, and airlines. Student-made photographs are valuable in a variety of contexts, including the development of visual literacy skills. This source has become more generally feasible because advances in photography have now made it possible to provide students with simple but reliable

cameras for as little as $2.00 to $8.00 each.

A very useful index to primary sources of picture materials is Catherine M. Williams, *Learning from Pictures,* 2nd ed., Assn. for Educational Communications and Technology, 1201 16th St., N.W., Washington, D.C. 20036. 1968, $4.50 (AECT was formerly DAVI, a department of the Natl. Education Association).

American Museum of Natural History, Central Park West at 79th St., New York, N.Y. 10024.

American Petroleum Institute, 1271 Avenue of the Americas, New York, N.Y. 10020.

Artex Prints, Inc., P.O. Box 70, Westport, Conn. 06880 (color art reproductions).

Audio-Visual Enterprises, 911 Laguna Rd., Pasadena, Calif. 91105.

Basic Skill Films, 1355 Inverness Drive, Pasadena, Calif. 91103.

Creative Educational Society, 515 North Front St., Mankato, Minn. 56001.

Denoyer-Geppert Co., 5235 Ravenswood Ave., Chicago, Ill. 60640.

Documentary Photo Aids, Inc., P.O. Box 2620, Sarasota, Fla. 33578.

Friendship Press, 475 Riverside Dr., New York, N.Y. 10027.

Hammond, Inc., 515 Valley St., Maplewood, N.J. 07040.

Hi-Worth Pictures, P.O. Box 6, Altadena, Calif. 91001.

Informative Classroom Picture Publishers, Inc., 31 Ottawa Ave., N.W., Grand Rapids, Mich. 49501.

The Instructor Publications, Inc., Dansville, N.Y. 14437.

International Communications Foundation, 870 Monterey Pass Rd., Monterey Park, Calif. 91754.

Jam Handy Organization, 2843 E. Grand Blvd., Detroit, Mich. 48211.

McGraw-Hill Book Company, Text-Film Division, 330 W. 42nd St., New York, N.Y. 10036.

Motion Pictures Association of America, Inc., 1600 Eye St., N.W., Washington, D.C. 20006.

National Aeronautics and Space Administration (NASA), Washington, D.C. 20546.

National Geographic Society, School Service Division, 16th and M Sts., N.W., Washington, D.C. 20036.

New York Graphic Society Ltd., 140 Greenwich Ave., Greenwich, Conn. 06830 (fine art reproductions).

A. J. Nystrom & Co., 3333 Elston Ave., Chicago, Ill. 60618.

Perry Pictures, Inc., 42 Dartmouth St., Malden, Mass. 02148.

Popular Science Publishing Company, Audio-Visual Division, 355 Lexington Ave., New York, N.Y. 10017.

Rand McNally & Company, P.O. Box 7600, Chicago, Ill. 60680.

Society for Visual Education, Inc., 1345 W. Diversey Parkway, Chicago, Ill. 60614.

United Nations, Public Inquiries Unit, Dept. of Public Information, New York, N.Y. 10017.

Free and inexpensive materials

COMMERCIAL SOURCES

Allied Chemical Corporation, Public Relations Department, 40 Rector St., New York, N.Y. 10002.

American Can Company, 100 Park Avenue., New York, N.Y. 10017.

American Telephone and Telegraph Company, 195 Broadway, New York, N.Y. 10007.

Boeing Company, P.O. Box 3707, Seattle, Wash. 98124.

Chrysler Corporation, Public Relations, P.O. Box 1919, Detroit, Mich. 48231.

E. I. DuPont de Nemours & Company, Public Relations Department, Wilmington, Del. 19898.

General Electric Company, Educational Relations, 570 Lexington Ave., New York, N.Y. 10022.

General Motors Corporation, Public Relations Staff, Detroit, Mich. 48202.

B. F. Goodrich Company, Public Relations Department, 500 S. Main St., Akron, Ohio 44318.

National Park Service, Department of Interior, Washington, D.C. 20240.

Shell Oil Company, 50 W. 50th St., New York, N.Y. 10020.

Standard Oil Company of California, Public Relations Department, 225 Bush St., San Francisco, Calif. 94120.

Swift and Company, Agricultural Research Division, 115 W. Jackson Blvd., Chicago, Ill. 60604.

Trans World Airlines, 1735 Baltimore Ave., Kansas City, Mo. 64108.

United Air Lines, School and College Service, P.O. Box 8800, O'Hare International Airport, Chicago, Ill. 60666.

United States Steel Corporation, Public Relations Department, 71 Broadway, New York, N.Y. 10006.

FILMS

American Automobile Association, Department of Public Education, 1712 G St., N.W., Washington, D.C. 20006.

American Iron and Steel Institute, 150 E. 42nd St., New York, N.Y. 10017.

Association-Sterling Films, Inc., 866 Third Ave., New York, N.Y. 10022.

Ruth H. Aubrey's Selected Free Materials for Classroom Teachers, Fearon Publishers, 2165 Park Blvd., Palo Alto, Calif. 94306 (1967), $1.75.

Bell Telephone Company. Check with your local telephone office.

Contemporary Films/McGraw-Hill, 330 W. 42nd St., New York, N.Y. 10036.

Films, Inc., 1144 Wilmette Ave., Wilmette, Ill. 60091.

General Electric Company, Educational Relations, 570 Lexington Ave., New York, N.Y. 10022.

General Motors Corporation, General Motors Building, Detroit, Mich. 48202.

Modern Talking Picture Service, 1212 Avenue of the Americas, New York, N.Y. 10036.

INDEXES

The following eight guides, which are revised annually, are all issued by the Educators Progress Service, Randolph, Wis. 53956:

Educators Guide to Free Curriculum Materials

Educators Guide to Free Films

Educators Guide to Free Guidance Materials

Educators Guide to Free Health, Physical Education, and Recreation Materials

Educators Guide to Free Science Materials

Educators Guide to Free Social Studies Materials

Educators Guide to Free Tapes, Scripts, and Transcriptions

Elementary Teachers Guide to Free Curriculum Materials

Catalog of Free Teaching Materials, 236 pp., Gordon Salisbury, P.O. Box 1975, Ventura, Calif. $1.85, revised regularly.

Free and Inexpensive Learning Materials, published by the Division of Surveys and Field Services, George Peabody College for Teachers, Nashville, Tenn. 37203; contains 258 pages and costs $3.00.

National Audio Tape Catalog provides a subject index of tape recordings including more than 5,000 titles listed for use from nursery school to graduate school. A small fee is charged for duplication. The catalog is available from the AECT Audio Tape, 1201 Sixteenth St., N.W., Washington, D.C. 20036, for $3.00.

SELECTED ORGANIZATIONS

Agency for International Development, U.S. Department of State, Washington, D.C. 20523.

American Dental Association, 211 E. Chicago Ave., Chicago, Ill. 60611.

American Gas Association, Educational Services, 605 Third Ave., New York, N.Y. 10016.

American Heart Association, 44 E. 23rd St., New York, N.Y. 10010.

American Iron and Steel Institute, Teaching Aids Distribution Center, Bedford Hills, N.Y. 10507.

American Library Association, 50 E. Huron St., Chicago, Ill. 60611.

American Medical Association, 535 N. Dearborn St., Chicago, Ill. 60610.

American Petroleum Institute, Education Department, 1271 Avenue of the Americas, New York, N.Y. 10020.

Austrian Information Service, 31 E. 69th St., New York, N.Y. 10021.

Automobile Manufacturers Association, Educational Services, 320 New Center Building, Detroit, Mich. 48202.

British Information Services, 845 Third Ave., New York, N.Y. 10022.

Bureau of International Education and Cultural Affairs, U.S. Department of State, Washington, D.C. 20520.

Canadian Government Travel Bureau, Ottawa, Ontario, Canada.

Chinese Information Service, 1270 Sixth Ave., New York, N.Y. 10020.

Danish Information Office, 280 Park Ave., New York, N.Y. 10017.

Embassy of New Zealand, 10 Observatory Circle, Washington, D.C. 20008.

Embassy of the Union of Soviet Socialist Republics, Press Department, 1706 Eighteenth St., N.W., Washington, D.C. 20009.

Federal Aviation Administration, Special Assistant, Aviation Education, Office of General Aviation Affairs, Washington, D.C. 20590 (FAA's Aviation Bibliography).

Food and Agricultural Organization of the United Nations, North America Regional Office, 1325 C St., S.W., Washington, D.C. 20437.

French National Railroads, 610 Fifth Ave., New York, N.Y. 10020.

German Tourist Information Office, 500 Fifth Ave., New York, N.Y. 10036.

Information Service of India, 2107 Massachusetts Ave., N.W., Washington, D.C. 20008.

International Labor Office, 917 Fifteenth St., N.W., Washington, D.C. 20005.

Italian Government Travel Office, 626 Fifth Ave., New York, N.Y. 10020.

Japan Information Service, Consulate General of Japan, 235 E. 42nd St., New York, N.Y. 10017.

Manufacturing Chemists' Association, 1825 Connecticut Ave., N.W., Washington, D.C. 20009 (Guide to Education Aids available from the Chemical Industry).

Mexican National Tourist Council, 2 E. 55th St., New York, N.Y. 10022.

Modern Language Association, 100 Washington Square N., New York, N.Y. 10003.

National Association of Educational Broadcasters, Public Relations Service, 1346 Connecticut Ave., N.W., Washington, D.C. 20036.

National Canners Association, Home Economics Consumer Service, 1133 Twentieth St., N.W., Washington, D.C. 20036.

National Cotton Council of America, P.O. Box 12285, Memphis, Tenn. 38112; Catalogue of Educational Materials on Cotton, National Council of Teachers of English, 704 S. Sixth St., Champaign, Ill. 61820.

National Dairy Council, 111 N. Canal St., Chicago, Ill. 60606.

National Education Association, 1201 Sixteenth St., N.W., Washington, D.C. 20036.

National Forest Products Association, 1619 Massachusetts Ave., N.W., Washington, D.C. 20036 (Lumber and Wood Products Literature).

National League for Nursing, 2 Park Ave., New York, N.Y. 10016.

National Wildlife Federation, Educational Servicing Section, 1412 Sixteenth St., N.W., Washington, D.C. 20036.

Pan American Health Organization, Pan American Sanitary Bureau, Regional Office of the World Health Organization, 525 Twenty-third St., N.W., Washington, D.C. 20037.

People-to-People, School and Classroom Program, 2401 Grand Ave., Kansas City, Mo. 64141.

Pharmaceutical Manufacturers Association, 1155 Fifteenth St., N.W., Washington, D.C. 20085. The Story of Health Society of American Foresters, 825 Mills Building, Washington, D.C. 20006.

Spanish National Tourist Office, 589 Fifth Ave., New York, N.Y. 10017.

Swedish Information Service, 161 E. 42nd St., New York, N.Y. 10017.

Swiss National Tourist Office, 608 Fifth Ave., New York, N.Y. 10020.

United States National Commission for UNESCO, Washington, D.C. 20250.

Weyerhaeuser Company, Visual Information Department, Tacoma, Wash. 98401 (Sources of Information about Forest Resources).

Furniture and facilities

ACOUSTICAL MATERIALS

Celotex Corporation, 120 S. La Salle St., Chicago, Ill. 60603.

Johns-Manville, Greenwood Plaza, Denver, Colo. 80217.

GENERAL SOURCES

Furniture that is both functional and relatively inexpensive is widely available. In addition to commercial sources, it may be worthwhile to consult local carpenters or building contractors. Also, furniture that is quite functional and very inexpensive may often be constructed. For example, cardboard, wooden boxes, or other inexpensive materials may be used to make student carrels when funds are limited. Once their value has been demonstrated, such temporary carrels may be replaced with commercial models.

Adirondack Chair Company, 276 Park Ave. S., New York, N.Y. 10010.

Advance Products Company, P.O. Box 2178, Wichita, Kans. 67201.

American Seating Company, 2930 Canton St., Dallas, Tex. 75226.

American Structural Products Company, Toledo, Ohio 43601.

Arlington Aluminum Company, 19303 W. Davison, Detroit, Mich. 48223.

Brunswick Corporation, School Equipment Division, 2605 E. Kilgore Rd., Kalamazoo, Mich. 49003.

Chester Electronic Laboratories, Inc., Winthrop Rd., Chester, Conn. 06412.

Fleetwood Furniture Company, Electronics Division, P.O. Box 58, Zeeland, Mich. 49464.

Foldcraft, Mendota, Minn. 55050.

Formica Corporation, 120 East 4th St., Cincinnati, Ohio 45202.

General Electric Company, 1 River Rd., Schenectady, N.Y. 12309.

Hauserman Co., 5711 Grant Ave., Cleveland, Ohio 44105.

Howe Folding Furniture, Inc., 360 Lexington Ave., New York, N.Y. 10017.

Magna Design, Inc., P.O. Box 606, Lynnwood, Wash. 98036.

Charles Mayer Studio, Inc., 776 Commins St., Akron, Ohio 44307.

Mobile Classrooms, Inc., 11400 Bluffton Rd., Rt. 1, Fort Wayne, Ind. 46809.

PPG Industries, Inc., The Library, One Gateway Center, Pittsburgh, Pa. 15222.

Radio Corporation of America, Audio-Visual Marketing Division, Front and Cooper Sts., Camden, N.J. 08102.

Toledo Metal Furniture Company, 1400 N. Hastings St., Toledo, Ohio 43607.

H. Wilson Corporation, 555 W. Taft Dr., South Holland, Ill. 60473.

The Worden Company, 199 E. 17th St., Holland, Mich. 49423.

LEARNING RESOURCES FACILITIES

American Library Association, 50 E. Huron St., Chicago, Ill. 60611.

Association for Educational Communications and Technology, 1201 Sixteenth St., N.W., Washington, D.C. 20036.

Educational Facilities Laboratories, 477 Madison Ave., New York, N.Y. 10022.

Educational Research Information Center (ERIC), U.S. Office of Education, Washington, D.C. 20202.

National Council on Schoolhouse Construction, 411 Erickson Hall, Michigan State University, East Lansing, Mich. 48823.

U.S. Office of Education, Washington, D.C. 20202.

Westinghouse Electric Corporation, P.O. Box J, Sea Cliff, N.Y. 11579.

LEARNING SYSTEMS

American Telephone and Telegraph Company, 195 Broadway, New York, N.Y. 10007.

Avedex, Incorporated, 7328 Niles Center Road, Skokie, Ill. 60076.

Behavioral Research Laboratories, Ladera Professional Center, P.O. Box 577, Palo Alto, Calif. 94302.

Cenco Instruments Corporation, Cenco Center, 2600 S. Kostner Ave., Chicago, Ill. 60623.

Educational Development Laboratories, Inc., Huntington, N.Y. 11743.

Grolier Educational Corporation, 845 Third Ave., New York, N.Y. 10022.

Norelco Training and Educations Systems, 100 East 42nd St., New York, N.Y. 10017.

Raytheon Learning Systems Company, 475 Dean St., Englewood, N.J. 07631.

Rheem-Califone Division, 5922 Bowcroft St., Los Angeles, Calif. 90016.

Switchcraft, Inc., 5555 N. Elston, Chicago, Ill. 60630.

Westinghouse Electric Corporation, P.O. Box J, Sea Cliff, N.Y. 11579.

White Electronic Development Corporation, 410 Jericho Turnpike, Jericho, N.Y. 11753.

LISTENING LABORATORIES

Audio Teaching Center, 137 Hamilton St., New Haven, Conn. 06511.

Audiotronics Corp., 7428 Bellaire Ave., N. Hollywood, Calif. 91603.

Avedex, Incorporated, 7328 Niles Center Road, Skokie, Ill. 60076.

Brunswick Corporation, 2605 E. Kilgore Rd., Kalamazoo, Mich. 49003.

Chester Electronic Laboratories, Winthrop Rd., Chester, Conn. 06412.

Educational Developmental Laboratories, Inc., Huntington, N.Y. 11743.

Hamilton Electronics Corporation, 2726 W. Pratt Ave., Chicago, Ill. 60645.

Instructomatic, Inc., 30625 W. 8 Mile Rd., Livonia, Mich. 48152.

Perma Power Company, Division Chamberlain Mfg. Corp., 5740 N. Tripp Ave., Chicago, Ill. 60646.

Radio Corporation of America, Audio-Visual Marketing Division, Front and Cooper Sts., Camden, N.J. 08102.

Switchcraft, Inc., 5555 N. Elston, Chicago, Ill. 60646.

Tandberg of America, Inc., 8 Third Ave., Pelham, N.Y. 10803.

Webcor Sales Co., 5610 W. Bloomingdale Ave., Chicago, Ill. 60639.

White Electronic Development Corporation, 410 Jericho Turnpike, Jericho, N.Y. 11753.

Wible Language Institute, 24 South Eighth St., Allentown, Pa. 18105.

ROOM-DARKENING EQUIPMENT

Alcan Building Products, Division of Alcan Aluminum Corporation, Box 6977, Cleveland, Ohio 44101.

Beckley-Cardy Company, 1900 N. Narragansett St., Chicago, Ill. 60639.

Clopay Corporation, Clopay Square, Cincinnati, Ohio 45214.

Colonial Drapery & Curtain Co., Colonial Plastics Corporation, 3 S. 12th St., Richmond, Va. 23219.

Draper Shade Company, 411 S. Pearl St., Spiceland, Ind. 47385 (drapes).

E. I. DuPont de Nemours & Company, Wilmington, Del. 19898.

Duracote Corporation, Ravenna, Ohio 44266.

Forse Manufacturing Company, 2347 Sullivan Ave., St. Louis, Mo. 63107 (drapes).

Lelelor-Lorentzen, 720 Monroe St., Hoboken, N.J. 07030.

Luxout Plastic Products, Inc., 1822 E. Franklin St., Richmond, Va. 23208 (room-darkening and light-control draperies).

Mackin Corp., 300 W. 6 St., Momence, Ill. 60954.

Plastic Products, Inc., P.O. Box 1118, Richmond, Va. 23208.

Games and simulations
See Simulations and games

Globes
See Maps, globes, and supplies

Graphic materials

When you prepare your instructional materials, many of the construction supplies may be found in local art, stationery, photographic, or drafting equipment supply stores. If you cannot locate a local distributor for a particular item, write to the manufacturer for the nearest outlet or request a catalog from a source listed below. Sign lettering and graphic materials may sometimes be secured from expendable displays set up by local retail outlets.

ADHESIVES

Addressograph-Multigraph Corp., Charles Bruning Division, 1555 Times Drive, Des Plaines, Ill. 60018 (striped adhesive wax coater).

Brandywine Photo Chemical Co., Inc., P.O. Box 298, Avondale, Pa. 19311 (Spray-Mount photo adhesive).

Chemex Industries, Inc., 2822 35th St., Tampa, Fla. (Base-Tape) 33605.

Daige Products, Inc., 160 Denton Ave., New Hyde Park, N.Y. 11040 (Daige Speedcote).

Ditto Division, Bell and Howell Company, 6800 McCormick Rd., Chicago, Ill. 60645.

Lea AV Service, 182 Audley Drive, Sun Prairie, Wis. 53590 (Bulletin Board *STYX*).

Letro-Stik Co., 3721 Broadway, Chicago, Ill. 60613 (Letro-Stik).

CHARTS AND GRAPHS

Aero Service Corporation, 210 E. Courtland St., Philadelphia, Pa. 19120.

American Forest Products Industries, 1816 N St., N.W., Washington, D.C. 20036.

American Museum–Hayden Planetarium, 81st St. and Central Park West, New York, N.Y. 10024.

American Petroleum Institute, 50 W. 50th St., New York, N.Y. 10020.

Clay-Adams, 299 Webro Road, Parsippany, N.J. 07054.

General Motors Co., Department of Public Relations, General Motors Bldg., 3044 W. Grand Blvd., Detroit, Mich. 48292.

National Forum Foundation, c/o American Guidance Service, Publishers' Building, Circle Pines, Minn. 55014.

National Industrial Conference Board, Inc., 845 3rd Ave., New York, N.Y. 10022.

U.S. Forest Service, Education Section, 12 Independence Ave., Washington, D.C. 20003.

Ward's Natural Science Establishment, Inc., 3000 E. Ridge Road, Rochester, N.Y. 14605.

CLIP ART SERVICES

Artype, Inc., 345 East Terra Cotta Ave., Crystal Lake, Ill. 60014.

Multi-Ad Service, 118 Walnut St., Peoria, Ill. 61602.

Tecnifax Corporation, 195 Appleton St., Holyoke, Mass. 01040.

Volk Corporation, Pleasantville, N.J. 08232.

COLORING AND SHADING MATERIALS

Bourges Color Corp., 84 Fifth Ave., New York, N.Y. 10011.

Cello-Tak Manufacturing, Inc., 35 Alabama Ave., Island Park, N.Y. 11558.

Chartpak, One River Road, Leeds, Mass. 01053 (Contak).

Craftint Manufacturing Co., 18501 Euclid Ave., Cleveland, Ohio 44112 (Craf-tone).

Mico/Tape, Inc., 7005 Tujunga Ave., North Hollywood, Calif. 91605.

Para-tone, Inc., 5227 So. Dansher, Countryside, Ill. 60525 (Zip-a-tone).

Peerless Color Laboratories, 11–13 Diamond Place, Rochester, N.Y. 14609 (transparent water colors).

GRAPHIC TAPES

Chartpak, One River Road, Leeds, Mass. 01053.

Craftint Manufacturing Co., 18501 Euclid Ave., Cleveland, Ohio 44112.

Deinco Educational Corp., P.O. Box 1488, Madison, Wis. 53701.

Labelon Corp., 10 Chapin St., Canandiagua, N.Y. 14424.

Mico/Tape, Inc., 7005 Tujunga Ave., North Hollywood, Calif. 91605.

Para-Tone, Inc., 5227 So. Dansher, Countryside, Ill. 60525.

LAMINATORS

General Binding Corp., 1101 Skokie Blvd., Northbrook, Ill. 60062.

Nationwide Adhesive Products, Inc., 19600 St. Clair Ave., Cleveland, Ohio 44117 (Transeal).

Seal, Inc., Roosevelt Drive & B St., Derby, Conn. 06418.

MOUNTING MATERIALS

Brooks Manufacturing Co., P.O. Box 41195, Cincinnati, Ohio 45241.

Cann-Lox Products, Henry H. Grant Co., P.O. Box 366, Redondo Beach, Calif. 90277;

Chartex Seal, Inc., Roosevelt Drive & B St., Derby, Conn. 06418.

SOS/Photo-Cine-Optics, Inc., 315 W. 43rd St., New York, N.Y. 10036.

Union Rubber and Asbestos Co., 232 Allen St., Trenton, N.J. 08618 (Best Test).

POLARIZING MATERIALS

Technamation, Inc., 112 Parkway Drive South, Hauppauge, N.Y. 11787.

Tecnifax Corporation, 195 Appleton St., Holyoke, Mass. 01040.

POSTERS

American Dental Association, 222 E. Superior St., Chicago, Ill. 60611.

American Humane Education Society, 180 Longwood Ave., Boston, Mass. 0215.

Argus Communications, 3505 N. Ashland Ave., Chicago, Ill. 60657.

Cunard Line, Ltd., 555 Fifth Ave., New York, N.Y. 10017.

French Line, Publicity Department, 555 Fifth Ave., New York, N.Y. 10017.

Hapag-Lloyd AG, c/o U.S. Navigation Company, Advertising Dept., 17 Battery Place, New York, N.Y. 10004.

National Safety Council, 425 N. Michigan Ave., Chicago, Ill. 60611.

Graphic tape
See **Graphic materials**

Graphics and charts
See **Graphic materials**

Hook-and-loop boards
See **Display surfaces and supplies**

Individualized instruction

Continuous Progress Plan Materials, Utah State Department of Public Instruction, Division of Research and Innovation, Salt Lake City, Utah 84101.

Environmental Studies, P.O. Box 1559, Boulder, Colo. 80302.

Hawaii English Project Materials, Office of Curriculum Development and Technology, 1750 Wist Place, Honolulu, Hawaii 96814.

An Individualized Spelling and Language Arts Program, Wilson School, Janesville, Wis. 53545, and Wisconsin Research and Development Center for Cognitive Learning, University of Wisconsin, Madison, Wis. 53706.

Individually Prescribed Instruction Materials, Learning Research and Development Center, University of Pittsburgh, Pittsburgh, Pa. 15213, and Research for Better Schools, Inc., 1700 Market Street, Philadelphia, Pa. 19104.

Lessons for Self-Instruction in Basic Skills, California Test Bureau, Del Monte Research Park, Monterey, Calif. 93940.

Project PLAN Materials, Westinghouse Learning Corporation, 100 Park Ave., New York, N.Y. 10017.

A Statement of Skills and Objectives for the Wisconsin Prototypic System of Reading Skill Development, Wisconsin Research and Development Center for Cognitive Learning, University of Wisconsin, Madison, Wis. 53706.

The Wilson Manual for Individually Guided Reading, Wilson School, Janesville, Wis. 53545, and Wisconsin Research and Development Center for Cognitive Learning, University of Wisconsin, Madison, Wis. 53706.

Winnetka Curriculum Materials List, Winnetka Public Schools, Winnetka, Ill. 60093.

Kits, multimedia
See **Multimedia equipment and materials**

Laboratories, language
See **Furniture and facilities: listening laboratories**

Laboratories, listening
See **Furniture and facilities**

Laminators
See **Graphic materials**

Language laboratories
See **Furniture and facilities: listening laboratories**

Learning resource centers.
See **Furniture and facilities: learning resources facilities**

Learning systems
See **Furniture and facilities**

Lettering

LETTERING EQUIPMENT
Dick Blick Company, P.O. Box 1267, Galesburg, Ill. 61401.
Carter's Ink Company, Cambridge, Mass. 02142.
Chartpak, One River Rd., Leeds, Mass. 01053.
E. Dietzgen Co., 2425 N. Sheffield Ave., Chicago, Ill. 60614.
Dri-Flo Pen Co., P.O. Box C, Detroit, Mich. 48213.
Embosograf Corporation of America, 38 W. 21st St., New York, N.Y. 10010.
Hunt Manufacturing Company, 1405 Locust St., Philadelphia, Pa. 19102.
Keuffel and Esser Company, 20 Whippany Rd., Hoboken, N.J. 07960.
Koh-i-noor, Inc., 100 North St., Bloomsbury, N.J. 08804.
Letterguide Co., 4247 O St., Lincoln, Neb. 68510.
Lockwood Co., 336 Boston Post Rd., Milford, Conn. 06460 (Dri-Rite Pen).
Magic Marker Corp., 84–00 73 Ave., Glendale, N.Y. 11227.

Mark-Tex Corp., 161 Coolidge Ave., Englewood, N.J. 07631 (Tech-pen for inking metal, porcelain, paper, plastic, cloth, etc., in colors; Action Marker).
Showcard Machine Company, 320 W. Ohio, Chicago, Ill. 60610.
Varigraph, Inc., P.O. Box 690, Madison, Wis. 53701.
Venus Esterbrook Corporation, Springplace Pike, Lewisburg, Tenn. 37091.
Wood-Regan Instrument Co. Inc., 184 Franklin Ave., Nutley, N.J. 07110 (Wrico).

LETTERS
Arthur Brown and Bros., Inc., 2 W. 46th St., New York, N.Y. 10036.
Artype, Inc., 345 East Terra Cotta Ave., Crystal Lake, Ill. 60014.
Cello-Tak Manufacturing, Inc., 35 Alabama Ave., Island Park, N.Y. 11558.
Chartpak, Inc., Leeds, Mass. 01053 (Deca-dry).
Demp-Nock Company, 21433 Mound Rd., Warren, Mich. 48090.
Gaylord Bros., Inc., P.O. Box 61, Syracuse, N.Y. 13201.
Naz-Dar Co. of California, Inc., Graphic Arts Center Division, 1534 W. 7th St., Los Angeles, Calif. 90052.
Graphic Products Corp., 3601 Edison Place, Rolling Meadows, Ill. 60008.
The Holes-Webway Co., Webway Park, 28th & Division, St. Cloud, Minn. 56301.
Instantype, Inc., 6553 W. Sunset Blvd., Los Angeles, Calif. 90028 (Instantype).
Manhattan Wood Letter Company, 151 W. 18th St., New York, N.Y. 10011.
Mitten Designer Letters, 39 W. 60th St., New York, N.Y. 10023.
Prestype Corp., 194 Veterans Blvd., Carlstadt, N.J. 07072.
Redikut Letter Company, 12617 S. Prairie Ave., Hawthorne, Calif. 90250 (cardboard letters and Plasti-Tak adhesive for mounting on changeable backgrounds).
Stik-a-Letter Company, Rt. 2, P.O. Box 1400, Escondido, Calif. 92025.
The Tablet and Ticket Company, 1021 W. Adams St., Chicago, Ill. 60607.

Libraries, audiotape
See **Audio equipment and materials: tape sources**

Light control
See **Furniture and facilities: room-darkening equipment**

Lighting
See **Photographic equipment**

Listening laboratories
See **Furniture and facilities**

Magnetic boards
See **Display surfaces and supplies**

Magnets
See **Display surfaces and supplies**

Maps, globes, and supplies
Aero Service Corp., 210 Courtland St., Philadelphia, Pa. 19120 (plastic relief maps).
Aldine Publishing Co., 529 S. Wabash Ave., Chicago, Ill. 60605.
American Map Company, 3 W. 61st St., New York, N.Y. 10023.
George F. Cram Company, Inc., 301 S. La Salle St., P.O. Box 426, Indianapolis, Ind. 46206.
Denoyer-Geppert Company, 5235 Ravenswood Ave., Chicago, Ill. 60640.
A. B. Dick Co., Audio/Visual Communications Systems, 5700 W. Touhy, Niles, Ill. 60648 (map stencils).
Farquhar Transparent Globes, 5007 Warrington Ave., Philadelphia, Pa. 19143.
Geographia Map Co., Inc., 220 W. 42nd St., New York, N.Y. 10036.
Graphics Institute, 42 W. 39th St., New York, N.Y. 10036.
Hammond, Inc., 515 Valley St., Maplewood, N.J. 07040.
McKinley Publishing Co., 112 S. New Broadway, Brooklawn, N.J. 08030 (desk and wall outline maps).
National Geographic Society, 16th and M Sts., Washington, D.C. 20036.
A. J. Nystrom and Company, 3333 Elston Ave., Chicago, Ill. 60618.
Pictograph Corporation, 175 Fifth Ave., New York, N.Y. 10010.

Rand McNally & Company, P.O. Box 7600 Chicago, Ill. 60680.
Replogle Globes, 315 N. Hoyne Ave., Chicago, Ill. 60612.
Weber-Costello Company, 1900 N. Narragansett Ave., Chicago Heights, Ill. 60639.

Microfilm and microfiche
Dennison Manufacturing Company, Framingham, Mass. 01701.
Eastman Kodak Company, 343 State St., Rochester, N.Y. 14650.
Microtext Publishing Corporation, 112 Liberty St., New York, N.Y. 10006.
NCR-Microcard Editions, 365 South Oak St., West Salem, Wis. 54669.
National Cash Register Co., 3131 S. Dixie Drive, Dayton, Ohio 45439.
Readex Microprint Corporation, 100 Fifth Ave., New York, N.Y. 10011.
University Microfilms, A Zerox Company, 300 N. Zeeb Rd., Ann Arbor, Mich. 48106 (microfilms).
University of Rochester Press, Micropublication Service, Rochester, N.Y. 14627 (microcards).

Microprojectors
See **Projectors**

Mimeograph machines
See **Reproduction equipment**

Models, 3–D
See **Three-dimensional materials**

Motion picture equipment
See **Photographic equipment**

Mounting materials
See **Graphic materials**

Multimedia equipment and materials
The local teacher is probably the best source of multimedia materials needed to meet the in-

dividual needs of his students (as for Individualized Instruction programs). As a teacher develops sets of slides, tapes, and programed materials of other types, he will find it helpful to keep records of materials and techniques used so they can be put back together again for later use. Over a period of years a file of such records can become a valuable resource for one's own use and the use of other teachers.

INSTRUCTIONAL KITS

Paul S. Amidon & Associates, Inc., Chicago Ave. S., Minneapolis, Minn. 55116.

Behavioral Research Laboratories, Ladera Professional Center, P.O. Box 577, Palo Alto, Calif. 94302.

Comspace Corp., 350 Great Neck Road, Farmingdale, N.Y. 11735.

Cathedral Films, Inc., 2921 W. Alameda Ave., Burbank, Calif. 91505.

Chandler Publishing Company, 124 Spear St., San Francisco, Calif. 94105.

Denoyer-Geppert Company, 5235 Ravenswood Ave., Chicago, Ill. 60640.

Educational Media Laboratories, 4101 South Congress Ave., Austin, Tex. 78745.

Flexible Learning Systems, Inc., Box 123, Chesterland, Ohio 44026.

D. C. Heath and Company, Division of Raytheon Education Co., 285 Columbus Ave., Boston, Mass. 02116.

Imperial Productions, Inc., 247 W. Court St., Kankakee, Ill. 60901.

Instructo Corporation, 1635 N. 55th St., Philadelphia, Pa. 19131.

Jayark Instruments Corporation, 10 E. 49th St., New York, N.Y. 10017.

Language Laboratories, Inc., 4823 Fairmont Ave., Bethesda, Md. 20014.

Learning Research Associates, 1501 Broadway, New York, N.Y. 10036.

McGraw-Hill Book Company, Webster Division, 330 W. 42nd St., New York, N.Y. 10036.

Media Associates, Inc., 525 Moorland Drive, East Lansing, Mich. 48823.

National Special Media Institutes, Instructional Media Center, Michigan State University, East Lansing, Mich. 48823.

Responsive Environments Corporation, 200 Sylvan Ave., Englewood Cliffs, N.J. 07632.

Sanderson Films, Inc., P.O. Box 13121, Wichita, Kansas 67213.

School House Visuals, Inc., 816 Thayer Ave., Silver Spring, Md. 20910.

See, Inc., 3 Bridge St., Newton, Mass. 02195.

Shorewood Reproductions, Inc., 724 5th Ave., New York, N.Y. 10019.

Teaching Technology Corp., 6837 Hayuen St., Van Nuys, Calif. 91406.

United Scientific Co., 216 South Jefferson St., Chicago, Ill. 60606.

Western Publishing Company, Inc., 850 Third Ave., New York, N.Y. 10022.

PROGRAMING EQUIPMENT

Arion Corporation, 825 Boone Ave. N., Minneapolis, Minn. 55427.

Eastman Kodak Company, 343 State St., Rochester, N.Y. 14650 (Programmer).

General Techniques, Inc., 1270 Broadway, New York, N.Y. 10001.

Intermedia Systems Corporation, 711 Massachusetts Ave., Cambridge, Mass. 02139.

Link Educational Laboratories, P.O. Box 11073, Montgomery, Ala. 36111.

Montage Productions, Inc., 49 W. 27th St., New York, N.Y. 10001.

North American Philips Corp., Training and Education Systems, 100 E. 42nd St., New York, N.Y. 10017.

Optisonics Corp., Montgomeryville Industrial Center, Montgomeryville, Pa. 18936.

Pro-Gramo, Inc., 44 W. 44th St., New York, N.Y. 10036.

Systems Technology, 5512 Dyer St., Dallas, Tex. 75206.

V-M Corp., 375 W. Main St., Benton Harbor, Mich. 49022 (V-M Synchronizer).

Museums

California Museum of the Sea Foundation, P.O. Box 20890, Long Beach, Calif. 90801 (*Queen Mary*).

Chicago Museum of Science & Industry, 57th St. and S. Lake Shore Drive, Jackson Park, Chicago, Ill. 60637.

Circus World Museum, Baraboo, Wis. 53913.

Museo Nacional de Antropología, Mexico City, Mexico.

Oregon Museum of Science and Industry, Portland, Ore. 97208.

Smithsonian Institution, Washington, D.C. 20560.

Networks, radio
See **Audio equipment and materials**

Networks, television
See **Television**

Offset reproduction machines
See **Reproduction equipment**

Opaque projectors
See **Projectors**

Overhead projectors
See **Projectors**

Photographic equipment

Most school systems have photography facilities and services for yearbook or newspaper publicity purposes. Check into the possible expansion of these services to include instructional functions such as assistance with visual literacy programs and procurement of inexpensive camera equipment. Also consult local camera clubs and professional photographers for information about possible equipment, supplies, costs, and instruction for your students.

LIGHTING
Brewster Corporation, 50 River St., Old Saybrook, Conn. 06475.
General Electric Company, Nela Park, Cleveland, Ohio 44112.
Mole-Richardson Co., 937 N. Sycamore Ave., Hollywood, Calif. 90038.
Smith-Victor Corp., Griffith, Ind. 46319.
Sylvania Electric Products Company, 730 Third Ave., New York, N.Y. 10017.
Westinghouse Electric Corporation, Lamp Division, 1 Westinghouse Plaza, Bloomfield, N.J. 07003.

MOTION PICTURE CAMERAS AND EQUIPMENT
Allied Impex Corporation, 168 Glen Cove Rd., Carle Place, N.Y. 11514.
Bell and Howell Company, 7100 McCormick Rd., Chicago, Ill., 60645.

Canon U.S.A., Inc., 64–10 Queens Blvd., Woodside, N.Y. 11377.
Eastman Kodak Company, 343 State St., Rochester, N.Y. 14650.
Ehrenreich Photo-Optical Company, Garden City, N.Y. 11533 (Fujica).
F&B/CECO Inc., 315 West 43rd St., New York, N.Y. 10036.
Fairchild Camera and Instrument Corporation, 75 Mall Dr., Commack, N.Y. 11725.
Alan Gordon Enterprises, 5362 Cahuenga Blvd., North Hollywood, Calif. 91601.
Harwald Company, The, 1245 Chicago Ave., Evanston, Ill. 60202.
Minolta Corporation, 200 Park Ave. S., New York, N.Y. 10003 (Minolta).
Paillard, Inc., 1900 Lower Rd., Linden, N.J. 07036.
Quick-Set, Inc., 8121 Central Park Ave., Skokie, Ill. 60076.
SOS/Photo-Cine-Optics, Inc., 315 W. 43rd St., New York, N.Y. 10036.

SLIDE COPIERS
Bogen Photo Corp., 232 S. Van Brunt Street, Englewood, N.J. 07631 (Bowens Illumitran).
Honeywell, Inc. Photographic Division, 5501 S. Broadway, Littleton, Colo. 80120.

STEREO EQUIPMENT AND MATERIALS
Canon U.S.A., Inc., 64–10 Queens Blvd., Woodside, N.Y. 11377.
Motiva Ltd., 155 East 55th St., New York, N.Y. 10022.
Realist, Inc., Megal Drive, Menomonee Falls, Wis. 53051.
Spindler and Sauppe, Inc., 1329 Grand Central Ave., Glendale, Calif. 91201.

STILL CAMERAS
Allied Impex Corporation, 168 Glen Cove Rd., Carle Place, N.Y. 11514.
Bell and Howell Company, 7100 McCormick Rd., Chicago, Ill. 60645.
Charles Beseler Company, 219 S. 18th St., East Orange, N.J. 07018 (Topcon).
Canon U.S.A., Inc., 64–10 Queens Blvd., Woodside, N.Y. 11377.
Eastman Kodak Company, 343 State St., Rochester, N.Y. 14650.

Ehrenreich Photo-Optical Company, Garden City, N.Y. 11533 (Nikon).

Graflex Division, The Singer Co., 3750 Monroe Ave., Rochester, N.Y. 14603 (Graflex).

Karl Heitz, Inc., 979 Third Ave., New York, N.Y. 10022.

Honeywell, Inc., Photographic Division, 5501 S. Broadway, Littleton, Colo. 80120.

Konica Camera Corporation, Box 1070, Woodside, N.Y. 11377 (Konica).

E. Leitz, Inc. 46 Park Ave. S., New York, N.Y. 10016 (Leica).

Minolta Corporation, 200 Park Ave. S., New York, N.Y. 10003 (Minolta).

Polaroid Corporation, Cambridge, Mass. 02138 (Polaroid Land).

Ponder and Best, 11201 W. Pico Blvd., Los Angeles, Calif. 90064 (Mamiya).

Carl Zeiss, Inc., 485 Fifth Ave., New York, N.Y. 10017 (Zeiss-Ikon-Contax).

Pictures
See **Flat pictures**

Planetariums

Astro-Tec Manufacturing, Inc., 231 Locust St., Canal Fulton, Ohio 44614.

Jack C. Coffey Co., Inc., P.O. Box 131, Waukegan, Ill. 60085.

Denoyer-Geppert Company, 5235 Ravenswood Ave., Chicago, Ill. 60640.

Farquhar Transparent Globes, 5007 Warrington Ave., Philadelphia, Pa. 19143.

Nova Laboratories, Union Hill Park, West Conshohocken, Pa. 19428.

Planetariums Unlimited, Inc., Broadway Ave., Holbrook, N.Y. 11741 (Apollo).

Trippensee Planetarium Company, 2200 S. Hamilton St., Saginaw, Mich. 48602.

Polarizing materials
See **Graphic materials**

Posters
See **Graphic materials**

Prints
See **Flat pictures**

Professional association
See **Free and inexpensive materials: selected organizations**

Programed instruction

Addison-Wesley Publishing Co., Inc., 2725 Sand Hill Road, Menlo Park, Calif. 94025.

Adler Educational Systems, 1 Fevre Lane, New Rochelle, N.Y. 10801.

Appleton-Century-Crofts, Lyons & Carnahan, 34 W. 33rd St., New York, N.Y. 10001.

Behavioral Research Laboratories, Ladera Professional Center, Box 577, Palo Alto, Calif. 94302.

Central Scientific Co., 2600 S. Kostner Ave., Chicago, Ill. 60623.

Doubleday & Company, Inc., 501 Franklin Ave., Garden City, N.Y. 11530.

Educational Development Laboratories, Inc., Huntington, N.Y. 11743.

Encyclopaedia Britannica Educational Corp., 425 Michigan Ave., Chicago, Ill. 60611.

Field Enterprises Educational Corp., Merchandise Mart Plaza, Chicago, Ill. 60654.

Ginn & Co., 125 Second Ave., Waltham, Mass. 02154.

Graflex, Division, The Singer Co., 3750 Monroe Ave., Rochester, N.Y. 14603.

Harcourt Brace Jovanovich, Inc., 757 Third Ave., New York, N.Y. 10017.

Carl H. Hendershot's Programmed Learning: A Bibliography of Programs and Presentation Devices, 1970 (Carl H. Hendershot, Bay City, Mich. 48706).

Holt, Rinehart and Winston, Inc., 383 Madison Ave., New York, N.Y. 10017.

Hughes Aircraft Co., Videosonic Systems Division, P.O. Box 3310, Fullerton, Calif. 92634

Kalart/Victor Corp., Hultenus St., Plainville, Conn. 06062.

McGraw-Hill Book Company, 330 W. 42nd St., New York, N.Y. 10036.

McMahon Electronic Engineering, 381 W. 7th St., San Pedro, Calif. 90731.

The Macmillan Company, 866 Third Ave., New York, N.Y. 10022.

Sargent-Welch Scientific Company, 7300 N. Linder Ave., Skokie, Ill. 60076.

Teaching Machines, Inc., 845 Third Ave., New York, N.Y. 10022.

Viewlex, Inc., Broadway Ave., Holbrook, N.Y. 11741.

John Wiley & Sons, Inc., 605 Third Ave., New York, N.Y. 10016.

Xerox-Education Group, 600 Madison Ave., New York, N.Y. 10022.

Programing equipment
See **Multimedia equipment and materials**

Programs, computer
See **Computers and programs**

Projectors

FILMSTRIP PROJECTORS

American Optical Company, Eggert Rd., Buffalo, N.Y. 14215.

Audio-Master Corp., 121 W. 45th St., New York, N.Y. 10036.

Bausch & Lomb, Inc., 626 St. Paul St., Rochester, N.Y. 14605.

Bell and Howell Company, 7100 McCormick Rd., Chicago, Ill. 60645.

Charles Beseler Company, 219 S. 18th St., East Orange, N.J. 07018.

DuKane Corp., 103 N. 11th Ave., St. Charles, Ill. 60174.

Eastman Kodak Company, 343 State St., Rochester, N.Y. 14650.

Graflex Division, The Singer Co., 3750 Monroe Ave., Rochester, N.Y. 14603.

Kalart/Victor Corp., Hultenus St., Plainville, Conn. 06062.

LaBelle Industries, Inc., 510 S. Worthington St., Oconomowoc, Wis., 53066.

E. Leitz, Inc., 46 Park Ave. S., New York, N.Y. 10016.

Standard Projector and Equipment Co., Inc., 1911 Pickwick Ave., Glenview, Ill. 60025.

3M Company, 3M Center, St. Paul, Minn. 55119.

Viewlex, Inc., Broadway Ave., Holbrook, N.Y. 11741.

MICROPROJECTORS

American Optical Company, Eggert Rd., Buffalo, N.Y. 14215.

Bausch & Lomb, Inc., 635 St. Paul St., Rochester, N.Y. 14602.

Bioscope Mfg. Co., P.O. Box 1492, Tulsa, Okla. 74101.

Karl Heitz, Inc., 979 Third Ave., New York, N.Y. 10022.

MOTION PICTURE PROJECTORS

8mm

Avis Films, Inc., 2408 West Olive Ave., Burbank, Calif. 91506.

Bell and Howell Company, 7100 McCormick Rd., Chicago, Ill. 60645.

Eastman Kodak Company, 343 State St., Rochester, N.Y. 14650.

Fairchild Camera and Instrument Corporation, 75 Mall Dr., Commack, N.Y. 11725.

Jayark Instruments Corporation, 10 E. 49th St., New York, N.Y. 10017.

Paillard, Inc., 1900 Lower Rd., Linden, N.J. 07036.

Technicolor, Inc., 299 Kalmus Dr., Costa Mesa, Calif. 92627.

16mm

Audiscan, Inc., P.O. Box 1456, Bellevue, Wash. 98005.

Bell and Howell Company, 7100 McCormick Rd., Chicago, Ill. 60645.

Eastman Kodak Company, 343 State St., Rochester, N.Y. 14650 (Pageant).

Graflex Division, The Singer Co., 3750 Monroe Ave., Rochester, N.Y. 14603

Harwald Co., 1245 Chicago Ave., Evanston, Ill. 60202.

Kalart/Victor Corp., Hultenus St., Plainville, Conn. 06062.

Movie-Mite Corp., 1004 E. Jefferson Ave., Detroit, Mich. 48207 (Movie-Mite).

Paillard, Inc., 1900 Lower Rd., Linden, N.J. 07036.

RCA Victor Division, Radio Corporation of America, Audio-Visual Marketing Division, Front and Cooper Sts., Camden, N.J. 08102.

Technicolor, Inc., 299 Kalmus Drive, Costa Mesa, Calif. 92627.

3M Co., Mincom Division (Wollensak Products) 220 E. 21st St., Chicago, Ill. 60616.

Victor Animatograph Corporation, Division of Kalart, Plainville, Conn. 06062.

OPAQUE PROJECTORS

American Optical Company, Eggert Rd., Buffalo, N.Y. 14215.

Bausch and Lomb Optical Company, 626 St. Paul St., Rochester, N.Y. 14605.

Charles Beseler Company, 219 S. 18th St., East Orange, N.J. 07018.

Keystone View Co., Hamilton & Crandall Sts., Meadville, Pa. 16335.

Projection Optics Co., Inc., 271 Eleventh Ave., East Orange, N.J. 07018.

Squibb-Taylor, Inc., P.O. Box 20158, Dallas, Tex. 75220 (Taylor Spotlight).

OVERHEAD PROJECTORS

American Optical Company, Eggert Rd., Buffalo, N.Y. 14215.

Bausch & Lomb, Inc., 635 St. Paul St., Rochester, N.Y. 14602.

Bell and Howell Company, 7100 McCormick Rd., Chicago, Ill. 60645.

Charles Beseler Company, 219 S. 18th St., East Orange, N.J. 07018.

Buhl Optical Co., 1009 Beech Ave., Pittsburgh, Pa. 15233.

Graflex, Division, The Singer Co., 3750 Monroe Ave., Rochester, N.Y. 14603.

Karl Heitz, Inc., 979 Third Ave., New York, N.Y. 10022.

Keystone View Company, Hamilton & Crandall Sts., Meadville, Pa. 16335.

Owens-Corning Fiberglas Corporation, Fiberglas Tower, Toledo, Ohio 43601.

Ozalid Division, General Aniline and Film Corporation, 140 W. 51st St., New York, N.Y. 10020.

Projection Optics Company, Inc., 271 11th Ave., East Orange, N.J. 07018.

Tecnifax Corporation, 195 Appleton St., Holyoke, Mass. 01040.

3-M Company, 3M Center, St. Paul, Minn. 55119.

Visualcraft, Inc., 12842 S. Western Ave., Blue Island, Ill. 60406.

SLIDE PROJECTORS

2 × 2

American Optical Company, Eggert Rd., Buffalo, N.Y. 14215.

Bausch & Lomb, Inc., 626 St. Paul St., Rochester, N.Y. 14605.

Bell and Howell Company, 7100 McCormick Rd., Chicago, Ill. 60645.

Eastman Kodak Company, 343 State St., Rochester, N.Y. 14650.

GAF Corporation, AV Products Division, 140 W. 51st St., New York, N.Y. 10020.

Graflex, Division, The Singer Co., 3750 Monroe Ave., Rochester, N.Y. 14603.

Kalart/Victor Corp., Hultenus St., Plainville, Conn. 06062.

Keystone View Co., Hamilton & Crandall Sts., Meadville, Pa. 16335.

LaBelle Industries, Inc., 510 S. Worthington St., Oconomowoc, Wis. 53066.

E. Leitz, Inc., 46 Park Ave. S., New York, N.Y. 10016.

Spindler and Sauppe, 1329 Grand Central Ave., Glendale, Calif. 91201.

Standard Projector and Equipment Company, 1911 Pickwick Ave., Glenview, Ill. 60025.

Viewlex, Inc., Broadway Ave., Holbrook, N.Y. 11741.

3¼ × 4

American Optical Company, Eggert Rd., Buffalo, N.Y. 14215.

Bausch & Lomb, Inc., 626 St. Paul St., Rochester, N.Y. 14605.

Charles Beseler Company, 219 S. 18th St., East Orange, N.J. 07018.

Keystone View Co., Hamilton & Crandall Sts., Meadville, Pa. 16335.

Radio networks
See **Audio equipment and materials**

Radio receivers
See **Audio equipment and materials**

Record players
See **Audio equipment and materials**

Records
See **Audio equipment and materials: recordings and transcriptions**

Recorders, tape
See **Audio equipment and materials**

Recorders, television
See **Television: videotape recorders**

Reproduction equipment

Addressograph-Multigraph Corp., Charles Bruning Division, 1555 Times Drive, Des Plaines, Ill. 60018 (Multilith; Bruning Copyflex).

American Photocopy Equipment Company, 2100 W. Dempster St., Evanston, Ill. 60204 (Super-stat).

Columbia Ribbon and Carbon Manufacturing Company, Herb Hill Rd., Glen Cove, N.Y. 11542.

Copy-Rite Corporation, 1203 W. Cortland St., Chicago, Ill. 60614 (Copy-Rite).

A. B. Dick Company, 5700 W. Touhy Ave., Niles, Ill. 60648 (mimeograph).

Ditto Division, Bell and Howell Company, 6800 McCormick Rd., Chicago, Ill. 60645.

Eastman Kodak Company, 343 State St., Rochester, N.Y. 14650 (Verifax).

Gestetner Corporation, 216 Lake Ave., Yonkers, N.Y. 10702 (mimeograph).

Keuffel and Esser Co., 20 Whippany Rd., Hoboken, N.J. 07960.

Ozalid Division, General Aniline and Film Corporation, 140 W. 51st St., New York, N.Y. 10020.

Standard Duplicating Machines Corporation, 1935 Revere Beach Parkway, Everett, Mass. 02149.

3M Company, 3M Center, St. Paul, Minn. 55119.

Viewlex, Inc., Broadway Ave., Holbrook, N.Y. 11741 (Viewfax).

Xerox Corporation, 701 S. Aviation Blvd., El Segundo, Calif. 90245.

Resources facilities, learning
See **Furniture and facilities**

Room-darkening equipment
See **Furniture and facilities**

Rubber cement mounting materials
See **Graphic materials: mounting materials**

Screens

Commercial Picture Equipment Co., 5725 N. Broadway Ave., Chicago, Ill. 60626.

Da-Lite Screen Company, Inc., P.O. Box 629, Warsaw, Ind. 46580.

Eastman Kodak Company, 343 State St., Rochester, N.Y. 14650 (Ektalite).

Hudson Photographic Industries, 2 S. Buckhout St., Irvington-on-Hudson, N.Y. 10533.

Knox Manufacturing Company, 111 Spruce St., Wood Dale, Ill. 60191.

Polacoat, Inc., 9750 Conklin Rd., Cincinnati, Ohio 45242.

Radiant Corp., 8220 N. Austin Ave., Morton Grove, Ill. 60053.

Trans Lux News Sign Corp., 625 Madison Ave., New York, N.Y. 10022.

Shading and coloring materials
See **Graphic materials: coloring and shading materials**

Simulation and games

A comprehensive bibliography including Simulation Games was published in the February 1969 issue of *Social Education,* "Foreign Policy Association Bibliography on Simulation."

Abt Associates, Inc., 55 Wheeler St., Cambridge, Mass. 02138.

Academic Games Associates, Center for Study of Social Organization of Schools, The Johns Hopkins University, 3505 N. Charles St., Baltimore, Md. 21212 (games of Consumer, Democracy, Disaster, Economic System, Life Career, and The Ghetto Game).

American Management Association, Saranac Lake, N.Y. 12983.

Amstan Supply Division, American Radiator and Standard Sanitary Corporation, 6587 Hamilton Ave., Pittsburgh, Pa. 15206.

E. M. Babb and L. M. Eisgruben, Purdue University Business School, Lafayette, Ind. 46207.

Colonel L. Baumann, Simulation and Computer Directorate, ICAF, Fort McNair, Washington, D.C. 20315.

Board of Cooperative Educational Services, 845 Fox Meadow Rd., Yorktown Heights, N.Y. 10598.

Milton Bradley Company, 74 Park St., Springfield, Mass. 01105.

Bureau of Business Research, University of Texas, Austin, Tex. 78712.

Burroughs Corporation, 460 N. Sierra Madre Villa Ave., Pasadena, Calif. 91109; Burroughs Machines Group, 6071 2nd Ave., Detroit, Mich. 48232.

Carnegie Institute of Technology, Schenley Park, Pittsburgh, Pa. 15213.

CBS Learning Center, 12 Station Dr., Princeton Junction, N.J. 08550 (games of Githaka and The Market Place).

C.E.I.R., Inc., Control Data Corp., Washington Systems Div., 901 S. Highland, Arlington, Va. 22903.

The Cities Game, 1330 Camino Del Mar, Calif. 92014.

Dr. Malcolm Collier, Director, ACS Project 5632 Kimbark Ave., Chicago, Ill. 60639.

Communications Workers of America, 85 Worth St., New York, N.Y. 10013.

Dayco Corporation, 333–7 West First St., Dayton, Ohio 45402.

Didactic Game Company, Education Services DW/RB, Enterprises, Inc., Box 500, Westbury, N.Y. 11590.

Educational Services, Inc., 15 Mifflin Place, Cambridge, Mass. 02138.

Free Press, 866 Third Ave., New York, N.Y. 10022.

Harvard Graduate School of Business, Information System for Vocational Decisions, 220 Alewife Brook Parkway, Cambridge, Mass. 02138.

High School Geography Project, P.O. Box 1095, Boulder Colo. 80302 (games of Section and Farming).

Holt, Rinehart and Winston, Inc., 383 Madison Ave., New York, N.Y. 10017.

Human Resources Research Office, George Washington University, 2029 G St., N.W., Washington, D.C. 20006.

Humble Oil and Refining Co., 30 Rockefeller Plaza, New York, N.Y. 10020.

Imperial Oil, Limited, Toronto, Canada.

Indiana University, School of Business, Bloomington, Ind. 47401.

Industrial Relations Center, University of Chicago, Chicago, Ill. 60637.

Institute of Defense Analysis, 400 Army-Navy Drive, S., Arlington, Va. 22202.

Instructional Simulations, Inc., 2147 University Ave., St. Paul, Minn. 55114.

Interact, P.O. Box 262, Lakeside, Calif. 92040 (games of Disunia, Division, and Sunshine).

International Academic Games, 440 Las Olas Blvd., Fort Lauderdale, Fla. 33301.

International Learning Corporation, 440 Las Olas Blvd., Fort Lauderdale, Fla. 33301.

Kaiser Community Homes, Kaiser Industries Corp., 4950 Wilshire Blvd., Los Angeles, Calif. 90005.

The Kroger Company, 1014 Vine St., Cincinnati, Ohio 45201.

The Learning Center, Social Studies Department, Princeton Public Schools, Princeton, N.J. 08540.

McKinsey and Co., 245 Park Ave., New York, N.Y. 10017.

Mental Health Research Institute, University of Michigan, Ann Arbor, Mich. 48104.

Professor E. S. Munger, Division of Humanities and Social Sciences, California Institute of Technology, 1201 E. California Blvd., Pasadena, Calif. 91109.

Office of Civil Defense, Shelter Management Instruction, Washington, D.C. 20305.

Pillsbury Company, Pillsbury Bldg., Minneapolis, Minn. 55402.

Proctor and Gamble Company, Educational Services Department, P.O Box 599, Cincinnati, Ohio 45201.

Project CONEX, L. P. Bloomfield, M.I.T., Cambridge, Mass. 02138.

Projects SIMILE, Western Behavioral Sciences Institute, 1150 Silverado Blvd., La Jolla, Calif. 92037 (games of Crisis, Napoli, and Plans).

Radio Corporation of America, Front and Cooper Sts., Camden, N.J. 08102.

Rand Corporation, 1700 Main St., Santa Monica, Calif. 90401.

Raytheon Company, Missile and Space Division, Bedford, Mass. 01730.

Remington Rand UNIVAC, 1290 Ave. of the Americas, New York, N.Y. 10019.

Science Research Associates, 529 East Erie St., Chicago, Ill. 60611 (games of Economic Decisions and Inter-Nation Simulation).

Scott Foresman & Co., 1900 E. Kale Ave., Glenview, Ill. 60025 (game of Dangerous Parallel).

Simulations Publications, Inc., 44 E. 23rd St., New York, N.Y. 10010.

Sloan School of Industrial Marketing, Massachusetts Institute of Technology, Cambridge, Mass. 02138.

C. N. Smith, College of Business, Northern Illinois University, De Kalb, Ill. 60155.

Systems Development Corporation, 5827 Columbia Pike, Falls Church, Va. 22041.

Systems Gaming Associates, A1–2 Lansing Apartment, 20 N. Triphammer Rd., Ithaca, N.Y. 14850.

Professor Hans B. Thorelli, Purdue University, Lafayette, Ind. 46207.

3M Company, Business Ventures Division, 3M Center, St. Paul, Minn. 55119.

Travelers Insurance Company, Educational Public Services Department, 277 Park Ave., New York, N.Y. 10017; The Travelers Corp., One Tower Square, Hartford, Conn. 06115.

U.S. Army Logistics, Army Center, Fort Lee, Va. 23801.

Washington Center for Metropolitan Studies, 1717 Massachusetts Ave., N.W., Washington, D.C. 20036.

Wayne State University, Detroit, Mich. 48202.

Wellesley Public School System, Wellesley, Mass. 01570.

Western Behavioral Science Institute, 1121 Torrey Pines Blvd., La Jolla, Calif. 92037.

Western Management Science Institute, c/o R. C. Henshow, UCLA, Los Angeles, Calif. 90024.

Western Publishing Company, Inc., School and Library Department, 850 Third Ave., New York, N.Y. 10022.

John Wiley & Sons, Inc., 605 Third Ave., New York, N.Y. 10016.

Professor Robert C. Wood, Department of Political Science, Northern Illinois University, De Kalb, Ill. 60115.

D. Yount, El Capitan High School, Lakeside, Calif. 92040.

16mm films
See Films

16mm projectors
See projectors

Slide and filmstrip projectors
See projectors

Slides

SOURCES

Since there is no master list of 2″ × 2″ slides, it is necessary to consult a wide variety of sources which specialize in slides for art, architecture, science, religion, medicine, travel, and space.

American Museum of Natural History, Central Park West at 79th St., New York, N.Y. 10024.

Clay-Adams, 299 Webro Rd., Parsippany, N.J. 07054.

Eastman Kodak Company, Motion Picture and Education Markets Division, 343 State St., Rochester, N.Y. 14650.

Meston's Travels, Inc., 3801 N. Piedras, El Paso, Tex. 79930.

Metropolitan Museum of Art, Fifth Ave. at 82nd St., New York, N.Y. 10028.

Museum of Modern Art, 11 W. 53rd St., New York, N.Y. 10019.

National Audubon Society, 1130 Fifth Ave., New York, N.Y. 10028.

Prothman Associates, Inc., 650 Thomas Ave., Baldwin, N.Y. 11510.

Society for Visual Education, 1345 W. Diversey Parkway, Chicago, Ill. 60614.

Ward's Natural Science Establishment, Inc., 3000 E. Ridge Rd., Rochester, N.Y. 14605.

STORAGE

Joshua Meier Co., Inc., 7401 Westside Ave., North Bergen, N.J. 07047 (Slide-Sho).

Plastican Corp., P.O. Box 157, Butler, N.J. 07405.

Plastic Sealing Corp., 1507 N. Gardner St., Hollywood, Calif. 90046 (plastic sheet slide holders).

Spirit duplicators
See Reproduction equipment

Stencil duplicating equipment
See Reproduction equipment

Stereo and 3-D projectors
See **Photographic equipment**

Tape adhesives
See **Graphic materials: graphic tapes**

Tape libraries
See **Audio equipment and materials: tape sources**

Tape manufacturers
See **Audio equipment and supplies**

Tape sources
See **Audio equipment and materials**

Tape recorders
See **Audio equipment and materials**

Television

CASSETTES

CBS Electronic Video Recordings, 51 W. 52nd St., New York, N.Y. 10119.

Panasonic VTR/CCTV (Matsushita Electric Corp. of America), 23–05 44 Rd., Long Island City, N.Y. 11101.

Sony Corp. of America, VTR Division, 47–47 Van Dam St., Long Island City, N.Y. 11101.

GENERAL INFORMATION

Adler Educational Systems Division, Litton Systems, Inc., 72 E. Main St., New Rochelle, N.Y. 10801.

Association for Educational Communications and Technology, 1201 Sixteenth St., N.W., Washington, D.C. 20036.

Children's Television Workshop, 1 Lincoln Plaza, New York, N.Y. 10023.

Committee on Television, American Council on Education, 1785 Massachusetts Ave., N.W., Washington, D.C. 20036.

GLP Division, Aerospace Group, General Precision, Inc., 63 Bedford Rd., Pleasantville, N.Y. 10570.

Great Plains Regional Instruction Television Library, University of Nebraska, Lincoln, Nebraska 68508.

Memorex Corporation, San Towas at Central Expressway, Santa Clara, Calif. 95052.

Microwave System, Micro-Link Division of Varian Associates, 1375 Akron St., Copiague, N.Y. 11726.

National Association of Educational Broadcasters, 1346 Connecticut Ave., N.W., Washington, D.C. 20036.

NET Film Service, Indiana University, Bloomington, Ind. 47401.

RCA Victor Division, Radio Corporation of America, Audio-Visual Marketing Division, Front and Cooper Sts., Camden, N.J. 08102.

Visual Educom Incorporated, 4333 S. Ohio St., Michigan City, Ind. 46360.

NETWORKS

American Broadcasting Company, 1330 Avenue of the Americas, New York, N.Y. 10019.

Columbia Broadcasting System, 51 W. 52nd St., New York, N.Y. 10019.

National Broadcasting Company, 30 Rockefeller Plaza, New York, N.Y. 10020.

Public Broadcasting Service, 955 L'Enfant Plaza North, S.W., Washington, D.C. 20006.

RECEIVERS

Admiral Corporation, 3800 W. Cortland St., Chicago, Ill. 60647.

General Electric Company, Television Division, College Blvd., Portsmouth, Va. 23705.

GPL Division, General Precision, Inc., 63 Bedford Rd., Pleasantville, N.Y. 10070.

Jerrold Electronics Corp., 401 Walnut St., Philadelphia, Pa. 19105.

RCA Victor Division, Audio-Visual Marketing Division, Radio Corporation of America, Front and Cooper Sts., Camden, N.J. 08102.

SC Electronics, Inc., 530 Fifth Ave., N.W., New Brighton, Minn. 55112.

Sony Corporation, 47–47 Van Dam St., Long Island City, N.Y. 11101.

Sylvania Commercial Electronics Division, 100 Endicott St., Danvers, Mass. 01923.

VIDEOTAPE RECORDERS

Ampex, 2201 Landmeier Rd., Elk Grove Village, Ill. 60007.

Concord Electronics Corporation, 1935 Armacost, Los Angeles, Calif. 90025.

Panasonic/Matsushita Electric Corporation, 23–05 44 Rd., Long Island City, N.Y. 11101.

Shibaden Corporation of America, 58–25 Brooklyn–Queens Expressway, Woodside, N.Y. 11377.

Sony Corporation, 47–47 Van Dam St., Long Island City, N.Y. 11101.

Westinghouse Electric Corporation, P.O. Box J, Sea Cliff, N.Y. 11579.

3 1/4 × 4 slide projectors
See **Projectors**

3–D projectors
See **Photographic equipment: stereo equipment and materials**

Three-dimensional materials

MODELS, etc.

Audio-Visual Enterprises, 911 Laguna Rd., Pasadena, Calif. 91105 (color study prints and historical models).

Bicknell Macalaster Co., 253 Norfolk St., Cambridge, Mass. 02139 (apparatus kits).

Robert Brunner Division, Cadan Corp., 635 Madison Ave., New York, N.Y. 10022 (cutout model of human brain).

Creative Playthings, Inc., P.O. Box 110, Princeton, N.J. 08540 (manipulatives for instructional materials centers and classrooms—kindergarten through grade 8).

B. F. Goodrich, Koroseal Division, Oak Grove, Marietta, Ohio 45750 (Koroseal flexible magnetic strip).

Imitation Food Display Co., 197 Waverly Ave., Brooklyn, N.Y. 11205 (models of food).

Louis Paul Jonas Studios, Inc., Box 59-A, R.D.1, Hudson, N.Y. 12534 (miniature animals).

Judy Company. *See* Silver Burdett Company (instructional toys, models).

A. J. Nystrom & Co., 3333 Elston Ave., Chicago 18, Ill. 60618.

Revell, Incorporated, 4223 Glencoe Ave., Venice, Calif. 90291.

Silver Burdett Company, A Division of General Learning Corporation, 460 So. Northwest Highway, Park Ridge, Ill. 60068.

Viking Importers, 113 S. Edgemont St., Los Angeles, Calif. 90004.

Weber-Costello Company, 1900 N. Narragansett Ave., Chicago Heights, Ill. 60639.

SCIENCE MATERIALS AND SPECIMENS

CCM: General Biological, Inc., 8200 S. Hoyne Ave., Chicago, Ill. 60620 (models, manikins, charts, Kodachrome slides, biological colored movies, plastic-embedded specimens).

Central Scientific Company, 2600 S. Kostner Ave., Chicago, Ill. 60623.

Clay-Adams, 299 Webro Rd., Parsippany, N.J. 07054.

Denoyer-Geppert Company, 5235 Ravenswood Ave., Chicago, Ill. 60640.

Hubbard Scientific Company, P.O. Box 105, Northbrook, Ill. 60062.

New York Laboratory Supply Co., 510 Hempstead Turnpike, West Hempstead, N.Y. 11552.

New York Scientific Supply Company, 28 W. 30th St., New York, N.Y. 10001.

Pacific Bio-Marine Supply Co., P.O. Box 536, Venice, Calif. 90291.

Sargent-Welch Scientific Company, 7300 N. Linder Ave., Skokie, Ill. 60076.

Stansi Scientific Division, Fisher Scientific Co., 1231 N. Honore St., Chicago, Ill. 60622.

Ward's Natural Science Establishment, Inc., 3000 E. Ridge Rd., Rochester, N.Y. 14626.

Transcribers
See **Audio equipment and materials**

Transcriptions
See **Audio equipment and materials**

Transparencies

MATERIALS

Charles Beseler Company, 219 S. 18th St., East Orange, N.J. 07018.

Arthur Brown and Bros., Inc., 2 W. 46th St., New York, N.Y. 10036.

Cousino Electronics Corp., 1941 Franklin Ave., Toledo, Ohio 43624.

Eastman Kodak Company, 343 State St., Rochester, N.Y. 14650.

Holson Co., Belden Ave., Norwalk, Conn. 06850 (clear acetate).

Keuffel and Esser Company, 20 Whippany Rd., Hoboken, N.J. 07960.

Labelon Corp., 10 Chapin St., Canandaigua, N.Y. 14424.

National Adhesive Products, Inc., 19600 St. Clair Ave., Cleveland, Ohio 44101.

Ozalid Division, General Aniline and Film Corp., 140 W. 51st St., New York, N.Y. 10020.

Seal, Inc., Roosevelt Dr. & B St., Derby, Conn. 06418.

Tecnifax Corporation, 195 Appleton St., Holyoke, Mass. 01040.

3M Company, 3M Center, St. Paul, Minn. 55119. VariTyper Corp., 11 Mt. Pleasant Ave., Hanover, N.J. 07936.

SOURCES

There is one reference to commercially prepared transparencies: Index to Overhead Transparencies, which covers over 18,000 transparencies (R. R. Bowker Co., 1180 Avenue of the Americas, New York, N.Y. 10036, $22.50).

Allyn and Bacon, Inc., AV Department, 470 Atlantic Ave., Boston, Mass. 02210.

Black Box Collotype Studios, Inc., 4840 W. Belmont Ave., Chicago, Ill. 60641.

John Colburn Associates, Inc., 1122 Central Ave., P.O. Box 236, Wilmette, Ill. 60091.

Creative Visuals Division, Games Industries Inc., P.O. Box 1911, Big Spring, Tex. 79720.

Encyclopaedia Britannica Educational Corp., 425 N. Michigan Ave., Chicago, Ill. 60611.

Ginn and Company, 125 Second Ave., Waltham, Mass. 02154.

Hammond, Inc., 515 Valley St., Maplewood, N.J. 07040.

The Instructo Corp., Paoli, Pa. 19301.

Keuffel and Esser Company, 20 Whippany Rd., Hoboken, N.J. 07960.

McGraw-Hill Book Company, Text-Film Division, 330 W. 42nd St., New York, N.Y. 10036.

Ozalid Division, General Aniline and Film Corporation, 140 W. 51st St., New York, N.Y. 10020.

Popular Science Publishing Company, Audio-Visual Division, 355 Lexington Ave., New York, N.Y. 10017.

Rand McNally & Company, P.O. Box 7600, Chicago, Ill. 60680.

Tecnifax Corporation, 195 Appleton St., Holyoke, Mass. 01040.

3M Company, Visual Products Division, 3M Center, St. Paul, Minn. 55119.

Tweedy Transparencies, 208 Hollywood Ave., East Orange, N.J. 07018.

United Transparencies, Inc., P.O. Box 688, Binghamton, N.Y. 13902.

Visual Materials, Inc., 2549 Middlefield Rd., Redwood City, Calif. 94063.

2 × 2 slide projectors
See **Projectors**

Videotape recorders
See **Television**

Wax adhesives
See **Graphic materials**

Index

Recording (*Continued*)
  methods of, 330–336
  videotape, 520–523
Records, long-playing (LPs), 338–339
Recycling, 76
Referent confusion, 23–24
  in reading, 24
Relief maps, 291, 294–295, 310, 313; *illus.,* 311
  three-dimensional, *illus.,* 294
Renshaw, Samuel, 423
Renshaw system, 423–424
Research surveys, 252–253
Resource persons, visits by, in community study,
  245
Responsive Environments Program Center, New
  York, 555
Retrieval, playback and, 336–351
Retrieval systems, storage information, 344
Road maps, 295
Rogers, C. R., quoted, 598
Role-playing, 583
Roy, Utah, High School, 607, 609
Rulon, Philip J., 466

Sabaroff, Rose, quoted, 305
St. Louis, science radio broadcast lessons in, 366
Saks, Lewis, 648–649, 651
  quoted, 180
Salt Lake City, Meadow Moor Elementary
  School in, 615, 617
San Carlos, Calif., Brittain Acres Elementary
  School in, 624
San Diego, "outdoor schools" in, 246
San Mateo, Calif., Hillsdale High School in, 607
Santa Clara, Calif., television instruction in, 524
Santa Monica, Calif., Systems Development
  Corporation in, 570
Satisfaction, sense of, 67
Sawyer's Rotomatic slide projector, *illus.,* 436
Scheepmaker, Bob, and Karl L. Zinn, quoted,
  571
Schenectady, N.Y., Niskayuna School District
  in, 615–616, 619–620
Schindel, Morton, quoted, 464
School administrators, exchange programs and,
  250
  planning of community study experiences by,
  254

School boards, liability of, in community study,
  262
  and planning of community study experiences, 246, 254
School buildings, design of, 194
  standardization of, 64
School camps, 239
School displays and exhibits, 186–188
School population, changing, 6–8
  growing, 5
School radio broadcasts, 364
  availability of, 366
  nature and advantages of, 364–366
School work, outside world in relation to, 85
Schools, and effective communication, 18
  hours spent in, 10, 17
  and population explosion, 6
  recent changes in, 194
  use of posters in, 125–126
Schramm, Wilbur, 33, 524–526
Science, audio-cued learning materials used in
  teaching, 370
  biological, films made for, 457
  changing curriculum for, 8–9, 271
  films made for teaching of, 458, 462
  filmstrips used in teaching, 404
  inquiry method for teaching, 11–12
  use of specimens in teaching, 163–164
Seeing, 25–26
Seeing efficiency, improvement in, 26
  for instructional television, 527
Self-accomplishment, 67
Self-critique or self-image teaching, 539
Self-directed Individualized Instruction, 607;
  illus., 608–609
Self-evaluation, 351
  audiotape playback for, 339–342
  through instructional television, 537–541
  tape recorder as instrument of, 350
Self-instruction, film learning and, 487–488;
  illus., 486
  individualized, *illus.,* 432
Self-realization, 234
Self-tutorial learning, 64
Self-tutorial multimedia programs, 37, 39
Sense of the World, 364
Sensorimotor apparatus, perception and, 26
Sensory mechanisms, 48–49, 51

DATE DUE

MAR 27 '79	MAR 27 '79		
APR 17 '79	MAY 2 '79		
GAYLORD			PRINTED IN U.S.A